ONE WEEK LOAN

PLANNING LAW AND PRACTICE

Third Edition

J Cameron Blackhall
BA (Hons), Dip Landscape Design, MRTPI, ALI

Cavendish
Publishing
Limited

London • Sydney • Portland, Oregon

To A, B and C

Third edition first published in Great Britain 2005 by Cavendish Publishing Limited,
The Glass House, Wharton Street, London WC1X 9PX, United Kingdom
Telephone: +44 (0)20 7278 8000   Facsimile: +44 (0)20 7278 8080
Email: info@cavendishpublishing.com
Website: www.cavendishpublishing.com

Published in the United States by Cavendish Publishing
c/o International Specialized Book Services,
5824 NE Hassalo Street, Portland,
Oregon 97213-3644, USA

Published in Australia by Cavendish Publishing (Australia) Pty Ltd
45 Beach Street, Coogee, NSW 2034, Australia
Telephone: + 61 (2)9664 0909   Facsimile: + 61 (2)9664 5420
Email: info@cavendishpublishing.com.au
Website: www.cavendishpublishing.com.au

British Library Cataloguing in Publication Data

Library of Congress Cataloguing in Publication Data
Data available

ISBN 1-85941-748-5

Printed and bound in Great Britain

PREFACE

The preface to the first edition of this book published in 1998, included the statement that 'nothing is permanent'. This is not only true of the use of land and buildings but also of legislation governing town and country planning and the interpretation of that legislation by the courts. This third edition deals with the recent changes and essentially provides an update on planning law and practice, as well as an opportunity to present the reader with additional material. I make no apology for retaining the original format which readers have acknowledged is successful and which resulted in the first edition being awarded the Chartered Institute of Builders 1999 Gold Award for the best reference book related to the work of the building industry.

The law relating to town and country planning directly or indirectly affects the life of each of us. The demands we place on the use of land for food, manufactured and processed products, places of employment, communications, shopping, recreation and our homes creates a complex system of inter-relationships which are in themselves constantly evolving and changing. Nothing is permanent and the rationale for town and country planning is that the change is inevitable. The resulting conflicting demands which affect the use of land should be foreseen (as far as is humanly possible), ordered in a rational manner and thereafter be the subject of control. This is not merely an academic exercise and must occur within the limits of what is acceptable politically, economically, environmentally and socially. That is not to suggest that there will ever be a consensus view on the desirability of achieving broader objectives while various groups within society legitimately seek to promote their own objectives. As individuals, it can reasonably be assumed that we agree that every family is entitled to a decent standard of housing, but when the provision of additional housing to meet this objective is proposed in our town or neighbourhood, we may not be enamoured with the proposal put forward by the local planning authority.

Whilst we all seek to take advantage of the rapidly developing technologies of the 21st century, which hopefully will lead to a higher standard of living for ourselves and our children, there is no consensus as to how this should be achieved. Planning, therefore, has to make balanced judgments on behalf of society as to what is acceptable after carefully weighing the arguments both for and against proposed changes and the likely impact of such change on an established area. Change, in whatever form or scale, is akin to throwing a stone into a tranquil pond. It creates 'ripples', that is, it disturbs the status quo, and it is the duty of planners to assess whether those 'ripples' – or the degree of disturbance which results from proposed change – are acceptable to society.

To achieve the objectives of planning, there is a complicated and ever-evolving foundation of primary legislation in the form of Acts of Parliament and secondary legislation in the form of orders and regulations. In writing this book, I have drawn upon my experiences as Senior Lecturer in the Department of Town and Country Planning, University of Newcastle-upon-Tyne, during which time I lectured on the subject of planning legislation to our own planning students, planning students in Shah Alam, Malaysia, and to those in Newcastle studying architecture, law, civil engineering and landscape architecture. In addition, I have lectured to, or advised, numerous civic groups on aspects of planning law. In each of these circumstances, the complexity of the subject has primarily demanded that the basic elements are clearly understood.

These experiences have led me to adopt the particular format of this book. The approach has been first to provide the reader with the basic elements of a particular aspect of planning law and then to elaborate on that aspect by providing details of how these elements have been interpreted by the Secretary of State or the courts; for example, Chapter 8 states the content of the Use Classes Order 1987 and Chapter 9 then deals with challenges to that Order which have assisted in clarifying the precise meaning of the Order. By adopting this method, it is felt that the reader will benefit from a level of understanding before embarking upon the detailed nuances contained in the legislation.

In the Table of Cases, it should be noted that the detailed references are contained within the main text. To facilitate ease of access to the details of cases referred to, the primary reference is, wherever possible, to the Journal of Planning and Environmental Law (JPL). This is followed by other sources of reference, and it should be noted that, in some instances, these may pre-date those provided by the JPL. Nevertheless, the JPL reference is given priority. Where the dates of two or more references are the same, the date appears only in relation to the first reference, for example: [1989] JPL 635; 21 P & CR 110.

The Table of Cases lists the chapter and paragraph in which the case is cited. Therefore, for example, by looking at the case *AG v Calderdale BC*, it will be noted that this occurs in Chapter 21, para 5, shown as 21.5. As shown on the contents page, Chapter 21 deals with listed buildings and conservation areas, it is, therefore, immediately apparent that this case deals with a conservation issue, and that para 5 deals with listed building enforcement notices. Similarly, the Table of Statutes is referenced on the basis of chapters and paragraphs.

My hope is that this book will provide each reader with a planned, structured, applied and controlled resource in his or her study which will permit them to both understand and operate successfully in the complex area of planning law.

J Cameron Blackhall

March 2005

ACKNOWLEDGMENTS

In preparing this third edition, I am particularly grateful to my publishers for their wholehearted support and advice and to those readers who have taken the trouble to forward very valuable suggestions for the inclusion of additional material.

I acknowledge the part played by countless numbers of students, both in my own University of Newcastle-upon-Tyne, and those studying at the Institut Teknologi Mara (ITM), Shah Alam, Malaysia, and members of civic societies and other groups who have, through their constant questioning of issues relating to planning law, provided the stimulus to write this text.

Two people in particular deserve my special thanks: my wife Angela, for her patience and critical proof reading, and Miss Chathuri Nugawela, LLB, without whose tenacity and hours of work the referencing of the case studies included in this book would never have been satisfactorily completed.

My thanks are also given to the university library staff and the Faculty of Law at the University of Newcastle for making the facilities freely available and, on occasions, literally pointing me in the right direction. I am indebted to the editors, contributors and publishers of the Encyclopedia of Planning Law and the Journal of Planning and Environmental Law, both for the legal content of this book and for many of the cases to which reference has been made.

CONTENTS

TABLE OF CASES

TABLE OF STATUTES

TABLE OF NOTES, CIRCULARS, PPGs, MPGs

TABLE OF STATUTORY INSTRUMENTS

TABLE OF EU LEGISLATION

TABLE OF ABBREVIATIONS

AAP	Action Area Plan
AC	Appeal Court
All ER	All England Report
AMR	Annual Monitoring Report
AONB	Area of Outstanding Natural Beauty
App Cas	Appeal Case
BC	Borough Council
BCN	Breach of Condition Notice
BLR	Building Law Report
BPEO	Best Practical Environmental Option
BPZ	Business Planning Zone
CA	Court of Appeal
CC	County Council
Ch D	Chancery Division
CLEUD	Certificate of Lawfulness: existing use or development
CROW	Countryside and Rights of Way Act
DC	District Council
DCMS	Department of Culture, Media and Sport
DEFRA	Department for Environment, Food and Rural Affairs
DETR	Department of the Environment, Transport and the Regions
DNPA	Dartmoor National Park Authority
DPD	Development Plan Document
DTLR	Department of Transport, Local Government and the Regions
ECHR	European Convention on Human Rights
EG	Estates Gazette
EGCS	Estates Gazette Case Summaries
EGLR	Estates Gazette Law Report
EGR	Estates Gazette Review
EIA	Environmental Impact Assessment
EIP	Examination in Public
ELM	Environment Law and Management
Env LR	Environmental Law Report
EPA	Environmental Protection Act
ESA	Environmentally Sensitive Area
EWCA	England and Wales : Court of Appeal
EWHC	England and Wales : High Court
EWHL	England and Wales : House of Lords
Ex D	Exchequer Division

Ex p	Ex-party
EZ	Enterprise Zone
GDO	General Permitted Development Order
GDPO	Town and Country Planning (General Development Procedure Order
GLC	Greater London Council
GPDO	Town and Country Planning (General Permitted Development Order
HLR	Housing Law Report
HMIP	Her Majesty's Inspectorate of Pollution
IDO	Interim Development Order
JEL	Journal of Environmental Law
JP	Justice of the Peace Report
JPL	Journal of Planning and Environmental Law
KB	King's Bench Division
LBC	London Borough Council
LBCAA	Listed Building and Conservation Areas Act
LDD	Local Development Document
LDF	Local Development Framework
LDO	Local Development Order
LDS	Local Development Scheme
LGC	Local Government Chronicle
LGLR	Local Government Law Report
LJ Ch	Lord Justices Report
lpa	local planning authority
LQR	Law Quarterly Review
MAWS	Minerals and Waste Scheme
MBC	Metropolitan Borough Council
MPA	Minerals Planning Authority
MPG	Minerals Policy Guidance
MR	Master of the Rolls
NPACA	National Parks and Access to the Countryside Act
NPC	National Parks Commission
ODPM	Office of the Deputy Prime Minister

P & CR	Property and Compensation Report
PAG	Planning Advisory Group
PCA	Planning and Compensation Act
PCN	Planning Contravention Notice
PCPA	Planning and Compulsoary Purchase Act
PLB	Property Law Bulletin
PLCR	Planning Law Case Report
PLR	Planning Law Report
PPG	Planning Policy Guidance Note
PPS	Planning Policy Statement
QB	Queen's Bench Division
RDA	Regional Development Agency
RDC	Rural District Council
RPB	Regional Planning Board
RPG	Regional Policy Guidance
RSPB	Royal Society for the Protection of Birds (RSPB
RSS	Regional Spatial Strategy
RVA	Relevant Valuation Date
SA	Sustainability Appraisal
SAC	Special Area of Conservation
SCI	Statement of Community Involvement
SDS	Spatial Development Strategy
SEA	Strategic Environmental Assessment
SJ	Solicitors Journal
SoS	Secretary of State
SPA	Special Protection Area
SPD	Supplementary Planning Document
SPG	Strategic Policy Guidance
SPZ	Simplified Planning Zone
SSSI	Site of Special Scientific Interest
TCPA	Town and Country Planning Act
TCP(CA) Regs	Town and Country Planning (Control of Advertisements) Regulations
TMA	Tenant Mix agreement
TPO	Tree Preservation Order
UCO	Use Classes Order
UDC	Urban Development Corporation
UDP	Unitary Development Plan

UFMS	Urban Fringe Management Scheme
UKHL	United Kingdom; House of Lords
WLR	Weekly Law Report

CHAPTER 1

DEVELOPMENT OF PLANNING LAW AND PRACTICE

1.1 INTRODUCTION

Planning is not a new human activity; nor is the planning of human settlements, which began as soon as man imposed himself upon the environment as distinct from living in and off the natural habitats. The larger settlements of the early civilisations demanded both physical and economic planning because a large number of human resources were often required to construct the 'new' urban environments. In other areas of the world, the growth of urban areas was incremental, but both developments created major problems. For example, early Rome required the introduction of traffic restrictions to overcome the difficulties of an inadequate road system in a densely populated city, and a decree by Queen Elizabeth I restricted development immediately outside London. The phenomenon of the city as a catalyst for growth is not new, but the Industrial Revolution in Britain proved to be the critical factor in establishing the town as a major unit of production, rather than a place associated with commerce, defence or religion.

1.2 THE INDUSTRIAL REVOLUTION

The description given to the change in methods of production, and the increasing specialisation of both factories and workers in the 19th century, is generally described as the 'Industrial Revolution'. In practice, it was an industrial 'evolution' which was dependent upon the earlier agricultural revolution. The agricultural revolution had resulted in greater levels of production which were needed, at least in the initial stages, to feed the growing industrial population. During the 19th century, the population of the UK increased from approximately 10.5 million to 37 million, and the growth centres of the newly established industries, the location of which was first dictated by the availability of water power, and then coal, led to the concentration of population in particular parts of the country. The urban problems associated with large concentrations of people requiring to be housed in close proximity to the point of production led inevitably to risks to health and, in particular, the periodic outbreaks of cholera and typhoid.

Over 100 years later, the perceived problems associated with high density urban living appear to condition the attitude of a large number of the population who see dispersal to outer, or rural, locations, as their aim. This presents a major current planning problem in terms of the need to regenerate the inner areas of many of our towns, and also the need to conserve resources and ensure, as far as possible, that development is sustainable. Ease of communications, changing methods of production, plus relatively cheap green field sites, have all contributed to the constant pressure for the outward movement of land uses, including industry, commerce and housing.

1.3   GOVERNMENT INTERVENTION IN THE 19th CENTURY

The 19th century was largely a period of *laissez faire* in terms of development. The traditional thinking is that the standard of housing provided for workers was inadequate, but this criticism must be tempered by the fact that the conditions existing in rural areas at that time were certainly no better; the problems of inner city living were accentuated by the density of living and working conditions which prevailed.

It is, therefore, understandable that the government's concern over the health problems in industrialised towns led to the appointment of a Royal Commission on the Health of Towns which published reports in 1844 and 1845. These reports were followed in 1848 by the passing of two Acts of Parliament, the Public Health Act and the Nuisance Removal and Disease Prevention Act. The former set up a General Board of Health with powers to create local boards where the death rate was above 23 persons per 1,000, or where a petition of 10% of the inhabitants of the district requested such a board. The boards were granted powers to ensure that both existing and new houses were provided with water and drainage. The second Act complemented the first by making it an offence to build a new house which would depend upon drainage into an open ditch.

The government's concern over conditions which prevailed led to the passing of two further Acts, the Nuisances Removal Act 1855 and the Sanitary Act 1886. Under the Nuisances Removal Act 1885, the justices were empowered to require the provision of sufficient privy facilities, and the means of drainage and ventilation to make a house safe and habitable, or if the house was declared unfit for human habitation, the justices could prohibit its use for that purpose. The Sanitary Act 1886 enabled the local council, or Board of Health, to deal with those houses lacking proper drainage and to compel the owner to connect the property to a public sewer, if it was within 100 feet of the property, or in any other situation, with a cesspool.

The Public Health Act 1875 consolidated other public health Acts and, in addition, local authorities were given the power to make bylaws regulating the minimum size of rooms, the space surrounding houses, and the width of streets. Provision was also made for the making up of unadopted streets and the provision of sewers at the expense of the owners of property fronting such roads. The minimum bylaw standards set by the local authority were, not surprisingly, adopted by developers as the maximum standard they were prepared to accept! This provision of the Public Health Act 1875 still has a dramatic effect upon the character of our industrialised towns with vast areas of identical terraced housing which now form part of the inner city. This is correctly termed 'bylaw housing' and should not be confused with 'back-to-back housing' which existed before the introduction of the minimum standards. The latter was housing in the form of two-storied developments where, in a single block, there were two party walls separating each unit, one at right angles to the terrace and one parallel to the frontage, thus dividing the block into four separate units, hence the term 'back-to-back'. The obvious problem was one of lack of cross-ventilation in individual units. Where these dwellings are still in existence, it is likely that they will now be listed buildings as they form part of the social history of the Industrial Revolution.

The Artisans and Labourers' Act 1868 extended the powers of local government to deal with individual insanitary dwellings which were further extended by the Artisans' and Labourers' Dwelling Improvement Acts 1875 and 1890. These Acts granted powers of slum clearance and the building of tenements and cottages for the housing of the working classes. The years 1888 and 1894 also saw reforms to local government with the setting up of county councils and urban and rural district councils. A number of enlightened industrialists were carrying out housing for their workers which showed the standards which could be achieved, for example, Bournville, New Lanark, Port Sunlight and Saltaire. These enlightened approaches to the housing of workers no doubt influenced Ebenezer Howard who, in 1899, published his book *Garden Cities of Tomorrow*. This book not only inspired the first Garden City at Letchworth, but has a continuing influence on the type of housing to which the vast majority of the population seek to aspire – low density suburban living which has been made possible by vastly improved communications and the increase in car ownership.

Throughout the 19th century, the main focus of government intervention related to public health issues and it was not until the beginning of the 20th century that land use planning was introduced. However, the Victorian attitude that physical illnesses and social problems could be eliminated by simply providing better housing conditions continued to prevail up to the 1960s and beyond.

1.4   THE EARLY 20th CENTURY

The link between the provision of adequate housing conditions and the right of local authorities to impose bylaw standards was further developed by Part I of the Housing, Town Planning etc Act 1909 which dealt with 'Housing of the Working Classes', and Part II which related to 'Town Planning' and granted powers (s 54) to local authorities to make a town planning scheme:

> ... as respects any land which is in the course of development or appears likely to be used for building purposes, with the general object of securing proper sanitary conditions, amenity and convenience in connection with the laying out and use of land and of any neighbouring lands.

A town planning scheme afforded an opportunity for greater flexibility than could be achieved by bylaws, and it could determine the number of buildings on a site, and the space around them, and also control their appearance. A scheme also allowed the definition of zones in which only certain types of buildings would be permitted. The use of 'zoning' has remained a popular means of planning in many parts of the world, but as discussed below, this was replaced in Britain by land 'allocation' which provides a greater degree of flexibility.

The Housing, Town Planning etc Act 1909 (s 54(2)) required any local authority wishing to make a town planning scheme first to gain the approval of the Local Government Board. The scheme could not take effect until it had been approved by the Board, or in some cases until it had been laid before Parliament (s 54(4)). As the preparation of a scheme was discretionary, it is not surprising that, given the complications of gaining approval, it was not a widely used piece of legislation. Ten years later, the Housing, Town Planning etc Act 1919 sought to overcome the problems associated with the bureaucratic provisions for approval. The need first to gain approval of the Local Government Board, and the necessity to lay the proposals before Parliament were removed in most cases by s 44. Schemes were to come into force immediately after approval by the Board.

Having at least partially removed the obstacles for the approval of town planning schemes, it was also made obligatory for authorities with a population of 20,000 or more to prepare schemes, and the Local Government Board could require an authority to prepare a scheme if it was satisfied that the particular circumstances warranted a scheme (s 47). Provision was also made for two or more authorities to prepare a joint scheme and to appoint a committee for that purpose (s 42).

The 1919 Act also introduced the concept of interim development control whereby a developer was not obliged to apply for permission, but if the development did not comply with a scheme as ultimately approved, he would forego his right to compensation (s 45).

Part II of the Housing etc Act 1923 amended the 1919 Act in providing that local authorities were empowered to withdraw or modify provisions contained in a scheme which had given rise to an award of compensation.

In 1925, the first piece of legislation was passed which related solely to town planning: the Town Planning Act 1925, which was largely a consolidating Act.

The Town and Country Planning Act (TCPA) 1932 was a particularly significant piece of legislation for a number of reasons:

(a) it introduced in its title for the first time the concept of planning in non-urban areas;

(b) it provided local authorities with the opportunity to prepare planning schemes for any land in England and Wales and not purely suburban land as in previous legislation; and

(c) it provided an opportunity to prepare schemes for developed areas in addition to green field sites.

Whilst the provisions of the Act were purely permissive, and approval was required from the Minster of Health, the approved scheme was binding on the local authority and those wishing to carry out development.

It was becoming apparent in the 1930s that the older industrial areas were experiencing a period of prolonged and, in some areas, severe economic depression. The gravity of the situation had been highlighted by the General Strike in 1926. The economic imbalance between the London metropolis, which continued to grow in a haphazard manner, and the rest of the country, led to the appointment of Commissioners for Special Areas to investigate the problems, and they reported that much of the growth was not based upon strictly economic factors. Their reports led to the Royal Commission on the Distribution of the Industrial Population (the Barlow Commission). The Barlow Report (Cmd 6153), published in 1940, found that the concentrations of industrial populations in the cities created dangers to the nation's life and development, and that action should be taken by the government towards remedying the situation. The report also drew attention to the serious loss of agricultural land and this was the subject of a setting up of a further committee on Land Utilisation in Rural Areas under the chairmanship of Scott LJ. The Scott Report (1942, Cmd 6378) urged that more attention should be given to the siting of development to preserve agricultural land, and both reports were critical of the operation of the 1932 Act which they argued was not capable of checking the outward spread of towns and the consequent tendency to increase central density and traffic congestion. Although planning legislation was radically altered by the later 1947 Act, these problems remain a constant problem for planners over 50 years later.

1.5 THE SECOND WORLD WAR

During the period of the Second World War (1939–45), little physical development was carried out unless it was directly connected with the paramount needs of equipping and defending the country. It was not until 1943 that the government turned its legislative attention to planning following the publication of the Barlow and Scott Reports. The Minister of Town and Country Planning Act 1943, appointed for the first time a minister who was:

> ... charged with the responsibility of securing consistency and continuity in the framing and execution of national policy with respect to the use and development of land throughout England and Wales [s 1].

A second Act in 1943, The Town and Country (Interim Development) Act, provided that all land in England and Wales be deemed subject to interim development control, provided by the 1932 Act, irrespective of whether or not the local authority had passed a resolution to prepare a planning scheme.

The TCPA 1944 made provision to deal with the extensive war-damaged areas (blitzed areas), in the towns and cities of the UK. With the end of the war in sight, the need to make provision for the redevelopment of these areas was becoming more urgent. The Act provided power for local authorities compulsorily to acquire these areas, as well as areas of poor layout and obsolete development, and, in addition, land which would be required to accommodate the relocation of uses (overspill areas). It also empowered local authorities themselves to carry out the redevelopment of these areas.

The publishing of the Abercrombie 'Greater London Plan' (HMSO) in 1945 had an immediate and lasting effect upon planning policies which were to be adopted when hostilities ceased. The main policies related to decentralisation of population and industry from overcrowded cities, the establishing of a series of 'self-contained' new towns designed to accommodate those to be moved out of the cities, and also a green belt to prevent the further outward sprawl of major towns. Of these three basic policies, that which related to green belts remains a major element in current planning; the continuing pressure for decentralisation is now frequently resisted because of the need to regenerate cities and also to encourage sustainable development.

1.6 THE IMMEDIATE POST-WAR PERIOD

The years immediately following the cessation of the Second World War heralded a period when not only was there a desperate need to rebuild the fabric of the country ravaged by six years of war, but also a national desire to build for the citizens 'a greater and better Britain'. This was to be achieved by a State-run economy which saw widespread nationalisation of public utilities, the coal, iron and steel industries, the railway system and also the setting up of the National Health Service and a new education system. Physical planning was also at the forefront of government thinking, and following the recommendations of the Barlow and Scott Reports, the New Towns Act 1946 provided a planned opportunity to carry out the dispersal of population and industry. The Act granted the minister the power to designate land for new towns, and also to set up State-appointed New Town Development Corporations to carry out the development subject to the approval of the minister.

This policy of new town development, which was based upon the success of the Garden Cities of Letchworth and Welwyn, and the philosophies of Ebenezer Howard, led to the creation of what were intended to be 'self-contained' new settlements built at relatively low residential densities. They also provided town planners with an ideal opportunity to progress principles of a balanced neighbourhood community (balanced in the sense of social groupings and also local facilities such as shops and schools), segregation of land uses, pedestrian and vehicular segregation both in town centres, for example, Stevenage, and in housing areas in accordance with the 'Radburn Principle' of segregation which involves vehicular access at the rear of houses, and an integrated system of landscaped footpaths giving pedestrian access to the front. This particular form of housing layout did not prove popular but nevertheless the overall influence of new towns on subsequent development elsewhere cannot be underestimated. Most public and private development since shows the influence of the early new towns, and the much maligned social engineering which was attempted by the creation of balanced neighbourhoods may yet reappear with the current efforts to ensure that large-scale residential development contain an element of low-cost housing.

The designation of new towns was also 'backed up' by 'Town Expansion Schemes' throughout the South East of England, whereby agreements were drawn up between market towns, which acted as the 'importing authorities', and London boroughs which were the 'exporting authorities' of sections of their population (largely young, mobile families).

The creation of extensive green belts was undertaken as envisaged in the Abercrombie Plan, by using planning powers in the TCPA 1947, to ensure that existing towns and cities, in particular London, did not continue to create fresh suburban sprawl which, if unchecked, was likely to result in the coalescence of existing settlements. This form of green belt differed both in extent and function from that envisaged in the Green Belt (London and Homes Counties) Act 1938 which allowed urban authorities to acquire land in adjoining rural areas to provide green spaces for recreational use by the urban population. The concept of a green belt, that is land surrounding a built-up area, is a British phenomenon which should be contrasted with the alternative 'Copenhagen finger plan' approach in Denmark where open land is retained which forms 'fingers' of space which penetrate into the city. Circular 42/55, Green Belts, issued by the then Minister of Housing and Local Government, made it clear that government policy was to encourage lpas to consider the provision of green belts which were to be several miles wide as a means of 'checking the unrestricted sprawl of the built-up areas, and of safeguarding the surrounding countryside against further encroachment' (para 1). Green belts are now a firmly established principle in town planning in England and Wales (there are none in Scotland), and are generally regarded by the public as inviolate. However, they exist only because of policies contained in plans prepared by lpas and, as such, declared boundaries of existing green belts can be altered if circumstances require such a change. Current government policy on green belts is contained in Planning Policy Guidance Note (PPG) 2 and retains the original objectives of green belts which were to:

(a) check the unrestricted sprawl of large built up areas;

(b) prevent neighbouring towns from merging into one another;

(c) assist in safeguarding the countryside from encroachment; and

(d) preserve the setting and special character of historic towns.

Current government policy includes a further objective which is to:

(e) assist in urban regeneration by encouraging the recycling of derelict and other urban land.

The TCPA 1947 provided the framework for the present form of planning law. It repealed all previous planning legislation with the important exception of the Minister of Town and Country Planning Act 1943, and set up a powerful and highly centralised system of control. This centralisation of control in the immediate post-war period can be justified by three main factors:

1   many of the new lpas, which were the county councils and county borough councils, had no real experience of planning as an activity of local government;

2   a drastic shortage of experienced and professionally qualified planning staff; and

3   the political thinking of the time was based upon a State run economy with a consequent high level of centralisation.

Following the Uthwatt Report (1942, Cmd 6386), which dealt with the vexed question of compensation and betterment arising from the changed value of land when it has the benefit of a planning consent, the 1947 Act nationalised the development rights to land. Prior to this legislation landowners enjoyed a right to develop land and an entitlement to compensation if permission was refused by the State, but the 1947 Act deprived owners of their previous rights. No landowner would retain the right to develop his land without gaining prior approval from the State; as a consequence, no compensation would be payable to the landowner if planning consent is refused since no individual rights remained to develop land. This removal of the right of the individual proved to be the most significant factor in the new planning legislation. (There were minor exceptions to this rule which related to permissions granted under the interim development control provisions contained in the 1932 Act.) It was also recognised that land enjoying the benefit of planning permission would immediately increase in value in the market and this 'windfall gain', that is the difference of the land with the benefit of planning permission and its existing use value. This increase was to be paid to the State in the form of tax, known as a development charge. Land bought by the State under compulsory purchase powers would be acquired at existing use value. It has been argued that this resulted in land not being brought forward for development as there was little or no financial incentive to the owner to release land to another party to carry out development.

Following the recommendation of the Barlow Commission, applications for planning permission to build factory premises also required a supporting certificate issued by the Board of Trade. These 'industrial development certificates' were aimed at directing new industrial development to those areas which were in decline, and to prevent further industrial growth in and around Greater London.

All lpas were required to produce plans at statutory approved scales: six inches to one mile in the case of built-up areas, known as town maps, and one inch to one mile in rural areas, known as county plans. The format of these plans were set out in minute detail by central government including the thickness of line, the precise colours to be used to denote land uses, and the gap between hatched lines. In addition to the plan itself, there was a plan showing the phasing of development and written documents covering survey and analysis, and the supporting written statement. The plan essentially 'allocated' land for primary land uses as distinct from the principle of zoning. This was an important departure from previous practice and ensured a degree of flexibility in the final form of development, for example, land allocated for residential development did not exclude other compatible uses such as shops, churches, etc. This concept of land allocation has continued to be the basis of plans prepared under the British system.

The resulting plans were the subject of public objections, all of which had to be heard and determined by the minister (now known as the Secretary of State for the Environment, Transport and the Regions). The principle of public participation had yet to establish itself in the planning system, and the only right granted to the individual was that of a formal objection to a plan conceived by the planning authority. In addition to the time required to prepare the plans in accordance with the strict requirements set down by central government, the inquiry procedure took months, and in some cases years, before final approval of the plan by the minister. Given all the constraints it is not surprising that progress to achieving statutory approved plans was painfully slow and many plans were out of date by the time they gained statutory approval.

Although the production of plans suffered major delays, the physical environment of vast areas of British cities was being changed beyond recognition by the government's policy on slum clearance. Two powers existed which could be used by local authorities in tackling the problems of slum clearance. The first was embodied in the TCPA 1944, which allowed authorities to acquire areas of bad layout and obsolete development and land for overspill; the second was by using powers under the Housing Act 1949 to acquire property classified as a 'slum' by the Public Health Inspector. The 1950s and 1960s was a period when local authorities were vying with one another to prove the effectiveness of their clearance and rehousing programmes. The result was that in many areas the general public became disillusioned by 'planning'. The largely unchallenged arguments for retaining high residential densities resulted in the erection of high-rise blocks of flats. This physical solution to the problems of rehousing slum dwellers was supported by the grant structure from central government, and the need to erect new dwellings speedily and cheaply by using largely untried methods of prefabrication. This was the period when almost all investment in housing and housing development was carried out by the local authority with subsidies from the State. The Victorian principles of dealing with social and health problems by a purely physical solution were apparent in this drive to provide new homes, irrespective of the fact that the families may have to be relocated on the periphery of existing towns, or that they would find difficulty in paying for the increased costs of transport to work and the new accommodation. The events in the recent past, including the demolition of tower blocks, or their sale to the private sector for £1, are evidence of the failure of this particular solution to the post-war housing problem.

The Planning Acts of 1953 and 1954 altered the financial provisions of the TCPA 1947, and the 1959 and 1960 Acts made three significant changes. First, they allowed a person to serve a purchase notice on the local authority in cases of planning blight, that is where an individual is unable to dispose of his property on the open market because of a declared intention of the local council to carry out a planning scheme in the area which affects that property (see Chapter 28, para 28.7). In many instances, these situations arose because of an impending slum clearance programme. Secondly, the 1959 Act marked a return to full market value, including the benefit of enhancement which came about because of land allocations in development plans. Thirdly, it made provision for appeals to the courts on points of law arising from the operation of the planning system.

1.7 THE 1960s AND 1970s

The 1962 Act was a consolidating Act, which effectively meant that the 1947 Act and the subsequent amendments were incorporated into the new legislation. The vexed question of 'windfall gains' arising from planning permissions was once again on the political agenda and prior to the 1964 General Election, the Labour Party's election programme contained a proposal to set up a Land Commission which would be given power to acquire all land required for development purposes on the basis of existing use value, plus an increment to the owner (assumed to be 60%). When elected, the Labour government found it impracticable to acquire all development land and therefore it announced it would set up a Land Commission which would have the power to acquire selected land at existing use value, plus part of the development value. Land not acquired by the Commission would change hands at market value and to overcome the problem of two price systems a levy of 40% of the net development value would be paid to the Exchequer. The Land Commission came into effect on 1 February 1967 but no betterment levy was payable on development commenced before 6 April 1967. The result was predictable: a vast number of hasty starts to development proposals ensued and, as a result, the actual sum collected was comparatively small. With a change in government the Act was repealed in 1970.

The early 1960s saw a growing demand from private developers to invest in the redevelopment of town centres which, in most cases, had not been the subject of major change since the 1930s. The statutory planning system which required that plans for urban areas should be produced at a scale of six inches to one mile proved incapable of providing the level of detail required for the planning of town centre renewal. The government, therefore, published advice on the redevelopment of town centres in 'Planning Bulletin No 1, Town Centres – Approach to Renewal' (1962, HMSO), which acknowledged the need to produce larger scale plans for such areas, that is, at a scale of 1/1250. As these larger scale plans did not constitute statutory plans, that is not at an approved scale of six inches or one inch to one mile, the formal right of objection to plans as embodied in the 1947 Act did not exist. The principle of public involvement during the preparation of the plan, rather than merely a right of formal objection to the final plan prepared by the local planning authority (lpa), was established in para 24 of the Bulletin:

> ... for this purpose (the town centre map) what is wanted is not a plan suitable for statutory submission to the minister ... If such a map is prepared and is used as the basis of planning in the central area and is available for public examination and discussion, the minister will take full account of it in any matter which comes to him for a decision.

The extension of this principle to public involvement in the preparation of statutory plans was included in the provisions of the 1968 Act (see below).

1967 saw the passing by Parliament of the Civic Amenities Act, which introduced the concept of conservation areas and also strengthened existing legislation in relation to the preservation of trees and buildings of architectural or historic interest.

The continuing slow progress in the approval of plans, required under the 1947 Act, led the government to appoint members to the Planning Advisory Group (PAG) whose brief was to review the system of town and country planning. Their report, published in 1965, accepted that the development control system was effective, but was critical of the plan production system which produced plans which were out of date and technically inadequate. The Group saw the need for a more flexible form of plan, and recommended that there should be broad structure plans which would require ministerial approval, and detailed local plans which would be approved locally. It was assumed by the Group that these plans would be produced by a single-tier planning authority.

The 1968 Act put these recommendations into effect, but only selected authorities were entitled to use these new forms of plan, and this was not on the basis of single-tier authorities as envisaged by PAG, but a two-tier basis whereby county councils would prepare structure plans and the district authorities would be responsible for the detailed local plans.

The Act also included legislation designed to ensure that the participation of the public was to take place in the formulation of the plans, and unless there was satisfactory evidence submitted to the Secretary of State (SoS) that the local authority had provided opportunities for adequate participation the SoS could refuse to consider the plan. The problem lay in the fact that although the minister could return a submitted plan on the basis that the accompanying statement showed that the lpa efforts to involve the public were in his view held to be inadequate, there was no guidance from central government as to what those requirements might entail. In an attempt to fill this gap the government set up a committee to look into the question of public participation in planning, which resulted in the publication of the Skeffington Committee Report, 'People and Planning' (1969, HMSO). In accordance with the political thinking of the time the use of the word 'participation' is relevant as it suggests a greater degree of public involvement. Whether this is a fact or not is a matter of continuing debate!

The election of a Labour government saw the enactment of the Local Government Act 1974, which heralded changes to both the structure and responsibilities of planning authorities by the provision of a two-tier structure for planning functions. The whole country was divided into new metropolitan counties and non-metropolitan counties, that is, the old county councils, each county being made up of constituent district councils which were also to have planning powers. The county councils were made statutorily responsible for the preparation of structure plans, whilst the preparation of detailed local plans was left entirely to the discretion of district councils.

This was followed by yet another attempt to deal with escalating land values as a result of the granting of planning permission. The Community Land Act 1975 had two main objectives which were set out in a White Paper (Cmd 5730):

1   to enable the community to control development of land in accordance with its needs and priorities; and

2   to restore to the 'community' the increase in value of land arising from its efforts.

The second objective relating to the 'community' was somewhat misleading as the money which accrued from the operation of the legislation was to be paid to the Exchequer and not the local authority. When fully operational, the legislation intended that all land would be acquired at existing use value and when land was sold by the local authority it would do so at market value.

1.8　THE 1980s

The election of a Conservative government in 1979 led to a series of reviews and changes to a planning system which was held to be responsible, in no short measure, for the delay in improving the economic well being of the country. The Local Government Planning and Land Act 1980 saw the first measure to speed up the planning process by the powers granted to the SoS to create Enterprise Zones (EZs), and to declare Urban Development Corporations, to ensure the redevelopment of inner city sites, the first of which were designed to tackle the problems of old dockland areas, for example, London Docklands and Liverpool Docklands. The principle of reduced planning involvement was part of the incentive offered to developers in EZs which was later expanded to apply to Simplified Planning Zones by the Housing and Planning Act 1986 (see Chapter 4).

The Community Land Act was repealed in 1980 but the development land tax was initially retained. It was, however, considered to be a discouragement to development and the Chancellor of the Exchequer finally abolished the tax in 1985.

As part of this continuing review, the planning responsibilities set out in the 1974 Act were considered to amount to an unnecessary duplication of control and the Local Government Act 1985 abolished the metropolitan county councils on 1 April 1986, thus leaving a system of single-tier authorities in metropolitan areas, and an unaltered two-tier system in rural areas. This is the system which operates at the present time and the number of single-tier authorities has been increased following the subsequent reorganisation of local government which took place in April 1996.

The Use Classes Order was reviewed in 1987, bringing it up to date and also providing opportunities for changes of use of buildings or land, without the need to gain planning consent. Likewise, the permitted development rights contained in the General Development Order were reviewed in 1988.

Central government also took steps to encourage private investment, and at the same time, to curtail local government expenditure. Partnerships between the private sector, and both central and local government, were seen as the most appropriate method of ensuring that development proceeded, particularly with the creation of new job opportunities, and the regeneration of the inner cities. Local authorities also became more aware of the possibility of tying the granting of planning permission to the provision of additional public facilities to be financed by the developer, that is, planning gain. Following the 1968 TCPA, agreements with developers to provide elements of 'planning gain' no longer required the prior approval of the minister, and this newly found freedom was actively pursued by those planning authorities where there was an ever growing pressure from the private sector to take advantage of opportunities for both development and redevelopment (see Chapter 15).

The principle of dispersal of industry and population, which was such an important element of planning policy in the immediate post-war period, was being questioned as large areas of cities were left in a derelict or semi-derelict state because of the success of that earlier policy. The need to obtain an industrial development certificate was abandoned and industry was free to locate where it considered there were economic advantages of land values, proximity to markets and where the skills demanded could be satisfied. The creation of out of town shopping centres and the movement of new 'high-tech industries' to 'green field' sites as a result of private initiatives was eventually realised to be a major factor in accentuating the problems of the inner city areas which successive governments had recognised required attention.

During this period, it is argued that planning was 'developer led' because of the government's determination that private investment initiatives should not be stifled by the planning system. Where lpas refused planning permission, their decisions were frequently overruled by the then SoS, Nicholas Ridley. During this period, many lpas failed to use their discretionary powers to prepare local plans for their areas but where a plan was produced the lpa and the SoS were simply required to 'have regard to the plan' in the determination of individual planning applications. The late 1980s saw a change in government policy resulting in greater a tightening of planning control within the existing planning legislation which serves to highlight the fundamental importance of government policies in relation to the operation of the planning machinery. This change in policy was to prove to be the beginning of a review of planning legislation which resulted in the TCPA 1990.

The TCPA 1990 and the Planning (Listed Buildings and Conservation Areas) Act 1990 saw the pendulum swing back in favour of greater planning control and the statutory requirement that district councils shall prepare local plans. The 1990 Act was almost immediately amended by the Planning and Compensation Act 1991, with changes designed to improve the enforcement procedures against breaches of planning control and, more importantly, the insertion of s 54A which now requires that planning decisions are made in accordance with the plan unless material circumstances suggest otherwise. Not only must lpas produce local plans but they are now required to make planning decisions based upon the content of the plan and not merely 'have regard' to it as was the case under earlier legislation.

The new emphasis was to control outward expansion and to place even greater emphasis on urban renewal and the redevelopment of 'brown field' sites rather than continuing outward expansion. This, in part, was the government's reaction to the growing environmental lobby both in the UK and at an international level. The planning system has taken on a new responsibility to give due weight to the issue of sustainability both in plan-making and in controlling development proposals.

The plan-making functions of local authorities, albeit with plans which have a different format and content, are now almost back to the situation which applied under the TCPA 1947. Once again, plans *must* be prepared by the relevant authority. The role of the plan in determining planning applications has, however, been enhanced as a result of s 54A. However, the immediate post-war problem of producing and adopting plans remains. There is complete coverage of those parts of the country covered by structure plans, that is, the shire counties, and most of the metropolitan districts have unitary development plans but, by 1997, it is estimated that less than 50% of districts have adopted local plans. The major contrast with the 1950s is that central government control over the preparation and adoption of local plans has been relaxed and in most instances they no longer require the approval of the SoS.

1.9   THE 1990s

Since the 1997 general election, the Labour government has pursued two main projects which directly affect the working of the planning system. The first includes devolution, following the establishment of the Parliament for Scotland, the Irish and

Welsh Assemblies, the setting up of Regional Development Agencies (RDAs) in England and the creation of a new planning authority for Greater London. The second is an ongoing review of the planning system following the publication in 1993 by the Department of the Environment, Transport and the Regions of their report, *Modernising Planning*. The general object of this report is the speeding up of the planning process, coupled with a firm commitment to utilise brown field sites and develop an integrated land use transportation policy within a general framework of sustainable development. As a result, a number of PPGs have been updated and further changes are anticipated with a number of draft documents in the pipeline. The continuing slow progress in the preparation of development plans remains a matter of major concern that has resulted in a revision of the steps required for the submission and approval of plans.

1.10   THE NEW MILLENNIUM

The new millennium heralded changes in both the structure of those departments of central government responsible for land use and also major changes in planning legislation. Following the government's return to office the Department of Environment, Transport and Planning (DETR) was abolished in June 2001 and replaced by the Department of Transport, Local Government and the Regions (DTLR). A second new ministry, the Department for the Environment, Food and Rural Affairs, replaced the Ministry of Agriculture Fisheries and Food with responsibility for environmental policy in addition to the former functions of its predecessor.

The DTLR proved to be one of the shortest-lived Departments as it was abolished in May 2002, ending the direct link between planning and transport in Whitehall. Following the demerger of the DTLR the new separate Department of Transport was created. The responsibility for regional and local government, planning, housing, and regeneration (including the social exclusion unit and neighbourhood renewal), was transferred to the Office of the Deputy Prime Minister. The Deputy Prime Minister is also a SoS and he is now styled in decision letters as 'the First Secretary of State'.

Changes in the administrative system have not been restricted to the machinery of central government. The Regional Development Agencies Act 1998 (s 11(1)) made provision for nine regions in England (including London) and the subsequent Regional Assemblies (Preparations) Act 2003 allows each of the English regions to establish an elected assembly if approved by a local referendum, the first of which was held in the North East of England in November 2004. This 'test case' for the setting up of the first elected Regional Assembly resulted in an overwhelming 'no' vote. Nevertheless the Act enables the government to specify further regions where referenda will be held should it choose to do so. It appears more likely that the government will accept that Regional Planning Bodies will remain unelected. It is required that not less than 60% of the body will be made up of members from district councils, county councils, metropolitan district councils, National Park Authorities and The Broads Authority: Planning and Compulsory Purchase Act 2004 (s 2(3), (4)).

Planning legislation has been the subject of major changes long heralded by the government. Following the publication of a Green Paper in December 2001 and, after a gestation period of almost two and half years, the Planning and Compulsory Purchase Act finally received Royal Assent on 13 May 2004. This Act amends the TCPA 1990 and introduces a new development plan regime, certain changes to the development control system and reform to compulsory purchase law. The government's stated objectives for the new Act are to speed up the planning system, to make it more predictable and fair and to improve public participation. In addition, as a general policy, tests are to be applied throughout in both plan-making and development control with particular regard to the principles of sustainable development.

The government's commitment to sustainable development was set out in 'A Better Quality of Life' (DETR May, 1999). This document sets four broad objectives: maintenance of high and stable levels of economic growth and employment; social progress which recognises the needs of everyone; effective protection of the environment; and prudent use of natural resources. A sustainability appraisal and strategic environmental assessment will be required to be integral processes in the Local Development Document assessing the impact of policies from environmental, economic and social perspectives.

CHAPTER 2

CENTRAL AND LOCAL GOVERNMENT

2.1   THE SECRETARY OF STATE

The planning of both town and country is a political process. Under the Town and Country Planning Act (TCPA) 1947, the then Minister for Town and Country Planning was charged with the administration of planning throughout England (Wales, Scotland and Northern Ireland had their own ministers). Over the years, the titles have changed but primary legislation refers to the Secretary of State (SoS). At the present time the post is occupied by the Deputy Prime Minister and in recent appeal decisions he is referred to as 'The First Secretary of State' whilst pronouncements on planning issues originate from the 'Office of the Deputy Prime Minister'.

The SoS is an elected member of Parliament chosen by the Prime Minister to head this particular department of government. It also provides the holder with a place within the Cabinet and, therefore, the postholder is directly involved in the policies adopted by the government including those related to the control and development of land. Whilst those involved in the planning profession frequently regard this post as purely carrying out the responsibilities for planning, there are other and equally onerous duties attached to the post, including local government, and particularly local government finance.

The post of SoS is essentially that of administering planning based upon the policies of the government and it is answerable to Parliament. This allows individual members to raise issues by means of formal parliamentary questions or by correspondence with the SoS. There are, however, two circumstances when it is *not* appropriate to raise issues with the SoS: the rules of *sub judice* must apply when the matter is the subject of an appeal to the SoS or when he has been called upon to make a determination. The fact that the duty is purely one of administering the planning process and is not a judicial process was established by the courts at a very early stage. In 1947, in the case *Franklin v Minister of Town and Country Planning* [1948] AC 87, which related to the New Town Act 1946, Lord Thankerton stated:

> … in my opinion, no judicial, or quasi-judicial duty, was placed upon the respondent, and any reference to judicial duty, or bias, is irrelevant in the present case. The responsible duties are, in my opinion, purely administrative, but the Act prescribes certain methods of, or steps in, discharge of that duty. I am of the opinion that no judicial duty is laid on the respondent in discharge of these statutory duties, that the only question is whether he has complied with the statutory directions to appoint a person to hold a public inquiry and to consider that person's report.

It is, therefore, clear that the SoS, in addition to being responsible to Parliament, can also be held to be responsible for his actions by the courts whose duty is to ensure that those actions are within the powers granted to the SoS by legislation, that is not *ultra vires*. The courts, in carrying out this duty, have a responsibility to consider the administrative process by which decisions are made but are not entitled to grant planning permission. Should they find against the SoS then the matter is referred back to him for reconsideration.

The duties and powers granted to the SoS can be summarised as follows:

(a) to ensure that local planning authorities carry out the duties placed upon them by the TCPA 1990 as amended by the Planning and Compulsory Purchase Act 2004;

(b) to prepare regional guidance which is to be incorporated in plans prepared by the responsible local authorities;

(c) to provide local planning authorities and others involved in the process of development with statements of current government policies;

(d) power granted under the Act to make delegated legislation;

(e) power to call in planning applications for his own determination rather than that of the local planning authority; and

(f) a quasi-judicial function in the determination of appeals against decisions made by local planning authorities.

The (SoS) survived a major challenge to his quasi-judicial functions following the Human Rights Act 1998 (s 6) which requires civil rights to be determined by a fair and public hearing before an impartial tribunal. Four cases collectively known as the *Alconbury case, R v Secretary of State for the Environment, Transport and the Regions ex p Holding and Barnes plc* [2001] PLR 58 were considered by the High Court. These involved decisions by the SoS in respect of two call-in applications, a decision under the Transport and Works Act 1992 and a decision regarding a compulsory purchase and highway orders. The High Court concluded that:

> In terms of Article 6 the decision on the merits, which usually involves findings of fact and planning judgement, have not been determined by an independent and impartial tribunal or anyone approaching this, but by someone who is obviously not independent or impartial.

Such was the importance and likely impact of this decision on the operation of the entire planning system that the matter was referred immediately to the House of Lords. In an unanimous decision the Law Lords restored the status quo finding that s 6 need not be applied at all stages of decision-making and following *Bryan v UK* [1996] JPL 386; EG 137, that it was sufficient that the citizen should be entitled at some stage to an independent tribunal. That need not be at the stage of determining the merits of the matter and it is sufficient that there is a right of judicial review of the merits of the decision.

As the SoS has overall responsibility for town and country planning it is inevitable that he should exercise control over the activities of local planning authorities. The SoS is responsible for publishing the guidance in the form of Regional Policy Guidance (RPG) after consultation with the constituent local planning authorities and other agencies likely to be involved in future development, for example, statutory undertakers, the House Builders' Federation, and Chambers of Commerce.

Under the legislation, the SoS has powers to formulate policies in relation to all matters provided that the policies are founded on considerations which are material in planning terms. Perhaps surprisingly, there is no requirement to formulate policies in any particular way, or indeed to have any policies at all. It has long been established by the courts that the SoS is responsible for the administration of planning functions but there are no formal requirements for the publication of government policy. Provided there is an accurate record of what has been said, the SoS may express himself in any way he may choose and the courts have accepted that policies can be expressed in the form of government White Papers, Circulars, Policy Guidance (Planning Policy

Guidance Notes (PPGs)), previous decisions (*North Wilts DC v Secretary of State and Glover* [1992] JPL 955; 3 PLR 113; (1993) 65 P & CR 137), written parliamentary answers (*R v Secretary of State ex p Surrey Heath BC* (1984) 16 HLR 7), and even after-dinner speeches (*Dimsdale Developments (South East) Ltd v Secretary of State and Hounslow LBC* [1986] JPL 276; 2 EGLR 183).

It is, however, more usual for the SoS to announce government land use policies by the publication of PPGs, Planning Policy Statements (PPSs), Minerals Policy Guidance (MPG) and by advising local planning authorities on the mechanics of the administration of their planning functions by means of circulars. These are not statutory documents. They are an indication of the government's policies which will be taken into account in any matter brought to the attention of the SoS, for example, development plans and the determination of planning appeals, and in the case of Circulars, the mechanics of operating and administering the planning system.

The SoS is also empowered under the Planning Acts to make rules and orders in respect of the administrative process of planning, for example, General Development Orders (GDOs) (see Chapter 10) and the Use Classes Order (UCO) (see Chapter 8). These are in essence additions to the primary legislation contained in the Act although they are technically 'laid before Parliament', rather than being the subject of debates in both Houses.

Under the Local Government Planning and Land Act 1980, power was granted to the SoS to declare Urban Development Corporations, for example, Thurrock Development Corporation (see Chapter 4, para 4.11) and Enterprise Zones (EZs), for example, Gateshead (see Chapter 4, para 4.2). Both are designed to promote the regeneration of urban areas. These initiatives were followed by an extension of the EZ principle by powers to encourage local planning authorities to consider, and also declare, the creation of Simplified Planning Zones (SPZs), for example, Derby (see Chapter 4, para 4.7), under the Housing and Planning Act 1986. In 1993, the powers of the SoS were further enhanced with the setting up of the Urban Regeneration Agency, now retitled English Partnership, under the Leasehold Reform and Urban Regeneration Act 1993 (see Chapter 4, para 4.16).

The SoS retains the power under the TCPA 1990 (s 2) to create a single body as the county planning authority for areas of two or more shire counties. Similarly, the power is granted to constitute a joint planning board for any two or more district councils. Such an order setting up a joint planning board first requires that a public inquiry is held unless the local government councils concerned consent to the making of the order (s 2(2)). This power was initially used in 1951 to create the Lake District Planning Board (SI 1951/1419) and the Peak District Planning Board (SI 1951/1533).

Reserve powers are also granted to the SoS to call in particular types of planning applications. These are normally applications which have either regional significance, or applications which prove to be highly controversial. In such cases, the decision by the SoS can only be given after a local inquiry. The same call in power extends to plans produced by local planning authorities. A further responsibility is to make decisions when an appeal is lodged against the decision of a local planning authority which the original applicant considers to be unreasonable. Under normal circumstances, the decision of the SoS is final in such appeals unless the matter is pursued through the courts on a point of law, that is, the SoS is charged with erring in the administration of the matter or his legal interpretation of the facts (see Chapter 17).

It should be noted that, whilst decisions taken on a day-to-day basis are the responsibility of the SoS, this function is, in most cases, delegated to civil servants employed at either the headquarters of the Department of the Environment, London, or the Government Regional Offices. Planning appeals are dealt with by the Appeals Agency in Bristol. The SoS is, however, held responsible to both Parliament and the courts for action taken either by himself in person, or others acting in his name.

2.2   NATIONAL PLANNING POLICY

Although the SoS is 'charged with the responsibility of securing consistency and continuity in the framing and execution of national policy' under the Minister of Town and Country Planning 1943 (s 1), this did not take the form of a national plan as in some other countries, that is, a plan for the development of land on a state-wide basis. The closest approach to some form of national plan is contained in Regional Planning Guidance (RPG) which provide broad planning frameworks for each region.

At a national level the government's planning policy guidance on particular planning issues have, until recently, been by way of PPGs. The government is currently revising all PPGs and MPGs and replacing them with PPSs with the stated intention to:

> seek to reduce the volume of guidance and increase its clarity; we will prescribe less policy at a national level and ensure that PPSs are more concise, clearer and better focused on implementation of policy objectives.

> (Sustainable Communities – Delivering through Planning para 18) (OPDM, 2002)).

Local planning authorities are charged with implementing these policies and, although they appear as 'guidance notes' or 'policy statements', the courts have held that as statements of government policy, they are material considerations which *must* be taken into account, where relevant, in decisions on planning application. If a local planning authority elects not to follow relevant statements of government policy, they must give clear and convincing reasons (see *Grandsen (EC) and Co Ltd v Secretary of State and Gillingham BC* [1986] JPL 519; (1987) 54 P & CR 86).

The main thrust of government policy is towards sustainable development, the protection of the environment and amenity and the need to minimise the need to travel. Urban regeneration remains an important objective as this is intended to re-use previously development land (brown field sites) which will assist in creating a more sustainable pattern of development coupled with the need to increase the density of housing. This emphasis on re-use is complemented by policies which are designed to ensure that the amount of agricultural land (green field sites) required for development is kept to a minimum. In rural areas it is accepted that the planning function is to integrate development necessary to sustain economic activity with the protection of the countryside.

Amplification of the general planning policies contained in PPS1 'Creating Sustainable Communities' is provided on the following planning issues:

PPG 2   Green Belts

PPG 3   Housing

PPG 4   Industrial Development

PPG 5   Simplified Planning Zones

PPG 6   Town Centres and Retail Developments

PPS 7   Sustainable Development in Rural Areas

PPG 8   Telecommunications

PPG 9   Nature Conservation

PPS 10   Planning and Waste Management

PPS 11   Regional Spatial Strategies

PPS 12   Local Development Frameworks

PPG 13   Transport

PPG 14   Development on Unstable Land

PPG 15   Planning and Historic Environment

PPG 16   Archaeology and Planning

PPG 17   Sport and Recreation

PPG 18   Enforcing Planning Control

PPG 19   Outdoor Advertising Control

PPG 20   Coastal Planning

PPG 21   Tourism

PPS 22   Renewable Energy

PPS 23   Planning and Pollution Control

PPG 24   Planning and Noise

PPG 25   Development and Flood Risk

Note: The advice contained in PPGs is constantly being added to and/or amended and revised documents are published as PPSs. It is the government's intention that PPGs will be superseded by a new series of PPSs and that these will be more streamlined and focused.

2.3   LOCAL GOVERNMENT

The units of local government and the functions they undertake are determined by Parliament: in other words, local government in Britain exists purely at the discretion of Parliament. Whilst the Planning and related Acts set down the responsibilities of 'planning authorities', this is a generic term. The units of local government and their functions (including planning responsibilities) are determined by the Local Government Act 1985, as amended by orders after the findings of the 1996 Commission on Local Government.

The 1985 Act resulted in major changes in the format of local government in England and Wales as a result of the government's decision to abolish the Greater London Council (GLC) and the six metropolitan councils by the bold statement contained in s 1 which states, 'they shall cease to exist'. Thus, the six metropolitan councils, created by the Local Government Act 1972, namely:

1   Greater Manchester;

2   Merseyside;

3   South Yorkshire;

4   Tyne and Wear;

5   West Midlands; and

6   West Yorkshire,

became purely postal addresses. The abolition of these six metropolitan councils was followed by the abolition of Cleveland County Council in 1996. In each case, the constituent district planning authorities became responsible for all local government functions within their area, including planning. Thus, a major distinction now exists in the planning functions of the metropolitan districts, which are now single-tier planning authorities, and the remaining non-metropolitan districts, or as they are generally known, 'shire counties', where planning functions are shared between the county council and the constituent district councils.

Section 1 of the TCPA 1990 states that:

(a) In a shire county, the county council shall be the county planning authority for the whole county and the shire district councils shall be the district planning authority for their own district.

(b) In a metropolitan county (which had ceased to exist on 1 April 1986), each of the metropolitan districts shall be the planning authority for their own district.

(c) In Greater London (which also ceased to exist), the London boroughs shall be the planning authority for their own borough. This includes the City of London. In April 2000, London re-established a two-tier system with the setting up of the Greater London Authority (see para 2.5).

For those who live in a shire county, there remain two planning authorities, that is, county and district councils, and in many areas there is a third tier of local government, namely, the parish council which is a rural phenomenon and does not exist in urban areas. They are not to be confused with ecclesiastical parishes. Parish councils are not planning authorities but, if they choose, they are entitled to be consulted about applications for planning permission in their area (s 1 of, Sched 1 to the TCPA 1990).

Each of the tiers of planning authority has plan-making responsibilities. Regional development bodies have responsibility for the preparation of Regional Spatial Strategies. Until the new planning system is fully operational county councils retain a structure planning function and thereafter will continue to be responsible for minerals and waste planning. District councils have responsibility for the production of the portfolio of local development plan documents (see Chapter 3). Single-tier metropolitan districts have sole responsibility for both local development documents and minerals/waste planning.

The question of the distribution of development control and enforcement functions in the two-tier shire counties is dealt with in Sched 1(1) to the TCPA 1990. The necessity to gain planning permission for development is contained in s 57 and all such applications are determined by the district council except in the case of a 'county matter' which is determined by the county council. Precisely what constitutes a 'county matter' is defined in Sched 1, para 1 to the TCPA 1990 as:

(a)   mineral working and any related development, including cement works;

(b)   any development which straddles a National Park boundary;

(c) any development prescribed in regulations made under the 1990 Act, which currently make applications for waste disposal a county matter, Town and Country (Prescription of County Matters) Regulation 1980 (SI 1980/2010).

Each planning authority has a duty to consider the appropriateness of enforcement action to ensure that development accords with the law. The exercise of this power is, however, discretionary (see Chapter 18 on enforcement).

2.4 REGIONAL DEVELOPMENT AGENCIES

The Regional Development Agencies Act 1998 established Regional Development Agencies (RDAs) in each of the nine English regions. They are government sponsored bodies with Boards which are business led and which reflect the perspectives and needs of each of the regions and the main interest groups within each region. The members of the Boards are not democratically elected and their appointment is a matter wholly for the SoS.

The prime objectives of the RDAs, as set out in s 4(1) of the Regional Development Agencies Act are:

(a) to further the economic development and the regeneration of its area;

(b) to promote business efficiency, investment and competitiveness in its area;

(c) to promote employment in its area;

(d) to enhance the development and application of skills relevant to employment in its area; and

(e) to contribute to the achievement of sustainable development in the UK where it is relevant to do so.

Section 4(2) makes it clear that the purpose of RDAs relates as much to the rural as well as to the urban parts of its area. To assist in this purpose, the rural regeneration programmes of the Rural Development Commission will be transferred to RDAs. No date for this transfer has been specified.

It should be noted that the RDAs do not have any planning powers and will require planning permission from the relevant local planning authority for any development they may wish to promote. Neither the RDA's own strategic plans, which are to be prepared under s 5 of the Regional Development Agencies Act 1998, nor the RPG will prevail over the other. Concurrence between the two documents is to be achieved by effective working relationships between the RDAs and the local planning authorities in their areas.

The government's intention was to replace these un-elected bodies with elected regional assemblies but following the over-whelming 'no' vote in the referendum held in the North East of England in 2004 it appears unlikely that this intention will be pursued. The existing non-elected bodies look likely to continue for the foreseeable future.

2.5   LONDON

In London, RDAs will be part of the Greater London Authority and are, therefore, established from April 2000 in accordance with the timetable for that authority. Under the Greater London Authority Act 1999, part of the new role of Mayor will be to produce a Spatial Development Strategy.

CHAPTER 3

DEVELOPMENT PLANS

3.1   INTRODUCTION

NB The 2004 Act is *not* a replacement Act and amends the Town and Country Planning Act (TCPA) 1990. All references in this chapter refer to the new Act.

Prior to the changes introduced by the Planning and Compulsory Purchase Act 2004, the hierarchy of plans involved Regional Planning Guidance prepared by the Regional Government Office. In two-tier authorities Structure Plans and District-wide local plans were prepared and in the case of a single-tier Metropolitan District a hybrid Unitary Development Plan was produced that combined the elements of Structure Plans and local plans. These statutory plans will continue to operate under the provisions of the Town and Country Planning (Transitional Regulations) (England) Regulations 2004 (SI 2004/2205) (see para 3.10 and Appendix 1). The new system requires the preparation of Local Development Frameworks (LDFs) that will integrate spatially with strategies having relevant implications outside traditional land use planning. Whilst the term LDF does not appear in the Act it is used to describe a portfolio of documents required to implement the new planning procedure and it contains:

(a) Local Development Scheme (LDS);

(b) Local Development Documents (LDDs);

(c) a Statement of Community Involvement (SCI);

(d) Annual Monitoring Report;

and *may* also include

(e) Area Action Plans (AAPs);

(f) Supplementary Planning Guidance (SPG);

(g) Simplified Planning Zones (SPZs);

(h) Local Development Orders (LDOs); and

(i) other Development Plan Documents (DPDs).

The rationale for the new system is that it will provide greater certainty for the decision-maker but with sufficient in-built flexibility to help deliver regeneration priorities. The other main objective is that the planning system should have the objective of achieving 'sustainable development'. Section 39(2) of the 2004 Act imposes a new duty on persons and bodies responsible for preparing Regional Spatial Strategies (RSSs) and LDDs in England and the Wales Spatial Plan or local development plan (in Wales):

> such person or body must exercise the function with the objective of contributing to the achievement of sustainable development.

3.2 REGIONAL PLANNING

Regional Spatial Strategies are to be prepared by the Regional Planning Boards (RPBs) for each of the eight English regions by the regional chambers whether elected or non-elected. These strategies are statutory, that is, they have a legal status, and it is intended that they should provide a broad development strategy for each region for a 15–20-year period.

An RSS will:

(a) provide a spatial framework to inform the preparation of development documents, local transport plans and regional and sub-regional strategies and programmes that have a bearing on land use activities with particular reference to housing, transport, economic development and the environment; and

(b) be consistent with the objectives set out in the Regional Sustainable Development Framework and with the Regional Transport Strategy.

In the preparation of an RSS the RPB must seek the advice of each authority in the region, namely:

(a) county council;

(b) metropolitan district council;

(c) district council; and

(d) a National Parks authority.

This advice may also relate to the inclusion in the RSS of specific policies relating to any part of the region and should this occur the different provision *must first* be made by a county council, metropolitan district council, or district council or National Park Authority as appropriate. When preparing a revision of the RSS the RPB *must* have regard amongst other matters to the desirability of making different provisions in relation to different parts of the region.

The RPB is required to prepare and publish a statement of its policies as to the involvement of persons who appear to the RPB to have an interest in the exercise of its functions.

The RPB must keep under review the RSS relating to matters which may be expected to affect the development in its region and the planning of development and publish an annual report on the implementation of the RSS. The RPB must also prepare a draft revision of the RSS when it appears necessary or expedient to do so, at such time as is prescribed or if it is directed to do so by the Secretary of State (SoS) (s 5). The draft revision of the RSS must be published and any person may make representations on the draft. The SoS may arrange for an examination in public to be held and in doing so regard must be given to the extent of the revisions, the level of interest shown and such other matters as he thinks appropriate (s 7).

In London the RSS is known as the Spatial Development Strategy (SDS) (or London Plan) which is prepared by the Mayor of London and the London boroughs have responsibility for the preparation of their own DPDs.

The RSS will replace Structure Plans, which will be 'saved' for a period of three years, during which time existing Regional Policy Guidance (RPG) will be revised to reflect the objectives in the emerging RSS.

LDDs must be in general conformity with the RSS.

3.3   LOCAL DEVELOPMENT FRAMEWORKS

Details of LDFs are contained in Planning Policy Statement 12: 'Local Development Frameworks' and these are to be prepared by each local planning authority and, whilst related to the development of land, they should not be restricted to implementation through planning. All policies and proposals in the development plan will be subject to Sustainability Appraisal (SA) and Strategic Environmental Assessment (SEA) to ensure that they reflect sustainable development principles. (NB Sustainable development is defined by the World Commission on the Environment and Development as:

> development that meets the needs of the present without compromising the ability of future generations to meet their own needs.

The requirement to carry out SEA/SA is contained in the European Directive 2001/42/EC and embodied in s 39 and the Environmental Assessment of Plans and Programmes Regulations 2004 (SI 2004/1633). The appraisals are required to consider the significant effects upon biodiversity, population, human health, fauna, flora, soil and water.

(a) **An LDS** The local planning authority *must* prepare and maintain an LDS which must specify (s 15(1)):

- the documents which are to be Local Development Documents (LDDs);
- the subject matter and the area to which it relates;
- the timetable for the preparation and revision of the documents;
- which documents (if any) to be prepared jointly with one or more local planning authorities (lpas);
- such matters as may be prescribed; and
- submit the scheme to the SoS and at the same time to the RPB.

(b) **Supplementary Planning Documents (SPDs)**, which are *not* subject to independent testing and whilst they do not have development plan status they should be the subject of rigorous procedures of community involvement (see para.3.6).

(c) **A Statement of Community Involvement (SCI)**, specifying how the authority intends to involve stakeholders and communities in the process of producing the LLDs. The SCI is subject to independent testing, although it is not a DPD and is required to ensure community involvement:

- appropriate to the level of planning;
- at the *beginning* of the plan preparation process and continuing throughout;
- is seen to be effective;
- is transparent and accountable; and
- is joined up with other community initiatives.

(d) **Annual Monitoring Report** setting out progress in terms of producing LDDs and implementing policies.

The SoS may direct the local planning authority to make such amendments to the scheme as he sees fit but must give reasons for such amendments (s 15(4), (5)).

County councils must prepare and maintain a minerals and waste scheme (MAWS) (s 16(1)).

The local planning authority is required to keep under review matters that may be expected to effect the development of their area or the planning of its development. These matters include:

(a) the principal physical, economic, social and environmental characteristics;

(b) principal land uses in the area;

(c) the size, composition and distribution of population;

(d) communications, transport system and traffic;

(e) any other considerations that may be expected to effect those matters;

(f) such other matters that may be prescribed by the SoS;

(g) changes which the authority think may occur in relation to any other matter; and

(h) the effect such changes are likely to have on the development of the authority's area or the planning of such development.

The local planning authority may also keep under review proposals in neighbouring authorities that are likely to have an effect upon their area and must consult with the local authority for the neighbouring area in question.

County councils must keep under review matters concerning development or the planning of development that relates to a county matter and any such matters that the SoS may require by regulations.

3.4   PROPOSALS MAP

All LDF policies and proposals are to be illustrated in a proposals map in such a manner that they can be understood by both the community and stakeholders. DPDs are to be prepared on an Ordnance Survey base map (at an appropriate scale) to indicate main proposals, designations and locations and areas to which specific policies will apply. It may also include inset maps and indicate where AAPs are to be prepared.

3.5   AREA ACTION PLANS

Area Action Plans can normally be prepared in parallel or subsequent to the preparation of core strategies but if there are relevant 'saved policies' in certain circumstances they can be prepared first. They will focus on implementation.

Area Action Plans or area strategies with a geographical or spatial dimension will be DPDs. It is anticipated that AAPs could be relevant in the following circumstances:

(a) in growth areas, for example urban expansion areas, new settlements and major areas of development potential within existing built-up areas. It would prioritise development objectives, specify phasing, co-ordinate new infrastructure and services as well as identifying broad planning obligations;

(b) in areas where development is not forthcoming but is desirable, for example regeneration areas. It would seek to identify opportunities, act as a catalyst for development and address problems likely to deter delivery;

(c) in areas particularly sensitive to change, for example those with significant natural or cultural heritage value;

(d) in areas in multiple ownership subject to development pressures, for example town centres, in order to attempt to resolve different stakeholders' objectives and also to provide a basis for compulsory purchase orders;

(e) in areas in multiple ownership subject to particular change, for example those benefiting from regeneration initiatives, Business Improvement Districts or Market Town Initiative funding;

(f) when focusing the delivery of area-based initiatives, for example delivery framework for regeneration where there are important land use and development issues; and

(g) when developing minerals and waste action plans, for example to integrate policies in areas of intense mineral working or to set out proposals for major new waste.

Joint AAPs may be prepared where change cuts across lpa boundaries. Where this occurs key milestones would need to be agreed at the outset so that they can be included in the respective LDS.

3.6   SUPPLEMENTARY PLANNING DOCUMENTS

SPDs elaborate on policy and proposals contained in DPDs and they are specified in the LDS in terms of their role and links to other LDDs. Although they do not have development plan status they have weight as a material consideration.

SPDs can include design guides, site development briefs, issue or thematic-based documents. They can also be produced in response to unforeseen events provided such a brief fits with the core strategy. If this cannot be demonstrated then a new amended DPD will be required.

3.7   LOCAL DEVELOPMENT SCHEME: EXAMINATION AND ADOPTION

Local planning authorities must submit the DPD, the Statement of Compliance with the SCI and the Final Sustainability Report to the SoS and arrange for the publication of all three documents.

There is a formal six-week consultation period following the publication of the documents. The lpa is then required to prepare a summary of the representations made on the submission and where such representations include proposals for alternative site allocations the lpa is required to publish these and invite representations in a similar manner to the submitted DPD.

Most representations are dealt with by means of written representations but there remains the right to exercise the right to an oral hearing. The inspector appointed to assess 'the soundness of the plan' has discretion as to which he/she considers the most appropriate means of considering oral representations. This can be by way of round table discussions, hearings or exceptionally by formal inquiry sessions. It is intended to adopt an inquisitorial rather than adversarial approach to dealing with oral representations. Representations or objections which relate to certain matters proposed under Highways Acts 1959, 1961, and 1980 or an Order made under the New Towns Act 1981 may be disregarded by the SoS or the lpa (s 32).

The assessment of 'the soundness of the plan' requires the application of tests set out in Planning Policy Statement 12, namely;

(a) it has been prepared in accordance with the requirements of s 19 and s 24(1) of the Act;

(b) it is consistent with national policy and in general conformity with the RSS and has regard to Community Strategy and other relevant strategies;

(c) it is founded on robust evidence, it is deliverable and there are the most appropriate strategies/policies/allocations; and

(d) there are clear mechanisms for monitoring.

After the examination the inspector is responsible for producing a report that is binding on the lpa. Should modifications be required the inspector's report gives precise recommendations as to how the DPD and the proposals map must be changed and unless the SoS directs otherwise formal adoption by the lpa is based upon this modified document (s 23(1), (2), (3), (4)).

An inspector may also report upon matters that need further consideration and should be brought forward as a review of the DPD, or as a separate DPD, that is, where evidential problems are revealed at the examination or where new sites were the subject of consideration and had not been the subject to SA or SEA.

3.8   ANNUAL MONITORING REPORTS

Each authority is required to prepare an AMR to assess the implementation of the LDS and the extent to which policies in the LDDs are being achieved (s 35(1), (2), (3)). This is to be submitted in December of each year.

3.9   GREATER LONDON

In accordance with the Greater London Authority Act 1999, in Greater London the development plan comprises:

(a) the SDS to be prepared by the Mayor, and

(b) the DPDs which have been adopted or approved in relation to that area.

The strategic overview of planning deals only with matters which are of strategic importance to Greater London (s 334(5)), including:

(a) transport;

(b) a London Development Agency strategy; this is the equivalent of the strategies required to be prepared by Regional Development Agencies (RDAs). (s 7 refers to the London strategy);

(c) a London biodiversity plan;

(d) a municipal waste management strategy;

(e) a London air quality strategy;

(f) a London noise abatement strategy; and

(g) a culture strategy.

Development control remains primarily with the London boroughs but the Mayor is a statutory consultee for a specific range of applications for planning permission that are considered to be of strategic importance and retains the power under s 74 (1990 Planning Act) to direct refusal of any planning application in circumstances when development is considered to be of potential strategic importance. The following categories of development are set out in the Town and Country Planning (Mayor of London) Order 2000 (SI 2000/1493);

3.9.1 Large scale development

Category 1A

1   Development which:

(a) comprises or includes provision for more than 500 houses or houses and flats, or

(b) comprises or includes houses and flats and the development occupies more than 10 hectares.

Category 1B

1   Development, (other than houses or flats) which comprises or includes the erection of a building or buildings:

(a) in the City of London with a total floorspace of more than 30,000 sq m;

(b) in Central London (other than the City) of more than 20,000 sq m;

(c) outside Central London of more than 15,000 sq m.

Category 1C

1   Development which comprises or includes the erection of a building in respect of one or more of the following conditions:

(a) more than 25 m high adjacent to the River Thames;

(b) more than 75 m high in the City of London;

(c) more than 30 m high outside the City of London.

2   A building is adjacent to the River Thames for the purposes of 1(a);

(a) if it is wholly or partly on a site which falls within the area identified as a Thames Policy Area in the development plan, or

(b) where no such area is defined the building is wholly or partly on a site which falls within the Thames Policy Area bounded by the outer edge of the red line on the 'Maps of the Thames Policy Area referred to in the Mayor of London Order 2000.'

Category 1D

1   Development which comprises or includes the alteration of an existing building where:

(a) it would increase the height of the building by more than 15 m and

(b) where the building on completion would be higher than the threshold set out in paragraph 1 of Category 1C.

3.9.2   Major infrastructure

Category 2A

1   Development which involves mining operations on land of more than 10 hectares.

Category 2B

1   Waste development to provide an installation with a capacity of throughput of more than 50,000 tonnes per annum of waste produced outside the land for which planning permission is sought. ('Waste development' is wholly or mainly involved in the treating, keeping, processing or disposing of waste or waste materials.)

Category 2C

1   Development to provide:

(a) an aircraft runway;

(b) a heliport (including a floating heliport or helipad on a building);

(c) air passenger terminal at an airport;

(d) a railway station;

(e) a tramway, an underground, surface or elevated railway or cable car;

(f) bus or coach station;

(g) an installation for use within Class B8 (storage and distribution) or the Schedule to the Use Classes Order where the development would occupy more than 4 hectares;

(h) a crossing over or under the River Thames; or

(i) a passenger pier on the River Thames.

2   Development to alter an air passenger terminal to increase its capacity by more than 500,000 passengers per year.

3.9.3   Development which may effect strategic policies

1   In this Part, land shall be treated as used for a particular use if:

(a) it was last used for that use, or

(b) it is allocated for that use in

   (i)   the development plan in force for the area in which the application site is situated,

(ii) proposals for such a plan, or

(iii) proposals for the alteration or replacement of such a plan.

Category 3A

1 Development which is likely to:

(a) result in the loss of more than 200 houses, flats or houses and flats (irrespective of whether the development would entail also the provision of new houses or flats); or

(b) prejudice the use of land which exceeds 4 hectares and is used for residential use.

Category 3B

1 Development

(a) which occupies more than 4 hectares of land which is used for use within Class B1, B2 or B8 of the Use Classes Order; and

(b) is likely to prejudice the use of that land for any such use.

Category 3C

1 Development which is likely to prejudice the use as a playing field of more than 2 hectares of land which:

(a) is used as a playing field at the time of the relevant application for planning permission is made, or

(b) at any time in the five years before the making of the application it has been used as a playing field.

Category 3D

1 Development

(a) on land allocated as Green Belt or Metropolitan Open Land in the development plan, proposal for such a plan or proposals for the alteration or replacement of such a plan; and

(b) which would involve the construction of a building with a floorspace of more than 1,000 sq m or a material change in the use of such a building.

Category 3E

1 Development which does not accord with one or more provisions of the development plan in force in the area in which the application is situated and:

(a) comprises or includes the provision of more than 2,500 sq m of floor space for a use falling within any of the following Use Classes:

(i) Class A1

(ii) Class A2

(iii) Class A3

(iv) Class A4

(v) Class A5

(vi) Class B1

(vii) Class B2

(viii) Class B8

(ix) Class C1

(x) Class C2

(xi) Class D1

(xii) Class D2

(for details of Use Classes see Chapter 8)

or

(b) comprises or includes the provision of 150 houses or flats or houses and flats.

Category 3F

1 Development for a use, other than residential use, which includes the provision of more than 200 car parking spaces in connection with that use.

3.9.4 Development on which the Mayor must be consulted by virtue of a Direction from the SoS

1 Development in respect of which the lpa is required to consult the Mayor by virtue of a direction given by the SoS under Article 10(3) of the Town and Country Planning (General Permitted Development) Order (GPDO)1995 (SI 1995/418).

3.10 TRANSITIONAL ARRANGEMENTS

Local Development Schemes were required to be submitted to the SoS by March 2005 indicating the milestones in the preparation of LDDs by March 2007. As a result a series of transitional arrangements are required to cover the period before the new plan-making is completed. Essentially, upon commencement, the following arrangements were put in place;

(a) in the first instance the existing Regional Planning Guidance will usually be translated into the new RSS but the SoS has power to determine which parts will be incorporated (s 12 (4));

(b) all adopted development plan policies are 'saved' for a period of three years;

(c) plans with an inspector appointed will continue to adoption under the old arrangements, that is Town and Country Planning (Development Plan) (England) Regulations 1999 (SI 1999/3280);

(d) plans that have reached at least the 'first deposit stage' will continue to adoption (Sched 8 to the Planning and Compulsory Purchase Act 2004) (PCPA 2004). They will require a further deposit and inquiry and a binding report with no modifications;

(e) plans that have not reached the first deposit stage lapse; and

(f) pre-commencement work on LDDs is allowed to 'count' subject to certain requirements (Sched 8 para 18 to PCPA 2004).

NB See Appendix 1 for details of plans referred to in the transitional arrangements.

CHAPTER 4

OTHER PLANS AND DEVELOPMENT AGENCIES

4.1   INTRODUCTION

This chapter deals with other forms of plans, which are prepared as part of the planning system, and also those government agencies set up with the object of promoting development without necessarily preparing an overall plan for land for which they are responsible.

Two types of plans are associated with the word 'zone' and this is of particular significance. In preparing plans, local planning authorities (lpas) continue the traditional approach, embodied in the Town and Country Planning Act (TCPA) 1947, of 'allocating' land for a primary land use which does not preclude development which incorporates complimentary land uses. This provides a degree of flexibility not afforded by zoning. For example, land shown on such a plan for residential use would not prevent the lpa from granting planning permission for shops, churches, open space or other uses associated with the primary use. The system of land use 'zoning', which is widely used throughout the world, has a much stricter interpretation. The plan consists of a series of 'zones' and is accompanied by a 'zoning ordnance' which prescribes in detail the acceptable use, or uses, density of development, which is usually determined by plot size, access arrangements and in some cases the materials to be used in the construction of property. Any use not contained in the zoning ordnance can only be established via an appeal. Conversely, any development which fully satisfies the requirements of the ordnance will be granted a permit to build.

The principles of 'zoning' have been adopted in British planning by the introduction of Enterprise Zones (EZs), Simplified Planning Zones (SPZs) and Business Planning Zones (BPZs).

PART A – ENTERPRISE ZONES

4.2   ENTERPRISE ZONES

Provision for the creation of EZs was established by s 179 and Sched 32 of the Local Government Planning and Land Act 1980 and this was referred to by the then Minister for Local Government and Environmental Services as:

> ... the bold new experiment of Enterprise Zones where business can be freed from much detailed planning control and from rates.

Subsequently, in 1981, a booklet entitled 'Enterprise Zones', was published by the Department of the Environment which includes the following statement:

> The government is setting up a number of Enterprise Zones. The idea is to see how far industrial and commercial activity can be encouraged by the removal of certain tax burdens, and by relaxing or speeding up the application of certain statutory or administrative controls. The zones will last for 10 years and it is hoped that the first ones will come into effect this summer. Eleven sites have been announced as prospective Enterprise Zones. They vary from about 50 to over 400 hectares.

Enterprise Zones are not part of regional policy, nor are they directly connected with other existing policies such as those for inner cities or derelict land. The sites chosen will continue to benefit from whatever aid is available under these policies.

The booklet then lists the benefits available to both new and existing industrial and commercial enterprises for a period of 10 years in declared EZs:

(i) exemption from development land tax (a short-lived benefit as it was abolished in the budget April 1985);

(ii) exemption from rates on industrial and commercial property (the local authority is reimbursed for the loss of income by the Treasury);

(iii) 100% allowances for corporation and income tax purposes for capital expenditure on industrial and commercial business;

(iv) applications from firms in EZs for certain customs facilities will be processed as a matter of priority and certain criteria relaxed;

(v) Industrial Development Certificates not needed (again a short-lived benefit as they were abolished in January 1982 in the Town and Country Planning (Industrial Development Certificates) (Prescribed Classes of Buildings) Regulations 1981);

(vi) employers to be exempt from industrial training levies and from the requirement to supply information to Industrial Training Boards;

(vii) NB a greatly simplified planning regime; development that conforms with the published scheme for each zone will not require individual planning permission;

(viii) those controls remaining in force will be administered more speedily; and

(ix) government requests for statistical information will be reduced.

Only certified bodies were invited by the Secretary of State (SoS) to draw up proposals for an EZ and these were:

(a) district councils;

(b) London boroughs;

(c) New Town Corporations; and

(d) Urban Development Corporations (UDCs) (see para 4.11, below).

It should be noted that county councils ('shire counties') are *not* included.

4.3   SETTING UP AN ENTERPRISE ZONE

There are three basic steps in the creation of EZs:

1   the invitation to prepare a scheme is given by the SoS (Sched 32, para 1(3), (4), (5)), and it must specify the area of the proposed zone (Sched 32, para 1(5)(a));

2   the preparation and adoption of the scheme which may include directions about the drawing up of the scheme (Sched 32, para 1(5)(b)); and

3   finally, the designation of the EZ (Sched 32, para 5(1), (2)).

The authority invited to prepare an enterprise scheme retains the right to decline the invitation, but if it accepts then it is obliged to do so within the terms of the invitation

(Sched 32, para 2(1)). Acceptance also requires the authority to give adequate publicity to the proposal so that representations may be made within a specified period on the ground that development within the area covered by the scheme should not be granted automatic planning permission in accordance with the terms of the scheme. At the end of this period of consultation, and having considered the representations, the authority may, by resolution, adopt the scheme (Sched 32, para 3(1), (2), (3)).

A copy of the scheme must be forwarded to the SoS and also be placed on deposit at the principal office of the body which prepared the scheme to enable the public to inspect the content of the scheme. Copies must also be made available at a reasonable cost (Sched 32, para 3(5)) so that persons interested can gain information as to what forms of development are, or are not, granted automatic planning permission.

The validity of the scheme may, within a period of six weeks, be questioned in the High Court by any aggrieved person (Sched 32, para 4(1) and s 4). The court may take one of two actions: it may order that the SoS shall not designate the area as an EZ or, that it shall not be designated until action has been taken to overcome substantial prejudice to the aggrieved person.

4.4 DESIGNATION OF AN ENTERPRISE ZONE

Once the scheme has been adopted by the authority, it is the SoS's decision as to whether to designate the scheme as an EZ. Before he can take such action, the SoS must gain Treasury consent because of financial implications to central government of setting up such a scheme. In accordance with Sched 32, para 5(4), the order must:

(a) specify the date of the designation taking effect (*apart from other reasons this is important for existing businesses who then benefit from the fiscal incentives*);

(b) specify the period for which the area is to remain an EZ;

(c) define the boundaries by means of a plan or map; and

(d) designate as the EZ authority the body which was invited to prepare the scheme.

Following designation, the scheme must be advertised in accordance with Sched 32, para 6 and the information must state that an EZ has been created and that copies of the scheme may be inspected at a stated place.

Once in place, it is possible to modify the designated EZ provided the SoS has Treasury approval, but he may not:

(a) alter the boundaries of the scheme;

(b) designate a different EZ authority to administer the zone; or

(c) reduce the period during which the zone will operate.

4.5 PLANNING CONTROL IN AN ENTERPRISE ZONE

The stated objective in physical planning terms is 'a greatly simplified planning regime' whereby development which conforms to the published scheme will not require individual planning permission – in other words – 'zoning'. The critical factor is, therefore, the degree to which freedom is granted under the scheme. Most schemes accept commercial and office development, and also certain classes of industrial use without the submission of a formal planning application, subject to the development conforming to set standards, for example, access arrangements and a declared maximum percentage of site coverage. Provided these standards are met, then automatic planning approval is granted. The EZ authority may, with the approval of the SoS, direct that permission shall not apply to specific uses (Sched 32, para 17(4), (5), (25)) in relation to:

(a) specified development;

(b) specified class(es) of development; and

(c) specified class(es) of development within a specified area of the EZ.

Issues such as landscaping are frequently reserved matters and will require the developer to submit a scheme for the consideration and approval by the relevant authority. Similarly, development which is not specifically included (or is excluded), will require the submission of a planning application in the normal manner in accordance with s 58(1)(b) of the TCPA 1990.

The content of the scheme is critical to planning control in EZs. The scheme is the equivalent of the zoning ordnance referred to in para 4.1, above. It provides a check list of those uses which are to be granted automatic planning permission, sets out the requirements which have to be met if that permission is to be forthcoming, and also reserves other issues for consideration and approval of the EZ authority.

4.6   ENTERPRISE ZONES AND LOCAL PLANS

The declaration of EZs may have a significant impact on proposals contained in an approved local plan and, therefore, any district authority within whose area an EZ has been declared, must consider whether they need to prepare proposals for the alteration or replacement of any local plan (s 52(1)).

PART B – SIMPLIFIED PLANNING ZONES

4.7   INTRODUCTION TO SIMPLIFIED PLANNING ZONES

During the 1980s, the government continued with its attempt to free enterprise by deregulation from what it regarded as unnecessary controls which, it argued, stifled investment in the UK. In July 1985, it published the White Paper 'Lifting the Burden' (Cmd 9571), which highlighted the government's intentions to seek to free enterprise from planning controls by the introduction of SPZs. Paragraph 3.6(i) states:

It is proposed to introduce new legislation to permit the setting up of Simplified Planning Zones which will extend to other areas the type of planning regime already established in Enterprise Zones. This will enable the local planning authority to specify types of development allowed in an area, so that developers can then carry out development that conforms to the scheme without the need for a planning application and the related fee. Planning permission for other types of development can be applied for in the normal way. This type of planning scheme has proved to be effective and successful in Enterprise Zones and can provide a real stimulus to the redevelopment of derelict or unused land and buildings in areas that are badly in need of regeneration. In addition to providing local planning authorities with powers to provide Simplified Planning Zones they will also be required to consider proposals for the establishment of Simplified Planning Zones initiated by private developers. The Secretaries of State would have reserve powers to direct the preparation of proposals for a Simplified Planning Zone, similar to those they already have to direct the preparation of alterations to development plans.

The intention set out in the White Paper resulted in the enactment of the Housing and Planning Act 1986, Part II of which related to SPZs.

The similarity between SPZs and EZs is that land will be *zoned* for particular uses by the preparation of a SPZ scheme. The essential differences are, first, that this new addition to the family of planning zones was not born with a silver spoon in its mouth! There is no provision for rate exemption or other financial incentives to developers (other than the exemption from the planning application fee) and, secondly, SPZs will be set up by the lpa and not declared by the SoS unless his reserve powers are invoked, and furthermore, any person may request that the lpa prepare a SPZ scheme for a particular area.

4.8   PREPARATION OF A SIMPLIFIED PLANNING ZONE SCHEME

Section 45 of the Planning and Compulsory Purchase Act 2004 requires that SPZs must relate to the spatial strategy and requires prior identification for such an SPZ in the Regional Spatial Strategy.

Each lpa is under an obligation to consider whether a SPZ scheme is considered desirable for any part of their area and shall keep that question under review (s 83(1) of the Housing and Planning Act 1980). This is reinforced in the strategic guidance, given by the DoE related to the preparation of local plans and also in PPG 5 'Simplified Planning Zones' (revised November 1992), which sets out the government's views of the benefits of SPZs and also the size and possible uses appropriate for an SPZ scheme. If the local authority consider that it is appropriate to declare a SPZ then they are required to do so (s 83(2)).

The government's enthusiasm for SPZs is not matched by lpas. During the first seven years of operation only 13 SPZs were commenced in England, only three of which were actually adopted, five were aborted and the remaining five were 'progressing' (Blackhall, JC, 'Simplified planning zones (SPZs) or simply political zeal?' [1994] JPL 117).

The power to establish SPZs is granted to metropolitan districts, London boroughs, and in the case of shire counties, the district planning authorities subject to certain restrictions as to the type of area, or land which may be included in a SPZ. These restrictions are listed in s 87(1):

(a) land in a National Park;

(b) land in a conservation area;

(c) land within the Broads;

(d) land designated as an area of outstanding natural beauty (s 87 of the National Parks and Access to the Countryside Act 1949);

(e) land within a green belt as defined in a development plan; and

(f) an area of special scientific interest (ss 28 and 29 of the Wildlife and Countryside Act 1981).

In the event of any land already included in a SPZ becoming land in any of the above descriptions, this does not exclude the area from the zone (s 87(2)).

PPG 5, para 2 includes other types of land which the SoS 'advises' should not form part of a SPZ and this includes the best and most versatile agricultural land, common land, greens, open space and heritage coast, other locally important areas of conservation interest, and land containing hazardous installations. Care should also be taken to avoid sterilising important mineral resources, and due consideration given to any land use constraints imposed by unstable land or contaminated land.

The procedure for making a SPZ scheme is set out in Sched 7 which contains the following requirements:

1   A scheme must consist of a map defining the area of the zone and a written statement along with such diagrams, illustrations and descriptive matter as the lpa may think appropriate for explaining or illustrating the provisions of the scheme. The scheme shall specify:

(a) the development or classes of development permitted by the scheme;

(b) the land in relation to which permission is granted; and

(c) any conditions, limitations or exceptions subject to which it is granted, and shall contain such other matters as may be prescribed.

2   The lpa shall inform the SoS of their decision to make or alter a SPZ and determine the date when they will begin to prepare the scheme, or its alteration.

3   The authority shall consult the SoS having responsibility for highways, and if it is a district authority, they shall consult both the county planning and county highways authority. PPG 5, para 3.9, also 'advises' that the Countryside Commission, English Heritage, National River Authority, HM Inspector of Pollution, and the New Towns Commission should be consulted when appropriate.

4   The authority shall take steps to publicise the matters which they intend to include in their proposals and after a six-week period has elapsed they shall consider any representations received.

5   If objections are made to the proposals, provision is made for the holding of a public local inquiry or hearing, but the lpa is not obliged to hold such an inquiry or hearing unless directed to do so by the SoS.

6   Before the proposal to make or amend a scheme is adopted by the lpa, the SoS may call in the proposals for his own approval.

7   If any person requests the lpa to prepare a scheme and they refuse to do so, or after a period of three months have failed to make a decision on the matter, the individual may require the lpa to refer the matter to the SoS. After the SoS has considered the matter, and any representations from the applicant and the lpa he shall notify both parties of his decision and may make a direction requiring the formulation of a scheme.

8   Where an lpa has been given a directive to prepare or amend a scheme, and the SoS is satisfied that the authority is not complying with that directive, he may himself make the scheme or invoke the alterations.

4.9 PLANNING CONTROL IN SIMPLIFIED PLANNING ZONES

Following the *adoption* of a scheme by the lpa, or *approval* by the SoS, planning permission is automatically granted (as for EZs) for any development which is specified in the scheme (s 58(1)). The scheme may specify conditions or limitations and exceptions ('zoning ordnance'), in which case planning approval will be necessary prior to the carrying out of such development (s 84). It is not possible for a scheme to grant planning permission for development which constitutes a 'county matter', that is, working of minerals and associated land and the waste disposal.

Should the lpa wish at a later date to amend the scheme to exclude land, withdraw planning permission or impose new conditions, the alterations cannot take effect until 12 months have elapsed since their adoption or approval (s 86(5)).

The lpa is required (s 69) to keep a register of applications for planning permission within the SPZ.

4.10 SIMPLIFIED PLANNING ZONES AND LOCAL PLANS

In the preparation of local development frameworks, the respective lpas are encouraged by central government policy in PPG 5 to give due consideration to the declaration of SPZs. Whilst it is recognised that there are separate procedures for the adoption of each type of plan, it is suggested that both SPZ proposals and local plan preparation could take place simultaneously. In such cases there would not be conflict between the plans. In the past, few, if any, authorities have chosen to adopt this approach, and most (in carrying out their duty to consider the desirability of adopting an SPZ), explain in the local plan why SPZs are not a suitable vehicle for overcoming their particular problems and/or the physical nature of their area.

In the limited number of instances where SPZs have been adopted at times when the plan is already in place, they relate to land which is already included in the plan for the specific land use which forms the basis of any scheme. In most instances this relates to land which is already allocated on the plan for industrial development and the benefit of declaring it to be an SPZ is largely a marketing device to attract industrial and other users. There is normally, therefore, no conflict with the aims and objectives of the local plan but *'where, exceptionally, proposals depart from the plan in such a way as significantly to prejudice its implementation, a local inquiry will be appropriate'* (PPG 5, para 7).

The preparation of an SPZ is seen as a duplication of effort on the part of authorities with the added complication of different methods of approval. An adopted local plan will contain land allocations for particular uses which ensure that planning permission for these uses will be forthcoming. This gives developers the certainty which they require, and many see little additional benefit arising from an SPZ.

From the developer's point of view, the possibility of requesting the local authority to prepare an SPZ risks an initial rebuff and further consideration by the SoS. Even if the request is supported by the SoS, the production of such a scheme takes time and it is likely to be quicker to submit a normal planning application and, if refused, pursue the matter via an appeal to the SoS (see Chapter 16).

PART C – URBAN DEVELOPMENT CORPORATIONS

4.11 INTRODUCTION TO URBAN DEVELOPMENT CORPORATIONS

The Local Government and Planning Act 1980 not only introduced the concept of EZs (see para 4.2, above) but also that of UDCs, which was the second part of the government's initiative to promote urban regeneration. In November 1980, the Minister for Local Government and Environmental Services stated:

> We shall shortly be bringing orders under the Local Government, Planning and Land Act to set up Urban Development Corporations as single-minded agencies to spearhead the regeneration of the London and Merseyside docklands (and to introduce the bold new experiment of Enterprise Zones).

The concept of development corporations had previously been used in 1945 with the setting up of New Town Development Corporations under the New Towns Act as the responsible body directly responsible to the minister and charged with the construction of the new town.

The SoS may designate an area of land as an urban development area (s 134(1)), but in accordance with the provisions of the 1980 Act, this power was restricted to the then metropolitan counties (subsequently abolished under the Housing and Planning Act 1986) and certain London boroughs. This restriction was removed by s 47 of the 1986 Act, and land anywhere in England can now be considered by the SoS as a potential UDC area. It is not necessary that the area so designated should form a single physical area and may constitute separate parcels of land (s 134(3)).

In selecting areas for UDC status, the SoS has to satisfy himself that it will be in the national interest (s 134(1)). When such a body is set up, the designated area is removed from the control of the local government authority and becomes the responsibility of the corporation which is charged with the task of regenerating the area (s 135(1)). The title of the corporation must be established by an order made by statutory instrument (s 135(1)) which requires the approval of both Houses of Parliament (s 135(3)).

The first orders were made in 1981 in respect of Merseyside and London Docklands. Subsequent orders were made in relation to Cardiff Bay, Central Manchester, Teesside, Leeds, Tyne and Wear, Sheffield, Trafford Park, Bristol and the Black Country, all of which have now been disbanded.

There are currently two Urban Development Corporations in operation, the London Thames Gateway UDC and the Northamptonshire UDC. The former is intended to play a major role in the regeneration of the Thames Gateway Project which extends on the north bank from the Isle of Dogs in London, 40 miles to Southend, Essex, and on the south to the Isle of Sheppey, Kent. Thurrock is a unitary planning authority and has handed powers for large development to the UDC. The Northamptonshire UDC covers 3 areas in the County in which it will assume responsibility for regeneration.

4.12 URBAN DEVELOPMENT CORPORATIONS

A UDC consists of a chairman, a deputy chairman and between five and 11 additional members, all of whom are appointed by the SoS (Sched 26, para 2(1)). None of the members of the board are elected but, in appointing members, the SoS must have regard to appointing persons who have a special knowledge of the locality and, before making such appointments, he must consult those local authorities who are concerned with the regeneration of the area (Sched 26, para 2(4)).

Land included within the area of the UDC is taken out of the control of the local authority and is controlled by a non-elected board. Members of the UDC are paid a remuneration by central government, details of which have to be approved by the minister charged with responsibility for the civil service (Sched 26, para 9). To assist in the carrying out of its duties, the corporation may, with the approval of the SoS, appoint staff and remunerate them (Sched 26, para 11).

The UDC, having been established, is required to prepare a code of practice within 12 months (s 140(3)) setting out the agreed method of consultation with all local authorities, the whole or part of which is incorporated in the UDC's area (s 140 (1), (2), (5)).

The object of the UDC is to secure the regeneration of the designated area for which it has responsibility by (s 136(2)):

(a) bringing land and buildings into effective use;

(b) encouraging the development of new industry and commerce;

(c) creating an attractive environment; and

(d) ensuring that housing and social facilities are available to encourage people to live and work in the area.

To achieve this object, the UDC may (s 136(3)):

(a) acquire, hold, manage, reclaim and dispose of land and other property;

(b) carry out building and other operations;

(c) seek to ensure the provision of water, electricity, gas, sewerage and other services;

(d) carry out any business or undertaking for the purpose of the object; and

(e) do anything necessary or expedient for the purposes of the object or purposes incidental for those purposes.

To this wide range of powers is added the further power, with the consent of the SoS, to make financial contributions (s 136(5)) towards:

(a) expenditure incurred or to be incurred by any local authority or statutory undertaker (now privatised industries) in the performance of their functions, including expenditure incurred in the acquisition of land; and

(b) the provision of amenities.

The SoS has the power under s 135 to exclude any of the above provisions in the making of the initial order setting up the UDC The UDC is *not* to be regarded as an agent for the Crown and, therefore, cannot claim any status, immunity or privilege associated with Crown land (s 135(6)).

4.13 THE FUNCTIONING OF URBAN DEVELOPMENT CORPORATIONS

To achieve the object of regeneration within the designated area, it is critical that a UDC has the ability to own and dispose of land. To achieve this, the SoS may by an order (s 141), vest land in the Development Corporation which is controlled by a local authority, statutory undertaker, or any other public body. Such an order requires the approval by resolution by both Houses of Parliament (s 141(6)), and has the same effects as a declaration under Part III of the Compulsory Purchase (Vesting Declarations) Act 1981. Compensation is paid on the basis of values current at the date of vesting (s 141(5) and Sched 27).

The corporation may also acquire land by agreement (ss 142(1), 144(1), (3) and Sched 28) or, if authorised to do so by the SoS, by compulsory purchase under s 142(1), (3), (4), s 144(1), (2) and Sched 28. In addition to land falling within the urban development area, the corporation may acquire under s 142(1) if it is:

(a)   land adjacent to the area which is required for purposes connected with the carrying out of the duties of the Development Corporation; or

(b)   land irrespective of whether it is adjacent to the area which it requires for the provision of services connected to the corporation's functions within the area.

Following the acquisition of land, Sched 28, Part III makes provision for the extinguishment of rights over land, overriding easements, the treatment of consecrated land including burial grounds, open spaces, overhead lines, and the rights of statutory undertakers and the extinguishing of public rights of way. In addition, a local highway authority can be authorised to acquire land compulsorily outside a Development Corporation's area to construct or improve an existing road if this will further the regeneration of the urban development area.

The sole object of regeneration is to be achieved, as far as possible, by the attraction and injection of private capital investment. Therefore, any land which has been vested in, or acquired by a UDC may, subject to any directions given by the SoS, be disposed of to such persons and in such manner subject to covenants and conditions as thought expedient by the corporation to secure the regeneration of the area (s 146(1)).

In disposing of land, the UDC has to have regard to the need to preserve features of special architectural or historic interest. In accordance with s 1 of the Planning (Listed Buildings and Conservation Areas) Act 1990 the SoS has a duty under s 148(3) of the Local Government, Planning and Land Act 1980 to give such directions as he thinks necessary, or expedient, to ensure the corporation discharges these obligations. The corporation also has a duty, as far as is practicable, to re-accommodate persons living or carrying out business in the area who wish to obtain accommodation on land belonging to the corporation (s 146(2)). The terms offered must have regard to the purchase price of land purchased from such persons by the corporation (s 146(2)), but at the same time such persons must comply with any requirement of the corporation as to the development or use of the land on which they are re-accommodated.

4.14   PLANNING FUNCTIONS OF URBAN DEVELOPMENT CORPORATIONS

Urban Development Corporations are not plan-making authorities. They are not required to prepare an overall plan for their area and rely upon private consultants to propose plans for different parts of their area (frequently known as 'flagship sites'). The Corporation then submits regeneration proposals for specific areas to the SoS (s 148(1)), who, after consulting the lpa within whose area the land lies and with any other lpa who appear to be concerned, approve such development proposals with or without amendments.

The SoS may then make a special development order under the TCPA 1990 (s 58), granting automatic planning permission for any development of land which is in accordance with the approved proposals (s 148(2)) subject to any conditions set out in the order. The order *may* require that the lpa be consulted on the details of the application, but the responsibility for approval lies with the board of the UDC. It is almost inevitable that, from time to time, the two authorities may disagree on the particular merits of a planning application falling within the jurisdiction of the UDC.

A decision by Teesside Development Corporation to allow a proposed hypermarket was the subject of a challenge by Redcar and Cleveland BC (reported in (1997) *Planning* 30 May). The High Court quashed the permission for the scheme and Sedley J, in what has been claimed to be a landmark judgment, stated that the Teesside Development Board had *'surrendered its judgment as a planning authority to its judgment as a Development Corporation'* and ordered that the scheme be reconsidered. After giving the matter due reconsideration, the UDC remained convinced that it was appropriate to grant planning permission for the hypermarket despite the continued opposition of the adjoining lpas At the time of writing, the SoS has called-in the application which means that there will be a local inquiry before he determines the matter.

To avoid conflicting proposals for the area controlled by a UDC, the SoS may direct that a local plan shall not be prepared or shall not operate within the area of an UDC (s 51A(2)).

A developer who wishes to carry out development which does not fall within the special development order will require planning permission. The determination of such an application will fall to the lpa *unless* the SoS has, by an order, declared the UDC to be the lpa for the area, or any part of their area (s 149(1). In most instances, the order makes provision for the UDC to act as the appropriate planning authority for development control purposes, although the actual decision notice is issued by the llpa whose area is covered by the UDC designation. In declaring the corporation, Sched 16 of the Local Government Act 1972 allows the highway authority, in certain circumstances, to impose restrictions on the grant of planning permission.

To facilitate the rapid regeneration of the UDC's area, the 1980 Act specifically provides further duties and powers in addition to the planning functions granted to the corporation. These are:

(a) building control (s 151);

(b) fire precautions (s 152);

(c) housing authority functions (s 153);

(d) rent rebates (s 154);

(e) adoption of highways (s 157);

(f) public health (s 159);

(g) loans for building to any person buying or renting UDC land (s 160);

(h) loans made by UDC in pursuance of building agreements (s 161);

(i) power relating to 'designated districts' under the Inner Urban Areas Act 1978 (s 162);

(j) supply of goods and services by a local authority to a public body (s 163);

(k) surveying of land (s 167); and

(l) service of notices (s 168).

4.15   DISSOLUTION OF URBAN DEVELOPMENT CORPORATIONS

As has been noted (para 4.11, above), UDCs are set up for a relatively short period. The 1980 Act provides that an UDC may transfer the whole or part of its undertaking by agreement made with any local authority and any statutory undertakers as approved by the SoS and with the agreement of the Treasury (s 165(1)). This agreement does not preclude the right of the UDC to dispose of any of its property including any trade or business in which it may be involved (s 162(2)).

In the case of liabilities, these will remain with the corporation and in such cases the SoS may vest such liabilities in himself (s 165(3)). Where the liability of the corporation is in respect of advances made by the SoS, he may, by order made with the consent of the Treasury, reduce this liability as specified in the order (s 165(7)) but this must be first approved by resolution of both Houses of Parliament (s 165(8)).

When all the property and other undertakings of the UDC have been transferred or otherwise disposed of, the SoS by order may dissolve it and responsibility for the area reverts to the original local authority. It is also possible that land in the ownership of the corporation may be transferred to English Partnerships.

PART D – ENGLISH PARTNERSHIPS

4.16   INTRODUCTION TO ENGLISH PARTNERSHIPS

The body known as the Urban Regeneration Agency was set up under Part III of the Leasehold Reform, Housing and Urban Development Act 1993 (s 158). This established 'the agency' which it was announced was to be known as English Partnerships. In November 1993, the SoS announced that its task was:

> ... to release the potential of 15,000 acres of vacant and derelict land in towns for any other use that will help to regenerate the area. It will also be responsible for reclaiming derelict land in rural areas.

The agency concentrates on relatively small sites and within these areas acts in a similar manner to UDCs. The SoS may by order vest land in the agency (s 161), and the agency may for the purpose of achieving its objects or for purposes incidental to that purpose, acquire land by agreement, or with authority to do so granted by the SoS, by compulsory acquisition (s 162(1)). In the case of the acquisition of any common, open space or fuel or allotment garden land, land must be provided in exchange (s 162(3)). The Act also dissolved the English Industrial Estates Corporation (s 184) and all properties, rights and liabilities of the Corporation were transferred to the agency.

The power of the SoS to set up an agency is contained in s 171, and, whilst the agency is an independent body, it is subject to close control by the SoS (s 167), and it is required to have regard to guidance from him as to which land is suitable for regeneration or development and how it should bring about that regeneration (s 167(1)). The SoS is also entitled to direct the agency as to how to exercise its functions (s 167(2)).

4.17 OBJECTS OF THE AGENCY

The main object of English Partnerships (s 159(2)) is to secure the regeneration of:

(a) land which is vacant or unused;

(b) land in an urban area which is underused or ineffectively used;

(c) land which is contaminated, derelict, neglected or unsightly; and

(d) land which is likely to become derelict, neglected or unsightly by reason of actual or apprehended collapse of the surface as the result of carrying out relevant operations which have ceased to be carried out (*'relevant operations' are defined in s 1 of the Derelict Land Act 1982*).

In doing so, it is required to:

(e) have regard to the guidance and directions given by the SoS (s 159(3)(a), (b)); and

(f) proposals which have the consent of the SoS (s 159(3)(c)).

These objects are to be achieved by the following means, or by such of them as are deemed appropriate in any particular case (s 159(4)):

(a) by ensuring that land and buildings are brought into effective use;

(b) by developing or encouraging the development of existing and new industry and commerce;

(c) by creating an attractive and safe environment; and

(d) by facilitating the provision of housing and social and recreational facilities.

The SoS may, with the consent of the Treasury, give financial assistance to any person in respect of the expenditure incurred in connection with activities contributing to the regeneration of an urban area (s 174).

4.18 FUNCTIONING OF THE AGENCY

The SoS is empowered to designate urban regeneration areas (s 170) in a similar manner to the designation of urban development areas but, in this case, the control of the area becomes the responsibility of English Partnerships rather than of a UDC. The consequences of designating the area are:

(a) powers of the lpa may be transferred to the agency (s 171);

(b) a UDC may exercise the function on behalf of the agency (s 177); and

(c) the agency given powers in relation to the adoption of private streets (s 172).

4.19 PLANNING FUNCTIONS OF THE AGENCY

The agency is designed to operate on a site-specific basis to carry out its function of regenerating the area in a short time period. It may be granted planning powers by the

SoS and, where this occurs, the agency is empowered to carry out the development control function both in terms of uses for the site, and the granting of planning permission. By its very nature, it is not a plan-making body in the local authority sense, but its function is to promote development by encouraging and, where appropriate, providing financial assistance to the private sector.

PART E – BUSINESS PLANNING ZONES

4.20   FORM AND CONTENT

The government's intention is to introduce a new concept of Business Planning Zones (BPZs) based upon the earlier concept of SPZs. These new zones would be identified in regional strategies and be designated by lpas in partnership with universities and leading high-tech companies who would be able to initiate proposals for the designation of such areas. Zones would be specific to types of businesses that have minimum impact on the surrounding area, do not have major infrastructure requirements or necessitate special environmental precautions.

CHAPTER 5

LEGAL CHALLENGES TO THE DEVELOPMENT PLAN

5.1   INTRODUCTION

The increasing emphasis on the plan as a major factor in the determination of planning applications resulted initially from the insertion of s 54A into the Town and Country Planning Act (TCPA) 1990. The repeal of Part 2 of the 1990 Act by the Planning and Compulsory Purchase Act (PCPA) 2004 resulted in the replacement of s 54A with a new s 38(6)) which states unequivocally that:

> If regard is to be had to the development plan for the purpose of determination to be made under the Planning Acts, the determination must be made in accordance with the plan unless material considerations indicate otherwise.

The dominance of the plan in determining proposals likely to gain planning permission has led to a greater number of challenges to the way in which the plan has been prepared and adopted by the planning authority. The introduction of the new plan-making functions contained in PCPA 2004 will require time to become fully operational and for the next three to four years a dual system will operate. Interim arrangements allow for the carrying forward of old style structure plans, unitary development plans and district plans. The old and the new systems of plan-making have essential differences both in their content and the procedural method of adoption. The special policy statement 'Sustainable Communities – Delivering through Planning' (18 July 2002) states the government's intention to;

> reform the process plan adoption, including the abolishing of the present two-stage process, promoting mediation, time-tabling the inquiry process, giving inspectors more control over the procedures and making them more informal and making the inspector's recommendations binding on the lpa.

The courts are not concerned with the merits on planning grounds but solely with the question of legality, which may be substantive or procedural. To mount such a challenge the objector must act within six weeks of the intention to adopt the plan by way of an application to the High Court under s 287 of the TCPA1990. The strict application of this 'six-week rule' is highlighted in *R v Secretary of State ex p Kent* (1988) 3 PLR 17, upheld by the Court of Appeal in [1990] JPL 124; [1990] 1 PLR 128. The applicant did not know until after the period that a planning appeal had been lodged with the Secretary of State (SoS). The courts held that the requirements of s 287 could not be circumvented.

There are two grounds for questioning the validity of the plan:

1   that it is not within the power conferred in Part II of the Act; or

2   that any requirement of that Part of the Act or any regulations made under it has not been complied with for the approval or adoption of the plan, or as the case may be, its alteration or replacement.

Following such an application the High Court may;

(a) suspend wholly or in part the operation of the plan generally, or in so far as it affects the applicant, until the proceedings are finally determined; or

(b) if it is outside the powers of the Act, or in the interests of the applicant have been substantially prejudiced by a failure to comply with the Act or regulations made under it, the court may quash the whole of the plan or any part of it or so much of the plan in so far as it affects the property of the applicant.

Note: Whilst the right of challenge remains in the immediate future it will be necessary to establish whether the proposed plan is currently with an inspector and was prepared under the Development Plan Regulations 1999 (SI 1999/3280). Plans that have reached at least the 'first deposit stage' will continue to adoption under transitional arrangements (Sched 8, P&CPA 2004). These will require a further deposit and an inquiry resulting in an inspector's binding report. Any other plans that have not reached the first deposit stage will lapse. It is important that the following sections are considered in relation to the 1999 Regulations.

5.2   CHALLENGES TO THE SECRETARY OF STATE

Under s 35(2) TCPA 1990, the SoS is empowered, at any time before the adoption of proposals, to issue a direction to a structure planning authority to modify its proposals in accordance with the contents of the directive. In December 1997, he issued such a directive to West Sussex County Council following the publication of the council's proposed modifications to the plan as a result of the report of the panel that conducted the Examination in Public (EIP). The panel concluded that housing provision should be made for an additional 58,700 dwellings during the period 1991–2011. Instead, the council proposed a figure of 37,900 and it was this that prompted the direction.

The council sought judicial review of the SoS's direction in *R v Secretary of State ex p West Sussex CC* [1998] JPL November Update, and the High Court dismissed the application. In doing so, the court stressed the breadth of s 35(2) and Scott Baker J commented:

> ... the power to intervene is by nature a default power, which allows the Secretary of State to correct a matter which would be adopted following normal procedure. It is unfettered in its terminology and, in my judgment, broad in its application. It is unsurprising that the Secretary of State should be given such broad power bearing in mind (i) his wide involvement prior to the enactment of s 35; and (ii) the fact that he has to consider a broader planning picture then the individual counties themselves.

One of the grounds of challenge to the direction relates to the SoS's actions in exercising his power to amend plans prepared by lpas. In *R v Secretary of State ex p Islington LBC* [1995] JPL 121, the SoS had issued a direction under s 17 TCPA 1990 requiring the removal of the plan's 'conservation area guidelines' because he considered them too detailed and prescriptive to be included in the body of the plan. The SoS did not seek to remove all mention of conservation area protection, merely that the council should reconsider the matter and produce a separate conservation area plan. The High Court accepted the use of the SoS's power to do so, and held that he had not acted perversely or misinterpreted or ignored his own policies.

The obligation which requires the SoS to provide proper and adequate reasons for his decision, and to deal with the substantive points raised in his consideration of the plan, was the subject of challenge in *Bradley (Edwin H) and Sons Ltd v Secretary of State* (1982) 266 EG 264. It was held by the court that the SoS is entitled to give short reasons, and furthermore, if the point is not substantive, he needs little or no reasoning. However, if he decides to approve an alteration which conflicts with his own policy guidance, he should refer to that policy guidance in his statement of reasons (see *Barnham v Secretary of State* [1985] JPL 861; (1986) 52 P & CR 10).

5.3   CHALLENGES ARISING FROM THE INSPECTOR'S RECOMMENDATIONS

There have also been a number of cases where challenges have been made to the process in adopting local plans. In *Electricity Supply Nominees Ltd v Secretary of State and Northavon DC and Kingswood BC* [1992] JPL 634; 2 PLR 70, the issue related to the consideration by the inspector at the local plan inquiry of competing proposals: one proposed by the developer and the other proposed by the planning authority in the local plan. The developer in support of his argument cited PPG 1, para 15 which refers to a presumption in favour of development, whilst the local planning authority (lpa) argued in favour of the site which formed part of their plan. Whilst the court accepted there was little to choose between the two proposals, the inspector had found in favour of the plan. The courts held that the planning authority had discretion in the content of its plan, provided it acted reasonably, and that the presumption in favour of development formed part of their consideration. The inspectorate, when faced with competing sites may, therefore, prefer that shown in the plan although there is nothing substantially wrong with the developer's proposal and he may find no substantial planning objections to the objector's site. The presumption in favour of development may be overruled in such cases. This case was decided in November 1991 prior to the introduction of s 54A of the TCPA 1990 which places emphasis on the plan as the primary factor to be taken into account in the determination of planning applications.

The consideration by the lpa of the inspector's report and recommendations has resulted in a series of challenges through the courts. In *Laing Homes Ltd v Avon DC* [1994] JPL 1010; 67 P & CR 34; (1993) 3 PLR 23, the lpa considered such a report which was acknowledged by both parties to be defective in that the inspector had not addressed all the relevant issues, particularly some relating to the green belt. The court had to decide to what extent, if at all, the local authority could deal with a defective report from the planning inspector. The court accepted that the council was the decision-making body, and in this instance they were left in the invidious position of being judges in their own cause as they were deprived of the benefit of an inspector's findings on issues which were clearly material to their consideration of the matter. The court noted 'there was no procedure by which any inquiry can be re-opened if an inspector falls down on his job and fails to make material considerations'. It went on to recommend that if the lpa could not rescue the situation, the SoS should have intervened. Presumably this would result in a new inquiry to deal with the issues omitted from the first consideration of the plan.

Two recent cases appear to indicate a stricter approach by the courts in assessing the lpa's reasons for departing from the inspector's recommendations. In *The Black Country Development Corporation v Sandwell MBC; Park Lane Property v Sandwell MBC and the Secretary of State* [1996] JPL B117, it was made clear that the reasons must deal with the main points raised by the inspector. In *Stirk et al v Bridgnorth DC* (1996) EGCS 159, the Court of Appeal upheld the decision of the lower court that the council's reasons must not be simply the same as those given at the public inquiry; they must give the matter fresh consideration. The court noted that the lpa were in a special situation, as both proposer and decision-maker, and accordingly had an enhanced obligation to deal thoroughly and fairly with any objection. In this instance, the authority's consideration of the inspector's report in relation to the applicant's objection, and the reason given for the decision were inadequate, amounting to a decision that was perverse and irrational. The lpa had also acted unfairly in deciding against holding a further inquiry into the objections made by the applicants to the adoption of the local plan.

In *Hall Aggregates (South Coast) Ltd v New Forest DC* (1996) EGCS 108, the court held that the council must state their reasons in sufficient detail to enable the reader to know what conclusion they had reached on the principal controversial issues. In this instance, the council's statement was considered to be inadequate and did not deal with the main issues in dispute. The court accordingly quashed that part of the local plan.

In *Modern Homes (Whitworth) Ltd v Lancashire CC* (1998) EGCS 73, the High Court reviewed the duties imposed upon a structure plan authority following an EIP. The court held that s 33(6) of TCPA 1990 prevented an authority from adopting their proposals until after they had considered any objections made in accordance with the regulations. This requirement imposed a wider obligation on the authority than they had previously been under at the EIP. The duty under reg 16(1) of the Development Plan Regulations 1999 (SI 1999/3280) to prepare a statement of the decisions reached by the authority, in the light of the report's recommendations, meant that the authority had to give reasons for their decision on each objection, whether or not it had been debated at the EIP.

In *Gillenden Development Company Ltd v Surrey CC* [1997] JPL 944, there were contradictory findings from two planning inspectors relating to land owned by the company which was included within the proposed green belt. The company objected to the proposal and following the inquiry the inspector reported to the council on 23 February 1994 and recommended that the plan be modified by the exclusion of the land from the green belt. A previous planning application, submitted by the company for residential development on the site, had been the subject of an inquiry and an inspector determined the appeal on 21 February 1994. In his decision letter, the inspector considered that the site fulfilled a green belt function and dismissed the appeal. In November 1994, the council published its statement on decisions following the inquiry into the local plan. The local plan inspector's recommendation was rejected and the council's statement referred to the decision of the s 78 TCPA 1990 appeal inspector who considered that the land did perform a green belt function.

Gillenden challenged the council's decision by application to the High Court and Malcolm Spence QC (sitting as Deputy Judge) quashed that part of the plan relating to the site. The council appealed to the Court of Appeal submitting that the judge had exceeded his function and based his decision upon his own view of the planning merits. For their part, the defendants argued that the recommendations of the local plan inspector should normally be accepted unless there were good reasons to the contrary. These points could not be dealt with simply by reference to the opinions of the s 78 appeal inspector but required adequate explanation as to what was wrong with the reasoning of the local plan inspector. In allowing the appeal, it was held that in making their decision the council had in mind both inspectors' opinions and they were entitled to prefer the views of the appeal inspector and to adopt his reasons as their own.

(The government has issued a current consultation document on speeding up the adoption of development plans, and it remains to be seen what changes, if any, will result from this consultation.)

5.4   APPLICATION FOR A SECOND INQUIRY

The issue of a second inquiry into a local plan was the subject of a challenge in the case of *British Railways Board v Slough BC* [1993] JPL 678; 2 PLR 42. Land owned by BRB was included in the local plan for a variety of alternative uses. At the inquiry, BRB argued that the site should be shown for residential development and was supported by the council who rejected two objections requesting that the land be left as open space on wildlife conservation grounds. The inspector duly supported the council in his report, and recommended that residential use be limited to part of the site. In May 1991, the council considered the inspector's report and also had before it a planning application submitted by BRB for residential development. At this stage, the council changed its mind and refused the planning application and resolved to designate all the land as a wildlife heritage. Not surprisingly, BRB objected to the proposed modification when it was advertised, and in addition, appealed against the refusal of planning permission. Their request for a fresh inquiry was refused by the lpa and BRB sought a judicial review of that decision.

It was accepted by the court that there was no requirement under regulations for the lpa to give any reason for rejecting the request for a second inquiry, but the court would consider whether such a decision was reasonable by applying the *Wednesbury* principles established in *Associated Picture Houses v Wednesbury Corporation* [1948] 1 KB 223; [1947] 2 All ER 680, that is:

(a) that they have taken into account irrelevant matters;

(b) that they have left out relevant matters; and

(c) that they have acted unreasonably, that is, reached a decision which no reasonable council could arrive at.

On the basis of 'reasonableness', the court stated that, 'fairness to persons affected is an important consideration in the exercise of discretion under the regulations, especially as the council are the confirming authority for their own plan', and the judgment was to quash that part of the plan.

The question of holding a second inquiry into a local plan was also the issue in *Harlowbury Estates Ltd and Another v Harlow DC* [1996] JPL B106; (1996) EGCS 28. The case involved two sites in the Harlow local plan one of which (Gilden Way) was included in the green belt. Following the local plan inquiry, the council rejected the inspector's recommendation that the site be removed from the green belt and retained the other site for housing. Harlowbury Estates objected to the proposed modifications to the plan, seeking the substitution of Gilden Way for the site favoured by the local authority, or alternatively, a second inquiry to assess the comparative merits of the two sites. The council rejected the request for a second inquiry and adopted the plan.

An application to the High Court to quash the relevant part of the plan was granted and the court held that the council had failed to give adequate reasons for the rejection of the inspector's recommendation and, therefore, was in breach of the 1982 reg 28(1) of the Development Plan Regulations (SI 1999/3280). The court decided it would not exercise its power to quash the plan on that ground, and went on to consider the fact that the local authority's preferred site had not been considered at the inquiry. Objections by the applicants involved new evidence which had not been presented previously and, therefore, had not formed part of the inspector's report or recommendations. The council had acted in breach of regulations in failing to have regard to material considerations and, therefore, the applicants had been substantially prejudiced. Accordingly, the plan was quashed in so far as it related to the council's preferred site which was introduced after the inquiry into the plan.

The general approach of the courts to applications for a second inquiry was indicated in the case of *Uttlesford DC v Birchanger, Felstead, Little Dunmow and Takeley Parish Councils* (1997) *Planning*, 27 June, where it was claimed a change in the housing requirements related to the proposed development of Stanstead Airport warranted a second inquiry. In giving the judgment dismissing the application to the Court of Appeal, Schiemann LJ noted that 'in the plan making process conflicts arise between the need to ensure that no-one is treated unfairly and reaching a decision swiftly. But these are matters which planning authorities are better placed to weigh up than the courts'.

In the case *Bersted Parish Council v Arun DC* [2003] EWHC 3419, the claimant applied under s 287 (TCPA 1990), claiming that the lpa had allocated land for housing following the inspector's report which amended the allocation proposed for the area 'subject to the local authority reviewing the infrastructure implications' of that increase. Following a planning officer's report which stated that objections relating to the modification of the policy were either resolved by the inquiry and the inspector's report or raised issues which could be dealt within the intended development brief, the local authority resolved to adopt the local plan. The basis of the parish council's challenge was that the local authority had erred in deciding not to hold a second inquiry and that furthermore it had misconstrued the inspector's report.

The High Court determined that the local authority had erred in the question of whether to hold a second inquiry and in the decision that the proposed modifications should stand and that the members did not have their attention drawn to all the considerations that were relevant at that time. The inspector had put forward a review of the infrastructure implications as a precondition of the inclusion of a higher housing allocation and this had not been undertaken and this constituted a material error. Accordingly the court granted relief by quashing the relevant part of the local plan.

5.5   CONFLICTING RESPONSIBILITIES

Local planning authorities are not only required to embark upon the lengthy procedure of preparing and adopting a plan for their area, which is likely to take years rather than months, but they have also a duty to determine planning applications on a day-to-day basis within the normal target time of eight weeks. It clearly is not possible to 'stop the world' until the plan is in place and this raises conflicting and incompatible timescales.

There are many instances where an objector to a plan is seeking to have his land included for a particular use. Should the inspector recommend the allocation of the site to the lpa as part of his recommendations, the applicant often follows this with the submission of a planning application. The question arises in such cases as to the extent the inspector's recommendations should be regarded as material considerations in the determination of the planning application. In *The Bath Society v Secretary of State* [1991] JPL 663; 62 P & CR 565; 1 WLR 1303; [1992] 1 All ER 28, an application for planning permission for residential development was refused in 1987, and an appeal was heard shortly before the local plan inquiry took place. The Bath Society had lodged an objection to the proposal. In July 1988 an inspector recommended that the SoS allow the appeal although he was aware of representations against the local plan. In August of the same year, the local plan inspector recommended that the site be retained as open space, and this was accepted by the lpa. However, in November of the same year, the SoS allowed the appeal against the refusal of planning permission.

The court quashed the SoS's decision on the basis that the inspector's local plan report was a material consideration and that the SoS should have known its contents. In doing so, the court did not challenge the SoS's right to determine the weight to be given to a material consideration. This is a planning matter which is to be determined by the SoS or the lpa. In this instance, the court was satisfied that:

> ... there is no evidence that anybody on behalf of the Secretary of State considered this matter at all. If this is correct, as is my view it is, then it is open to the court to decide whether the recommendation was a material consideration.

The later decision of the House of Lords in the case *Tesco Stores v Secretary of State* [1995] 1 WLR 759; 2 All ER 636, reaffirmed that whether something is a material consideration is a matter of law. The weight given to that material consideration is, however, a planning judgment to be taken by the SoS.

The *Bath Society* case also involved the likely impact of the proposed development on the character of a conservation area and further discussion of this aspect is to be found in Chapter 21, para 21.11.

In the case *Jeantwill Ltd v Secretary of State and Cherwell DC* [1993] JPL 445; (1992) ECGS 128, following the local plan inquiry held in June 1989, the inspector's report was considered by the council in the following November. The inspectors recommended modification of the policy which related to the provision of new hotels, motels, guesthouses and restaurants by the addition of the sentence, 'this policy will apply except where it can be demonstrated that development would meet regional and strategic need which could not be met in a less sensitive area'. This proposed amendment was rejected by the authority. Subsequently, a planning application for a hotel was refused and was the subject of an appeal to the SoS who overruled his inspector and refused permission in January 1991. The appellants were clearly of the opinion that the amendment to the policy as recommended by the inspector should have been taken into account and would have enhanced their case for gaining planning permission and sought a judicial review.

The plan was eventually adopted in June 1991, five months after the SoS's appeal decision. The court took the view that the inspector's recommendation had been rejected by the council before the appeal was heard although at that stage the plan as such had not been formally adopted and that:

> ... it would be confusing for the Secretary of State to consider recommendations which had in fact been rejected. Were it otherwise, decisions on policy would never be settled but would be re-opened, thereby destroying the value of such policies in providing a framework for planning control.

In the *Jeantwill* case, the lpa were held to have completed all the necessary steps to have effectively rejected the inspector's recommendation but a subsequent case, *Ravebuild Ltd v Secretary of State and Hammersmith and Fulham London BC* [1996] JPL 107, once again raised the critical issue of the timing and progress of the lpa's response to an inspector's report. In this instance, the authority were in *the process of* considering responses to the proposed modifications to the Unitary Development Plan at the time the inspector announced his decision on the planning appeal. The appeal inspector's report noted that the authority had rejected the local plan inspector's recommendation and, therefore, in accordance with *Jeantwill*, he considered it was not a material consideration.

The court, however, took a different approach to the question of whether the recommendation had in fact been rejected by the authority. The court took the view that:

> ... there was still opportunity for Ravebuild Ltd to have sought to persuade the council that the local plan inspector's recommendations should be accepted. It could not be treated as dead and buried as in the case of *Jeantwill*. Local planning authorities can be relied upon to consider very carefully any representations which are made under Reg 16(4) ... it would not have been enacted if the opportunity to make such representations could be dismissed as a mere formality. So it seems to me that the position here is that the policy position was not 'settled' as it was in *Jeantwill* and the local plan inspector's recommendations were a most material consideration which should have been taken into account by the inspector.

The court therefore quashed the SoS's decision letter relating to the planning appeal.

Perhaps the most contentious case arising from the duality of responsibilities exercised by lpas in determining their reaction to recommendations from a local plan inspector and, at the same time, determining planning applications is that highlighted by the case of *R v Hammersmith and Fulham LBC ex p People Before Profit* [1981] JPL 869; (1983) 45 P & CR 364. In this case, the local authority's plan proposed the development of what was known as 'Site 93'. People Before Profit objected to this proposal during the public inquiry, and London Transport then submitted a planning application for the development of the site. The inspector's report recommended that the site should not be developed. The authority considered the report and decided to reject the recommendation and at the same meeting granted planning permission for the London Transport proposal.

People Before Profit then took the matter to the High Court in an attempt to have the decision of the lpa quashed. An application for leave for judicial review was reluctantly refused and the judge indicated that 'one of the consequences of this unhappy case is to lead me to believe that public inquiries very often may have no useful purpose at all', and he went on to remark that he was:

> ... slightly perturbed to think that a public inquiry of up to a month's length can take place and its findings be so unfavourable and yet the local authority could dismiss it

virtually out of hand ... but it is only fair to point out with regard to the borough and London Transport that, in my judgment, they have the law on their side ... to the extent that they may make individuals incredulous. It ought to be said in favour of the council that of course a public inquiry with its recommendations cannot bind them. The council have had to have regard to the report and they have taken this into account, they have considered this report and that was that.

The issue of duality of responsibility, in terms of the production of plans, was considered in *Nottinghamshire CC v Secretary of State* [1999] JPL June Update. The inspector had reported to the SoS in 1997, but it took a year for the SoS to issue a decision that simply adopted the inspector's report without alteration. During that period, the county council had adopted its minerals plan which became part of the statutory development plan. The SoS conceded that the decision on the appeal was flawed and should be quashed. The developers opposed this, arguing that the inspector had taken into account the policies contained in the draft minerals plan which had not changed prior to adoption. The court held that there was a clear difference between a statutory obligation to determine an appeal, as set out in s 54A (TCPA 1990), and an obligation to bear in mind emerging policies and material considerations even if the emerging policies were accorded considerable weight. There was now a policy conflict and the inspector had attached particular importance to the extent to which the two proposals were or were not in conflict with development plan policy.

5.6 PREMATURE PERMISSION

So far, the cases in this section have dealt with planning applications which have been determined during the authority's consideration of the reports from local plan inspectors. The following case refers to issues which are raised when a planning application is submitted during the later stages of the production of a local plan and risks being refused on the basis of prematurity. This was considered in the case of *Leigh Estates (UK) Ltd v Secretary of State and Woking BC* [1996] JPL 217. The SoS's advice on the matter of prematurity is set out in PPG 1 'General Policy and Principles', para 33, which states:

> The weight to be attached to emerging development plans which are going through the statutory procedures towards adoption, depends upon the stage of preparation; the weight will increase as successive stages are reached ...

> It may be justified to refuse planning permission on grounds of prematurity in respect of development proposals which are individually so substantial, or likely to be so significant cumulatively, as to pre-determine decisions about scale, location or phasing of new development which ought properly to be taken in the development plan context.

In the *Leigh Estates (UK)* case, a planning appeal was heard before the local plan inspector's report was made public and the SoS had refused permission on the grounds of prematurity. He had been forwarded a copy of the local planning inquiry inspector's report after the closure of the inquiry, but he felt it was appropriate to refuse the appeal and then allow the lpa to consider the inspector's report. The court was not impressed with the SoS's approach and indicated:

... on the basis of the Secretary of State's comments, it would appear arguable that any proposal which would involve consideration of a site, considered by a local plan inspector before the authority had yet to consider the local plan inspector's report would automatically be premature. This is not the understanding of policy as set out in PPG 1.

The court rejected the SoS's approach as being outside his own policy and found that he had also failed to explain why he had chosen to depart from his policy. He also failed to explain the circumstances whereby the granting of planning permission would have prejudiced the development plan process. PPG 1 makes it clear that the refusal of planning permission on the ground of prematurity is only acceptable in exceptional circumstances:

This (prematurity) *may* be appropriate in respect of development proposals which are individually so substantial, or whose cumulative effect would be so significant, that to grant permission would prejudice the outcome of the plan process by pre-determining decisions about the scale, location or phasing of new development which ought to properly be taken in the development plan context [para 47].

Other than in the circumstances described above, refusal of planning permission on the ground of prematurity *will not usually be justified* (para 48 of PPG 1).

5.7 FORM AND CONTENT OF THE PLAN

The Court of Appeal upheld the High Court's ruling in *Peel Investments (North) Ltd v Bury MBC* [1999] JPL 74; (1998) EGCS 67 concerning the process of adoption of the plan and failure to provide adequate reasons. It was held that the authority had failed to give proper reasons for allocating certain land in the green belt. Laws LJ observed:

Where its [the plans] allocation to the green belt risks causing or exacerbating a housing shortfall, the very question for decision will be whether its green belt merits are so great as to be given overriding weight. The balance, of course, is for the council to strike. In my judgment, in such a case, their duty to give reasons must require them to identify the overriding considerations leading to their decision.

The council had failed to identify the above considerations and, as a result, substantial prejudice had been suffered by the applicants. The Bury UDP was quashed with regard to the retention of the applicant's land in the green belt.

The issue of a council failing to give adequate reasons for its decision for rejecting the recommendations of the inspector was also raised in *Bovis Homes Ltd v New Forest DC* [2002] EWHC 483. The High Court held that the authority's decision to exclude land was vitiated by apparent bias. The chairperson was a member of the New Forest Committee and there was a real danger of bias. It could also be inferred that her views would be influential, particularly as there had been no dissent from a single member of the committee. The court also addressed the implications of the Human Rights Act 1998 for plan-making activity and concluded:

(a) Art 6(1) of the Treaty was not engaged because a civil rights issue was not being determined in contract to an enforcement appeal or determination of a planning application;

(b) a pecuniary impact does not in itself demonstrate that the proceedings are determinative of civil rights;

(c) the local plan does not in itself determine property rights because planning applications remain a discretion of the decision-maker;

(d) however, the designation of land which led to statutory or non-statutory blight might determine human rights; and

(e) even if human rights were being determined via a local plan the process of preparation, application and adoption is indistinguishable for human rights purposes from the process applicable to planning appeals (see *Alconbury* case at para 2.1).

In *Reigate and Banstead BC v Secretary of State* [1996] JPL 307; (1995) 3 PLR 1, the issue was whether the glossary of terms, which was contained in a local plan, could be construed as forming a part of the plan's policies and proposals, or whether it should be regarded as explanatory material. The High Court held the latter to be the case, and that the planning inspector had been correct in concluding that the glossary could not expand or restrict the scope of a policy. A definition contained in the glossary was not an explicit or integral part of the relevant policy.

The High Court in *Cooper v Secretary of State and Harlow DC* [1996] JPL 945, B76; 71 P & CR 529 dealt with a similar issue to that above. In this case the conflict was between a policy contained in the structure plan and the textual support of it contained in the plan's explanatory memorandum. The court concluded that, for the purposes of construing s 54A (of TCPA 1990), the relevant parts of the plan were the actual policies and not the preceding text. There was also the wider question of whether the construction of a development plan policy is a matter of law. The court took the view that it was not, particularly as the meaning or scope of a policy will often require the exercise of planning judgment. Planning policies are distinct from statutes or contracts and are not intended to provide detailed frameworks which govern the relationship between public bodies and individuals. This was made clear in the statement by Lord Scarman in his determination in *Westminster City Council v Great Portland Estates plc* [1985] JPL 108; AC 661, where he stated that personal circumstances are not to be ignored in the administration of planning control (see Chapter 13, para 13.15.2).

CHAPTER 6

DEVELOPMENT

6.1   INTRODUCTION

The preparation of plans by local planning authorities is designed to provide the framework for development in their areas. This is achieved by allocating land for particular uses and the plan includes statements of policies and may include supplementary planning guidance which is to be applied to ensure that the development is in accordance with the plan's objectives. The successful implementation of the plan is totally dependent upon the ability to control and promote 'development'. This is a fundamental basis of planning.

The plan, as an element in the day-to-day decisions on proposals to carry out development, was originally given greater importance by the introduction of s 54A into the Town and Country Planning Act (TCPA) 1990. The repeal of Part 2 of the 1990 Act by the Planning and Compulsory Purchase Act (PCPA) 2004 resulted in the replacement of s 54A with a new s 38(6), the spirit of which remains the same, namely:

> If regard is to be had to the development plan for the purpose of any determination to be made under the Planning Acts, the determination must be made in accordance with the plan unless material considerations indicate otherwise.

6.2   THE MEANING OF 'DEVELOPMENT'

The definition of what is, or is not, regarded as development is critical to the operation of the entire planning system. The original definition of development appeared in the TCPA 1947 and this has been carried forward to s 55(1), (3), (4), (4A) and (5) of the 1990 Act. These sections should be read in conjunction with s 336(1) (TCPA 1990) which elaborates on the precise definition of terms for planning purposes. The definition is as follows:

> The carrying out of building, engineering, mining and other operations, in, on, over or under land, or the making of a material change in the use of any buildings or land.

On first reading the definition may appear to be all embracing but there have been a great number of challenges since the 1947 Act, particularly as to the precise meaning of 'operations', 'land', 'material change' and 'buildings' (see Chapter 7 for details).

It is important to appreciate that the definition includes two distinct forms of development: 'operations' and 'use'. To prevent confusion in the interpretation of these specific terms, particularly by way of overlap, s 336(1) states that 'use' in relation to land 'does *not* include the use of land for the carrying out of any building or other operations thereon'. Conversely the Act recognises that the enjoyment of a building erected following the grant of planning permission will almost inevitably result in a change of use of the land on which it is built. Section 75(2) TCPA 1990 provides that:

Where planning permission is granted for the erection of a building, the grant of permission may specify the purposes for which the building may be used.

Where no purpose is so specified s 75(3) makes it clear that:

If no purpose is so specified the permission shall be construed as including permission for the use of the building for the purpose for which it is designed.

Whilst the two terms 'operations' and 'use' refer to distinct activities this does not preclude the possibility of a single process which comprises both. In *West Bowers Farm Products v Essex CC* [1985] JPL 857; 50 P & CR 386, Nourse LJ stated:

The planning legislation is not impressed by the indivisibility of single processes. It cares only for their effects. A single process might for planning purposes amount to two activities. Whether it did so or not was a question of fact and degree. If it involved two activities, each of substance, so that one is not merely ancillary to the other, then both required planning permission.

Section 55(4) (TCPA 1990) further defines 'mining operations' as including:

(a) the removal of material of any description from:

(i) a mineral working deposit;

(ii) a deposit of pulverised fuel ash or other furnace ash or clinker; or

(iii) a deposit of iron, steel or other metallic slags; and

(b) the extraction of minerals from a disused railway embankment.

TCPA 1990 specifically states that four matters *shall* constitute development:

1 the use of a single dwelling house for the purposes of two or more separate dwelling houses (s 55(3)(a));

2 the deposit of refuse or waste materials on an existing dump if either

(a) the superficial area of the dump is extended; or

(b) the height of the dump is extended and exceeds the level of the land adjoining the dump (s 55(3)(b));

3 the placing or assembly of a tank in any inland waters for the purpose of fish farming (s 55(4)(A));

4 the display of an advertisement on the external part of a building not normally used for such a display (s 55(5) and s 222).

The Act also specifically states that certain matters *shall not* constitute development (s 55)(2)):

(a) internal and external improvements, alterations or maintenance works (not constituting making good war damage), none of which materially affects the external appearance of a building so treated, provided that any works begun after 5 December 1968, for the alteration of a building providing space below ground will constitute development (s 55(2)(a)), and provided further that, in the case of a listed building, internal improvements, alterations or maintenance works will require 'listed building consent' even though they do not materially affect the external appearance of the building.

Note 1: Although internal improvement and alterations do not constitute 'development', s 45 (PCPA 2004) amends the definition of development in s 55(2) of TCPA 1990, so as to bring the creation of additional floor space within a building under planning control. This will allow the Secretary of State (SoS) at a future date to determine the thresholds for such development by an amendment to the General Permitted Development Order. This change in definition was brought about by the creation of mezzanine floors in supermarkets which were capable of doubling the stores' existing floor space.

Note 2: See details of listed buildings in Chapter 20.);

(b) maintenance or improvement works carried out by a local highway authority to, and within the boundaries of a road (s 55(2)(b));

(c) breaking open of streets for the inspection, repair or renewal of sewers, mains, pipes, etc by a local authority or statutory undertaker (s 55(2)(c));

(d) the use of any buildings or other land within the curtilage of a dwelling house for any purpose incidental to the enjoyment of the dwelling house as a dwelling house (s 55(2)(d));

(e) the use of land for agriculture or forestry (including afforestation) and the use for such purposes of any building occupied with the land so used (s 55(2)(e));

(f) in the case of buildings or other land used for a purpose of any class specified in an order made by the SoS, the use for any other purpose of the same class (s 55(2)(f));

(g) the demolition of any description of building specified in a direction from the SoS to the local planning authorities generally or a particular local planning authority (lpa) (s 55(2)(g));

(h) the resumption, where planning permission to develop land subject to limitations has been granted by a development order, of the normal use of the land, provided that such normal use does not contravene Part III of TCPA 1990 or previous planning control (s 57(3));

(i) the resumption, after the issue of an enforcement notice in respect of any unauthorised development of land, of the use of the land for the purpose for which, under Part III of TCPA 1990, it could lawfully be used if the unauthorised development had not been carried out (s 57(4)).

TCPA 1990 (ss 90 and 220) also specifically states that, whilst the following matters *do* constitute development, planning permission in respect of them shall be deemed to be granted when:

(a) there is the display of an advertisement in accordance with regulations made under the Act (see Town and Country Planning Advertisement Regulations 1989 (SI 1989/1810) and Chapter 24); and

(b) certain development by a local authority or statutory undertaker has been authorised by a government department.

6.3 CERTIFICATE OF LAWFULNESS: EXISTING USE OR DEVELOPMENT

The commencement date of TCPA 1947 was 1 July 1948, and on that date uses of both land and buildings were 'frozen', that is, any 'development' after that date would fall to be considered by the lpa.

Fifty years later, the use on the appointed day may be lost in the mists of time, and the present owner, or other persons interested in the land or building, may wish to establish the current legal use of the land. Provision is made under s 191(1) (TCPA 1990), as amended by the Planning and Compensation Act 1991, for any person who wishes to ascertain whether:

(a) the existing use of buildings or other land is lawful;

(b) any operations which have been carried out in, on, over or under land are lawful; or

(c) any other matter, constituting a failure to comply with any condition or limitation subject to which the planning permission has been granted is lawful,

to apply to the lpa specifying the land and describing the use or other matter. This provision is of particular significance when contemplating the purchase of property which may, or may not, enjoy legal status for its present use. The lpa is required to consider the application and issue a certificate, or refuse the application (s 191(4)). The certificate may accept the matters described in the application or may modify or substitute those statements and must give reasons for the determination. The applicant has the right to appeal to the SoS if he wishes to challenge the findings of the lpa.

Uses and operations are lawful at any time if:

(a) no enforcement action may be taken in respect of them, that is, they did not involve development, or because the time for enforcement action has expired or for any other reason; and

(b) they do not constitute a contravention of any requirements of any enforcement notice then in force.

(*Note*: For enforcement details see Chapter 18.)

Under s 191(6), the certificate has the same effect as the granting of planning permission except in those instances which require a licence to operate in addition to planning permission, that is, for the purpose of gaining:

(a) a caravan site licence;

(b) a waste disposal licence;

(c) a waste management licence;

(d) a licence for the sale of alcohol, gambling and a sex shop.

(See Chapter 30, para 30.7 for details.)

The establishment of a use of land or buildings is obviously the prime factor in establishing its value in the market. Any person who attempts to gain a certificate by the use of false statements or documents, or withholds material information, is liable on summary conviction to a fine of £2,000 or, on conviction on indictment, to imprisonment not exceeding two years, or an unlimited fine, or both (s 194(1), (2)).

The lpa has no discretion as to whether or not a certificate is issued if the applicant can satisfactorily prove the lawfulness of the development carried out. The onus of proving lawfulness rests with the applicant and the courts have taken the view that the relevant test of the evidence is 'the balance of probability'. Furthermore the courts have held that the applicant's own evidence does not have to be corroborated by other 'independent' evidence in order to be accepted. If the lpa has no evidence of its own, or from other parties, to make the applicant's evidence less probable then there is no good reason to refuse the application.

In *Panton & Farmer v Secretary of State for the Environment, Transport & the Regions and Vale of White Horse DC* [1999] JPL 461 the High Court gave guidance as to the approach the decision-maker should adopt in considering an application. The first and critical question is 'when did the material change specified in the application occur?' To succeed this must be prior to 1 July 1948, that is, the date of the operation of the 1947 Act, by 31 December 1963 or at least ten years prior to the application being made. Should this be the case then the question should be considered as to whether the use specified has been lost either by abandonment, the formation of a new planning unit or by way of a material change of use either as a result of the implementation of a further planning permission or otherwise.

Section 191(6) (TCPA 1990) provides that once lawfulness has been established it is not possible for the lpa to take enforcement action against any use, operations or other matter specified in the certificate. As there is no provision for a certificate of lawfulness of an existing use or development to be revoked it is, therefore, important that in accordance with s 191(5) that the lpa specifies the land to which the certificate relates the uses, operations or other matter in question and give reasons for determining the matters to be lawful and specify the date of the application for the certificate. However, following *R v Epping Forest BC ex p Philcox* [2000] P & CR 57 it is within the lpa's power subsequently to issue another certificate covering a larger area of land than that covered by the original certificate.

6.4   CERTIFICATE OF LAWFULNESS: PROPOSED DEVELOPMENT

There is now provision in s 192(1) (TCPA 1990) whereby any person who wishes to ascertain whether any proposed development for the use of buildings or land, or any operations which are proposed in, on, under, or over land, would be lawful, may submit an application to the lpa. The application must specify the site and give details of the proposal. In other words it cannot be used hypothetically as a method simply to 'test' the development control powers of a planning authority.

If the lpa is provided with adequate information, and is satisfied that the proposed development would be lawful, they must issue a certificate to that effect (s 192(2)), or alternatively refuse the application. The certificate may be issued in respect of the site or part of the site, and where the application specifies two or more uses, it may relate to all or some of those uses. Under s 192(4), the lawfulness of any use specified in the certificate shall be conclusively presumed unless there is a material change before the development is commenced.

There is a right of appeal to the SoS in the same manner as for a certificate for existing use, and the same conditions apply in the event of an applicant submitting false documents or information, or withholding material information. A certificate may also be revoked if it is gained by means of false information (s 193(6), (7)).

CHAPTER 7

CHALLENGES: THE MEANING OF DEVELOPMENT

7.1   INTRODUCTION

Chapter 2 explained the Secretary of State's (SoS's) responsibility for carrying out an administrative process in relation to planning and, although he determines appeals in a quasi-judicial capacity, judicial actions are the responsibility of the courts. The basis for the control of development vested in the SoS and local planning authorities is contained in the definition of development (s 55(1) of TCPA 1990) which includes a number of words which have been the subject of challenges in the courts to establish their precise legal interpretation. For ease of reference the definition of development is repeated below:

> The carrying out of building operations, engineering operations, mining operations and other operations in, on, over, under land, or the making of any material change of use of any buildings or other land.

The remainder of this chapter highlights those cases which are important in understanding the legal interpretation of the elements contained in the definition of what constitutes 'development'.

7.2   OPERATIONS

There is an important distinction between 'operations' and 'use'. 'Operations' was held in *Cheshire CC v Woodward* [1962] 2 QB 126; 1 All ER 517; 13 P & CR 157, which involved the installation of a coal hopper mounted on wheels, to be an act which changes the physical characteristics of the land, or what is under it, or in the air above it, whereas 'use' refers to the purposes to which a building or land are devoted. In dismissing the appeal Lord Parker's judgment appears to suggest that an object may be affixed to the land and not be a building, or not affixed to the land and be a building. He stated;

> The mere fact that something is erected in the course of a building operation which is affixed to the land does not determine the matter ... equally the mere fact that it can be moved and not affixed does not determine the matter. There is no one test and ask in all the circumstances is it to be treated as part of the reality? One must look at the whole of the circumstances including the permanency which is affected.

This definition was further refined in *Parkes v Secretary of State* [1979] JPL 33; [1978] 1 WLR 1308 by Lord Denning who stated:

> ... it seems to me that the first half 'operations' comprise activities which result in some physical alteration to the land which has some degree of permanence in relation to the land itself, whereas the second half, 'use' comprises activities which are done in, or alongside the land but do not interfere with the actual physical characteristics of the land.

The *Woodward* decision was later considered in *Barvis Ltd v Secretary of State for the Environment* [1971] 22 P & CR 710 which arose from an enforcement notice served by the local planning authority (lpa) following the erection of a 89-ft-high crane which ran on a track permanently fixed to the land by concrete. Following the appeal the notice was upheld and the appellant company challenged the decision of the High Court arguing that the crane was intended to be moved on and off the land and its degree of permanence was slight and furthermore that it had not altered the physical character of the land. In dismissing the appeal Bridge J did not question the validity or usefulness of the test propounded by Lord Parker CJ in what he regarded as the borderline *Woodward* case. In his judgment he stated:

> Building includes any structure or erection. If as a matter of impression one looks objectively at this enormous crane, it seems impossible to say that it did not amount to a structure or erection. It was no less a structure or erection by reason of its limited degree of mobility, nor by reason of the circumstances that at some future date, uncertain when it was erected, the appellants contemplated it would be removed.

This case highlighted the tests of whether something is a building or not: size, permanence and physical attachment to the land. (See also *Cardiff Rating Authority v Guest Keen Baldwin Iron and Steel Company Ltd* [1949] 1KB 385.)

The question of permanence was considered in *Skerritts of Nottingham Ltd v Secretary of State for the Environment, Transport and the Regions* [2000] JPL 281. The issue involved the annual erection of a large marquee that remained on site between February and October. An enforcement notice, served by the lpa requiring its removal, was upheld by the inspector acting on behalf of the SoS having decided the marquee was a building.

7.3 DEMOLITION – AN OPERATION?

The question as to whether demolition constitutes an 'operation' remained largely unresolved until 1991. Except in particular circumstances involving a listed building or conservation areas, previous Acts had not imposed a clear prohibition on demolition. The High Court handed down a decision in *Cambridge CC v Secretary of State* [1992] JPL 644; [1991] 1 PLR 109 which held that the demolition of two substantial dwelling houses amounted to a 'building operation' because it was an activity normally undertaken by a person carrying out the business of a builder. Therefore, such demolition would require planning permission. The SoS lodged an appeal against this ruling, and the Court of Appeal [1992] 3 PLR 4, overturned the decision in finding that the judge had made a finding of fact that he was not entitled to make and went on to rule that the works of demolition were not an 'other operation on, over or under land'.

The matter did not rest there. Whilst awaiting the outcome of the Court of Appeal the government introduced further provisions in the Planning and Compensation Act (PCA) 1991 designed to restrict to a narrow set of circumstances those circumstances when it is a requirement to gain planning permission prior to demolition. The SoS used his power (s 29(g) 1991 Act) to direct (under the Town and Country Planning (Demolition – Description of Buildings) Directive 1995, subsequently published as Appendix A to Circular 10/95) that the following are not to be taken to involve development:

(1) (a) any building which is a listed building;
    (b) any building in a conservation area;
    (c) any building which is a scheduled monument.

NB The above have their own safeguards re demolition: see Chapter 20)

> (d) subject to para (2) any building other then a dwelling house or building adjoining a dwelling house;
>
> (e) any building, the cubic content of which, measured externally, does not exceed 50 cubic metres;
>
> (f) the whole or any part of any gate, fence, wall or other means of enclosure.
>
> (2) A building is not to be regarded as a dwelling house for the purposes of para (1)(d) if the use of that building or part of that building as a dwelling house, is ancillary to any non-residential use of that building or other buildings on the same site.

The effect of the Direction was to make the demolition of all houses, whether in a terrace or a semi-detached dwelling, subject to control. As the demolition of most houses does not justify the full application of these new controls the SoS, with one exception, exercised his power in relation to the Town and Country Planning (General Permitted Development Order) (GPDO) to grant permission for the demolition of all buildings not already excluded from control. The one exception is where a building has been made unsafe or uninhabitable either through deliberate action or neglect by anyone having an interest in the land upon which the building stands where it cannot be made secure by temporary repairs or support. The demolition of the dwelling or of a building adjoining the dwelling house is permitted by virtue of Part 31 (Sched 2) to the Order. However, before such permitted development rights can be used the developer must first apply to the lpa for a determination as to whether prior approval of the authority is required as to the *method* of the proposed demolition and any proposed restoration of the site. The lpa has 28 days in which to consider the matter and failure to inform the applicant within that period gives deemed consent. Should the authority require prior approval the only remedy available to the owner/developer is to seek prior approval, and if this is not given, to appeal to the SoS. It is stressed that the prior approval requirement is to give the lpa an opportunity to minimise the impact of the act of demolition on local amenity and the need to seek prior approval does not prevent demolition from taking place. In order to prevent demolition there must be in place an Article 4 Direction (GPDO) withdrawing that permitted development right.

The prior approval procedure does not apply where demolition is:

(a) urgently required in the interests of health or safety;

(b) on land which is the subject of a planning permission for the redevelopment of the land;

(c) required or permitted under any enactment, for example anenforcement notice; or

(d) required by virtue of a relevant obligation, for example a s 106 agreement.

7.4 BUILDING OPERATIONS

The term 'building operations' is clearly intended to relate to work carried out involving work to a building defined in s 366(1) and 55(1)(A) (TCPA 1990) as:

> any structure or erection, and any part of a building as so defined, but does not include plant or machinery comprised in a building.

and also includes:

(a)   the demolition of buildings (subject to the limitations listed above para 7.3;

(b)   rebuilding;

(c)   structural alterations and additions to buildings; and

(d)   any other operations normally undertaken by a person carrying out business as a builder.

The effect of 55(1)(A) is reduced by s 5(2)(a) which excludes from the above definition:

The carrying out of works for the maintenance, improvement or other alteration of any building of works which:

(i)   affect only the interior of a building; or

(ii)   do not materially affect the external appearance of the building, and are not works for making good war damage or works begun after 5 December 1968 for the alteration of a building by providing additional space in it underground.

The inclusion of the word 'erection' expands the operation beyond that normally associated with the normal use of the word 'building' and includes walls, fences, masts etc associated with the building per se. Machinery housed in the open does constitute a building but not if the same machinery is housed within a building. Moveable objects such as caravans and vending machines are not normally regarded as buildings (and, therefore, a building operation for the purposes of planning control) but nevertheless they may involve a change of use and thereby require planning permission. In *Bendles Motors Ltd v Bristol Corporation* [1963] 1All ER 578 the court held that the minister was entitled to find the installation of an egg-vending machine in the forecourt of a garage to be a material change of use and, therefore, constituted development.

The scale of the building operation is irrelevant in determining whether or not the operation requires planning permission as in the case of *Buckingham CC v Callingham* [1952] 2 QB 515; 1 All ER 1166 where is was held that a model village constructed to scale was a structure or erection and, therefore, subject to planning control.

7.5   EXTERNAL APPEARANCE

The permission granted to developments which 'do not *materially* affect the external appearance of a building' gives rise to contentious issues. What is 'material' is largely a question of aesthetic judgment based upon the twin tests of *fact* and *degree* which involves the nature of the proposed change, the character of the building and its setting. For example, the enlargement of window frames on a detached house on a 'traditional' housing estate is likely to be acceptable whereas a similar proposal in a terrace of identical properties may require the submission of a planning application for consideration by the lpa. The interpretation of s 55(2)(a) (TCPA 1990) as to the affect of a proposal on the external appearance of a building is left to be determined by the lpa.

In *Royal London Borough of Kensington and Chelsea v CG Hotels* [1981] 41 P & CR 40, it was made clear that the effect has to be more then *de minimus* (see Chapter 21, para 21.4).

7.6   MAINTENANCE AND IMPROVEMENT

All buildings will, at some time, require maintenance and many will also be the subject of proposals for improvement, but how far is it possible to carry out relatively major works and remain within the limits set by s 55(2)(a) (TCPA 1990)?

In the case of case of *Street v Essex CC* [1965] 193 EG 537, the appellant had commenced repair work and found it necessary to demolish the building down to the damp proof course and begin 'maintenance' from that level. The court held that whether the work could fairly be said to amount to maintenance, or more properly be called reconstruction, was a matter of fact and degree and on this point upheld the SoS's contention that in this case the nature of the work amounted to reconstruction.

In *Larkin (CW) v Basildon DC* [1980] JPL 407, the developer was advised that he could rebuild two walls without the need to gain planning permission, and, having completed the work, proceeded to rebuild the remaining two walls. The Divisional Court upheld the SoS's decision that the construction of these walls, as distinct from the replacement of one or two of them, were not works of 'maintenance, improvement, or other alteration' within the meaning of s 55. The principle of rebuilding a property in stages has now been upheld as falling outside the limits of s 55(2)(a) following a further decision by the Court of Appeal in *Hewlett v Secretary of State* [1985] JPL 404; [1983] JPL 105.

7.7   ENGINEERING OPERATIONS

Section 336(1) (TCPA 1990) provides little guidance as to what may constitute an engineering operation and simply states that such operations include, 'the formation or laying out of means of access to highways'. Furthermore s 55(2)(b) and(c) of the 1990 Act specify operations which are not to be taken to involve the development of land:

(a)   the carrying out within the boundaries of a road by a local highway authority of any works required for the maintenance or improvement of the road, but in the case of works which are not exclusively for the maintenance of the road, not including any works which may have significant adverse effects on the environment.

(b)   the carrying out by a local authority or statutory undertakers of any works for the purpose of inspecting, repairing or renewing any sewers, mains, pipes, cables or other apparatus, including the breaking open of any street or other land for that purpose.

Clarification of what constitutes an engineering operation was provided by the decision in *Fayrewood Fish Farms Ltd v Secretary of State for the Environment* [1984] JPL 2667. The SoS was of the opinion that the removal of topsoil to extract underlying gravel constitutes an 'engineering operation'. In remitting the matter back to the SoS Mr. Widdicombe QC stated that in his view 'engineering operations' should be interpreted as 'operations of the kind usually undertaken by engineers, that is, operations calling for the skills of an engineer'. These would be normally be civil engineers, but could be traffic engineers or other specialist engineers who applied their skills to land. It did not mean that an engineer must be actually engaged in the project, simply that it was the kind of operation on which an engineer could be employed, or which would be within his purview.

Although the deposit of refuse or waste materials on land is regarded by the 1990 Act as a change of use, it was suggested by the High Court in *Ratcliffe v Secretary of State for the Environment* [1975] JPL 728 that depositing refuse could amount to an engineering operation.

The Court of Appeal, in holding a contrary view to the finding of the High Court, in *RFW Copper (Trustees of Thames Dutton Lawn Tennis Club) v KF Bruce-Smith* [1998] JPL 1077 held that the proposed breaking up of a tennis court was more aptly considered to be an engineering or other operation rather than demolition and a building operation.

The installation of fish tanks, that is, cages in inland waters, raised the question of whether it was the subject of planning control as an engineering operation over land. This led to the introduction in s 14 (PCA 1991) to the insertion in s 55 (TCPA 1990) of a new subsection (4A) which made the placing or assembly of fish tanks development. However, Part 6 (Sched 2) of the GPDO provides that such activity should be permitted development when carried out outside national parks, provided a person wishing to exercise this right gives prior notice to the lpa. This allows the authority 28 days in which to decide whether or not they wish to make the proposal the subject of their prior approval. If the authority does so decide then they have the right to exercise control over the siting and appearance of the development.

7.8   MINING OPERATIONS

In s 366(1) (TCPA 1990) mining operations are defined to include 'all minerals and substances in or under land of a kind ordinarily worked for removal by underground or surface working, except that it does not include peat cut for purposes other than sale'. This definition was amended by the Town and Country Planning (Minerals) Act 1981, and is now contained in s 55(4), which states:

(a)   the removal of material of any description from:
   (i)   a mineral working deposit;
   (ii) a deposit of pulverised fuel ash or other furnace ash or clinker; or
   (iii) a deposit of iron, steel or other metallic slags; and
(b)   the extraction of minerals from a disused railway embankment.

7.9   OTHER OPERATIONS

There is no definition of 'other operations' but the term is all embracing and there must, therefore, be some restrictions on the use of the words. The House of Lords in *Coleshill and District Investment Co. Ltd v Minister of Housing and Local Government* [1969] 1 WLR 746 pointed out that the use of the words 'building, engineering, mining and other operations' makes it clear that not every operation constitutes development, since to hold otherwise would render the use of the terms building, engineering and mining superfluous. Lord Pearson suggested that although no single genus would fit all three preceding words, it was possible that there were three separate genera and that 'other operations' would connote an activity similar to 'building operations, engineering operations or mining operations'.

Two ministerial decisions provide an indication of what may be construed as 'other operations'. An inspector held that the deposit of waste material on land to make it suitable for agricultural use was not a building or engineering operation, but an 'other operation' for which planning permission was required. [1982] JPL 267. A further case reported [1985] JPL 129 related to the installation of a protective grill over a shop window and door as this was regarded by the inspector as an 'other operation'.

7.10 LAND

The entire planning system operates on the basis of planning the future use of land and controlling the development of land. The basic question is: what is land? 'Land' is defined in s 336(1) (TCPA 1990) as, 'any corporeal hereditament, including a building, and, in relation to the acquisition of land under Part IX, includes any interest in or right over land'. The banks of a river constitute a corporeal hereditament but not the flow of water.

The case of *Thames Heliport v Tower Hamlets LBC* [1997] JPL 448, involved an application for a number of declarations to determine whether planning permission was required to operate helicopters from a vessel floating on the River Thames and also whether the use for 28 days during a year was permitted under the General Development Order 1988, Art 3(1) and Sched 2, Part IV Class B, for each of the proposed 20 different sites from which the helicopters might take off and land, or whether it was restricted to the whole length of the river on which the activity might take place. The High Court decided that planning permission was required and the 28 days permitted use would relate to the whole of the river. On appeal the Appeal Court was only prepared to grant a declaration that the use of the vessel could constitute a change of use under s 55 (TCPA 1990), and was of the opinion that whether a change of use was material or not is the responsibility of the local planning authorities. Similarly the court also refused to rule on the question of whether the 28-day permitted use covered the whole of the river likely to be used for the activity as again this was a matter of fact and degree to be determined by the lpa.

Despite the lack of a ruling Ward LJ observed that 'land' could only be the river bed and the river banks, not the flow of water. There was an ancillary use which was the exercise of rights of passage through it but the use of a vessel as a heliport was not such an incidental use because it involved holding the vessel in a stationary position during flight movements rather then moving up and down the river. The stationary vessel was not navigating, it was an obstruction to navigation. The helicopter taking off and landing would make use of the airspace above the river and that planning legislation is not simply concerned with the use of land, it is concerned with the area affected by an activity. The operation of helicopters was capable of having a considerable impact over a wider area that that occupied by the vessel and hence the proposal was capable of amounting to a material change of use.

7.11 CHANGE OF USE

The previous sections of this chapter have dealt with the first part of the definition of development. This paragraph deals with the change of use as defined in the second part of the definition, '... the making of any *material* change in the use of any buildings or other land'.

'Development' in this context does not require any physical change to the land or building itself but is purely related to the change in the use of the land or building. For example a building occupied as a private dwelling house could change its use to an office without any change to the structure but this would rightly be regarded as a change of use requiring planning permission.

Equally important is the fact that the change of use has to be regarded as '*material*' before the need for planning permission arises. The TCPA 1990 does not contain any definition of the expression 'material change'. Section 55(3) does, however, give two examples of what does constitute a material change of use, namely the use of a single dwelling house for the purpose of two or more separate dwellings and the deposit of waste materials which extend the superficial area or the height of the dump above adjoining ground level.

It is difficult to impose a general set of criteria that can be applied in any circumstance to define what is meant by the word 'material'. In the example above of a change of use from a dwelling to an office this obviously involves a change of use and therefore planning permission is required. What is the situation where part of the building is used as an office and the rest remains in residential use? Would it require planning permission, or not? The question of what amounts to a material change of use, as distinct from a change of use, is determined by applying two tests in any given situation, those of *fact* and *degree* (see *Barling (David W) Ltd v Secretary of State and Swale DC* [1980] JPL 594). Once the facts have been established the degree of use is essentially an assessment of the likely impact of that part of the building being used as an office and would raise issues concerning the amount of traffic generated by the partial use of the building for office purposes and the levels of noise and general disturbance to the immediate area.

A further hypothetical example could be two shops trading in the same high street each selling snacks. One provides the choice of hot or cold snacks, for example pies and pasties that are heated when requested by the purchaser by use of a microwave oven. The second shop, no doubt reacting to the competition, decides to offer the attraction of chips that are cooked in a deep-fat frying pan on the premises. Both premises are, therefore, selling hot food to be eaten off the premises and this would normally require planning permission (see Chapter 8 para 8.2) but does this apply to both premises? The tests of fact and degree must be applied. In the case of the first shop the installation of a microwave oven is not likely to have any material effect upon the number of customers or the surrounding property. On the other hand the installation of a deep-fat fryer equipped with suitable outside ventilation is likely to result in smells which may well affect the occupiers of surrounding properties and therefore planning permission may well be required.

The critical issue is that a *material* change of use must involve a new use that is substantially different from the old use, sufficient to change the character of that use in planning terms. Not surprisingly there are a considerable number of cases that have resulted in appeals to the courts. In determining such cases the attitude of the courts was made clear in the case of *Bendles Motors Ltd v Bristol Corporation* [1963] 1 WLR 2247 which arose after the local authority had issued an enforcement notice requiring the removal of an egg-vending machine from the garage forecourt. On appeal the minister upheld the notice on the ground that the stationing of an egg-vending machine on the site involved a change of use of the land on which it stood as the nature of the use was that of a shop and that it attracted customers not necessarily concerned with the service provided by a garage. The owners appealed to the High Court and in dismissing the appeal Parker CJ quoted his own words in an earlier appeal *East Barnet UDC v British Transport Commission* [1962] 2 QB 484:

> It is a question of fact and degree in every case and the court is unable to interfere with a finding on such a matter unless it can be said that they, (the local planning authority or the Minister), could not have properly reached that conclusion. This court can only interfere if satisfied that it is a conclusion that he could not, properly directing himself as to the law, have reached.

He went on to comment:

> It is surprising, and it may be, if it was a matter of my own personal judgement, that I should feel inclined to say that the egg-vending machine was *de minimus*, but it is not a question of what my opinion is on the matter, it is for the Minister to decide.

The limited ability of the courts to intervene was further indicated in *Moore v Secretary of State for the Environment, Transport and the Regions* [1998] JPL 877 by Nourse LJ:

> A question of fact and degree, although it is a question of fact, involves the application of a legal test. If the Secretary of State applies the correct tests, the court, on appeal under s 289, can only interfere with his decision if the facts found are incapable of supporting it. If, on the other hand, he applies the incorrect test, then the court can interfere and itself apply the correct test to the facts found.

In *Marshall v Nottingham Corporation* [1960] 1 WLR 7071; All ER 659; 11 P & CR 270, the site was used for the sale and small scale manufacture of garden sheds some of which were imported to the site. The site was tarmacadamed and then used for the sale of caravans not manufactured on the premises. It was found that there was no material change of the use and in his judgment Glyn-Jones J stated;

> Moreover if the business of a retailer is being carried on in any particular building, it may be that there is a change of use if, for example, that the business of a baker is substituted for a different business for example, that of a grocer: but I am unable to see why or how such a change can be material from any point of view which could legitimately be taken by the planning authority. The mere fact that a dealer in the course of his business begins to deal in goods in which he had not dealt with before does not necessarily involve a change, still less a material change, in his use of the land and premises where the business is carried on.

However, in *Miller (TA) Ltd v Minister of Housing and Local Government* [1968] 1 WLR 992; 2 All ER 633, it was held that a change from a plant nursery to a garden centre did constitute development. In this case the tests of fact and degree related to the likely increase in traffic and the fact that the form of sales was materially different.

The issue of whether it is proper to consider the off-site effects of a change of use in determining whether or not the change is 'material' was addressed in the case of *Blum (Lilo) v Secretary of State for the Environment and Richmond-on-Thames LBC* [1987] JPL 278. It was found that the inspector had rightly addressed the extent to which the additional use when livery stables were added to an existing riding school. It would involve additional staff and facilities, more horse activity, more rides out of the premises, more car traffic, more car parking as well as the introduction of a sanded paddock to be used for instructional purposes. He was entitled to assess the overall impact of the introduction of a new use on the overall character of the land. Similarly in *Forest of Dean DC v Secretary of State* [1995] JPL B 184, when the SoS's decision in respect of an enforcement notice relating to the change of use of a caravan park from holiday use to a permanent residential use was remitted to the court it was found that the inspector had failed to take account of the relevance of the off-site effects in determining whether or not a material change of use had taken place.

The problem of defining 'material change' where the change in character occur within the same general purpose was addressed in *Gray v Oxfordshire CC* [1963] 186 EG 19, where a block of lock-up garages was used to house a coach fleet and three minibuses. This was held to be a material change of use on the basis that the new use was sufficiently different although the general purpose remained the same. A further case *Miller Mead v Minister of Housing and Local Government* [1963] 2 QB 196; WLR 225; All ER 459, involved the change from the use of land for caravan storage to use of land for residential caravans. This was held to be a material change of use. (*Note*: This dealt solely with the planning aspects of the case but the proposed use would also have required a site licence: see Chapter 26.) However, in *Lewis v Secretary of State* [1972] 23 P & CR 125, the courts upheld the SoS's decision that a change of use from a repair garage carrying out repair work for a single company to a garage carrying out repairs available to member of the general public, was not a material change of use. Lord Widgery CJ stated:

> It is not my understanding of the law that, if the activity is exactly the same throughout the relevant period, a material change of use merely occurs because of a change in the identity of the person carrying out that activity. Similarly, I am not prepared to accept that, if the use through the relevant period is for the repair of motor vehicles, a material change of use occurs merely because the ownership and source of supply of those motor vehicles has changed.

Whilst the clientele may change without a material change of use having occurred, the method of trading can result in such a change as indicated in *Hidderley v Warwickshire CC* [1963] 61 LGR 266; 14 P & CR 134. The appellant had established a business selling farm eggs to the general public from his farmstead and in 1961 he provided an egg-vending machine immediately adjoining the main road. On appeal to the court, the appellant argued that he had an existing use right to sell eggs and only the method of sale had changed, which he argued was not a material change of use. Lord Parker CJ accepted that a mere change in the method of sale would not in itself constitute a material change, but in this case the change was of such a kind and degree that a material change of use had occurred. There was a difference between allowing the public to come to your door and selling on the main road.

7.12 INTENSIFICATION OF USE

So far this chapter has concentrated on issues where there has been an alleged change of use. This leaves an unresolved problem - can an existing use so change its character by intensification that it may constitute a material change of use by virtue of the additional impact it has either on the site itself or its surroundings?

Intensification of the degree of use on the same site may constitute a material change of use as exemplified in *Guilford DC v Fortescue and Penny* [1959] 2 QB 112; 2WLR 643; 2 All ER 111. There had been eight caravans on the site on 1 July 1948 (the appointed day for commencement of the TCPA 1947), and 21 when the enforcement notices were served, which rose to 27 before the hearing. The Court of Appeal held that this was a matter of fact decided at the lower court but Lord Evershed MR did not accept the argument that mere intensity of use, or occupation, could never be relevant as it could result in a substantial increase in the burden of services which the local authority supply. He went on to state:

> Mere intensity of user may (it seems to me; but I must not be taken as deciding this point) affect a definable character of the land or its use – or one of them.

(See, also, *James v Secretary of State for Wales* [1996] 1 WLR 135; *Esdell Caravan Parks Ltd v Hemel Hempstead DC* [1965] 3 WLR 1238; *Peake v Secretary fo State for Wales* [1971] 22 P & CR 889.)

In the case of *Birmingham Corporation v Minister of Housing and Local Government & Habib Ullah* [1964] JPL 394; 1 QB 178; [1963] 1 All ER 668; 3 WLR 937, an enforcement notice was served alleging a material change of use had occurred as a result of a single dwelling house being used as a house let to lodgers. The court held that, in law, the minister had erred in quashing the enforcement notice on the basis that as the house remained in residential use. This was a matter of fact and degree (see also, *Borg v Khan* [1965] 63 LGR 309; 17 P & CR 144).

A later case, *Clarke v Minister of Housing and Local Government* [1966] 18 P & CR 82, reinforced the fact that intensification of the same use can result in a 'material change' of use. The site comprised a large house and a lodge and in 1953 the house was sold and was converted into a hotel. In 1963 the hotel owners acquired the lodge and used the premises to accommodate staff working in the hotel. An enforcement notice was served alleging there had been a material change of use of the lodge from that of use by a single family to that of multiple accommodation for hotel staff. In dismissing the appeal from the decision of the Minister, Lord Parker CJ stated:

> I cannot see anything in law which prevented the Minister from saying that there was a change, and that that was a material change from the planning point of view.

The critical issue of precisely when does intensification of use amount to a material change of use was addressed in the finding of Donaldson LJ in *Royal London Borough of Kensington and Chelsea v Secretary of State for the Environment* [1981] JPL 50. The local authority had served an enforcement notice alleging a material change of use after a garden adjacent to a restaurant was used as a restaurant. On appeal the notice was quashed as the inspector had decided that the planning unit comprised the restaurant and the garden and therefore no change of use had occurred. The local authority did not appeal against that part of the inspector's decision but argued that he had erred in failing to consider the council's alternative argument that a material change of use had occurred as a result of the intensification of the use as a restaurant. Donaldson LJ drew attention to the ordinary use of the word 'intensification' and the different meaning ascribed by planners;

> In ordinary language, intensification meant more of the same thing or possibly a denser composition of the same thing. In planning language, intensification meant a change to something different … it had to be clearly understood by all concerned that intensification which did not amount to a material change of use was merely intensification and not a breach of planning control.

He further expressed the hope that those involved in planning would get away from the term and try to define what was a material change of use by reference to the *terminus a quo* (the starting point) and *terminus ad quem* (the end point). If planners were incapable of formulating what was the use prior to and as a result in alleging intensification, and thereby a material change of use, then there had been no material change of use. Thus, the intensification of the degree of the same use on the same site may constitute a material change in the use as exemplified in *Guilford RDC v Fortescue and Penny* [1959] 2 QB 112; 2 WLR 643. There had been eight caravans of the site on 1 July 1948 (the commencement day for the TCPA 1947), and 21 when the enforcement notices are served, a figure which rose to 27 before the date of the hearing. The Court of Appeal held that this was a matter of fact decided in the lower court but Lord Evershed MR did not accept the argument that mere intensity of use, or occupation, could never be relevant as it could result in substantial increase in the burden of services which the local authority supply.

7.13   MULTIPLE USE OF A SITE

The examples above have all dealt with issues relating to changes to a single use within a defined site. The question remains, what if there are two or more uses occupying the same site? Where two uses co-exist in one building or site, the question is raised whether one is ancillary to the other, or should each be assigned a definite part of the premises? It is frequently difficult to determine which of these circumstances exists and this provides potential pitfalls in deciding whether or not a change of use had occurred on the site.

In *Vickers Armstrong Ltd v Central Land Board* [1957] 9 P & CR 33, the appellant's administrative block had been destroyed by enemy action and the issue was whether, for valuation purposes the replacement building would be regarded as office or industrial use. The court found that the administrative block was incidental to the use of the industrial unit.

In a later case, *Trentham (Percy) Ltd v Gloucestershire CC* [1966] 1 WLR 506; 1 All ER 701; (1967) 18 P & CR 225, the appellants had purchased 1.5 acres of land which included a farmhouse and farm buildings, which had previously been part of a 75-acre farm. They then proceeded to use the premises for the storage of materials, plant, equipment and vehicles, and were served with an enforcement notice to discontinue the use. The Court of Appeal held that the buildings were never a repository, and that it was essential to look at the whole unit which had previously been a farm and the buildings had been used for agricultural purposes. The determination of the issue was clearly stated by Lord Denning MR based upon a judgment by Diplock LJ:

> What is the unit which the local authority are entitled to look at and deal with in an enforcement notice for the purpose of determining whether or not there had been a material change in the use of buildings or other land? As I suggested in the course of the argument, I think for that purpose what the local authority are entitled to look at is the whole area which was used for a particular purpose, including any part of that area whose use was incidental or ancillary to the achievement of that purpose. I think, therefore, they are entitled here to select as a unit the whole hereditament acquired by the appellants, and looking at that, ask themselves was there any material change in the uses of it? It is, I should have thought, as plain as a pikestaff that there is a change of use from an agricultural use as farm buildings to a storehouse for other purposes.

In his statement in *Brazil Concrete Ltd v Amersham RDC and another* [1967] 65 LGR 365; 18 P &CR 396, Lord Denning quoted the *Trentham* case and added:

> Take for instance Harrods store. The unit is the whole building. The greater part is used for selling goods; but some parts are used for ancillary purposes, such as offices and for the packing of articles for dispatch. The character of the whole is determined by its primary use as a shop. It is within Class I (now Class A3) of the Use Classes Order. The ancillary use of part as an office does not bring it within Class II (now Class B1); and the ancillary use for packing does not make it a light industrial building within Class III (now also Class B1).

The right to use land or a building for a dominant or primary use also includes the right to use it for any purpose which is ancillary to the dominant use and therefore the introduction of an ancillary use cannot be regarded as a material change of use, nor can the substitution of one ancillary use for another. If, however, an ancillary use becomes the dominant use then a material change of use may have taken place. In *Jillings v Secretary of State for the Environment* [1984] JPL 32, land and building in the Norfolk Broads had been used for the purpose of boat-hire with an ancillary use of boat building. The boat building activity expanded to the point that it became the primary purpose with boats for sale as well as the continued use for boat hire. One use had given way to two and the Divisional Court upheld the validity of the enforcement notice alleging that a material change of use had taken place.

In practice, determination of change in the use of land or buildings is dependent upon the evaluation of the twin tests of fact and degree. There is no rule book. The guidance from the courts over the years has proved invaluable to those making decisions on an array of complex areas, and there is no doubt the courts will be continually called upon by appellants to untie this Gordion Knot.

The issue of what constitutes an ancillary use was considered by the High Court in *Main v Secretary of State* [1999] JPL 195; (1998) 77 P & CR 300. The court held that a planning inspector had erred in treating 'ancillary' as meaning relatively small as opposed to being functionally related to the use of the premises. The haulage activities, which were not properly connected to the main use of the premises as a scrap yard, could not be regarded as ancillary to that main use.

7.14   THE PLANNING UNIT

What constitutes a planning unit is often a major factor in determining whether or not there has been a material change of use and is also a major factor in the enforcement of planning control (see Chapter 18). Is a purpose-built shopping centre a planning unit or each individual shop within the centre a planning unit? This question was addressed in *Church Commissioners v Secretary of State for the Environment* [1995] 71 P & CR 73. It was held that a shop in the Metro Centre, Gateshead, constitutes a individual planning unit and therefore planning permission was required to change the use from A1 to A3.

The judgment of Bridge J in the case of *Burdle v Secretary of State for the Environment* [1972] 1 WLR 1207; 3 All ER 24, provided guidance in the determination of what constitutes a planning unit. The problem addressed involved a site used as a car-breaking yard and spare parts from the car-breaking were sold from a lean-to building. The question was whether the sale from that building of imported spare parts

introduced a material change of use in terms of a shop. Although the court was unable
to come to a conclusion on the basis of the material before them, sending the matter
back to the SoS for his reconsideration, his Lordship set out three criteria to be used to
determine the correct planning unit:

1   Whenever it is possible to recognise a single main purpose of the occupier's use
     of his land to which secondary activities are incidental or ancillary, the whole
     unit of occupation should be considered.

2   Secondly, it may be equally apt to consider the entire unit of occupation even
     though the occupier carries on a variety of activities and it is not possible to say
     that one is incidental to another. This is well settled in the case of a composite use
     where the component activities fluctuate in their intensity but different activities
     are not confined within separate and physically distinct areas of land.

3   Thirdly it may frequently occur that within a single unit of occupation two or
     more physically separate and distinct areas are occupied for substantially
     different and unrelated purposes. In such a case each area used for different
     purposes (together with its incidental and ancillary activities) ought to be
     considered as a separate planning unit.

The second criteria was applicable in *Wipperman v Barking LBC* [1965] 17 P & CR 225,
where the occupier of land was using it for a number of different and unrelated
purposes. None of the uses were ancillary to a primary use and they were not confined
to any particular part of the overall site. In such a case the planning unit is the whole of
the site.

The application of the third criteria occurred in *Fuller v Secretary of State for the
Environment* [1987] 2 EGLR 189. The land being farmed by the appellant comprised a
number of scattered farms, some up to eight miles apart. The question arose as to
whether the SoS was correct in finding that the agricultural unit comprised a number
of separate planning units. In upholding the SoS's decision, Stewart-Smith J held that
there was material evidence in terms of fact and degree on which the decision was
based. He went on to quote Glidwell J in *Duffy v Secretary of State* [1981] JPL 811:

> In my judgment when buildings lie on opposite sides of a road, at some distance from
> each other, separated by properties, that geographical separateness must be a major,
> and may be the main factor in deciding whether they form one planning unit.

7.15   SEPARATE AND CONCURRENT USES

The problem becomes more complicated when there are two separate and concurrent
uses are established and exist in their own right on one physical area. In the case of
Williams v Minister of Housing and Local Government (1967) 65 LGR 495; 18 P & CR 514, a
shop sold produce from a nursery garden. Applying the tests above, it is clear that the
whole unit was considered as a nursery garden so the use was 'agriculture'. The sale of
imported produce from the shop was a material change of use. Had the sale of
imported produce been ancillary to the 'whole', that is the nursery, no permission
would have been required, but this was not the case as the shop existed in its own
right.

Situations arise when an area of land is in the occupation of two or more people. In *Rawlings v Secretary of State of the Environment and Tandridge DC* [1990] 60 P & CR 413, it was found that the determination of a planning unit was a matter of fact and degree and that the inspector had not erred in dismissing an appeal against an enforcement notice in respect of a piece of land which had been divided into small plots for the occupation of caravan dwellers.

The case of *Ralls v Secretary of State for the Environment* [1998] JPL 444, involved five parcels of land, some of which were not contiguous and in different ownerships (the appellant had owned five parcels prior to there disposal of some of the parcels). The Court of Appeal, in upholding the inspector's finding, emphasised that the proper planning unit was a matter of fact and degree for the decision-taker and occupation and ownership were not conclusive. He had come to the view that the coordinated land use for the holding of a market in excess of 14 days in any calendar year overcame the separate physical separation of the various parcels and their separate occupancy.

Where there are dominant and ancillary uses, this can only apply to activities within the same planning unit as made clear in the case of *Westminster City Council v British Waterways Board* [1985] AC 676. Lord Bridge of Harwich stated:

> The concept of a single planning unit used for a main purpose to which other uses carried on within the unit are ancillary is a familiar concept in planning law. But it is a misapplication of this concept to treat the use or uses of single planning unit as ancillary to activities carried on outside the unit altogether. (see also *Essex Water Co. v Secretary of State for the Environment* [1989] JPL 914).

Land constituting a planning unit can, and frequently does, include a dominant and ancillary use or uses. If land on which there is a secondary use is sold, the use becomes a dominant use for that area of the site and as such planning permission is required. It would appear that this does not apply to the sale of land comprising the dominant use as no change of use or status is involved.

In *Wakelin v Secretary of State for the Environment* [1978] JPL 769, a house in large grounds was granted planning permission to provide additional residential accommodation subject to a condition that it was occupied by a close relative or a member of the household staff. Later this accommodation was converted into self-contained flats and the issue was whether the change to separate accommodation involved a change of use. The Court of Appeal ruled that it did and Lord Denning MR was in no doubt that the division of a single planning unit into two separate units involved a material change of use.

7.16   ABANDONMENT

The concept of whether a use once established can be abandoned has, over the years, proved a contentious issue for the courts.

It was the issue in *Fyson v Buckinghamshire CC* [1958] 1 WLR 634. From 1943 to 1949 land had been used for storage purposes but from 1949 to 1956 the land was not used at all with the exception of a brief period from the end of 1953 to March 1954. In 1956 the land was once again used for storage purposes and an enforcement notice was served requiring that the use for storage purposes should cease on the ground that in 1956 a material change had been made in the use of land without the necessary planning permission. On appeal to the magistrates' court, the justices found that that no material change of use had taken place since 1949 and therefore no planning permission was required to carry on the storage use. Arising from this decision by the justices, the Divisional Court held that the decision was sound. It was pointed out that since 1943 there had never been any use of the land other than for storage and all that had happened was a long interruption of the storage use without any change having taken place.

The possibility of abandonment was also one of the issues addressed in *Webber v Minister of Housing and Local Government* [1967] 19 P & CR 1. The appellant owned a four-acre field which from 1960 was used between Easter and the end of September for camping after which period it reverted to land used for grazing. Shortly before the campers were due to depart in September 1965 the local authority served an enforcement notice requiring the removal of the tents, caravans and dormobiles within 28 days. Prior to 1968 the local authorities were required to serve an enforcement notice within four years of the alleged breach of planning control and the appellant maintained that as he had been using the land since 1960 it was no longer open to the authority to take enforcement action. For their part, the local authority maintained that the change of use was being made twice a year and since planning permission had not been granted for the last change to a camp site and therefore they were within the four-year period. The Court of Appeal held that the normal use of the field had to be looked at in terms of its normal use year to year over a considerable period of time. In doing so this established that the normal use of the field was for two purposes, camping in summer and grazing in winter and so long as this continued there could not be a material change of use.

The courts finally addressed the issue of abandonment in *Hartley v Minister of Local Government* [1970] QB 413; 2 WLR 1; (1969) 3 All ER 1658. Hartley appealed to the High Court and then to the Court of Appeal which held that the minister was entitled to find that the use for car sales had been abandoned and that once so abandoned, it cannot be resurrected without gaining planning permission. There were originally two distinct uses on the site, car sales and a petrol filling station and the car sales ceased in 1961. Car sales were resumed in 1965, but this was held to be development requiring planning permission. In his judgment at the Divisional Court, Ashworth J set out four propositions to assist in determining whether change of use had taken place under such circumstances:

(1) if the sole use to which the land had been put is suspended and thereafter resumed without there having been any intervening use, prima facie the resumption does not constitute development;

(2) there may be cases in which the period of suspension is so long that the original use can properly be described as having been abandoned;

(3) if land is put to more than one use, the cessation of one of the uses does not itself constitute development; and

(4) if one or two composite uses is discontinued and thereafter resumed, the question whether such a resumption constitutes a matter of fact is to be determined in all the relevant circumstances.

With the recognition that use can be abandoned it follows that the land would have no planning use other than agriculture or forestry which do not involve development. The argument by the appellant, that there could be no material change of use between the 'nil' use of land, that is, after alleged abandonment, and the resumption of the previous use for car sales unless there was an opposite material change of use when the use of the land for car sales ceased was not accepted by the courts. According to Lord Denning MR it is open to the lpa and the minister to conclude a use has been abandoned if land has remained unused for a considerable period of time. In such circumstances that a reasonable man might conclude the use had been abandoned. He also thought that the date for determining whether or not a use had been abandoned was when the new use was started.

The question of abandonment can reasonably be related to the intention of the party concerned and the weight that should be attributed to this fact. In *Hall v Lichfield DC* [1979] JPL 246, a residential property in the green belt had been occupied since 1935 but in 1961 the occupant entered hospital as a voluntary patient where she remained until her death in 1974. During her years in hospital she had made occasional visits to her home until about 1968 after which she was not able to continue her visits. On the advice of the local authority her dependants removed the furniture from the house to avoid attracting chargeable rates with the intention of returning the property should the owner recover sufficiently to return to her home. This never occurred and the property (albeit it in a dilapidated condition) was put on the market. The local authority took the view that even if the residential use had not been abandoned the major works required could constitute a rebuilding operation. Counsel advising the dependants sought a declaration that the residential use had not been abandoned and that declaration was duly granted.

Whilst the intentions of the party is one factor, it has to be taken into account with all the other relevant factors. In *Trustees of the Castell-y-Mynach Estate v Secretary of State for Wales* [1985] JPL 40, the Queen's Bench Divisional Court, in considering whether or not the resumption of residential use of a derelict house required planning permission, decided on the issue of abandonment that it was necessary to take into account:

(a) the physical condition of the building;

(b) the period of non-use;

(c) whether there had been any intervening use;

(d) evidence of the owner's intention.

7.17 USES WHICH DO NOT CONSTITUTE DEVELOPMENT

Finally, this chapter addresses the issues which arise from s 55 TCPA 1990 (see Chapter 6, para 6.2 for details) which states that certain matters shall not constitute development and includes:

(a) the use of any buildings or other land within the curtilage of a dwelling house used for any purpose incidental to the use of the dwelling house as such; and

(b) the use of land for agriculture or forestry (including afforestation) and the use for any of those purposes of any building occupied together with the land so used.

It should be emphasised that this exemption from planning control *only* relates to the *use* of buildings or other land and any building or other operation will require planning consent in the normal way.

The issue of what can be regarded as the curtilage of a dwelling house was considered in *McAlpine (The Hon David) v Secretary of State and Wycombe DC*[1994] JPL

B43 when a swimming pool was constructed without prior consent in the grounds of a listed building. The court found that there were three relevant characteristics determining a curtilage:

1   it was confined to a small area about the building;

2   it has an intimate association with the building; and

3   it was not necessary for there to be a physical enclosure of that land but the land, at least in law, must be regarded as part of one enclosure with the house.

(See, also *James v Secretary of State and Chichester DC* [1991] JPL 550; 1 PLR 58; 61 P & CR 234.)

The question of what constitutes 'the use of any buildings or other land within the curtilage of a dwelling house for any purpose incidental to the enjoyment of the dwelling house as such' was the issue in *Wallington v Secretary of State for Wales and Montgomeryshire DC* [1990] JPL 112; [1991] JPL 942. The householder kept 44 dogs on the premises, not for commercial gain but as a hobby, and the lpa served an enforcement notice (presumably because of the level of noise). This notice was appealed against and following the dismissal of the appeal by the SoS for Wales, the matter eventually was taken to the Court of Appeal. In dismissing the appeal, Farquarson LJ considered it to be sensible to consider what would be a 'normal' use of a dwelling house, although he did not necessarily regard this as the determinative factor. The word 'incidental' meant subordinate in land use terms to the enjoyment of the dwelling house and a hobby 'might be of such a kind and requiring such space that the enjoyment of the dwelling house became subordinate to the indulgence in the hobby'.

Farquarson LJ was of the opinion that the location of the dwelling house, its size and how much land was included in the curtilage, the nature and scale of the activity, and the disposition and character of the occupier were matters to be considered. However, Slade LJ was more emphatic that an objective standard had to be applied, namely, that one should have regard to what people normally did in a dwelling house.

The *Wallington* case raises the question of the role of planning enforcement not only against the private rights of the individual but also as an alternative to the method available to neighbours to resolve such issues by seeking an injunction. It can only be assumed that the lpa took action on the basis of the alleged nuisance arising from the keeping of 44 dogs on the property, in which case an application could have been made to the court to curtail or prevent the activities which were the cause of concern (see Chapter 30, para 30.2).

The issue of agricultural development (embodied in (2) above) has to be considered within the definition of agriculture contained in s 336(1) of TCPA 1990, which states:

> Agriculture includes horticulture, fruit growing, seed growing, dairy farming, the breeding and keeping of livestock (including any creature kept for the production of food, skins, fur, or for the purpose of farming the land), the use of land as grazing land, meadow land, osier land, market garden and nursery grounds, and the use of land for woodlands where that use is ancillary to the farming of land for other agricultural purposes.

In *Belmont Farm Ltd v Minister of Housing and Local Government* (1962) 13 P & CR 417, it was held that the breeding and training of horses for show jumping was not an agricultural activity, as the words 'breeding and keeping of livestock' were qualified by the parenthesis which refers to 'creatures kept for the production of food, skins, fur or for the purpose of farming the land'.

In *Sykes v Secretary of State* [1981] JPL 285; 42 P & CR 19, DC, a contrary decision was reached. It was held that the use of land for the grazing of racehorses and point-to-point ponies was agricultural because the grazing of land was not qualified by the words in parenthesis. A further judgment may finally determine the issue.

The question of what constitutes a lawful agricultural use was the subject of further consideration in *Millington v Secretary of State* [1999] JPL 644; 1 PLR 36. The applicant had a vineyard planted in 1991 that occupied approximately one-fifth of his total holding of 9.3 hectares. In 1993, he applied for a certificate of lawful use as viticulture – the breeding of sheep and lavender cultivation. Incidental to the agricultural uses, approximately 20–25 persons per week paid to visit the site to view ancient remains, the vineyard and the lavender. Farm sales included free-range eggs, lavender and wine, with limited hospitality in the form of free wine tasting. The certificate was refused and, on appeal, was granted with the exclusion of the sale of wine and visits by the general public.

In 1994, the appellant sought planning permission for a change of use of existing agricultural buildings to provide facilities for the making and storing of wine, the sale of light refreshments, agricultural products and for use by fee paying members of the public. An enforcement notice was then issued requiring Mr Millington to stop selling wine, light refreshments and to cease permitting visits by fee-paying members of the public. The notice did not require him to stop *making* wine. An appeal was lodged with the SoS against the enforcement notice and against the refusal of planning permission to change the use of existing agricultural buildings to use for making wine from grapes grown and sold on the holding. An application was also made for a certificate of existing use and development. The appeal was dismissed in relation to the enforcement notice. However, planning permission was granted for the use of existing buildings for the making of wine from grapes grown on the holding but preventing its sale. In relation to the certificate of existing use, the SoS allowed the appeal in part by certifying the 'agricultural use and a use incidental to agricultural use including the sale of eggs and lavender' ('agriculture' includes viticulture) and this did not amount to development, therefore.

The Millingtons challenged these decisions in the High Court which held that, in construing the term 'agriculture', it was not appropriate to include activities which went beyond the growing of crops. This excluded the processing of food and similarly went beyond the growing or cropping of fruit. It could not be said to be for the purposes of agriculture, nor incidental or ancillary to agricultural use and, therefore, constitutes a change of use. Consequently, the court (a) held that the enforcement notice prohibiting the sale of wine and light refreshment was valid; and (b) refused to quash the refusal of the SoS to grant a certificate for the use of the land for public visits to the site and for the sale of wine.

Mr Millington then appealed to the Court of Appeal. The fundamental question was whether wine making is one of the uses of land or a building that is occupied with land used for agriculture, which does not involve development by virtue of s 55(2)(e) (TCPA 1990) being the use of land for the purposes of agriculture as defined by s 336(1) (TCPA 1990). Schiemann LJ stated that there was no clear legal authority on whether the SoS was right in his contention that, where land is used for the creation of a new product from produce grown on the land, the land in question is, therefore, no longer used for agricultural purposes and thus exempt from planning control. The proper approach was to consider whether the activities could, having regard to ordinary and reasonable practice, be regarded as ordinarily incidental to the growing of grapes for wine, or whether the operations could reasonably be said to be consequential on the agricultural operation of producing a crop. The SoS's decision on the enforcement appeal was quashed.

(There is a marked difference in the approach taken by the High Court and the Court of Appeal. This decision presumably relates to the scale of the operation. Judge Rich *did* hold that, generally, agriculture does not extend to the further processing of crops. It would seem to follow equally that the making of wine from grapes on any substantial scale will involve a change of use, just as the making of beer from hops.)

One issue which has been resolved is that of the status of allotments which were held to fall within the statutory definition of agriculture (see *Crowborough Parish Council v Secretary of State* [1981] JPL 281; (1982) 43 P & CR 229).

It is clearly stated that the use of land for agriculture does not include the erection of buildings but leaves unresolved the question of the stationing of caravans, vehicles and pieces of equipment which are ancillary to agricultural operations. In *Wealdon DC v Secretary of State and Day* [1988] JPL 268; 1 PLR 87, a caravan was placed on land for the purpose of storing cattle food and providing shelter for the farmer whilst he mixed the food. The lpa issued an enforcement notice which was quashed by the planning inspector on the grounds that the caravan was ancillary to the agricultural use. The council unsuccessfully appealed to the High Court where Kennedy J stated:

> The fact that an item which is brought on to the land is aesthetically objectionable does not of itself cast any light on the question of whether the land is being used for the purposes of agriculture and whether the item complained of is contributing to that purpose.

This judgment was upheld in the Court of Appeal where it was stated:

> There is, in planning law even with reference to the most beautiful parts of our countryside, no basis for excluding from the notion of ordinary equipment a useful and suitable article such as a caravan on the ground only that it was not traditional in construction or appearance for the particular purposes for which Mr Day had applied it.

7.18   CERTIFICATE OF LAWFULNESS

In the case of *Bailey and Bailey v Secretary of State ex p Sedgemoor DC* [1994] JPL B52; (1995) 69 P & CR 617, the issue before the Court of Appeal was whether an application for an existing use certificate was prevented by the issuing of a temporary planning permission which had expired. The appellants acquired a site in 1981 which had been used for the repair, maintenance and storage of vehicles from a date before the end of 1963. The fact that the use started prior to the end of 1963 made it immune from enforcement action under the provisions of previous planning Acts, which were subsequently amended by the 1991 Act. No planning permission had been granted for the change of use of the land or for the buildings which were subsequently erected on the land. In 1987 the appellants applied to the lpa for planning permission for the continued use of the site and were granted temporary planning permission which expired on 30 April 1989. In February 1989, the appellants applied for a further planning permission to continue the use of the site. This was refused and an enforcement notice was served by the lpa. Although the appellant's site had an established use for the repairing and storing of motor vehicles under the old provisions, that is, which required the use to have been established prior to 1963 (now superseded by the '10-year rule') (see Chapter 18), that entitlement had been destroyed by the grant of a two-year, temporary planning consent granted in 1987. The effect of that grant of permission had been to make the use lawful for the period of the consent, that is, a two-year period (1987–89), after the expiry of which the use became unlawful. The Court of Appeal, therefore, dismissed the appeal on this ground.

In *Panton and Farmer v Secretary of State and White Horse Vale DC* [1999] JPL 461, the point at issue was whether the reference in s 191(1)(a) TCPA 1990 to 'existing use' meant that, to obtain a certificate of lawful use, the uses had to be continued at the time of the application. The Deputy Judge held that a use could be existing as long as that use has not been lost in the sense that the resumption of that use would be a material change of use. Provided the use had not been abandoned, extinguished, or changed to another use, it remained lawful, even if the use was dormant and physically non-existent.

CHAPTER 8

THE USE CLASSES ORDER 1987 AS AMENDED

8.1   INTRODUCTION

The Use Classes Order 1987 places groups of uses, known as 'classes', together and provides the opportunity to change from one use to any other *within* that particular group without the need to gain express planning permission. The Town and Country Planning General Permitted Development Order (GPDO) 1995 (see Chapter 10) authorises changes *between* use classes in certain cases. The rationale for the groupings is first, that the uses contained within them are similar in planning terms, and secondly, that the flexibility to change from one class to another is on the basis of a 'trade-up' in that the new class is more acceptable in planning terms. The flexibility afforded by the UCO and GPDO also reduces the number of planning applications which would otherwise fall to be determined by the local planning authority and should, at least in theory, assist in speeding up the planning process.

The original order was made in 1948; this was replaced by a further order made in 1972 which was very similar to the original. A review of the 1972 UCO was undertaken by the Property Advisory Group (not to be confused with the *Planning* Advisory Group: see Chapter 1, para 1.7), of the Department of Environment, whose brief was:

> To reduce the number of classes to a minimum compatible with keeping within specific control changes of use which, because of their environmental consequences or relationships to other uses, need to be the subject to prior authority; to permit, without the need for specific application, changes in the proportion or 'mix' of uses of different kinds within a single building; and, where possible, to permit change of uses to a less noxious one. Overall, the intention is to enable the occupiers of land and buildings to enjoy the maximum practical flexibility in the use of their property free from public control.

In 1985, a radical revision of the order was undertaken which reflected the government's desire to give greater freedom to developers to change the use of buildings or other land (or part thereof) and was part of the government's expressed intention of reducing the bureaucratic burden of planning amongst other forms of control. The White Paper, *Lifting the Burden* (1985, Cmd 9571), stated in para 3.1:

> The town and country planning system has not changed in its essentials since it was established in 1947. In many ways it has served the country well and the government has no intention of abolishing it. But it imposes costs on the economy and constraints on enterprise which are not always justified by any real public benefit ... Too often the very wide discretionary power that the system affords is used to apply excessively detailed and onerous controls of a kind that would not be tolerated in general legislation.

The new UCO was introduced in 1987 (SI 1987/764), and this has been amended on several occasions, in particular by the Town and Country Planning (Use Classes) (Amendment) Order 1995 (SI 1995/297), which added to the 'development' which can be undertaken without first gaining planning consent and by the Amendment Order 2005 (SI 2005/84).

It must be stressed that this freedom relates only to the *use* of land or buildings, and does *not* include any building or other operations which will require planning permission in the normal way. It does not follow that change of use not authorised by the Order necessarily requires planning consent because, as explained in Chapter 7:

(a) whether a change of use occurs is a matter of fact and degree;

(b) many primary uses have ancillary uses; and

(c) it should be noted that the majority of uses of land and buildings are not included in the UCO and they are *sui generis*, that is, they 'stand on their own'.

Under Art 3(5) of the Order no class as specified in the Schedule includes use:

(a) as a theatre;

(b) as an amusement arcade;

(c) as a launderette;

(d) for the sale of fuel of motor vehicles;

(e) for the sale or display of motor vehicles;

(f) for a taxi business or business for the hire of motor vehicles;

(g) as a scrap yard, or a yard for the storage or distribution of minerals or the breaking of motor vehicles;

(h) for any work registrable under the Alkali etc Works Regulation Act 1909;

(i) as a hostel;

(j) as a waste disposal installation for the incineration, chemical treatment (as defined in Annex IIA to Directive 75/442/EEC, D9) or landfill of waste to which Directive 91/689/EEC applies;

(k) as a retail warehouse club being a retail club where goods are sold, or displayed for sale, only to persons who are members of that club; or

(l) as a nightclub.

Therefore any change of use involving those uses not included in the order will continue to require an express grant of planning permission.

8.2 CONTENT OF THE ORDER

8.2.1 Class A.1 Shops

(a) Retail of goods other than hot food;

(b) post office;

(c) ticket sales, travel agency;

(d) sale of sandwiches or other cold food to be consumed off the premises;

(e) hairdressing;

(f) direction of funerals (not chapels of rest);

(g) the display of goods for sale;

(h) hiring of domestic or personal goods or articles;

(i) washing and cleaning of goods on the premises (not launderettes);

(j) reception of goods to be washed, cleaned or repaired; and

(k) internet café; where the primary purpose of the premises is to provide facilities for enabling members of the public to access the internet.

Provision is also made in the GPDO (Sched 2, Part 3) to allow for mixed uses primarily within a Class A.1 to use as a shop and a single flat. This also applies to Class A.2 and any change from Class A.2 to A.1 which has a window at ground level. These changes are also reversible.

8.2.2 Class A.2 Financial and professional services

(a) financial services;

(b) professional services (other than medical);

(c) any other service, including betting offices, appropriate in a shopping area,

where the services provided are principally to members of the general public.

8.2.3 Class A.3 Restaurants and cafés

(a) food and drink for consumption *on* the premises.

In addition to change within the same class, for example, hairdresser to travel agents (which are both A.1 uses), the following changes across classes do not require planning permission:

A.2 (where there is a window at ground level) to A.1;
A.3 to A.1;
A.3 to A.2; and
sale of motor vehicles (*sui generis*) to A.1.

8.2.4 Class A.4 Drinking establishments

(a) Use as a public house, wine bar or other drinking establishment.

Changes to A1, A2, A3 do not require planning permission.

8.2.5 Class A.5 Hot food takeaways

(a) Use for sale of hot food for consumption off the premises.

Changes to A1, A2, A3 do not require planning permission.

8.2.6 Class B.1 Business

This includes:

(a) use as an office which is not within Class A.2, research and development; and

(b) any industrial processes subject to the test that it is a use, 'which can be carried out in any residential area without detriment to the amenity of that area by reason of noise, vibration, smell, fumes, smoke, soot, ash, dust or grit'.

8.2.7 Class B.2 General industrial

Carrying out of an industrial process other than one which is within Class B.1 above.

8.2.8 Class B.8 Storage and general distribution

(*Note*: Classes B.3–B.7 contained in the previous order were revoked (Town and Country Planning (Use Classes) (Amendment) Order 1995 (SI 1995/297)).

The GPDO (Sched 2, Part 3) also permits changes between B.1, B.2 and B.8 subject to limitation as follows:

B.1 to B.8 (subject to a maximum of 235 sq m);
B.2 to B.1 (no restriction);
B.2 to B.8 (subject to a maximum of 235 sq m); and
B.8 to B.1 (subject to a maximum of 235 s m).

8.2.9 Class C.1 Hotels

Use as a hotel or boarding or guest house. (*Note*: No significant element of 'care' is to be provided. 'Care' relates to persons in need because of old age, disablement, alcohol, drugs, or mental disorder.)

8.2.10 Class C.2 Residential institutions

Use for the provision of residential accommodation and care for people in need of care (excluding Class 3, below), or as a hospital or residential school, college or training centre.

8.2.11 Class C.3 Dwelling houses

Use as a dwelling house (whether or not as a sole or main residence) by a single person or by people living together as a family (unrestricted in size), or by not more than six residents living together as a single household, including a household where care is provided for the residents.

8.2.12 Class D.1 Non-residential institutions

This class contains any medical or health services, except those *attached* to the residence of a consultant or practitioner; a crèche, day nursery or day centre. A 'day centre' is defined in Art 2 as 'premises which are visited during the day for social or recreational purposes, or for the purpose of rehabilitation or occupational training at which care is also provided'.

It also includes the provision of education, the display (*not* sale) of works of art, museums, public libraries or reading rooms, public halls or exhibition halls, and for or in connection with, public worship or religious instruction.

8.2.13 Class D.2 Assembly and leisure

Use as a cinema, concert hall, bingo hall or casino, dance hall, swimming bath, skating rink, gymnasium or other *outdoor* sports or recreation, *not* involving motorised vehicles or firearms.

CHAPTER 9

CHALLENGES TO THE USE CLASSES ORDER

9.1   INTRODUCTION

The interpretation of the content of the Use Classes Order (UCO) is subject to challenge by both planning authorities and developers, each for contrasting reasons: local planning authorities (lpas) frequently seek to narrow the degree of flexibility in changes of use which is provided; developers seek maximum 'elasticity'. These diametrically opposed approaches have led to a number of cases which have required interpretation by the courts.

9.2   BASIC CHALLENGES

The fundamental question raised by lpas has been whether they are entitled to restrict the benefits of movement within a particular use class. As a result of the decision in *Corporation of City of London v Secretary of State and Another* (1971) 23 P & CR 169, which required the premises be used for no other use than that of an employment agency, an lpa may, on the granting of planning permission, impose conditions which will preclude the use of the building or land changing from the use permitted to any other use within the same use class. However, the Secretary of State (SoS) has established a presumption against the use of such conditions. There must be clear evidence that:

> ... the uses excluded would have serious adverse affects on amenity, or the environment, that there were no other forms of control, and that the condition would have a clear planning purpose. (Circular 11/95, para 87, 'The Use of Conditions in Planning Permissions').

The effect of the order is entirely permissive and it does not necessarily follow that a change of use not specified by the order must necessarily constitute development, *Rann v Secretary of State and Thanet Business Council* [1980] JPL 109; 40 P & CR 113. In this case, a three-storied property had been used as holiday flatlets and in November 1975 planning permission was granted for use as a hotel/guest house. The property was actually used as a holiday home for mentally handicapped persons and in March 1976 the lpa requested a planning application on the basis that there had been a change of use within Class XIV of the UCO 1972: 'use as a home or institution providing boarding care and maintenance of children, old people or persons under disability, a convalescent home, a nursing home, a sanatorium or a hospital'. An enforcement notice was also served alleging an unauthorised change of use. On appeal, the enforcement notice was upheld but the SoS nevertheless considered it appropriate to grant planning permission subject to a condition that the use should cease before 30 December 1981.

The decision that there had been a material change in the use of the land or building was then the subject of an appeal to the High Court The SoS's decision was quashed in the High Court, and Sir Douglas Frank QC stated in his judgment that:

> The purpose of the Use Classes Order is not to define *what is development* but rather *what is deemed not to be development*.

... the Order of 1972 is being borrowed in this case for a purpose for which it was not intended. Its intended purpose is to put outside the ambit of the Act a change of use that has taken place within the same use class. I think it is inherent in the words used that the care and maintenance referred to is of a special nature ... the basic feature of a guest house as the word is used in the English language, however, is that it contains a transient population because it is there to serve people travelling who require short stays only ... I hold that the Secretary of State wrongly construed the use in this case.

In determining the character of the use, the factors to be taken into account are the effect of the change on the neighbourhood and/or the additional burden on local services (see *Guilford RDC v Fortescue & Penny* [1959] 2 QB 112; 2 WLR 6430; 2 All ER 111. If this is not the case, the application of the UCO is irrelevant.

The Order also relates to the primary use of premises and not some ancillary use. Thus a commercial use contained in Class B.1 (business class) may also include a staff canteen, and this would not constitute a separate use for the purposes of Class A.3 (food and drink). The canteen could be changed to the primary use, or vice versa without any planning consent being required.

The effect of the Order is not limited to buildings, and in some instances the use may take place entirely in the open. Where a building is erected on the site and the land is used for the same purpose, then this forms one planning unit.

There is no specific requirement in the Order which requires that the rights conferred are restricted to existing land uses which are lawful. If enforcement action is still possible against the unlawful use (subject to time limits (see Chapter 18, para 18.5)), then it is equally enforceable against the use introduced by virtue of the UCO. The converse is equally true: if enforcement action is not possible against the 'unlawful' use, then the benefits of change within the UCO cannot be challenged.

Changes of use authorised by the UCO are all bilateral, that is, a change within one use class can always be reversed without constituting development. This does *not* necessarily mean that it is possible to change from one class into another and then revert to the original class. In *Cynon Valley BC v Secretary of State (Wales) and Oi Mee Lam* [1986] JPL 760; (1987) 53 P & CR 68, an end-of-terrace shop with residential accommodation was granted permission in 1958 for the use of the shop premises as a fish and chip shop and this permission was implemented. In 1978, Mrs Lam acquired the property as a going concern with the intention of continuing the business but was unable to do so due to ill health. She therefore let the premises on a temporary basis for use as an antique shop until in 1983, having recovered from her illness, she recovered possession of the premises. She was informed that a fresh planning permission was required for the proposed use and her application was refused on amenity grounds in May 1983. On appeal to the SoS, the inspector appointed to determine the case held that no development requiring planning permission was involved on two grounds: first, that resumption of the use was permitted by s 23(8) of the Town and Country Planning Act (TCPA) 1971; and, secondly, that the 1958 permission was not spent.

Cynon Valley BC then applied to the High Court for an order to quash the inspector's decision. The court dismissed the application and in doing so supported the inspector's finding that the change of use to an antiques shop did not mean that the premises had lost the benefit of the 1958 planning permission for a fish and chip shop. The decision of the court supported ground two but not ground one of the inspector's finding.

Leave was granted to take the case to the Court of Appeal which upheld the decision of the lower court but on a different and narrower ground. The court determined that the 1958 permission *was* spent but that that s 23(8) did apply and therefore there had been no material change in use of premises which changed from a fish and chip shop (A.3) to an antique shop (A.1) and then reverted to a fish and chip shop (A.1–A.3). These changes did not involve development as the former use, that is, the fish and chip shop, was lawful.

This decision largely negated the ratchet effect, that is, moving to a more acceptable use in planning terms, but the problem may have been overcome by the introduction of the word 'exceptions' in the GPDO 1995, Sched 2, Art 3(2) which makes it clear that in the case of permitted development it is subject to any exception limitation or condition specified in Sched 2.

9.3   WHAT IS A SHOP?

In *Cawley v Secretary of State* [1990] JPL 742; 2 PLR 90; 60 P & CR 492, the High Court held that the word 'shop', as used in the order, showed an intention to restrict the operation to within buildings. The Order, therefore, did not authorise the use of land for the sale of caravans in connection with the use as a garden centre.

In *R v Kensington and Chelsea Royal London Borough ex p Europa Foods Ltd* (1996) EGCS 5, the proposed use of the premises as an auction room, to be combined with an existing adjoining auction room, was refused by the court. It was held that although goods would be sold it was a question of fact and degree and did not meet the requirements of a normal shop which was taken to be a 'shop' that might be found in a typical high street.

Similarly in *R v Thurrock Council ex p Tesco Stores* [1994] JPL 328; (1993) 3 PLR 114, it was found that a 'warehouse club' was not a shop for the purposes of Class A.1 as there was a restriction on those who were entitled to purchase goods and, therefore, it was not *prima facie* for the sale of goods to the visiting public.

Neither a bureau de change (which falls more appropriately under Class A.2: *Palisade Investment Ltd v Secretary of State and Westminster City Council* [1991] JPL 331; (1994) EGCS 188 CA), nor the showing of films in coin-operated booths (*Lydcare v Secretary of State and Westminster City Council* (1985) 49 P & CR 186) have been found to be within Class A.1.

The development of large shopping malls has resulted in the question as to whether the mall itself is one planning unit, or whether each individual unit within the mall is the appropriate planning unit. This matter was addressed in *Church Commissioners v Secretary of State* (1995) (unreported) and involved a change of use of a single unit in the Metro Centre, Gateshead, which had been constructed in an Enterprise Zone without express planning consent. The question was whether planning permission would be required to change the use of a single retail unit (Class A.1) to a restaurant (Class A.3). The landowners argued that the whole of the Metro Centre was the appropriate planning unit, in that it was an area of land in one occupation and comprised a single building. On this basis the use of any part of the Metro Centre was not a change of use of the planning unit but the adjustment of ancillary uses as could occur in any multiple store. After reviewing the relevant cases, including *Burdle v Secretary of State* [1972] 1 WLR 1207; 3 All ER 24 and *Johnston v*

Secretary of State (1974) 28 P & CR 424, the court upheld the approach of the SoS which was to accept that although for certain purposes the landlord was in occupation of the whole Metro Centre, but for the purpose of planning control it was nevertheless appropriate to identify each individual shop as a planning unit. This decision reduces the flexibility to change uses within established shopping malls which previously had been assumed to be a matter of landlord control over the mix of uses.

9.4   WHAT ARE FINANCIAL AND PROFESSIONAL SERVICES?

The critical test of an A.2 use is whether the service is provided principally for members of the general public. In *Kalra v Secretary of State* (1994) 2 PLR 99; (1995) EGCS 163, the Court of Appeal drew a distinction between different types of solicitors. In some cases, the office is open to members of the general public and in others the nature of the work undertaken was primarily by correspondence and telephone. This latter category would more appropriately fall into Class B.1. This does leave the problem of a solicitor who, over a period of time, changes the emphasis on the type of work carried out by the firm. One who genuinely falls within Class A.2 by providing a service to members of the general public, may (inadvertently) become B.1 and, therefore, require planning permission to continue to operate from the same site; likewise there is no provision for a B.1 user to change the emphasis of the business to meet the requirements of the general public without first gaining planning permission.

9.5   WHAT IS A B.1 USE?

The old class of 'light industry' has been omitted from the current UCO and the problem relating to new B.1 uses arises from the definition which is:

> Any industrial process, being a use which can be carried out in *any residential area* without detriment to the amenity of the area by reason of noise, vibration, smell, fumes, smoke, soot, ash, dust or grit.

The reference to 'any residential area' is a notional concept. The precise location of the use is irrelevant. The industry may be within a noisy area, or one which has all the characteristics of a major industrial area, but the test is whether the use would be satisfactorily accommodated in a hypothetical residential area (see *Lamb (WT) Properties Ltd v Secretary of State and Crawley BC* [1983] JPL 303).

The definition focuses on the impact of the use and not the proposed industrial process. In theory any use contained within a building which is fully equipped to deal with noise, vibration, smell, fumes, etc, could well fall within the B.1 class. The lpa is, therefore, placed in the position of having to evaluate the likely future impact from an industrial process prior to accepting an industry into this class of development (see Chapter 30, para 30.6).

The inclusion in Class B.1 of office and research and development uses has also created problems for lpas in attempting to establish industrial employment uses within their areas. Office use will, in most circumstances, increase the value of a building and, therefore, there has been a fear expressed by authorities that the industrial uses they seek to promote will be lost because of the flexibility afforded by

B.1. Some are, therefore, seeking to restrict that flexibility by the imposition of conditions (see para 9.2 above).

A further potential problem is the change in use to offices which may take place in already well established B.1 industrial areas. This issue was the subject of an adjournment debate in the House of Commons (*Hansard*, 5 February 1987) when John Wheeler MP for Westminster (North), raised the issue of the tailors established in Saville Row, London. His argument was that the location in Saville Row was part of an integrated series of land uses in and around the area, and that if the tailoring community were forced to move away from the centre of London, their departure would damage that areaaand, in particular, the commercial activity of the City of Westminster. Wheeler failed to get the then proposed business B.1 class changed, and in reply to the arguments mounted on behalf of the tailoring community, the government took the approach that planning should not be concerned with property values or rents.

9.6   WHAT IS A B.2 USE?

The 1995 UCO deleted special industrial use classes B.3–B.7 which had previously formed a part of the 1948 and the original 1987 UCOs. (Hence, we now move directly from B.2 to B.8.) These original use classes included what may be regarded as offensive, or bad neighbour, uses such as smelting, burning bricks or pipes, producing or using cellulose, blood boiling and the breeding of maggots from putrescible matter. To answer the question, 'what is a B.2 use?', it is simply any industry or industrial process which does not comply with the requirements of Class B.1.

The government's rationale for deleting the uses B.3–B.7 is based upon consideration of two factors. First, it was argued that it would benefit industry by providing greater flexibility, and, secondly, it was considered that the new pollution control legislation brought into effect since 1987 will maintain control over these industries. This switch from planning to pollution control as a mechanism for providing adequate environmental safeguards is addressed in PPG 23, 'Planning and Pollution Controls' (see Chapter 30 and, also, Blackhall, JC, 'Planning control and special industrial uses: B.2 or not 2.B' [1995] 3 JPL).

9.7   WHAT CONSTITUTES STORAGE OR A DISTRIBUTION CENTRE?

This wording in B.8 replaced that in the 1972 Order which read 'use as a wholesale warehouse or repository for any purpose.' The change is significant as a 'wholesale warehouse' will generally fall within A.1 shops however much floorspace is used for storage purposes. There is no implied use of the premises for a shop except to a limited incidental extent (see *Decorative and Caravan Paints Ltd v Minister of Housing and Local Government* (1970) 214 EG 1355; *Monomart Warehouses Ltd v Secretary of State* (1977) 34 P & CR 305). By the same token, it would not include a cash and carry warehouse (*LTSS Print and Supply Services v London Borough of Hackney* [1976] 1 QB 663; 1 All ER 311; 2 WLR 253).

The Court of Appeal in *Crawley BC v Hickmet Ltd* [1998] JPL 210 held that there is a clear distinction between car parking and commercial storage. A site, which had the benefit of an established user certificate for commercial storage, had become an off-airport car park at Gatwick. The court held that the difference was a matter primarily of law and not exclusively one of fact; neither was it simply a matter of degree. The two activities of parking and storage were distinct and mutually exclusive. Storage connoted taking a car off the road while it was not in current use, whilst parking was an incident of use. The court granted an injunction prohibiting the continuance of the car parking use on the site.

It is also important to note that the new uses may be carried out on open land and do not necessarily require a building to establish the use class.

9.8   WHAT IS A HOTEL?

Class C.1 was introduced in April 1994 and subsequently included in the UCO. Prior to that, the use class included a hostel, which is now deliberately excluded as the SoS regarded this flexibility as a potential threat to the amenities of tourist areas from the establishment of hostels which frequently attracted large numbers of social benefit claimants. The distinctive features of a hotel, or guest house, are dealt with in *Panyani v Secretary of State* [1985] JPL 783; 50 P & CR 109, and in *Mayflower Cowbridge Ltd v Secretary of State* (1975) 30 P & CR 28 where the change from a hotel to bed-sitting rooms was held to be a material change of use, as was a change to a residential club (*English Speaking Union v Westminster LBC* (1973) 26 P & CR 575). However, the redistribution of an ancillary activity, for example, the bar area within an established hotel, does not require planning permission (*Emma Hotels Ltd v Secretary of State* [1979] JPL 390).

9.9   WHAT IS A DWELLING HOUSE?

The definition in Class 3 includes an arbitrary figure of 'not more than six persons living together as a single household', that is, sharing the common facilities. This raises the question regarding whether any number in excess of six will take the property out of this use class. The figure is arbitrary, and the question will only arise if the numbers increase to such an extent that it can be said that the use has intensified to such a degree as to alter the character of the premises – once again a question of fact and degree. However, if the occupants, irrespective of the number, do not live as a household the use may then fall to be regarded as hostel use, or a house let in lodgings.

The court has confirmed that, where care is provided for residents, this does not require that the staff providing that care are themselves residents in the same dwelling (*R v Bromley LBC ex p Sinclair* (1991) 3 PLR 60).

The question of conflict between two legislative provisions relating to occupancy of dwellings was addressed by the High Court in *Hyde Park Residence Ltd v Secretary of State* [1999] JPL 897; 4 CL 493 QBD. Under s 3 of the Greater London (General Powers) Act 1973, the use of residential accommodation in London for the purpose of providing 'temporary sleeping accommodation' involves a material change of use. The

UCO 1987, Class 3, deems there to be no development when the old and the new use constitute the use of a dwelling house.

The court concluded that the changes that had occurred would not generally be regarded as development. However, it went on to hold that, in London, the position was reversed and that the 1987 UCO could not override the 1973 Act.

The Court of Appeal in *Secretary of State for the Environment, Transport and the Regions v Waltham Forest LBC* [2002] EWCA, held that an inspector was wrong to find that under Class C3, where the use of a single dwelling house was increased to eight residents living together as a single household from not more than six, that there was no material change of use.

9.10 CONDITIONS RESTRICTING PERMITTED DEVELOPMENT

The grant of planning permission for the erection of a building will automatically place the subsequent building within a particular use class, unless the proposed use of the building is a *sui generis*, for example, planning permission for a shop would allow change of use within Class A.1. As has been noted above in *Corporation of the City of London v Secretary of State and Another* (see para 9.2), provided there is a clear planning purpose this right to change the use may be restricted by means of a planning condition. This early judgment has recently been upheld in *Camden LBC and PSP (Nominees) v Secretary of State* [1989] JPL 613; (1990) 59 P & CR 117; 2 PLR 79 wherein it was held that a condition could be imposed to preclude the right under Class B.1 to change from light industry to offices.

In the case of *sui generis* use, in this case, a car showroom, the question raised in *Dunoon Development Ltd v Secretary of State and Poole BC* [1992] JPL 936; 2 PLR 128; (1993) 65 P & CR 101 was whether that use can take advantage of a UCO to change its use to a shop. In 1956, planning permission was granted for the erection of a car showroom, subject to a condition that the use of the premises should be limited to the display and sale of cars and associated activities; no heavy repairs or noisy activities were to be carried out. The reason for the condition was to preserve the amenities of the residential area. In 1990 the premises were acquired and the new owner opened an indoor market, relying on the interpretation of the UCO. It was held that this change was permitted and that the 1956 condition delimited or circumscribed the ambit of the then permitted use and no more. It was not apt to prevent development under any existing or future order.

CHAPTER 10

TOWN AND COUNTRY PLANNING (GENERAL PERMITTED DEVELOPMENT) ORDER 1995 AND LOCAL DEVELOPMENT ORDERS

10.1   INTRODUCTION

Prior to 1995, there was a single General Development Order, the content of which was effectively split into two parts by the introduction of the Town and Country Planning (General Permitted Development) Order (GPDO) 1995 (SI 1995/418) and the Town and Country Planning (General Development Procedure) Order (GDPO) 1995 (SI 1995/419). These orders are applicable to all land in England and Wales. The 'sections' comprising these Orders are referred to as 'Articles'.

The Secretary of State (SoS) is *required* (s 59 of the Town and Country Planning Act (TCPA) 1990) to make a Development Order providing for the grant of planning permission. Such an Order may either grant planning permission itself or provide for the granting of planning permission by the local planning authority (lpa) on an application made in accordance with the provisions of the order. The GPDO meets the SoS's statutory requirements in this regard; likewise the GDPO sets out the statutory procedures to be followed by lpas when determining planning applications (see Chapter 12, 'Planning Applications').

Article 3, sub-s 5, contains an overriding condition which applies to all permitted development classes to the effect that nothing in the Order authorises any development 'which requires or involves the formation, laying out or material widening of the means of access to an existing highway which is a trunk or classified road, or creates an obstruction to the view of persons using the highway used by vehicular traffic so as to be likely to cause danger to such persons'.

Article 4(1) of the Order gives lpas the power, subject to approval by the SoS, to make a Direction which has the effect of withdrawing permitted development rights, as specified in the Direction. Under Art 4(2) local authorities can make orders, without reference to the SoS, withdrawing permitted development rights from dwellings in Conservation Areas, where the development would front a highway, waterway or open space.

10.2   ARTICLES COMPRISING THE TOWN AND COUNTRY PLANNING (GENERAL PERMITTED DEVELOPMENT) ORDER

Permitted development is defined in Sched 2 of the GDPO, which provides details of development which can be undertaken without the need to seek planning permission.

Article 1 provides a comprehensive list of extended definitions of planning terms.

Article 3 grants planning permission for the categories of permitted development set out in Sched 2 and also sets out the limitations where permitted development will not apply:

(a) to provisions in the Conservation (Natural Habitats, etc) Regulations 1994 (SI 1994/2716);

(b) to limitations or conditions attached to planning permissions;

(c) to unlawful building operation, or unlawful use of land;

(d) with the exception of Parts 9, 11, 13 or 30, to authorise any development which would result in the formation, laying out, widening of a means of access to a highway which is a trunk or classified road;

(e) to the granting of permission for pipelines other than gas;

(f) except as provided in Part 31 to the demolition of a building ('building' does not include part of a building); and

(g) if it conflicts with the Town and Country Planning (Assessment of Environmental Effects) Regulations 1988 (SI 1988/1812).

Article 4 provides for Directions by which an lpa may withdraw or restrict the scope of Sched 2 permitted development rights within defined areas (in other words they will require applications for planning permission in the normal way (see Chapter 12 for those changes so restricted). Restrictions under Art 4 cannot be applied to development proposed by statutory undertakers.

Article 5 (paras 3 and 4) specifies that Art 4 Directions shall not require the approval of the SoS when related to:

(a) a listed building;

(b) a building which is notified to the SoS as a building of architectural or historic interest;

(c) development within the curtilage of a listed building;

(d) any development permitted by Parts 1–4 or Part 31 of Sched 2, that is, development within the curtilage of a dwelling house, minor operations, changes of use, temporary building and uses and demolition of buildings.

In all other cases, the SoS's approval must be granted before the Order is confirmed and, should the direction not be approved within six months, it automatically lapses (Art 5(1)).

Once any direction has been made under Art 4(2), the lpa is required to advertise the fact in a local newspaper and also serve notice on the owner and occupier of every dwelling house within the area in so far as this is practicable. Such persons affected shall be given 21 days in which to make representations which must be considered by the lpa before confirming the Order (Art 6).

Under the notification procedure which relates to minerals covered by Sched 2, Part 22 (Class B) or Part 23 (Class C), a minerals authority (shire county or metropolitan district), under Article 7, may, within 21 days, restrict the development permitted under Sched 2 in relation to land:

(a) within a National Park, including the Broads;

(b) in an area of outstanding natural beauty (AONB);

(c) which is a site of archaeological interest, or a site of special scientific interest (SSSI);

(d) which adversely affects the setting of a Grade I listed building;

(e) which is likely to create a nuisance to occupiers of residential building, hospital or school; or

(f) which may endanger aircraft using an airfield.

The SoS may within 28 days disallow the Direction, and Art 8 grants power to cancel or vary a direction previously issued.

10.3   SCHEDULE 1 TO THE TOWN AND COUNTRY PLANNING (GENERAL PERMITTED DEVELOPMENT) ORDER

This, the first of two schedules, specifies geographical areas within which stricter limits apply to certain permitted development rights granted under Sched 2 (see para 10.4, below).

Article 1(4):   lists particular counties in England and Wales.

Article 1(5):   relates to land within:

(a) a National Park;

(b) an area of outstanding natural beauty;

(c) an area designated as a conservation area under s 69 of the Planning (Listed Buildings and Conservation Areas) Act 1990;

(d) an area specified by the SoS or DEFRA for the purpose of s 41(3) of the Wildlife and Countryside Act 1981, specifically to enhance and protect the natural beauty and amenity of the countryside; and

(e) the Broads.

Article 1(6):   lists parishes within or adjoining national parks.

10.4   SCHEDULE 2 TO THE TOWN AND COUNTRY PLANNING (GENERAL PERMITTED DEVELOPMENT) ORDER

This schedule provides details of development which can be undertaken without the need to seek planning permission within defined limits. It comprises the following 33 Parts, each of which contains a series of classes which deal with a particular type of development:

1   **Development within the curtilage of a dwelling house.**

2   **Minor operations.**

3   **Changes of use.**

4   **Temporary buildings and operations.**

5   Caravan sites.

6   Agricultural buildings and operations.

7   Forestry buildings and operations.

8   Industrial and warehouse development.

9   Repairs to unadopted streets and private ways.

10   Repairs to services.

11 Development under local or private Acts or Orders.

12 Development by local authorities.

13 Development by highway authorities.

14 Development by drainage authorities.

15 Development by National Rivers Authority.

16 Development by or on behalf of sewerage undertakers.

17 Development by statutory undertakers.

18 Aviation development.

19 Development ancillary to mining operations.

20 Coal mining development by the Coal Authority and licensed operators.

21 Waste tipping at a mine.

22 Mineral extraction.

23 Removal of material from mineral-working deposits.

24 Development by telecommunications code system operators.

25 Other telecommunications development.

26 Development by the Historic Buildings and Monuments Commission for England.

27 Use by members of certain recreational organisations.

28 Development in amusement parks.

29 Driver information systems.

30 Toll road facilities.

31 Demolition of buildings.

32 Schools, colleges, universities and hospitals.

33 Close-circuit television cameras.

(*Note*: A full explanation of the 33 Parts is not possible in a book of this length and only those in bold above will be dealt with in detail as these are probably the most frequently used provisions of this Schedule. For a resume of the GPDO see Appendix II.)

It is stressed that each class of permitted development is restricted to clearly defined tolerances. If these limits are exceeded in any particular case this will take the development out of the permitted development classification and will require express grant of planning permission from the lpa.

Furthermore the Town and Country (Environmental Impact Assessment) (England and Wales) Regulations 1999 (SI 1999/293) may require an Environmental Impact Assessment (EIA) to be submitted to the local authority in spite of the permitted development rights contained in the GPDO.

10.5 PART 1: DEVELOPMENT WITHIN THE CURTILAGE OF A DWELLING HOUSE

As explained in para 10.4, above, Part 1 is taken as an example of the operation of the permitted development under Sched 2 because it is probably the most frequently used of the schedules and it also provides a very good example of the parameters set out in each class. To a member of the general public posing the question, 'Do I need planning permission to alter my house?', there is no simple or easy answer. A series of tests must be applied before the planning officer can provide the answer to what may appear to be a deceptively simple request.

Part 1 contains eight classes (or sub-ss) one or more of which may have to be consulted to determine whether or not a proposal affecting a dwelling house will fall within permitted development rights. The first question, 'Is the property a "dwelling house"?' is defined in Art 1(1) and 'does not include a building containing one or more flats, or a flat contained within such a building'. Assuming the property passes this critical test, and is a dwelling house, then the following classes apply:

Class A the enlargement, improvement or other alteration;

Class B the enlargement consisting of an addition or alteration to its roof;

Class C any other alteration to the roof;

Class D erection or construction of a porch outside any external door;

Class E provision within the curtilage of any building or enclosure, swimming or other pool, required for a purpose incidental to the enjoyment of the dwelling house as such, or the maintenance or other alteration of such a building or enclosure;

Class F provision of any hard surface for any purpose incidental to the enjoyment of the dwelling house;

Class G erection or provision of a container for the storage of oil for domestic heating;

Class H installation, alteration or replacement of a satellite antenna on a dwelling house or within the curtilage.

Each class defines limits beyond which planning permission *will* be required.

Class A

Development is not permitted by Class A if:

A.1

(a) the cubic content of the resulting building would exceed the cubic content of the original house (measured externally and including the roof space);

    (i) in the case of a terraced house or dwelling on Art 1(5) land by more than 50 cu m or 10% whichever is the greater;

    (ii) in any other case more than 70 cu m or 15%;

    (iii) in any case by more than 115 cu m;

(b) any part would exceed the highest part of the roof of the original dwelling;

(c) any part of the building enlarged, improved or altered would be nearer to any highway than that part of the original dwelling house nearest to the highway or 20 m from that highway, whichever is the nearer;

(d) any part of the building enlarged, improved or altered would be within 2 m of the boundary of the curtilage and would exceed 4 m in height;

(e) the total area of ground covered by buildings within the curtilage (other than the original house would exceed 50% of the total area (excluding the ground area of the original house);

(f) consists or includes the alteration or replacement of a satellite antenna;

(g) the erection of a building within the curtilage of a listed building; or

(h) it would consist of or include an alteration to any part of the roof (see Classes B and C below).

Note: The enlargements referred to above relate *only* to the *original* dwelling which is that granted planning permission if constructed after 1948, or in the case of dwellings constructed before that date, the dwelling as it existed on the appointed day, that is, 1 July 1948. Once the permitted development rights have been exercised, there is no further opportunity to enlarge, improve or alter the building without first gaining planning consent.

A.2 Where a dwelling house is located on Art 1(5) land (see above) development is not permitted by Class A if it would consist of or include the cladding of any part of the exterior with stone, artificial stone, timber, plastic or tiles.

A.3 The erection of any new building with a cubic content greater than 10 cu m is treated as the enlargement of the dwelling house where the dwelling is on Art 1(5) land, or in any other case where any part of that building would be within 5 m of any part of the dwelling house. If the building is within 5 m of the dwelling house then it is treated as forming part of the original building and, therefore, forms part of the cubic content which is regarded as permitted development.

Class B

Class B deals with the enlargement consisting of an addition or alteration to the roof. Development is *not* permitted if:

(a) any part of the works would exceed the existing height of the roof;

(b) the result of the works would extend beyond the plane of any existing roof slope which fronts a highway;

(c) it would increase the cubic content of the house by more then 40 cu m in the case of a terraced house, and 50 cu m in any other case;

(d) the cubic content of the resulting building would exceed the cubic content of the original by more then 50 cu m, or 10%, whichever is the greater in the case of a terraced house, or in any other case by 70 cu m or 15% whichever is the greater; or

(e) the dwelling is on Art 1(5) land.

Class C

Class C relates to any other alteration to the roof, and development is not permitted which would result in a material alteration to the shape of the roof.

Class D

Class D deals with the erection or construction of a porch outside any external door. This is not permitted if:

(a) the ground area of the porch exceeds 3 sq m (measured externally);

(b) any part of the structure would be more than 3 m above ground level; or

(c) any part would be within 2 m of any boundary of the curtilage which fronts a highway.

Class E

Class E relates to the provision of any building or enclosure within the curtilage, swimming or other pool required for the incidental enjoyment of the dwelling house, for the maintenance, improvement or other alteration of such a building or enclosure.

E.1 Development is *not* permitted under Class E if:

(a) it relates to a dwelling or a satellite antenna (see Class H.1 below);

(b) any part of the building or enclosure would be nearer any highway bounding the curtilage than the nearest part of the original house, or any point 20 m from the highway, whichever is the nearer;

(c) any building would have a cubic content of more than 10 cu m;

(d) the height of the building or enclosure would exceed 4 m if it has a pitched roof or 3 m in any other case;

(e) the total ground area covered by the buildings or enclosure would exceed 50% of the total area of the curtilage excluding the original dwelling; or

(f) in the case of Art 1(5) land, or land within the curtilage of a listed building, it would involve a building with a cubic content greater than 10 cu m.

'A purpose incidental to the enjoyment of the dwelling house as such' includes the keeping of poultry, bees, pet animals, birds or other livestock for domestic needs or personal enjoyment of the occupants.

Class F

Class F allows the provision within the curtilage of a hard surface for any purpose incidental to the enjoyment of the dwelling house.

Class G

Class G erection/provision of a container for the storage of oil for domestic heating is not permitted if:

(a) the capacity is more than 3,500 litres;

(b) any part is more than 3 m above ground level; or

(c) any part is nearer the highway than the original dwelling or at any point 20 m from the highway, whichever is nearer.

Class H

Class H installation, alteration or replacement of a satellite antenna on a dwelling house or within the curtilage.

H.1 Development is *not* permitted if:

(a) the size of the antenna (excluding brackets, etc) when measured in any direction would exceed:

    (i)   45 cm if installed on a chimney;

(ii)   90 cm if attached to the dwelling or within the curtilage on Art 1(4) land (other than the chimney); or

(iii) 70 cm in any other case;

(b) the highest part of the antenna would when installed exceed the highest point of the roof or chimney;

(c) there is any other antennae on the dwelling house or within its curtilage;

(d) in the case of Art 1(5) land it would consist of the installation on a chimney, or a building which exceeds 15 m in height, or on a wall or roof which fronts a highway or waterway in the case of the Broads.

Development under Class H is permitted subject to the condition that it is sited so as to minimise the visual impact, as far as is practicable, and that any antennae no longer in use shall be removed as soon as reasonably practicable.

10.6   PART 2: MINOR OPERATIONS

This part has general application, including development related to a dwelling house.

Class A

The erection, construction, maintenance, improvement or other alteration of a gate, fence, wall or other means of enclosure.

A.1 Development is not permitted if:

(a) the height of any gate, wall, fence or means of enclosure adjacent to a highway used by vehicular traffic would exceed 1 m above ground level

(*Note*: A highway is land over which the public have the right to pass and re-pass);

(b) in any other circumstances would exceed 2 m;

(c) the height maintained, improved or altered would, as a result of the development, exceed its former height or the height referred to in (a) and (b) above; or

(d) it would involve development within the curtilage of, or to a gate, fence, wall, or other means of enclosure surrounding a listed building.

Class B

The formation, laying out and construction of a means of access to a highway which is not a trunk road or a classified road, where that access is required in connection with development permitted by any class in this Schedule (other than Class A of this Part).

(*Note*: A 'classified road' is a motorway, and 'A', 'B' and 'C' class roads.)

Class C

The painting of any exterior of any building or work.

This is *not* permitted where the painting is for the purpose of an advertisement, announcement or direction.

It will now be appreciated that the answer to the apparently simple question, 'Do I need planning permission to extend my dwelling?' requires a great deal of research by the planning department. 'Is it a flat?', 'Is it in a terrace?', 'Is it a listed building, or within Art 1(5) land?', 'What is the cubic content of the dwelling?', 'Has the original building been extended in the past?', 'Where do you propose to extend the building?' are the basic questions to which there must be answers before any decision can be made.

The apparent complexity of the classes is designed to safeguard the amenities of adjoining properties which would result from over-development within a curtilage, and also addresses the visual amenity of the general street scene, hence the limitations on changes which front a highway.

There has been a proposal to establish a new permitted development right which would allow the extension of a domestic garden onto surrounding land without first requiring planning permission for change of use. The extension would be only for purposes incidental to the enjoyment of the dwelling house as such, and the land would benefit from the existing permitted development rights set out in Parts 1 and 2 of Sched 2. It is not proposed to restrict the area which could be added to the curtilage but at the present time there is considerable opposition to this proposal and the eventual outcome remains uncertain.

10.7   PART 4: TEMPORARY BUILDINGS AND USE OF LAND

Class A

The provision on land of buildings, moveable structures, works, plant or machinery required temporarily in connection with and for the duration of operations being carried out on, in, under or over land or on land adjoining that land.

Development is *not* permitted if:

(a) the operations are mining operations; or

(b) planning permission is required for those operations but is not granted or deemed to be granted.

After completion of the works, the building, etc, are to be removed and any adjoining land shall, as soon as reasonably possible, be reinstated to its previous condition.

Class B

ClassB.1: The use of any land for any purpose for not more than 28 days in total in any calendar year, of which not more than 14 days in total may be for the purposes referred to in B.2, and the provision of any moveable structure for the purposes of the permitted use.

Development is *not* permitted if:

(a) the land in question is a building or within the curtilage of a building;

(b) the use of the land is for a caravan site;

(c) the land is, or is within, a site of special scientific interest and the use of the land is for:

(i)   a purpose within B.2(b) or other motor sports;

(ii) clay pigeon shooting;

(iii) any war game; or

(iv) the land is used for the display of an advertisement.

Class B.2: Restricts the following uses to a period of 14 days in any one calendar year in relation to:

(a) the holding of a market; or

(b) motor car/cycle racing including trials of speed (includes practising).

The remaining 31 Parts are similar in their content in that they set out particular changes which are permitted development and then provide parameters within which that permission may be exercised.

10.8 LOCAL DEVELOPMENT ORDERS

Section 40 of the Planning and Compulsory Purchase Act (PCPA) 2004, allows lpas to expand the national permitted development rights by making a local development order (LDO) to implement policies in one or more of the development plan documents prepared under Part 2 of the 2004 Act, or in any local development plan.

A local development order may grant planning permission (s 61A) for:

(a) development specified in the order;

(b) development of any class so specified;

and may relate to

(a) all the land in the area of the relevant authority;

(b) any part of that land; or

(c) a site specified in the order.

The authority may make different provision for different description of land and may specify any area or class of development in respect of which an LDO must not be made. It is clear that LDOs will need to be confined so as to accord with Environmenal Impact Assessment principles. Prior to the adoption of an order the SoS may direct that the order (or any part of it) is submitted for his approval. Planning permission granted by a LDO may be granted unconditionally or subject to conditions or limitations specified in the order.

An LDO may be revoked by the lpa at any time, or by the SoS (s 61B(8) TCPA 1990) but this will not affect any previous planning permission or rights which have arisen by reason of the commencement of development. It is open to the local authority to serve a discontinuance order (s 102) for which compensation is payable for loss of value. Where development has not commenced revocation may still carry a liability to compensation under s 108 (as amended by s (2)(h)) where the owner applies successfully within a year of the modification. Should the LDO be revoked by the SoS the payment of compensation falls to the local authority.

An LDO must require that an application for planning permission of such description as specified in the order be accompanied by such of the following as is so specified (as substituted in s 62 TCPA 1990);

(a) a statement of the design principles and concepts that have been applied to the development; and

(b) a statement about how issues relating to access to the development have been dealt with.

Permission granted by a LDO may be granted unconditionally to subject to such conditions or limitations as are specified in the order (s 61C). The applicant retains the right of appeal against conditions imposed by the lpa (s 61C(2)(e)).

CHAPTER 11

LEGAL CHALLENGES TO THE CONTENT OF THE TOWN AND COUNTRY PLANNING (GENERAL PERMITTED DEVELOPMENT) ORDER 1995

11.1 INTRODUCTION

As with the Use Classes Order, the Town and Country (General Permitted Development) Order (GPDO) 1995 provides details of 'development' which fall within the limits of permitted development, and there is an obvious temptation to attempt to take full advantage of these rights by seeking to widen their interpretation where possible. It should be understood that development which exceeds the limits is not necessarily unacceptable; it does, however, require the submission of a planning application in the normal way.

11.2 REMOVAL OF RIGHTS

By a direction made under Art 4, the local planning authority (lpa) can restrict the scope of permitted development rights within a defined area. This does not amount to prohibition but it is pre-emptive as it requires the submission of a planning application for the development proposals. In these circumstances, it is not required that a planning application fee be payable (see Chapter 12, para 12.4 for details). If permission is refused, or granted with conditions which are other than those in the Order, the landowner and tenant are entitled to compensation under ss 107 and 108 of the Town and Country Planning Act (TCPA) 1990. In *Pennine Raceway v Kirklees Metropolitan Council* [1982] JPL 780; [1993] QB 382, CA the right to compensation was extended to persons who had a contractual right to use the land.

In *Thanet DC v Ninedrive* [1977] JPL 718; [1997] 1 All ER 703 Walton J stated that:

> The planning authority may either ban all, or any development or ban specific development, that is to say, it can either sweep the board clean or be as extremely selective as it chooses.

(*Note*: 'ban' in a pre-emptive sense.)

The lpa need not serve individual notice of the Order on the owners or occupiers of property if they consider this to be impracticable or it is difficult to identify or locate them. In *Spedeworth v Secretary of State* (1972) 116 SJ 426, the Court of Appeal held that a direction withdrawing permitted development rights 'except as a caravan site' was a general direction and that the service of notice on individuals was not required. This decision of the Court of Appeal remains despite the suggestion by the Lands Tribunal in *Carter v Windsor and Maidenhead Royal Borough Council* (1988) 3 PLR 6; (1989) 57 P & CR 480 that there is a requirement to serve notice upon individuals.

The issue of compensation payable arising from an lpa's attempt to remove permitted development rights was considered in *Bolton v North Dorset DC* [1997] JPL May Update; (1997) 74 P & CR 73. An Art 4 Direction was served on the applicant withdrawing permitted development rights for the holding of motorcross meetings, that is, GPDO Part 4, Class B.2 which permits use for 14 days per year. An application for planning permission was refused but the Secretary of State (SoS) also refused to confirm the Order as he was not satisfied that all other avenues had been explored to reach a mutual agreement. Subsequently noise abatement notices were served under the Environmental Protection Act 1990 and upheld on appeal. The Lands Tribunal held that the applicant was entitled to compensation under s 107 since he had been precluded by the Art 4 Direction from holding any events on his land over a six month period.

11.3   ISSUES RELATING TO DEPOSIT OF WASTE MATERIALS

Under Class D, Part 8, development involving the deposit of waste material is permitted if it arises from an industrial process on any land which was in use for that purpose prior to 1 July 1948. In *Kent CC v Secretary of State* (1997) EGCS 64, the Court of Appeal upheld the decision of the High Court that demolition was an industrial process, as involving 'the breaking up or demolition of any article' and that a building and its component parts were capable of amounting to an 'article' for these purposes.

11.4   ISSUES RELATING TO DWELLING HOUSES

In spite of what may appear to be a clear and concise definition of a dwelling house in Art 1(2):

> ... it does not include a building containing one or more flats, or a flat contained within such a building,

there remain areas of doubt which have been challenged in the courts. If the dwelling forms part of the same building, which is divided vertically, then it becomes a semi-detached house; it becomes a terraced house if there are three or more dwellings joined by party walls, or having adjoining walls. Once the dwelling is classed as a terraced house, the lower permitted development limits apply. The term 'flat' includes properties occupying one floor and also maisonettes which may occupy two or more floors within a building. In either case, the accommodation is divided horizontally.

The definition of Class C3 (dwelling house) was challenged in *R (on application for Hossack) v Kettering BC* [2002] JPL 1206; 14 EGCS 125. The use of three adjoining, but not interlinked, terraced houses, were used as temporary accommodation for homeless young people. The landlord selected the tenants, allocated rooms and decided how long they should remain in occupation with a maximum of five persons per dwelling. They shared cooking, food storage and dining facilities and had locks on their bedroom doors. The High Court found no relationship between the occupiers and that the properties had the characteristics of a hostel and therefore fell outside Class A3. This judgment was overturned by the Court of Appeal as it was considered that the lower court had gone too far in deciding that residents coming to a house neither as a pre-formed group nor for a predetermined period could ever be a single household. The case was, therefore, remitted to the council for further consideration.

Whatever the nature of the physical division, it must essentially be a house for dwelling in. In *Gravesend BC v Secretary of State and Michael O'Brien* [1983] JPL 307; (1984) 47 P & CR 142, it was made clear that the common feature of all buildings used as dwellings is that they afforded the facilities required for day-to-day domestic residence. Nevertheless, the court upheld the finding of the SoS that the small holiday chalet comprising a living room, kitchen and bedroom did constitute a dwelling house, although lacking a bathroom and toilet, because it did provide for the main activities associated with a residence.

There is apparently a distinction between the physical use of dwelling houses for mixed use and the use of premises which, whilst involving a secondary activity, does not amount to a physical change. In *Surlock (Grace) v Secretary of State for Wales* [1976] JPL 431; (1997) 33 P & CR 202; 1 WLR 707, the owner operated an estate agent's office on the ground floor of a three-storied Georgian property and lived in the upper two floors. The owner altered two windows to make one large picture window and contended that the premises were in residential use and therefore she did not require planning permission. An enforcement notice was served and confirmed by the SoS on appeal. The appellant then applied to the High Court for the order to be quashed. The main issue to be decided by the court was whether the alterations amounted to permitted development under Class I, Sched 1 (Town and Country General Development Order 1973). To fall within Class I the building must be regarded as a 'dwelling house'. The court confirmed the SoS's finding that the building had dual use and could not be regarded as a dwelling under Class I and therefore the residential accommodation constituted a flat in accordance with the definition.

The growing desire for a sector of the population to live in rural areas has resulted in a number of cases which deal with the issues of derelict houses or cottages in what are now regarded as desirable locations. In the case involving *Trustees of the Earl of Lichfield's Estate v Secretary of State* [1985] JPL 251, it was found that there must be a structure which is sufficiently intact to warrant the description of a dwelling, and not merely ruins of a former dwelling. If there is insufficient structure at the outset, it will take more than the permitted development works of 'enlargement, improvement or other alteration' to make it into a dwelling.

11.5   ISSUES RELATING TO CURTILAGE

Many of the permitted development rights contained in the GPDO (Sched 2, Part 1) are restricted to the curtilage of the dwelling house. Under normal circumstances, this is not a difficult concept to apply as it will relate to the garden or outdoor area attached to the dwelling. There are, however, instances where the matter becomes highly complex not only in connection with to permitted development rights but also, particularly in the case of listed buildings (see Chapter 20).

In *Dyer v Dorset CC* [1988] 3 WLR 213; (1989) EGCS 15, the Court of Appeal did not accept that a house within, but on the edge of, the grounds of a college was within the curtilage of any relevant building. Nourse LJ stated that the definition contained in the *Oxford English Dictionary* was adequate for most purposes:

> A small court, yard, garth, or piece of land attached to a dwelling house and forming one enclosure with it, or so regarded by the law; the area attached to and containing a dwelling house and its outbuildings.

There is no prior requirement that the land should be enclosed or marked off in any way. In *Sinclair-Lockhart's Trustees v Central Land Board* (1951) 1 P & CR 320, it was stated that 'it is enough that it serves the purpose of the house or building in some reasonably useful way'.

The fact of ownership is, in itself, not enough to establish land within the curtilage of a building. In *Collins v Secretary of State and Epping Forest DC* (1989) EGCS 15, an area of rough grass which lay beyond well-maintained lawns near a dwelling house was found not to form part of the curtilage. Similarly, in *James v Secretary of State* [1991] JPL 550; 1 PLR 58, the court held that a tennis court some 100 m from the house was not within its curtilage.

The matter is further complicated in the operation of planning law by the concept of the 'planning unit' which deals with land use(s), whereas curtilage relates to a building. It is quite common, for example, for an industrial building to have an established curtilage, but the curtilage itself may contain one or more planning units and this principle was also applied in the case relating to the constituent parts of a major shopping mall (see Chapter 9, para 9.3, *Church Commissioners v Secretary of State* (unreported)). However, in the case of dwelling houses, this principle may not be held to apply. In *Wood v Secretary of State and Others* [1973] 1 WLR 707; 2 All ER 404, Lord Widgery CJ stated that:

> In no case known to me, however, has it been said that, unless the circumstances are highly special, it is permissible to dissect a single dwelling house into separate parts and treat them as different planning units for this purpose. Indeed, as far as authority goes, it all seems to me to go the other way.

This case is at variance with the *Collins* case quoted above where the planning unit could be argued to include the rough area of land beyond the maintained lawns but was held to be outside the curtilage. (Perhaps this can be regarded as an example of 'highly special circumstances' referred to by Lord Widgery.) What is clear, however, is that where land has been unlawfully appropriated into the curtilage, there can be no reliance on the permitted development rights because the use is unlawful unless, or until, the period for taking enforcement action has lapsed.

In *R v Sevenoaks DC ex p Palley* [1995] JPL 915, a neighbour succeeded, by means of an application for judicial review, in quashing two decisions by the lpa relating to the erection of a glasshouse which had been constructed in purported reliance upon the permitted development rights under the 1988 GDO (Sched 2, Part 6). In 1992, the lpa wrote to the landowner confirming that his proposal to erect a greenhouse constituted permitted development and, therefore, no application for planning permission was required. The High Court considered that the evidence indicated that the lpa had given little or no consideration of the question of whether the land was used at that time for agricultural purposes, and it was not properly open to them to conclude on the meagre material available that the land was in use for agriculture. They considered 'that there was every likelihood that such income as might be derived from the only agricultural activities described was so small as to be no more than pocket money' and therefore did not come within Part 6.

The second determination by the lpa, which was the subject of a challenge, related to the authority's decision not to take enforcement action. The court held that this action (or inaction) was also flawed because the advice given to the planning committee by its officers had been based on the assumption that the earlier determination was valid.

In *Rambridge v Secretary of State* [1997] JPL May Update, the issue arose as a result of an application for a certificate of lawful proposed use (s 192) and was whether permitted development rights under Sched 2, Part 1, Class E conferred permission for the construction of 'a substantial building at the end of the garden for use as a residential annex'. It would appear that the application was an attempt to exploit a loophole in the content of the schedule. The court upheld the inspector's ruling that Class E does not include a building which is designed from the outset as primary residential accommodation. Such a proposal would fall into Class A. There is a fundamental difference between making a change in the use of an existing building and the operation of erecting a new building within a residential curtilage. The court rejected the proposition that the owner could erect his building for a purpose incidental to the enjoyment of the dwelling house and then 'have a change of mind' and use it later for primary residential use. Notwithstanding that planning permission is not required for a change of use from incidental residential use to primary residential use it was considered that such a sham would not be genuinely in accordance with Class E. The court, however, conceded that it would be different if the owner really did build the building for a purpose which was incidental to the dwelling house and then had a change of mind.

Permitted development allowing 'the use of any buildings or other land within the curtilage of a dwelling house for any purposes incidental to the enjoyment of house as such' was at issue in *Croydon LBC v Gladden* [1994] EGCS 24, where it was held that 'no matter how exquisite the personal pleasure that might be derived, the concept of the enjoyment of the dwelling house as such embraced an element of reasonableness and could not rely wholly on the unrestrained whim of the occupier.'

11.6   ISSUES RELATING TO ABANDONMENT

The problem of dereliction is inextricably linked to the question of abandonment. This question is whether a planning permission, once activated, can be abandoned by non-use of the permission so that the permission cannot enure for the benefit of the land or for any successor in title to the land. The issue was resolved after a number of years by the decision of the House of Lords in *Pioneer Aggregates v Secretary of State* [1984] JPL 651; 2 All ER 358, AC 132. Planning permission had been granted for the erection of a dwelling house and it was deemed to include permission for its use as such and the question of abandonment did not arise. The Law Lords held, unanimously, that there is no principle in planning law that a valid planning permission capable of being implemented according to its terms can be abandoned. Lord Scarman in his judgment declared:

> On the question of abandonment, he [Lord Scarman] agreed with both courts below that there was no such general rule in planning law.

He went on to state that:

> In certain exceptional circumstances not covered by legislation, the courts have held that a landowner by developing his land can play an important part in bringing to an end or making incapable of implementation a valid planning permission.

This serves to highlight the fact that the planning permission has not been abandoned, it is simply incapable of being implemented as a direct result of subsequent development.

Abandonment of planning permission is one aspect of the problem, the other is the abandonment of a use which was in existence when planning control over development was introduced when the TCPA 1947 came into force on 1 July 1948, that is, it does not have the benefit of a subsequent planning permission. In *White v Secretary of State and Congleton BC* [1989] JPL 692; 58 P & CR 281 the Court of Appeal held that a dwelling which existed prior to 1948 was capable of being abandoned.

This leaves the question of what constitutes abandonment. This has to be decided by drawing inferences from the fact that the building, or land, and as stated by Lord Denning MR in *Hartley v Minister of Housing and Local Government* (see Chapter 7, para 7.13):

> ... has remained unused for a considerable period of time, in such circumstances that a reasonable man might conclude that the previous use had been abandoned.

In such cases, the tests are once again those of 'fact and degree' which take into account both the physical state of the property, the removal of essential fixtures in the case of residential property and plant and machinery where industrial units are concerned.

In a recent case, *Hughes v Secretary of State* [1999] JPL July Update, the court accepted that the four relevant criteria were those spelled out by Nolan J (as he then was), in *Trustees of the Castell-y-Manach Estate v Secretary of State for Wales and Taff Ely BC* [1985] JPL 40. The tests are: (a) the physical condition of the property; (b) the period of non-use; (c) whether there had been any other use; and (d) evidence regarding the owner's intention. The fourth criterion referred to all the evidence other than that in the other three criteria. In any given case, evidence under the first three criteria may outweigh such statements of intention.

11.7   ENFORCEMENT

Where development has taken place which purports to be within the limits granted under the GPDO, but is subsequently found to exceed those limits, the lpa now has the discretion not to require the total demolition but to require steps to be taken which will make the development comply with the limitations. In issuing an enforcement notice, the authority must identify the breach which involves development without permission rather than a breach of the limitation (see, also, Chapter 18).

11.8   ENLARGEMENT OF THE DWELLING

Where an extension to the dwelling would bring it within 5 m of an existing building, then that building is required to be included in calculating the cubic capacity of the extension (Class A.3). For example, if the householder decides to extend the dwelling by providing a covered area between the existing house and a garage sited within 5 m of the dwelling, the existing garage would form part of the calculation of cubic content permitted under Class A.3.

In *Richmond-upon-Thames LBC v Secretary of State and Neale* [1991] JPL 948; 2 PLR 107; 62 P & CR 350, the council served an enforcement notice on Mr Neale regarding the erection of parapet walls around two of the flank walls on a flat roof extension to the rear of the house. On appeal the inspector in his decision letter made his finding that:

I consider that the development enforced against can properly be described as: 'The enlargement of a dwelling house consisting of an addition or alteration to its roof', therefore falling to be assessed against the criteria of Sched 2, Part 1, Class B of the 1988 GDO.'

He went on to find that the development had not infringed the conditions of Class B and therefore found the development did not constitute a breach of planning control, the permitted development being the enlargement of a dwelling house consisting of an additional alteration to its roof. The council challenged this decision in the High Court contending that the inspector had erred in law and in suggesting that the erection of a parapet wall was an enlargement of the dwelling house. The contention was that to be an enlargement one had to increase the volume or usable area within the dwelling house and the erection of a wall would not achieve that. Henry J considered that the erection of a parapet to a roof is undoubtedly an addition or alteration to the roof, and in the ordinary sense of the words it is an enlargement of the dwelling house as it makes the dwelling house bigger or taller. The difficulty is drawing a line of distinction between:

Class B: 'The enlargement of a dwelling house consisting of an addition or alteration to its roof' which is not permitted if it exceeds the highest part of the existing roof, extends the plane of an existing roof fronting a highway, increases the cubic content beyond the limits set out'; and

Class C: 'Any alteration to the roof of a dwelling house' where development is not permitted if it would result in a material alteration to the shape of the dwelling house'.

The question of whether the erection of the parapet walls formed an enlargement of the dwelling house depended on whether one had regard only to the external appearance of the house or whether one judged it by the amount of internal closed space. From the external appearance the building was undoubtedly enlarged because the north and west walls were higher but there was no more usable space within the house. It was held to be an enlargement of the dwelling under Class B although it did not provide additional enclosed accommodation for the occupier. The issue of height restriction did not apply in this case as the roof of the existing dwelling was higher than that of the parapet walls, therefore the appeal failed.

In *Hammersmith and Fulham LBC v Secretary of State and Davison* [1994] JPL 957, this point was reinforced and the decision confirmed that 'the existing roof' referred to the highest part of the house as a whole irrespective of the complex nature of any particular roof structure.

Following the *Richmond-upon-Thames* case, the SoS, in an appeal decision ([1996] JPL 68), ruled that a proposal to create extra accommodation in the roofspace of a dwelling house fell to be considered under Class B (enlargement consisting of an addition or alteration to the roof), notwithstanding that a significant change to the shape of part of the roof would be involved which falls within Class C (development is not permitted which would result in a material alteration to the shape of the roof). However, the requirements of sub-para (d) that 'the resulting building not to exceed the cubic content of the original dwelling house by more than 70 cubic metres', was not satisfied because of the construction of a detached garage in 1987 within 5 m of the dwelling house. The increases in cubic content were not to be treated as separate entitlements, but as a cumulative control total for Part 1.

11.9 FRONTAGE TO A HIGHWAY

For largely aesthetic reasons, the permitted development rights contained in Sched 2, Part 1 are restricted in relation to works which front a highway. Classes A, E and G remove permitted development rights where:

... the part of the building enlarged, etc, would be nearer to the highway which bounds the curtilage of the dwelling house than (i) the part of the original dwelling house nearest to the highway; or (ii) any point 20 metres from the highway.

Class B relates to:

... any part of the dwelling house which would, as a result of the works, extend beyond the plane of any existing roof slope which fronts a highway.

Part 2, Class A relates to:

... the height of any gate, fence, etc, erected or constructed adjacent to a highway used by vehicular traffic which would, after the carrying out of the development, exceed one metre above ground level.

A highway is land over which the public have the right to pass and re-pass and includes footpaths and bridleways. It also follows that a private road or footpath does not fall into the definition of a highway as there is no general right granted to members of the general public. The permitted rights do not relate to a separate building within the curtilage, for example, a garage, but only to the line of the dwelling house itself. The problems previously associated with stone cladding, which had been held to extend beyond the wall of the existing dwelling, have been removed by the omission of the word 'wall' from the 1988 Order and the current Order. That part of the dwelling house nearest a highway can now be construed as the eaves of the property and, therefore, the addition of stone cladding is unlikely to place it outside the permitted development (see *Bradford MBC v Secretary of State* [1978] JPL 177; 35 P & CR 387).

The addition of stone cladding remains excluded in sensitive areas by virtue of Class A.2, but the list of materials is incomplete as brick, glass and other materials are not included, and in the case of *Tower Hamlets LBC v Secretary of State and Nolan* [1994] JPL 1112, pebbledash was held not to fall within the list of excluded forms of cladding and was, therefore, permissible.

11.10 REPAIRS TO UNADOPTED STREETS AND PRIVATE HIGHWAYS

The Court of Appeal in *Cowen v Peak District National Park Authority* [2000] JPL 171; 3 PLR 108, held that the scope and significance of the word 'improvement' in Part 9 was contextually conditioned. Whether the construction of a hard surface was an 'improvement' deemed to be permitted by the Order was not a matter for the subjective opinion of the person who carried out work on the track or those who used it. Rather, it was a matter of fact and degree. In this case there was clearly a relationship between Parts 6 and 9 which pertains to the formation and alteration of private agricultural ways and the owner should have given prior notice to the lpa. The inspector appeared to have assumed that the way to reconcile the two was to conclude that works of a certain magnitude should be referred to the lpa and thus be regarded as falling within Part 6. In doing so, he had taken a narrow view of the permitted rights under Part 9.

Henry LJ remarked that there is no overriding policy or planning objective which would justify giving the words in Part 9 a narrower meaning than they ordinarily bear. The ordinary meaning of 'improvements' is limited to changes which do not alter the basic character of that which is improved. Part 9 is not limited to improvements which do not alter the surface or the method of construction. 'Improvement' is permitted as well as 'maintenance' and the provision was clearly concerned with the surface of the way. The permitted works could only affect the surface and foundations of the way and they could not widen or alter its route. The creation of a hard surface was, therefore, capable of being an improvement that would not alter the character of the way.

11.11 MINOR OPERATIONS (SCHEDULE 2, PART 2)

In *Prengate Properties Ltd v Secretary of State* (1973) 25 P & CR 311, Lord Widgery considered 'a wall' to be governed by the words 'other means of enclosure', which means that a free-standing wall constructed in the middle of a garden was not permitted as it fails to provide any form of enclosure. Similarly, in *Ewen Developments Ltd v Secretary of State and North Norfolk DC* [1980] JPL 404, it was found that some embankments within a caravan site were not within Class A of Part 2 as they were intended merely as landscaping.

In *Shepherd v Secretary of State for the Environment and Three Rivers DC* [1997] JPL 764, the High Court held that Class B was not confined to the formation of a means of access to a highway which was adjacent to land on which the permitted development was to take place. The right existed even when there was intervening land between the highway and the site of the permitted development.

11.12 DEVELOPMENT BY STATUTORY UNDERTAKERS

Prior to 1968, land acquired by statutory undertakers for the purpose of undertaking development automatically became operational land with the benefits of permitted development rights. This right was curtailed by s 264 TCPA 1990which now requires that, before any land acquired by statutory undertakers can be regarded as operational, there must be specific planning permission for its development for the purpose of the undertaking. The question which arose in *Adur DC v Secretary of State* [1999] JPL B99; PLCR 295 was whether the status was activated by the grant of a temporary planning permission. The court found that it did.

However, the court did *not* find that the consequence was that statutory undertakers then enjoyed full permitted development rights to use the site. In addition to a condition which required the use to cease at the end of the period, there was a second condition which required that 'notwithstanding the GPDO the site shall be used solely for the storage of cars'. The court held that this condition remained effective beyond the period for which the temporary planning permission had been granted. The inspector and the SoS had been wrong in finding that the second condition did not prevent the exercise of permitted development rights.

11.13 TEMPORARY BUILDINGS AND USES

The permission granted for the temporary use of land for either a period of 28 or 14 days (under GPDO Sched 2, Part 4) raises two issues:

1   When does the 28-day or 14-day period start?

2   Can an intended permanent use take advantage of these periods?

On the first point, the Court of Appeal in *AG's Reference No 1* (1996) EGCS 164 was asked to rule on the effect of an enforcement which was intended to restrict a landowner to the permitted extent of his temporary use rights in terms of shooting for a period of up to 28 days in any one calendar year (GDPO Sched 2, Part 4, Class B). The notice took effect during a calendar year, and the question was whether, in calculating the 28 days, the court should include four days for which the land had already been used for shooting. The court reaffirmed that, for the purposes of the GDPO, a calendar years runs from 1 January to 31 December, hence any shooting days which had occurred before the date specified for compliance with the notice should be taken into account in calculating compliance within the 28-day limit.

The second point considered the issue of distinguishing between a genuine temporary use of land or that which may be intended as a permanent change. The commencement of an activity which it is intended to establish as a permanent use constitutes a breach of planning control from the start, and the provision under Part 4 does not offer a period which provides immunity from challenge. If the lpa are of the opinion that the change of use is intended to be permanent, they are entitled to take enforcement action (see *Tidswell v Secretary of State* [1977] JPL 104; (1977) 34 P & CR 152 and *Stoke-on-Trent City Council v W and J Wass Ltd* (1992) 2 PLR 22). It is then a matter for the developer to challenge the authority's actions by means of an appeal against the enforcement notice by bringing evidence to prove that the use is temporary.

Ramsey v Secretary of State [1997] JPL B122 involved land which was being used for vehicular sports and leisure activities. Whilst the activities themselves were restricted to 14 days per year, the site, when not in use, retained the physical characteristics of the use, that is, tyres embedded in the ground and pits and mounds used as a vehicle obstacle course. The High Court refused to interfere with the finding of the planning inspector that the use of the land had all the attributes of a permanent rather than a temporary use and therefore fell outside the permitted development right granted by the GPDO.

The possibility also arises of an owner seeking to use up the full annual permission on one part of his land and then move it to another to recommence the use. Such movements are likely to be regarded by the courts as unreasonable exploitation of the rights under Part 4 and the planning unit which will normally be the whole unit in the same occupation. It is nevertheless possible that, where a farm comprises land separated from other land in the same occupation by land in different ownership, each site may constitute a different planning unit (see *Fuller v Secretary of State* [1987] JPL 854; (1988) 1 PLR; 56 P & CR 84, CA). This has led some 'resourceful' landowners to sub-divide their land and place each unit in a separate ownership so that use can be made of the temporary period of 28 days, or 14 days where this is applicable, on each unit of land. The lpa could consider the use of an Art 4 direction to overcome such a problem but there is the risk to the authority that it may have to pay compensation.

In *Fitzpatrick v Secretary of State* [1988] JPL 564; (1990) 1 PLR 8, it was held that a car-boot sale could be described as a market and thereby restricted to 14 days per year. The fact that a market is held under a market franchise granted by the Crown will not extend Crown immunity from planning control (*Spook Erection v Secretary of State* [1988] JPL 821).

The case of *R v Sheffield City Council ex p Russell* [1996] JPL 123 raised the issue of the temporary use of land and application for an established use certificate (prior to the provision relating to certificates of lawful development introduced by the Planning and Compensation Act 1991). The council granted an unrestricted certificate for the use of the land for clay pigeon shooting, and three local residents applied for judicial review to have the certificate set aside. Whilst the three persons lived in the parish they did not represent a local conservation society or the parish council, but were members of the Grenoside Action Group formed to make the application to challenge the certificate. The court rejected a challenge from the landowners to the applicants' *locus standi* following *Covent Garden Community Association v GLC* [1981] JPL 183. The court also examined the nature of an application for an existing use certificate. Only the applicant for the certificate had a right to make representations to the lpa, which is in direct contrast to the position in relation to an application to develop land. The issue of a certificate is conclusive for the purposes of an enforcement appeal, and it is a declaration that no development has taken place and, therefore, no permission is required before the land is put to the established use. While there is no right granted to any person, other than the applicant to make representations, it is open to the lpa to require the applicant to provide 'such further information as may be required to enable them to deal with the application'. Given the conclusive nature of the certificate, the court accepted that if a certificate is granted in terms that are wider than those necessary to describe accurately the established use, it will have the effect of gaining additional user rights but without those parties involved in a planning application having had an opportunity to be consulted. Hence the applicants did have a sufficient interest to apply for judicial review.

The court concluded that there was no evidence on which the local authority could have concluded that the existing use of the land for clay pigeon shooting was on a daily and day-long basis, and their failure to impose any conditions to restrict the level of use constituted an error in law. The notice was quashed. (It should be noted that the applicants for the certificate do, however, retain their rights to temporary use of the land for clay pigeon shooting in accordance with the provisions of the GPDO (see Chapter 10, para 10.6)).

The Court of Appeal in *South Buckinghamshire DC v Secretary of State for the Environment* [1989] JPL 351, held that with the temporary use provision, that is, 28 or 14 days, the effect was to grant as many planning permissions as there were changes of use. In the case of a Sunday market a change of use occurred every time the market was held. This ruling is of particular significance as it enables a local authority to issue an Art 4 Direction withdrawing permitted development rights even when the landowner has started to use the temporary permission but has not yet exhausted the 28 days.

11.14 TELECOMMUNICATIONS DEVELOPMENT

Under Sched 2, Part 24, the automatic character of the grant of planning permission was considered by the court in *R v Staffordshire Moorlands DC ex p Bartlam* [1998] PLCR

385. The applicant maintained that, because the authority had admittedly failed to follow its declared policy of public consultation, it had thereby defeated Bartlam's legitimate expectation of consultation. Without determining whether there was such an expectation, the court held that the local authority's failure could not prejudice the working of the Order once the 28-day period had expired without anything happening. The planning permission granted by the Order thus became effective.

11.15 AGRICULTURAL BUILDINGS AND OPERATIONS

Permitted development rights under Class A of Part 6 are restricted to building operations 'reasonably necessary to the purposes of agriculture within that unit'. It was held in *Clarke v Secretary of State for the Environment* [1992] 65 P & CR 85, that the buildings do not have to be reasonably necessary for the activities undertaken at the time the building is erected provided the building is designed for the purposes of agriculture within the unit.

CHAPTER 12

PLANNING APPLICATIONS

12.1   INTRODUCTION

As explained in Chapters 8 and 10, there are some forms of development which do not require planning permission, either because they are excluded by the Act itself, or they fall within the provisions of the Use Classes Order 1987 or the Town and Country Planning (General Permitted Development) Order (GPDO) 1995 (SI 1995/418) or a Local Development Order (s 40 Planning and Compulsory Purchase Act (PCPA) 2004). A person who is contemplating carrying out 'development' is, therefore, first advised to check whether the proposal actually requires planning permission by consulting these documents, or by seeking independent professional advice or that of the local planning authority (lpa). In particularly complicated cases it is also possible to make a formal request for a determination by the submission of an application for a certificate of lawfulness (see Chapter 6, para 6.4).

12.2   THE TOWN AND COUNTRY PLANNING (GENERAL DEVELOPMENT PROCEDURE) ORDER 1995

In Chapter 10, para 10.1, it was explained that, prior to 1995, there was a single General Development Order but this was effectively 'split' into two separate Orders: the GPDO (SI 1995/418) and the Town and Country Planning (General Development Procedure) Order (GDPO) (SI 1995/419). The latter Order is a technical document which sets out the procedure to be adopted by lpas in carrying out their statutory functions. It comprises 28 Articles and five Schedules, and the paragraph below highlights *only those which are in general use*.

Article 1:   Provides definitions which are to be read in conjunction with Art 1 of the GDPO.

Article 3:   Outlines planning applications: this allows lpas to grant permission subject to condition(s) specifying reserved matters for the authority's subsequent approval. The lpa is also entitled to request a full application when it feels this is appropriate, but it must do so within one month of receipt of the outline application. When notifying the applicant, the further details required by the authority must be specified.

Article 4:   An application for the approval of reserved matters shall provide sufficient information to identify the outline permission and be accompanied by such plans and drawings as are required to deal with the reserved matters.

Article 6:   An applicant for planning permission must give notice of the application to the owner of the land or the tenant.

Article 7:   The applicant is required to certify that the requirements of Art 6 have been met.

Article 8: Publicity for planning applications.

Article 10: Consultations to be undertaken by the lpa before the granting of planning permission: this contains a list of 25 consultees whom the lpa *shall* consult before granting planning permission. Those consulted on any one planning application will depend upon the nature of the proposal. The Amendment Order 1996 (SI 1996/1817) introduced a new consultation requirement whereby lpas are to consult the appropriate Sports Council before granting planning permission which is likely to prejudice the use, or lead to the loss of use, of land being used as a playing field. Amendment Order 1997 (SI 1997/858) requires lpas to consult the British Waterways Board where development is likely to affect specified inland waterways, reservoirs, canal feeder channels, let-offs and culverts within areas notified by the Board to the local authority.

The Schedules to SI 1995/419, which are also included within the GDPO, contain various forms to be used by lpas in carrying out their statutory duties.

Whilst SI 1995/419 is a technical 'operational' Order, the content of the articles is particularly important when lodging a planning application (see below) or considering an appeal against the decision taken by the lpa (see Chapter 16).

12.3   THE PLANNING APPLICATION FORM

Although the legislation governing the need to gain planning permission operates nationally, there is, perhaps surprisingly, no standard application form available for use by applicants. Each planning authority produces its own application forms which, whilst similar in content, are only applicable to that authority. Most district authorities provide two types of application form: one for what is termed 'householder development', that is, minor matters relating to domestic property; and a standard application form for all other types of development, excluding minerals applications. The minerals authorities, that is, shire counties and metropolitan districts, provide special application forms for this type of development.

Most forms include, or have attached, certificates to confirm that the applicant is the owner of all the land which is the subject of the planning application (Certificate A), or that he has informed the owner of the application (Certificate B) and that, if appropriate, the agricultural tenant has been informed (see para 12.4, below for details).

Note: 'owner' for the purpose of a planning application is a person having a freehold, or leasehold with at least seven years remaining.

The number of copies of the form to be returned to the individual planning authorities varies from authority to authority. They are to be forwarded to the authority responsible for making the decision on the particular type of application, that is, minerals, waste disposal and processing applications should be forwarded directly to the shire county.

12.4   THE PLANNING APPLICATION

A planning application consists of:

(a) the required number of the completed application forms;

(b) the required number of plans (usually at a scale of 1/1250) to identify the site;

(c) the required number of other plans and drawings necessary to describe the development;

(d) the relevant certificates;

(e) the appropriate planning application fee; and

(f) any other information which it is felt will assist the planning authority in making a determination on the application.

The site identification plan is required to show the site of the planning proposal outlined in red. Any other land adjoining the application site and which is in the ownership of the applicant is shown outlined in blue. This 'blue land' may have particular significance as s 72(a) TCPA 1990 allows conditions to be imposed upon:

> ... any land under the control of the applicant (whether or not it is the land in respect of which the application was made), or requiring the carrying out of works on any such land, so far as it appears to the local planning authority to be expedient for the purposes of or in connection with the development authorised by the permission.

The application must be accompanied by a certificate, in a form prescribed in Sched 4 (GDPO), that the applicant has satisfied the requirement to inform the owners of the land of the planning application. There are four certificates to meet the following requirements:

Certificate A: 21 days before the date of the application no one other than the applicant owned the land, or any part of the land, which is the subject of the application;

Certificate B: the applicant has informed the person(s) who, 20 days before the application, was (were) the owner(s) of the land;

Certificate C: the applicant is unable to discover all the persons with an interest in the land; and

Certificate D: the applicant is unable to ascertain the name of any person who has an interest in the land.

In the cases of Certificates C and D, the applicant is required to advertise the planning application in a local newspaper. In *all* cases, the applicant must either certify that none of the land forms part of an agricultural holding or, if it is part of such a holding, that the tenant farmer has been informed of the application.

The appropriate planning application fee (determined by regulations made by the Secretary of State (SoS) under s 303 TCAP 1990) must accompany the application and is payable to the local authority determining the application. The precise fees are revised annually (and upwardly!) and are assessed either on the basis of area or the number of units. For example, an outline application for residential development is currently charged (2004) on the basis of £220 per 0.1 hectare up to a maximum of £5,500, and a full application at £220 per house unit up to a maximum of £11,000. The application fee is non-refundable, and the application will not be registered by the lpa until the appropriate fee is paid.

A planning application fee is *not* required if the application would normally have permitted development rights which have been removed by an Art 4 direction (see Chapter 10); neither is a fee payable if the application is for listed building consent (see Chapter 20).

When submitting a planning application, it is advisable for the applicant or his agent to retain copies of the application form, plans, certificates and any accompanying material as these will be required if, in due course, a planning appeal is to be lodged against the decision of the lpa (see Chapter 16).

The government has stated its commitment to the electronic delivery of local authority services by 2005, although currently only about 5% of authorities allow the full submission of planning applications electronically. In England a previous impediment to the use of e-mail services was removed by the Town and Country Planning (Electronic Communications) (England) Order 2003 (SI 2003/956). This amends the relevant planning legislation to enable the term 'writing' and other equivalent expressions to include electronic communication. There is no requirement for applications or other documents submitted online to be signed electronically or otherwise.

NB This provision does NOT relate to enforcement matters.

12.5   OUTLINE APPLICATION

An outline permission is defined in Art 2 of the Town and Country Planning (Applications) Regulations 1988 (SI 1988/1812) to mean:

> Planning permission for the erection of a building subject to a condition requiring the subsequent approval of the local planning authority with respect to one or more reserved matters.

Reserved matters are then defined as:

(a) siting;

(b) design;

(c) external appearance;

(d) means of access; and

(e) the landscaping of the site.

The lpa may consider that it cannot determine an outline planning application without first being provided with details relating to some or all of the reserved matters and can require the applicant to provide such detail as required prior to the consideration of the application. This is frequently the case involving development in conservation areas.

Applicants frequently submit details of the proposed development 'for illustrative purposes only'. Should the 'status' of such details not be made clear by the applicant the lpa should consider the detail as part of the proposed development and cannot reserve the matter by the use of a condition for subsequent approval.

Under s 73 (TCPA 1990), as amended by PCPA 2004, a developer may seek permission to carry out development without compliance with one or more conditions set out in the original outline planning consent but the provisions under s 51(3) of PCPA states;

> Planning permission must not be granted under this section to extent that it has effect to change a condition subject to which a previous planning permission was granted by extending the time within which
>
> (a) the development must be started
>
> (b) an application for the approval of reserved matters (within the meaning of s 92) must be made.

The effect of this new provision is that it is no longer possible to extend the life of either full or outline planning permission via a s 73 application and the applicant must make an application for planning permission in the normal way.

12.6 OUTLINE OR FULL APPLICATION?

If the application involves the erection of a building or buildings, then it is possible to consider whether it is appropriate or desirable to submit an outline planning application to establish the principle of the development. Outline applications are *not* accepted for changes of use or other forms of 'development' which do not involve buildings. An outline application affords two distinct benefits:

1 it prevents abortive expenditure on professional fees which may be required to prepare a full application; and

2 it establishes the principle of use and is, therefore, frequently used to establish land value prior to sale.

The appropriateness of submitting an outline application may, in part, be determined by the content of the district-wide plan. If the particular site is allocated on the plan for a specified use, then this, in effect, amounts to an outline consent and there is nothing to be gained by submitting an outline planning application for the same use of the land.

12.7 OFFICER ADVICE

Prior to the lodging of a planning application most planning authorities encourage the developer to hold discussions with officers of the authority. These pre-application discussions are intended to assist the developer in a variety of ways, for example ascertaining whether planning permission is required; the likelihood of planning permission being granted; the need for an environmental assessment and the relevant planning policies of the authority which should be taken into account, including any planning obligations which would relate to the proposed development (see Chapter 15 Planning Obligations). It should be noted that under the provisions of the Local Government Act 2003 (s 93) 'Best Value authorities', as defined in the Local Government Act 1999 (s 1), *may* charge for discretionary services.

Delegated powers to determine a wide range of types of planning applications are now granted to named officers of the council in an attempt to speed up the planning process. The precise details of the delegated functions vary throughout authorities but the government's intention is that up to 90% should be dealt with in this manner. The decision of the level of delegation is a matter for elected representatives who remain responsible for the functioning of the authority as well as determining non-delegated applications.

This does not absolve officers of the council from making statements or taking actions which amount to malpractice. Two cases determined in July 1966 should serve as a salutary warning to both officers and their employers. These cases are discussed in Chapter 13, para 13.10.

12.8   PROCESSING THE PLANNING APPLICATION

The lpa must check that the application is complete in terms of the required elements listed in para 12.4, above. If it is defective in any way, or incomplete, then the lpa will refuse to register the application. An erroneous certificate is not a matter for the lpa and will not affect the determination of the application, but the applicant remains liable for action through the courts by the *bona fide* land owner.

On receipt of a complete application, the lpa must enter it in a register which is available for inspection by the general public in accordance with Art 25 (GDPO), and on a map register which is used for office purposes. The lpa must also acknowledge receipt of the application and give the date by which the decision should be forthcoming, which is normally eight weeks from the date of registration, or 16 weeks if an environmental assessment is required (Art 20). (See para 12.12 below for details of environmental assessments.) These are 'target dates' and the time may be extended subject to the applicant's agreement in writing.

The lpa is also entitled to request further information if this is felt to be necessary to allow consideration of the application (Art 3). The authority may refuse to determine a planning application (s 70A TCPA 1990) if:

> ... within a period of two years ending with the date of receipt of the planning application, the Secretary of State has refused a *similar* application following an appeal, and where, *in the opinion of* the local planning authority, there has been no significant change in the development plan or any other material considerations. [See Blackhall, JC, 'So what is different?' [1991] JPL 1113.]

Normally, decisions on planning applications are made by the lpa, but the SoS retains the power (s 77 TCPA 1990) to call in any application and to direct that it shall be referred to him for a decision. It is entirely at the SoS's discretion as to whether he chooses to take this action, but if he does so, the parties have the right to be heard at a local public inquiry or other hearing.

Section 44 (PCPA 2004) gives a specific statutory power to the SoS to call in applications which he considers to be of 'national or regional importance'. There is also a procedural structure for 'lead' inspectors to be appointed together with additional inspectors. The additional inspectors can hear the evidence of the issues and they then report to the lead inspector who, in turn, reports to the SoS.

12.9 INVOLVEMENT OF THE SECRETARY OF STATE

In addition to the power granted to the SoS under s 77 (TCPA 1990), he may also give directions restricting the grant of planning permission by an lpa, either indefinitely or during such period as may be specified in the directions (Art 14, GDPO).

Article 15 requires the local authority to consult the SoS in the case of development affecting trunk roads and certain other major highways, whether existing or proposed, and he retains the right to direct the authority either to refuse the application or to impose conditions on the granting of consent. This provision applies to the formation or laying out of an access, or alteration to an existing access to a highway and any development within 67 m of the centre of the highway, where there is likely to be an increase in the volume of traffic or a material change in the character of the traffic. What constitutes 'increase' or 'character' is left to the local authority's planning officer to decide.

The lpa must not grant planning permission in certain instances for development which does not accord with the provisions of the development plan without first complying with the procedures laid down in the Town and Country Planning (Development Plans and Consultation) Directions 1992. (For details of development involved, see Chapter 3, para 3.20.)

12.10 CONSULTATIONS BY THE LOCAL PLANNING AUTHORITY

Consultations carried out by the lpa fall into two categories:

1   statutory consultations, that is, those that are required by law (see Art 10 GDPO); and

2   non-statutory consultations, that is, those at the discretion of the authority.

The parties consulted will depend upon the location and the type of application. This requires a degree of skill on the part of the officer concerned. However, failure to carry out consultations of either type could result in the lpa being charged with maladministration. Consultees are given 21 days in which to make their comments to the lpa, with the exception of parish councils, which are restricted to 14 days.

Prior to introduction of s 65 into TCPA 1990 by the Planning and Compensation Act 1991, there was no legal requirement on the part of lpas to give publicity to planning applications other than those which were classified as 'bad neighbour uses'. Although many authorities had previously adopted informal schemes of notification, it was made clear in *R v Secretary of State ex p Kent* [1990] JPL 124; [1988] 3 PLR 17 that this did not give rise to any legitimate expectation of notification. Where publicity takes the form of an advertisement in a local newspaper, the courts will not insist upon exhaustive coverage (*McMeechan v Secretary of State* (1974) 232 EG 201).

Publicity for *all* planning applications is now required by s 65, and Art 8 (GDPO) sets out the manner of this publicity. For the first time, members of the general public are statutory consultees in the determination of planning applications. The meaning of the word 'consultation' was analysed by Webster J in *R v Secretary of State for Social Services ex p Association of Metropolitan Authorities* [1986] 1 WLR 1, where he stated:

> In any context, the essence of consultation is the communication of a genuine invitation to give advice and a genuine consideration of that advice. In my view, it

must go without saying that to achieve consultation, sufficient information must be supplied by the consulting party to the consulted party to enable it to tender helpful advice. Sufficient time must be given by the consulting to the consulted party to enable it to do that, and sufficient time must be available for such advice to be considered by the consulting party. Sufficient, in that context, does not mean ample, but at least enough to enable the relevant purpose to be fulfilled. By helpful advice, in this context, I mean sufficiently informed and considered information or advice about aspects of the form or substance of the proposals, or their implications for the consulted party, being aspects material to the implementation of the proposal as to which the Secretary of State might not be fully informed or advised and as to which the party consulted might have relevant information or advice to offer.

(*Note*: This observation is quoted at length because it has particular significance in the consideration of public involvement discussed in Chapter 30.)

Details of the forms of publicity required are set out in Art 8 (GDPO), and this varies according to the type of application being considered. In the following cases:

1   where an application is accompanied by an *environmental statement*;

2   where it does *not accord* with the provisions of the development plan; or

3   where it affects a *right of way* to which Part III of the Wildlife and Countryside Act 1981 applies,

the lpa *must*:

(a) place a site notice at one or more places on the site or adjoining land for 21 days; *and*

(b) advertise the application in the local press.

When an application is not within the type outlined above, but the application is a major development, that is minerals, waste, more than 1 hectare, more than 10 houses, or 0.5 hectare if the number of houses is not known, or more than 1,000 sq m, the lpa is required to:

(a) place a site notice at one or more places on the site, or adjoining land for 21 days; or

(b) serve a notice on any adjoining land owner *and* advertise in the local press.

In all other cases, the lpa *must*:

(a) place a site notice at one or more places; or

(b) serve a notice on any adjoining owner or occupier.

Where a notice is 'without any fault or intention of the lpa, removed, obscured or defaced before the period of 21 days has elapsed', the authority shall be treated as having complied with the requirements of the relevant paragraph (Art 8(6)).

12.11 CONSIDERATION OF THE APPLICATION BY THE LOCAL PLANNING AUTHORITY

The first test must be: is planning permission required for the proposed development? When the officer responsible is satisfied that this is the case, the following steps should be undertaken:

1 The lpa *must*, in considering a planning application, have complied with the directions given by the SoS.

2 Government policy as expressed in Planning Policy Guidance Notes (PPGs) and Planning Policy Statements must be taken into consideration.

3 The provisions of the development plan must be taken into account. The determination will be in accordance with the development plan unless material considerations indicate otherwise.

4 Any views from other government departments or other bodies, including members of the public, whom the lpa is required to consult, and from any other interested parties must be considered. (*Note*: Section 54 (P&C Act) places a new requirement on those bodies which are required to be consulted, prior to the determination of an application to respond within a prescribed period of time.) In an attempt to speed up the process the requirement to consult an authority or body is waived if that authority or body has up-to-date standing advice. Statutory consultees must update their standing advice, or verify the information is still up-to-date, at least every two years (Art 4, GPDO (Amendment) Order 2003 (SI 2003/2047)).

5 When required, in accordance with the Town and Country Planning (Environmental Impact Assessment) (England and Wales) Regulations 1999, the environmental assessment has to be evaluated.

6 The Regional Development Agency must be consulted before the grant of planning permission for certain categories of development (Art 3, GPDO (Amendment) Order 2003) which relate to strategic infrastructure projects or strategic regional investment or employment policies.

12.12 TOWN AND COUNTRY PLANNING (ENVIRONMENTAL IMPACT ASSESSMENTS) (ENGLAND AND WALES) REGULATIONS 1999 (SI 1999/293)

Circular 2/99 gives policy guidance on the implementation in England (separate advice for Wales WO Circular 11/99) of the amendments made to the original European Directive. Paragraph 15 makes it clear that an Environmental Impact Assessment (EIA) refers to the whole process by which environmental information is collected, publicised and taken into account in reaching a decision on a relevant planning application. This process was formally referred to in the UK as an Environmental Assessment (EA). Generally it will be the responsibility of the lpa in the first instance to determine whether a proposed development requires an EIA. Attention is drawn to the fact that changes or extensions to existing uses contained in the schedules may also fall within the scope of these regulations. The characteristics to be considered by the lpa when screening the Sched 2 development (below) are set out in Sched 3 of the Regulations and must include:

(a) the size of the development;

(b) the cumulation with other development;

(c) the use of natural resources;

(d) the production of waste;

(e) pollution and nuisances; and

(f) the risk of accidents having regard, in particular, to substances and technologies used.

The information the developer shall provide include, as appropriate:

(a) a description of the physical characteristics of the whole development and the land-use requirements during the construction and operational phases;

(b) a description of the main characteristics of the production process, for example, the nature and quantity of materials used;

(c) an estimate by type and quality of the expected residues and emissions (water, air and soil pollution, noise, vibration, light, heat radiation, etc);

(d) a description of the aspects of the environment likely to be significantly affected by the development including population, fauna, flora, soil, water, air, climatic factors, material assets (including the architectural and archaeological heritage, landscape and the inter-relationship between these factors);

(e) a description of the likely significant effects of the development on the environment which should include direct effects and any indirect, secondary, cumulative, short-, medium- and long-term, permanent and temporary, positive and negative effects of the development, resulting from the existence of the development; the use of natural resources; the emissions of pollutants; the creation of nuisances; and the elimination of waste;

(f) a description by the applicant of the forecasting methods used to assess the effects on the environment;

(g) a description of the measures envisaged to prevent, reduce and, where possible, off-set any adverse effects on the environment;

(h) an indication of any technical difficulties or lack of know how encountered by the applicant in compiling the required information; and

(i) a non-technical summary of the information provided.

Where a Member State is aware that a project is likely to have a significant impact on the environment of another Member State, or where a State requests information, it shall be sent and will serve as a basis for consultations between the States.

Annex I sets out projects which are to be the subject of EIAs:

1 crude oil refineries and installations for gasification and liquefaction of more than 500 tonnes of coal or bituminous shale per day;

2 thermal power stations with a heat output of 300 megawatts or more, and nuclear power stations and other nuclear reactors;

3 installations for the reprocessing of irradiated nuclear fuel;

4 works for the initial smelting of cast iron or steel or the production of non-ferrous crude metals from ore;

5 installations for the extraction or processing of asbestos,

6 integrated chemical installations;

7 construction of lines for long distance rail traffic and airports with a basic runway length of 2,100 m or more;

8 construction of motorways and express roads of four or more lanes or widening of an existing road to four or more lanes if over more than 10 km in continuous length;

9 inland waterways and ports for inland traffic, ports, piers connected to land (excluding ferry piers) which permit vessels of over 1,350 tonnes;

10 waste disposal installations for incineration, or chemical treatment or landfill of hazardous waste (see Council Directives 75/442/EEC and 91/689/EEC);

11 waste disposal for incineration, or chemical treatment of non-hazardous material with a capacity exceeding 100 tonnes per day;

12 groundwater abstraction or artificial recharge schemes where the annual volume of water exceeds 10 million cu m;

13 works for the transfer of water resources, other than piped drinking water, between river basins if in excess of 100 million cu m per year, or where in the basin of abstraction flow exceeds 2,000 million cu m per year and where the transferred water exceeds 5%of the flow;

14 waste water treatment plants with a capacity exceeding 150,000 population equivalent;

15 extraction for commercial purposes of petroleum in excess of 500 tonnes per day and natural gas in excess of 500,000 cu m per day;

16 dams and other installations where new or additional water held back exceeds 10 million cu m;

17 pipelines for gas, oil or chemicals with a diameter of more than 800 mm and a length of more than 40 kilokmetres;

18 installations for the intensive rearing of poultry or pigs with more than; 85,000 places for broilers or 60,000 places for hens; 3,000 places for pigs over 30kg or 900 places for sows;

19 industrial plants for production of pulp from timber or similar fibrous materials or the production of paper or board exceeding 200 tonnes per day;

20 quarries and open-cast mining where the surface of the site exceeds 25 ha, or peat where exceeds 150 ha;

21 installations for the storage of petroleum, petrochemical or chemical products with a capacity of 200,000 tonnes or more.

Annex II of the Direction provides a comprehensive list of activities that may require the preparation of an EIA. These are too comprehensive to set down in detail but relate to the following:

1 certain agricultural operations, including use of uncultivated land, water management, intensive livestock and fish farming, reclamation from the sea;

2 extractive industries;

3 energy industries, including wind farms;

4 processing of metals;

5 minerals industries, for example, coke ovens, asbestos production, ceramic products;

6 chemical industries;

7 food industries, for example, vegetable and animal fats, dairy products, brewing, fish ;

8 textile, leather, wood and paper plants;

9 rubber industries;

10 industrial estates, shopping centres, sports centres, leisure centres;

11 railways, roads, motorway service areas, airfields, harbours;

12 permanent racing tracks;

13 installations for waste disposal and water treatment;

14 test benches for engines, turbines and reactors;

15 ski-runs, ski-lifts; and

16 marinas, holiday villages, golf courses.

The Directive's requirements were originally brought into force in England and Wales by the Town and Country Planning (Assessment of Environmental Effects) Regulations 1988 (SI 1988/1199) with accompanying advice in Circular 15/88. A new s 71A of TCPA 1990, inserted as a result of the Planning and Compensation Act 1991(s 15), grants power to the SoS to make regulations for the purposes of implementing any EU obligation.

A person intending to apply for planning permission may ask the lpa to state in writing whether in its opinion the proposal falls within a description mentioned in Scheds 1 and 2 (reg 5(1)) and thereby requires the submission of an environmental statement. Whether Sched 2 provisions require the submission of an environmental statement in a particular circumstance is a matter of judgment by the lpa, but this can be challenged in the courts. In the first *Royal Society for the Protection of Birds* (RSPB) case [1991] JPL 39, the judgment of the lpa was challenged, and the court decided that the RSBP had a legitimate expectation of being consulted. However, provided the local authority is satisfied that it has been supplied with sufficient information, within three weeks or such period that may be agreed, the lpa shall inform the person of its decision by means of a written statement which clearly and precisely sets out the full reasons for the conclusion that the development requires environmental analysis and, therefore, that the developer must submit an environmental statement. Where the local authority indicates that it requires an environmental statement, or has failed to respond within the period, the person may apply to the SoS for a direction on the matter.

Where a planning application is accompanied by an environmental statement, the lpa is required to publicise both the application and the statement (Art 12B, GPDO) by placing a notice on the site and advertising the proposal in a local newspaper. If the statement is submitted after the application, then this responsibility falls to the applicant (reg 13). The period for the determination of such applications is extended to 16 weeks, during which time the lpa must consult with various government departments and public bodies including the Countryside Commission and English Nature (see Art 18, GPDO). A copy of the application and the statement must also be forwarded to the SoS who has the right to call in the application for his determination (regs 8 and 14).

If an application is granted without an environmental statement, where this is required, this constitutes a breach of reg 4, and the validity of the permission may be challenged in the High Court (s 288 TCPA 1990). Similarly, should an lpa fail to require an environmental statement when it would be appropriate to do so, or fails to take any action, the remedy would be an application to the High Court for a judicial review.

The following cases highlight examples of the interpretation by the courts in relation to the actions by lpas in interpreting the requirements of the Directive on EA.

In *Berkeley v Secretary of State* (1997) EGCS 49, the High Court rejected an application made by a community group under s 288 to set aside a decision by the SoS to grant planning permission and listed building consent for the provision of new stands at Fulham Football Club. The applicants claimed that the decision was flawed, as neither the SoS nor his inspector had considered the need for an EA, and that the proposal constituted an 'urban development project' for the purpose of Sched 2 Environmental Assessment Regulations 1988 (SI 1988/1199) and Circular 15/88. The court held that, in applying the circular, no EA was required because the site, which did not exceed 2.5 hectares, largely consisted of land which had previously been developed.

In *Twyford Parish Council v Secretary of State (Environment) and Secretary of State (Transport)* (1992) Env LR 37, it was held that the applicants were among those whom the Directive was intended to benefit. Whilst the provisions of the Directive were considered to be both unconditional and precise, the court was not convinced that the applicants had suffered damage. It was also made clear that the Directive does not apply to 'pipeline projects', that is, projects in respect of which the application for planning permission was already under consideration when the Directive came into force on 3 July 1988. The Scottish Court of Session, in *Kincardine and Deeside DC v Forestry Commission* (1993) Env LR 151, held that whilst the Directive was capable of having a direct effect in relation to Annex I projects, in the light of the mandatory nature of Art 4.1, it nevertheless gave Member States broad discretion in relation to Annex II projects.

The amendments to the Environmental Assessment Directive (85/337/EEC), which were adopted in March 1997, now require not only that shall certain projects be the subject of an assessment, but also that there is a requirement for development consent. This will have implications for afforestation in the UK, which at present does not require consent. The assessment is used only for the purpose of obtaining grant aid (see Environmental Assessment (Afforestation) Regulations 1988) (SI 1988/1207)).

12.13 THE LOCAL PLANNING AUTHORITY'S DECISION

The decision of the local authority may be delegated to named officers, who are acting on behalf of that authority or to elected representatives acting as a planning committee. In the later case the decision is taken after consideration of the recommendation provided by the professional planning staff, but elected representatives are not bound to follow the advice given by officers. The decision may grant permission unconditionally, or subject to such conditions as they think fit, or they may refuse permission (s 70(1)(a) TCPA 1990).

The term 'unconditional' grant of consent is somewhat misleading as it is subject to s 91 and 92 TCPA 1990, which mandate that every permission must have a condition which limits its duration to three years (s 51 PCPA 2004). In granting permission the local authority is also required to state its reasons for doing so in accordance with Art 5 GPDO (Amendment) Order 2003 (SI 2003/2047).

The extremely wide remit to impose conditions, 'as they think fit' is subject, amongst other things, to the requirement that each condition serve a planning purpose and that a reason be stated for the imposition of each condition (see Chapter 14, para 14.15 *et seq*).

The determination of a planning application is an administrative act and whilst there is no general obligation to afford a hearing to the applicant or objectors most authorities do afford such an opportunity conditional upon the statements being brief, for the obvious reason that the committee has only limited time to deal with its agenda. In *Gaiman and Others v National Assembly for Mental Health* [1971] Ch 317; [1970] 3 WLR 42, Megarry J pointed out that thousands of planning applications are determined every year without an opportunity for the parties to be heard, '... yet I know of no suggestion that the local planning authorities are thereby universally acting in contravention of the principles of natural justice'. However, when making decisions, the local authority must be seen to act fairly. In *R v Great Yarmouth BC ex p Botton Brothers Arcades Ltd* [1988] JPL 18; 56 P & CR 99, potential objectors did not make their views known because they were aware of a strict policy adopted by the authority which was designed to prevent any further development of amusement arcades in a particular area of the town. The application was refused in accordance with this policy, but the applicant's agent later addressed the committee, which recommended that permission should be granted. The potential objectors became aware of this change of mind by the committee but failed to persuade the committee to defer a decision until after they too, had an opportunity to put forward their case. The court quashed the decision ruling that whilst the potential objectors, even if they did not have a legitimate right to be heard, were nevertheless entitled to be treated fairly by the granting of an opportunity to address the committee.

If the lpa refuses permission or imposes conditions, then it must state clearly and precisely its full reasons in the notice of its decision, which must be given in writing (GDPO, Art 22). Although the council or authorised committee effectively may grant planning permission, it is held in law that no permission exists until the applicant is in receipt of the decision notice.

The Local Government Act 1972 (s 101) enables a council to delegate planning functions to a named officer or officers of the authority. This is frequently adopted by authorities to speed up the planning process, and the level of delegated responsibility varies. Most authorities appear to restrict delegated power to the approval of minor applications.

Should an applicant wish to challenge the decision of the lpa to refuse permission or to impose conditions upon a grant of permission, then he may appeal to the SoS (s 78(1) TCPA 1990) and, if the authority has failed to make a decision within the prescribed period, the applicant is entitled to lodge an appeal with the SoS against a deemed refusal (s 78(2)). (See Chapter 16.)

The lpa is empowered to decline to determine applications under s 43 (PCPA 2004) where:

(a) it has refused two similar applications and there has been no appeal to the Secretary of State in the preceding two-year period, and

(b) they think that it is similar to another application which has not been finally determined either by the lpa or the SoS.

12.14 CONDUCT OF THE COMMITTEE

The conduct of members of a committee charged with the responsibility to determine planning applications was the subject of a recent challenge by way of a judicial review in *R v Secretary of State and Another ex p Kirkstall Valley Campaign Ltd* [1996] 3 All ER 304. In 1995, the Leeds Urban Development Corporation (UDC) (since dissolved, hence the respondent to the application was the SoS) granted outline planning permission for a retail development on part of the land owned by a local rugby club. The appellant company, which was a local community action group concerned with the interests of local residents, applied for a judicial review by way of an order of certiorari to quash the decision and the reserved matters decision on the ground that they were vitiated by the participation of three members and an officer of the corporation who had pecuniary or personal interests amounting to apparent bias.

In an application for judicial review, the court may grant one or more of the following remedies known as 'prerogative orders':

1   certiorari – which quashes an unlawful decision of a public authority;

2   prohibition – which prohibits an unlawful act which a public authority is proposing to perform; or

3   mandamus – which compels a public authority to perform a public duty.

It was alleged those interests included the undeclared interest of the chairman of the corporation relating to land which would increase in value if the rugby club sold its existing site and moved to a nearby site, and the association of other members of the corporation with the rugby club either as members, vice-presidents or professional adviser; hence an application for certiorari.

The principle held – that a person be disqualified from participation in a decision if there was a real danger that he or she would be influenced by a pecuniary or personal interest in the outcome – is of general application in public law. In applying this principle to town and country planning law, it was recognised that members would take office with publicly stated views on a variety of policy issues, and in the case of UDCs that the SoS would have regard, in making his appointments to the Board, the desirability of securing the services of persons having a special knowledge of the area. The court therefore was concerned to distinguish legitimate prior stances or experiences from illegitimate ones.

The court then proceeded to give advice to members of committees, accepting that there was a constant risk that a planning authority would have to decide matters where a member happened to have a pecuniary or personal interest. That interest had to be declared, and the member concerned should not participate in the decision unless it was too remote or insignificant to matter. There is no rule requiring a member who has an interest to be declared to absent himself from the meeting while the matter was being discussed, but since participation is a matter not of form but of substance, withdrawal is generally wise.

The Nolan Committee's report 'Standards of Conduct in Local Government in England, Scotland and Wales in Public Life' (Cmd 3702), published in July 1997, contains a number of recommendations which are directly related to the work of those elected members of the local authority who form the planning committee. The report concluded that planning is not an exact science and there are no 'right answers', and in broaching the central issue of the political role of councillors and their role as members of a planning committee, the report states (vol 1, para 290):

> It is significant that planning decisions are taken in committee or in council, not by councillors sitting in any form of court or tribunal. Planning decisions are not legal judgments. They are administrative decisions, taken within the framework of law and

practice, and this view has been upheld by the courts. The effect of this is not that planning decisions are freed from legal constraints, but that the constraints are different. Decisions must still be free from bias caused by personal interest. But in our view they need not be decisions which are taken judicially, based solely upon a rational and impartial assessment of the evidence. On the contrary, councillors must bring to planning decisions a sense of the community's needs and interests. That is why they are there. Theirs is sometimes a difficult task of marrying their duty to represent the interests of the community with their obligation to remain *within the constraints of planning law*, and only to take account of relevant matters. If they do either to the exclusion of the other they are equally at fault. [Author's emphasis.]

This led directly to Recommendation 34, which states:

All members of an authority's planning committee (or equivalent) should receive training in the planning system, either before serving in the committee or as soon as possible after their appointment to the committee.

The Nolan Committee appeared to have overlooked further constraints and complexities faced by councillors. In making decisions they are obliged to take into account the Regional Policy Guidance, PPGs – both issued by central government – and local policies embodied in the development plan. Frequently they will be faced with the need to pursue objectives, for example housing targets set out in the Structure Plan, which will often be in conflict with the wishes of the local community.

12.15 REFERENCE OF APPLICATION TO THE SECRETARY OF STATE

The SoS is empowered under s 77 (TCPA 1990) to issue directions requiring applications for planning permission to be referred to him instead of being dealt with by the lpa. A direction under this section may be given:

(a) to a particular lpa or lpas generally; and

(b) may relate either to a particular application or to applications of a Class specified in the direction.

Before determining an application referred to him under these powers, the SoS shall (if either the applicant or the lpa wish), give each an opportunity to appear at a local inquiry. The decision of the SoS on any application referred to him under this shall be final.

Note: See para 3.21 which sets out the SoS's involvement in the determination of planning applications in accordance with the Town and Country Planning (Development Plans and Consultations Direction) 1999.

It is anticipated that Part IV of the Planning and Compulsory Purchase Act 2004 will become operative in September 2005. This will require amendments to Articles 3 and 4 of the Town and Country Planning (General Development Procedure) Order 1995 relating to applications for outline planning permission. Outline applications will have to include information about the use, quantum, layout, scale parameters and indicative access points. Reserved matters will deal with layout, scale, appearance, access and landscaping.

12.16 MAJOR INFRASTRUCTURE PROJECTS

Section 76A (PCPA 2004) was added to allow the SoS to call-in major infrastructure projects. Under 76(A)(4)(b), having called-in such a project, the SoS may appoint a 'lead inspector' and direct him to consider such matters related to the application as are prescribed. After considering any recommendation from the 'lead inspector' the SoS may appoint additional inspectors as he thinks appropriate and direct them to consider such matters as the lead inspector decides (see Town & Country Planning (Major Infrastructure Project Inquiry Rules Procedure) (England) Rules 2002 (SI 2002/1223)).

12.17 REVOCATION AND MODIFICATION OF PLANNING PERMISSION

In what may be regarded as exceptional circumstances, the lpa has the power under s 97(1) (TCPA 1990) to revoke or modify any permission which it has previously granted, providing that the permission has not been completed in the case of building or other operations, or before any permitted change of use has taken place. The lpa has no power simply to withdraw permission unilaterally and Orders under this section require confirmation by the SoS. The lpa will also be responsible for paying compensation under s 107.

The power to revoke or modify a planning permission is also vested in the SoS under s 100(1). Before making such an order, the SoS must consult the lpa and the authority may request to appear before and be heard by an appointed person (s 100(5)). The lpa has more than a passing interest in such Orders by the SoS as it falls to it to pay any compensation which may result from his action (see para 14.26).

12.18 TIMETABLE FOR THE SECRETARY OF STATE'S DECISION

Schedule 2 (PCPA 2004) applies to decisions made by the SoS under s 77 (call-in) and s 78 (planning appeals) (TCPA 1990), and requires the SoS to make and publish one or more timetables setting out the time within which the decision, or any other steps, must be taken. The timetable is not legally binding and may be varied, but not retrospectively and the SoS is required to provide written reasons why the timetable was not adhered to and to provide an annual report to Parliament on his performance.

12.19 RESUBMISSION OF APPLICATION

Following the refusal or withdrawal of an application, (for which there is no reimbursement of the planning application fee), the same applicant for the same site and the same development is entitled to submit a second application without the payment of a second application fee (Town and Country Planning (Fees for Applications and Deemed Applications) Regulations 1989 (SI 1989/193), reg 8(2)(f)). In the case of the application having been withdrawn, the second application must be submitted within 12 months of the date of the submission of the first. In the case of a planning refusal the 12-month period runs from the date of the local authority's decision (reg 8(2)(a)(i)).

12.20 CROWN DEVELOPMENT

Previous planning Acts did not bind the Crown but the Planning & Compulsory Purchase Act 2004, Part 7, ends Crown immunity in the planning system and makes special provision in relation to certain applications by or on behalf of the Crown and in respect of enforcement of planning control in relation to the Crown. Government Departments and the Queen must now make applications, rather than follow the previous procedure set out in Circular 19/84, and enforcement action will apply to Crown land. The exemption from criminal sanctions, however, is to remain.

12.21 DEVELOPMENT BY LOCAL AUTHORITIES

Local authorities are required to obtain planning permission for development which they wish to carry out but certain development is permitted under the General Development Order. Section 316 (TCPA 1990) empowers the SoS to make regulations governing the development by local authorities (currently the Town and Country Planning General Regulations 1992 (SI 1992/1492)) in which Reg 3 states:

> Subject to reg 4, an application for planning permission by an interested planning authority to develop any land of that authority, or for development of any land by interested planning authority or by an interested planning authority jointly with any other person, shall be determined by the authority concerned unless the application is referred to the Secretary of State under s 77 of the 1990 Act for determination by him.

Regulation 4 states;

> Reg 3 does not apply where:
>
> (a)   the authority do not intend to develop the land themselves or jointly with any person, and
>
> (b)   if it were not such land the application would fall to be determined by another body.

12.22 DEVELOPMENT BY STATUTORY UNDERTAKERS

The term 'statutory undertaker' is defined in s 262(1) of TCPA 1990 as:

> persons authorised by any enactment to carry on any railway, light railway, tramway, road transport, water transport, canal, inland navigation, dock, harbour, pier, or lighthouse undertaking or any undertaking for the supply of hydraulic power and a relevant airport operator.

In addition to which, under the Act's provisions, also included are:

> any gas supplier, water or sewerage undertaking, the National Rivers Authority, the Post Office and the Civil Aviation Authority are deemed to be statutory undertakers.

Planning permission for types of development are granted under the General Development Order and modification of the 'normal' procedures relate to the development of 'operational land' of such bodies. Should an appeal be lodged following the planning authority's refusal of proposed development on operational land or if the matter is called-in by the SoS, the decision is to be taken jointly with the appropriate Minister responsible for the operations of the particular statutory undertaker.

12.23 MAJOR PUBLIC WORKS

The Transport and Works Act 1992 (s 1, 2 and 3), gave the SoS power to make orders relating to a variety of modes of transport and s 5 includes such provisions as the application, modification or exclusion of other statutory provisions; the acquisition of land whether by agreement or compulsorily; the extinguishments of rights over land; the abrogation and modification of agreements relating to land; the payment of compensation the charging of tolls etc and the making of bylaws and their enforcement. Planning permission is deemed to be granted by the SoS when making the order.

Under s 11, provision is made for any person to object to a draft order and the Secretary if State is obliged to hold a public inquiry if objections to the order are submitted by statutory objectors, lpas or landowners whose land is proposed to be acquired. Other objectors have their objection heard by way of a hearing conducted by a person appointed by the SoS.

Parliamentary approval is only required for those proposals which, in the opinion of the SoS, are of national significance. In such cases proposals must be approved under s 9 by both Houses of Parliament.

Planning permission must be obtained before the proposals contained in the order can be implemented, but prior to applying for an order the applicant is required to obtain a statement form the lpa or authorities as to whether the proposal is consistent with the planning policies in the development plan and also giving details of any extant planning permissions. The SoS also has the power to grant permission for any development involved in the implementation of the order under s 90(A) which states:

> On making an order under sections 1 and 3 of the Transport and Works Act (1992), the Secretary of State may direct that planning permission for the development shall be deemed to be granted, subject to such conditions (if any) as my be specified in the direction.

Although the use of this power is discretionary it seems inconceivable that, having approved an order, the SoS would consider withholding planning permission.

CHAPTER 13

LEGAL CHALLENGES TO THE CONSIDERATION OF PLANNING APPLICATIONS

13.1   INTRODUCTION

The determination of planning applications invariably involves the weighing of conflicting interests, and each application involves an attempt by the applicant to carry out some form of development, the rights for which are vested in the State as a result of the Town and Country Planning Act (TCPA) 1947. The re-establishment of this 'right' by the granting of planning permission is, in many cases, contentious. The individual's wishes have to be weighed against the broader objectives of the planning system which is designed to safeguard the needs and wishes of the general public.

In determining planning applications, local planning authorities (lpas) are also obliged to carry out the procedures set out in Chapter 12. Failure to do so may result in a challenge in the courts by way of an application for judicial review on the ground that there has been a disregard of some procedural requirement causing substantial prejudice. This is described as 'procedural *ultra vires*'.

This chapter focuses on these procedures and legal challenges to the manner in which decisions are taken. It is stressed that normally the aggrieved applicant's first recourse is to appeal to the Secretary of State (SoS), and that persons other than the aggrieved applicant only have recourse to the courts on a matter arising from the lpa's decision.

Unless otherwise stated, all sections referred to relate to the TCPA 1990.

13.2   PRE-APPLICATION DISCUSSIONS

Intending applicants are encouraged by the SoS to discuss the content of their proposals with officers of the council prior to the formal submission of the planning application. The House of Lords held, in *McCarthy and Stone (Developments) Ltd v Richmond-on-Thames LBC* [1992] JPL 467; [1991] 4 All ER 897, that local authorities are not entitled to charge a fee for the officer's time spent discussing an impending application. (See, also, para 13.20, below, relating to estoppel.)

13.3   DETERMINATION OF THE VALIDITY OF APPLICATIONS

Determination of the validity of applications for planning permission has tacitly been assumed to accord with s 62(b) which states that '... any application for planning permission ... shall include such particulars and be verified by such evidence as may be required by regulations or directions given by the local planning authority under them'. This interpretation was challenged in *R v Secretary of State ex p Bath and North East Somerset DC* [1999] JPL B160. The case raised the issue of whether an lpa was the sole arbiter of what constitutes a valid application and, on appeal to the SoS, whether a valid application had been submitted in the first instance.

In the opinion of the lpa, simultaneous applications relating to proposed change of use and listed building consent required the submission of further details. The applicant did not consider that it was appropriate to go to the expense of providing the level of detail required until the matter of the proposed change of use had been settled.

In refusing the application, the court held, first, that the interpretation of Art 20(3)(b) of the General Permitted Development Order (GPDO) 1995, requires that the date of receipt of an application should be the date when the material required in reg 3(1)(a) and (b) have been provided, that is:

> ... an application for planning permission shall be made on a form provided by the local planning authority and include particulars specified in the form and be accompanied by a plan which identifies the land to which it relates and any other plans and drawing and information necessary to describe the development.

Secondly, Art 20 of the GPDO 1995 does not prescribe who is to determine the question of validity. The decision by an lpa is not determinate (see *Geall, Marc John v Secretary of State and Lewes DC* [1999] JPL 909). It is, therefore, open to the inspector to make a determination when required to address the problem.

The requirement to submit further details in relation to both a planning application and an application for listed building consent did not invalidate the applications but merely required supplementary information before there could be proper determinations.

13.4 DUTY OF CARE

The general rule that the lpa is not liable to neighbouring landowners in negligence for granting planning permission for development which adversely affects the plaintiff's interests has been upheld in the Court of Appeal in *Lam v Brennan* (1997) 3 PLR 22. Although safety to a person and property may be a material consideration, it was clear that the policy of the Act, in conferring broad discretionary power under s 70, was not to make a duty of care at common law which would make the public authority liable to pay compensation for the foreseeable loss caused by the exercise or non-exercise of power.

13.5 DUTY OF FAIRNESS

The case of *R v Rochdale MBC ex p Brown* [1997] JPL 337 has significant general implications for the process of development control, although the case arose as a result of an application for the renewal of an Interim Development Order consent under Sched 2(1) to the Planning and Compensation Act 1991. The prime issue was the extent of the duty placed upon members to give proper consideration to representations made to them before determining the application. In this particular case there was pressure to determine the application because of the three-month rule (Sched 2(1)(5)(b)), which meant that, if the decision had not been taken on that evening, the period available to the council would have expired. The applicant to the court lived close to the quarry and represented local community organisations. He maintained that the council had unreasonably denied him access to documents submitted by the owners in support of proposed conditions until it was too late for him to make effective use of the documents. There appears to have been a request from the applicant on 28 February 1996 for a copy of documentation, which was reinforced by a further letter dated 10 April 1996. The council responded on 12 April. As a result, the applicant's final written representations and accompanying expert's report were not laid before the committee. He managed to submit representations, including a consultant's report, to the council's officers two hours before the meeting, but the members did not have access to the documents, nor was any summary available to them.

In the judgment of the court, the applicant had been entitled to the documents when first requested, and not having received them, he was deprived of an opportunity to make proper, full and meaningful representations. The council had also failed to comply with an undertaking given to members of the public that representations from them would be reported in summarised form to the meeting. The council's assurance had created a legitimate expectation which had been denied. Whilst the court acknowledged that councillors justifiably and lawfully placed considerable reliance on their officers' views, this did not permit them to abrogate their responsibility to give adequate consideration to the gist of any objections.

The court dismissed the submission that, if the decision was quashed under the 1991 Act (Sched 1), there would be no determination, with the effect that the quarry owner's suggested conditions would then become the operative ones. The decision was quashed and the council was instructed promptly to rehear and determine the application in the proper manner and inform the owner immediately following the decision.

13.6   THE DECISION-MAKING BODY

As noted above, the lpa may delegate responsibility to officers to determine planning applications (s 101 of the Local Government Act 1972). The responsibility given to one person does not extend to an authority acting under its own standing orders to delegate responsibility to the chairman of its planning committee. Delegation to a single individual other than an officer is not in accordance with s 101(1), as there is no concept in law of a committee of one. In *R v Secretary of State ex p Hillingdon LBC* [1987] JPL 717; [1986] 1 WLR 807, the action of the chairman was held to be *ultra vires*, as were the council's standing orders which conferred this power to the chairman.

13.7   COUNTY AND DISTRICT RESPONSIBILITIES

The development control responsibilities of the county and district authorities are set out in what may appear to be a clear-cut manner, with the county councils being responsible for mineral and waste applications. However, this is perhaps not so clear-cut as one may imagine, as in the case of *R v Berkshire CC ex p Wokingham DC* (1995) EGCS 57. The planning application, which led to a determination by the Court of Appeal, was for 'B.1(c) and B.2 units, recycling and transfer stations, access road, parking and landscaping'. (See Chapter 8, para 8.2, for definitions of B.1(c) and B.2 units.) There was no argument that the waste station and ancillary development amounted to a county matter, but the industrial units constituted a form of development which was appropriate for determination by the DC, which sought a declaration that the county council had no power to determine the application in so far as it related to industrial units.

The court held that, since the major part of the proposed development, in terms of size, was the waste recycling and transfer station, with associated buildings and access road, it clearly constituted a county matter. The Court of Appeal applied to the question the tests appropriate to determine the appropriate planning unit. Where it was possible to recognise a single, main purpose of the occupier's use of land to which secondary activities were incidental or ancillary, the whole unit of occupation should be considered. It might equally be apt to consider the entire unit of occupation, even though the occupier carried out a variety of activities and it was possible that one was not incidental or ancillary to another. Although parts of a single unit of occupation could be considered as separate planning units, the test to be applied was whether there were two or more physically and distinct areas which were used for substantially different and unrelated purposes.

13.8   FAILURE TO COMPLY WITH A DIRECTION OR REGULATION

The GPDO 1995 requires that certain steps are taken if the application is a departure from the plan, including publicity and the forwarding of the application to the SoS for his consideration. The question is raised about the validity of any permission granted without observing the requirements of the direction. In *Co-operative Retail Services Ltd v Taff-Ely BC* (1979) 38 P & CR 156; (1981) 42 P & CR 1, HL, it was held that the procedure laid down by the direction then in force was merely directory and not mandatory. Subsequently, in *R v St Edmundsbury BC ex p Investors in Industry Commercial Properties Ltd* [1986] JPL 38; [1985] 3 All ER 234, it was held that the failure to comply with the direction did not render the application null and void.

In *R v Lambeth LBC ex p Sharp* [1987] JPL 440; 55 P & CR 232, the Court of Appeal considered the procedure to be followed by the lpa under s 270 of the TCPA 1971 and reg 4 of the Town and Country Planning (General) Regulations 1976 rather than a direction. In this instance it was proposed to construct a floodlit athletics track within an area of parkland forming part of a designated conservation area. The regulations provided that, unless the SoS called in the application, the council should pass a resolution to seek planning permission for the proposed development and then *had to* publicise the intended development and invite public comment. After due consideration of any public comment, the authority was then required to pass a second resolution and under the terms of reg 4(5), which provided that, if all the required steps had been undertaken in a proper manner, planning permission should be deemed to be granted by the SoS.

To meet the requirement to advertise the proposal, Lambeth Council posted a notice of intent on the park gates and advertised the proposal in a newspaper circulating in the area inviting public comment. Alas, what the council failed to include in either notice was the date by which representations were to be submitted to the council! In the view of the court, it followed that the period might not have ended, since no time limit had been specified. Failure to abide by the regulations, which set out the requirements for advertising planning applications (which include a date by which representations must be submitted) was the reason for the judgment to dismiss the appeal.

13.9   CONSIDERATION OF PLANNING POLICY GUIDANCE

Planning decisions by both lpas and the SoS are required to take into account both the content of policies contained in the development plan (s 54ATCPA 1990) and also current Central Government Policy Guidance in the form of Planning Policy Guidance Notes (PPGs). A number of cases have come before the courts to determine the interpretation of this Guidance and, perhaps not surprisingly, a number of them relate to proposed supermarket developments and to PPG 6, 'Town Centres and Retail Developments', 3rd edn, 1996.

The sequential tests set out in PPG 6 came in for careful scrutiny in two High Court cases, the first of which was *R v Hambleton DC ex p Somerfield Stores Ltd* [1998] JPL 307; [1999] EGCS 155. The court rejected the submission that the lpa should first have considered whether there was a need for the development. If need were to be a material consideration in assessing all applications for planning permission for new retail development, one would expect reference to be made to it in the PPG. If need were a precondition to the granting of permission it would undermine one of the stated objectives of the PPG, which is to maintain an efficient and competitive retail market.

Where out-of-town development was proposed, the meaning of the term 'impact' was relevant to the extent of any likely harmful effect upon the town centre. It could not be read as requiring an assessment of the benefit of the proposed development for an existing town centre. However, it did not follow that an authority would ignore beneficial effects, simply that PPG 6 did not require beneficial impacts to be shown, nor that it would be a material consideration in all cases.

The second case that determines the interpretation of current Central Government Policy Guidance is *Michael Shanley Group Ltd v Secretary of State* (1998) EGCS 142, where the court allowed an application to set aside an inspector's decision on the ground that he had misapplied the Guidance and failed to give proper reasons for his decision. During the local plan inquiry, the suitability of the site had been considered, but the inspector had felt unable to recommend it because there was insufficient evidence to demonstrate that the development would be compatible with the residents' interests. The applicant then sought planning permission for the appeal site and at the inquiry the council argued that, whilst they were not contending that other sites were suitable, they had begun to investigate whether two other sites could be said to be so. The inspector rejected the appeal on this ground as he considered that it would not be sensible to permit an out-of-town-centre foodstore given the possibility of a better site being identified in the future.

The court rejected the approach that, unless there was a finding that a site otherwise meeting the criteria was likely to become available within a reasonable period of time, the decision-maker was obliged to give appropriate consideration to sites that were out of town. This approach was considered to be too narrow.

The sequential test was considered in *Budgens Stores Ltd v Secretary of State* (1998) EGCS 28. If a site was determined to be too far out to be an 'edge of centre' site, and there was a barrier between the site and the town centre, the inspector was correct in concluding that it could not be considered under the category of 'town centre' and, under the sequential approach, the next appropriate category for it was 'out of centre'.

The Hambleton case and others led the government to issue further clarification which should be taken into account by lpas when applying the policy tests contained in PPG 6. The clarification is contained in a written parliamentary answer on 11 February 1999. The Minister for Planning advised that decisions on applications for retail and leisure development outside town centres should take into account the following:

(a) in preparing planning strategies and policies, consideration should be given to the need for new retail and leisure facilities over the lifetime of the plan. Demonstration of need should not be regarded as being fulfilled by simply showing that there is a physical capacity or demand in terms of available expenditure within the proposal's catchment area. Whilst the existence of capacity or demand may form part of the demonstration of need, the significance in any particular case will be a matter for the decision maker;

(b) proposals for retail and leisure development which accord with an up-to-date plan, or are within an existing centre, should not be required to demonstrate that they satisfy the test of need; but

(c) in other cases, it will be necessary to demonstrate need and also that a sequential approach has been applied in selecting the location of the site; and

(d) the Guidance should be applied equally to proposals for extending existing edge of centre and out of centre development that creates additional floor space.

13.10 PUBLICITY AND CONSULTATIONS

Prior to the introduction of s 65 into the 1990 Act by the Planning and Compensation Act 1991 (see Chapter 12, para 12.10), there was no legal requirement on the part of lpas to give publicity to planning applications other than those which were classified as 'bad neighbour uses' or where development was proposed which affected a listed building or a conservation area (see Chapter 20).

Although many authorities had previously adopted informal schemes of notification, it was made clear in *R v Secretary of State ex p Kent* [1990] JPL 124; (1988) 3 PLR 17 that this did not give rise to any legitimate expectation of notification. Where publicity takes the form of an advertisement in a local newspaper, the courts will not insist upon exhaustive coverage (*McMeechan v Secretary of State* (1974) 232 EG 201).

In *R (on application of Gavin) v Haringey LBC)* [2003] EWCH 2591, the court considered the consequences of an lpa failing adequately to publicise a planning application. Although others had been notified by letter, a solicitor working directly opposite the application site had not been informed and a site notice had not been posted. Planning permission had been granted in September 2000 but the claimant had not been made aware of this until operations began in March 2003 and he received confirmation of the permission by the lpa in April 2003, following his request for information. The commencement of judicial proceedings commenced some 32 months after the grant of planning permission and this proved to be a critical factor. In the view of Richards J the planning authority had failed to publicise the application properly or carry out the requisite Environmental Impact Assessment (EIA) obligations and were it not for the delay he would have quashed the permission. The judge emphasised that the developer was entitled to rely upon the lpa to discharge the publicity requirements under the GDPO and was not obliged to monitor the steps taken by the lpa to comply with those requirements. Third parties were entitled to reply upon information in the planning register and in consequence quashing a planning decision long after it had been made would be detrimental to good administration as well as causing hardship and prejudice to the developer.

NB A growing number of lpas are now incorporating details of current planning applications on their web sites as a means of giving further publicity.

13.11 NOTIFICATION TO OWNERS

Whilst it is not necessary for the applicant to have a legal interest in the land or building for which he is seeking planning permission, he is required either to inform the owner (Certificate B) or, when the owner or owners are not known, to advertise the application in a local newspaper (Certificate C or D). The completion of the certificate certifies that the appropriate action has been undertaken.

Section 65(6) TCPA 1990 provides that if any person who issues a certificate, the content of which he knows to be false or misleading in a material particular, he is liable on summary conviction to a fine not exceeding level 5 on the standard scale. This leaves the question of what effect, if any, does a false, misleading or inaccurate statement have on any planning permission which had been granted? In *R v Bradford-upon-Avon UDC ex p Boulton* [1964] 1 WLR 1136, an application was made for an order of certiorari to quash a permission for residential development because the certificate was signed by the applicant stating he was the owner of the fee simple of the land (Certificate A). At that time he was negotiating the purchase of the land and the actual owner was aware of his interest. In refusing to grant the order the Divisional Court held that a planning authority had jurisdiction to entertain an application for planning permission and that a factual error in the certificates did not deprive the authority of that jurisdiction. The decision appears to have been influenced by the fact that planning permission 'runs with the land' and in this case could benefit the rightful owner who retained the right to convey the land or not to another party (see also *Main v Swansea City Council* [1985] JPL 558).

The previous cases were held not to involve dishonest actions. In *English v Dedham Vale Properties Ltd* [1978] 1 WLR 93, the circumstances were somewhat different. The application was signed by the employee of the prospective purchaser who stated himself to be the vendors' agent and who requested that the decision notice be forwarded to him at the purchaser's address. The vendors were unaware of this activity as the submission of Certificate A precluded them from being rightfully being informed by means of a Certificate B. Still unaware of the existence of a planning consent, the vendors subsequently sold the land to the applicant company at a price which was claimed to be lower than they would have done had they known the true position. The surviving vendor brought action against the purchaser claiming, *inter alia*, damages for fraudulent misrepresentation in obtaining planning permission and an account of the profits which had accrued to the purchasers following their acquisition at a lower cost. Slade J held that whilst there had not been any misrepresentation by the purchaser, as to the prospects of gaining planning permission he was absolved from any charge of fraud but was accountable to the vendors for the profit he had received as a result of making the planning application. This was because in relation to the application he had assumed the position of a self-appointed agent for the vendors and, as a result, had placed himself in a fiduciary relationship with them.

The decision in *R (on Application of Pridmore) v Salisbury DC* [2004] JPL 784 relates to a claim that a certificate B had been served on the owner of adjacent land. A Mr Docking had applied for planning permission to construct a new bungalow in his garden with an access which involved a widened splay. The applicant certified that all the land was in his ownership but in fact part belonged to the claimants. When the lpa became aware of the situation they invited the applicant to withdraw his application, with a view to resubmission, or that a notice be served upon the claimants. Mr Docking in submitting an amended plan accompanied by a Certificate B certifying that the claimants had been informed. The lpa reasonably assumed the previous error had been corrected and granted planning permission for the amended proposals. In fact no such action had been taken by Mr Docking. In quashing the decision Newman J took the view that it was necessary to ensure that the mandatory scheme of the legislation could not be undermined. It was one thing to fail to give notice to an unidentified owner as in the case of *Main v Swansea CC* [1985] 49 P&CR 26 but it was quite another to certify that the prior notice had been given when it had not been given. Furthermore it was certified that the notice had been given on a stated date when no notice had been given at all.

13.12 THE TIMESCALE FOR A DECISION

Unless the applicant subsequently agrees to an extension of the time period for the consideration of the planning application, the lpa should make its determination within eight weeks of receiving it, 16 weeks if an environmental statement is required, or such time as agreed with the applicant in writing. These periods do not distinguish between a small-scale application or a multimillion-pound proposal, and during this time the lpa is required to carry out those statutory consultations required under Art 10(1). Given that statutory consultees have 21 days in which to make their observations, the possible complexity of the application, and the fact that in most cases the decision has to be taken by the appropriate elected body which only meets at regular intervals, this is a short time span. It was held by the Court of Appeal in *ADC Estates v Camden LBC* [1991] JPL 327 that the date on which a planning application is made is the date when it is received by the lpa.

Any application not determined within the time period prescribed or agreed may be treated by the applicant as a deemed refusal which gives rise to the right of appeal to the SoS (see Chapter 16). Provided an appeal has not been lodged on the basis of a deemed refusal, the local authority is not absolved from its duty to determine the application simply because the time period has expired (see *James v Minister Housing and Local Government* [1968] AC 409).

13.13 OUTLINE APPLICATIONS

Article 3 of the 1995 GDPO makes provision for the submission and consideration of outline planning applications which were first introduced in the 1950 General Development Order. It allows an lpa to give a decision in principle and, at the same time, to reserve details for subsequent approval. Outline applications, defined in Art 1(2), *can only* be considered when the proposal involves the erection of a *building* as defined in s 336(1) TCPA 1990. The scope of an outline permission was the issue in

Hargreaves Transport v Lynch [1969] 1 WLR 215; 1 All ER 455. The lpa must guard against giving a blanket permission for, say, industrial development, and thus effectively lose control over the amount of development which it has approved in outline. This was explained in Circular 87/50, which states that:

> The application should indicate the character and approximate size of the building to be erected, and the use to which it will be put, for example, a three bedroomed house, a two storied factory with an aggregate floorspace of 'x' square feet.

The Court of Appeal overturned the decision of the lower court in *R v Newbury DC ex p Chieveley Parish Council* [1998] JPL 679; 10 CL 490. Whilst upholding the first instance of the decision, particularly the statement that an lpa has no power to reserve any matter for which details have been supplied as part of the planning application, the court disagreed with Carnwath J's view that the size and scale of the development could be treated as reserved matters. In their view, by virtue of Art 1 of the GDPO 1995, there is no power to reserve matters of which details have been given in an outline planning application. The applicant retains the right to amend the application by withdrawing details and it is up to the lpa to require further details. There is also no objection to the practice of including details 'for illustrative purposes only'.

The submission of a fully detailed application does not prejudice the power of an lpa to impose a condition(s) for its subsequent approval. In *Sutton LBC v Secretary of State* (1975) 29 P & CR 350, the authority, having received a detailed application for full permission, nevertheless reserved for subsequent approval the type and treatment of materials to be used on the exterior of the building.

Once an outline consent has been granted, the submission of reserved matters must take place within three years, or such period as determined by the lpa (s 92(2) TCPA 1990). The lpa is also empowered to specify different periods in relation to separate parts of the application in order to allow control over the phasing of the development (s 92(5)). Failure on the part of the applicant to meet any of these requirements results in the lapsing of the consent, but the lpa may chose to treat any 'late submission' as a fresh application for full permission (*Cardiff Corporation v Secretary of State (Wales)* (1971)115 SJ 1817; 22 P & CR 718). In *R v Secretary of State ex p Corby BC* [1995] JPL 115; (1994) 1 PLR 38, the High Court confirmed that an application to vary a standard condition, which requires the submission of reserved matters within three years, is acceptable under s 73 provided the application is lodged prior to the expiry of the permission. Where authorities cannot demonstrate that harm would be caused by allowing the same development in the future, as was approved in the recent past, they may well be the subject of a challenge in the courts if they refuse applications under s 73 to extend the time periods (see *Allied London Property Investment Ltd v Secretary of State* [1997] JPL 199; (1996) EGCS 52).

Provided details of the reserved matters have been submitted within the timescale set by the lpa, it has been held in *Inverclyde DC v Secretary of State (Scotland)* 1982 SLT 200, that these details may be amended provided the character of the application is not altered. However, it is essential that the submission of reserved matters be within the limits imposed by the outline planning consent. In *Calcaria Construction Co (York) v Secretary of State* [1974] JPL 287; 27 P & CR 435, the company was granted outline consent for a warehouse, and their eventual detailed submission took the form of an outof-town shopping centre and associated car parking, which was refused.

In *Shemara v Luton Corporation* (1967) 18 P & CR 520, outline permission was granted for three five-storied blocks of flats with garages and, although the number of units remained the same, the detailed application consisted of four four-storied blocks with garages. The revised form of the detailed application was considered by the authority to prejudice the development of adjacent sites and the authority's refusal of the revised detailed application was upheld by the court. The omission of a use included in the original outline consent may prove acceptable unless it is closely linked with the other uses, or there was a condition which required that all the uses should be developed (*R v Hammersmith and Fulham LBC ex p GLC* [1986] JPL 528; 51 P & CR 120).

It is possible to submit piecemeal applications to satisfy the requirements contained in the reserved matters (*R v Secretary of State ex p Percy Bilton Industrial Properties* (1976) 31 P & CR 154), but it remains possible for the lpa to withhold permission if, in its opinion, on planning grounds the reserved matters should be considered as a whole (*Heron Corporation v Manchester City Corporation* [1978] JPL 471; 1 WLR 937; 3 All ER 1240).

13.14 THE IMPORTANCE OF THE PLAN

Section 54A of the TCPA 1990, replaced by s 38(6) of the Planning and Compulsory Purchase Act (PCPAPCPA) 2004 is to be read in conjunction with s 70(2), and requires lpas to make decisions in accordance with the development plan, unless there are material circumstances which 'indicate otherwise'. Section 70(2), which has *not* been repealed by s 54A, states that, in determining applications, the authority 'shall have regard to provisions of the development plan, so far as material to the application and to any other material considerations'. The effect is to introduce a presumption in favour of development which is in accordance with the plan, and, at the same time, place the onus on developers to provide convincing reasons why the plan should not prevail. The High Court considered the implications of the new section in *St Alban's DC v Secretary of State* [1993] JPL 374; 66 P & CR 432; (1992) EGCS 147. David Widdicombe QC held that, undoubtedly, the section did provide for a presumption in favour of the plan, but he rejected the submission that the plan should prevail unless there were strong, contrary, planning grounds. He preferred to adhere to the words of the section which made it clear that the presumption may be rebutted if there were 'material considerations' which 'indicated otherwise'.

In *R v Leominster DC ex p Patricia Pothecary* [1997] JPL 835, the applicant applied to the High Court to quash the decision of the lpa to grant retrospective planning permission for a livestock shed sited within the Kingsland Conservation Area. The original permission granted was for the erection of a steel-framed, polythene lambing cover, but a livestock shed had been erected instead, hence the application for retrospective permission. Mrs Pothecary objected to the application, but the council resolved to grant a conditional permission. Her application to the High Court was based upon two main submissions: first, that the committee had failed to determine the application in accordance with the development plan in breach of s 54A, and, secondly, that the committee had failed to discharge its duty under s 72 Planning (Listed Buildings and Conservation Areas) Act 1990 to pay special attention to the desirability of preserving the character of the conservation area. The application to quash the decision was allowed, and it was held that it was completely manifest that the proposal did not accord with the local plan and that the officers and the members of the committee had paid no regard to their duty under s 72 to give special attention to the desirability of preserving the character and appearance of the conservation area.

The court in *Cranage Parish Council v Secretary of State* [2004] EWCA 2949 considered the issue of the meaning of words included in a policy document which the planning authority is bound to take into account and, in doing so, adopted the approach outlined by Brooke LJ in *R v Derbyshire County Council ex p Woods* [1997] JPL 958. It is the function of the court to determine as a matter of law what the words are capable of meaning. Should the decision maker attach meaning to the words they are not capable of bearing then they have made an error in law. The court accepted that policies were often loosely drafted and were not intended to be legally binding documents in the strict sense and resort will be needed to elements of value judgment. (eg) 'existing town centre' or 'institutions standing in extensive grounds'. Nevertheless the courts must be wary of an approach 'whereby decision makers can live in a planning world of Humpty Dumpty, making a particular planning policy mean whatever the decision maker decides it should mean'. The court set out the following four guidelines:

(1) As Brooke LJ made clear the court will assess, as a preliminary matter, whether the interpretation is one that the words used are in law properly capable of bearing.

(2) If in any particular planning case one meaning is from any standpoint, highly probable, but a counter meaning is advanced by the decision maker which can at best be regarded as 'tenuous' they should not be surprised if the court choose to adopt a robust approach.

(3) There may be circumstances where even if the words of the policy are taken on their *prima facie* value support the interpretation by the decision maker, consideration of the purpose and underlying objective of the policy in question may show that such interpretation simply will not accurately represent the true policy.

(4) Decision makers need to bear in mind that adoption of a particular interpretation of policy in a development plan in respect of a particular case will make it difficult, in the absence of a convincing explanation, for them to adopt a different interpretation in another case without attracting a challenge on the ground of arbitrariness or collateral purpose or the like.

However, the lpa may well find itself in the position where it does not have a formally adopted plan. In such cases, it may have a plan at one of the various stages of preparation. If this plan is accepted as the basis for a decision on a planning application which conforms to the emerging plan, the authority may be tempted to grant consent, but to do so would pre-empt possible objections to the plan. This issue was addressed in *R v City of London Corporation ex p Allan* (1980) 79 LGR 223. A planning application was received for the redevelopment of a large area shown in the draft plan which was, however, the subject of objections to be heard at the public inquiry. The application was referred to the SoS who declined to call in the application, and, as the Corporation seemed likely to grant permission, the objectors sought an order of prohibition to prevent the permission from being granted.

Woolf J said that, once an lpa had publicised the proposals in the draft plan, the authority should take the objections into account, and were they left with alternative courses of action, they could either deal with the application at this stage or they could refuse the application on the grounds of prematurity. (The possibility of refusing an application on the grounds of prematurity is limited; see PPG 1, para 33, and Chapter 5, para 5.6.) He concluded that there was nothing to suggest that the corporation would not give proper consideration to relevant matters and dismissed the application for an order of prohibition.

13.15 MATERIAL CONSIDERATIONS

13.15.1 Introduction

The requirement placed upon planning authorities to take into account 'material considerations' when determining planning applications begs the question: what are material considerations? The basic principle is that these considerations must be related to the objects of planning legislation. This, in turn, requires further definition: what are the objects of planning? In *Stringer v Minister of Housing and Local Government* [1971] JPL 114; 1 All ER 65; [1970] 1 WLR 1281, Cooke J said that 'any consideration which related to the use and development of land was capable of being a planning consideration'.

This wide interpretation by the courts has continued, and in a more recent case, *Northumberland CC v Secretary of State and British Coal Corporation* [1989] JPL 700; (1990) 59 P & CR 468, the *dictum* of Cooke J was held to be 'still good law'. In this case, it was held that the SoS had not erred in law in permitting an opencast mine because of the financial benefit to deep mining, even though no particular deep mine had been identified.

The scope of planning has increased over the years, and this broadening of issues which are accepted as part of the role of planning has been matched by a liberal attitude by the courts in determining what can legitimately be considered as material factors (see Purdue, M, 'Material considerations: an ever expanding concept?' [1989] JPL 156). Whether a particular issue can be regarded as material may well depend upon the circumstances of the individual case and on an increasingly liberal approach by the courts. Having established that an issue is a material consideration, the question is raised as to how much weight should be given to that issue in the determination of a planning application or following the lodging of a planning appeal. Lord Hoffman in the *Tesco Stores v Secretary of State* case (see Chapter 5, para 5.5) stated:

> The law has always made a clear distinction between the question of whether something is a material consideration and the weight which it should be given. The former is a question of law and the latter is a question of planning judgment, which is entirely a matter for the planning authority. Provided that the planning authority has regard to all material considerations, it is at liberty (provided that it does not lapse into *Wednesbury* irrationality) to give them whatever weight the planning authority thinks fit or no weight at all. The fact that the law regards something as a material consideration therefore involves no view about the part, if any, which it should play in the decision making process.

13.15.2 Personal circumstances

Lord Scarman in *Westminster City Council v Great Portland Estates plc* [1985] JPL 108; AC 661 defined a material consideration by whether it served a planning purpose, and whether that planning purpose was related to the use and character of land, and added:

Personal circumstances of the occupier, personal hardship, the difficulties of business which are of value to the character of a community are not to be ignored in the administration of planning control. It would be inhuman pedantry to exclude from the control of our environment the human factor. The human factor is always present, of course, indirectly as background to the consideration of the character of land use. It can, however, and sometimes should, be given direct effect as an exceptional or special circumstance. But such circumstances, when they arise, fall to be considered not as a general rule but as exceptions to a general rule to be met in special cases. If a planning authority is to give effect to them, a specific case has to be made and the planning authority must give reasons for accepting it.

The question of personal circumstances was given further consideration in *Tameside Metropolitan BC v Secretary of State* [1984] JPL 180 when Webster J stated:

> ... arguments of this kind (personal hardship) must always be considered, but they will seldom outweigh the more general planning considerations. If the development proposed entails work of a permanent kind, it should be borne in mind that it will remain long after the personal circumstances of the applicant have ceased to be material. If there are substantial planning objections to the development, they will therefore prevail. But if the case is more finely balanced and there are no decisive planning objections to the proposal, a genuine plea of hardship may tip the scale in the applicant's favour.

In *Essex County Council v Secretary of State* [1989] JPL 187, the case related to the relocation of a small business to a rural area. The financial aspects of running a small business which would have to pay high rents had the move been made to an industrial estate was considered to be a material factor.

13.15.3 Financial considerations

The issue of cost was also raised in *Murphy J and Sons Ltd v Secretary of State* [1973] 2 All ER 26. The London Borough of Camden wished to build flats on a site which adjoined the company's industrial premises on one side and a railway line on the other. The council admitted that the proposal would be very expensive, and the company, which wished to acquire the site, objected to the council's proposal. Ackner J, in upholding the SoS's decision, said: 'What the planning authority is concerned with is how the land is going to be used. The planning authority exercises no paternalistic or avuncular jurisdiction over would-be developers to safeguard them from their financial follies.'

In 1977, the prospective cost of the development was found to be relevant in *Niarchos (London) Ltd v Secretary of State* [1978] JPL 247; 35 P & CR 259. The development plan provided that the temporary use of houses should not be renewed as offices as they could reasonably be used or adapted for residential use. It was held that, in deciding whether the premises could be reasonably used or adapted, the SoS should have had regard to the cost of reconverting them to residential use.

In 1989, the issue of the relevance of financial considerations was considered once again in *R v Westminster City Council ex p Monahan* [1989] JPL 107; 3 WLR 408; [1990] 1 QB 87. This judgment of the Court of Appeal must be considered as a definitive statement because the House of Lords refused leave to appeal. In their application, the Trustees of the Royal Opera House sought to extend and improve the Opera House and to erect office accommodation on part of the site. The modernisation of the Opera House was a feature in the local plan, but no provision was made in the plan for the erection of offices. Westminster City Council accepted the argument of the need to build the offices to provide funds for the improvements to the Opera House which were unobtainable by any other means.

The Covent Garden Community Association challenged the council's decision on two grounds: first, that to permit the commercial development of part of the site for purely financial reasons, whatever their purpose, was not a material consideration the council was entitled to take into account; and secondly, that the council was bound to investigate whether the offices were in fact necessary to achieve the objectives of modernising the Opera House. It was held that the fact that the finances available from the commercial development would enable the improvements to be carried out was capable of being regarded as a material consideration in that it related to the use and development of land, particularly as they occupied the same site and all formed part of one proposal. It was also held that the council had adequately investigated the question of whether the office development was necessary to achieve the proposed improvement to the Opera House.

The issue of the weight given to financial aspects is one which the courts have determined in a variety of ways, and it appears that an increasingly liberal approach is being adopted. Personal circumstances of the applicant may be found to be the material factor which 'tips the balance' in exceptional circumstances, and in the case of the Opera House, two factors appear to have been considered: the 'social need' to update the premises and the fact that the modernisation was an element in the local plan.

13.15.4 Precedent

When considering a planning application, it is by no means unusual for the authority to consider that the granting of planning permission would create a precedent which might make it difficult to refuse further similar applications and that this, therefore, should be a material consideration. This view was upheld in *Collis Radio v Secretary of State* [1975] JPL 221; 73 LGR 211; 29 P & CR 390 by Lord Widgery CJ, who said:

> Planning is something which deals with localities and not individual parcels of land and individual sites. In all planning cases it must be of the greatest importance to ask what the consequences in the locality will be – what are the side effects which will flow if such a permission is granted?

The law on this point was refined in *Poundstretcher Ltd v Secretary of State and Liverpool City Council* [1989] JPL 90; (1988) 3 PLR 69, where David Widdicombe QC stated:

> The mere fear or generalised concern about creating a precedent was not enough; there had to be evidence in one form or another for reliance on precedent ... in some cases, the facts might speak for themselves; for instance, in the case of the rear extension of one house in a terrace of houses, it might be obvious that other owners in the terrace would want extensions if one was permitted.

13.15.5 Unexplained inconsistency

In *R v East Hertfordshire DC ex p Beckman* (1997) EGCS 104 it is likely that, for the first time, the High Court (Lightman J) has set aside a planning permission issued by the lpa on the ground of inconsistency with past decisions. The ruling has implications for the manner in which planning committees conduct their business and the nature of the minutes of their meetings.

The applicant sought an order to quash a planning permission for the erection of a detached house on a neighbouring property. Two identical applications had previously been refused on the site and, with no relevant change in circumstances, the third application succeeded against the advice of officers. The sub-committee's minutes disclosed that they believed there had been a change in circumstances in that the police supported the application on the grounds of security. This matter had already been taken into account when the second application was rejected.

In an attempt to justify its position, the council submitted an affidavit sworn by the chairman of the committee which varied from the recorded minutes:

> Whilst during the discussion by members the point had been made that the support of the police was a new factor to be taken into account, by the time we came to our decision, having heard from the planning officer, we were well aware that the police neither supported nor objected to the proposal.

The court found this submission was unimpressive, and Lightman J said:

> I find it highly unsatisfactory that the council's approved minute, which stands as at least an unofficial record of the gist of the reasoning for the council's decision and is verified by the officer charged with its making, should be capable of being seriously qualified or displaced, at the stance of the council, by an affidavit subsequently sworn by a member of the committee. This is particularly unsatisfactory where that member of the committee was, as I understand the case here, one of those persons who was a party to the approval of the minute at a later meeting.

On the basis of these findings, the court concluded that the council must have taken into account a factor which was totally incorrect and irrelevant. Even if there were doubt of that, there was clear confusion in the mind of the committee, as evidenced by the minutes and the affidavits. The court then went on to observe:

> Where a council's decision seriously affects the citizen, the council minute of the decision should be prepared with care and only approved after careful consideration whether it is clear and correct. Approval should not be an empty ritual undertaken blind ... Where a decision of the council is made to reverse a position taken twice in so recent a period, fairness and good administration require that the reasoning advanced by the council should be clear and unambiguous; it should not be contradictory, unsatisfactory or pregnant with possibilities of error.

13.15.6 Public concern

Fear of crime has been recently considered as being capable of being a material consideration in *West Midlands Probation Committee v Secretary of State* [1997] JPL 323. The court upheld the inspector's decision to dismiss a planning appeal against the refusal to allow the extension of an existing bail hostel. It was accepted that annoyance to the public might well be a matter of concern which was material to planning control, and if fear of crime was justified in relation to the proposed use or its effects, that, too, could be a material consideration. In this particular case, there was evidence which included fighting, robbery, and incidents of drunken, intimidating or loutish behaviour.

However, in *Newport County BC v Secretary of State (Wales)* [1997] JPL June Update, the court awarded costs against the lpa who had taken into account local public concerns about the safety of the proposed development. The SoS's approach was that fears on the part of the public, unless objectively justified, could never amount to a material consideration.

In a third case, *R v Broadland DC ex p Dove* [1999] JPL 397; [1998] PLCR 119; 4 CL 521, anti-social behaviour by residents was held to be a material planning consideration. The officer's advice to his committee was that concerns over safety to school children, leading to increased journeys to and from a nearby primary school, and the nature and character of potential residents, were not planning matters. The court held that there was a heavy burden on the applicants despite the officer's advice and Bartlett QC went on to state:

> ... while it is reasonable to infer that the council accepted the advice about materiality, I see no reason to conclude that they stopped short at that point and did not go on to consider the concerns of local residents and whether that would affect their decision.

The court did not find it necessary to address the distinction between matters which concerned local residents and the concerns themselves in upholding the decision.

13.15.7 Previous permission

In *South Oxfordshire DC v Secretary of State* [1981] JPL 359; 1 WLR 1092, it was held that a previous planning permission is capable of being a material consideration even if it has expired. A lpa may change its mind but it is required to show the changed circumstances which have led to the reversal of a previous decision.

13.15.8 Alternative sites

In considering a planning application for a use which the authority considers is necessary in a particular area, it has been held that the authority is entitled to consider an alternative site as a material consideration even if the alternative site is not specified. In *Trusthouse Forte Hotels Ltd v Secretary of State and Northavon DC* [1986] JPL 834; (1987) 53 P & CR 293, the authority accepted the need for a hotel development, but considered the need should not be met on the application site but on some other unspecified site.

In *GLC v Secretary of State and London Docklands Development Corporation and Cablecross Projects Ltd* [1986] JPL 193, the Court of Appeal dismissed an appeal against the SoS's granting of planning permission for office and residential development. One of the arguments put forward by the appellants was that the SoS had failed to consider whether the site provided significant facilities for passenger interchange or access, hence the need, in their view, to look at alternative sites. In dismissing this argument, the court provided a detailed test as to when the existence of an alternative site is a relevant factor in the determination of a planning application:

(a) the presence of a clear public convenience or advantage in the proposal under consideration;

(b) the existence of inevitable adverse effects or disadvantages to the public or some section of the public in the proposal;

(c) the existence of an alternative site which would not have those effects, or would not have them to the same extent;

(d) a situation in which there could only be one permission granted for such development, or at least only a very limited number of permissions.

The issue of the consideration of alternative sites as a material consideration is dependent upon a number of 'tests'. If the proposal is to develop land in a way which is acceptable in planning terms then the existence of other land which is more acceptable does not justify refusal of planning permission. However, where there are clear planning objections or inevitable adverse effects it may be relevant to consider alternative sites. The courts consider that it is the council's responsibility to decide what is a material consideration and will only interfere if that decision was perverse.

13.15.9 Expert advice

In *R v Tandridge DC ex p Mohamed Al Fayed* [1999] JPL 825; 2 CL 433, the High Court rejected an application for judicial review of a grant of planning permission for a radio telephone tower. It was argued, on behalf of the applicant, that the lpa wrongly thought that they were bound by the views of the Health and Safety Executive on the effects of electromagnetic fields. The court accepted that, if the lpa had acted in that way, its decision would be challengeable, but it was correct that they should give great weight to the advice of experts. Furthermore, if the authority were to depart from national planning policy guidance, they ran the risk of the decision being overturned and costs awarded against them.

In arriving at its decision, the court referred to *Newport County BC v Secretary of State (Wales)* [1998] JPL 377, where it had been accepted that decision-makers might take into account genuine issues of public safety even when not wholly supported by technical evidence. This did not, however, make it necessarily reasonable for permission to be refused on the basis of unsubstantiated fears.

13.15.10 Applicant's fall-back position

It is not unusual for an appellant to argue that planning permission should be granted for development in order to avoid the greater harm which would result from the resumption of some lawful use of the site. In *South Buckinghamshire DC v Secretary of State* [1998] JPL August Update, the court ventured the view that the decision-maker, in deciding whether planning permission should be granted, should consider the likelihood of such resumption taking place. It would be '*Wednesbury* unreasonable' to take potential harm into account if there was no realistic possibility of it being caused and because it also posed the question of the probability of the harm that the use would cause. The inspector had failed to consider whether there was any particular degree of probability that the unauthorised use would be resumed. This constituted an error of law which undermined the basis of his decision. (See also *Snowden v Secretary of State* [1980] JPL 749; *Burge v Secretary of State* [1988] JPL 497; and *Brentwood BC v Secretary of State* [1996] JPL 939; (1995) 72 P & CR 61.)

Nolan v Secretary of State (1998) EGCS 7 confirms the need to have regard, when determining a planning application, to what the applicant may be able to do without planning permission. In rejecting an enforcement appeal against a requirement to remove a wall that was 4 m high, the inspector had failed to consider allowing the appellant to retain the wall at 2 m, given the permitted development rights under GPDO, Sched 2, Pt 2, Class A.

13.16 APPROVAL OF RESERVED MATTERS

An outline planning permission is a planning permission granted subject to the approval of reserved matters. Although the applicant must gain further approval before acting upon it, an outline permission can be revoked only in accordance with statutory procedures. These normally involve the SoS and the payment of compensation by the council to the applicant (see *Hamilton v West Sussex CC* [1958] 2 QB 286; 2 WLR 873). When considering an application to meet these reserved matters, the authority cannot frustrate the earlier grant of planning permission (see *Medina BC v Proberun Ltd* [1991] JPL 159). Nor does it entitle the applicant to raise matters which do not fall within the content of the outline permission.

However, as a result of the decision in *R v Hammersmith and Fulham LBC ex p GLC* [1986] JPL 528; (1985) 51 P & CR 120, it appears that the application can remove elements from the outline planning consent. In this case, the outline application included the provision of a bus station and a library, both of which were omitted from the application for the approval of details. This was held to be in order as the omission of these elements did not put the application for detailed consent outside the ambit of the original outline planning permission. A similar situation occurred in *Sunland Development Co v Secretary of State and Lewes DC* [1986] JPL 759, in which outline consent was granted for 44 houses, but only 35 were the subject of the application for the approval of reserved matters. If such situations are to be prevented, the planning authority must grant outline permission with a condition designed to ensure that all the elements will be included in the subsequent application for the approval of reserved matters.

The precise wording and content of conditions attached to outline permissions has particular significance if the local authority is to avoid problems at the later stage. This is exemplified in *R v Secretary of State ex p Slough BC* [1995] JPL 135; [1996] JPL B8. The High Court was invited to overturn the SoS's finding that an application for the approval of reserved matters fell within the scope of the outline planning permission although the applicants proposed a building of 1,530 sq m as against the 1,055 sq m which appeared in the original application. It was held that the application had not been incorporated in the outline consent, notwithstanding that it had been referred to by number and reference to the development being approved 'in accordance with the accompanying particulars and plans'. In the view of the court, the outline permission was clear: it imposed no limits on the permitted floor area.

Following the approval of reserved matters, the applicant is permitted to submit further, revised, details under the original grant of outline permission (see *Heron Corporation Ltd v Manchester City Corporation* [1978] JPL 47; 1 WLR 137).

13.17 ISSUING THE PLANNING DECISION

It had always been assumed that the date of the planning decision was that of the resolution of the authorised committee, or the council itself. However, in *R v Yeovil BC ex p Trustees of Elim Pentecostal Church* (1972) 23 P & CR 39; 70 LGR 142, the Divisional Court took a different view. In this case, the committee resolved to authorise the town clerk to grant planning permission for a youth hostel once an agreement had been reached about carparking facilities. Before such agreement was reached, the council changed its mind and resolved to refuse the application. The court decided there could be no planning permission until written notice of the council's decision had been given to the applicant.

Where a planning application consists of a number of separate elements, it is lawful for the planning authority to deal with them separately by only granting permission for so much of the development as it considers should be permitted (see *Kent CC v Secretary of State* [1976] JPL 755; 241 EG 83).

Following the introduction of Art 22(1)(a) to the General Development Order 1995 by the Town and Country Planning (General Procedure) (England) Amendment Order 2003 there is a duty placed upon lpas to provide summary reasons for the granting of planning permission or the approval of reserved matters in the decision notice. Following a successful challenge by an adjoining neighbour to a proposal involving a replacement apartment block in *R (on Application of Wall) v Brighton and Hove CC* [2005] JPL 747, Sullivan J set out guidance as follows as to how this should be provided:

> The new requirement does not impose an undue burden upon lpas. Officers' reports customarily include recommended reasons for refusal of planning permission or the imposition of conditions ... When officers recommend the grant of planning permission there is no reason why their reports should not similarly contain recommended summary grounds for the granting of planning permission. The members will be able to adopt or amend the officers' summary grounds but the requirement to set out summary grounds in the decision notice will ensure that the members decide in public session why they wish to grant planning permission.

> The new requirement to give summary reasons for the grant of planning permission will be particularly valuable in cases where members have not accepted officers' advice, where the officer has felt unable to make a recommendation, where the officers' report fails to take account of a material consideration but that omission is said to have remedied by the members in the course of their discussions, or where an irrelevant factor has been relied upon by some members during the course of their discussions and it is important to ascertain whether it was one of the committee's reasons for granting planning permission. In such cases, and I emphasise they are only examples, there would have to be very powerful reasons for not quashing a decision notice which did not include the lpa's summary reasons for granting planning permission. To allow extrinsic post hoc evidence as to what the lpa's reasons were in such cases would perpetuate the very problems Parliament intended the susbtituted Art 22(1) to address.

13.18 SPLIT DECISIONS

Following an appeal, the SoS is empowered (s 79(1) TCPA 1990) to issue a split decision where the proposed development is clearly divisible into two distinct elements. This was supported in the judgment in *Glacier Metal Co Ltd v Secretary of State for the Environment and London Borough of Hillingdon* [1975] JPL 165. Such severability may be not only on a physical basis but can include uses proposed on the same land at different times.

In determining a planning application lpas may grant a lesser planning permission than that applied for (*Kent CC v Secretary of State for the Environment and Burmah-Total Refineries Trust Ltd* [1976] JPL 755; 33 P & CR 70). Before doing so, the local authority should enquire first whether the applicant wishes to make any representations.

Applications for express consent for the display of advertisements may result in split decisions under the powers given in the Town and Country Planning (Control of Advertisements) Regulations 1992 (SI 1992/656).

13.19 OFFICER ADVICE

In giving advice to their elected members, developers and members of the public, officers must act both fairly and with a duty of care. Recent cases have highlighted these requirements.

The first such case was *Slough Estates plc v Welwyn and Hatfield DC* (1996) EGCS 132. The allegation, which was upheld by the court, was that the council's officers and members had deliberately deceived the plaintiffs and induced them to embark upon a retail development scheme which incurred significant losses. The court initially awarded the company damages amounting to £48 million, which later resulted in a negotiated settlement of £29.5 million. Slough Estates commenced building a retailing complex known as the Howard Centre in 1989, which opened in August 1991, and which incorporated part of the railway station at Welwyn Garden City. Prior to the commencement of development, in 1984 Slough Estates Centre learned of the council's intention to build a second retail complex called the 'A1 Galleria' one mile from their complex. The council, as head leaseholder, had a financial interest in the second scheme, and was proposing to enter into a development agreement which would provide 200,000 sq ft of retail floorspace. Slough Estates were concerned that the area could not sustain two such large retail developments in such close proximity. To overcome any potential problems, and to encourage Slough Estates to proceed with their development proposal, the council undertook to include, and to enforce, a Tenant Mix Agreement (TMA) with Carrolls, who were the developers of 'A1 Galleria', which opened in November 1991. This was designed to cover a five-year period and limit the occupation of the scheme to 'leisure occupants' and not allow traditional 'high street' shops which would be in competition with those established in the Howard Centre. Such an agreement was entered into, but subsequently there was a secret agreement with Carrolls to relax the terms of the agreement without the knowledge of Slough Estates.

The court found that:

> In July 1987, the full Welwyn and Hatfield DC (WHDC) resolved upon specific advice from its most senior officers to agree to Carrolls' request to relax the 'TMA' as to 85,000 square feet but to keep its relaxation secret and to pretend to all other parties, including Slough Estates, that the TMA was still in place and that it was their intention to enforce it. The council's specific intention as far as Slough Estates were concerned was to induce them to continue with the Howard Centre with the knowledge that, if they learned of the relaxation, they probably would not continue. WHDC wanted both 'A1 Galleria' and the Howard Centre to be built. They had a strong financial interest in the 'A1 Galleria'.

The court concluded that the council had made, or had continued, representations regarding the TMA to Slough Estates plc and others on at least 22 separate occasions between 1984 and 1990, and that the council's intention quite obviously was to induce Slough Estates to continue with the Howard Centre. There was also a continuing misrepresentation by silence.

The second case, *Welton v North Cornwall DC* [1997] JPL February Update, directly relates to the duties of an officer who is acting on behalf of his council. The Court of Appeal upheld the award to the plaintiffs of damages amounting to £34,000, after an environmental health officer had negligently required the owner of food premises to undertake works which were unnecessary to secure compliance with the Food Act 1990. The plaintiffs undertook the works as a result of pressure exerted by the officer, and it was clear that the officer knew that what he said would be relied upon by the plaintiffs without independent inquiry. He proceeded to inspect and approve the works as they were being carried out.

In delivering the leading judgment, Rose LJ was of the view that, on the basis of these facts, there had been an assumption of responsibility by the officer and hence a duty of care owed by him. The basis of the liability was the common law duty of care within the ambit of the doctrine in *Hedley Byrne and Co v Heller and Partners Ltd* [1964] AC 465; [1963] 3 WLR 101; 2 All ER 575 relating to negligent misstatement. There are three categories of local authority conduct in the planning system which might give rise to common law liability, namely:

1   Conduct, specifically directed to statutory enforcement, such as the institution of proceedings, the service of improvement notices and the obtaining of closure orders.

    Such conduct, even if careless, would only give rise to common law liability if the circumstances were such as to raise a duty of care at common law, and such a duty was not raised if it was inconsistent with, or had a tendency to discourage, due performance of the statutory duty.

2   The offering of an advisory service.

    In so far that it was merely a part and parcel of the local authority's system for discharging its statutory duties, liability would be excluded so as not to impede the due performance of those duties. But in so far as it went beyond that, the advisory service was capable of giving rise to a duty of care; and the fact that the service was offered by reason of the statutory duty was immaterial.

3   To conduct, such as that in the present case, namely, the imposition by the officer, outwith the legislation, of detailed requirements enforced by threat of closure and by close supervision.

    The existence of the local authority's statutory powers and duties afforded no reason why it should not be liable at common law for this type of conduct by its servant.

The issue of whether the local authority has a duty of care was considered in *Lambert v West Devon BC* [1997] SJ 621. The property owned by the plaintiff was within the Dartmoor National Park Authority (DNPA) and, although West Devon BC was the lpa, it had delegated its development control powers within the park area to the DNPA, while retaining its responsibility for granting building regulations approval. The plaintiff applied to the district council for planning permission for the redevelopment of his property, and the application was duly forwarded to the DNPA, which granted planning permission.

Subsequently, the plaintiff decided he wished to amend the plans approved by the DNPA by redesigning the shape of the roof of the property. The plaintiff approached the senior building control officer employed by the district council, who informed him that he would not only deal with the variation of the building regulation consent but also that he was in a position to amend the planning permission and that work should proceed with the development. On this basis, the work was commenced. The DNPA then took enforcement action against the plaintiff, which was upheld at appeal, and the plaintiff was prosecuted on two occasions for failing to comply with the DNPA's requirements under the enforcement action.

The plaintiff claimed damages for the alleged negligence of the district council in relation to the advice given by its officer. The court held that it was reasonable for the plaintiff to rely on the advice given to him. Accordingly, the council was liable, as a duty of care arose between the parties in line with the *Hedley Byrne* case. The council had breached that duty of care when its officer informed the plaintiff that he could proceed with the development when in fact the officer did not have the power to resolve the issue himself.

This case reiterates the fact that the courts are willing, in certain circumstances, to infer a that a duty of care exists between a local authority and members of the public and that an authority can be held as being negligent where that duty is breached.

In *R v Oldham MBC ex p Bentley* [1996] JPL B119; EGCS 109, the planning committee was wrongly advised by its officers as to a material fact. Planning permission was granted for 120 houses, and the planning committee was advised in making that decision that an earlier permission relating to the site had been implemented by the commencement of development. However, the work that had been undertaken on the site was in breach of conditions attached to the earlier permission, and could not, therefore, be properly be described as commencing development, as it was unlawful. Accordingly, as the decision was based upon wrongful advice given to the committee, the decision was quashed by the court.

13.20 THE QUESTION OF ESTOPPEL

The doctrine of estoppel was developed towards the end of the 19th century, and in a leading case, *Hughes v Metropolitan Railway Co* [1887] 2 App Cas 439, Lord Cairns set out the principle of estoppel as follows:

> It is the principle upon which all the Courts of Equity proceed, that if parties who entered into a definite and distinct terms involving certain legal results … afterwards by their own act or with their own consent enter into a course of negotiations which has the effect of leading one of the parties to suppose that the strict rights *arising under the contract* will not be enforced or will be kept in suspense or held in abeyance the person who might otherwise have enforced those rights will not be allowed to enforce them where it would be inequitable, having regard to the dealings which have thus taken place between the parties.

It is important to understand that the principle of estoppel arises from rights under a contract and this highlights the distinction between public and private law. Whilst the principle of estoppel remains essentially a private law remedy this has not prevented it being used by parties involved in decisions related to planning matters. Developers and objectors have drawn upon the doctrine of estoppel to mitigate the effects of the changes of mind by lpas. Conflict can arise between the objective of the court, which is to prevent an individual from being treated unconscionably, and the broader planning interest, which is to act on behalf of the general public.

In *Tidman v Reading BC* (1994) 3 PLR 72, the issue was the giving of informal advice over the telephone. The giving of informal advice certainly does not constitute a contractual situation between the parties, and therefore the issue of estoppel cannot arise. It was found that the council had no duty of care in these circumstances, notwithstanding that it published a document encouraging persons involved in planning matters to seek advice and guidance. The court held that it is reasonable to assume that the individual would seek proper advice of his own from persons who were conversant with the requirements of planning legislation and practice. But in *London Borough of Camden v Secretary of State* [1994] JPL 403, an applicant's architect sought approval for 'minor alterations' to an approved plan and, in due course, received a written reply signed by a planning officer stating that '... in my view the variations are minor and would not constitute development requiring planning permission'. Later, the council served an enforcement notice, which was quashed by the inspector who took the view that the officer's letter had been clear and unambiguous and furthermore that the signatory had conveyed ostensible authority. The court agreed with the inspector's findings and, moreover, that the authority, in its statement, had not mentioned that only the head of planning had delegated responsibility and not the officer concerned.

In *Wells v Minister of Housing and Local Government* [1967] 1 WLR 1000; 2 All ER 1041, the Court of Appeal determined that a letter from the council relating to a planning proposal was a valid determination, although here had not been an application for a determination as such. Lord Denning MR expressed the view that

> a public authority cannot be estopped form doing its public duty, but I do think it can be stopped from relying on technicalities.

A later case (*Brooks and Burton Ltd v Secretary of State for the Environment* [1976] 35 P & CR 27) sought to limit the scope of the doctrine. Lord Widgery CJ stressed the importance of planning officers being able to help applicants

> without all the time having the shadow of estoppel hanging over them and without the possibility of their immobilising their authorities by some careless remark which produces such an estoppel.

Similarly in *Western Fish Products v Penwith DC* [1978]JPL 623; [1979] 38 P & CR 7; [1981] 2 All ER 204, the Court of Appeal restricted estoppel in determinations on the need to gain planning permission (subsequently removed by the formal procedures contained in s 192 of the TCPA 1990, which deals with determinations of existing and proposed uses).

The decision of the House of Lords in *R v East Sussex CC ex p Reprotech (Pebsham) Ltd* [2002] JPL 821; UKHL 8 attempted to resolve finally the use of the principle of estoppel in planning. Lord Hoffman complained that it was unhelpful to introduce private law concepts of estoppel into planning law and stated;

> it seems to me that in this area, public law has now developed whatever is useful from the moral values which underlie the private law concept of estoppel and the time has come for it to stand on its own two feet.

It is very important to note that this decision is restricted to so-called estoppel by representation and it has no impact on issue estoppel, or *res juducata* as in the case of *Thrasyvoulou v Secretary of State for the Environment* [1990] 1 All ER 65. In this case enforcement proceedings had been brought unsuccessfully a local authority was prevented from issuing a fresh notice in relation to the same alleged breach.

The *Reprotech* case was applied in the High Court in *Henry Boot Homes Ltd v Bassetlaw DC* [2002] JPL 1173; 1224; 1269; 1472, where a dispute arose about the status of an informal agreement between the developers and the lpa as to whether development required compliance with a planning condition forming part of an outline consent. It was held that such an 'agreement' could not provide exemption from statute as s 191A(1)(b) (T & CP Act 1990) made it clear that failing to comply with any condition constituted a breach of planning control. Nevertheless, Sullivan J was willing to accept that established public law principles, such as legitimate expectation, were in principle applicable to town and country planning, but given the comprehensive nature of the statutory code it might be difficult in practice to establish any expectation.

Such expectation was found to be justified in *Downderry Construction Ltd v Secretary of State for Transport, Local Government and the Regions and Caradon DC* [2002] JPL 380; 509; 1173. Two separate outline permissions were granted in 1979 for two different phases of house building. The first phase was completed in 1978, and full planning permission granted for the second phase in the same year. This lapsed, however, because no material operations were commenced within the required period. However, in correspondence between the developer and the local authority there was a letter from the Director of Planning Services stating that the commencement on the first phase kept the second phase 'alive.' This statement was clearly incorrect but the land was sold in 1995 on reliance of the letter and the local authority then claimed that the second permission had indeed lapsed. This prompted an application by the new owners under s 192 for a certificate that it would be lawful to proceed under the 1978 permission, but the application was refused and on appeal the decision of the authority was upheld by an inspector who took the view that experienced developers should not be expected to rely totally upon an officer's reply. Richards J held that the inspector had erred in law in that estoppel cannot be defeated on the basis that the reliance was unreasonable.

13.21 DIRECTIVE ON ENVIRONMENTAL ASSESSMENT

It is the responsibility of the lpa, before determining an application to assess whether the nature of the proposed development should be the subject of an EIA. The Town and Country Planning (Environmental Impact Assessment) (England & Wales) Regulations 1999 (SI 1998/293), require notice to be given, to the SoS in writing and the general public by local newspaper advertisement, of the determination of EIA applications. The lpa must also maintain for public inspection;

(a) the content of the decision and any conditions;

(b) the main reasons and considerations on which the decision is based; and

(c) a description, where necessary, of the main measures to avoid, reduce, and if possible, offset the major adverse effects of the development.

A number of cases have been brought before the courts concerning the authority's screening of applications for this purpose and *R (on application of Goodman) v Lewisham LBC* [2003] JPL 1309, showed that the courts are prepared to intervene to determine that the lpa has wrongly applied the Town and Country Planning (Environmental Impact Assessment) (England & Wales) Regulations 1999. The Court of Appeal, whilst accepting that the responsibility was essentially that of the planning authority, stated that (per Buxton LJ):

> However sensitive such a determination may be, it is not simply a finding of fact, nor of discretionary judgement. Rather, it involved the application of the authority's understanding of the meaning of the law of the expression used in the Regulations. If the authority reaches an understanding of those expressions that is wrong as a matter of law, then the court must correct that error; and in determining the meaning of the statutory expressions the concept of reasonable judgements embodied in Wednesbury simply has no part to play.

The Court of Appeal considered that whether an EIA was required fell to be made by the lpa according to its judgment and opinion. This was also considered in *R (on application of Jones) v Mansfield DC* [2003] JPL 1148; 1 P & CR 31. Jones challenged the decision on the basis that, despite the uncertainties about environmental impact, the council had, unlawfully, left the assessment to be undertaken after outline planning permission had been granted for use as an industrial estate in open countryside near his home. The decision of the court was in the absence of a direction from the SoS under reg 2(2) of the Regulations, the decision as to whether the development was likely to have significant effects on the environment was one for the lpa. A local authority was not bound to require an EIA where it was not confident or positively satisfied that there would be no significant effects. Although a planning authority could not rely on undertakings and remedial measures as a surrogate for the EIA process, the question of whether there were likely to be significant effects on the environment was one of degree and the proposed remedial measures could be taken into account to a certain extent.

The case of *R v Rochdale Metropolitan BC ex p Tew* [2000] JPL 54, was of particular significance in the operation of the planning system within the framework of European environmental law. The issue concerned the validity of an outline application and the level of detail the applicant must provide. The application was for permission for a 'proposed business park consisting of general and light industry, offices, distribution and storage, research and development with associated complimentary retail, leisure, hotel, and housing land'. Planning permission was granted subject to conditions, one of which was that the development should be carried out in accordance with the mitigation measures set out in the environment statement, unless otherwise provided. There was also a further condition which required that the development should not be commenced until a scheme had been submitted and approved showing the overall design and layout of the application site. Judicial review of the permission was sought by local residents primarily on the ground that the application was invalid because it failed to specify the scale of the development. Within the planning system the court concluded that it was not necessary in every case to specify the scale, in terms of space, in order to fulfil the requirement under Reg 3 of the Town and Country Planning (Environmental Impact Assessment) (England & Wales) Regulations 1999 (SI 1998/293). It was for the lpa to decide whether the description of the application was sufficient, given the characteristics of any particular matters of concern, such as height limitation. The fact that Reg 3 was in mandatory terms did not affect this. It would be, observed Sullivan J:

> ... an unduly literal meaning of Reg 3 to construe it so as to require the applicant to provide particulars merely because a question was asked on a local authority's application form which had been prepared for a very wide range of applications for

planning permission, if the local planning authority itself did not require those particulars in the circumstances of the applicant's case.

In the judgment of the European Court of Justice in *R (Delena Wells) v Secretary of State for Transport, Local Government and the Regions* [2004] JPL 400; 1161; 1481, questions were raised relating to the proceedings between Mrs Wells and the SoS concerning the grant of a new consent for mining operations without an EIA having first being carried out. The court confirmed that the decisions, the effect of which was to allow resumption of mining operations, did comprise development consent within the meaning of the Directive. There was a second issue, which was that the SoS had, on appeal, imposed 58 conditions on the consent, some of which required the further approval of the minerals authority. Should the planning authority have considered the need for an EIA in considering those subsequent approvals? The court considered that the approvals process must be taken as a whole and that the imposition of new conditions and the subsequent approval of matters reserved by those conditions constituted a new consent for the purposes of the Directive. The environmental assessment must, in principle, be carried out as soon as was possible to identify and assess all the effects on the environment. Only if the effects are not identifiable until a later stage in the procedure should be they be carried out in the course of the procedure. The UK government was required to ensure the revocation or suspension of the consent in order to carry out an assessment of the environmental effects and to make good any harm caused by the failure to carry out an earlier assessment, or, if the individual concerned agreed, to establish whether it was possible for the person to claim compensation for the harm suffered.

Applications under s 73 TCPA 1990 that is, to vary conditions, are subject to the Town and Country Planning (Environmental Impact Assessment) (England & Wales) Regulations 1999 (SI 1998/293) and this was endorsed by Ouseley J in *R (on the application of Hammerton) v London Underground Ltd* [2003] JPL 984; EWHC 2307. However, this was contested by the lpa and the developer of Battersea Power Station in *R (on application of Hautot) v London Borough of Wandsworth* [2003] JPL 935; EWHC 900, where permission was granted for a judicial review to a resident who claimed that the application should have been screened for EIA purposes. As a result of the judicial review the consent issued was quashed by Collins J (see also *R (on an application of Prokopp) v London Underground Ltd* [2003] EWHC 960).

The content of the lpa register of EIA development consents was challenged in *R (on application of Richardson) v North Yorkshire CC* [2003] EWCA 1860. This case concerned what the claimant regarded as inadequate reasons for the grant of permission for a quarry. On appeal Brown LJ took the view that the procedural error was still capable of being remedied by placing a substitute notice on the register and rejected the argument that the court could not be permitted to regard a breach of SI 1998/293 as curable other then by outright quashing of the permission. The same point was taken in *R (on the application of Burkett) v Hammersmith & Fulham LBC* [2003] EWCH 1031.

In *Twyford Parish Council v Secretary of State (Environment) and Secretary of State (Transport)* [1992] Env LR 37 it was held that whilst the applicants were those whom the Directive was intended to benefit, the court was not convinced that the applicants had suffered damage. It was also made clear that the Directive did not apply to 'pipeline projects', that is, projects in respect of which the application for planning permission was already under consideration when the Directive came into force on 3 July 1988.

13.22 THE OMBUDSMAN

The Parliamentary Commissioner Act 1967 created the office of Parliamentary Commissioner for Administration, or 'Parliamentary Ombudsman', appointed by the Crown with the duty to investigate complaints of injustice arising from maladministration by government departments.

In *R v Parliamentary Commissioner for Administration ex p Morris and Balchin* [1997] JPL 917, the applicants, Mr and Mrs Balchin, purchased property known as 'Swans Harbour' in 1984, and at that time the land search did not reveal any road proposals which might affect their property. In 1996, the county council adopted a preferred route for a proposed bypass, and this was followed by the purchase of an immediate neighbour's property. The applicants requested that the council acquire Swans Harbour, which they claimed was severely blighted by the proposed bypass, but the council declined to do so on the basis that the applicants had no statutory right to insist that the property be acquired. When the council served a compulsory purchase order related to land required for the bypass, the applicants protested about the scheme because of the effect upon the value of their property and again requested that the council acquire the property. The request was again turned down. Following a public inquiry into the scheme, the inspector's report accepted that the proposal would have an adverse effect upon the Balchins' property and, in sympathising with their predicament, expressed a hope that the council would deal with the matter sympathetically. Sympathy was not forthcoming! The council considered that it did not have a legal duty to buy houses on the basis of sympathy.

When the SoS for Transport confirmed the road orders in respect of the bypass, the applicants complained of maladministration founded on the failure of the SoS to obtain assurance from the county council that the applicants would be given adequate compensation. The Parliamentary Ombudsman found that the issue arising from the confirmation of an order is not a matter for the SoS and could not, nor should not, be conditional upon any settlement in relation to compensation. In other words, he saw nothing wrong with the action taken by the SoS.

The applicants applied to the court to quash the decision of the Parliamentary Ombudsman, based upon three issues:

1   the Parliamentary Ombudsman had failed to address the key issue revealed by the investigation;

2   he had posed the wrong question of law in reaching his conclusion on the question of maladministration; and

3   he had reached a conclusion which was unsustainable in the face of the facts found by the commissioner himself.

The court held that, in relation to the first submission, the whole of the findings had to be taken together, and these included consideration of more than the legal obligations of the department. This submission failed. The third submission also failed, as there was nothing in the decision which could be regarded as irrational. However, on the second submission, the court allowed the application, as the court concluded there was maladministration in declining to consider the propriety of the county council's negative attitude to the use of its compensatory powers under s 246(2) of the Highways Act 1980, and the possibility of correction by the Department of Transport. This was a decisive element in the consideration of the question of injustice to the applicants in their dealings with the county council.

The Local Government Act 1974 extended the concept of an ombudsman by the introduction of the Commissioner of Local Administration, which provided for local 'ombudsmen' on a regional basis. Complaints relating to maladministration may be forwarded direct to the local ombudsman, but he or she is specifically excluded from dealing with matters where the complainant has a right of appeal or a right of redress in the courts.

'Maladministration' is not defined in either of the Acts, but it is held to relate to the way in which the decision has been arrived at (see *R v Local Commissioner for the North and Northeast of England ex p Bradford MBC* [1978] JPL 767; [1979] QB 287; 2 WLR 1). Many complaints lodged against the action of local authorities relate to alleged delay, the giving of wrong advice, lack of, or misleading, information, and the lack of consultation. Planning departments of local authorities appear to feature highly in this respect, perhaps partly because of the legal requirement to encourage public participation. In investigating the alleged maladministration, the local ombudsman is not empowered to vary the decision taken by the local authority; his powers are purely persuasive. The report from the ombudsman must be publicised at a local level and, where the finding is against the local authority, it may recommend an *ex gratia* payment to individuals. The sums are usually small, but payment is at the discretion of the authority. It would appear that it is the embarrassment to the local authority of having been charged with maladministration which is the main sanction.

Two cases discussed below were reported in [1997] JPL 160, and serve to illustrate the type of planning matters brought before the local ombudsman and, more importantly, the response by authorities to recommendation from local ombudsmen.

In the first case, a complaint was lodged about the way in which the council had granted planning permission for residential development, which, it was alleged, had an adverse effect on the amenities of the complainants' home. During a visit to the planning department to inspect the plans for the proposed development, it was claimed that the officer showed Mr Z and Mr Y the plans of an earlier application to which they had raised no objection. This had the effect of denying the complainants the opportunity to comment on the finally approved plans, and the ombudsman held that this amounted to maladministration. If objections had been lodged, this may have resulted in the council seeking more detailed information, and might have resulted in the developer modifying his proposals. Thus it was held that the complainants had suffered an injustice, and the ombudsman recommended that the council pay each complainant £1,000 in compensation. However, the council disagreed with this finding and refused to accept the recommendation to make a payment to each of the persons concerned as, in the council's opinion, there had not been maladministration or, even if maladministration had occurred, the complainants had not suffered an injustice. A further report from the ombudsman indicated that the council should reconsider its decision, but to date no payment has been made.

The outcome of the second case contrasts with the first. Mr A complained that there was maladministration on the part of the council which served a Planning Contravention Notice (PCN) (see Chapter 18, para 18.2) following repair to a drive leading across common ground to his home by the installation of concrete kerbs and the laying of a hoggin surface. The ombudsman accepted the government advice that it is sufficient to suspect a breach of planning control to justify the issuing of a PCN, but that suspicion must be reasonable and the authority is required to take reasonable steps to establish the facts before issuing such a notice. The authority should have considered whether the action by Mr A amounted to development by a proper reading and understanding of the GPDO which grants permitted development rights to the maintenance and repair of unadopted streets. Furthermore, the council took an unreasonable period of time to reply to the complainant when asked to provide details of the relevant legislation which led to the action. Subsequently, the council decided not to proceed with enforcement action. The ombudsman considered that the council's actions amounted to maladministration resulting in Mr A incurring legal fees, inconvenience and anxiety. It was recommended that the council pay the cost of reasonable legal fees plus £250 for the inconvenience and anxiety Mr A had suffered, and a further £250 for his time and trouble in pursuing the complaint. The council paid the complainant £1,346.79 plus VAT and interest. (No information is forthcoming on the career prospects of the officers who failed to understand the basic content of the GPDO in relation to permitted development rights!)

CHAPTER 14

THE NATURE AND SCOPE OF PLANNING PERMISSION

14.1 INTRODUCTION

Planning decisions are taken by elected representatives advised by their professional officers or by named officers who are authorised to act on behalf of the authority by way of delegated powers. The democratic process vests in the elected representatives the right to vary or ignore the recommendations of their professional staff. In considering planning applications the elected body, or those acting on its behalf, can take one of three actions (s 70(1) of the Town and Country Planning Act (TCPA) 1990):

1   grant planning permission unconditionally, that is, subject only to a time limit for commencement (usually three years) (s 51(1)(a) of the Planning and Compulsory Purchase Act (PCPA) 2004);

2   grant conditional permission; or

3   refuse permission.

If conditions are imposed the reason for each condition must be stated and, following the amendment to the Town and Country Planning (General Development Procedure) Order (GDPO) 1995 (SI 1995/419) in 2003, the authority is required to provide a summary of the reasons for the grant of planning permission. In making decisions the authority must be aware that in the case of a refusal of planning permission or the imposition of conditions either action may result in an appeal and the award of costs against the local authority (see Chapter 16). Appeals against the decision of the local planning authority (lpa) must be lodged within six months of the date which appears on the decision notice.

Where no decision has been communicated to the applicant within eight weeks in the case of 'normal applications', 13 weeks for 'major applications', or 17 weeks where an Environmental Impact Assessment is required, the applicant has the right of appeal to the Secretary of State (SoS) on the basis of a deemed refusal. Section 50 (PCPA 2004) provides a new provision to allow a period of 'dual jurisdiction' between the SoS and the lpa where an appeal has been made under these circumstances. The intention is to allow the authority the opportunity to overcome the automatic transfer of jurisdiction to the SoS during which time the authority could issue its decision even though the appeal has been lodged. (It is not clear why this provision has been introduced and one must assume it is an attempt to reduce the number of appeals dealt with by the Planning Inspectorate.) If the local authority refuses permission then the appeal will progress in the normal manner. However, if permission is given the appellant may either;

(a) withdraw the appeal;

(b) proceed with the appeal; or

(c) proceed with an appeal upon revised grounds, for example only against a condition or conditions which may have been imposed.

In making decisions, the council must be aware that, in the case of conditional consent or the refusal of planning permission, the action may result in an appeal to the SoS and an award of costs against the local authority (see Chapter 16). The council, however, does *not* have to justify its reasons for the granting of planning permission. In *R v Aylesbury Vale DC ex p Chaplin* (1996) (unreported), the High Court reaffirmed this general rule. In this case, the planning committee resolved to refuse the application in January and, in August of the same year, to grant permission for the same development. The court recognised the theoretical possibility that in some cases the basic principles of fairness might require reasons to be given but was of the opinion that requiring reasons in what it regarded as 'certain ill-defined cases' would not only make the work of planning committees more difficult but it could put at risk the planning permission granted to a third party who was not at fault. The finding in the *Aylesbury Vale* case was not supported in *R v East DCex p Beckman* [1998] JPL 55. (See Chapter 13, para 13.15.5.)

The grant of planning permission does not guarantee that development will occur. Changes to the economic viability of a project or to the economic circumstances of the individual may result in the permission remaining unacted upon. In this event, the permission will lapse (see para 14.5, below) and may not be renewed if there has been a change in policies adopted by the lpa (see *Medhat Nawar v Secretary of State*, Chapter 17, para 17.7.7). In some instances, planning permission is sought purely to establish the potential value of the land. This is usually achieved by the submission of an outline planning application which does not require the presentation of detailed matters and is, therefore, relatively inexpensive (see para 14.14, below).

14.2   THE PLANNING APPLICATION

When planning applications are submitted, the applicant is required to specify the nature of the development (s 62 TCPA 1990). The question arises as to whether the lpa must consider the grant of planning permission solely within the terms of the application, or whether it can rightly grant permission for something which is substantially the same. In *Bernard Wheatcroft Ltd v Secretary of State* [1982] JPL 37; (1980) 257 EGR 934, the application was to erect 420 houses on 35 acres of land, and planning permission was granted to develop only 250 houses on 25 acres. The court held that it is permissible to grant planning permission subject to a condition which reduced the development to be carried out *provided* such a reduction did not differ substantially from the development proposed in the original planning application.

However, where a planning authority grants itself planning permission, this is not the case. Following the Town and Country Planning (General) Regulations 1992 (SI 1992/1492), as amended by SI 1998/2800, the permission enures only for the benefit of the authority or, in the case of joint development, the authority and the other person(s) specified in the application for planning permission as a joint developer (reg 9).

14.3   PLANNING PERMISSIONS

A grant of planning permission normally ensures for the benefit of the land and those persons having an interest in the land (s 75(1) TCPA 1990). It is, therefore, a commodity that may be bought and sold.

There is nothing to prevent the existence of more than one permission in respect of the same piece of land at any point in time. The grant of planning permission does not revoke earlier consents which may relate to the site. Any number of consents which have not been acted upon may remain valid even if they are mutually inconsistent (*Pioneer Aggregates (UK) Ltd v Secretary of State* [1984] JPL 651; AC 132; 2 All ER 358). The owner retains the choice as to which, if any, he will activate.

There is a potential problem if an owner decides to activate, not one, but two or more consents on the same land. In *Pilkington v Secretary of State* [1973] JPL 153; 26 P & CR 508; [1974] 1 All ER 283, the owner was granted planning permission for a bungalow, and a condition attached to the permission stated that it should be the only house to be built on the site. Later, the owner began to activate an earlier permission, which related to a bungalow on another part of the site, and was served with an enforcement notice. It was held that the effect of building the first bungalow was to make the earlier permission incapable of being implemented, and that the erection of two bungalows on the site had never been sanctioned.

In the case of *Durham CC v Secretary of State and Tarmac Roadstone Holdings Ltd* [1990] JPL 280; 60 P & CR 507, the issue of the validity of two consents was further explored. In this case, a 1947 permission for quarrying on the site was granted and was actively carried out until 1956. In 1957, a further planning permission was granted for the tipping of household refuse, and this continued until 1976, by which time just over 40% of the site covered by the 1947 consent had been subjected to tipping. In 1986 Tarmac recommenced extraction operations, relying on the original 1947 consent. Neil LJ explained that, where development consisted of making a material *change of use* of the land, the permission was spent when that change of use was implemented. In these circumstances, the owner could not revert to the original use. However, when permission was for *operational development*, the permission was not spent when the development began. This was the case here, and the following was the question for consideration: 'Was it possible to carry out the development covered by the permission on which it was now sought to rely, having regard to that which had been done or authorised to be done under a permission which had already been implemented?' On the facts submitted, it *was* possible, and the inspector found that the extraction of sand and gravel from areas covered subsequently by tipped material and by natural overburden would be both practicable and viable. The 1947 permission was still capable of being implemented.

It is also possible for a developer to rely on two permissions which are compatible, one for part of the site, and the second for another part of the same site. In *Lucas (F) and Sons v Dorking and Horley RDC* (1966) 17 P & CR 111; (1964) 62 LGR 491, the plaintiffs were granted planning permission in 1952 to develop 28 houses in accordance with a layout which showed 14 houses on each side of a cul-de-sac from a main road. In 1957, they obtained permission to develop the same land by building six houses fronting the main road and proceeded to build two houses in accordance with this permission. They then proposed to construct 14 houses along one side of the cul-de-sac, relying upon the 1952 permission. The council contended that the 1952 permission was no longer valid, and this was challenged by the plaintiffs. In granting the declaration, Winn J accepted that the 1952 permission was not conditional upon the developer completing the whole of the approved development; it was a permission for any of the development comprised therein. To prevent such circumstances occurring, the authority can legitimately attach a condition to a later permission which prevents the exercise of the earlier consent, or which prevents the earlier consent being combined with the later permission.

In exceptional circumstances, permission may be conditioned so that it enures for the sole benefit of an individual or for a particular type of individual, for example, persons employed in agriculture (see para 14.15, below). In such cases which enure for the benefit of a named individual, the personal circumstances of the applicant may be regarded as an important, material factor, or it may be designed to prevent further intensification of what is an acceptable level of use by a particular person. It is, however, possible, in exceptional circumstances, for an lpato grant permission which is restricted by condition to enure solely for the applicant. In *Knott v Secretary of State and Carrodon DC* [1997] JPL 713, planning permission was granted for the erection of a dwelling within an area of outstanding natural beauty subject to a condition that 'the permission shall enure solely for the benefit of Mr and Mrs Knott'. The Knotts started the construction of the property and then applied under s 73 of TCPA 1990 to develop the land without complying with the condition. The eventual appeal was dismissed by the SoS who construed the condition to be similar to those regarding agricultural occupancy conditions. The Knotts claimed that their case was exactly the same as at a previous appeal on another nearby property which had been allowed by the SoS, and they applied to the High Court under s 288 (TCPA 1990) for the decision to be quashed. It was held that there was a material difference between the granting of permission to a named person and that which restricted occupancy to persons engaged in agriculture, and the SoS had erred in law in construing the condition in the way in which he had done. The latter might form a class of their own, whereas, under the terms of the condition in the Knotts' case, use by anyone else would be materially different. However, the finding of the court was that the condition which was to enure only for their benefit did not prevent the making of a material change of use from their use without involving development or without breaching the condition. The SoS's decision not to remove the condition was based upon an error in law, and he therefore did not choose to grant planning permission subject to different conditions by exercising his powers under s 73(2)(a). The case was dismissed and the condition retained, but, as pointed out, this does not prevent other persons from occupying the dwelling once construction has been completed by the applicants who have the sole right to implement the planning permission.

The act of 'development' does not in itself constitute a breach of planning law if undertaken without the benefit of planning consent, unless and until the authority takes action to enforce against the breach (see Chapter 18). It is possible that development which has taken place without the benefit of planning consent can be authorised by the submission and approval of a retrospective planning application. The planning application form provides the opportunity to rectify an unauthorised permission by asking the applicant if the permission sought is 'to retain buildings or works already constructed or carried out, or a use of land already instituted as described in this application and the accompanying plans'.

14.4   TWIN-TRACKING

Until the introduction of a new s 70B into the TCPA 1990 local authorities could be faced with two identical detailed planning applications submitted at the same time by the same developer. This was known as 'twin tracking' the purpose of which was to establish a decision at the earliest possible date. In the event of the applications not being determined within the specified period an appeal would be lodged in relation to one application and the other would be left 'to run'. The appeal machinery was thus brought into operation and should the second application be granted permission by the lpa the appeal would then be withdrawn. Section 70B allows authorities to decline to determine overlapping applications for planning permission, listed building consent and conservation area consents when a similar application:

(a) is still under consideration by the local planning authority and the determination period has not expired;

(b) is still under consideration by the SoS (on appeal or call-in) and no decision has been issued; or

(c) has been determined by the local planning authority or the determination period has expired without it being determined, and the time within which an appeal could be made to the SoS has not expired.

14.5   TIME LIMITS ON PLANNING CONSENTS

Once permission is granted and acted upon, that becomes the established use of the land. Conversely, if no action is taken to implement a consent, it will lapse after three or five years depending on whether it constituted an outline or full planning permission, provided no change has been effected to the original use. A full planning permission for development is granted, or is deemed to be granted, subject to a condition that the development is commenced within five years (s 91(1),(2),(3) TCPA 1990) or within such period as the authority may direct (s 93(1)). This does not apply to following categories of development (s 91(4)):

(a) any permission granted under a development order;

(b) any permission granted under s 63 on an application relating to buildings or works completed, or use of the land instituted before the date of the application;

(c) any permission granted for a limited period under s 72(1)(b) and s 92;

(d) certain permission relating to minerals;

(e) any permission granted by an Enterprise Zone;

(f) any permission granted in a Simplified Planning Zone; and

(g) any outline permission as defined by s 92.

In the case of an outline permission, it is granted, or is deemed to be granted (s 92(2)(3)) subject to:

(a) an application for the approval of any reserved matter for later approval must be made within three years of the grant; and

(b) the development itself must be begun within five years of the grant or two years of the final approval of any reserved matter, whichever of these periods is the longer.

The authority may vary these time limits as it thinks appropriate (s 94(4)).

14.6 COMMENCEMENT OF DEVELOPMENT

The time limits for the activation of a planning consent (set out above) raise the question: what constitutes the commencement of development? A start is deemed to have taken place if any one of the following 'material operations' has taken place (s 56(1)(2) and (4) TCPA 1990):

(a) any work of demolition of a building;

(b) any work of construction in the course of the erection of a building;

(c) the digging of a trench which is to contain the foundations, or part of the foundations, of a building;

(d) the laying of any underground main or pipe to the foundations, or part of the foundations, of a building;

(e) any operation in the course of laying out or constructing a road or part of a road; or

(f) any change in the use of any land, where that change constitutes 'material development'.

In *Malvern Hills DC v Secretary of State and Robert Barnes Ltd* [1982] JPL 439; (1983) 46 P & CR 58; 81 LGR 13, it was held that the marking out of the line and width of a proposed road was sufficient to activate a planning consent. It is quite obvious that, with the minimum of effort on the part of the developer, a planning consent can be secured against expiry. To counter the possibility of a planning consent activated in this way continuing indefinitely, the authority has the power to serve a completion notice (s 95) (see para 14.7, below).

In a decision of the SoS ([1996] JPL 65), he took the view that development may be commenced for the purposes of implementing planning permission under s 56 notwithstanding that the works carried out could also have been implemented as permitted development under the GDPO 1995. Planning permission related to all the elements of the scheme including those which would otherwise have been permitted under the GDPO.

In a more recent case, *R v Arfon BC ex p Walton Commercial Group Ltd* [1997] JPL 237, the High Court was asked to deal with three interrelated issues as to what amounted to the commencement of development. Planning permission was originally granted in 1958 for housing development, and this was followed in 1967 by a further detailed permission for the first phase of the development which amounted to 21 houses. The issue was whether they were still extant or had expired as a result of the introduction of the time limiting restrictions introduced by the Town and Country Planning Act 1968. The 'commencement' involved the digging of a trench and the construction of part of a road early in 1967 in anticipation of the betterment levy which was to become effective on 6 April 1967.

The local authority contended, first, that these actions were carried out in breach of conditions which required certain approvals before development took place. The court accepted that argument. Secondly, part of the site had since been taken for road works and this made it impossible to implement the permission, following *Pilkington v Secretary of State* (see para 14.3, above). The court accepted that, as a result of a dual carriageway running through the site, the conditions attached to the permission could no longer be complied with, and that it was not physically possible to build anything which could be regarded as an implementation of the permissions. Thirdly, the works carried out had been for the sole purpose of avoiding betterment levy, and further development of the site had not followed. In accordance with *Malvern Hills DC v Secretary of State* (see above) and *Spackman v Secretary of State* [1977] JPL 174; 1 All ER 257, the court held that the burden of proof lay with the applicants to show that the physical steps relied on were taken with the intent of developing the land. Where the purpose of the work was simply to preserve a permission, or seek to fix the value of land, then that act could not be accepted as 'beginning development'.

In *Leisure Great Britain plc v Isle of Wight Council* [1999] JPL August Update, the High Court reviewed whether, and in what circumstances, development following a planning permission could be said to have begun as a result of work carried out in breach of a planning condition. Physical works had been carried out but without compliance with condition 12 which required that:

> ... the sequence of operations during the implementation of the permission hereby granted shall be as may be approved by the local planning authority and a programme of working shall be submitted to the local planning authority for approval before any operations are commenced on the site.

Likewise, there had been no compliance with a condition which related to fencing.

The court held that the situation was comparable to that arising where there has been no approval of reserved matters under an outline planning permission, but it was also similar to cases where the necessary approval had been given but there had been a failure to satisfy some other condition. There was, therefore, no valid distinction to be drawn between non-compliance in these different types of condition. There was a breach of condition and therefore a breach of planning control.

In the opinion of the court, the applicants had rightly argued that there were certain exceptions and that it was necessary to look at all the circumstances. These circumstances, it was argued, included the importance and nature of the condition; the reasons for the breach; the knowledge or agreement of the lpa in relation to the breach; and the age of the permission. However, it was not the function of the court simply to look at all the circumstances and determine whether it was fair that the breach of condition should stand in the way of the works being regarded as the commencement of development.

The court accepted that some established exceptions are cited in the *Encyclopedia of Planning* 2005 update: Sweet & Maxwell, including: *Platt (Daniel) Ltd v Secretary of State* [1997] JPL 349; 1 PLR 73, where developers had done all they could to satisfy the condition; *Whitley FG and Sons v Secretary of State (Wales)* (1992) 3 PLR 72, where approval was subsequently given so that the work done before the deadline was made lawful; *Agecrest Ltd v Gwynedd CC* [1998] JPL 325, where the lpa had agreed that the development could commence without full compliance with the relevant conditions; and *R v Flintshire CC ex p Somerfield Stores Ltd* (1998) EGCS 53, where the condition had been complied with, in substance, but had not been completed prior to the start of work on the site. The court found that there was no justification for recognising a fresh exception in the present case.

The validity of old planning permissions which pre-dated the statutory time limits introduced in 1968 was considered in *Field v First Secretary of State* [2004] EWHC 147. In 1967 planning permission had been granted which authorised the demolition of certain cottages and the erection of two bungalows. The cottages were demolished in

1970 and the question was whether the bungalows could be erected in reliance on the permission. The court held that the authorised demolition had constituted development for the purposes of planning legislation and hence it constituted the beginning of development.

14.7   COMPLETION NOTICES

If the development has begun and is not completed within the specified time period, and the lpa is satisfied that the development will not be completed within a reasonable period, it *may* consider serving a completion notice. The notice must be confirmed by the SoS, and will state that, if the development is not completed within a specified period (which must exceed 12 months), the planning permission will cease to have effect. Before confirming the notice, the SoS must grant the person on whom the notice is served an opportunity to appear at a public local inquiry or hearing. Assuming the notice is confirmed, the developer has a choice either to complete the work within the specified period or allow the permission to lapse. If the latter is chosen, the permission will be invalidated except in so far as it authorises development carried out in the meantime (ss 94 and 95 TCPA 1990).

The threat of a completion notice may be sufficient to persuade a developer to complete the development unless there are local circumstances which suggest that the development is inappropriate at that time. The SoS, in overruling his inspector, refused to confirm a notice issued by Burnley BC (see [1979] JPL 184) where he was satisfied that the development of a 10-acre site for housing had been actively pursued by the developer, but there were problems with regard to access and the uncertain state of the property market in the area.

In a second case, a completion notice issued by Montgomeryshire DC in relation to the development of a bungalow, garage and new driveway (see [1979] JPL 480) was confirmed by the SoS, and once again he overruled his inspector. The owners of the site were given the minimum period of 12 months to complete the work.

14.8   RENEWAL OF TIME-LIMITED PERMISSIONS

Section 5 of the PCPA 2004 amends ss 73, 51, 52 (TCPA1990) and as a result the relevant period of the validity of the time limit set out in the original planning permission can only be extended following the submission of a new application.

14.9   TEMPORARY PLANNING PERMISSIONS

In considering a planning application, it is possible for the authority to consider the granting of permission for a restricted period of time, but it has been made clear by the SoS that such action can only be justified in exceptional circumstances. The planning authority cannot use this device simply to defer taking a decision on what would justifiably be a permanent planning consent. Instances where this may be appropriate are where the applicant indicates that the use of land or buildings is required on a temporary basis, for example, the stationing of a caravan whilst constructing a permanent dwelling on the site.

Circular 11/95 (para 109) sets out three main factors that should be taken into account in deciding whether a temporary permission is appropriate. First, it will rarely be appropriate to grant a temporary permission where the applicant wishes to carry out development that is in accordance with the development plan; secondly, it is undesirable to impose a condition requiring demolition after a stated period for what is clearly intended to be a permanent building; and, thirdly, material considerations to which regard must be made in granting any permission, are not limited or made different to a decision to make a permission temporary.

A High Court decision in *I'm Your Man Ltd v Secretary of State* [1998] JPL B85, provides a salutary warning to lpas who seek to grant temporary planning permissions. In 1995, permission for the use of buildings for 'sales, exhibitions and leisure activities for a temporary period of seven years' was granted on appeal, but no condition was imposed requiring the cessation of the use at the end of that period. The owner later applied for permanent permission for the same use and this was refused. The appeal was dismissed and the matter referred to the High Court. The deputy judge identified two fundamental questions. First, is there an implied power to impose limitations on permissions granted otherwise than by a development order? and, secondly, what is the effect of a use permitted on an application expressed to be for a limited period? With regard to the first question, the deputy judge decided that there is no general power to impose limitations except by a development order. With regard to question two, he referred to s 72(1)(b) which provides that, to create a temporary consent, conditions must be attached 'requiring discontinuance of any use of land so authorised at the end of the specified period'. It had been open to the inspector who granted the original permission to impose a condition requiring discontinuance but he had chosen not to do so.

A further case, *Tarmac Heavy Building Material Ltd v Secretary of State* (1999) EGCS 97, also serves to draw attention to pitfalls which befall lpas in attempting to enforce conditions relating to temporary use of land. In 1947, or earlier, a plant existed on a site for the production of ready made concrete. In 1952, permission was granted for the extraction of sand and gravel subject to a condition that, on completion of all extraction, all buildings on the site were to be removed and the land restored to agriculture. In 1986, Tarmac took over the production of concrete and decided to replace the old plant with a new one. An application was submitted to determine whether planning permission was required for the new plant. It was declared to be permitted development, but the company was informed that the council regarded the plant to be subject to conditions contained in the 1952 permission. Extraction of material ended in 1996 and, because Tarmac refused to dismantle the plant, the county council, as minerals authority, served an enforcement notice requiring them to do so. The subsequent appeal was dismissed and Tarmac brought proceedings in the High Court to quash the decision of the SoS. Tarmac alleged that, first, the disputed condition was void, at least in so far as it related to the plant, and, secondly, even if it was valid, it did not cover the new plant built in 1986. The court held that the power of the council in 1952 to impose conditions must be 'for the purpose of, or in connection with, development authorised by the permission'. The permission granted in 1952 was for the extraction of sand and gravel and not the concrete plant which was permitted development as it pre-dated the 1947 Act. The condition, therefore, did not fairly and reasonably relate to the development permitted by the planning permission and was void in so far as it purported to affect the concrete plant.

The validity of a temporary planning permission was challenged in *R v King's Lynn and West Norfolk BC* (1996) Env LR D36, where the applicants sought judicial review of a temporary planning permission to retain a general agricultural building to rear free-range chickens. They argued that the condition was temporary only to the use of the building rather than the construction of the building. The court rejected the application, holding that it was reasonable and lawful to grant permanent permission for a building but to require a trial period in relation to its use.

The issue of whether a temporary planning permission prevented the grant of an existing use certificate was addressed by the Court of Appeal in *Bailey and Bailey v Secretary of State and Sedgemoor DC* [1994] JPL B52; (1995) 69 P & CR; LGR 248. The appellants acquired a site in 1981 which, since before 1963, had been used for the repair, maintenance and storage of motor vehicles, and included a workshop originally erected in 1970. The building was converted into a more substantial structure by the appellant in 1986. No planning permission for the use of the land or the construction of the building had been granted. In January 1987, the appellants applied to the lpa for planning permission for continued use of the site, presumably as a result of pressure from the authority, and temporary planning permission was granted in April for a period of two years, that is, to expire on 30 April 1989. In February, the appellants submitted a further planning application to continue the existing use of the site. This was refused and, in June, the authority served an enforcement notice against the continued use of the site. An appeal was heard against the refusal of planning permission and the enforcement notice, and both were dismissed by the SoS.

The decision was upheld in the High Court, and leave was granted to appeal to the Court of Appeal which held, in dismissing the appeal, that an existing use certificate could not be granted if a temporary planning permission had at some stage been granted for that use. The established use of the land required the grant of a certificate (s 191 TCP 1990) which was necessarily a lawful one. The effect of the grant of temporary planning permission was to render that which had been unlawful, lawful, and thus bring to an end the use under s 191 terminating the entitlement to grant of an established use certificate.

14.10 ABANDONMENT OF PLANNING PERMISSION

The abandonment of a planning permission should *not* be confused with the abandonment of *use* of land. In *White v Secretary of State and Congleton BC* [1989] JPL 692; 58 P & CR 281, the Court of Appeal held that the use of land which was in existence on 1 July 1948 was capable of being abandoned. In such a case, the resumption of the use would constitute development, and planning permission would be required (see, also, *Hartley v Minister Housing and Local Government* [1970] 1 QB 413; [1969] 3 All ER 1658; 2 WLR 1).

In a situation where a planning permission has been activated, and the lpa has taken no action to serve a completion notice, can that permission ever be regarded as having been abandoned? This issue was finally resolved in *Pioneer Aggregates (UK) Ltd v Secretary of State* (see para 14.3, above), in which the House of Lords arrived at a unanimous decision that there is no principle in planning law that a valid planning permission, capable of being implemented according to its original terms, can be abandoned. The important basis of this judgment are contained in Lord Scarman's comments, which made it clear that, on the question of abandonment, he agreed with both courts below that there was no such general rule in planning law. In certain exceptional circumstances not covered by legislation, the courts have held that a landowner, by developing his land, can play an important part on bringing to an end, or making incapable of implementation, a valid planning permission.

He went on to comment that:

> ... planning control is a creature of statute. It is a field of law in which the court should not introduce principles or rules derived from private law unless it be expressly authorised by Parliament or necessary in order to give effect to the purpose of the legislation. Parliament has provided a comprehensive code of planning control currently found in s 75(1) of the Town and Country Planning Act.

The judgment reinforced the principle that, unless the lpa grants a temporary, time-limited consent or takes action to revoke or modify a previous planning permission, the act of granting permission to develop land enures for the benefit of the land and persons having an interest in the land.

14.11 REVOCATION OR MODIFICATION OF PLANNING PERMISSION

In exceptional circumstances, an lpa may consider it necessary to revoke or amend an earlier planning permission (s 97 TCPA 1990). Unless the order is unopposed (s 99), it will require confirmation by the SoS, who must afford the owner and occupier of the land affected by the order an opportunity of being heard at a public local inquiry or hearing. The order revoking or modifying the planning permission must be served either:

(a) before building operations have been completed, in which case it will not affect so much of the building operations as have been carried out; or

(b) before the change of use takes place.

Compensation may become payable on revocation or modification of a valid planning permission (see Chapter 28).

14.12 DISCONTINUANCE OF USE

As explained in the previous section, the revocation or amendment powers under s 97 relate to planning permissions which have not been fully implemented. Further powers are granted to lpas under s 102 to discontinue the established use of land or to impose conditions relating to the continued use of land. Such an order must be confirmed by the SoS (s 103) and compensation may be payable.

14.13 REFUSAL OF PLANNING PERMISSION

PPG 1, 'General Policies and Principles', makes it clear (para 5) that the planning system:

... should operate on the basis that applications for development should be allowed, having regard to the development plan and all material considerations, unless the proposed development would cause demonstrable harm to interests of acknowledged importance,

and, in para 6:

... it is not the function of the planning system to interfere with or inhibit competition between users and investors in land, or to regulate the overall provision and character of space for particular uses for other than land use planning reasons. Where development is acceptable, it is a matter for landowners, developers and/or tenants as to whether or not to proceed with it.

The statistics quoted in PPG 1, para 13 give a clear indication that local authorities are following this advice:

Currently, over 500,000 planning applications are received by English local authorities annually, and nearly 40,000 by those in Wales. About 80% are granted.

In refusing planning permission, the lpa must have regard to the plan, in so far as it is relevant to the application, and to any other material considerations. These requirements are set out in s 54A (TCPA 1990):

Where, in making any determination under the planning Acts, regard is to be had to the development plan, the determination shall be made in accordance with the plan unless material considerations indicate otherwise,

and, in s 70(2), which is yet to be repealed following the introduction of s 54A into the 1990 Act by the Planning and Compensation Act 2004:

In dealing with such an application, the authority shall have regard to the provisions of the development plan, so far as material to the application and to any other material considerations.

The decision must be communicated in writing and the lpa 'shall state clearly and precisely their full reasons for the refusal' or any condition imposed (Art 22(1)(a) of the GDPO). In doing so, the authority will, in some instances, enable the applicant to submit an amended proposal which is more acceptable to the planning authority. The reason or reasons for refusal must also be capable of justification, not only in the event of an appeal against the decision, but also in relation to the possible award of costs against the authority (see Chapter 16).

14.14 OUTLINE PLANNING PERMISSIONS

The grant of outline permission places upon the recipient of the notice, or the person seeking to activate the consent, the responsibility to provide subsequent details relating to reserved matters for approval by the lpa. The High Court in *Braintree DCv Secretary of State* [1996] JPL B56; [1997] JPL 217 held that the question of whether details submitted for approval as reserved matters are within the ambit of the outline consent is a matter of fact and degree. Where outline permission included, *inter alia*, a 'local centre', that meant a centre designed to serve an area of new housing, and not some wider area. It was not enough to argue that the centre would serve not only the new housing but also a wider area. Had the SoS construed the words properly, he could not have come to the conclusion that the schemes fell within the outline planning permission. Furthermore, the SoS had not furnished adequate reasons that led him to conclude that they were within the scope of the outline permission. The court quashed the SoS's decision and awarded costs to the local authority.

The submission of details must be in accordance with the requirements of the reserved matters and should not include matters not actually reserved by the outline permission, such as a new means of access (see *Chalgray Ltd v Secretary of State* [1977] JPL 176; 33 P & CR 10). This places an onus both upon the planning authority to ensure that the reserved matters will result in a satisfactory form of development, and upon the developer to adhere to the requirements attached to the original outline consent.

In *R v Secretary of State ex p Slough BC* [1995] JPL 135, the Court of Appeal upheld a finding of the SoS that an application for a reserved matter fell within the scope of the outline permission, notwithstanding that it proposed 1,530 sq m of floorspace as against 1,055 sq m which appeared on the original application. The court held that the application had not been incorporated into the outline permission although it had been referred to both by number and reference, and that the application was approved 'in accordance with the accompanying particulars and plans'. The court held that this was not sufficient to inform a reasonable reader that the application formed part of the permission, and that there were substantial disadvantages in making it necessary always to refer back to the application rather than being able to read the permission at face value. In the view of the court, the outline permission was clear, and it imposed no limit on the area of floorspace permitted.

The degree of flexibility afforded by an outline planning permission, as indicated above, is a matter which requires careful consideration by lpas who may wish to ensure that the final form of development reflects that proposed at the outline stage. Clear and unequivocal reference must be made to the original submission. The High Court in *R v Bolsover DCex p Ashfield DC* [1996] JPL 400 B2; (1995) 70 P & CR 507 upheld the council's decision to approve reserved matters relating to an outline application for the construction of a retail park incorporating five units, notwithstanding that it was the developer's intention to subdivide these into 70 units.

The issue of whether an application for approval of reserved matters can itself be the subject of further conditions was determined in *R v Newbury DC ex p Stevens and Partridge* [1992] JPL 1057; 3 PLR 34; (1993) 65 P & CR 438. The court ruled that conditional approval of a reserved matter in a planning application was legitimate, and that the lpa or the SoS could impose such conditions provided they did not materially derogate from the permission which had already been granted.

14.15 THE GRANT OF CONDITIONAL PLANNING PERMISSION

Planning permissions are rarely granted without some kind of condition or conditions being attached to the notice of approval. The planning authority has a very wide remit and is entitled to grant permission, 'subject to such conditions as they think fit' (s 70(1)(a) TCPA 1990). This power is not completely unfettered and must be read subject to the requirements of the general law, and in particular that statutory powers must be exercised only for the purpose of the statute concerned.

The Court of Appeal in *Mixnam's Properties v Chertsey UDC* [1965] AC 735; [1964] 1 QB 214 stated four general limitations to which the imposition of planning conditions is subject:

1   conditions must not effect a fundamental alteration to general law;

2   conditions must be limited to reference to the subject matter of the statute;

3   conditions must not be unreasonable; and

4   conditions must be sufficiently certain and unambiguous.

Planning law relates to the control of land use and, therefore, conditions should not 'trespass' into other areas of law, for example, it is not accepted that an lpa could place a condition on a planning consent which restricted the sale of alcohol, this being a matter properly dealt with by the licensing justices and not the planning department.

'As they think fit' must be construed as 'what they think fit for *planning purposes*'. The principles of planning control were effectively defined by the courts in *Pyx Granite Co Ltd v Minister Housing and Local Government* [1958] 1 QB 554, reversed in part [1960] AC 260, and later in *Fawcett Properties v Buckinghamshire CC* [1961] AC 636; [1960] 3 All ER 503; 3 WLR 831 and *Newbury DCv Secretary of State* [1980] JPL 325; [1981] AC 578; [1980] WLR 379; 1 All ER 732; 78 LGR 306; 40 P & CR 148. The *Fawcett* case considered a number of points relating to planning conditions and the following principles were established. A condition:

(a) must serve some useful planning purpose;

(b) must fairly and reasonably relate to the permitted development;

(c) must not be manifestly unreasonable;

(d) may be imposed restricting the user according to the personal circumstances of the occupier; and

(e) may be declared invalid on the ground that its meaning is uncertain.

These principles are further reinforced in Circular 11/95, 'The Use of Conditions in Planning Permissions', which sets out the following tests to be applied when considering planning conditions:

(a) Is it necessary in relation to the development proposed?

(b) Is it relevant to planning?

(c) Is it relevant to the development proposed?

(d) Is it enforceable?

(e) Is it precise? and

(f) Is it reasonable?

The circular acknowledges that the power to impose conditions is very wide and makes it clear that:

> If used properly, conditions can enhance the quality of the development and enable many development proposals to proceed where it would otherwise be necessary to refuse planning permission. The objectives of planning, however, are best served when the power is exercised in such a way that conditions are clearly seen to fair, reasonable and practicable.

14.16 RELATIONSHIP TO THE DEVELOPMENT PROPOSED

A condition will be void if it does not 'fairly and reasonably relate to the permitted development', as stated by Lord Denning in *Pyx Granite v Minister of Housing and Local*

Government (see above). In *Newbury DC v Secretary of State* [1981] AC 578, the *dictum* of Lord Denning was taken further following the decision of the House of Lords to uphold the SoS's decision in this case.

In 1962, the International Synthetic Rubber Co Ltd was granted planning permission to use two hangars on a disused airfield for storage purposes. The permission had attached a condition which required the removal of the hangars by 31 December 1972. The company failed to comply with this condition and was served with an enforcement notice requiring their removal. On appeal, the inspector accepted that the hangars were large, prominent and ugly, and certainly did not add to the visual amenity of the rural area, but nevertheless he considered the condition to be void. The condition appeared to arise from a desire to restore the area rather than from any planning need arising from the actual purpose for which the permission was sought in the first instance. It was not necessary for that purpose, nor to the protection of the environment in the fulfilment of that purpose; it was a condition extraneous to the proposed use.

The question of the validity of a planning condition which relates to land outside the application site and not in the ownership of the applicant was addressed in *Davenport v London Borough of Hammersmith and Fulham* [1999] JPL 1122. Planning permission for motor vehicle repairs had been granted subject to several conditions, including one stating that 'no vehicles which are left with or are in the control of the applicant shall be stored or parked on Tasso Road'. Tasso Road is a public highway and, therefore, not owned or controlled by the applicant. The court noted that, in *Mouchell Superannuation Fund Trustees v Oxfordshire CC* (1992) 1 PLR 97, p 105, Glidewell LJ had said:

> A condition purporting to require the carrying out of works on land neither within the application site nor within the control of the applicant is outside the powers of the 1990 Act.

Glidewell LJ's decision had been based on a planning condition that required the applicant to secure more than he could be assured of achieving. By contrast, in this case, the applicant was able to comply with the condition and in order to do so did not have to have control over the land. There was nothing to show that a condition relating to land outside the application site, or outside the control of the applicant, was invalid unless the condition could not be assured of compliance. (See also *Grampian Regional Council v City of Aberdeen* [1984] JPL 590.)

14.17 CONDITIONS RELATING TO OTHER LAND

Under s 72(1)(a) (TCPA 1990) a condition may be imposed on the grant of planning permission to:

> regulate the development or use of any land under the control of the applicant (whether or not it is land in respect of which the application was made) or requiring the carrying out of works on any such land, so far as appears to the local planning authority to be expedient for the purposes of or in connection with the development authorised in the permission.

This is frequently described as 'blue land' because applicants are required to outline such land in blue as distinct from red, which is used to denote the application site itself, when submitting an application. The inclusion of 'blue land' does not necessarily require an applicant to own an estate or interest in the land. Sir Douglas Frank QC held in *George Wimpey & Co Ltd v New Forest DC* [1979] JPL 313 that whether the land was in the applicant's control was a matter of fact and degree and the SoS's determination of these tests was the determining factor.

Atkinson v Secretary of State for the Environment [1983] JPL 599 illustrates the situation where the land over which the condition is to be imposed is clearly not in the control of the applicant. It was argued by the appellants that a condition that outbuildings should be demolished and an access widened could not be properly imposed as the land was not in their ownership. The SoS argued that s 70(1), which states that a planning authority may grant permission 'subject to such conditions as they think fit', provided the necessary authority. Woolf J, whilst agreeing with the SoS, expressed concern that if a condition could not be complied with it would be unreasonable to enforce a condition on a wholly innocent neighbour. The permission should make it clear that before the benefit of the permission could be exercised the developer must have actually secured his ability to comply with the condition himself. Such a condition should specify that the construction of the houses should not commence until after the access had been constructed. (Whilst this is a logical approach the fact that planning permission has been granted leaves the applicant in the difficult position of negotiating a price for the additional land if he wishes to carry out the development.)

The ability of the lpa to use the power under s 70(1) to impose conditions on land not under the control of the applicant was again raised in *Grampian Regional Council v City of Aberdeen DC* [1984] 47 P & CR 633. The application for the use of agricultural land for industrial use resulted in appeal to the SoS against the non-determination by the local authority. The reporter, that is, the inspector, took the view that traffic generated by the proposed use would create hazardous conditions for other road users but considered that hazard could be removed if an existing road could be closed. He concluded, however, that it would not be competent to grant planning permission subject to a condition requiring the closure of the road as it was not in the power of the respondent to secure the closure. This would require confirmation by the SoS and would not necessarily be granted. He therefore dismissed the appeal. The First Division of the Inner House of the Court of Session allowed an appeal by the first respondents on the ground that, whilst a condition requiring the closure of a road on land not within the control of the first respondents was incompetent, a condition requiring that no development could be commenced until the road was closed was competent. The appellants appealed arguing that the imposition of a negative condition related to occurrence of an uncertain event was unreasonable and therefore invalid and furthermore that in any event it was undesirable that there was likely to be a period of prolonged uncertainty as to whether any development would be able to take place. The House of Lords in dismissing the appeal held the latter to be enforceable whereas the former is not.

Since the determination of this case the use of negative conditions, particularly in relation to highway works necessary on other land, has been used more frequently. However, their use was restricted by Appendix A, PPG13, *Highways Considerations in Development Control*, which suggests that their appropriateness is restricted to situations where the works are likely to be carried out within a reasonable period of time, usually the normal lifetime of a planning permission (now three years).

However, the House of Lords in *British Railways Board v Secretary of State for the Environment* [1994] JPL 32, were of the opinion that the mere fact that a desirable condition appeared to have no reasonable prospects of fulfilment did *not* mean that planning permission must be necessarily be refused. Lord Keith stated:

> The function of the local planning authority was to decide whether the proposed development was desirable in the public interest. The answer to that question was not to be affected by the consideration that the owner of land was determined not to allow the development so that permission for it, if granted, would not have reasonable prospects of being implemented. That did not mean that the planning authority, if it decided the proposed development was in the public interest, was absolutely disentitled from taking into account the improbability of permission for it, if granted, being implemented. For example, if there were a competition between two alternative sites for a desirable development, difficulties in bringing about the implementation of on one site which were not present in relation to the other might very properly lead to the refusal of planning permission for the site affected by the difficulties and the grant of it to the other. But there is no absolute rule that the existence of difficulties, even if apparently insuperable, had to necessarily lead to the developer might be faced with difficulties of many different kinds, in the way of site assembly or securing the discharge of restricted covenants. If he considered it was in interests to secure planning permission notwithstanding the existence of such difficulties, it was not for the planning authority to refuse it simply on their view of how serious the difficulties were.

This statement by Lord Keith was subsequently translated into Circular 11/95 (para 40) with a note clearly intended to restrict the broad view expressed in the judgment:

> The House of Lords established the mere fact that a desirable condition, worded in a negative form, appears to have no reasonable prospects of fulfilment does not means that planning permission must refused a matter of law. However, the judgement leaves open the possibility for the Secretary of State, to maintain as a matter of policy that there should be at least reasonable prospects of the action in question being performed within the time-limit imposed by the permission.

In *Millington v Secretary of State for the Environment, Transport and the Regions* [1999] JPL 644, the Court of Appeal accepted the legal right of the SoS to state policy as contained in the footnote to para 40 of the Circular.

The issue was raised once again in *Merritt v Secretary of State for the Environment, Transport and the Regions* [2000] JPL 371. The court found that an inspector had erred in law in rejecting a Grampian condition because he was not convinced that there was a reasonable prospect that the condition would be fulfilled within the time limit imposed upon the permission. In doing so the court found that the inspector had simply applied the policy as a mandatory requirement and had not considered whether there was scope for the exercise of discretion. He should have considered the actual implications of imposing a *Grampian* condition and whether it would, in fact, cause demonstrable harm. His Honour Judge Rich also drew attention to the danger that, in promulgating a policy in absolute form, a decision-maker may regard himself as bound to follow that policy.

14.18 PERSONAL PERMISSION

Normally planning permission 'runs with the land', that is, it is a commodity which can be transferred to another person, but under exceptional circumstances it is possible for a permission to enure for the benefit of a particular individual or company. Section 75(1) (TCPA 1990) states:

> ... any grant of planning permission to develop land shall (except in so far as the permission otherwise provides) enure for the benefit of the land and of all persons for the time being interested in it.

Although rarely used, this provision allows planning permission to be granted in a case of personal hardship (see Circular 11/95, The Use of Conditions in Planning Permissions, para 93).

In *Knott v Secretary of State for the Environment and Caradon DC* [1997] JPL 713, the local authority used this provision to grant permission for a dwelling, the occupation of which was to benefit the Knotts alone. The High Court held that once the house had been constructed the condition did not prevent other persons from occupying the dwelling. Faced with this apparent rebuff the district council reacted by deciding to make revocation and discontinuance orders requiring the removal of the partially completed dwelling. Both orders were confirmed by the SoS and this required the district council to pay compensation. The council then became aware that the house was being erected outside the boundaries of the application site and went on to serve an enforcement notice on the ground of a breach of planning control. It also meant that the compensation, which would have been payable following the confirmation of the revocation, no longer applied. The Knotts then went back to the High Court seeking to quash the enforcement notice on the grounds that it was contrary to law (*R v Caradon DC ex p Knott* [2000] 80 P & CR 154). In quashing the enforcement notice Sullivan J was of the opinion that the authority had not served the enforcement notice to secure any planning objective as that had already been achieved by the serving of the revocation and discontinuance orders. Furthermore under the doctrine of estoppel the authority was barred from taking enforcement action.

14.19 TESTS OF REASONABLENESS

The planning authority is not at liberty to use its powers to achieve some ulterior object, no matter how desirable or beneficial that may be in the public interest. If the authority misuses its powers, the courts can, and frequently do, intervene. In *Hall and Co Ltd v Shoreham UDC* [1964] 1 WLR 240; 15 P & CR 119, a condition which required the landowners to build a road on their own land and to grant a right of way over it without compensation was held by the Court of Appeal to be so unreasonable as to be *ultra vires*. The proper course would be for the local authority to use its powers under the highways legislation to acquire the land after paying proper compensation and then to construct the road at public expense.

Similarly, in *R v Hillingdon LBC ex p Royco Homes* [1974] 1 QB 721; 2 WLR 805; 28 P & CR 251, a condition attached to the planning consent required that the houses erected as a result of the permission should first be occupied by persons on the council's waiting list, and should, for a period of 10 years, be occupied by persons enjoying protection under the Rent Act 1968. The Divisional Court held that these conditions were unreasonable, since, in effect, they required Royco Homes to take on, at their own expense, part of the duty of the council as a housing authority. (*Note*: Had this requirement taken the form of a 'planning agreement', then the court would not have been involved and the developer would have been responsible for the provision of housing in accordance with the authority's wishes. See Chapter 15.)

It has been held to be unreasonable to impose a condition on land which is not in the control of the applicant. In *Peak Park Joint Planning Board v Secretary of State and ICI Ltd* [1980] JPL 114; 39 P & CR 361, a condition placed on a permission for quarrying, which required the applicants to carry out extensive landscaping which was not on land under the control of the applicants, was held to be *ultra vires*. This type of condition is also held to be *ultra vires* even if the applicant has expressed a willingness to accept such a condition. In *Bradford MBC v Secretary of State and McLean Homes Northern Ltd* [1986] JPL 598; (1987) 53 P & CR 55, the local authority granted consent for housing development subject to a condition requiring the widening of an existing road which the applicants had included for that purpose in a revised plan. It appears that the applicants were inviting such a condition by including the land. However, they subsequently appealed on the ground that they did not own the land affected by the condition. The SoS's decision that the condition was *ultra vires* was upheld by the Court of Appeal, and Lloyd LJ explained:

> If the proposed condition was manifestly unreasonable, then it was beyond the powers of the planning authority to impose it; and if it was beyond the powers of the planning authority to impose the condition, then it was beyond their powers to agree to impose it, even if the developer consented ... *vires* could not be conferred with consent.

There is no doubt in the cases outlined above that the local authorities were endeavouring to achieve objects which were in the interests of the general public. However, irrespective of the benefits which may be seen to have accrued, the lpa is restricted to that which is reasonable. This can cause a dilemma for authorities which may wish to grant planning permission but are unable to do so until access to a site is improved. This has been overcome by the imposition of a negative condition, which has the effect of delaying the development until such times as the improved access has been achieved, relating to land not in the control of the applicants. Such a condition has been approved by the House of Lords in *Grampian Regional Council v City of Aberdeen* [1984] JPL 590; 47 P & CR 633. It was held not to be unreasonable to leave the applicants to negotiate with the other parties to satisfy the requirements of the planning condition. Only when these negotiations had succeeded would the planning permission be capable of being exercised.

The *Grampian* condition was subsequently modified in *Jones v Secretary of State for Wales and Another* [1990] JPL 907. The Court of Appeal, in reversing a decision of the High Court, held that, in any *Grampian* condition, there must be a reasonable chance that the applicant can fulfil the requirements of the condition. If no such chance existed, then the condition would be unreasonable and accordingly would fail.

The *Jones* case was later held to have been wrongly decided and was overruled by the House of Lords in *British Railways Board v Secretary of State* [1994] JPL 32. The fact that such a condition had no reasonable prospect of fulfilment did not mean that the condition was invalid and that planning permission should be refused. As a result of this decision, there is an apparent discrepancy between policy guidance and the judicial decisions on this issue.

There are also situations where the lpa may seek to impose conditions which effectively remove the applicant's existing use rights which are not necessarily incompatible with the proposed development. In *Allnatt London Properties Ltd v Middlesex CC* (1964) 15 P & CR 288; 62 LGR 304, it was held at that time that such a condition is unreasonable. However, in 1974, in the case of *Royal London Borough of Kingston-on-Thames v Secretary of State* [1974] 1 All ER 193; [1973] 1 WLR 1549; 26 P & CR 480, Lord Widgery CJ said there was no principle in planning law which requires an authority to refrain from imposing conditions which abrogate existing use rights.

14.20 TESTS OF UNCERTAINTY

In attaching conditions to a grant of permission, the wording of the condition must be unambiguous; and, when refusing permission, the lpa must make clear the reasons for its actions. In *Great Portland Estates Ltd v Westminster City Council* [1985] JPL 108; AC 661; [1984] 3 WLR 1035, Lord Scarman stated:

> When a statute requires a public body to give reasons for a decision, the reasons must be proper, adequate and intelligible.

He then went on to quote Megaw J from *Poyser and Mills Arbitration* [1964] 2 QB 467:

> ... the reasons that are set out must be reasons which will not only be intelligible but which deal with the substantial points that have been raised.

If the wording of a condition is ambiguous, the court can determine which is the correct meaning; but a condition may be so ill worded that the court cannot resolve the doubt. In *R v Secretary of State ex p Watney Mann (Midlands) Ltd* [1976] JPL 368, the local justices made an order under the Public Health Act 1936 which required the abatement of a nuisance caused by music played in a public house, stating that the noise level should not exceed 70 decibels. The Divisional Court found that the order was void as it did not specify the position at which the measurement of the noise level should be taken.

In *Shanley (MJ) v Secretary of State and South Bedfordshire DC* [1982] JPL 380, the appellants offered a condition that the first opportunity to buy houses should be given to local people in an attempt to overcome green belt objection to their proposal. The SoS considered that such a condition would be invalid and unenforceable. This decision was upheld in the High Court, as the condition did not give any indication of the method or terms upon which the first opportunity was to be offered. (Had the offer by the applicant been in the form of a planning obligation, which was accepted by the authority, then it is possible that planning permission would have been granted by the lpa (see Chapter 15.)

However, in *Fawcett Properties v Buckinghamshire CC* (see para 14.15, above), the planning authority had granted planning consent for two cottages in the green belt subject to a condition which required that:

> The occupation of the houses shall be limited to persons whose employment or latest employment is or was in agriculture as defined in s 119(1) of the Town and country Planning Act 1947 [now s 336(1)] or in forestry or in an industry mainly dependent upon agriculture and including also the dependants of such persons as aforesaid.

The House of Lords held that the condition was not void on the basis of uncertainty. It was not necessary that the condition should identify all the persons who might be eligible to occupy the houses; it was the owner's obligation to satisfy himself that any proposed occupier would come within the definition.

Note: This particular condition is now widely used in the case of the grant of permission for dwellings in the green belt, or areas of open countryside, where the general policy is to restrict residential development. The currently suggested wording of the condition is contained in Circular 11/95, para 45:

> The occupation of the dwelling shall be limited to a person solely or mainly working, or last working, in the locality in agriculture or in forestry, or the widow or widower of such a person, and to any resident dependants.

The introduction of 'last working' is intended to cover the cases where the person is temporarily unemployed or is no longer able to work because of old age or illness. This does not necessarily exclude persons who are engaged in either part-time or temporary employment (if that person can be regarded as a farm worker or retired farm worker) but a person who now works on a permanent basis in non-agricultural or forestry employment would not satisfy the condition. The introduction of the words 'in the locality' is designed to restrict occupation to those persons needing to live in that particular area.

In the case *R v Bristol City Council ex p Moira Anderson* [2000] JPL January Update, the Court of Appeal determined whether a planning condition was legally invalid because of uncertainty and also whether the welfare and support of students was a planning issue. The decision was on appeal from a judgment of Collins J who quashed a grant of planning permission and conservation area consent. He held that a condition which required that, prior to occupation, full details of the proposed management system and system for the control over the keeping of motor vehicles by the occupiers should be submitted to and approved by the local authority was legally invalid. It was too uncertain and, in part, at least, had nothing to do with planning purposes.

It was held on appeal that a condition is only likely to be held void for uncertainty if its words can be given no sensible meaning. In arriving at this decision, the court had regard to the House of Lords' ruling in *Newbury DC v Secretary of State* [1980] JPL 325; [1981] AC 578; [1980] ? WLR 379; 1 All ER 732; 78 LGR 306; 40 P & CR 148 which set the test of legality. The test stipulates that the condition:

(a) must fulfill a planning purpose;

(b) must fairly and reasonably relate to the development permitted; and

(c) must not be manifestly unreasonable.

The maintenance of support to students and the promotion of their welfare was objectively linked to the effects of this development upon neighbours and other interests. The amenities provided for the student occupiers would affect both the students and have consequences for their impact upon the neighbourhood. Therefore, there was no failure to fulfill the first of the *Newbury* criteria, and the condition should be upheld. The condition was not uncertain and a management agreement was plainly needed.

14.21 PREVIOUS PLANNING PERMISSIONS

In determining planning appeals, the issue is raised of whether existing but inactivated planning permission is a material consideration. The High Court in *Brentwood BC v Secretary of State* [1996] JPL 939/B115; (1995) 72 P & CR 61 followed established case law in determining that decision-makers must have regard to the applicant's 'fall-back position', that is, his entitlement to an existing or deemed permission for alternative development. The prospects for the fall-back development actually occurring must be real and not merely theoretical. It has been made clear that the weight to be attached to such a consideration is a matter for the decision-maker and not one for the courts. (See also *New Forest DC v Secretary of State* [1996] JPL 935.)

14.22 APPLICATION TO DEVELOP WITHOUT COMPLYING WITH EARLIER CONDITIONS

Two decisions relating to applications (s 73 TCPA 1990) to carry out development without complying with conditions attached to earlier consents have been considered by the courts. In *R v London Docklands Development Corporation ex p Sister Christine Frost* [1996] JPL July Update, the court accepted that an application to extend the time limits for two outline consents could be dealt with under s 73 rather than by a formal application for renewal. The question of whether the planning permission should be allowed to continue beyond the original dates posed the same question which would have arisen if a formal application for renewal had been submitted, that is, that it had to be judged in the current situation. Under s 73, the planning authority was not confined to dealing with a particular conditions or conditions which the applicant wished to have changed or discharged; the authority was entitled to look at other conditions attached to the original consent, and to add new conditions.

In the second case, *Allied Property Investment v Secretary of State* [1997] JPL 199; (1996) EGCS 52, the High Court reinforced the fact that only the conditions could be considered, and the authority could not go back on its original decision to grant planning permission. Whilst an lpa review of conditions may result in a variation which makes the development more acceptable in relation to the development plan and other material considerations, it was *not* open to local authorities to reconsider the acceptability of the development as a matter of principle. The inspector had taken such a view and, therefore, the decision was quashed.

The apparent conflict between the two decisions referred to above has been resolved by the High Court in *Pye v Secretary of State and North Cornwall DC* [1998] JPL B135; 9 CL 486. Outline planning permission was granted in 1992, subject to a number of conditions, the second of which required the submission of detailed plans and particulars within three years from the date of the permission. A s 73 application to extend this period was refused by the council and an inspector on appeal. The applicant applied to the court to have the decision quashed.

The High Court started from the basic proposition that a s 73 application was an application for planning permission and it was the authority's duty to determine it in accordance with the development plan, unless material considerations indicated otherwise. The court accepted that, although s 73 applications were commonly referred to as 'amendments' to conditions attached to a planning permission, they actually tended to leave the original planning permission unaltered. This was the case whether planning permission had been granted unconditionally or subject to conditions. In such circumstances, a developer may implement either the original permission or the new amended permission. Under s 73, it was not possible to revoke the original permission.

When considering whether to extend the time limit for the approval of reserved matters, s 73 contained nothing that allowed the planning authority to ignore any practical consequences of granting the application. They have a stated duty to have regard to all the factual circumstances which had existed when it made its decision and this included the acceptability of the development as a matter of principle. Therefore, if the original permission had been incapable of being implemented, they were also obliged to consider this fact.

The court went on to state that, as the practical effect of s 73 was to grant a new permission, the lpa could apply the guidance in Circular 11/95 (para 60) relating to the renewal of permission. This advises that such applications should only be refused when there has been a material change in planning circumstances. Continued failure to begin the development will contribute to an unacceptable level of uncertainty about the future pattern of development; or the application is premature because the permission still has a reasonable time to run. This finding was applied in *R v London Borough of Wandsworth and others* [2003] (unreported) which held that the Town and Country Planning (Environmental Impact Assessment) (England and Wales) Regulations 1999 (SI 1999/293) applied to a s 73 application as they did to any other application for planning permission.

14.23 APPLICATION TO DISCHARGE A PLANNING CONDITION

The provision exists (s 73 TCPA 1990) which allows the holder of a planning permission to apply at any time for the removal of a condition attached by the lpa, provided it is not a condition which relates to the time in which the development was to be begun, and that time has expired without development taking place. In *Knott v Secretary of State and Carrodan DC* [1997] JPL 713 (see para 14.3, above), an application for the removal of a condition was refused by the authority. The issue was whether the lpa is only entitled to consider the question of the condition, or whether it can look at the wider considerations affecting the original grant of permission. It was held that the wording of s 73 makes it clear that the authority is entitled to consider the wider implications, and the only requirement is that the original permission should be left intact. The lpa may:

(a) grant permission subject to conditions differing from those attached to the original consent; or

(b) grant permission unconditionally.

14.24 STRIKING OUT VOID CONDITIONS

If a condition or conditions are found to be void, what effect, if any, does this have on the original grant of permission? In *Hall and Co Ltd v Shoreham UDC* (see para 14.17, above), the conditions in question were fundamental to the whole of the permission, in that the lpa would not have granted planning permission without them. On this basis, the council was granted a declaration that the permission was subsequently null and void.

In later cases, the permission has been allowed to stand, as it has been found that it is permissible to sever the offending condition if it were merely trivial or unimportant. This was the case in *Allnatt London Properties v Middlesex CC* (see para 14.17, above).

When the issue of severance of conditions was raised again in *Kent CC v Kingsway Investments (Kent) Ltd* [1971] AC 72; [1970] 2 WLR 397; 1 All ER 70, the Court of Appeal held that, having declared the condition void, the permission remained in force. Winn LJ went further, and in his opinion, 'if [the condition] is void, it can have no effect on the force of the permission itself'. However, in the House of Lords, the majority held that the condition was valid, but their Lordships went on to consider whether the permission would have stood if they had decided otherwise. It was said that there might be cases in which unimportant or incidental conditions were superimposed on the permission, and, if such conditions were held to be void, the permission may be allowed to survive.

The answer would appear to be that the condition must be of such importance that the lpa would not have considered the grant of permission without it before the permission is declared invalid.

14.25 IMPLIED CONDITIONS

The actual wording on the grant of planning permission may be held to circumscribe the permission. In *Wilson v West Sussex CC* [1963] 2 QB 764; 1 All ER 751; 14 P & CR 301, CA, a planning application for what was stated to be 'an agricultural cottage' was granted consent in the terms of, and subject to compliance with, the details specified in the application and on the plan and other relevant correspondence. The wording 'agricultural cottage' was held by the Court of Appeal to limit the user of the building who must, therefore, be someone engaged in agriculture. In the absence of a *Fawcett* condition (see para 14.15, above), the court was not prepared to indicate whether occupation by a person not engaged in agriculture would be a material change of use.

Chapter 16 deals with the methods of appeal against the decision of lpas in terms of rights to challenge the refusal of planning permission, deemed refusal of planning permission, and the complex nature of planning conditions as outlined in this chapter.

In the case of *Sevenoaks DC v Secretary of State and Pedham Place Golf Centre* [2004] JPL 1176, the issue was the absence of a specific construction condition. The golf club successfully appealed against an enforcement notice in respect of the construction of earth mounds on the golf course. A condition on the grant of permission was that details of the engineering works had to be submitted and approved. The details were subsequently submitted but the earth mounds, as constructed, were not in accordance with the details. The SoS considered that in the absence of a construction condition he could not imply into any condition a requirement that any construction had to be in accordance with the details. The decision of the High Court, in dismissing the appeal, set out the following tests to be applied to conditions:

(a) In the absence of a specific construction condition an inspector could not imply into a condition for details of engineering works a requirement that any construction had to be in accordance with such details.

(b) Planning permission is not considered by reference to the intention of the applicant or the lpa as it was a public document. It was essential that any condition was clearly and expressly imposed.

(c) It is not possible for a condition to be implied, nor was it possible for an obligation to be implied into a condition as that amounted to an implied condition. In the instant case the planning permission was clear and unambiguous and the SoS was correct to quash the notice.

14.26 REVOCATION OF PLANNING PERMISSION

The issue of the revocation of planning permission and the consequent payment of compensation was the issue in *R v Secretary of State ex p Alnwick DC* [1999] JPL September Update. The granting of planning permission results in property rights and, should the lpa or the SoS wish to interfere with those rights, compensation is payable by the local authority.

The *Alnwick* case raised two significant issues. The first is the extent of the SoS's discretion when he determines to revoke a planning permission. The second is a policy issue. In this case, the application had been properly notified to the SoS, as required by the Shopping Direction, and at that stage he chose not to intervene. Is it proper that he should later seek to intervene after permission had been granted by the lpa?

The inspector took the view that the potential liability of the lpa to pay compensation was not a land use planning matter and, therefore, did not fall to be considered. In upholding the inspector's approach, the court took the view that, whilst the decision-maker will often be entitled to take into account the financial consequences of his decision because of the consideration of the effect on others, the generality must, however, yield to the statutory context (see *R v Westminster City Council ex p Monahan* [1989] JPL 107; 3 WLR 408; [1990] 1 QB 87; *Sosmo Trust Ltd v Secretary of State* [1983] JLP 806; and *Northumberland CC v Secretary of State* [1989] JPL 700; (1990) 59 P & CR 468). Richards J observed:

> I see no warrant for treating cost as a permissible consideration even where it is not a 'material consideration' within the meaning of the legislation. It is wholly consonant with the statutory purpose that decisions under ss 97 and 100 should be guided only by planning considerations. It cannot have been the legislative intention, in introducing provision for the payment of compensation, that the impact of such payment upon a local planning authority's financial position should condition the exercise of powers to revoke or modify planning permissions. Payment of compensation enters into the picture only after a decision to revoke or modify has been made.

The court gave no opinion or guidance on the SoS's responsibility for the events that had occurred. In terms of statute law, he has no responsibility for the payment of compensation, leaving Alnwick DC with a likely bill in excess of £4 million.

CHAPTER 15

PLANNING OBLIGATIONS

15.1 INTRODUCTION

The Town and Country Planning Act (TCPA) 1947 (s 25) permitted local authorities to enter into agreements with any person with an interest in land in their area:

> ... for the purpose of restricting or regulating the development or use of the land ... and any agreement may contain such incidental and consequential provisions (including provisions of a financial character) as appear to the local planning to be necessary or expedient for the purpose of the agreement.

All such agreements required the approval of the Minister of Town and Country Planning, and the provision under s 25 was used infrequently. During the four years 1956–59, the number approved by the minister was 83, and in the 1960s, the number did not exceed 157 in any one year (see article by P Jowell [1977] JPL 423). The removal of the requirement to gain ministerial approval following the TCPA 1968 resulted in many authorities taking the opportunity to obtain 'gains' from developers which could not be obtained by planning conditions and which were considered to be of benefit to the community. The removal of the need for prior consent from the Secretary of State (SoS) opened up a legal Pandora's Box, the contents of which are constantly being produced. The critical issue is whether such agreements lead to, or can be construed as, the selling of planning permission by the local authority or, through offers made by developers, the buying of planning permission.

The most recent concern has been expressed in the report in July 1997 of the Nolan Committee, 'Standards of Conduct in Local Government in England, Scotland and Wales' (Cmd 3702). On the evidence available, the committee was satisfied that three criticisms of the process are valid:

1   Inappropriate planning permissions were being granted because of infrastructure improvements offered by developers.

2   Developers were held to ransom or involved in auctions to get planning permissions.

3   The detail of negotiation was covered in a cloak of commercial confidentiality which excluded local people, and sometimes their councillors, from the process.

Whilst the criticisms are no doubt justified, the recommendations to overcome them appear to rely on two main improvements to the system:

(i)   All potential developers should be operating on the basis of equality ... although clearly the precise details of any agreement must be the subject of direct negotiation; [vol I, para 318] and

(ii) It is entirely unacceptable for negotiation between a public body like a local authority and a commercial developer to be hidden either from local people or councillors. We recognise, of course, that elements of a planning gain agreement may be commercially sensitive, but these should be kept to a minimum ... confidentiality should cease well before a final decision is taken by the authority [vol I, para 319].

The first recommendation could be seen to relate to the content of local plans in which authorities may set out the anticipated planning gain in terms of requirements for particular types of development (see the *Crest Homes* case, para 15.10, below). The question of accountability in relation to commercial negotiations is likely to remain a sensitive issue which is not helped by the government's previous reluctance to allow planning obligations to be placed in the planning register and thereby open to public inspection.

The Fourth Report of the House of Commons Environment Committee on Shopping Centres makes two important procedural recommendations in respect of Circular 1/97 'Planning Obligations' (which supersedes Circular 16/91):

(a) that guidance was still needed on the apportionment of cross-boundary planning gain; and

(b) that copies of planning obligations should be kept in the planning register together with the permissions to which they relate, thus facilitating public access.

15.2   TOWN AND COUNTRY PLANNING ACT 1990

During the development boom of the 1970s, this form of planning bargaining became widespread and was undertaken under the power granted to local planning authorities under s 52 of the TCPA 1971.

Section 106 of the TCPA 1990 simply re-enacted s 52 of the previous 1971 Act. However, this section has been replaced by new ss 106, 106(A) and 106(B) by virtue of s 12 of the Planning and Compensation Act (PCA) 1991. This introduced the concept of 'planning obligations' which replaced the previous concept of 'planning agreements' as a mechanism for securing 'planning gain'.

This is not merely a semantic change of title, as the new provisions allow proposals to be offered unilaterally by a developer when seeking planning permission. The offer must be considered as part of the overall package constituting the planning application and, in the event of an appeal to the SoS, the obligation offered will be taken into account in arriving at the final decision.

15.3   THE BARGAINING PROCESS

Bargaining, or 'to come to terms', is a long-established principle. The submission of a planning application may be preceded by the developer seeking the advice of the planning officer as to the likelihood of a proposal gaining planning consent. This approach was recommended in Circular 22/83, 'Planning Gain' (now superseded by Circular 1/97 'Planning Obligations'). Changes suggested by the officer to the form and content of the application may make it more acceptable to the local authority, but there is no certainty. As explained earlier, the council is the decision-making body, and the officer's role is normally that of offering professional advice to the elected members.

Following the freedom granted in 1968 to act without the SoS's prior approval, those authorities which were under great development pressure sought the opportunity to obtain planning gain for the community which is not possible to achieve by means of conditions attached to the grant of planning permission. In the development boom of the late 1960s and 1970s, many developers were only too willing to agree to provide 'gains' in the form of dedicated open space, provision of community facilities, restoration of listed buildings, and housing to meet local authority requirements, etc. Many of these 'gains' went far beyond the amenity and land use considerations which apply to the imposition of planning conditions (see Chapter 14). The benefit to the developer was the granting of a planning consent, rather than the risk of a refusal or a delay which would arise if there was an appeal to the SoS. To the developer, time is money!

There is little doubt that, in some instances, local authorities were abusing their power to seek planning gain, but an 'agreement' was required by both parties. On the other hand, many gains for the community resulted in the provision of improved access to sites and the provision of infrastructure which involved the carrying out of works on land not under the control of the applicants. The argument was one of the legitimacy of requiring work and expenditure which directly related to the site to be developed and other less well justifiable forms of 'gain' (see *Barber v Secretary of State and Horsham DC* [1991] JPL 559; 2 PLR 20). Local planning authorities were accused, on the one hand, of 'selling' planning permissions and, on the other, of legitimately requiring the developer to finance the costs of the development which would otherwise fall to be paid out of public money.

Likewise, developers were accused of attempting to 'buy' planning permissions by offering to finance development projects which were, in some cases, unrelated to the proposal for which they were seeking planning permission, for example, the offer to construct a sports hall which cannot be reasonably linked to the erection of a supermarket! The possibility of benefits which may accrue to local authorities from 'gain' are largely dependent upon the pressure for development in particular areas of the country. Where there is little or no development pressure, the authority's task is to promote interest in development opportunities rather than to require additional gains.

The whole process of negotiating planning gain raised questions about the fundamental principle of planning permission, which is that it should not be bought or sold by the responsible authority. As a result of the controversy brought about by the use and abuse of power, the SoS requested the Property and Advisory Group to investigate and report on the matter, which resulted in the publication of their report 'Planning Gain' (1991). The report regarded the practice of bargaining for planning gain as unacceptable, and recommended that it should be discouraged except in exceptional circumstances. However, the government did not fully accept this recommendation and, in Circular 22/83 (superseded by Circular 16/91, which in turn has been replaced by Circular 1/97, see below), it was stated that obligations should only be imposed where it would be unreasonable to grant planning permission without such an obligation. Wholly unacceptable development should not be permitted because of extraneous community benefits offered by the developer.

15.4   PLANNING AND COMPULSORY PURCHASE ACT 2004

In an attempt to bring greater transparency to the issue of planning obligations and also to give clearer guidance to developers, s 46 of the Planning and Compulsory Purchase (PCPA) Act 2004 grants the SoS the power to make regulations for the making of a planning contribution in relation to the development or use of land in the area of a local planning authority (lpa). To date no such regulations have been made but it is intended that they should allow a contribution to be made:

(a) by prescribed means,

(b) by compliance with the relevant requirements, or

(c) by a combination of such means and compliances.

It is intended that the regulations may require the lpa to include in the development plan document a statement of:

(a) the developments or uses to which they will consider accepting a planning contribution;

(b) a statement for development or use which they will not consider accepting a contribution by prescribed means;

(c) the purpose to which receipts from payment are (in whole or in part) to be put; and

(d) the criteria by reference to which the value of a contribution made by the prescribed means is to be determined.

The prescribed means are:

(a) the payment of a sum the amount and terms of the payment determined in accordance with criteria published by the lpa;

(b) the provision of a benefit in kind the value of which is so determined, or

(c) a combination of such payment and provision.

Section 47 (PCPA 2004) provides for regulations which will prescribe the maximum and minimum amounts of payment and enables periodic adjustments of the criteria set out and may also require the lpa to publish an annual report containing such information in relation to the planning contribution as is prescribed.

15.5   THE SCOPE OF SECTION 106 OF THE TOWN AND COUNTRY PLANNING ACT 1990

The new ss 106, 106(A) and 106(B), inserted in the TCPA 1990 by s 12(1) of the PCA 1991, introduced the concept of 'planning obligations' whereby the local authority and the developer may agree to enter into an obligation, or by which the developer may unilaterally offer an obligation as part of the planning application to be considered by the lpa.

Section 106(1) provides that any person interested in land in the area of the lpa may, by agreement or *otherwise*, enter into an obligation (to be referred to as a 'planning obligation'):

(a) restricting the development or use of land in any specified way;

(b) requiring specific operations or activities to be carried out in, on, under or over the land;

(c) requiring the land to be used in a specific way; or

(d) requiring a sum or sums to be paid to the authority on a specified date or dates or periodically.

Note: The use of the word 'otherwise' in the definition (s 106(1)) allows for unilateral action by the developer.

Sub-section (2) provides that a planning obligation may:

(a)   be unconditional or subject to conditions;

(b)   impose any restriction or requirement mentioned in sub-s (1)(a)–(c) above either indefinitely or for such periods as may be specified;

(c)   if it requires a sum or sums to be paid, require the payment of a specified amount determined in accordance with the instrument by which the obligation is entered into and, if it requires payment of periodic sums, require them to be paid indefinitely or for a specified period.

Sub-section (3): a planning obligation, is enforceable by the local authority (subject to sub-s (4) below) against:

(a)   the person entering into the obligation; and

(b)   any person deriving title for that person.

Sub-section 4:

(a)   an obligation entered into may provide that a person shall not be bound by the obligation in respect of any period during which he no longer has a legal interest in the land.

Sub-section 5:

(a)   a restriction or requirement imposed under a planning obligation is enforceable by an injunction.

Section 106(A)(1):

... a planning obligation may not be modified or discharged except:

(a)   by agreement between the authority and the person, or persons, against whom the obligation is enforceable;

(b)   in accordance with s 106B.

Sub-section (2):

... an agreement entered into under s 1 shall not be entered into except by deed.

Sub-section (3):

... a person against whom an agreement is enforceable may, at any time after the expiry of the 'relevant period' for the obligation, apply to:

(a)   have effect subject to modifications to be specified; or

(b)   be discharged.

Note: 'relevant period' means such period as may be prescribed, or if no period is prescribed, the period of five years after the obligation is entered into.

Section 106(B):

Where a local planning authority:

(a)   fails to give notice within the prescribed period following such an application; or

(b)   states that the obligation shall continue without modification,

the applicant may appeal to the Secretary of State.

15.6 JUSTIFICATION FOR PLANNING OBLIGATIONS

Planning obligations are entered into 'voluntarily' by the parties. Because of this, controls over the development of land can be achieved by the planning authority which are outside the powers of control imposed by attaching planning conditions, which are constrained by the law (see Chapter 14). Nevertheless, Circular 1/97 emphasises that, if there is a choice between imposing a planning condition or entering into an obligation, the imposition of a condition is to be preferred because it allows the developer the opportunity to appeal to the SoS.

Unrelated benefits should not be allowed to determine the grant of permission for unacceptable development, nor should acceptable development be refused permission because the applicant is unable, or unwilling, to offer unrelated benefits. The test of reasonableness of seeking a planning obligation is set out in Annex B10 and B11 of Circular 1/97, as follows:

1   Is it needed to enable the development to go ahead, for example, the provision of adequate access or car parking?; or

2   in the case of financial payment, will it contribute to meeting the cost of providing such facilities in the near future?; or

3   is it otherwise so directly related to the proposed development and to the use of land after its completion, that the development ought not to be permitted without it, for example, the provision, whether by the applicant or by the local planning authority at the applicant's expense, of car parking in or near the development, or reasonable amounts of open space related to the development, social, educational, recreational, sporting or other community provision the need for which arises from the development?; or

4   is it designed, in the case of mixed development, to secure an acceptable balance of uses; or to secure the implementation of local plan policies for a particular type of development, for example, the inclusion of affordable housing in a larger residential development?; or

5   is it intended to offset the loss of, or impact on, any amenity or resource present on the site prior to development, for example, in the interests of nature conservation?

Annex B12, 13 and 14 provides further tests to be applied if one of the tests above is satisfied:

1   the extent of what is required is to be fairly and reasonably related to the scale of the proposed development; and

2   the costs of subsequent maintenance and other recurrent expenditure should normally be borne by the authority, and the local planning authority should not attempt to impose commuted maintenance sums when considering the planning aspects of the development. Exceptions may be made where, for example, additional highway works are a prerequisite to the granting of planning permission, and an agreement specially providing for maintenance payments is made under s 278 of the Highways Act 1980, or in the case of open space or landscaping, which is principally of benefit to the development itself rather than the wider public.

15.7 UNILATERAL UNDERTAKINGS

The new provisions allow a developer to offer to make a unilateral undertaking by promising to do, or not to do, certain things conditional upon the granting of planning consent. It is made clear in Circular 1/97 'Planning Obligations' that unilateral undertakings are not intended to replace the use of agreements. They will be appropriate where negotiations are being unnecessarily protracted, or when unreasonable demands are being made by the lpa. It is anticipated that they will be principally used at an appeal where there are planning objections which cannot be overcome without an agreement, but where the parties cannot reach such an agreement. Any such undertaking should be relevant to planning and should resolve the planning objections to the development proposal, for example, the provision or financing of off-site works such as highways, or a financial contribution to enlargement of sewage disposal facilities. If the undertaking is not relevant to the planning issues, then it will not be considered as a material consideration at an appeal. Similarly, if the undertaking would resolve the planning objection to the proposal, but also contains unrelated benefits, it will only be taken into account in so far as it overcomes the planning issues.

15.8 PLANNING OBLIGATIONS AND PLANNING PERMISSION

The Court of Appeal in the case of *R (on application of Kebbell Development Ltd) v First Secretary of State* [2004] JPL 376 addressed the extent to which entering into a planning obligation creates a legitimate expectation that planning permission will be granted. Before the grant of planning permission the owners of the appeal site had entered into an agreement by deed under s 106 (TCPA 1990) to transfer land to the parish council, and this transfer had subsequently taken place. Surprisingly this was not made conditional on outline planning permission being granted for the proposed development, but the local authority had indicated that the proposal was likely to be approved. Outline planning permission was granted but no application for the approval of reserved matters was submitted within the required period. The developer made an application under s 73 for an extension of time for the approval of these matters. Unfortunately for the developers there had been a change in planning policies and permission was refused and this refusal was upheld on appeal.

The critical issue was, therefore, to what extent, by taking benefit of the obligation, was the local authority required to look favourably on the application to extend the life of the original permission. Sir Richard Tucker, although he did not go so far as to state that the council were bound to extend the time limit, held that the inspector had not given full consideration to this continuing obligation, that the claimants had a legitimate expectation of a substantive benefit and it would be unfair to frustrate that expectation without giving full consideration to it before reaching a decision.

15.9 ENFORCEMENT OF OBLIGATIONS

A planning obligation is executed as a deed and must identify the land, the person entering into the obligation and his interest in the land, and the local authority by which the obligation is enforceable. It is enforceable against the person entering into the deed and his successors in title (s 106(3) TCPA 1990), unless the deed provides that a person shall not be bound by the obligation in respect of any period during which he no longer has an interest in the land (s 106(4)).

The enforcement of obligations is by means of a court injunction (s 106(5)) rather than by taking enforcement action via the Planning Acts (see Chapter 18). The local authority has additional powers if any works required by the obligation have not been carried out. After giving 21 days' notice, the lpa may enter the site and carry out the works and recover the costs from the other party (s 106(6)). Any financial obligations on the part of the developer can be recovered as a civil debt (s 106(12)).

Entering into a planning obligation involves the planning authority and a developer. Both are required to fulfil their part of the agreement. In the case of *Patel v Brent London Borough Council* [2004] EWHC 763 the court upheld a claim for the return to the developer of a sum paid to the local planning authority on the ground that the authority had failed to carry out the highway improvements and traffic management measures for which the sum had been paid by the date specified in the agreement. The court was of the opinion that it was nonsense to suggest that their obligations ceased at that date and thereafter they were entitled to sit on the money until they chose to do something or the claimants made an application to discharge the planning obligation. The authority was not entitled to put forward the argument that its own organisational inadequacies as an excuse for non-compliance.

15.10 MODIFICATION OF AN OBLIGATION

Section 106(4) (as set out above in para 15.4) allows any person against whom a planning obligation is enforceable to apply for the obligation to be modified or discharged. On receipt of such an application the lpa may determine:

(a) that the planning obligation shall continue to have effect without modification;

(b) if it no longer serves a useful purpose it shall be discharged; or

(c) if it continues to serve a useful purpose, but would serve that purpose equally well subject to the modifications specified in the application, it shall continue to have effect subject to those modifications.

An application for the discharge or modification of an obligation under s 106A(3) may be submitted to the lpa at any time after the expiry of 'the relevant period', that is, such period as may be prescribed in the obligations, or if no period is prescribed, after a period of five years beginning with the date on which the obligation was entered into. Such applications are dealt with in a similar manner to a normal planning application. A special form is available from the local authority, and any other persons against whom the obligation is enforceable must be notified; the authority must publicise the application (s 106(9) and Planning Obligations Regulations 3, 4, and 5). As with a normal planning application, the planning authority has eight weeks in which to make a determination, and there is a right of appeal to the SoS. The SoS's decision on the appeal is final, but he does not have any jurisdiction to impose his own modifications (s 106(B)(6)). If the proposed modifications in the application are unacceptable, then it must be rejected.

In *R (on application of Garden & Leisure Group Ltd) v North Somerset DC* [2003] EWHC 1605, the High Court considered the statutory test to modify a planning obligation.

The issue arose as a result of an application by a garden centre operator challenging the council's decision in principle to grant an application for an extension to the range of goods (to include swimming pools, china, clothing, gardening equipment, Christmas decorations etc) to be sold from a neighbouring centre which was located in the countryside and was subject to more restrictive local plan policies than its rival. These policies included policy S 5 which was designed to apply to the type of goods sold from agricultural/horticultural units. Richards J took the view that the council's committees had failed properly to consider whether the obligation could continue to secure compliance with policy S 5. Section 106A(6) does not require that the obligation continues to serve its *original* purpose but whether the obligation continues to serve a *useful* purpose. The range of goods covered by the modification application went well beyond what was capable of being sold from agricultural/horticultural units and would result in large-scale retailing which policy S 5 sought to prevent. The resolution was quashed.

Situations can occur where the grant of planning permission creates a need to modify a planning obligation. In *R (on application of Batchelor Enterprises Ltd) v North Dorset DC* [2003] EWHC 3006, planning permission had been granted for five houses on the site of an old service station enclosed by two accesses to a main road. The developer entered into an obligation to maintain a grassed area but it was found that the development could not proceed without blocking a public highway. To overcome this problem the developer submitted a revised scheme involving the stopping up of the old accesses and the creation of a single new access. This application was refused as the loss of the grassed area was opposed. On appeal permission was granted even though its implementation would be in contravention of the s 106 agreement, the SoS concluding that this was a legal matter for the council and the developer to resolve. The council refused to agree to a modification of the agreement and this decision was challenged by way of judicial review. In quashing the decision Sullivan J held that the authority was not bound to modify the agreement because of the view of the SoS but they had failed to deal with the SoS's view that the grassed area was not necessary in planning terms as it did not serve a useful planning purpose. Furthermore, under legislation, after five years the developer could apply to have the agreement modified and there was a right of appeal should this be refused. Given the SoS's views such an appeal would be very likely to succeed and only two years remained before this modification could be requested.

15.11 LEGITIMACY OF OBLIGATIONS

It is hardly surprising that the bargaining associated with planning gain is a matter which has been brought before the courts over the years and has resulted in varying interpretations as to what may be legitimately be regarded as planning gain. These judgments have, in turn, led to a series of reviews of government guidance in the form of circulars.

The judgment in the case of *R v Plymouth City Council ex p Plymouth and South Devon Co-operative Society* [1993] JPL 553 provided a wide interpretation of what a local authority can reasonably expect from a developer. In this instance, the authority was asked to determine three separate applications for supermarkets submitted by the Co-operative Society, Sainsbury and Tesco in 1991–92. The Co-operative Society's application related to a proposed store in an expanding district centre which was broadly in accordance with the planning policy for the area on the outskirts of Plymouth. The other two applications were adjacent to a roundabout on the A38 and were contrary to the policies in the adopted local plan, which was largely out of date and the content of which had been overridden by other factors in a series of appeals.

Emerging local plan policies suggested that the A38 site was suitable for only one store on the grounds of retail impact and road traffic. Thus, Sainsbury and Tesco saw themselves as in competition for the single planning permission. The council proposal, that each of these two applicants should submit a package of 'benefits' which would enhance the retail facilities was accepted. These 'benefits' would then be taken into consideration in drawing a distinction between the merits of the two sites. The proposed benefits brought forward by the two competitors included bird hides on the site, water sculptures, contribution towards servicing industrial land and crèches off-site. Faced with this embarrassment of riches, the authority decided to approve both stores! At the same committee meeting, the council deferred consideration of the Co-operative Society's proposal and sought a reduction in the size of the development, given the retailing capacity of the two favoured sites. The Co-operative Society refused to amend its proposal and it, too, was eventually granted planning permission in August 1992.

Perhaps not surprisingly, the actions of the local authority were the subject of a challenge by the Co-operative Society, citing Circular 16/91 (para B7), which states:

> Planning obligations should only be sought where they are necessary to the granting of planning permission, relevant to planning and relevant to the development to be permitted.

Both the High Court and the Court of Appeal rejected this argument. In the court's view, the case to be determined was whether the benefits were 'material considerations' within s 70(2) of TCPA 1990. In the view of the court, the proposed benefits *did* have a planning purpose and they *did* relate to the development being considered by the council. Bird-watching hides and water sculpture were within the application site, and Hoffman LJ stated: 'I do not see how it can be possibly be said that such embellishments did not fairly and reasonably relate to the development.'

This view was supported by Russell LJ, who said: 'They made the development more attractive and that must surely be in the public interest.'

It should be noted that their Lordships were not necessarily concerned with any connection between the uses, but rather that the on-site benefits would be in 'the public interest'. The off-site benefits which included the servicing of industrial land and the provision of crèche facilities, also proved to be acceptable to the courts despite a rather tenuous linkage between that offered and the development proposed. The payment towards the servicing of industrial land was seen as a 'contribution towards restoring the balance disturbed by the grant of permission', and the crèche facilities were accepted by the High Court on the basis that the employees at the new stores would benefit from such facilities.

This judgment highlighted the apparent conflict between government policy, as expressed in circular advice, and the scant regard given to it by the Court of Appeal, and is now frequently regarded as the low point in judicial decisions on planning gain.

The guidance tests laid down in Circular 16/91 (the predecessor to Circular 1/97) and their interpretation by lpas also formed part of the basis for the House of Lords' decision in *Tesco Stores v Secretary of State* [1995] 1 WLR 759; 2 All ER 636. At the end of the judgment in the Court of Appeal, Sir Thomas Bingham MR stated that the case involved:

> ... a question of unusual public importance bearing on conditions which can be imposed and obligations which can be accepted on the grant of planning permission and the point at which the imposition of conditions and the acceptance of obligations overlaps into the buying and selling of planning permission which are always agreed to be unacceptable.

This case also involved three companies that applied to build retail food stores on different sites in Whitney, Oxfordshire. Tesco's site was described as the 'Henry Box site', and that of Tarmac (in association with J Sainsbury plc) the 'Mount Mills site'. The third site did not figure in the proceedings.

At a previous local plan inquiry, a proposed new road known as 'the West Link Road' was discussed, and the inspector approved this proposal in her recommendations. She did not make any formal recommendations about the shopping sites, but held that one would be beneficial and expressed a preference for the Tesco site. Furthermore, she expressed the view that the funding for the link road was unlikely to come from the Oxfordshire County Council (as the highway authority), and recommended a policy statement including reference to the district council's intention to negotiate with a developer for a major contribution towards the funding for the new road.

Tarmac's application was not determined within the eight-week period, and was the subject of an appeal to the SoS, who then called in the Tesco application. In July 1992, a joint inquiry was held, at which Oxfordshire County Council contended that, without the construction of the West Link Road, there was a fundamental constraint on the development of a superstore, and that private funding, at a cost of £6.6 million, must be provided. This view was supported by both the district council and Tesco, who offered to provide full funding. (Although it is not directly alluded to in the inspector's report, during the inquiry, Tesco offered to enter into a s 106 obligation with the county council to pay £6.6 million if planning permission was granted for the development of the Henry Box site.)

The inspector recommended that Tesco's application should be granted and Tarmac's dismissed. She rejected the proposition for the need for the link road on the basis that, whilst the superstore would generate more traffic at peak times, that is, Friday evenings and Saturday mornings, even the worst peak traffic flows would be well below 10% over and above the traffic generated by B1 office use, for which planning permission had already been granted. The inspector then referred to Circular 16/91 and observed that such obligations should relate to land, roads, etc, provided there was a direct relationship with the site. She went on to say:

> In this case, there is some relationship, in that the superstore would slightly worsen conditions. The relationship is, however, tenuous.

The inspector also drew attention to the fact that the Circular states that the extent of what is required must fairly and reasonably relate in scale to the proposed development. In her view, the full funding of the road was *not* fairly and reasonably related. On the planning merits of the two sites, she found them finely balanced, but, having regard to the local plan and the local inspector's preference for the Tesco site, decided in favour of that site.

However, in April 1993, the SoS issued his decision letter which rejected the inspector's recommendation, allowed the Tarmac appeal and rejected the Tesco appeal on the basis that:

(a) Tesco's funding offer was not a good ground for granting planning permission, or for dismissing Tarmac's appeal;

(b) the local plan inspector's informal preference for the Tesco site should receive only limited weight; and

(c) on planning grounds, Tarmac's site was to be preferred.

Perhaps not surprisingly, Tesco took proceedings in the High Court against the SoS to quash the decision letter on the grounds that:

(a) he had wrongly discounted the preference of the local plan inspector and the authority's support for the site; and

(b) in discounting their offer to fund the road, he had failed to take account of a material consideration.

In giving judgment, the court found in favour of Tesco and quashed the decision letter. On the first ground, the application failed, but the second ground was accepted, the court holding that the SoS had wrongly failed to treat Tesco's funding as a material consideration.

Following this decision by the High Court, Tarmac appealed to the Court of Appeal (1994) which allowed the appeal and reinstated the SoS's decision, holding that he had not failed to have regard to Tesco's offer of funding, nor treated it as immaterial, but simply declined to give it significant weight, as he was entitled to do.

Not to be outdone in this battle of giants, Tesco then appealed to the House of Lords, the thrust of their argument being that the offer of funding was a material consideration and that the SoS had failed to have regard to it as required under s 70 (TCPA 1990). The Master of the Rolls stated:

> ... 'material' meant 'relevant', and if the decision maker wrongly takes the view that some consideration is not relevant, and therefore had no regard to it, his decision cannot stand and he must be required to think again.

The content of Circular 16/91 under General Policy B5 makes it clear that inspectors and the SoS will have regard to circumstances where the benefit sought is related to the development and necessary to grant permission. Local authorities should ensure that the presence of extraneous inducements or benefits do not influence their decisions on planning applications. They are reminded that their decision may be challenged in the courts if they are suspected of having been improperly influenced. The Lords then reviewed the SoS's decision letter, the main points of which were:

(a) to accept that the development of any sites would increase traffic by 10%;

(b) given the distance of the link road from the sites, the relationship is tenuous;

(c) there is an existing permission for B1 use, and no contributions to highway improvement were sought in granting the permission; and

(d) full funding of the road is not fairly and reasonably related in scale to the proposed development, nor is partial funding.

The Law Lords determined that a planning obligation which has nothing to do with the development, apart from the fact that it is offered by a developer, will plainly *not* be a material consideration and could be regarded as an attempt to buy planning permission. If it has some connection with the development which is not *de minimus*, then regard must be given to it. But the extent, if any, to which it should affect the decision is a matter entirely for the decision-maker and, in exercising that discretion, he is entitled to have regard to his established policy, that is, Circular 16/91. Accordingly, the Law Lords agreed unanimously that the SoS had not disregarded Tesco's offer of funding as being immaterial; that he had given full and proper consideration; and that his decision is not open to challenge. The appeal was dismissed.

In making this final decision, the Law Lords reinforced the fact that the decision taker retains his right of discretion as to what weight, if any, should be given to obligations offered by a developer. This discretion includes the right of local authorities to consider such matters in the determination of planning applications. Although the 'rules of the game' are set out in s 106 (TCPA 1990), and currently amplified in Circular 1/97, the decision whether or not to accept a planning obligation offered by a developer is at the discretion of the lpa.

In *R v Kingston-upon-Hull City Council ex p Kingswood Development Co Ltd* (1996) EGCS 200, the High Court dismissed an application by a competing developer to quash the grant of planning permission which was coupled with a s 106 obligation offered by a rival. The authority had invited applications for proposals to provide for the development of a major shopping precinct within the city, and eventually considered four competing locations. They chose a site which would involve the removal of an existing factory to a new site, with the creation of an additional 100 jobs, and which would be financed by the sale of the applicant's existing site with the benefit of planning permission for retail development. The applicants offered an arrangement through a planning obligation in which they undertook not to open any retail units until the new factory was completed and partly operational. The court held that the authority was entitled to take the provision of an additional 100 jobs into account, and that the financing of the company's relocation was, therefore, a material planning consideration.

In *Wiggins v Arun DC* [1997] JPL May Update; (1996) 74 P & CR 64, a s 52 (TCPA 1971) agreement executed in 1981 was superseded by a new agreement in 1987 which was accompanied by a side letter which gave assurance to the landowner that 'the use of these premises as a garden centre includes the sale of a range of products identified in the current planning agreement'. It specified three types of product the sale of which was permitted by the agreement, provided the sale of the items related to the use of the whole site as a garden centre. In the Court of Appeal, it was stated that the letter was not an enforceable agreement and could not make deletions from an agreement under seal executed four days later. The court upheld the injunction granted by the county court.

15.12 LEGITIMACY OF OBLIGATIONS PROPOSED BY A LOCAL AUTHORITY

So far, this chapter has dealt with the legitimacy of obligations offered by developers as part of their proposals to gain planning permission. Local planning authorities are also entitled to propose agreements without which the authority would otherwise refuse planning permission. This has also proved to be a contentious area of planning control, as circular advice is that if there is a choice between a planning condition or entering into an obligation the former is to be preferred, as it allows the developer the opportunity to appeal to the SoS.

This advice formed the basis of the challenge in the case of *Good and Another v Epping Forest DC* [1994] JPL 372. The plaintiffs wished to gain planning permission to erect a house required for an agricultural worker on their pig farm. As the site was within the green belt, the lpa took two precautions to safeguard the principles of restricting any development in the green belt, first by imposing a generally applied condition restricting the occupancy to a person wholly or mainly employed in agriculture, or the dependant of such a person and, secondly, by requiring the applicant to enter into s 52 (TCPA 1971 now s 106 of TCPA 1990, as amended by s 12 of PCA 1991) agreement which provided:

(a)   that the said dwelling house when erected shall only be occupied by a person wholly or mainly employed in agriculture together with the spouse, other dependants of that person; and

(b)   that the said dwelling house shall not be sold away or otherwise alienated from the remainder of the application site.

The matter at issue was that, at the time of the proposed agreement, there was no right of challenge as exists with a planning condition. The introduction of s 106(B) (into TCPA 1990), which now allows an appeal to the SoS where, after an application to modify or remove the obligation, an lpa states that the obligation shall continue, does not, however, work retrospectively.

In dismissing the appeal, the court took the view that there would be little point in enacting s 52 (of TCPA 1971 (now s 106 TCPA 1990) if agreements were confined to those matters which could be dealt with by way of conditions. Given the wide list of matters which can be the subject of planning obligations, it has been put forward by some commentators that it suggests that a condition, which may be invalid on the grounds of unreasonableness, would not necessarily be invalid as a planning obligation.

The *Good* case was followed by that of *R v Northamptonshire DC ex p Crest Homes plc* [1995] JPL 200, which challenged the lpa's efforts to ensure that the cost of the provision of infrastructure and community facilities for major new housing provision were to be the subject of s 106 agreements. The draft local plan incorporated a policy designed to ensure that developers were required to make a payment towards the cost of these facilities by contributing a percentage of the enhanced value of the land to the local authority, that is, 20% for residential and 17.5% for commercial development. Over a period of three years, it proved impracticable to proceed with a single agreement with the consortium of developers, and therefore it was decided that there should be individual, legally binding agreements imposing s 106 obligations on each developer. Planning permissions were granted to some members of the consortium, the lpa having taken into account the s 106 agreements. The appellants, after withdrawing from a consortium, sought to gain planning permission on one site and had not entered in to a s 106 agreement. Planning permission was refused and a subsequent appeal to the SoS was dismissed.

The appellants then sought a comprehensive challenge to the legality of the council's decisions, including the council's policy as expressed in the draft local plan, and to the s 106 agreements made with the other developers which formed part of the original consortium, plus the fact that an agreement could not lawfully require the developer to transfer land to the local authority. Central to all these issues was the allegation that the council was selling planning permissions or had introduced its own local development land tax.

In dismissing the appeal, the Court of Appeal was satisfied that the council's policy as stated in the local plan was lawful and paid due regard to PPG 12 and the then current Circular 16/91 (now replaced by Circular 1/97). Where residential development made additional infrastructure necessary, there was nothing wrong in requiring major developers to contribute to the costs of infrastructure related to their development. On the issue of the use of a formula which related to the increase in value of the sites, whilst the court acknowledged that any formula which relied on the increase in land value was not directly based upon the cost of the provision of infrastructure and did not link the individual development with any specific community project, nevertheless, the court was satisfied that there was no risk of any disproportionate gain and that a unified approach was legitimate. In the judgment on the land transfer obligation, it was considered that such a requirement was valid under s 106(1)(a).

A second case, *Jelson Ltd v Derby City Council* [2000] JPL 201; (1999) 39 EG 149, arose from the lpa's local plan provision for affordable housing. In this case, two adjoining sites were suitable for residential development, one owned by Jelson and the other by Davis, and the local plan's provisions was that the total of the sites should yield 30 affordable dwellings. Whilst Jelson did not wish to provide any affordable housing on his land, Davis was willing to provide 32 affordable houses. Nonetheless, Jelson signed a s 106 agreement with the council agreeing to allocate an area for affordable housing and to transfer that part of the site to a housing association at a discounted price. The agreement released Jelson from that obligation in the event of the council entering into an agreement with Davis for at least 30 affordable houses on his site. A s 106 agreement was subsequently signed with Davis, but it only committed him to the provision of 15 affordable houses and this, therefore, did not release Jelson from their obligation. Jelson maintained that their s 106 agreement failed to reflect the clear-cut agreement between the council and Jelson that Davis would provide all the affordable housing.

They also argued that it was void in whole or in part by reason of s 2 of the Law of Property (Miscellaneous Provisions) Act 1989. The Act requires that a contract for sale, or other disposition of interests in land, can only be made in writing and only by incorporating all the items that the parties have expressly agreed in one document or, where the contracts are exchanged. Jelson maintained that clause 9, of s 106 agreement contained an express obligation to transfer the site for affordable housing to a nominated association at a price and on terms and conditions ascertainable from the schedules to the agreement. However, no housing association could be nominated until Jelson had begun to develop the site and there was, therefore, no signature, nor could there be a signature, to the Jelson agreement. Hence, the contract for the disposition of an interest in land was invalid because it lacked the signature of one of the parties. The court concluded that s 2 had to be complied with and failure to do so meant that the s 106 agreement was void and unenforceable. The findings in this case have significant implications for both policies related to the provision of affordable housing and for the general drafting of s 106 agreements. Despite the statutory character of a s 106 agreement, it remains subject to the usual rules of contract law.

15.13 ENFORCEABILITY OF EARLIER AGREEMENTS

The High Court in *Wycombe DC v Williams* (1995) 3 PLR 19 considered the enforceability of an agreement entered into under s 52 of the then TCPA 1971, which required the demolition and removal of an existing dwelling house not later than one month after the occupation of a new dwelling house on the site. The court was asked to consider the submission that the obligation fell outside s 52 and that the replacement of s 52 by the new s 106 (TCPA 1990) had the effect that the agreement was no longer enforceable. The court, in considering the Interpretation Act 1978 (s 16), determined that there was a right to:

(a) enforce agreements already entered into;

(b) sue in respect of a breach of agreement which had already occurred; and

(c) continue proceedings already commenced under an agreement in respect of such a breach.

15.14 AWARD OF COSTS

Where application for the award of costs is made at an inquiry, it falls to the inspector to determine whether the claim by one or more parties is justified. In *R v Secretary of State ex p Wakefield MBC* (1996) (unreported), the High Court rejected an application by the council to set aside the award of costs made against it by the planning inspector. The main issue related to the council's refusal to enter into a planning agreement or to consider a unilateral undertaking offered by the applicants. On this point, the court commented that:

> Wakefield adopted a stiff necked approach, unwilling to negotiate, unwilling to make constructive suggestions, and ready only to find fault and be unco-operative. One had only to read the correspondence to see that the inspector was fully entitled to say that, in relation to this matter, Wakefield were guilty of unreasonable conduct.

The court accepted that the appellants, when faced with a refusal to negotiate, were intending to offer a unilateral undertaking but were unable to do so pending negotiations with English Nature, and only after the appeal was heard were they in a position to make such an offer. The inspector accepted the argument that, with the active co-operation of the council, the process could have been undertaken more efficiently and would have brought the matter to a speedier conclusion prior to the inquiry. Such action would have had a consequent saving in time and expenditure. Because of the lpa's intransigence, it was determined that costs awarded to the appellant were justified.

15.15 HIGHWAYS AGREEMENTS

The decision of the High Court in *R v Warwickshire CC ex p Powergen plc* [1997] JPL 843 related to highway works which required an agreement under s 278 of the 1980 Highways Act, but the ruling will have implications for the manner in which local planning authorities exercise their functions in relation to planning s 106 obligations.

Powergen submitted an outline planning application for a supermarket development which was refused by the district council after it had carried out consultations with the county council, as the highway authority. At the subsequent appeal against this refusal, Powergen was granted outline permission which included a condition requiring the carrying out of highway works, which in turn, required an agreement to be entered into under the Highways Act 1980 (s 278).

The county council submitted that the discretion afforded to it as to the public benefit did not bind it to enter into such an agreement. The court did not accept this submission, and held that the benefit to the public of proposed highway works had been fully considered and determined in the planning process. This consideration resulted in planning consent being properly obtained and, therefore, the highway authority's discretion whether to enter into the agreement would necessarily be somewhat limited.

Forbes J held that:

> In my opinion, where the benefit to the public of a proposed highway work, in respect of which an agreement with the highway authority is sought under s 278 of the 1990 Act, has been fully considered and determined in the planning process, because the highway works in question formed a detailed and related aspect of the application for development of land in respect of which planning consent has been properly obtained through the planning process, then the highway authority's discretion whether to enter into a s 278 agreement will necessarily be somewhat limited.

The court, therefore, held that in this case the refusal to enter into the agreement was unlawful and unreasonable.

The introduction of the opportunity granted to a developer to offer unilateral planning obligations (s 106 TCPA 1990) was, in part, an attempt to overcome the problem of local planning authorities that refused to enter into statutory agreements necessary to give effect to planning permissions granted on appeal, given that the SoS himself has no powers to enter into such obligations. The 'Powergen doctrine', whilst limited to matters which have already been determined through the planning process, will allow the presentation of a unilateral obligation as a means of overcoming an authority's refusal to negotiate or to agree to appropriate terms.

In *Wards Construction (Medway) Ltd v Kent CC* (1997) EGCS 67, the county council had entered into a s 278 (Highways Act 1990) agreement with Wards Construction to ensure that road improvements in connection with the proposed development were carried out by Wards. Under the terms of an agreement, the developers were to contribute 65% of the road-widening and other off-site costs. Additional land was required to construct a roundabout, and after the owners had rejected an offer of £10,000, the land was purchased compulsorily by the county council. The value of the site was assessed by the Land Tribunal as £2,160,000, which took into account its ransom value, that is, the fact that the development could not proceed without the acquisition of the land and the construction of the necessary road works. The High Court held that, whilst it was legitimate in a s 278 agreement to imply the power to acquire land for the purposes of the agreement as well as to carry out the actual works, the county's exercise of compulsory purchase powers under s 239 was contrary to the limitations in s 278(5), which states:

> Where for the purpose of executing any works to which an agreement under this section relates a highway authority has a power to acquire land either by agreement or compulsorily and they not need to exercise that power for the purpose *had they not entered into an agreement* under this section they shall not exercise their power to acquire land compulsorily for that purpose. [Author's emphasis.]

In this case, the agreement had *not* been signed prior to the compulsory purchase action by the county council, and the court held that it was the clear intention of the highways authority to perform that part of the contract by illegal means, and this rendered the agreement illegal so far as it required Wards to pay any part of the costs of the acquisition.

CHAPTER 16

APPEALS RELATING TO PLANNING APPLICATIONS

16.1 INTRODUCTION

The right of the individual to challenge decisions on planning applications taken by a local planning authority (lpa) has always been embodied in planning legislation, and any applicant who is aggrieved by the decision taken by the lpa, and who wishes to challenge that decision, must, in the first instance, appeal to the Secretary of State (SoS).

16.2 PLANNING APPEALS

In the event of an lpa:

(a) refusing planning permission;

(b) granting planning permission subject to conditions;

(c) refusing, or granting permission subject to conditions, any approval required by the lpa as set out in the grant of outline planning;

(d) refusing, or granting subject to conditions, any approval of the authority required under a development order; or

(e) failing to give a decision within the requisite period of eight or 16 weeks,

the applicant has the right of appeal (s 78(1) and, in the case of (e) above, under s 78(2) of the TCPA 1990). The right to appeal is *limited to the applicant*, even where the applicant is not the owner of an interest in the land. There is no provision for the owner or a third party to lodge an appeal, hence the significance of legal challenges under s 288 (TCPA 1990) or by judicial review (see Chapter 13).

An appeal should be lodged within *six months* of the date of the decision notice 'or such period as the Secretary of State may allow' (Art 23 of the Town and Country Planning (General Development Procedure) Order (GDPO) 1995 (SI 1995/419)). The SoS 'allows' a period of six months and any appeal lodged after that date will be disregarded. It is also important to note that the relevant date is *not* the date on which the decision is received: it is the date which appears on the decision notice. This can be an important factor in ensuring that the appeal is lodged within the stated period, particularly as not all local authorities forward the decision notice immediately after the decision notice is prepared. A 'month' is not defined in the GDPO but, in accordance with the Interpretation Act 1978 (Sched 1, s 5), a month means a calendar month. In a case where the lpa fails to give a decision, the six-month period starts on the date by which the authority should have made a decision.

Notice of appeal must be given on Form TCP 201 which is available from:

The Planning Inspectorate
4/09 Kite Wing
Temple Quay House
2 The Square
Temple Quay
Bristol BS1 6PN

or by electronic mail (www.planning-inspectorate.gov.uk.), with whom the appeal has to be lodged. The Welsh equivalent is:

Room 1-004
Cathays Park
Cardiff
CF1 3NQ

(www.Wales@pins.gsi.gov.uk). It is also possible to submit an appeal using electronic mail.

Following receipt of an appeal, the SoS may deal with the matter as if it had been submitted to him in the first instance (s 79(1) TCPA 1990). The SoS may dismiss or allow the appeal, or he may reverse or vary any part of the lpa's decision. It is important to realise that, in lodging an appeal against planning conditions, the SoS is entitled to look at the whole of the application and may refuse it outright, or add more onerous conditions than were placed on the conditional consent issued by the planning authority.

Before embarking on an appeal, it is recommended that reference should be made to 'Planning Appeals – A Guide', published by the Department of the Environment and available free of charge from:

Department of the Environment
2 Marsham Street
London
SW1P 3EB.

16.3 DETERMINATION OF APPEALS

The determination of appeals is part of the quasi-judicial function carried out by the SoS and, in most instances, his decision is final. It is only when the decision of the SoS is challenged on a point of law that the matter is brought before the courts (s 288 TCPA 1990). An application to the High Court against the SoS's decision can proceed on the ground that:

(a) it was outside the powers conferred under the planning Acts;

(b) it had not taken into account considerations not relevant to planning;

(c) it failed to take into account relevant considerations;

(d) it imposed or upheld an improper condition;

(e) there was a breach of the rules of natural justice in the handling of the appeal, or other procedural irregularity; or

(f) on the basis of *Wednesbury*, it was unreasonable.

The High Court may grant leave to appeal to the Court of Appeal and, in a relatively small number of cases, the matter may be referred to the House of Lords. The judiciary are *not* allowed to grant planning permission and, if they find against the SoS, the matter is referred back to him for his further consideration.

16.4   LODGING AN APPEAL

Before deciding an appeal, the SoS must afford the parties an opportunity to be heard by a person appointed by him, if either the appellant or the lpa so requests. This can take the form of a local inquiry or, if the SoS considers it appropriate, the parties may be offered a 'hearing' (see para 16.9, below). The SoS retains the right to decide that there shall be a local inquiry if it is considered that the matter has aroused a great deal of public interest or that the issues are likely to be complex.

Initially, the choice of method to be adopted in pursuing the appeal is taken by the appellant, who may elect either for a local inquiry or for the matter to be dealt with by 'written representations' (see para 16.9 below). If the choice is the latter, this has to be agreed with the lpa. There is a strong emphasis in Circular 15/96, 'Planning Appeal Procedures' and in the Department of Environment publication, 'Planning Appeals – A Guide' (see 16.3, above), on the suggested use of written representations as a method of dealing with appeals, on the grounds that it is both cheaper for all the parties involved and provides a quicker decision. Paragraph 2.10 of the publication makes the statement (in bold type):

> To avoid significant costs and to obtain a decision most speedily, appellants will usually ask for a hearing or inquiry only if that course is considered necessary. The written method is the most common.

In completing the appeal form, the appellant must set out his statement of case as fully as possible, giving his reasons for disagreeing with the authority's reason for not granting permission, or for the need or appropriateness of planning conditions attached to the permission. It is not enough simply to state that the appellant disagrees with the reasons or conditions put forward by the lpa. Other matters which the appellant considers to be important, for example, similar development nearby, can also be included, and this will provide the planning authority with an opportunity to consider these issues in its statement. Together with the completed appeal form and statement of case, the following items must be included as part of the submission to the SoS:

(a) an appeal certificate covering the ownership of the land;

(b) a copy of the original application to the lpa;

(c) a copy of the original certificate of ownership which accompanied the planning application;

(d) copies of all other relevant correspondence (including any letters or drawings sent to the lpa amending the application);

(e) a copy of the authority's decision letter (if any);

(f) a plan showing the relation of the site to two well established named roads; and

(g) (if applicable) a copy of the original application for outline planning permission, the plan and the outline permission.

A copy of the appeal form, statement of case, and any material which is not already in the possession of the lpa, must also be forwarded by the appellant direct to the authority.

16.5   PRE-INQUIRY PROCEDURE

Appeals determined by way of an inquiry are governed by the Town and Country Planning (Inquiries Procedure) Rules 2000 (SI 2000/1624). On receipt of the appeal, the inspectorate will notify the appellant and the planning authority that an inquiry will take place. This letter establishes 'the relevant date' from which subsequent actions are timed in accordance with the rules. The actual date for the inquiry shall not be later than 20 weeks from the relevant date for appeals to be decided by inspectors, and 24 weeks if the appeal is to be decided by the SoS; but the SoS has discretion to extend these periods. Either of the main parties, that is, the appellant or the lpa, will normally be allowed to refuse one date, and they are entitled to at least 28 days' notice of the inquiry arrangements.

No later than *six weeks* from the relevant date, the local authority is required to send the appellant a statement of the case it intends to make at the inquiry, and this statement must be available for public inspection.

Likewise, no later than *nine weeks* from the relevant date, the appellant is required to make a statement of case, and this *must* be sent to the inspectorate, the lpa, and any other parties as indicated by the inspectorate. In complex cases, the SoS may require a pre-inquiry meeting to be held (reg 5), to resolve issues or agree facts, in which event the local authority is responsible for publishing a notice in a local newspaper giving details of the meeting. The power to hold a pre-inquiry meeting is extended to the inspector appointed to conduct the inquiry, who must give the parties *two weeks'* written notice of his intention to do so (reg 7).

The advance exchange of proofs of evidence is designed to help the efficient conduct of the inquiry, and if it is intended to read, or call any other person to read, a written statement at the inquiry, a copy must be forwarded to the inspectorate and to the other party(ies) no later than three weeks before the inquiry date. Where the evidence contains more than 1,500 words, a summary of the content will also be required, although the witness may be examined on the statements contained in the full proof unless they specifically state that they only wish the summary to be considered as their material evidence (reg 12).

The SoS may decline to determine an appeal (s 79(6)) if he is satisfied that planning permission for the proposed development:

(a) could not have been granted at all; or

(b) could have been granted subject only to the conditions on which the complaint is made.

The SoS may also dismiss an appeal if he considers that the applicant is 'responsible for undue delay in the progress of the appeal' (s 76(6A)(b)), but he must first give the appellant a period of time in which to expedite the appeal (s 76(A)(a)).

16.6   PROCEDURE AT THE INQUIRY

The persons entitled as of right to appear at an inquiry are:

(a) the appellant;

(b) the lpa; and

(c) the following bodies if the land is within their area, but for which they are not the relevant planning authority:

- county or district council;
- National Park Committee;
- Urban Development Corporation (UDC);
- Commission for New Towns;
- Enterprise Zone authority;
- Broads Authority;
- a housing action trust;
- a statutory party;
- parish council; and
- any other person served with a statement of case.

In addition to the above parties who have a right to appear, the inspector *may* allow any other person to appear, and this permission shall not be unreasonably withheld (reg 11(2)). A person entitled or permitted to appear may be represented by counsel, solicitor or any other person (reg 11(3)).

The applicant may, not later than 32 weeks prior to the inquiry, apply to the SoS for a representative of a government department to attend the inquiry, but that person shall not be required to answer any question which, in the opinion of the inspector, is directed at the merits of government policy (reg 12).

The conduct of the inquiry is determined by the planning inspector in accordance with reg 14. Unless agreed to the contrary by both the main parties, the appellant has the right to make an opening statement and the final right of reply. The appellant, lpa, and s 65 (TCPA 1990) parties, that is, the landowner, a tenant with less than a seven-year lease, and any agricultural tenant, have the right to give evidence and cross-examine witnesses of the other parties. The right of cross-examination *may* be extended to other persons attending the inquiry at the discretion of the inspector. In practice, this is rarely denied. The usual order of presentation of evidence is:

(a) opening statement on behalf of the appellant;

(b) calling of witnesses on behalf of the appellant;

(c) cross-examination of witnesses;

(d) opening statement on behalf of the lpa;

(e) calling of witnesses on behalf of the authority;

(f) cross-examination of local authority's witnesses;

(g) statement by interested parties;

(h) final statement on behalf of the lpa; and

(i) closing statement on behalf of the appellant.

The inspector may refuse to accept the giving of evidence which is considered irrelevant or repetitious, but where he refuses to permit the presentation of oral evidence, that person may submit that evidence in writing before the close of the inquiry. Any written evidence submitted to the inspector before the opening of the inquiry has to be disclosed at the inquiry.

The inspector is entitled to adjourn the inquiry and, if the date, time and place of the adjourned inquiry are announced at the inquiry, no further notice shall be required. Once the inquiry is formally closed, the inspector is normally not permitted to receive additional evidence. If he does intend to take into account new evidence, or a new issue of fact, he must not do so without first giving the parties 21 days in which to make further representations or to ask for the inquiry to be reopened.

16.7 SITE INSPECTIONS

The inspector may make an unaccompanied inspection of the site but is not allowed to enter a site which constitutes private property. Viewing of the site is, therefore, restricted to any vantage point to which the general public have access. The inspection may take place before or during the inquiry without giving notice to the parties at the inquiry. The inspector may also inspect the site after the closing of the inquiry, and must do so if requested by the appellant or the lpa during the inquiry. On such occasions, the inspector will be allowed to enter the site if accompanied by the owner or a person with a legal interest in the land.

16.8 DETERMINATIONS

Whilst appeals are lodged with the SoS, the actual determination of most appeals is made by the inspector appointed to hear the case in accordance with the Town and Country Planning Appeals (Determination by Inspectors) (Inquiries Procedure) Rules 1997 (SI 1997/402). The SoS delegates the responsibility to make decisions to his planning inspectors who act in his name, but he retains the power to take over any planning appeal for decision; in practice, he does so in less than 2% of cases, which are normally important or controversial. In cases which are to be determined by the SoS, the inspector prepares a report which usually includes a recommendation, which is forwarded to the SoS for his consideration. Should the SoS wish to vary the recommendation of his inspector he is entitled to do so, but he is required to present arguments to justify his action.

The decision letter must enable the appellant to understand fully the grounds upon which the appeal has been decided, and provide sufficient detail to enable him to establish the conclusions reached by the inspector the matters which were in dispute. In clear-cut cases, the inspector may offer the parties an early decision within 24 hours by means of an 'advanced decision letter' which indicates the decision to dismiss the appeal or allow it with or without conditions. The formal decision letter, which includes reasoned justification for the decision, will follow at a later date.

16.9 HEARINGS

The appellant may express a wish to have an appeal determined by means of a hearing, or the SoS may settle on this as an alternative method in cases where he considers that the holding of a local inquiry cannot be justified. Hearings are conducted in accordance with a Code of Practice (Annex 2, Circular 15/96), rather than the regulations which govern other forms of appeal, and they are intended to be conducted in a less formal atmosphere than a local inquiry, involving an open discussion led by the inspector. It is not usual for either of the parties to be legally represented, and cross-examination of witnesses does not take place. They are not considered suitable for complex or controversial issues, or those which have aroused a lot of local interest which could result in large numbers of people wishing to be present.

The parties set out their case in writing at least *three weeks* before the date for the hearing and forward a copy to the inspectorate and the other party. Having received and considered the evidence in advance, the inspector therefore starts the proceedings by outlining what he considers to be the major issues to be determined. The issues are then used as a focus for discussion rather than an adversarial approach adopted at public inquiries. The appellant usually has the right to start the discussion and to make any final comments, as in the case of a public inquiry. This method is relatively quick and cheap in comparison with a public inquiry.

16.10 WRITTEN REPRESENTATIONS

The third and most popular method of appeal to the SoS involves the use of written representations. If this method of lodging an appeal is chosen, then, subject to the agreement of the SoS and the lpa, the grounds of appeal as set out in the appeal notice are considered to constitute the appellant's case. It is particularly important that the appellant includes all the grounds at this stage of the appeal process if it is intended to use this method of appeal.

A copy of the appeal form (which includes the grounds of appeal) and the documents listed in para 16.4, above, have to be forwarded to the Planning Inspectorate and the lpa. Acknowledgment of the appeal by the inspectorate is the 'relevant date' for the purpose of the timetabling of steps to be taken in progressing the appeal. The local authority is then required to complete a questionnaire and forward it to the SoS and the appellant with the following documents supporting their decision:

(a) copies of relevant correspondence with statutory agencies and interested parties;

(b) the planning officer's report to the planning committee (if available);

(c) any relevant committee minute; and

(d) extracts from the relevant plans and policies on which the decision was based.

The lpa is also required to indicate whether it intends to provide a further written statement, and if so, this should be forwarded within 28 days of the 'relevant date'.

The appellant then has 17 days in which to comment on the content of the authority's statement of case.

The inspector appointed to deal with the appeal is given the appeal papers and may make an unaccompanied site visit, if the land can be viewed from accessible places available to the general public. If entry onto the site is required, the appellant will have to arrange access and be present with a member of the lpa staff. At either type of site visit, the purpose is only to allow the inspector to familiarise himself with the site and its surroundings, and it is not an opportunity to discuss the merits of the appeal or listen to arguments from any party.

The benefits of written representations are that the appellant is put to minimum cost in bringing the matter to the attention of the SoS and, as detailed arrangements are not required as with local inquiries or hearings, the matter can be dealt with relatively speedily.

16.11 FINALITY OF THE DECISION

The decision of the SoS on an appeal 'shall be final' (s 79(5) TCPA 1990). Notwithstanding this statement, a 'person aggrieved' may, 'within *six weeks*, challenge the decision on a point of law in the High Court' (ss 284(1)(f), (3)(b) and 288(1)(b)). An lpa may not be regarded in this context as 'an aggrieved person', but it is able to challenge the decision on the ground that it is 'directly concerned with the action on the part of the SoS' (s 288(2) and (10)(b)). (See Chapter 17.)

16.12 THE AWARD OF COSTS

In most circumstances, the costs involved in an appeal to the SoS are borne by the parties themselves, and the granting of permission following an appeal to the SoS does not automatically mean that costs are awarded against the local authority. Whilst the possibility of claiming costs has existed in post-war planning legislation on the basis that a party had acted 'unreasonably, vexatiously, or frivolously', very few cases were reported; but this changed dramatically as a result of government policy as outlined in Circular 2/87, 'The Award of Costs'. This Circular has been replaced by Circular 8/93, 'Award of Costs Incurred in Planning and Other (Including Compulsory Purchase Order) Proceedings'. The power to award costs is contained in s 322A (TCPA 1990).

An application for an award of costs is restricted to appeals determined either by an inquiry or hearing and is *not* available in the cases dealt with by written presentations, with the exception of enforcement appeals dealt with by this method and cases in which the appeal is not determined because of the withdrawal of one party during the proceedings. Circular 8/93 sets out a summary of criteria of what may be considered as unreasonable behaviour which could result in the award of costs. The appellant's attention is drawn to the following situations which may entitle the lpa to seek costs:

(a) failure to comply with the procedural arrangements related to the submission of statements;

(b) failure to pursue an appeal;

(c) the introduction of new grounds of appeal or new issues;

(d) withdrawal of the appeal after being notified of the inquiry; or

(e) pursuing an appeal which has no reasonable prospect of success.
    Local planning authorities are at risk if they:

(a) fail to comply with procedural requirements;

(b) fail to provide evidence on planning grounds, or to substantiate each of their reasons for refusing planning permission;

(c) fail to take into account government advice;

(d) refuse to discuss a planning application or provide requested information;

(e) refuse a modified scheme when an earlier appeal indicated this would be acceptable;

(f) fail to carry out reasonable investigations of fact or care before issuing an enforcement notice;

(g) introduce at a late stage an additional reason for refusal or abandon a reason for refusal;

(h) impose conditions which are unnecessary, unreasonable or unenforceable, imprecise or irrelevant;

(i) pursue unreasonable demands or obligations in relation to the application;

(j) fail to renew an extant or recently expired planning permission without good reason; or

(k) unreasonably refuse to grant planning permission for reserved matters or pursue issues settled at the outline stage.

Claims for costs should normally be submitted to the inspector at the inquiry or hearing, and this will not affect the inspector's appeal decision in any way, for example, the appellant may have his appeal dismissed but be awarded partial costs against the lpa or vice versa. The SoS or his inspector is empowered to make orders as to the costs of the parties at an inquiry, or hearing (s 250(5) TCPA 1990) in 'relation to the proceedings before him'. This does not extend to compensation for indirect losses, such as those which may be attributed to the delay in gaining planning permission. The party awarded costs should, in the first instance, submit details of their costs to the other party with a view to reaching agreement. Failure to agree results in the case being referred to the Taxing Officer of the Supreme Court.

In the limited number of cases where the application for costs applies to appeals dealt with by written representation, applications should be submitted to the SoS.

16.13 THIRD PARTIES

Third parties are entitled to claim an award of costs and may have an award made against them but, in either case, this is likely to be in exceptional circumstances, such as unreasonable conduct which has the effect of prolonging the inquiry or hearing because of an unnecessary adjournment.

16.14 PLANNING INQUIRY COMMISSIONS

Planning inquiry commissions (s 101 (TCPA 1990) are designed to 'provide a more satisfactory means of investigating development proposals of a far reaching or novel character' (Circular 67/68). In particular, they are intended to be used where the development could be carried out 'where the use of two or more alternative sites is prima facie possible'. It is envisaged that the commission's investigations will comprise two distinct phases, the first of which will involve witnesses giving written evidence on technical matters, and the second of which will be a local inquiry if this is requested by either of the parties. The inquiry will be conducted by one or more members of the commission, and where two or more sites are proposed, the inquiry may be adjourned and moved from place to place.

The provision for a Planning Inquiry Commission was first embodied in the 1968 Act, and has been retained in the 1990 Act, although it has never been used; nor does it appear that the government has any intention of using it in the future. In 1978, the then SoS reported that he perceived the procedure to be defective ('Current topics' [1978] JPL 731) in that the first investigative stage was bound to reach conclusions, but that the arguments of policy and principle, as well as local issues, would also arise at the second stage of the public local inquiry, and that members of the public would not feel they had had a fair hearing. This view was reiterated in 1986 in the government's response to the House of Commons Environment Committee's recommendation that the Planning Inquiry Commission procedure should be reactivated.

Major developments, such as the proposed additional terminal at London Heathrow Airport and the Sizewell B nuclear power station, have been dealt with via the normal public local inquiry method, and there is no reason to suppose that the government will change its attitude towards the Planning Inquiry Commission. Therefore, we are left with the alternative of 'normal' planning inquiries as the means of investigating and deciding upon major planning applications which are called in by the SoS. The adoption of the 'normal' inquiry system has resulted in a lengthy process. Inquiries in the Sizewell B power station and the more recent Heathrow Terminal Inquiry have taken years!

16.15 MEDIATION

In 1999, the Department of the Environment, Transport and the Regions (DETR) and the Planning Inspectorate introduced a pilot scheme as an option for settling planning disputes without recourse to an appeal. A disagreement between the lpa and an applicant could be the subject of mediation by a neutral party appointed by the Planning Inspectorate. This might occur:

(a) prior to an application being put forward to the lpa's planning committee;

(b) following the refusal of planning permission, either before or after an appeal has been lodged; or

(c) when planning permission has been granted subject to a condition or conditions which the applicant finds unacceptable.

The initiative for mediation lies with the lpas who inform the Planning Inspectorate of cases which they consider could benefit from such an approach. Both parties must agree to mediation and, in signing an agreement, the parties accept:

(a) the confidential nature of mediation and the restrictions necessary to keep confidentiality;

(b) that prior to mediation they will produce a brief written statement of their argument; and

(c) that the parties will pay their own costs, including any professional advisors they may choose to bring.

There is no fixed procedure. The parties do not have to reach a settlement and the mediator is not empowered to impose a solution. Should the process fail, then the applicant's statutory rights, including the right of appeal, are unaffected.

16.16 CORRECTION OF ERRORS

Part 5, s 56 (PCPA 2004) provides a new limited regime for the correction of errors made by the SoS or an inspector in decision letters where the document contains a 'correctable error'. A 'correctable error' is defined as one which is contained in any part of the decision document but is not part of any reasons given for the decision.

The SoS or the inspector may only correct an error when requested to do so in writing or where, on their own initiative, within the period during which an appeal may be made to the High Court, they have written to the applicant explaining that such a correction is being considered. The correction can only be made where consent in writing has been obtained from the applicant/owner and after the lpa has been informed of the intended correction. Notification of the correction notice in accordance with s 57(2) (PCPA 2004) must then be forwarded to the applicant/owner, the lpa and any other person requesting a copy of the notice.

Section 58(1) provides that where a correction has been made to the original decision that decision will be treated as though it had never been made. The statutory period for challenging the decision will run from the date of the corrected decision.

CHAPTER 17

LEGAL CHALLENGES TO THE SECRETARY OF STATE'S DECISION-MAKING

17.1 INTRODUCTION

The Secretary of State (SoS) carries out a quasi-judicial function in relation to the operation of planning legislation since he deals with the planning merits of cases and also the law relating to planning (see Chapter 2). The courts are responsible for ensuring that the SoS does not abuse or misuse the powers granted to him by statute, and that includes the methods adopted in determining issues which are brought before him or before inspectors making decisions in his name.

Legal challenges to decisions taken by the SoS may be made within six weeks of the decision on a point of law and can be mounted by 'a person aggrieved', that is, the applicant, or in certain cases by third parties (ss 284(1)(f), (3)(b) and 288(1)(b), (3), (4), (5) and (7) of the Town and Country Planning (TCPA) 1990). It is *not* the intention that any person who feels strongly about the matter should have the right of challenge, and an individual must show that he has 'sufficient interest' (that is, *locus standi*), to entitle him to apply for a judicial review.

Historically, the courts have taken a restricted view of 'persons aggrieved' as in *Buxton v Minister of Housing and Local Government* [1961] JPL 359; 1 QB 278; [1960] 3 All ER 408, where Salmon J held that adjoining landowners were not persons aggrieved. However, in *Turner v Secretary of State and Another* (1974) 28 P & CR 123, Ackner J held that persons attending an inquiry who were allowed to address that inquiry as a result of the inspector exercising his right under the Inquiries Rule Procedures to invite third parties to do so, had sufficient *locus standi* under s 288. This liberalisation of approach has been continued (see *Bizony v Secretary of State* [1976] JPL 306 and *Wilson v Secretary of State* [1988] JPL 540).

The lpa may not necessarily be 'a person aggrieved' but may nevertheless be able to challenge the decision on the ground that the authority is 'an authority directly concerned with the action on the part of the SoS' (s 288(2) and (10)).

17.2 GROUNDS FOR REVIEW

Chapter 13 dealt with failure to carry out particular procedural requirements in the lpa's determination of planning applications which may result in a challenge in the courts on the basis of 'procedural *ultra vires*'. This may also apply to decisions taken by the SoS, and it is possible to mount a challenge on the ground that:

(a) it exceeds the statutory powers conferred on the body making the decision, that is, 'substantive *ultra vires*';

(b) there has been an abuse of discretionary power, that is, unreasonableness;

(c) there is an error in law;

(d) there has been a breach of the rules of natural justice; or

(e) alleged bias.

Examples of challenges are dealt with below.

17.3   SUBSTANTIVE *ULTRA VIRES*

In the case of substantive *ultra vires*, the action taken is in excess of the statutory power. The question of whether the power granted under legislation has been exceeded is a matter of interpretation by the courts of the purpose which Parliament was seeking to achieve in formulating the legislation. In the case of *Stringer v Minister of Housing and Local Government* [1971] JPL 114; 1 All ER 65; [1970] 1 WLR 1281, the lpa entered into an agreement with Manchester University which was to resist development in the vicinity of the Jodrell Bank telescope. An application to erect 23 houses was refused by the lpa on the ground that the development would interfere with the telescope. The minister dismissed an appeal on the same ground. On a motion to quash the minister's decision, the court held that the agreement was *ultra vires* as it was intended to bind the authority to disregard the considerations to which s 17 of the TCPA 1962 required it to have regard, that is, '... shall have regard to the provisions of the development plan, so far as material to the application, and to any other material considerations' (now superseded by s 54A). The authority's decision was void as it intended to honour the agreement but, in his consideration of the appeal, the minister was not influenced by the agreement and, while he was entitled to have a policy about Jodrell Bank, it did not preclude him from considering the appeal on its merits. Cooke J stated:

> It seems to me that the general effect of the many relevant authorities is that a minister is charged with the duty of making individual administrative decisions in a fair and impartial manner may nevertheless have a general policy in regard to matters which are relevant to those decisions provided that the existence of that general policy does not preclude him from fairly judging all the issues which are relevant to each individual case as it comes up for decision.

A further example of action which is beyond the powers granted by Parliament is for a planning officer to grant planning permission without the delegated power to do so (see *Co-operative Retail Services v Taff-Ely BC* (1979) 38 P & CR 156; (1981) 42 P & CR 1, HL).

In *R v Secretary of State ex p Harrow LBC* (1994) *The Times*, 5 May, the planning inspector, in dismissing an appeal against the refusal of planning permission because of an unsatisfactory access to the site, went on to suggest an alternative access in his decision notice. This matter of an alternative access had not been the subject of any representations or submissions during the appeal. The court indicated that the lpa should not accord it too much weight in determining any subsequent application relating to the site. Because of this, the court would not grant leave for the authority to challenge the inspector's decision by judicial review. The matter was entirely one to be judged by the lpa, and the court expressed the view that judicial review should be used sparingly and should not be used to improve the reasoning behind a decision where the decision itself was unobjectionable.

17.4   UNREASONABLENESS

The High Court, in the case of *Keen v Secretary of State* (1996) 71 P & CR 543, quashed the decision of a planning inspector solely on the ground of 'unreasonableness'. The court took the view that the inspector had rejected arguments for the need for an agricultural dwelling on what were described as 'a number of what proved to be unjustifiable and inconsistent hypotheses', and had failed to deal with the issue of availability of suitable alternative accommodation. The test of what is reasonable or unreasonable in the actions of an authority and the role of the courts is set down in *Associated Picture Houses Ltd v Wednesbury Corporation* [1948] 1 KB 223; [1947] 2 All ER 680:

> The court is entitled to investigate the action of the local authority (or another authority) with a view to seeing whether they have taken into account matters which they ought not to have taken into account, or, conversely, have refused to take into account or neglected to take into account matters which they ought to have taken into account. Once that question has been answered in favour of the authority, it may be possible to say that, although the authority have kept within the four corners of the matters which they ought to consider, they have nevertheless come to a conclusion so unreasonable that no reasonable authority could ever have come to it.

Expressed simply, this *Wednesbury* definition of 'unreasonableness' is equivalent to irrationality in the decision making process.

17.5   NATURAL JUSTICE

The concept of natural justice is embodied in English law but, whilst the phrase is frequently used, it is rarely defined. In the *Council of Civil Service Unions v Minister for the Civil Service* [1985] AC 374; [1984] 3 WLR 1174; 3 All ER 395 Lord Roskill provided the following definition:

> ... the use of the phrase [natural justice] is no doubt hallowed by time and much judicial repetition, but it is a phrase often widely misunderstood and therefore often misused. The phrase might be allowed to find a permanent resting place and be better replaced by speaking of a duty to act fairly. But the latter in its turn must not be misunderstood or misused. It is not for the courts to determine whether a particular policy or particular decision taken in fulfilment of that policy are fair. They are only concerned with the manner in which those decisions have been taken and the extent of the duty to act fairly will vary a great deal from case to case, as indeed the decided cases since 1950 consistently show. Many features will come into play including the nature of the decision and the relationship of those involved on either side before the decision was taken.

There are three elements to the rule of natural justice:

1   there is a right to be heard;

2   no person shall be judge in his own cause; and

3   the rule against bias.

The rules are now regarded as a general duty to act fairly when making a determination on planning appeals.

The secondary planning legislation, that is, the Town and Country Planning (Inquiries Procedure) Rules 1992 (SI 1992/2038) and the Town and Country Planning Appeals (Determination by Inspectors) (Inquiries Procedure) Rules 1992 (SI 1992/2039), is drafted so as to avoid a breach of rules of natural justice. As noted in Chapter 16, para 16.9, whilst there are no rules which relate to the conduct of hearings, there is an established Code of Practice which is designed to ensure that the rules of natural justice are observed.

In *The Lake District Special Planning Board v Secretary of State and Another* [1975] JPL 220; (1979) 77 LGR 689, the Board, in granting planning permission to station caravans and tents on a site, imposed a time limitation. The company objected and, following a local inquiry, the inspector recommended rejection of the appeal, but the minister did not accept the recommendation and waived the condition. The Lake District Special Planning Board sought an order under s 254(4)(b) of TCPA 1971 to quash the minister's decision on the ground that the decision was contrary to natural justice as the minister had not disclosed to the Board correspondence between him and the company after the inquiry closed.

In the High Court, Kerr J, in dismissing the application, said that the complainant faced a heavy burden in seeking to establish a breach of natural justice when the allegation related to something which was comprised within the scope of statutory procedure, that is, r 12(2) of the Town and Country Planning (Inquiries Procedure) Rules 1974 (SI 1974/419).

A breach of natural justice was not *ipso facto* made by the mere receipt by the minister of further representations and the failure to circulate them to everyone concerned. Nor would there by a 'technical' breach of natural justice. *Local Government Board v Arlidge* [1915] AC 120 showed that, in administrative procedures, the question had to be approached on broad lines. The test was whether a reasonable person, viewing the matter objectively, and knowing all the facts, would consider that there was a risk that injustice or unfairness had resulted. It was a question of fact and degree in the administrative process whether the rules of natural justice had been broken. Applying this test it was impossible to accept that there was a risk.

In *Hitchens (Robert) Ltd v Secretary of State and Another* (1995) EGCS 101, the applicants also challenged an appeal decision on the ground that the SoS had acted in breach of the rules of natural justice by taking into account post-inquiry representations without affording the company a prior opportunity to make representations. The court concluded that, by the application of the relevant principles drawn from *Hibernian Property Co Ltd v Secretary of State* [1973] 1 WLR 751; (1974) 27 P & CR 197 and *Performance Cars Ltd v Secretary of State* [1976] JPL 370; (1977) 34 P & CR 9, it was clear that there was no such thing as a technical breach of natural justice. The receipt by the SoS of post-inquiry representations, and the failure to circulate them to Hitchens, did not in itself constitute a breach of the principles of natural justice. It was necessary to show that substantial prejudice had thereby been caused to Hitchens, in accordance with the tests set down in the case of *The Lake District Special Planning Board v Secretary of State* (see above). The court reviewed all the post-inquiry correspondence and found nothing which would prejudice the applicants and, furthermore, found that the SoS had been entitled in the exercise of his discretion to refuse to reopen the inquiry.

In *Rydon Homes Ltd v Secretary of State and Sevenoaks DC* [1997] JPL 145, the High Court was asked to consider the applicability of the rules of natural justice to informal hearings. The court accepted that the procedure at such inquiries was intended to be 'inspector-led' and to follow an inquisitorial rather than an adversarial pattern. It was also clearly intended that the rules of natural justice should be observed and that the inspector's decision letter would include an adequate statement of reasons for his decision. In this case, the inspector seemed to have made an unjustified assumption regarding whether a proposed road would be pervious and its implications for nearby trees. The decision was set aside for redetermination (see also *Orchard v Secretary of State and Stroud DC* [1991] JPL 64).

17.6   LEGITIMATE EXPECTATIONS OF THE PARTIES

Local planning authorities are encouraged to allow objectors the opportunity to appear both when an application is determined by the committee and also in the event of an appeal against the decision of the local authority. The issue of expectation on behalf of an objector was raised in *R v First Secretary of State, Harlow LBC, Mr and Mrs Dubiner* [2004] JPL 1317, concerning the rights of objectors to be informed on an appeal. Mr Rubin, a neighbour, had not been informed of a hearing against a refusal of planning permission and was therefore unable to make his views known. He had been informed of a previous planning application but not that which was refused and this was an error on the part of the lpa. Consequently he made no representations to the lpa and, as a result under rule 4 of the Town and Country Planning (Hearings Procedures) (England) Rules 2000 (SI 2000/1626), which only requires a neighbour to be informed of a hearing where the person had made representations at the application stage. Pitchford J held that Mr Rubin did have a legitimate expectation that he would be informed of the application and therefore had been unfairly treated. He stated;

> There were no promises to notify Mr Rubin, but it seems to me that there was an established practice. It went wrong because of a clerical error. The existence of the practice is important because it removes from the individual the necessity to make constant checks of his own in the local newspaper and on the site. There can hardly be a more sensitive area of relations between neighbours than the prospect that the development of one will affect the amenity of the other. Mr Rubin was thus deprived of the opportunity of attending the hearing and being heard.

Pitchford J then went on to quash the decision on the grounds that there was a real prospect that the decision made by the inspector might have been different. He pointed out, however, that it was important to show that the particular individual concerned had already benefited from the practice in the past and therefore grown to rely upon being notified or consulted.

17.7   ERRORS IN LAW

17.7.1 Inspector's reasoning

In *Banks (HJ) and Co v Secretary of State* [1996] JPL B68, B102; EGCS 171, the Court of Appeal considered the role of the courts related to the judgment of the inspector. The appellants owned Nailsworth Colliery which was in production between 1865 and 1991. In 1992, planning permission was granted to recover coal from waste heaps, subject to a condition for the restoration to woodlands and grasslands, which was due for completion by spring 1995.

In 1993, an application was made for development described as 'the restoration to informal recreation and industrial use by infilling with controlled waste'. The application was refused and an inquiry held into the appeal. The SoS, in accepting his inspector's conclusions and recommendation in their entirety, dismissed the appeal. The inspector concluded that the appeal proposals would delay final restoration by up to 12 years, and that the delay in itself would constitute a breach of policy to treat the site as a Priority Area, that is, one in which support for redevelopment and regeneration is to be focused.

The High Court had set aside the inspector's decision to refuse permission and held that there had been an error in the inspector's reasoning, as any environmental improvement that came after a 12-year delay is a material consideration and it had not been taken into account in balancing of need against a breach of policy. The decision of the High Court was reversed by the Court of Appeal, which emphasised that, in drawing the necessary balance between policies and priorities, it was the judgment of the inspector, and not that of the judge, which was relevant.

In the case of written representations, there is a duty placed upon the inspector to give reasons for his decision (see *Sir George Grenfell-Baines v Secretary of State and Sheffield City Council* [1985] JPL 256).

The question of whether it was necessary for an inspector or, when appropriate, the SoS, to actually cite government policy in order to demonstrate that it has been taken into account appears to be resolved. In *Boulevard Land Ltd v Secretary of State* [1998] JPL 983, the court was faced with conflicting *dicta*. In the first instance, in *Hatfield Construction Ltd v Secretary of State* [1983] JPL 605, Widdicombe QC is reported as saying:

> Policy documents such as Circular 22/80 and the Development Control Policy Notes were the background to every planning appeal and it could be assumed that they had been taken into account, unless it could be clearly demonstrated that they were ignored.

However, in a similar case determined the previous year, *JA Pye (Oxford) Estates Ltd v Secretary of State* [1992] JPL 577, the same judge had been reported as saying that the SoS had not referred to Circular 22/80 and:

> ... if he'd had it in mind he was sure that he would have referred to it, and in his judgment it was left out of the account.

The court felt that it was appropriate to take a fresh approach and to discard doctrine regarding assumptions or burdens of proof. The simple absence of reference to a particular policy would be unlikely to be sufficient in itself to show that it had been left out of the account.

However, in this particular case, the inspector, in dismissing an appeal on grounds of prematurity, was apparently acting contrary to the policy advice in PPG 1, 'General Policies and Principles'. In view of the fact that the issue had hardly been touched upon at the inquiry, there must be some real doubt regarding whether the inspector had taken the policy into account, and viewed the case as one where an exception should be made, or whether he had simply failed to have regard to it.

17.7.2 Inspector's action: simultaneous appeals

In *Dixon v Secretary of State and Gateshead MBC* [1997] JPL 346; (1995) EGCS 185, planning permission had been granted for three different premises on the same redevelopment site. In each case, the permission was subject to a condition restricting the hours of working, and three appeals by written representation were lodged to have the conditions varied. This resulted in refusal to vary the conditions by notification in a single decision letter. The court held that this was lawful as the inspector was aware that there were three appeals in respect of the properties, and there were considerable similarities in respect of the appeals.

17.7.3 Importance of the plan

Jones v Secretary of State (1977) EGCS 9 involved a third party challenge by a neighbour to the inspector's decision granting further residential development within the curtilage of an existing dwelling house, having taken into account that the proposal was not 'backland development', and that it would not result in serious harm to the character and setting of the locality. The High Court noted there was no finding by the inspector as to whether the scheme was in accordance with the development plan. Although an inspector was not required to make express mention of s 54A (TCPA 1990), his decision letter had to contain a clear finding of whether the proposal accorded with the plan or not. This he had failed to do and the decision was therefore quashed.

The extent to which an emergent plan is to be regarded as a material consideration arose in *R (Pembrokeshire Coastal National Park Authority) v National Assembly for Wales* [2003] EWHC 2105. The High Court upheld an inspector's decision which had applied policies in the development plan in preference to those in an emergent replacement plan which sought to reserve housing land for local residents and/or essential need. The authority had refused permission on the ground that the development would be premature and would prejudice the outcome of the adoption process of the emergent plan. In performing his function under s 54A the inspector had taken into account the assertion that the emerging policy should take precedence over the development plan.

A second case, *R (Taussig) v First Secretary of State* [2003] EWHC 3281, concerned the question of the status of supplementary planning guidance as a material consideration. The court quashed an inspector's decision for failure to take into account the lpa's relevant policy contained in supplementary planning guidance. Although reference had been made to the supplementary guidance its content and status had not been made clear and therefore the inspector felt unable to take it into account. In the decision of the court, although acknowledging that the Strategic Policy Guidance had not been placed before the inspector, it was a matter on which, given her reference to it, the inspector should have required further information.

17.7.4 Decision letter: material error

In the case of *Scott v Secretary of State* (1996) (unreported), the court addressed once again the issue of mistakes in decision letters. In this instance, the inspector erroneously referred to evidence showing that 41 planning permissions had been granted in the area for agricultural dwellings in the past three years, when the only evidence related to a period of 10 years. The court accepted that the correct approach in dealing with errors of fact occurring in inspectors' decision letters was:

1 to ask whether the mistake was material in the sense that it could affect the mind of the decision-maker, or a mere clerical error or obvious linguistic inaccuracy. If it is not material in this sense, then there is no error in law; and

2 following *R v London Residuary Body ex p Inner London Education Authority* (1987) *The Times*, 24 July, if the error is material it will only vitiate the decision if:

   (a) the fact is a condition precedent to an exercise of discretion; or

   (b) the fact was the only material evidential basis for a decision; or

   (c) the fact was a matter which expressly or impliedly had to be taken into account.

The court held that the mistake in this case was not a clerical or trivial error but that it went to the heart of the matter and was, therefore, of substance and was material and, therefore, fell within category 2(c) above. It was possible that the inspector might have come to a different conclusion had he not approached the case in a muddled fashion, and it was appropriate for the court to quash the decision.

17.7.5 Decision letters: duty to furnish reasons

The leading case relating to the duty of the SoS to give adequate reasons to support his decision is *Bolton MBC v Secretary of State and Others* [1995] JPL 1043; [1996] 1 All ER 184. The House of Lords held that:

> In making planning decisions, the Secretary of State had to state his reasons in sufficient detail so as to enable the reader to know what his conclusion was on the *principal important controversial issues*. Where the Secretary of State stated his conclusion, right or wrong, on *vital issues* they were adequate, even though they were not very full and were in certain respects badly expressed.

In the light of this ruling by the House of Lords, the duties of inspectors to consider issues raised at the inquiry were also addressed in *MJT Securities Ltd v Secretary of State* [1997] JPL 53; (1996) EGCS 85. The *Bolton* case had confirmed that there was nothing in the statutory language which required an inspector to deal specifically in his reasons with every material issue. However, in this instance, it was made clear that *Bolton* should not be taken as an indication to inspectors on smaller applications that they could omit issues where it was clear that the matter in question was fundamental to the decision. In the present case, the inspector had made no express mention of a matter which was common ground, namely, that if there was a need for a petrol filling station, then there was no other site available. The inspector should have had regard to that issue as a material consideration and given his reasons for dismissing it when refusing permission.

In *Save Britain's Heritage v Secretary of State, Number 1 Poultry Ltd and City Acre Investment Trust Ltd* [1991] JPL 831; 2 All ER 10; 3 PLR 17 (see Chapter 21, para 21.7 for further details), the Court of Appeal regarded that the crucial principles were the duty to give reasons for the decision and the need to have regard to material considerations. It was generally accepted that the inspector's reasoning was clear but the SoS, in his decision, whilst specifically agreeing with parts of his inspector's reasoning, left his position unclear regarding other points of the reasoning. In allowing the appeal, the court considered that the decision letter of the SoS was flawed through lack of intelligible reasons. This decision was reversed by the House of Lords on the ground that the courts are not involved in the planning merits of cases brought before them; the intrepretation of planning merits is purely a matter for the SoS.

17.7.6 Planning conditions

The case of *Ayres v Secretary of State for the Environment, Transport and The Regions* [2002] EWHC 295, involved the use of land by a gypsy for two mobile homes. Whilst involving a number of human rights arguments, the case has a wider significance. The main ground of challenge was that the inspector should have considered imposing a condition for a five-year temporary permission in the light of the Ayres' personal circumstances but at no time during the proceedings did the appellant or his representative seek a time-limited permission. Silber J quoted the statement of Mann LJ in *Top Deck Holdings Ltd v Secretary of State for the Environment* [1991] JPL 961:

> ... an Inspector should not have imposed upon him an obligation to cast about for a conditions not suggested before him

and a comment by Forbes J in an earlier case:

> ... if a party to an appeal wanted the appeal to be considered on the basis that some condition would cure the planning objection put forward, then it was incumbent upon the applicant to deal with that condition at the inquiry. Unless such a condition has been canvassed the Secretary of State was not at fault in not imposing such a condition.

The Court of Appeal in *Redrow Homes v First Secretary of State* [2003] EWHC 3094, considered that the SoS had erred in law in imposing a condition on a grant of planning permission because the condition amounted to a modification of the permission. Outline planning permission had been granted in 1957 for commercial and industrial development which allowed for the construction of access points onto an existing highway subject to a condition requiring prior approval of their location. The application was not considered in time and the applicant appealed to the SoS on the basis of a deemed refusal. Permission was granted for the proposed access points subject to a condition which limited its use to public service vehicles. The High Court had held the imposition of the condition was wrong in law as it modified and derogated from the conditions imposed in the 1957 permission. This decision was upheld as the 1957 condition had shown no restriction was to be imposed on the type of traffic using the access points. Accordingly the SoS had been wrong to impose a condition which sought to restrict the use to public transport vehicles.

17.7.7 The planning unit: extant permission and changed policies

In *Medhat Nawar v Secretary of State* [1997] JPL 153, the Court of Appeal was asked to determine three related issues arising from an inspector's decision to refuse planning permission for two applications related to the same dwelling which, at the time of the appeal to the SoS, had the benefit of an extant planning permission. The first appeal was against the granting of planning permission on 30 April 1992, by Ealing London Borough Council subject to a condition that the construction of the dwelling be commenced not later than 28 August of the same year. The second appeal was against the failure of the council to determine in time, that is, eight weeks, an application to construct a dwelling.

Both applications related to the same site, which was part of what was a large garden attached to the house. The original owner of the house and the garden area had applied for, and was granted in August 1987, planning permission for one dwelling on that part of his garden. This consent was subject to the standard condition which required development to commence within five years, that is, by August 1992. The plot was subsequently fenced off, and that part of the land which had the benefit of the planning permission was acquired by the appellant, who did not immediately commence development. In the autumn of 1991, realising that the consent would expire in August 1992, he applied for a larger house on the site rather than applying for renewal of the approved scheme. Planning permission was granted for the new form of development, but subject to a condition requiring construction to commence before August 1992, which was the date specified in the original consent. Mr Nawar appealed against this condition by means of written representations, and after the appeal decision was announced, which dismissed his appeal, an application was made to the High Court to quash the SoS's decision. The Department of Environment conceded that the decision was unlawful, and it was quashed. Thus, by May 1993, Mr Nawar still had an appeal against the condition outstanding following the decision of the court to quash the SoS's earlier decision and, in August, he submitted an application which was identical to that granted planning permission in 1987 and which had been submitted by the original owner of the site.

The lpa argued that the adoption of new policies in the emerging Ealing UDP should be applied, and they were designed to ensure that:

> ... any loss of garden or other green space around existing buildings will only be permitted if the development results in compensatory benefit for the local area in environmental and landscape terms, and safeguards the amenity of the local area.

On behalf of Mr Nawar, it was argued that the fencing off of his property from the original garden had created a separate planning unit and that, therefore, the policy did not apply.

The inspector's decision in the appeal relating to the condition was that the condition was unreasonably restrictive, but he dealt with the application *de novo* (as if it had been made to him in the first instance) under s 79(1) (TCPA 1990) and refused permission. He then went on to dismiss the second appeal.

The basic issue before the Court of Appeal was whether the inspector and the lower court were correct in deciding that the erection of a fence had failed to create a new planning unit. The court held that:

> ... [a planning unit] is a concept, not statutory but the result of judicial interpretation, which has come into use when consideration is being given to the question of whether there had been a material change of use.

The earlier decisions were supported by the court, and if the question of the planning unit has any relevance, the inspector was correct in regarding the unit as comprising the original site before the sub-division took place.

The inspector was also entitled to consider the relevant policy relating to the loss of open areas which was contained in the emerging plan, and to apply the policy to the whole site. Sir Iain Glidewell went on to state that:

> ... the loss of open space had not been caused by the earlier permission, had not been caused by the erection of a fence, and had not been caused by allowing the site to become overgrown. It had not happened at all yet. It would be caused at the time the inspector heard this appeal, and if and when the construction of a dwelling house took place on the site.

For these reasons, the court dismissed the appeal. There is also the lesson arising from the judgment highlighting the problems which may ensue if there is a delay in carrying out development and of using s 78 (TCPA 1990) rather than s 73 in challenging the merits of a condition. An lpa, in dealing with a subsequent application following the granting of an earlier consent for the same development, is entitled to consider the new application in relation to current planning policies rather than those which applied when the original consent was granted.

17.7.8 Alternative proposals

The Court of Appeal in R *(on application of Mount Cook Land Ltd and Another) v Westminster City Council* [2204] JPL 470, resolved the extent to which the possibility of an alternative proposal for the same site is a material consideration in the consideration of a planning application. The claimant was the freeholder of the building in a conservation area and the interested party held a 999-year leasehold which did not expire until 2912 and the application was to carry out relatively minor physical alterations. The claimant had, in parallel, commissioned a number of design options which it was claimed would not only provide additional accommodation but would further enhance the conservation area. These proposals had been put before the council but no formal planning application was submitted. The council submitted that it had been entitled to disregard the alternative proposals as irrelevant and, having regard to the development plan and what were regarded as other material considerations, the application was found acceptable and, therefore, the council was bound to grant planning permission.

Auld LJ held that:

> ... where application proposals, if permitted and given effect to, would amount to a preservation or enhancement in planning terms, only in exceptional circumstances would it be relevant for a decision maker to consider alternative proposals, not themselves the subject of a planning application at the same time. And, even in an exceptional case, for such an alternative proposals to be a candidate for consideration as a material consideration, there must be a likelihood or real possibility of them eventuating in the foreseeable future if the application were to be refused.

In dismissing the case the court went on to find that, in the circumstances of the case, the claimant's alternative proposals were not material considerations, or if they were, they were of such negligible weight that the court was entitled to refuse permission to claim judicial review. This decision should make it clear to developers that, should they wish to make alternative proposals, they would be well advised to put them forward by means of a formal planning application.

The findings in this case were followed by the High Court decision in *Jodie Phillips v First Secretary of State and others* [2004] JPL 613. This involved the siting and appearance of a mobile phone mast close to Ms Phillips' home. The case was dismissed relying upon the decision in *Mount Cook Land Ltd*.

17.7.9 Alternative future uses

The issue of alternative uses, as distinct from alternative sites dealt with above, was the central issue in *Blue Circle Industries plc v Secretary of State for Wales* [1996] JPL 939; EGCS 26. It was submitted that the inspector, before rejecting the application for landfill use of an existing quarry, on the ground of potential danger to aircraft using an adjacent airfield by attracting gulls and other birds, should have taken into account the number of birds likely to be attracted to the site if the existing permission for the restoration of the land to agricultural use were to be implemented. The court rejected the challenge and accepted that the inspector had considered the point but had come to the conclusion that it was fraught with practical difficulties in establishing the necessary background reference point.

17.8 INSPECTOR: ALLEGATION OF BIAS

In the case of *Fox v Secretary of State and Dover DC* [1993] JPL 448, an allegation of bias was made against the planning inspector who determined an appeal against the failure of the lpa to determine an outline application for four dwellings. The appeal was heard at a one-day inquiry where the appellant appeared in person without professional representation. At the luncheon break, the inspector left the inquiry room with one of the council's witnesses and had lunch in the authority's canteen. The appellant did not go with him. At the close of the inquiry, the inspector travelled to the site by car driven by one of the council's witnesses and accompanied by the second witness. The appellant did not travel with them. After the site visit, the inspector left in the car of one of the council's witnesses and the appellant did not travel with them. The inspector had, however, asked the appellant if he had any objection to him travelling with someone from the council.

The appellant appealed to the High Court, alleging breach of the rules of natural justice in that the inspector had 'acted so as to create a reasonable suspicion of bias'. The deputy judge considered that the appellant raised three essential and separate questions:

1 What was the principle of law raised by the appellant by the allegation?
2 Was there any test that the court should, as a matter of law, apply to determine the allegation?
3 Having regard to the answers to the first two questions, did the facts of this case reveal an error of law?

He found no difficulty in answering the first question. In *Sneddon Properties Ltd v Secretary of State* (1981) 42 P & CR 26, Forbes J enunciated a number of principles, one of which was that the SoS, in exercising his powers, should not depart from the principles of natural justice. In *R v Sussex Justices ex p McCarthy* [1924] 1 KB 256, Stewart LJ made the classic statement of law that '... justice should not only be done, but should manifestly and undoubtedly be seen to be done'. Concerning the role of the inspector at a planning inquiry, held under planning legislation, there was little, if any, real difference in the standard to be expected of him and that expected in a court of law (see *Simmons v Secretary of State* [1985] JPL 253).

In turning to the allegation of a breach of natural justice, the deputy judge applied three tests:

1 What would a reasonable man think if he were in the appellant's shoes?
2 The reasonable man was generally to be regarded as forming his view with no inside knowledge.
3 The court, in certain circumstances, might take into account an innocent explanation of facts which were at first sight suspicious.

On the facts presented, there was dispute arising from the affidavits from both sides in the dispute and the deputy judge had not been asked to resolve the dispute by permitting or requiring the cross-examination of the parties (see paragraph below). On the affidavit evidence of the inspector, corroborated to some extent by an officer of the local authority, the appellant was plainly asked if he had any objection to the inspector's travelling by car with a representative of the lpa. The deputy judge considered that he could not, without hearing that witness in cross-examination, reject the evidence. Hence the appellant had failed to make out his case on the facts and failed accordingly to prove breach of natural justice. The deputy judge went on to say that he was disturbed by the facts and doubted the wisdom of an inspector asking an unrepresented appellant whether he objected to him travelling without the appellant in a car with the council's representative.

Under normal circumstances, it is usually held that it is undesirable for a person holding a quasi-judicial office to be exposed to cross-examination (see *Richard Read Transport v Secretary of State and Forest of Dean DC* [1996] JPL 485). However, the Court of Appeal in *Jones v Secretary of State* (1995) *The Times*, 6 February, held that the court should allow the cross-examination of a planning inspector on the content of his affidavit where there was written evidence before the court which, unless satisfactorily explained, could lead to an inference of improper behaviour on the inspector's part. The court was of the opinion in that case that by simply reading the affidavits, which it accepted were given in good faith, they were not satisfied as the evidence tendered by the inspector and the applicants amounted to no more than differences in recollection of the facts.

17.9   INSPECTOR: REFUSAL OF ADJOURNMENT

In *R v Secretary of State ex p London Borough of Croydon* [1999] JPL September Update, the High Court dismissed an application for judicial review to quash an inspector's decision to refuse to adjourn a public inquiry. The matter arose following the initial failure of officers to report an Art 14 Direction (that is, call in by the SoS), to their committee. When the matter was eventually reported, the committee decided not to contest the appeal and went on to recommend approval to a second application which was in similar terms. The officers sought an eight-week adjournment because they had no authority to represent the authority at an inquiry. The inspector had properly balanced the public interest in ensuring that sound decisions are made in avoiding unnecessary delay. The court concluded that the lpa was responsible for the predicament in which it found itself.

An inspector's refusal to allow an adjournment was, however, regarded as a breach of natural justice in *West Lancashire DC v Secretary of State* [1999] JPL 890; (1998) EGCS 33. The High Court allowed an appeal against an inspector's decision on an enforcement appeal on the grounds that he wrongly refused to adjourn an inquiry that the council's noise witness was unable to attend because of illness. The court found that the witness's evidence was central to the case and should not have been considered by the inspector without her being properly cross-examined.

17.10 INSPECTOR : ROLE AT INFORMAL HEARINGS

The decision of the Court of Appeal in *Dyason v Secretary of State and Chiltern DC* [1998] JPL 778; 2 PLR 54; 75 P & CR 506 turned on the issue of whether a fair hearing had been conducted and whether the inspector should have adopted a more inquisitorial role at the hearing. The inspector had not permitted an expert witness the opportunity, on the day of the hearing, to consider evidence submitted by the appellant in the form of a business plan for his ostrich farm. As an informal hearing normally precludes

CHAPTER 18

ENFORCEMENT

18.1 INTRODUCTION

Any legal system is dependent upon powers which can be enforced against those who may transgress, and the planning system is no exception. Parliament has always taken the view that a breach of planning control is not, in the first instance, an offence punishable by the courts. Instead, the power to take enforcement action is vested in lpas which *may* require the owner or occupier to remedy the situation. Only in circumstances where the requirement of the enforcing authority is ignored *may* local authorities seek to prosecute the offender. Both actions, that is, enforcement and prosecution, are *discretionary*.

Since the Town and Country Planning Act (TCPA) 1947, enforcement had been regarded as the weak link in the planning chain. There are a number of factors which made effective enforcement action difficult, which included:

(a) the problem of gaining evidence to support action against an alleged breach;

(b) the legal requirements being seen as inflexible and overly technical;

(c) the time limits within which enforcement action was possible after the initial breach of planning control. The 1968 TCPA established that unauthorised changes of use occurring before 1964 became established uses as a result of the passage of time and were immune from enforcement action; and

(d) no quick and effective means of dealing with breaches of planning conditions, as opposed to development without planning permission.

As a result of the operational problems outlined above, Robert Carnwarth QC was appointed by the Secretary of State (SoS) to examine the effectiveness of the enforcement system and to make recommendations for its improvement. The Carnwarth Report, 'Enforcing Planning Control', was published in 1989, and most of the recommendations were accepted and form the basis for the new system of enforcement in the Planning and Compensation Act 2004.

The sections referred to in this chapter relate to the TCPA 1990.

18.2 PLANNING CONTRAVENTION NOTICE

The Planning Contravention Notice (PCN) was introduced by ss 171C and 171D (TCPA 1990) and allows lpas to serve the notice whenever it appears to the authority that there may have been a breach of planning control in its area, that is, carrying out development without the required planning permission, or failing to comply with any condition or limitation attached to a planning consent (s 171A(1)). The notice is served on the owner or occupier of land, or any person who has an interest in it, and may also be served on any person carrying out operations on the land or using it for any purpose (s 171C(1)).

The PCN requires the recipient to provide specific information on the following matters:

(a) whether the land is in fact being used, or operations or activities being carried out, as alleged in the notice, or whether it has been so used in the past;

(b) when any use or activity began;

(c) particulars of any person known to use, or to have used, the land for any purpose, or to be carrying on or to have carried on, any operations or activities on the land;

(d) any information about the planning permission in relation to the land or why the recipient contends planning permission is not needed; and

(e) what interest the recipient has in the land and the particulars of anyone else known to have an interest.

The PCN may also invite the recipient to attend a meeting with the lpa to discuss the matter with a view to agreeing the appropriate action to be taken. This could include (s 171(4)):

(a) the possibility of applying for a retrospective planning consent where the lpa would find this acceptable. Such action would also enable the authority to place conditions or limitations on the use if it were to grant planning consent;

(b) the recipient to agree to refrain from carrying out the activities, or to undertake remedial work; or

(c) an opportunity for the recipient to make representations about the notice.

The notice *must* (s 171C(5)):

(a) draw attention to the likely consequences of failure to comply with the notice within 21 days, that is, a fine; and

(b) draw attention to the fact that the serving of the notice does not prejudice the lpa's power to take enforcement action.

It is also an offence for a person to make false or misleading statements about the notice (s 171D(5)).

The PCN, therefore, serves two purposes:

1 it provides the recipient with a warning which hopefully may be sufficient to deter a continuing breach of planning control had it actually occurred; and

2 it is a means whereby the lpa can establish the facts relating to the matter which are required if subsequent enforcement action is to be taken.

The serving of a PCN is discretionary, and the lpa is entitled to proceed directly with the issue of an enforcement notice if it feels this is the most appropriate action to be taken.

18.3   BREACH OF CONDITION NOTICE

The introduction of the Breach of Condition Notice (BCN) (s 187A TCPA 1990) is designed to overcome the problem that, prior to its introduction, the only recourse open to an lpa was to take enforcement action against a breach of condition. The problems associated with taking such action (see para 18.1, above) meant that some developers tended to be lax in complying with conditions as a breach of planning control is not in itself an offence.

Where a planning application has been granted, subject to conditions interpreted to include 'limitations' (s 187A(13)(a)), and they have not been complied with, the lpa may serve a BCN on any person who is carrying out, or has carried out, development, or is the person in control of the land. The notice must specify the steps which the local authority requires to be taken to fulfil the conditions specified in the notice (s 187(A)(5)). A period of not less than 28 days must be given to comply with the requirements of the notice, beginning with the date of the service of the notice. The period may be extended by a further notice (s 187A(7)).

18.4 NON-COMPLIANCE WITH A BREACH OF CONDITION NOTICE

There is no right of appeal against a BCN. The logic which denies the opportunity to appeal is that the applicant had the right to challenge any condition or conditions within six months of the date of the decision notice granting conditional planning consent. Having failed to do so, it is, therefore, reasonable to assume that the person accepted the condition and, in so doing, fully intended to comply with the requirements. Should the lpa serve a BCN to enforce an invalid condition (see Chapter 14, para 14.22), the notice will presumably not apply as such a condition is unenforceable. An lpa may withdraw a BCN by serving notice on the person responsible, but this does not prejudice the authority's right to serve a further notice. The Department of Environment envisages that a challenge to the validity of a BCN, or the authority's decision to serve it, may be made by way of a judicial review or by defence submissions in the magistrates' court (see Circular 17/92, Annex 2).

An offence will be committed if the notice is not complied with within the period set out in the notice, or the notice as subsequently extended. There are only two defences against the alleged offence (s 187A(11) TCPA 1990):

1 that the person can show that he took all reasonable steps to secure compliance with the requirements of the notice; or

2 that he no longer has control of the land.

Persons convicted of an offence are liable to a fine up to level 3 on the standard scale, as determined by the Criminal Justice Act 1982 (s 37) (currently £1,000), and may also be subject to continuing daily fines (s 187A(10) and (11)).

The notice will cease to have effect when, after a BCN has been served, the person has complied with the requirements of the notice. However, the fact that the BCN has wholly or partly ceased to have effect does not affect the liability of any person for an offence in respect of the previous failure to comply, or to secure compliance with the notice (s 180(1)(2) and (3)).

18.5 TIME LIMITS

There are time limits beyond which a breach of planning control becomes immune from the possibility of enforcement action, that is, the serving of a BCN or enforcement notice:

(a) enforcement of control relating to 'operations' must be taken within four years from the substantial completion of the operations (s 171B(2) TCPA 1990);

(b) similarly, the change of use to a single dwelling house is restricted to four years (s 171B(2));

(c) a limitation of 10 years commencing with the date of the original breach applies in all other cases (s 171B(3)).

The TCPA 1990 also specifies that service of a BCN is not prevented where an enforcement notice in respect of the breach is in effect (s 171(B)(4)(a)).

The introduction of the new 10-year rule immunity provision, which was recommended in the Carnwarth Report and subsequently incorporated in the legislation, was considered to be:

> ... long enough for any offending use to come to light, and short enough to enable evidence to be obtained without undue difficulty.

There is a further important element which directly results from the introduction of the time limits set out in the Act: once the period for taking enforcement action has lapsed, the uses and operations become *lawful* as distinct from merely immune from enforcement (s 191(2)).

18.6 ENFORCEMENT NOTICES

As stated above, the power granted to lpas to take enforcement action is *discretionary*. The TCPA 1990 itself (s 172(1)(b)) requires that they should be satisfied that it is expedient to issue a notice having regard to the provisions of the development plan and any other material considerations.

The discretionary nature of the power is also drawn to the attention of authorities in PPG 18, 'Enforcing Planning Control' (para 5):

> 3   In considering any enforcement action, the decisive issue for the local planning authority should be whether the breach of control would unacceptably affect public amenity or the existing use of land and buildings meriting protection in the public interest;
>
> 4   enforcement action should always be commensurate with the breach of planning control to which it relates (for example, it is usually inappropriate to take formal enforcement action against a trivial or technical breach of control which causes no harm to the amenity in the locality of the site).

PPG 18 (paras 14 and 18) also suggests that the lpas should give very careful consideration to the desirability of taking enforcement action in the case of small businesses, or unauthorised development by private householders.

The law requires that an enforcement notice shall state (s 173(1)):

(a) the matters which appear to the authority to constitute a breach of planning control; and

(b) whether, in the opinion of the authority, the breach consists of the carrying out of development without the required planning permission, or the failure to comply with any condition or limitation subject to which the planning permission was granted (s 173(1)(b)).

Further, the notice shall specify:

(c) the steps which the authority requires to be taken, or the activities which the authority requires to cease, in order (wholly or in part) to remedy the breach of planning control, or to remedy any injury to amenity caused by the breach (s 173(3));

(d) the date on which the notice is to take effect (s 173(8));

(e) the period at the end of which the notice must have been complied with (s 173(9));

(f) the reasons why the authority considers it expedient to issue the notice (s 173(10)); and

(g) the precise boundaries of the land to which the notice relates, whether by reference to a plan or otherwise (reg 4, Town and Country Planning (Enforcement Notices and Appeal) Regulations 2002 (SI 2002/2682).

A copy of the enforcement notice must be served not later than 28 days after the date of its issue and not less than 28 days before the date on which it is to take effect, subject to an appeal to theSoS (s 172(3)) (see Chapter 19, para 19.2).

It is important to note that the notice must specify two dates: the date of its issue; and the date on which it is to come into effect. The date when it takes effect must take into account a reasonable period of time to allow the recipient to comply with the requirements of the lpa as specified in the notice. In the event of the enforcement notice relating to a breach of planning control which involved the demolition of a building, the lpa may require the construction of a 'replacement building' which is as similar as possible to the demolished building (s 173(6)(7)). When the requirements of the notice have been complied with, planning permission shall be treated as having been granted for the replacement building (s 173(12)).

Compliance with the terms of an enforcement notice does not discharge the notice (s 181(1)). Any attempt to resume the use after that use has been discontinued in compliance with a notice will constitute a further contravention. Similarly, where the notice requires the reinstating or restoration of buildings which have been demolished or altered, the enforcement notice is deemed to continue to apply to such reinstated building or works.

As a result of the EU Directive on Environmental Assessment (58/337/EEC) (see Chapter 29, para 29.4), there are two new obligations placed upon lpas. They are required to inform the recipient of an enforcement notice that they consider the matter to constitute development to which the Town and Country Planning (Assessment of Environmental Effects) Regulations 1988 (SI 1988/1199) would have been applied, and that any appeal to theSoS must be accompanied by an environmental statement unless theSoS directs otherwise. All such appeals are to be determined by theSoS and not by a planning inspector (Determination of Appeals by Appointed Persons (Prescribed Classes) Amendment Regulations 1995 (SI 1995/2259)).

18.7   ISSUING THE NOTICE

Once issued, the notice, in accordance with s 172(2) TCPA 1990, is required to be 'served' on:

(a) the owner of the land to which it relates; and

(b) any other person having an interest in the land, being an interest which, in the opinion of the local planning authority, is materially affected by the notice

Where a person who is entitled to be served with a notice is not in receipt of that notice the SoS may disregard that fact if neither the appellant nor the person concerned has been substantially prejudiced by this failure (s 176(5)). This provision was introduced to overcome the problem of transfers of ownership 'engineered' prior to the notice being served. It does not, however, deal with circumstances where an innocent purchaser, who without knowledge of the notice, is unable to appeal to the SoS before the notice takes effect. Section 285 provides that the embargo on questioning the validity of a notice shall not apply when a person has:

(a) held an interest in the land prior to the enforcement notice being issued;

(b) did not have a copy of the enforcement notice served upon him; and

(c) satisfies the court that:

(i) he did not know and could not have reasonably have been expected to know that the enforcement notice had been issued; and

(ii) that his interests have been substantially prejudiced by the failure.

18.8 NON-COMPLIANCE WITH AN ENFORCEMENT NOTICE

If the steps required in the enforcement notice are not carried out, the person who was the owner of the land at the time of the serving of the notice is in breach of the notice (s 171(1) (TCPA 1990), and thereby guilty of an offence for which he is liable on summary conviction to a fine not exceeding £20,000. In determining the amount of the fine, the court shall in particular have regard to any financial benefit which has accrued or appears likely to accrue to him in consequence of the offence (s 179(9)). Such a person may plead as a defence that:

(a) he did everything reasonably possible to secure compliance with the notice (s 179(3)); or

(b) he was not aware of the existence of the notice (s 179(7)).

Any person other than the owner who has control of or interest in land to which the notice relates must not carry on any activity required to cease in accordance with the notice, nor must he cause or permit such activity to be carried on. If he does, then he too is liable (s 179(5)) and on summary conviction may be fined.

In preparing evidence for the prosecution of offenders, the lpa is obliged to comply with rules contained in the Code of Practice published by the Home Office, which applies to all criminal investigations begun after 31 March 1997. The minimum essential requirements are:

(a) proof that the accused was the owner of the land at the date of the alleged contravention, which should be obtained from the Land Registry or the accused's return of a PCN;

(b) formal proof that the enforcement notice has been issued and served in accordance with the provisions of the TCPA 1990;

(c) whether there has been an appeal to the SoS against the enforcement notice and, if so, the outcome of the appeal;

(d) the precise date on when the enforcement notice should have been complied with; and

(e) proof that the notice has not been complied with after the end of the compliance period.

If photographs are to be used in evidence, then it is vital that there is proof of when and where and by whom the photographs were taken. Any evidence of conversations between the accused and the planning officer relating to the alleged offence may be considered inadmissible if the accused was not made aware by 'cautioning' beforehand.

If the steps required by the enforcement notice are not taken within the period specified in the notice, the authority may enter on to the land and take the steps itself (s 178(1)(a)), and recover reasonable expenses from the owner of the land for doing so (s 178(1)(b)).

18.9 FINES FOR NON-COMPLIANCE WITH AN ENFORCEMENT NOTICE

Under the provisions of s 179(9) (TCPA 1900), in determining the amount for any fine which is to be imposed on a person convicted, 'the court shall in particular have regard to any financial benefit which has accrued or appears likely to accrue to him in consequence of the offence'. The Court of Appeal in *R v Browning* (1996) 1 PLR 61 set aside a fine of £25,000 imposed by the Crown Court, and emphasised that the amount of the fine should not be fixed solely by reference to the accrued benefit. There should also be consideration of ability to pay. When imposing a fine, regard must be given not only to the seriousness of the offence, but also to the financial circumstances of the offender, which is a statutory obligation under the Criminal Justice Act 1991 (ss 18(2) and (3)). In this case, the defendant had erected an unauthorised building, and it was estimated that this action might have increased the land value by at least £80,000. However, no future gain was likely as the building would be demolished if the enforcement action was carried through, and that would cause the defendant further loss. The court accepted that a substantial fine was still appropriate, given that there had been such a flagrant breach of the law, and a fine of £1,000 was substituted.

In a second case, *Kent CC v Brockman* (1996) 1 PLR 1, the question of whether lack of funds can be regarded as a valid reason for not complying with an enforcement notice was considered by the Divisional Court. Although the court was willing to accept that personal circumstances of a defendant can fall within s 179(3), that is, 'it shall be a defence for him to show that he did everything he could be expected to do to secure compliance', there was concern that the magistrates should not too readily accept a claim of financial hardship as a defence. Simon Brown LJ observed:

> It is clearly imperative that land should not be left in an unsatisfactory state, perhaps a public eyesore, unless the owner has taken every practical step to overcome his financial problems in complying with the requirements of the enforcement notice, to the extent, if need be, of selling his land, if that is possible, to ensure it will be put into a proper state.

Buckley J also noted that s 179 makes no provision for inquiry as to the financial means of the defendant; the onus was on the defendant, and he would be very surprised if magistrates were satisfied 'simply by the defendant waving a blank statement in front of them showing an overdraft or mere assertion by him that he was impecunious'.

A further consideration was that the council could enter on to the land and carry out the necessary works and seek to recover its costs from the defendant, which might be a suitable remedy if they were unconvinced by his protestations of impecuniosity.

If the use is continued after conviction, a further offence is committed as in *Backer v Uckfield RDC* [1970] 114 SJ 666; P & CR 526. The defendant, having been served with an enforcement notice requiring the discontinuance of the use of land for the stationing of lorries, was convicted of contravening the notice. After the conviction, the parts of two vehicles were left on the land although the chassis of one had been removed and neither vehicle had any wheels. As a result, he was further convicted of continuing the unauthorised use and he appealed to the Divisional Court. The court dismissed his appeal, holding that the question was not whether the remains of lorries left on the site were vehicles for the purposes of the Road Traffic Acts but whether they were offending objects referred to in the enforcement notice.

18.10 STOP NOTICES

The issuing of an enforcement notice may result in an appeal against the notice (see Chapter 19), and such action suspends the operation of the notice until such time as the appeal has been determined. In the meantime, the operation or activity to which the notice relates can continue without penalty. There may be particular situations where the local authority considers that urgent action should be taken to prevent the continuation of the alleged breach during the period specified for compliance with the enforcement notice.

In such circumstances, the lpa may issue a stop notice at the time of, or subsequent to, serving the enforcement notice. A stop notice is essentially a supplement to an enforcement notice, and *cannot* be served independently (s 183(1) TCPA 1990). A stop notice must refer to the enforcement notice to which it relates and must have a copy of that notice attached to it (s 184(1)). The lpa must also display a 'site notice' on the land giving particulars of the stop notice, the date when it takes effect, and the requirements called for in the notice (s 184(6)). The notice cannot take effect until the date specified in the notice (s 184(2)), which may not be earlier than three or later than 28 days from the day on which it is served, unless there are exceptional circumstances, which must be stated when the notice is served (s 184(2), (3)(a)), in which case it can take effect immediately.

A stop notice *cannot*:

(a) prohibit the use of any building as a dwelling house; or

(b) prohibit the carrying out of any activity which has been carried out for more than four years ending with the date of the service of the notice (s 183(5)); but this does not extend to any activity which consists of, or is incidental to, building, engineering, mining or other operations, or the deposit of refuse or waste (s 183(5)(A)).

18.11 TEMPORARY STOP NOTICES

Section 52 of the Planning and Compulsory Purchase Act (PCPA) 2004 (inserting ss 171E–171H into the TCPA 1990) provides a new power for lpas to issue temporary stop notices which have effect up to 28 days. The temporary notice takes effect immediately and there is no requirement to serve an enforcement notice beforehand. Essentially it provides the local authority with an opportunity to decide whether further enforcement action should be taken and the form it should take. However, similar provisions to those contained in the 1990 Act exist relating to compensation in the event that activities prevented by the temporary notice are, in fact, lawful.

Such a notice may not relate to the use of a building as a dwelling house or the carrying out of an activity of such description as prescribed (NB as yet unknown, but will be defined in regulations issued by the SoS), or any activity which has been carried out (whether or not continuously) for a period of four years ending with the day on which the notice is displayed. A second or subsequent temporary notice must not be issued for the same activity unless the lpa has first taken enforcement action in relation to the activity alleged to be a breach of planning control.

18.12 NON-COMPLIANCE WITH A STOP NOTICE

Any person who contravenes the provisions of a stop notice is guilty of an offence (s 187(1)(1A) TCPA 1990) and is liable to a fine not exceeding £20,000, or on conviction, on indictment to a fine of an unlimited amount. The only defence is for the person to prove that he was not served with the stop notice and that he did not know, or could not reasonably be expected to know, of its existence (s 187(3)).

18.13 COMPENSATION FOR LOSS DUE TO A STOP NOTICE

Compensation for loss or damage which is directly due to a stop notice may be claimed by any person who has an interest in, or occupies, the land to which the stop notice relates (s 186(2) TCPA 1990), and this may include payment arising from a breach of contract caused by taking the action necessary to comply with the notice (s 186(4)). In the past, local authorities were often reluctant to serve stop notices because of the liability to pay compensation, but the Planning and Compensation Act 1991 made significant changes to the extent of that liability.

As a result of the 1991 Act, compensation will be payable (s 186(1)) *only* when:

(a) the enforcement notice to which the stop notice relates is quashed on grounds other than that planning permission should be granted, or the condition or limitation should be discharged (s 174(2));

(b) the enforcement notice is varied other than as in s 172(2) above;

(c) the enforcement notice is withdrawn by the local authority for reasons other than that planning permission has been granted or the conditions or limitations removed; and

(d) the stop notice itself is withdrawn.

Compensation is *not* payable:

(a) in respect of any activity which constitutes a breach of planning control (s 186(5)(a)); or

(b) where the claimant has failed to provide information thereby causing loss or damage which he could have avoided (s 186(5)(b)).

Claims for compensation due to a stop notice must be made to the local authority within six months from the date of the decision which gives rise to the claim (s 186(3)).

18.14 RIGHTS OF ENTRY

Any person duly authorised in writing by the lpa may enter any land at any reasonable hour and without a warrant (s 196A(1) TCPA 1990) to:

(a) ascertain whether there is or has been any breach of planning control;

(b) determine whether any of the powers conferred on the lpa in relation to enforcement should be exercised in relation to the land or any other land;

(c) determine how much power should be exercised in relation to the land or any other land; and

(d) ascertain whether there has been compliance with any requirement imposed as a result of any such power having been exercised in relation to the land or any other land.

There is one exception to the extensive powers of entry, and that relates to a dwelling house. In this case, 24 hours' notice of any intended entry must be given to the occupier of the house (s 196A(4)).

18.15 REGISTER OF ENFORCEMENT AND STOP NOTICES

An lpa is required to keep a register containing information about enforcement and stop notices in its area (s 188), which is to be available for public inspection at all reasonable hours (s 188(3)).

18.16 INJUNCTIONS

Prior to the introduction of s 187B into the TCPA 1990, the courts were not sympathetic to requests for injunctions which involved a breach of planning control, preferring the lpa to use the powers conferred upon it by the Planning Acts. The new power granted to lpas is all-embracing and, where they consider it necessary or expedient to do so, an lpa may apply to the High Court or the county court for an injunction to restrain a breach of planning control. This applies to an apprehended as well as an actual breach of control, and an injunction can be used either as a supplement to the use of existing powers or as an exclusive remedy.

Where an injunction is granted upon an application by the lpa, the landowner would have to pay the authority's costs. Likewise, lpas should take into account that, when seeking injunctive relief, an undertaking in damages is usually given to the court by the local authority to protect the person against whom the action is being taken. If that person is successful in showing that no breach of planning control took place, damages will be payable by the local authority for any loss or damage caused as a result of the injunction. However, the court has a discretion whether or not to require an undertaking in damages from the lpa where an injunction is sought to restrain a breach of planning control which is undertaken in the public interest (see *Kirklees MBC v Wickes Building Supplies Ltd* [1992] 3 All ER 717).

18.17 UNTIDY SITES AND BUILDINGS

Under s 215 (TCPA 1990), the lpa is empowered to take action to ensure that the owner or occupier of land or a building, the condition of which adversely affects the amenity of the area, takes action to remedy the situation. For details of the application of s 215, see Chapter 22, para 22.11.

CHAPTER 19

ENFORCEMENT APPEALS AND LEGAL CHALLENGES

19.1   INTRODUCTION

Enforcement action by local planning authorities (lpas) can be undertaken by the issuing of:

(a) an enforcement notice;

(b) a Breach of Condition Notice (BCN);

(c) a stop notice; or

(d) an injunction.

The recipient of an enforcement notice is required by the lpa to take action to overcome the alleged breach of planning control within a specified period of time, which can be as short as 28 days after the notice has been served. At this stage, it is an *alleged* breach of planning control and is, therefore, open to challenge by lodging an appeal to the Secretary of State (SoS). In the event of an appeal being lodged, the immediate effect is to extend the period for compliance stated by the lpa in its notice until the matter has been decided by the SoS and, in the meanwhile, the alleged breach can continue unless the local authority issues a stop notice (see Chapter 18, para 18.10).

In the event of the serving of a BCN, there is no right of appeal to the SoS (see Chapter 18, para 18.4). The only course open to the recipient is to challenge the notice in the courts by way of judicial review under s 288 or s 289 (Town and Country Planing Act (TCPA) 1990) (see para 19.5, below).

The Town and Country Planning (Enforcement Notices and Appeals) Regulations 2002 intend to speed up the enforcement appeal process. The main elements are that:

(a) the lpa is required to provide a list of all directly relevant development plan policies;

(b) appeal forms are to be submitted simultaneously to the SoS and the lpa;

(c) the SoS is to inform the appellant and the lpa that an appeal has been made and the date of the letter would be the 'start date';

(d) a planning application would only be deemed to be made where ground (a) is pleaded;

(e) the lpa is to submit the completed questionnaire within 14 days of the 'start date' and forward a copy to the SoS and the appellant;

(f) within six weeks of the 'start date', the lpa is to submit two copies of their statement of case and the appellant is to submit any further representations;

(g) both parties are to submit comments on the other party's representations within nine weeks from the 'start date';

(h) lpas are to give notice to third parties within two weeks of the 'start date' and third party representations are to be submitted within six weeks of that date;

(i) each of the main parties are to submit two copies of their statement within six weeks of the starting date of the appeal or four weeks after a pre-inquiry meeting; and

(j) the main parties are required to send a 'statement of common ground' to the Secretary of State no later than four weeks before the inquiry.

19.2   APPEALS AGAINST ENFORCEMENT NOTICES

Under the provisions of s 174(1) (TCPA 1990), a right of appeal is conferred on any person having an interest in the land or on a 'relevant occupier', that is, a person who occupies the land by virtue of a licence at the time at which the notice was served and has continued to do so at the time the appeal is lodged. It is not necessary for the person lodging the appeal to have received a copy of the enforcement notice.

Whilst TCPA 1990 clearly defines 'the owner' in s.172(2) it fails to define the term 'occupier' and this has led to a number of cases in the courts. Two cases relating to caravan dwellers resulted in conflicting judgments. In an early case, *Munnich v Godstone RDC* [1966] 1 WLR 427, it was found that they did not enjoy the status of 'occupiers'. Subsequent decisions in *Stevens v Bromley LBC* [1972] 2 WLR 605; 23 P & CR 142 and *Scarborough Council v Adams* [1983] JPL 673, determined that they did.

Unlike appeals against lpas' decisions on planning applications (see Chapter 16), an appeal against an enforcement notice must be lodged within the period specified on the notice which sets out when the notice becomes effective. Furthermore, the grounds of appeal are restricted (s 174(2)) to any one, or combinations, of the following:

(a) that, in respect of any breach of planning control which may be constituted by the matters stated in the notice, planning permission ought to be granted or, as the case may be, the condition or limitation concerned ought to be discharged;

(b) that the matters alleged have not occurred;

(c) that the matters (if they occurred) do not constitute a breach of planning control;

(d) that, at the date when the enforcement notice was issued, no enforcement action could be taken in respect of the breach of planning control which may constitute those matters, that is, a period of four years or 10 years had elapsed (see Chapter 18, para 18.5);

(e) that copies of the enforcement notice were not served as required by s 172;

(f) that the steps required by the notice to be taken, or the activities required by the notice to cease, exceed what is necessary to remedy any breach of planning control which may be constituted by those matters or, as the case may be, to remedy any injury to amenity which has been caused by any such breach;

(g) that any period specified in the notice for compliance with the notice falls short of what should reasonably be allowed.

In the case of ground (a) being included as a ground of appeal, the appellant is required to pay the Department of Environment the appropriate planning fee and the same amount to the lpa, as no previous planning consent has been sought.

An appeal against an enforcement notice must be lodged in writing to the SoS within the period specified in the notice as to the date on which it will take effect, which could be as little as 28 days. This was confirmed by the Court of Appeal in *Howard v Secretary of State for the Environment* [1975] QB 325. After that date, if no appeal has been lodged within the specified period the notice will come into effect.

The question of where the burden of proof lies in an enforcement appeal was addressed in *Nelsovil Ltd v Minister of Housing and Local Government* [1962] 1 All ER 423;

1 WLR 404; 13 P & CR 151, where the issue was whether a material change of use had occurred more than four years prior to the serving of the notice. Widgery J stated:

> I should have thought that a person given a right to appeal on certain specified grounds is the person who has to make good those grounds and is the person on whom the onus rests ... I can see no sort of hardship in requiring that the onus shall lie on the appellant in such a case.

In *R v Teinbridge DC ex p Teignmouth Quay Co Ltd* [1995] JPL 828; (1994) EGCS 203, the High Court held that an lpa was not entitled to serve a planning contravention notice simply at the request of residents who objected to the proposed development. In order to exercise its function properly, it had to appear to the authority that a breach of planning control had occurred. Accordingly, the court quashed the notice.

In the case of *Kerrier DC v Secretary of State, Brewer and Another* [1981] JPL 193; 41 P & CR 284, in May 1973, planning permission was granted for a bungalow sited on an agricultural holding of 5.3 acres, subject to an 'agricultural occupancy condition', that is, restricting the occupation to a person mainly employed in agriculture or the dependent of such a person. When the bungalow was built, the design differed from the approved design in that a basement was added. In March 1974, the planning department requested amended plans. No fresh application was submitted and the relevant committee considered the amended plan and approved it as a retrospective amendment to the original planning permission. In July 1975, the second and third respondents, Mr and Mrs Brewer, bought the property. In June 1979, the council served an enforcement notice alleging that the owners failed to comply with the agricultural condition and giving six months to cease occupation. In determining the appeal against the enforcement notice, the SoS stated:

> As a matter of fact, the dwelling house actually built differed materially from that shown on the plans ... in these circumstances, it is considered the dwelling was built without planning permission. [See *Copeland BC v Secretary of State and Others* (1976) 31 P & CR 403.]

The court considered that the lpa had no power retrospectively to approve a material amendment to the plans. The view was taken that the 1973 planning permission has not been *implemented* and therefore no beach of condition of that permission had occurred, as alleged in the enforcement notice. The enforcement notice must therefore be quashed, with the result that the owners benefited from the breach of permission, as the unlawful building is immune from further enforcement action under the four-year rule, whereby enforcement control relating to operations must be taken within four years from the substantial completion of the operations (s 171B(2) TCPA 1990). The normal alternative action which can be undertaken within a period of 10 years to enforce a condition (s 171(B)(1)) is not available to the lpa. Thus, the occupier of a dwelling which is constructed in accordance with a planning permission, and who then flouts a condition, is in a worse position than a person who carries out unlawful development.

The case provides two salutary warnings to lpas: first, that *material* amendment to an approved plan requires the submission of a fresh planning application (what is 'material' is a question of fact and degree), and secondly that, whilst development may be carried out, it does not necessarily follow that it accords with the planning permission and is thereby *implemented*.

The Court of Appeal in *Handoll v Warner Goodman Streat (a firm)* [1995] JPL 930; 1 PLR 40 held that a planning condition which is imposed on a permission cannot apply to a building which is not authorised by that permission. A bungalow was erected about 90 ft from the location approved by the lpa, and the court held that it was not permitted by that planning permission and that, therefore, the works were unlawful. As the building was unlawful, this meant that the agricultural occupancy condition attached to the consent was also inapplicable. In coming to this decision, the court accepted the submission that underlay the earlier *Kerrier* case but, in this instance, in determining the case, the court concluded that 'on a correct analysis, the occupier would be worse off since he would remain in breach of planning control'. It would appear that the court may be basing this judgment on a presumption that the occupier remains in breach of planning permission. The lpa is restricted to a period of four years in which enforcement action may be taken after the substantial completion of an unlawful erection (s 171(B)(3)).

The issue of the effect, granting a temporary planning permission upon subsequent enforcement action was addressed in *Creswell v Pearson* [1997] JPL 860. Mr and Mrs Creswell (the appellants) owned land in East Sussex and, in August 1986, Horsham District Council issued two enforcement notices requiring the unauthorised use of land for the parking and storage of commercial vehicles to cease and associated stored plant and machinery to be removed. Following an appeal, the period for compliance was extended until March 1988 and the appellants failed to comply with the notices which rendered them liable to prosecution. On 19 July 1989, the council granted them temporary planning permission authorising the use of the land for the purposes stated in the original enforcement notice until 31 July 1991. The appellants continued to use the land for the same purpose after that date and, in October 1996, they were convicted by Horsham magistrates' court of two offences of contravening the enforcement notices as at July 1995. In making this conviction, the justices interpreted s 180(1) of the TCPA 1990 to mean that the two notices ceased to have effect only during the period when temporary planning permission was granted for the uses. The central issue was not whether temporary planning permission caused the enforcement notices to cease to exist, but whether it caused them to go into a state of suspended animation, and were, therefore, capable of being revived when the temporary permission came to an end. In allowing the appeal, the court was quite clear that the words 'cease to have effect' adopted in s 180(1) meant exactly what they said. They did not mean 'go into suspended animation' nor did they mean 'have no effect for so long as the temporary planning permission is in being'. The enforcement notices ceased to have effect as at 19 July 1989 when the temporary planning permission was granted.

In the case of *R v Wicks* [1996] JPL 743; [1997] All ER 801, the House of Lords provided some practical procedural guidance to those wishing to challenge an enforcement notice as *ultra vires* and, in doing so, re-emphasised the requirement to challenge decisions by means of planning legislation. Wicks had undertaken some building work for which he thought planning permission was not required. The lpa disagreed (as, in its opinion, the work undertaken substantially changed the nature of the building) and wrote to Mr Wicks threatening the service of an enforcement notice. This was eventually served and, when it became clear that the work had not been stopped, the lpa issued a summons under s 179(1).

Wicks elected to be tried on indictment and argued in the Crown Court that the authority had acted in bad faith in serving the notice and had taken into account considerations which were not material. These allegations do not constitute a ground of appeal under s 174, and the lpa argued that such a challenge must be brought by an application for judicial review rather than as a defence in criminal proceedings. This contention was accepted by the judge. Wicks then appealed to the Court of Appeal which dismissed the appeal on the basis that, unless the order was clearly a nullity, the defence in a criminal trial could not go behind it. Wicks then appealed to the House of Lords.

The judgments of Lords Nicholls and Hoffman made it clear that, in the first instance, the appropriate method of challenging the lawfulness of an order made under statutory powers was the statute itself, that is, s 174. Equally, it is possible for a statute to demand that the court considers and rules on the validity of an administrative action. In such a case, if the order had not been quashed by judicial review, the matter would not ordinarily be considered by the criminal courts. Arguments concerning the wider validity of the notice could not constitute a defence, so the Crown Court had been correct to refuse to hear arguments on the basis of bias, bad faith or immaterial considerations. The appeal against the conviction was dismissed.

19.3 LODGING AN APPEAL

An appeal to the SoS against an enforcement notice (s 174(3) TCPA 1990), usually by means of the completion of an enforcement appeal form available from the Appeal Branch, must state the grounds of appeal ((a)–(g), see para 19.2, above) and *must* either:

(a) give written notice *before* the date on which the notice is due to take effect; or (presumably to deal with the vagaries of the postal system);

(b) send the notice in a properly addressed and stamped envelope at such a time that, in the ordinary course of the post, it would be delivered to him *before* that date.

The timing of the lodging of the appeal is critical. In *Lenlyn Ltd v Secretary of State* [1985] JPL 482, the notice came into effect on 16 February, and all the requisite appeal documents were posted on that date. The SoS declined to deal with the appeal as it had not been received by him before the date on which the notice took effect.

The appellant must also submit to the SoS a statement in writing specifying the details in support of his grounds of appeal. This may be done at the time of lodging the appeal, or not less than three weeks prior to the appeal being heard (reg 5 of the Town and Country (Enforcement Notices and Appeals) Regulations 1991 SI). Failure to do so within the time limit may result in the SoS dismissing the appeal forthwith and likewise, if the lpa fails to take similar procedural steps required of it, the SoS may allow the appeal (s 176(3)).

The SoS has no power to reinstate an appeal when it has been validly withdrawn, and the enforcement notice will remain in operation and will thereafter take effect (*R v Secretary of State ex p Monica Theresa Crossley* [1985] JPL 632).

The importance of using the appeal machinery which is part of the planning process, as distinct from relying upon the magistrates' court to determine the validity of an enforcement notice, was highlighted in *Vale of White Horse DC v Treble-Parker* [1996] JPL B113; EGCS 40. The respondents had withdrawn their appeal against an enforcement notice which alleged that there had been a change of use of their land from agricultural to business use. They proceeded to present a case to the magistrates based upon their submission that the use had been established for a period of more than 10 years before the serving of the enforcement notice. The magistrates upheld this submission. The Divisional Court ruled that it was not open to the magistrates to make such a decision, and the proper remedy was for the respondents to appeal to the SoS against the enforcement notice. They had failed to do so by withdrawing their appeal and were now precluded from raising these arguments in defence of prosecution by s 285(1).

The primacy of an enforcement notice and the need to challenge the validity of the notice, if at all, by an appeal to the SoS, was reasserted by the Queen's Bench Division in *R v Dacorum BC ex p Cannon* [1996] JPL B138; EGCS 97. The applicant claimed that he had been granted permission to carry out works on a listed building; that at least part of the building was not listed; that the works did not affect the character of the building; and, further, that the remedial steps required would not restore the character of the building. The court dismissed the application, as s 64 of the Planning (Listed Buildings and Conservation Areas) Act 1990 prevented the applicant from challenging the validity of the notice other than by an appeal to the SoS.

19.4   THE POWERS OF THE SECRETARY OF STATE

The SoS may uphold, quash, or vary an enforcement notice, and he may grant planning permission for the development to which the notice relates, or he may determine the lawfulness of any development on the land and issue a certificate of lawfulness.

He is also empowered to correct any defect, error or misdescription in the enforcement notice or vary the terms of the notice if he is satisfied that the correction or variation will not cause injustice to the appellant or the lpa (s 176(1) TCPA 1990). This provides a wide remit for the SoS, and the courts have regarded these provisions as enabling the SoS to amend fundamental mistakes by the lpa in describing the alleged breach of planning control.

In *R v Tower Hamlets LB ex p Ahern (London) Ltd* [1989] JPL 757; 2 PLR 96; (1990) 59 P & CR 133, the company had temporary planning permission for a waste skip transfer station, and the application to continue the use was refused and an enforcement notice served. On appeal, the inspector decided that the notice was so defective as to be invalid and was incapable of correction without injustice; he quashed the notice. The company, which wished to have a speedy decision and did not want to be forced to go through the whole procedure for a second time, applied to the High Court. It was the company's contention that they would have suffered no injustice as they knew precisely what was being alleged against them and the steps the authority required them to take. It was held that the inspector was wrong in deciding that the error was incapable of being corrected and in considering that an injustice would be caused. The learned judge was of the opinion that '… the law had progressed to a point where the pettifogging had stopped, where artificial and nice distinctions understood by lawyers no longer prevailed'.

This decision contrasts with earlier cases where enforcement notices were held to be invalid because they were imprecise (see *Miller Mead v Minister Housing and Local Government* [1963] 2 QB 196; 2 WLR 225; All ER 459; *Burgess v Jarvis and Sevenoaks Rural*

District Council [1952] 2 QB 41; 1 All ER 592; 2 P & CR 377; and *Metallic Protectives v Secretary of State* [1976] JPL 166).

There has also been a significant change in the power granted to the SoS under s 191(2) whereby, when the time has expired for taking enforcement action, that is, the four- or 10-year rule, the uses become *lawful*. This reverses the rule set down in *LTSS Print and Supply Services Ltd v London Borough of Hackney* [1976] 1 QB 663; 2 WLR 253; 1 All ER 311 which established that an established use was not *lawful* but merely *immune from enforcement*.

The power granted to the SoS to vary or correct an enforcement notice under s 176(1) is constrained only by the requirement that he should be satisfied that his correction or variation does not cause injustice. In *Lynch, Patrick Charles v Secretary of State* [1999] JPL 354, the relevant part of the notice required the removal of a mobile home (see, also, para 19.10 below). The inspector amended the notice to mobile homes. This required the appellant to do more than would have been required had he not lodged an appeal and it was submitted that it was not open to the SoS to extend the requirements of the notice as this would involve an injustice. The court rejected these arguments and accepted that the SoS can widen or extend the scope of an enforcement notice providing that *he* is satisfied that it does not cause an injustice.

19.5 CHALLENGES TO THE SECRETARY OF STATE'S DECISION

The SoS's decision following an appeal against an enforcement notice may be referred to the courts under either s 288 or 289 (TCPA 1990). The two sections are subtly different and give rise to some confusion. Section 288 provides for an application to the High Court for the decision to be quashed, and s 289 for an appeal seeking that the matter be referred back to the SoS. It is of particular significance that the time limits for applications to the court differ. In the case of s 288, the period allowed is six weeks, whereas s 289 requires action within 28 days. In the case of s 288, a challenge be made by any person who is aggrieved, whereas under s 289 this right is restricted to the person who appealed to the SoS, the lpa or any other person having an interest in the land to which the notice relates.

For a fuller explanation of the operation of these sections, see Petchey, P, 'What a difference a day makes: a consideration of sections 288 and 289' [1997] JPL 511.

19.6 INSPECTOR'S ACTION: MULTIPLE ENFORCEMENT NOTICES

In *Bruschweiller v Secretary of State* [1996] JPL 292; (1994) EGCS 20; (1995) 70 P & CR 150, five separate enforcement notices were served relating to different parts of a group of redundant agricultural buildings. The inspector, in making his decision, considered the five notices collectively rather than dealing with each separately. His failure to look at each notice individually was regarded by the court as an error in law, and the matter was remitted to the SoS for further consideration.

19.7 STEPS TO REMEDY A BREACH OF CONTROL

One of the grounds of appeal against an enforcement notice is that the steps required by the lpa exceed what is necessary to rectify the breach (see ground (f), para 19.2, above). The principle that requirements should not be excessive is found in *Mansi v Elstree RDC* (1965) 16 P & CR 153; (1964) 62 LGR 172. Land was used as a plant nursery and included a number of greenhouses, one of which had been used since 1922 for the retail sale of products from the nursery. In 1959, the use of the greenhouse was intensified to the point that it became primarily a shop. The lpa served an enforcement notice requiring the discontinuance of the use for the sale of goods and, on appeal, the enforcement notice was upheld. The minister's decision was overruled in the courts on the grounds that he should have recognised that a notice which required the discontinuance of the sale of goods went too far. There was a need to safeguard the established right to carry on a retail trade in the manner and to the extent that it was carried on in 1959.

The *Mansi* principle is now well established in the law relating to enforcement, but there remained the question of whether a local authority could *under-enforce*, that is, the scope for discretion in specifying the steps to be taken to overcome the breach of control. In *Iddenden v Secretary of State* [1972] 3 All ER 883; 1 WLR 1433, it was clear that the lpa does have discretion, and, as in this case, it does not have to insist that the land is restored precisely to its previous condition. Under the 1990 Act (s 173(3)), provision is made for the local authority to specify steps to be taken or the activities which the authority requires to cease in order *wholly or partly* to achieve any of the following purposes:

(a) remedying the breach by making any development comply with the terms of any planning permission which has been granted in respect of the land, by discontinuing any use of the land or by restoring the land to its condition before the breach took place; or

(b) remedying any injury to amenity which has been caused by the breach.

The expression 'wholly or partly' is an addition to the powers previously granted to lpas, and effectively allows under-enforcement. The enforcement notice may also specify different periods for taking different steps (s 173(5)).

19.8 DATE OF EFFECTIVENESS OF AN ENFORCEMENT NOTICE

An enforcement notice must include a date on which the notice becomes effective but, in the event of an appeal, the date when the notice takes effect will await 'the final determination of the appeal' (s 175(4) TCPA 1990). This raised the problem: when and what is a final determination? When the SoS dismisses an appeal, should this be regarded as the commencement date? Or should allowance be made for an appeal to the courts on a point of law under s 289?

In *R v Kuxhaus* [1988] QB 631, it was reluctantly acknowledged that where an appeal was made to the court it had the effect of suspending the operation of the enforcement notice until the matter was finally determined by the courts. To deal with the problem of extending the time taken before the notice could become effective, sub-section (4A) was inserted in s 289 (TCPA 1990). Where an appeal is made to the courts against a decision of the SoS in relation to an enforcement notice, the High Court or the

Court of Appeal may order that the notice shall have effect as may be specified in the order, pending the final determination of the proceedings. This includes the remitting of the matter to the SoS for his re-hearing and re-determination because the courts have no power to quash or set aside an enforcement notice.

Clarification of this matter was achieved in *Dover DC v McKeen* [1985] JPL 627; 50 P & CR 250 when it was held that, if the appeal against the enforcement notice has been dismissed by the SoS, the enforcement notice took effect from that date of dismissal, and not at some future date when the time for appealing to the High Court had expired. This ruling from the court has been a further 'tightening' of the enforcement procedure. In *Bown (Roger) v Secretary of State* [1996] JPL B130, the applicant had started his activities without seeking planning permission, although he had had clear warnings from the lpa. The local authority alleged that the activity caused considerable harm in terms of safety and damage to the environment. In this instance, the court used its power (s 289(4A)) to direct that an enforcement notice should take effect pending the final determination of an appeal to the court against the SoS's decision to uphold the notice.

On occasions attempts have been made to stave off the effect of an enforcement notice by lodging a planning application for the contravening development. On prosecution in the magistrates' court for failure to comply with the enforcement notice, the individual would request that the criminal proceedings be adjourned pending the determination of the planning application. In *R v Beaconsfield Magistrates ex p South Buckinghamshire DC* [1993] 157 JPN 652, Straughton LJ stated:

> As a general rule magistrates should proceed to hear and determine the guilt or innocence of the defendant, not withstanding that a planning application has been recently presented. If the defendant has a defence or claims to have a defence, it should be tried and determined whether he is guilty or not ... where the planning application is to be determined shortly, the magistrates should also deal with the sentence in such cases and not adjourn them. They can, of course, take into account in considering the severity or lenience of any penalty the fact that a planning application is pending.

19.9   TWO ENFORCEMENT NOTICES ON LAND IN SAME OWNERSHIP

This issue of whether two enforcement notices can co-exist on land in the same ownership was raised in *Biddle v Secretary of State and Wychavon DC* [1999] JPL 835. The lpa served an enforcement notice in relation to the stationing of caravans and mobile homes on land for residential purposes. The appellant subsequently acquired land outside the scope of the first notice and this raised fears in the lpa that compliance with the notice would be achieved by moving the offending caravans and portacabins to the newly acquired site. The lpa, therefore, served a second notice covering what had now become the appellant's total land holding. The appellant's appeal was dismissed and it was argued in the High Court that no second notice could be validly served when there had been no breach on the newly acquired area of land and that two enforcement notices could not co-exist.

These arguments were rejected by the court. It was held that, in respect of the breach which had already been committed, there was no reason why there should not be a notice served in respect of the whole land which was the correct planning unit, even though a previous notice had been served. The court also held that there was no reason why two enforcement notices should not co-exist.

19.10 THE FOUR-YEAR IMMUNITY RULE

The application of the four-year immunity rule as it applies to dwellings was the issue in *Sage v Secretary of State* [2003] UKHL 22; 2 P & CR 346, which was finally resolved by the House of Lords as to when operations are substantially completed for the purpose of s 171(b) (TCPA 1990). Mr Sage started to build a house without applying for the necessary planning permission and in 1994, while the house was still incomplete, he ceased work. In 1999 the lpa issued and served an enforcement notice and on appeal Mr Sage argued (amongst other matters) that the enforcement notice had been served outside the four-year time limit. The inspector, in dismissing the appeal, concluded that the building was in the course of construction and the four-year period could only begin to run when the building was substantially completed. The High Court, in October 2000, held that the building works were only complete when the activities requiring planning permission were complete and quashed the inspector's decision on the ground that he had failed to consider whether the works needed to complete the dwelling amounted to 'development' as defined in s 55(2)(a) (TCPA 1990). The Court of Appeal agreed with the lower court and the matter was then taken to the House of Lords. The Law Lords unanimously disagreed with the earlier decision holding that the substantial completion of a building pursuant to s 171(b) is not dependent upon whether or not works which amount to 'development' remain to be carried out. Rather, the question is one of fact and degree as to whether the operation has been substantially completed and if so, when? The maintenance and improvement operations defined under s 55(2)(a) as not involving 'development', that is, the interior of a building or not materially affecting its external appearance can only be relied upon once a structure is complete.

Whilst a change of use to a single dwelling house becomes immune after four years, and this also applies to unauthorised change of use of a single dwelling house to self-contained flats, there is one exception. The ten-year immunity rule applies if the change of use was to a house in multiple occupation (see *Van Dyck v Secretary of State and Southend-on-Sea BC* [1993] JPL 565).

19.11 THE 10-YEAR IMMUNITY RULE

The 10-year immunity rule was the second issue arising from *Lynch, Patrick Charles v Secretary of State* [1999] JPL 354 (see para 19.4, above). The appellant acquired the land in 1985 and began to use it for his haulage recovery business and for his hobby of restoring old vehicles. In the late 1980s, the use of the land changed to include the stationing of caravans and portacabins which was more intensive and covered a greater part of the site. The appellant did, however, continue to use the land for his recovery vehicle business and his hobby. On appeal to the court, it was argued on behalf of the appellant that the vehicle recovery use and the hobby use should be excluded from the scope of the enforcement notice as they enjoyed immunity, having continued for 10 years.

The court did not agree with the appellant and held that these uses were superseded by the change of use that occurred in the late 1980s. This decision is, therefore, authority for the important proposition that, where there is a material change of use from a single use A to a mixed use A/B, such material change of use prevents time running in favour of A as a single use.

One of the anomalies of planning law results from the definition of 'material use' as modified by the Greater London Act 1973 (s 25) whereby use as temporary sleeping accommodation of any residential premises in Greater London involves a material change of use of the premises and each part thereof which is so used. The High Court decision of *R (on the application of Fairstate Ltd) v First Secretary of State, Westminster City Council* [2004] JPL 1636; EWHC 1807, the question arose as to how this affected the 10-year rule. An enforcement notice had been served alleging there had been a change of use with planning permission from permanent residential accommodation to short-term letting purposes, that is, temporary sleeping accommodation. There was an appeal on ground (d), that is, no enforcement action could be taken in respect of such a breach after the end of the period of ten years, beginning with the date of the breach.

The inspector had accepted that as at 3 January 1999 there had been a continuous breach of planning control for ten years during which period the premises had been used for temporary sleeping accommodation and thus it had become lawful. As there had been a change back to residential accommodation of a more permanent nature this immunity from enforcement had been lost and enforcement action could be taken against a change back to temporary sleeping accommodation. Sullivan J accepted that in a normal case this would only be so if the change back was itself a material change of use and he went on to say:

> If the change of use from X to Y is not material then, in the normal course of events, there would equally be no material change of use from use Y to use X. There would therefore, in those circumstances, be no development within the previous ten years on which any enforcement notice could bite.

However he went on to state on the basis of s 25 (Greater London Act 1975) that:

> Whether or not a change of use from Y to X amounts to a material change of use, the subsequent change from Y back to X is deemed to be a material change of use by virtue of the provisions of s 25. Thus there is a fresh change of use on which an enforcement notice can bite. It was therefore necessary for the inspector to decide whether the change in occupation was a material change of use ... he was correct to conclude that the change of use was material.

19.12 'SECOND-BITE' ENFORCEMENT ACTION

Section 171B(4)(b) (TCPA 1990) allows an authority a period of four years to take further enforcement action outside the four- and 10-year limits if they have already taken enforcement action within the initial time limits. This 'second-bite' action must be in respect of the same breach of planning control. Clarification of this requirement was given in *Jarmain v Secretary of State and Welwyn Hatfield DC* [1999] JPL 1106.

The appellant had temporary planning permission for a mobile home which he had transformed into a single-storey dwelling in 1993 without the council's knowledge. Subsequently, the temporary planning permission ran out in 1996 and the council issued an enforcement notice against him retaining the mobile home. In 1998, the council made a further discovery – the mobile home had become a permanent single-storey dwelling! They withdrew the first notice and issued a second alleging the unauthorised erection of a single-storey dwelling.

An appeal was lodged on the basis that the second notice was out of time and that the council could not rely on s 171(B)(4)(b) because the second notice had not been issued in respect of the same breach of planning control. The inspector dismissed the appeal. The court upheld the inspector's decision and stated that the sub-section did not require the breach to be identically described in both enforcement notices. It could *not* be used to cover two different developments or two different changes of use, but it *could* be used, as in this case, to cover two different descriptions of the same development.

19.13 THE EFFECT OF UNDER-ENFORCEMENT

Section 173(11) (TCPA 1990) provides, in effect, that planning permission is deemed to be granted for any development in respect of which enforcement action could have been taken, but was *not* taken under the same breach of planning control, provided that all the requirements of the notice have been complied with. The interpretation of this section was one issue addressed together with the validity of enforcement notices in *Tandridge DC v Verrechia* [1998] JPL B1, B27; [1999] 3 All ER 247.

The appellant carried on a dual use of his land for commercial car parking and waste dumping. The district council enforced against the car parking use and this action was upheld by the inspector and also through the courts. The county council enforced against the dumping of waste. Following the subsequent appeal, the inspector curiously decided to amend the notice to include car parking in the breach of control and, having done that, failed to specify any steps to remedy the car parking breach. It was argued on behalf of Mr Verrechia that the effect of this omission was to grant him planning permission for car parking use under s 173(11). He accordingly applied to the court to be released from the undertaking he had given to the district council not to continue this use. This was a sound argument and no doubt would have prevailed had the Court of Appeal not found that the notice which failed to specify any steps to remedy a specified breach of planning control could not be a valid enforcement notice. It therefore followed that the inspector's amendment to the notice was ineffective.

Whilst the case of *R v Rochdale MBC ex p Tew* [2000] JPL 54 primarily concerned a judicial review of matters related to the need, or otherwise, for an environmental statement (see Chapter 29, para 29.4), it also dealt with the enforceability of planning conditions. The applicants did not own all the land included in the outline planning application and it was envisaged that it would be necessary to make a Compulsory Purchase Order to assemble various ownerships. The objectors claimed that several conditions attached to the outline planning permission were invalid because they were unenforceable against these other landowners. In the view of the court, the right approach was to consider enforceability, not on the basis of what was theoretically possible, but on the basis of whether a person could reasonably be expected to comply with it. It was inconceivable that a landowner who derived no benefit from the development, and would be vigorously opposed to it, should be required to comply with an enforcement notice relating to that development affecting his land. The conditions in the present case were not unenforceable because of 'framework document (masterplan) which would ensure that the conditions could be enforced when the time came'.

19.14 THIRD PARTY APPLICATION FOR JUDICIAL REVIEW

If a member of the public wants to challenge a planning decision made by a government body and that person has sufficient standing they must file the claim promptly, or in any event, within three months of the decision being made. Prior to the decision of the House of Lords in *R (on application by Burkett) v Hammersmith and Fulham LBC* [EWHC 1031; [2004] 1 P 7 CR 7, it had been argued that the claim had to be submitted within three months of the date of the resolution of planning committee to grant planning permission. The House of Lords determined that the three-month time limit runs from the date of the permission.

The Court of Appeal in *R v Secretary of State ex p Chiltern DC Baber and Others* [1996] JPL 1034 dismissed an appeal against the High Court's decision upholding an application for a judicial review which was made by neighbours. The neighbours claimed that they were affected by the grant of planning permission by an inspector following an enforcement appeal relating to five enforcement notices, four of which involved the use of Shardeloes Farm, owned by Mr Williams, where it was alleged that an unauthorised change of use had occurred from agriculture to use as an equestrian centre. Appeals against all the enforcement notices were by way of written representations.

Mr Baber and 12 other respondents, who were owners and occupiers of properties in the neighbouring hamlet of Woodrow, had submitted written objections to use of the land as an equestrian centre. The inspector's decision was to grant planning permission for the centre. Mr Baber and the other respondents applied for leave to move for a judicial review of the decision on the basis that the inspector had erred in law by not considering an earlier appeal decision on a neighbouring farm where an application for an equestrian centre had been recently dismissed on appeal. They had no statutory right to appeal under s 289 (TCPA 1990) which is restricted to the appellant, the lpa or any person having an interest in the land. The application for judicial review under s 288, which is open to any person aggrieved and can include third parties, was dismissed. In upholding the decision of the lower court, the Court of Appeal held that the third parties have *no* statutory right of appeal under s 289. In passing comment on the case, Glidewell LJ stated that it is logical that, in enforcement appeals, those likely to be affected by the outcome should be able to challenge its legality in the courts, and he suggested that it would be a useful amendment to allow interested parties to use the provisions of s 289. To date, no action has been taken to amend the legislation as suggested by Glidewell LJ.

19.15 STOP NOTICES

There is no right of appeal against a stop notice, and failure to comply is a punishable offence. However, there remains the right to appeal against the enforcement notice, though this does not allow any person to act against the requirements of a stop notice.

There is, therefore, a general duty placed upon the authority to state precisely what activities are prohibited, but this may prove difficult where there is an alleged change of use.

In *R v Runnymede BC ex p Seehra* [1987] JPL 283; 53 P & CR 281, the authority issued an enforcement notice alleging a material change of use of the house to mixed residential and religious use. The enforcement notice prohibited the use for religious purposes 'otherwise than as incidental to the enjoyment of the dwelling house as such'. This was followed by a stop notice which reinforced the same restriction on the use of the premises. The problem is that participation in religious devotions by visitors may, up to an undefined point, be incidental to the enjoyment of the dwelling house. Mr Seehra complained that the stop notice placed him in a very difficult position: if he came to the wrong judgment, he might well be prosecuted; if he erred on the side of caution, he may deprive himself of something he was entitled to do. Schiemann J accepted that these were well-founded worries, but held that the notice was not null and void as it did give the applicant an indication of what he may, or may not do.

19.16 COMPENSATION FOR STOP NOTICES

The case of *Sample J (Warkworth) Ltd v Alnwick DC* [1984] JPL 670; 48 P & CR 474 is one of few cases involving compensation arising from the serving of a stop notice. In this instance, the builder was contracted to build a house at a fixed price for his clients. The council served an enforcement notice alleging that the erection of the dwelling had been undertaken without planning permission and required that it be demolished. A stop notice was served on the same day prohibiting any further building work on the site. The council subsequently granted planning permission, but did not withdraw either the enforcement or the stop notice. The enforcement notice was later quashed on appeal and, as a result, the stop notice ceased to be effective.

The Lands Tribunal held that compensation was payable for any loss directly attributable to the stop notice, which included:

(a) cost of idle time when the work force was taken off site;

(b) work required to rectify deterioration caused by delays;

(c) loss of interest on the purchase price of the house pending completion; and

(d) payments made by the claimants for temporary accommodation for their clients.

19.17 BREACH OF CONDITION NOTICES

As explained above, there is no right of appeal to the SoS against the serving of a BCN (see Chapter 18, para 18.3) and, after the period for compliance expires, failure to comply becomes a criminal offence punishable by a fine in the magistrates' court. The process would seem to be very straightforward and was designed to overcome the necessity to take action by the issuing of an enforcement notice. Unfortunately, in practice, this is not always the case. Circular 17/92, Annex 2, para 20 states:

> ... the validity of the notice or the validity of the local planning authority's decision to serve it may be challenged by application to the High Court for judicial review or by submissions to the magistrates' court in the event of prosecution of an offence. This

emphasises the advisability of only using the BCN when the contravening planning condition is legally valid; satisfies the criteria for the imposing of conditions stated in DoE Circular 1/85 (now replaced by Circular 11/95); and clearly, on the evidence available, has been breached. Failure to make certain that the condition in question is both valid and enforceable, before serving a BCN, may result in protracted litigation ... where the local planning authority foresees any scope for argument ... it is suggested that the issue of an enforcement notice may be more appropriate than the use of the BCN procedure.

In *R v Royal Borough of Kensington and Chelsea ex p Lawrie Plantation Services* [1997] JPL B128, the respondent council had issued a BCN in respect of two flats. When the planning permission for the conversion of the property into flats was granted in 1987, it was subject to a condition which required that:

The premises subject to this permission shall not be used at any time for any purpose specified in s 25 of the Greater London Council (General Powers) Act 1973 ...

The section provides that:

The use as temporary sleeping accommodation of any residential premises in Greater London involves a material change of use of the premises,

and defines 'use as temporary sleeping accommodation' as:

... use as sleeping accommodation which is occupied by the same person for less than 90 consecutive nights and which is provided (with or without services) for a consideration arising either:

(i)   by way of trade for money or money's worth; or

(ii) by reason of the employment of the occupant, whether or not the relationship of landlord and tenant is thereby created.

The issue to be determined by way of judicial review was whether the use of the flats as sleeping accommodation for occupation by employees of the applicant or its group for less than 90 days involved a breach of condition, and in particular whether the accommodation was provided for a consideration arising by reason of the employment of the occupant. There was no contractual right of occupation and there was no payment or other direct consideration provided for the occupation of the flats.

It was held, in quashing the notices, that the provision of accommodation as a gratuitous award for past performance did not constitute a valuable consideration for the purposes of the section, unless in a particular case there was evidence that earlier work, or service, had been carried out in consideration of the future provision of accommodation. Similarly, the judgment did not consider that the generalised objective of boosting company morale, or goodwill of the staff, would suffice as 'a consideration arising by reason of the employment of the occupant'. Leave to appeal was granted.

The appropriate time limits for enforcement action was the issue in *Bloomfield v Secretary of State* [1999] JPL October Update; 2 PLR 79. Planning permission was granted in 1992 which allowed the original building to be retained but to be used 'solely for recreational purposes during the months of April to October inclusive and shall not be used at any time for permanent residential accommodation'. The question was whether the unauthorised permanent use as a dwelling house was a material change of use or a breach of condition, for the purposes of s 171B(2) (TCPA 1990). That sub-section draws a distinction between the change of use of a building to use as a single dwelling house, for which the enforcement period is four years, and other non-operational breaches, for which the period is 10 years.

The court held that, given the physical characteristics of the building, it was clearly a dwelling house (see *Moore v Secretary of State* [1998] JPL 877; 2 PLR 65) and, following completion, it would have permission under s 75(3) for the purpose for which it was designed. Therefore, the breach of planning control was not a change of use to a dwelling house but a breach of the condition attached to the 1992 permission. This was governed by s 171B(3) rather than 171B(2) and was, therefore, subject to the 10-year rule.

The issue of time limits for enforcement action was also addressed in *Nicholson v Secretary of State* [1998] JPL 553. The High Court held that the relevant time for determining whether the time for taking enforcement action had expired is the time of the application under s 191. In this instance, it was necessary to find a continuous breach over a 10-year period. If non-compliance ceased by the discontinuance of the offending activity, the breach was at an end. If there was subsequently renewed non-compliance that would constitute a fresh breach.

If a successful challenge is made to the serving of a BCN, then the embarrassment of the lpa may be compounded by the award of costs against it.

It is not possible to take any action relating to a breach of condition where the planning permission has not been implemented (see *Handoll*, para 19.2, above).

19.18 INJUNCTIONS

The introduction of s 187B (TCPA 1990) marked a change in the attitude of the courts, which had previously been reluctant to issue injunctions in matters they considered were more properly dealt with under the enforcement powers specifically granted to lpas to take action against breaches of planning control. In *Harwood v Runnymede BC* [1994] JPL 724; 1 PLR 22, in the leading judgment by Dillon LJ, it was stated:

> The enactment of the section followed recommendations in the Carnwath Report. It is an important extension to the powers of the court and of the powers of planning authorities to enforce planning control in that it is exercisable whether or not the authority has exercised, or is proposing to exercise, any of their statutory powers.

In other words, the court only had to consider whether the criteria of s 187 had been satisfied, that is, whether the lpa considers it necessary or expedient for any actual or apprehended breach of planning control to be constrained by injunction.

The lpas' recourse to the use of injunctions was given further encouragement as a result of the Court of Appeal findings in *Hambleton DC v Bird and Another* (1995) 1 PLR 22; EGCS 67. In this case, gypsies had moved onto a site and established a camp without planning permission, and an enforcement notice was served and subsequently ignored after it had been upheld on appeal. The council applied to the county court for an injunction and failed as the judge took into account the following factors:

(a) the length of time the gypsies had occupied the site;

(b) the absence of alternative sites;

(c) a further planning application to remain on the site which had not yet been determined; and

(d) the public benefit which might be served from the grant balanced against the private harm which would result.

The Court of Appeal took a fundamentally different approach, and Pill LJ said:

> The granting of an injunction in any particular case is dependent upon the court's discretion. This does not, however, entitle a judge, in the present context, to act as a Court of Appeal against a planning decision or to base a refusal to grant an injunction upon his view of the overall public interest ... The learned judge was taking upon himself the policy function of the planning authorities and housing authorities and their powers and duties.

He concluded:

> I have no doubt the injunction should be granted. The respondents have demonstrated a plain and consistent intention to remain in residence on the farm and thereby break the law and continue to do so. This cannot, in the circumstances of this case, be tolerated.

These cases have marked a dramatic shift in the attitude of the courts to the granting of injunctions to overcome problems of planning enforcement. Injunctions are now an effective device for lpas, and equally they are difficult to resist from the point of view of landowners.

The issues arising from the actions of an lpa seeking an injunction as a supplement to enforcement action was addressed in *South Hams DC v Halsey* [1996] JPL 761. Three issues were raised in the consideration of this case:

1 whether the defendant could assert that the enforcement notice was a nullity;

2 whether the fact that he had been acquitted in the Crown Court on a prosecution under s 179 meant that the council's application for an injunction was an abuse of the process; and

3 whether the court lacked the power under s 178 to issue a mandatory injunction.

On the first point, it was accepted that the defendant could not attempt to show that the notice was invalid in his grounds of appeal to the SoS. For a claim to be admissible, there must be a defect in the notice which did not occur in this case. The further argument submitted by the defendant was that the notice was a nullity because it required him to carry out works which were unlawful, that is, the demolition of part of a listed building which had become listed after the enforcement notice had been served. The court drew attention to s 179(3), which provides as a defence that the defendant had done all he could be expected to do to ensure compliance, and in this case the action open to him was to apply for listed building consent.

On the second point, the High Court 'pulled rank' and merely commented that 'a wrong decision on a question of law in the Crown Court cannot bind the High Court, nor can it be an abuse of process for the council to seek an injunction'.

The third point was dismissed, and the court was clear that s 187B conferred a wider scope and application than was the case under the previous common law, and was wide enough to allow the grant mandatory injunctions.

In *R v Leeds City Council ex p Rodgers* [1997] JPL June Update, the applicants sought leave to appeal for judicial review of a resolution of the council to institute proceedings for an injunction against them under s 187B. The court refused leave as the council had clearly taken into account all the relevant matters, including the planning merits, and the council's procedures were in accordance with its duties. It was held that it was undesirable that judicial review proceedings should be used to duplicate, and very probably delay, the injunctive proceedings which had already been instituted. Moreover, the application had not been made promptly The resolution had been made in July 1996 and the application was not made until the following November, when the administrative decision had been taken by the council to implement the resolution. It was clear that it was the resolution to which a challenge should be made, and not the later decision.

The Court of Appeal, in upholding the injunctions in the case of *Croydon LBC v Gladden* [1994] JPL 729, made it clear that s 187(B) (TCPA 1990) permitted either a *mandatory* injunction used to prevent any future use or development in those circumstances where further breaches are apprehended, or the use of a *restraining* injunction used to restrain any existing use or development. The case involved a traditional semi-detached property occupied by Mr Gladden who, over a period of time, sought to make it distinctive by adding certain 'features' by way of:

- a 3.5-m-long fibre glass shark fixed to the roof;
- a large wooden replica of a spitfire aircraft, also fixed to the roof;
- outsize Christmas decorations (for a temporary period);
- large replicas of a military tank and a rocket missile in the front garden;
- a large inflatable figure of Sir Winston Churchill, which was also in the front garden;
- large notices which were described as offensive to the council (it is not clear whether it was the size or the content which caused offence, or both!).

Given the history of added 'features', the lpa was not surprisingly concerned as to what the future held, and were successful in obtaining injunctions restraining Mr Gladden from causing or permitting any structural alterations or additions to be affixed to the exterior of the building.

Useful guidance on the question of how an order must be framed was given in *Kettering BC v Perkins* [1999] JPL 166. An enforcement notice required the defendant to stop using his land for retail sales to the public of second-hand vehicle parts, save for sales at such a level as would be ancillary to the permitted use of vehicle dismantling and storage. An injunction was sought in the same terms and it was argued on behalf of the defendant that this was too vague and that the order should be delineated in terms of time and/or space, or otherwise. The High Court held that the injunction should be granted in the terms sought. Planning legislation provided a statutory scheme to control the use of land and that did not admit of absolute precision in all cases. There were many cases in which subjective judgments as to the ancillary nature of use might need to be considered.

The permissible territorial scope of planning injunctions was considered by the Court of Appeal in *Wealdon DC v Kruschandal* [1998] JPL October Update. This case concerned a mobile home stationed on land for residential purposes which was moved from one location to another by the landowner to evade restrictions placed upon its siting. The judge granted an injunction restraining the defendant from siting the mobile home for residential purposes on any land within the administrative area of the council without the benefit of planning permission.

In *Tandridge DC v Delaney* [1999] JPL 1074, B183, B185, one of the questions for the High Court was whether, having regard to Art 8 of the European Convention on Human Rights, an injunction should be granted.

The council sought a permanent injunction to prevent the defendants from using certain land for the stationing of mobile homes and caravans. There had been a five-day planning inquiry and the inspector concluded that the public interest should outweigh the defendants' interest and, therefore, upheld the enforcement notice. The court noted the ruling by the European Court of Human Rights in *Buckley v UK* [1995] JPL 633; JPL 1018. It was relevant to consider the exercise of the court's discretion as to whether an injunction to enforce confirmed enforcement notices would be in breach of Art 8, but at the same time the court must be careful not to usurp the functions of lpas and the SoS. The court found that the issuing of an injunction would not be disproportionate to the harm done because there was otherwise little, if any, prospect of compliance.

The House of Lords' judgments in *South Bucks DC v Porter*; and *Wrexham County BCv Berry* [2003] UKHL 26; 2 WLR 1547, clarified the impact of the Human Rights Act 1998 on councils' decisions whether to grant an injunction. Lord Bingham offered clarification on a number of points which the courts should consider when dealing with s 187B applications. His broad conclusion was;

> It is, however, ultimately for the court to decide whether the remedy sought is just and proportionate in all the circumstances.

He then went on to suggest four matters which merit attention:

(a) an injunction should not be granted if the court would be unwilling to imprison a defendant who subsequently breached the order, for example on grounds of ill health or being elderly;

(b it should be seen as a last-resort remedy;

(c) a court should not concern itself with matters of planning policy or jurisdiction vis-à-vis s 87B (TCPA 1990) but the court is not precluded from entertaining issues not related to planning policy or judgment.

(d) personal circumstances of an occupier, for example personal hardship. The difficulties of businesses which are of value to the character of a community are not to be ignored in the administration of planning control.

The Court of Appeal in *South Cambridgeshire DC v Persons Unknown* [2004] EWCA 1280 granted an injunction allowing the local authority to take action against unauthorised caravans occupied by travellers. In overturning the decision of the lower court Brooke LJ decided that although the case concerned what he described as a 'stricky area of law' the courts did have power to grant such an injunction.

CHAPTER 20

LISTED BUILDINGS AND CONSERVATION AREAS

20.1   INTRODUCTION

In this chapter, unless specified, all references relate to the Planning (Listed Buildings and Conservation Areas) Act (LBCAA) 1990 and the Planning (Listed Buildings and Conservation Areas) Regulations 1990 (SI 1990/1519). Further advice is contained in PPG15, 'Planning and the Historic Environment'.

The latter half of the 19th century saw the beginnings of a movement to ensure the protection of ancient buildings, structures and monuments. In 1877 William Morris founded the Society for the Protection of Ancient Buildings, and this led to the first measure of statutory protection, the Ancient Monument Protection Act 1882. The protection of buildings in daily use, as distinct from ancient monuments, was not afforded until the Planning Act 1932. Subsequent planning Acts included measures for the protection of individual buildings, but it was not until the Civic Amenities Act 1967 that protection was afforded to areas subsequently known as 'conservation areas'. This provision resulted to a large extent from a Court of Appeal decision (see *Earl of Iveagh v Minister of Housing and Local Government* 1 QB 395; [1963] All ER 817), which held that a building might be of special interest by reason of its setting as one of a group.

It is stressed that the listing of a building extends control over activities which would otherwise be exempt from control under s 55 of the Town and Country Planning Act (TCPA) 1990. Listing requires consent for the demolition of a listed building, or its alteration or extension in any manner likely to affect its character as a building of architectural or historic interest. The listing of a building at a date after the granting of an extant planning permission does not invalidate the need to seek listed building consent for works yet to be completed.

20.2   LISTING OF BUILDINGS

Following proposals set out in the consultation document 'Protecting the Historic Environment' in July 2003, the Department for Culture, Media and Sport (DCMS) published a paper, 'Review of Heritage Protection: the Way Forward' in June 2004. Many of the changes proposed will require amendment to primary legislation with government scheduling parliamentary time sometime in 2006/7! Fortunately not all the proposals require amendment to primary legislation and there are a number of measures that have already been introduced including:

(a) The assumption of the day-to-day administration of the system (but not the designation decisions) by English Heritage from April 2005. Changes to the list will remain subject to the approval of the Secretary of State (SoS).

(b) A review of the criteria for listing by the (DCMS)and English Heritage.

(c) The creation of a comprehensive pack for owners, including a 'summary of importance' setting out the reasons for listing, a map which indicates the extent of the listing and general information on designation and seeking planning consent. (Initially this will apply only to new listings).

The criteria for listing buildings are set out in PPG15 and if met, the SoS has no choice but to list the building. Under the Ancient Monuments and Archaeological Areas Act 1979 and PPG 16, more discretion is afforded as to whether to schedule a site meeting in order to assess the criteria for designation. This had been found to serve a useful purpose, as in many cases a management agreement or other voluntary agreement with the owner serves to secure the future of the site without the need for scheduling.

Although the SoS is empowered to act on his own initiative he relies heavily upon llpas, local amenity groups and individuals to inform him of buildings which may be considered for listing.

When considering whether to list a building, the SoS may consider not only the building itself but also:

(a) the contribution which the exterior makes to the architectural or historic interest of a group of buildings; and

(b) the desirability of preserving any feature fixed to the building or contained within its curtilage (s 1(3)).

Circular 8/87, 'Historic Buildings and Conservation Areas – Policy and Procedures' (Appendix I) sets out the principles for the selection of buildings to be considered for listing. These are:

(a) all buildings built before 1700 which survive in anything like their original condition;

(b) most buildings built between 1700 and 1840; and

(c) only buildings built between 1840 and 1914 which have definite quality and character, but selection should include works of the principal architects.

A number of outstanding buildings erected after 1939 are also listed, and particular attention is paid to:

(a) architectural or planning reasons, or illustrating social and economic history, for example, industrial buildings, schools, theatres, town halls;

(b) technological innovation or virtuosity, for example, cast iron, prefabrication;

(c) association with well known characters;

(d) the group value, especially as examples of town planning, for example, squares, terraces and model villages.

The buildings are classified in grades to show their relative importance, as follows:

• Grade I – buildings of exceptional interest;

• Grade II* – particularly important buildings of more than special interest;

• Grade II – special interest.

In considering the listing of a building the SoS may also take into account (s 1(3) LBCAA 1990):

(a) any respect in which its exterior contributes to the architectural or historic interest of any group of buildings of which it forms part, and

(b) the desirability of preserving, on the ground of its architectural or historic interest, any feature of the building consisting of a man-made object or structure fixed to the building or forming part of the land and comprised within the curtilage of the building.

Section 1(5) also provides that listing may apply to:

(c)   any object or structure within the curtilage of a building which, although not fixed to the building, forms part of the land and has done so since before July 1948.

The government's proposals suggest an amalgamation of Grade I and Grade II* to be renamed Grade I and the current Grade II will remain. It is likely that the majority of previous Grade II* buildings will be designated as Grade I, but some may be recategorised as Grade II.

At the present time when a building is considered for listing, scheduling or registration, the SoS is not required to inform the owner of his intention to do so, and there is no formal right of appeal at this stage. An owner who feels aggrieved can pursue the matter via an informal mechanism by requesting a second opinion from an inspector other than the one who made the original recommendation.

It is proposed that in the future (as yet unspecified) there should be a statutory right of appeal to the SoS for owners against the decision to designate or not to designate.

(NB For a full explanation of the government's proposals, see [2004] JPL 1360–1376.)

As stated above, when a building is considered for listing, the SoS is *not* required to inform the owner of his intention to do so, and there is no right of appeal at this stage. The 'secrecy' surrounding the inclusion of a building on the list is required as, with any prior notification, there is a distinct possibility that, in some cases, the building would 'disappear'. The SoS informs the lpa that the building is included on the list, and the authority is required to inform the owner and occupier. Once the building is listed, the only recourse open to the owner to challenge the listing is on appeal to the SoS following the refusal of listed building consent. which presents an opportunity to argue that the building was not worthy of listing in the first instance (see para 20.4, below).

Some protection against this current 'secret' method of listing is afforded to purchasers and intending developers as a result of s 6 of the LBCAA 1990. Where a planning application has been submitted, or permission has been granted for development involving the demolition or alteration of a building, an application may be made to the SoS for a certificate that he does not intend to list the building. If the SoS grants a certificate, he is precluded from listing the building within five years. This section has particular significance for developers who seek an opportunity to carry out redevelopment. It is not unknown for a scheme of redevelopment to be prepared which involves the demolition of a building or buildings, only to find that at the eleventh hour one or more buildings were included in the list of buildings to be conserved. The problem was compounded for the developer if he had actually acquired the buildings for the purpose of carrying out a redevelopment proposal and then found that he was responsible for their retention.

The whole purpose of the listing of a building is to prohibit demolition or alteration, without the applicant first gaining listed building consent from the lpa, and for the local authority to give special consideration to the effect upon listed buildings which could arise from nearby development.

Circular 14/97 provides for changes in the notification procedure in relation to Grade II non-starred buildings. English Heritage are to be notified at an earlier stage about major changes to such buildings and various minor changes are no longer notifiable.

20.3   ECCLESIASTICAL BUILDINGS

The Ecclesiastical Exemption (Listed Buildings and Conservation Areas) Order 1994 (SI 1994/1771) provides exemption for buildings of the Church of England, Church of Wales, Roman Catholic Church, Methodist Church, the Baptist Union of Wales and the United Reformed Church (Art 4) and university chapels, Church of Scotland, Free Church of Scotland and the Free Presbyterian Church (Art 6). The exemption granted under s 60(1) is restricted to 'any ecclesiastical building which is for the time being used for ecclesiastical purposes' and relates to any:

(a) church building;

(b) object or structure within a church;

(c) object or structure fixed to the exterior of a church (unless it is a listed building in its own right); or

(d) object or structure within the curtilage of a church which, although not fixed to the building, forms part of the land (unless it is a listed building in its own right) (Art 5.3).

The exemption granted means that any ecclesiastical building which may be listed in the normal way is not subject to the controls under the Act so long as it remains in that use. It is, however, not exempt from the requirement under the Act to obtain planning permission for works which constitute 'development'.

The 1994 Order removed the ecclesiastical exemption from religious organisations which did not subscribe to the following Code of Practice agreed by the SoS:

1   All proposals for:

   (i)   internal and external works for the demolition, alteration or extension of a listed church building which would affect its character as a building of architectural or historic interest; and

   (ii) works of demolition affecting the exterior of an unlisted church building in a conservation area,

   should be submitted for approval to a body which is independent of the local congregation or community proposing the works.

2   The decision-making body, when considering the proposals for works, should be under a specific duty to take into account, along with other factors, the desirability of preserving church buildings, and the importance of protecting features of architectural or historic merit.

3   The body should include, or have arrangements for obtaining advice from, persons with expert knowledge of historic church buildings.

4   The process should make provision for:

   (a) consultation with the local planning authority, English Heritage, national amenity societies, etc, giving 28 days in which to comment;

   (b) proposals to be advertised by means of a site notice and a similar notice in a local newspaper circulating in the area; and

   (c) in cases of demolition, notification to the appropriate Royal Commission on Historical Monuments, whose comments are to be taken into account before the decision is made.

5   There should be a clear and fair procedure for settling disputes between the local congregation and the decision-making body.

6   The procedures set up by the church authority should include arrangements for dealing with any breach of the control system, including provision for the reinstatement of works to historic church buildings carried out without consent.

7   To permit effective monitoring, the church body should make arrangements for recording for each proposal how the above procedures were implemented, and the nature of the decision taken.

Similarly, the provisions of the Act also do not apply to ancient monuments (s 61(1) LBCAA 1990). It is possible that a building may be both listed under the Act *and* be a scheduled monument under the Ancient Monuments and Archaeological Areas Act 1979. Where such situations occur, the provisions of the 1979 Act take precedence. Under that Act, it is an offence, without prior grant of scheduled monument consent, to carry out any:

(a) works resulting in the demolition or destruction of or any damage to a scheduled monument;

(b) works for the purpose of removing or repairing a scheduled monument or any part of it, or making alterations or additions; and

(c) flooding or tipping operations on land in, on or under which there is a scheduled monument.

20.4   LISTED BUILDING CONSENT

When a building is listed (s (5) LBCAA 1990), in addition to the exterior and interior (s 1(5)) of the building itself, the following are to be treated as part of the building:

(1) any object or structure fixed to the building; and

(2) any object or structure within the curtilage of the building.

It is an offence to execute any works for the demolition of a listed building, or for works which would affect its character as a building of special architectural or historic character, without first obtaining listed building consent (s 9). In other words, one should 'not touch a hair on the maiden's head' without first gaining prior approval.

Listed building consent (s 10(1)) is quite distinct and separate from the need to gain planning permission, which may be required if the proposal amounts to 'development' (see Chapters 6 and 7). In such cases, simultaneous applications will be required by the lpa, but listed building consent does not require the submission of an application fee. There is a special form to be used in making an application for listed building consent (ss 10 and 11). Where it is proposed to demolish, extend or alter a Grade I or Grade II* building, a notice must be given to English Heritage to enable them to inspect and record details of the building. This requirement is mandatory, and failure on the part of the lpa to inform English Heritage will result in the grant of listed building consent being quashed.

The prohibition also applies to works which would affect the character of the building, which do not fall within the definition of development or constitute permitted development (see Chapter 10). As noted above, the listing of a building also extends to its interior and, therefore, the prohibition could apply to any action which would affect the internal character. This is particularly difficult to police, and there is no formal machinery which would allow the owner or occupier to request a determination as to whether the lpa consider the proposed action would, in its opinion, affect the character of the building.

Applications for listed building consent must be made to the lpa on a form available from the authority and must be accompanied by a plan identifying the building and such other plans/drawings as are required to describe the proposed works. It is *not* possible to submit an outline application. Following the receipt of an application for listed building consent the lpa is responsible for publicising the application in a local newspaper and placing a notice on or near the site and must take account of any representations received before determining the application. The local authority may grant listed building consent subject to conditions reserving details of the works for their subsequent approval (s 17(2)). Such conditions may only be discharged, or a variation of condition sought, by a person having 'an interest in the listed building'. Without prejudice to this general power s 16(1) listed building consent may be granted subject to conditions which relate to:

(a) the preservation of particular features of the building, either as part of it or after severance from the building;

(b) the making good after the works are completed of any damage caused to the building by the works; and

(c) the reconstruction of the building or any part of it following the execution of works with the use of original materials as far as is practicable and with such alterations of the interior of the building as may be specified.

Application for the demolition of a listed building or a building in a conservation area may be granted subject to conditions which require that:

(a) a contract for the carrying out of works for the redevelopment of the site has been made prior to demolition; and

(b) planning permission has been granted for the redevelopment for which the contract provides.

As with planning permissions, listed building consents must be begun within a period of three years or such other period as the local authority consider appropriate. Similarly appeals against the refusal of listed building consent, or against any condition attached to the consent, must be lodged within six months of the decision.

The SoS has power to direct lpas to notify specific persons of any applications for listed building consent and to inform them of their decision (s 15(5)) and this is in addition to the provisions of s 13 which requires the local authority to inform the SoS of any listed building application which they proposed to grant. This general requirement is limited by Circular 14/97 which absolves the local authority from notifying the SoS of applications relating to Grade II buildings unless there are major works, for example the demolition of an external wall.

20.5 BUILDING PRESERVATION NOTICE

If it appears to an lpa that a building which is not listed is in danger of demolition or alteration in a manner which will affect its character, the authority may serve on the owner and occupier a building preservation notice (s 3(1) LBCAA 1990). In cases of urgency, the local authority may fix the notice to the building instead of a serving notice (s 3(2)). The notice comes into force immediately and shall remain in force for six months, and shall cease to remain in force when either the SoS includes the building on the list or notifies the lpa that he does not intend to do so (s 3(3)). If the SoS fails to make a determination within six months, the notice automatically lapses (s 3(3), (4)). If the SoS states that he does not intend to confirm the notice or fails to take any action, the lpa shall serve a notice that, within a period of 12 months from the date of notification, no further building preservation notice will be served (s 3(7)).

20.6 REVOCATION AND MODIFICATION

The lpa or the SoS may revoke or modify a listed building consent if they consider it expedient to do so, having regard to the development plan and any other material considerations, but this only applies where the works authorised by the listed building consent have not been completed (s 23). If this action is taken by a local authority, it must submit it to the SoS for confirmation, and he is required to hold a public local inquiry or other hearing before deciding what action to take (s 24). In the case of an unopposed order, the local authority is required to advertise the order to give other parties the opportunity to object and be heard by the SoS (s 25). If there are no objections, the order is confirmed by the lpa.

Where an order is confirmed, the lpa is liable to pay compensation for abortive expenditure and for any other loss directly attributable to the revocation (s 28). Compensation is not payable to persons who did not object to the making of the order.

20.7 ENFORCEMENT

An lpa may issue a listed building enforcement notice specifying the steps to be taken (s 38 LBCAA 1990);

(a) for restoring the building to its former state; or

(b) where such restoration would not be reasonably practicable, or would be undesirable, such works as the lpa consider necessary to alleviate the effect of the works carried out without consent; or

(c) for bringing the building to the state it would have been in if the terms and conditions of the listed building consent had been complied with.

Copies of the notice are to be served on the owner and occupier of the building and any person having an interest in the building (s 38(4)). Any of these persons may appeal to the SoS against the notice on the grounds that (s 39(1)):

(a) the building is not of special architectural or historic interest;

(b) the matters alleged do not constitute a contravention or do not involve a contravention;

(c) the contravention alleged has not taken place;

(d) the works were urgently necessary in the interests of health, safety or the preservation of the building;

(e) the listed building consent should be granted or the relevant condition discharged;

(f) copies of the notice were not served as required by s 38(4);

(g) the requirements of the notice exceed what is necessary to restore the building to its condition before the works started;

(h) the period allowed falls short of what may be reasonably allowed;

(i) the steps required for the purpose of restoring the building would not serve that purpose; or

(j) the further works required to alleviate the effect of the works carried out exceed what is necessary.

The appeal must be lodged with the SoS before the date on which the enforcement notice takes effect.

The demolition or alteration of a listed building without consent, or in breach of conditions attached to a consent, is a punishable offence either by way of fine and/or imprisonment. This contrasts with the carrying out of development without prior planning permission, which only becomes an offence if and when the lpa institutes its enforcement powers. The 1991 Planning and Compensation Act increased the level of fine to £20,000, and the maximum term of imprisonment to two years. In determining the amount of any fine, the court is to have regard to any financial benefit accruing from the offence.

20.8   REPAIR AND ACQUISITION OF LISTED BUILDINGS

The owner of a building which is listed does not have direct obligation to repair the building, but the lpa or the SoS are empowered to take action if the building falls into disrepair. Under s 54 (LBCAA 1990), the lpa may take emergency action where a listed building, which is wholly or partly unoccupied, requires repair. After giving seven days' notice (s 54(6)) of the work required to the owner, the local authority may enter the building and carry out the necessary repairs of that part which is unoccupied (s 54(4)). The local authority may subsequently serve a notice on the owner to recover the cost of the works. This notice can be appealed against within 28 days of its receipt on the ground that some or all of the works were unnecessary, that the amount specified is unreasonable, or that recovery of that amount would cause financial hardship.

It is also possible for the SoS or the lpa to use powers under s 47 compulsorily to acquire a listed building which is not kept in a reasonable state of repair, whether that building is occupied or not. The SoS or the local authority must have served a repairs notice on the owner specifying the works required to ensure proper conservation at least two months before commencing compulsory purchase action (s 48). The notice does not impose any obligation on the owner to carry out the works, but it does provide an indication of the likely costs which could be involved, and no doubt this would be taken into account in establishing the value of the property if the compulsory purchase action is carried out. Alternatively, it provides a check as to whether reasonable steps have been taken by the owner if he decides to carry out the work. The amount of compensation will be reduced where the owner had deliberately allowed the building to fall into disrepair to justify its demolition with the intention of redeveloping the site. In these circumstances, the acquiring authority may request the

SoS to issue a 'direction for minimum compensation'. This would only apply if there is no likelihood of planning permission and/or listed building consent being granted for the redevelopment of the site. There is a right of appeal to the magistrates' court, which may quash the direction.

Compulsory purchase action must follow the requirements set down in the Acquisition of Land Act 1981, and the owner or lessees have a right of objection (s 47(2)). There is also the right of appeal to the magistrates' court on the ground that reasonable steps are being taken properly to preserve the building and, if the magistrates are persuaded that this is the case, the compulsory purchase order will be stayed (s 47(4)).

20.9   PURCHASE NOTICE

If the refusal of listed building consent renders the land incapable of any beneficial use, the owner may be able to serve a 'listed building purchase notice' on the lpa. This can only be done when the owner claims that the following conditions are satisfied:

(a) the land has become incapable of reasonably beneficial use in its existing state;

(b) if consent was granted with conditions, that the land cannot be rendered capable of reasonably beneficial use by carrying out the works required by these conditions; or

(c) that the land cannot be rendered capable of any beneficial use by carrying out any other works for which listed building consent has been granted.

The Court of Appeal in *Braun v First Secretary of State and Another* [2003] JPL 1536; EWCA 665, highlighted the possibility that purchasers of listed buildings may have to restore works carried out by previous owners without consent. The case arose following the serving of an enforcement notice requiring new owners to remedy not only recent alterations carried out by themselves but also works completed by the previous owners in 1970. In reversing the decision of the High Court Simon LJ advised prospective purchasers of listed buildings to check that all the necessary consents had been obtained for any work. Nevertheless, the court quashed the enforcement notices on the grounds that it was not sufficiently clear in informing the owners that it related to all unauthorised works and not just those that they had carried out.

20.10 CONSERVATION AREAS

The Civic Amenities Act 1967 introduced the concept of 'conservation areas', and lpas were required to consider which parts of their areas were of special architectural or historic importance. This concept is now embodied in the LBCAA 1990 (s 69(1)), which requires that, from time to time, an lpa is to consider which parts, if any, of its area should be declared a conservation area (s 69). It should be noted that the Act does not require an lpa to *declare* conservation areas; it requires authorities to *consider* whether they wish to declare such areas. Nevertheless, there has been an enthusiastic response which, no doubt, reflects the growing interest in the environment displayed by politicians and public alike. In addition to district councils, county councils may declare conservation areas, but they are required to consult with the district authority

(Sched 4, para 4(2)). In London, English Heritage operates concurrent powers with the London borough councils (s 70(1)).

The procedure for declaring conservation areas is very simple. After defining the boundaries of the area on a map, the planning authority can determine, by resolution of council, that the area is a conservation area. The SoS's approval is *not* required, but the lpa must give him formal notice of an area designated as a conservation area, and publish the notice in the *London Gazette* and a local newspaper (s 70(5)). This method of approval differs from that required for the approval of local plans 3.11 and it is for this reason that conservation area designation cannot occur as part of the process of local plan preparation.

Although the method of designating a conservation area is quite independent of the adoption of a local plan, it is vitally important that the two are considered as an integral part of the proposals for an area if the object of preserving and enhancing the character and appearance of the conservation area is to be achieved. It is important that the overall plan for an area should encourage the continued uses within the area to be conserved and, furthermore, to encourage investment in such areas if the building fabric is to be maintained. The survival, let alone the preservation and enhancement, of many such areas will only be achieved if the economic circumstances are created to ensure continuing investment.

Conservation areas are defined as (s 69(1):

... areas of special architectural or historic interest the character or appearance of which is desirable to preserve or enhance.

Having declared a conservation area, it is the duty of the authority to (s (71(1)):

... formulate and publish proposals for the preservation and enhancement of any parts of their area which are conservation areas.

The proposals must be published and submitted to a public meeting in the area and, before finalising the proposals, the lpa must have regard to any views expressed at that meeting (s 72(2) and (3)). The authority may, if it so wishes, subsequently decide to cancel the designation of a conservation area simply by resolution of the council (s 70(5)).

Having declared a conservation area, the lpa is encouraged, but not obliged, to establish a conservation area advisory committee, which should mainly consist of persons who are not elected members of the council, and to refer to them for advice on applications which the authority consider are likely to have an effect upon the conservation area. It is also suggested that the advisory committee could have a role in helping to formulate policies for the enhancement of the area (see Circular 8/87, 'Historic Buildings and Conservation Areas').

Land in a conservation area may not be included in a Simplified Planning Zone (s 87 TCPA 1990).

20.11 DEVELOPMENT CONTROL IN CONSERVATION AREAS

Applications for planning permission which are likely to affect the character or appearance of a conservation area must be advertised by the lpa (s 73 LBCAA 1990) by a notice on the site and an advertisement in a local newspaper. When considering the application, the lpa must pay special attention to the desirability of preserving or enhancing the character or appearance of the area (s 72).

20.12 ADVERTISEMENTS IN CONSERVATION AREAS

The general regulations in relation to advertisements are made by the SoS under powers granted by s 220 of the TCPA 1990, and s 221 gives further power to make different advertisement regulations for different areas, and in particular may make special provision (s 221(1)) with respect to:

(a) conservation areas;

(b) areas defined for the purposes of the regulations as experimental areas; and

(c) areas defined for the purposes of the regulations as areas of special control.

Experimental areas are defined for a prescribed period for the purposes of assessing the effect on amenity or public safety of advertisements of a prescribed description (s 221(2) TCPA 1990).

An area may be defined as an area of special control (s 221(3)) if it is:

(a) a rural area; or

(b) an area which appears to the SoS to require special protection on the grounds of amenity.

The Town and Country Planning (Control of Advertisements) Regulations 1992 (SI 1992/666) make provision for the designation of areas of special control but do *not* make special provision for conservation areas. There is, however, no reason why a conservation area cannot be designated as an area of special control (see Chapter 24, para 24.6).

20.13 TREES IN CONSERVATION AREAS

The designation of a conservation area automatically provides protection for most trees within the area irrespective of whether they are the subject of Tree Preservation Orders (TPOs). For details of TPOs and trees in conservation areas, see Chapter 22, para 22.7.

20.14 CONTROL OF DEMOLITION

Within a conservation area, there may well be listed buildings which are subject to control as outlined above (para 20.2) and which cannot be demolished without the grant of listed building consent. There will, however, be many buildings within the conservation area which are not worthy of listing in their own right but the demolition of which would have an adverse affect upon the general character of the area. Control over demolition of buildings within a conservation area is, therefore, extended (ss 74 and 75 LBCAA 1990) to all buildings within the area and 'conservation area consent' is required before demolition can proceed.

The following exemptions were introduced by Circular 14/97, para 28:

(a)   any building with a total cubic content not exceeding 115 cubic metres (measured externally) or any part of such building, other than a pre-1925 tombstone;

(b)   any gate, wall, fence or means of enclosure which is less than one metre high where abutting on a highway (including a public footpath or bridleway), waterway or open space, or less than two metres high in any other case;

(c)   any building erected since 1 January 1914 and in use, or last used, for the purposes of agriculture or forestry;

(d)   any building required to be demolished by virtue of an order made under s 102 of the principal Act;

(e)   any building required to be demolished by virtue of any provision of an agreement made under s 106 of the principal Act;

(f)   any building in respect of which the provisions of an enforcement notice issued under s 172 of the principal Act, or s 38 or 46 of the Act requiring its demolition, in whole or part, however expressed;

(g)   any building required to be demolished by virtue of a condition of a planning permission granted under s 70 or s 177(1) of the principal Act;

(h)   any building required to be demolished by virtue of a notice served under s 215 of the principal Act;

(i)   any building to which a demolition order made under Part IX of the Housing Act 1985 applies;

(j)   any building included in a compulsory purchase order made under the provisions of Part IX of the Housing Act 1985 and confirmed by the Secretary of State; and

(k)   any redundant building (within the meaning of the Pastoral Measure 1983) or part of such a building where demolition is in pursuance of a pastoral redundancy scheme (within the meaning of that scheme).

20.15 DEVELOPMENT IN CONSERVATION AREAS

Once a conservation area has been designated by an lpa, it falls within the definition of Art 1(5) of the Town and Country Planning (General Permitted Development) Order (GPDO) 1995 (SI 1995/418) (see Chapter 10). The lower limits of permitted development will apply, and the lpa may also further restrict permitted development rights by the use of powers granted under an Art 4 Direction (see Chapter 10, para 10.2).

In conservation areas, the intention is to 'conserve' and not necessarily 'preserve', all the existing buildings within the area. In considering development proposals within conservation areas, lpas are charged to ensure that (s 72(1) LBCAA 1990):

... special attention shall be paid to the desirability of preserving and enhancing the character and appearance of that area.

Planned change is perfectly acceptable, and PPG 15, 'Planning and the Historic Environment', provides useful guidance for lpas in determining planning applications within such areas. The status as a conservation area is a material consideration in determining planning applications within the area, and, therefore, the lpa should seek to ensure that any new development accords with the area's special architectural and historic interest. PPG 15 provides the following advice:

Many conservation areas will have gap sites, or buildings which make no positive contribution to, or indeed detract from, the character and appearance of the area; their replacement should be a stimulus to imaginative, high quality design, and be seen as an opportunity to enhance the area [para 4.17].

If any proposed development would conflict with that objective (preserving and enhancing), there will be a strong presumption against the grant of planning permission, though in exceptional circumstances the presumption may be overridden in favour of development which is desirable on the ground of some other public interest [para 4.19].

The lpa is required to advertise in the local press applications for development which it considers will affect the character and appearance of the area (s 73) and to display a notice on or near to the land to which the application relates. The public have the right to inspect the details of the application and to make representations to the lpa, which should be considered before the application is determined.

20.16 ANCIENT MONUMENTS AND ARCHAELOGICAL SITES

Protection for ancient monuments and archaeological sites is afforded under the Ancient Monuments and Archaeological Areas Act 1979, which defines a monument as any:

(a) building, structure or work, whether above or below the surface of land and any cave or excavation;

(b) site comprising the remains of such a building, structure or work or any cave or excavation;

(c) comprising or comprising the remains of, any vehicle, vessel, aircraft, or other moveable structure or part thereof which neither constitutes nor forms part of any work which is a monument within paragraph (a) above.

Under s 3 of the Ancient Monuments and Archaeological Areas Act 1979 the SoS may make an order allowing the execution of works and s 5(1) allows the SoS to enter a site and carry out necessary works at his own expense. He is also given the power to acquire such sites or alternatively he may assume responsibility for the site without disturbing the existing ownership.

In the preparation of a development plan lpas should include policies for the protection, preservation and enhancement of archaeological sites (see PPG 16, 'Archaeology and Planning'). Where development is proposed involving a site which is not scheduled as an ancient monument the lpa may impose a negative condition preventing development until such time as an archaeological investigation has taken place (see PPG 16 for a model condition). Alternatively the developer may enter into an obligation under s 106 (TCPA 1990) for the purpose of restricting the development or use of the land and he may also undertake to provide funding for the facilities to allow an investigation of the site.

20.17 HISTORIC PARKS, GARDENS AND BATTLEFIELD SITES

English Heritage has compiled a Register of those parks and gardens which form an important part of the cultural heritage of England, and they are categorised in the same manner as listed buildings. The Register does not, however, provide additional powers of control but Art 10(1), para (6) GDPO 1995 requires that the lpa consults English Heritage before granting planning permission for any development affecting Grade I or Grade II* historic parks and gardens.

There is a similar Register compiled by English Heritage for battlefields and the fact that they appear in the Register requires that they should be a material consideration in determining planning applications which affect them.

20.18 WORLD HERITAGE SITES

Perhaps surprisingly there are no special controls over World Heritage Sites other than the legal protection afforded by listing or the establishment of conservation area status and the preparation of a management plan. The outstanding international importance of such sites must be taken into account as a material factor by lpas in determining planning applications affecting such sites.

20.19 FINANCIAL ASSISTANCE

Limited financial assistance is available from central government for the preservation and enhancement of conservation areas. English Heritage (in Wales, the SoS) may make a loan or grant for work which makes a significant contribution towards preserving or enhancing the character or appearance of a conservation area (s 77 LBCAA 1990). Such financial assistance is usually related to work:

(a) involving a building of particular architectural or historic importance for which the lpa has been invited to submit a programme of conservation work;

(b) involving a scheme of conservation work prepared by lpas, amenity groups, preservation societies or a group of private owners; or

(c) where there is a 'town scheme' in operation.

The provision for 'town schemes' is contained in s 79. The scheme takes the form of a partnership agreement between English Heritage and the district and county council. Under the agreement, the parties will set aside a specified annual sum of money to be used for making grants for the repair of buildings included in the town scheme. When a grant or loan is made, the owner of the property is required to carry out the work in accordance with specifications laid down by the local authority. The fact that the sum is agreed annually and, therefore, varies from year to year, can cause problems in the selection of projects, as it is often difficult to programme the priority to be given to a particular project.

CHAPTER 21

LEGAL CHALLENGES TO LISTED BUILDINGS AND CONSERVATION AREAS

21.1 INTRODUCTION

Although the concept of conserving the environment is now widely accepted both by the government and the general public, the legislation designed to achieve this object has over the years been the subject of many legal challenges, partly because the listing of buildings and the declaration of conservation areas may well involve a degree of subjective judgment. What may be a distinctive building in one area may well be of lesser significance in another and, likewise, what is regarded as an area worth conserving will vary according to the location and general character of the surroundings. There are also fundamental questions relating to listed buildings and conservation areas on which the courts have been required to pass judgment.

Unlike other areas of planning control (see Chapter 18) there is no time limit for enforcing against breaches of listed building control and successive owners are not immune from such action.

21.2 WHAT IS A BUILDING?

To qualify for listing, the 'object' must qualify as 'a building which is of special architectural or historic interest'. This begs the question: what is a building? The Town and Country Planning Act (TCPA) 1990 provides a wide definition of a 'building' (s 336(1)):

> ... *any* structure or erection, and any part of a building, as so defined, but does not include plant or machinery comprised in a building.

As a result, a wide variety of 'structures and erections' have qualified for listing, and these include village pumps, milestones, Automobile Association boxes and lych gates.

The fact that any building can be listed was made abundantly clear in *Amalgamated Investment and Property Co v John Walker and Sons Ltd* [1976] 3 All ER 509, when Buckley J stated:

> It seems to me that the risk of property being listed as property of architectural or historic interest is a risk which inheres in all ownership of buildings.

21.3 THE EXTENT OF LISTING

In addition to the building, the Secretary of State for Culture, Media and Sport may take into account:

> The desirability of preserving, on the ground of its architectural or historic interest, any feature of the building consisting of a man-made object or structure fixed to the building or forming part of the land and comprised within the curtilage of the building [s 1(3)(b) Planning (Listed Buildings and Conservation Areas) Act (LBCAA) 1990],

and that the following should be treated as part of the building:

(a)   any object fixed to the building; and

(b)   any object or structure within the curtilage of the building, but only if it has been within the curtilage since before 1 July 1948 [s 1(5)].

The listing of a building requires a record of the description of the building and the significance of the wording of the description was considered by the House of Lords in *City of Edinburgh v Secretary of State for Scotland* [1997] 3 PLR 71, where it was held that the description does no more than provide an aid to its identification and any features not noted in the description are nevertheless part of the listing.

The need for precise interpretation of these sections has resulted in numerous appeals to the courts to determine the meaning of 'fixed' and 'curtilage'. Perhaps fortunately, there does not appear to have been a challenge on the issue of what is 'man-made'! The principle is that every part of a listed building is, in law, equally listed, not merely the exterior. All the features in the interior which are regarded in law as 'fixed' are included in the listing, irrespective of whether or not they were added later and are attractive or unattractive elements, or may even be considered to detract from the character of the interior.

In *Corthorn Land and Timber Co Ltd v Minister of Housing and Local Government* (1965) LGR 490; (1966) 17 P & CR 210 a building preservation order requiring that a mansion should not be demolished also listed items which should not be altered or removed, and these included portrait panels, carved oak panels, a large wood carving and a large wooden equestrian figure on the main landing. The court rejected the application by the owner to quash the order, holding that all the items were fixtures as that phrase was commonly applied in law, that is, definitely affixed to the building and, therefore, not easily removed.

In *R v Secretary of State for Wales ex p Kennedy* [1996] JPL 645; 1 PLR 97, the High Court upheld enforcement notices requiring the return and restoration *in situ* of a carillon clock and three chandeliers. The court accepted that the definition of a 'fixture' was the same for the purposes of a listed building as for any other area of law and, hence, the relevant tests were the degree and purpose of annexation of the article to the land or to the structure of the building. The court also held that the submission that the clock should be regarded as an item of 'machinery', and, therefore, excluded from the definition of a building under s 336(1) (TCPA 1990), was untenable.

The degree and purpose of the annexation was the issue in the controversy over the removal of the statue known as 'The Three Graces' from the tempietto at Woburn Abbey. The Secretary of State (SoS) indicated that he did not intend to take listed building enforcement action. Save Britain's Heritage then applied to the court for a judicial review of the decision. The matter was referred back to the SoS who took further advice and concluded:

> The tests, although easily stated, are not so easily applied. The degree of annexation was not great. The plinth upon which the statue stood was fastened to the floor, but apparently not in such a way as to make the removal particularly difficult. The statue itself was free-standing. As to the purpose of annexation, the Secretary of State now takes the view that even accepting that the tempietto was specifically built or modified to house the statue, that does not of itself mean that the statue became part of the building ... it seems to him that the object or purpose of installing the statue in the tempietto was not to dedicate it to the land or incorporate it into the land, but to show off the statue.

Whether the removal or alteration of a fixture requires listed building consent will depend upon whether the works will affect the character of the building as a building of architectural or historic interest and this remains an area of concern as exemplified by the following two cases.

A Ministerial decision upheld an enforcement notice issued by Harborough District Council to secure the reinstatement of seven paintings by the Italian artist Pannini in Noseley Hall ([1991] JPL 1145). He accepted the inspector's conclusion that the fixing of paintings with screws and similar fixing or the possible embedding of the paintings into the mantel plaster provided sufficient connection to the building. Furthermore their purpose had been to enhance the beauty of the study and they were integrated into the internal décor of the 18th century study and thereby became part of the building and as such were regarded as part of the listing. However, a further enforcement notice with regard to two 18th century paintings was quashed. Whilst the inspector found they passed the test of 'attachment' they had not been installed 'for the purpose of creating a beautiful room as a whole'.

21.4   LISTED BUILDING CONSENT AND PLANNING PERMISSION

The problem of reconciling a local planning authority's (lpa's) use of development control powers in accordance with s 54A of the TCPA 1990 with its duties under s 66(1) LBCAA 1990, is highlighted in *Heatherington (UK) Ltd v Secretary of State and Westminster City Council* [1995] JPL 228. The property, 48 Park Street, is a Grade II listed building comprising a basement, ground floor and four upper floors. The basement, ground floor and first floor were used as offices, and the remaining floors were residential. A further complication was that the basement and ground floor had the benefit of permanent planning permission for office use, whilst the first floor had been granted a series of temporary planning permissions for office use which expired on 31 December 1990, but which had continued to be used as an office after that date.

In due course, Westminster City Council served an enforcement notice alleging a breach of condition by virtue of the continuation of the office use. The notice was the subject of an appeal to the SoS, who dismissed the appeal on the ground that the office use was contrary to policies contained in the Westminster District Plan adopted in 1982, which 'normally requires the reversion to residential use of formally residential premises in temporary office use at the expiry of the temporary planning permission', that is, the application of the principle established by s 54A. In addressing the issue of the physical changes to the property required to allow the reversion to residential use, the inspector accepted that the proposal to continue the office use would result in the preservation of the special features of the first floor and so accord with the adopted policy on alteration to listed buildings, whilst the council's policy to promote residential reversion recognises that it may result in some compromise to a listed building.

In further consideration of this apparent conflict between s 54A (TCPA 1990) and s 66(1) (LBCAA), the court determined that the appeal be allowed and the matter remitted to the SoS in relation to the performance of the statutory duty imposed by s 66(1). Mr David Keene QC pointed out that the statutory requirement to 'have special regard' would suggest that more weight should be given to the listed building aspects than to the planning aspects. Whilst development plan policies should be considered first, they are not always of primary importance.

In *Burroughs Day v Bristol City Council* (1996) EGCS 10, the issue was whether internal works to a listed building also constituted development requiring planning permission. The works included the installation of a lift shaft housing which involved alteration to the roof, and the replacement of windows to the front elevation of the building. The court held that it was not sufficient that the works should affect the external appearance of the building; the test was whether 'they would *materially* affect the external appearance'. It was ruled that what must be affected is 'the external appearance' and not 'the exterior'. This implied that the change must be visible from a number of normal vantage points and not merely from the air, or from a single building.

The change in the external appearance must be judged in relation to the building as a whole, and not by reference to any part of the building taken in isolation in judging whether a building will be 'materially affected'. The effect has to be more than *de minimus*, as judged in the decision in *Royal London Borough of Kensington and Chelsea v CG Hotels* (1981) 41 P & CR 40. Floodlights had been installed on the ground and first floor balconies of the Prince of Wales Hotel. They were unnoticeable during daylight hours, and, in the inspector's judgment, they did not materially affect the building. This decision was upheld by the Divisional Court. The lpa's complaint was related to the effect that the floodlighting had at night, but the use of electricity does not constitute development, although it may have a major impact on the external appearance of the building!

The painting of the exterior of a listed building was the subject of an appeal decision in favour of the appellant, Mr Braunholz, whose original retrospective application had been refused in *West Dorset DC* ((1996) *The Times*, 23 April). Mr Braunholz had painted the exterior of his listed building lilac, and the SoS, in allowing his appeal, observed that, irrespective of whether he liked the particular colour, it did not spoil the attractiveness of the neighbourhood and should be allowed. This decision is being interpreted as allowing freedom to owners of listed buildings and buildings in conservation areas to paint their properties the colours of their choice, thus preventing lpas from interfering on the ground of taste alone.

In attempting to conserve listed buildings, lpas are frequently required to consider linked proposals for new development profit which could assist in the retention and refurbishment of a listed building. This is often described as 'enabling development'. The Court of Appeal in *R v West Dorset DC ex p Searle* [1999] JPL 331 upheld, by a majority decision, the council's approach in granting planning permission for such a scheme of enabling development. The proposals involved the erection of eight houses and garages in the grounds and the conversion of the listed building into five residential units. The majority rejected the submission from the applicants who argued that the council was not entitled to grant planning permission on the basis of the material before them and that the council ought to have tested the developer's financial case for erecting so many houses.

Aldous LJ was persuaded of this case. However, Schiemann LJ and Beldam LJ believed that the case was one entirely for the lpa. Schiemann LJ went on to observe:

> Any developer would only be prepared to do the work if he considered that the totality of what he was allowed to do on the site would show him sufficient profit to make it financially worthwhile. In the context of the present case, he would almost

inevitably ask to be permitted to do work which would, on the one hand, harm the setting of the Hall but which could, on the other hand, finance the preservation of the building. So there was a tension between these two desiderata. This leaves the council with complex judgments to make. How adverse is the effect of the proposed development in the grounds on the setting of the Hall? Is the developer bluffing when he sets out what he claims are his minimum terms? Can he be trusted to fulfill his engagements? Is it sensible to reject the so called minimum terms and hope that some other solution which is more acceptable in planning terms? Will the owner just let matters continue to slide? Is the building in danger of further serious harm while an ideal situation is sought? Will the search for the best inhibit the achievement of the good?

Schiemann LJ pointed out that these were all matters for the council and the only responsibility for the court was to ensure that they did not fail to take into account a material consideration.

The Court of Appeal in *Skerrits of Nottingham Ltd v Secretary of State for the Environment, Transport and The Regions* [2000] JPL 281 held that it was not an essential feature of the curtilage that it be small, and that in the context of the LBCAA 1990 the curtilage of a substantial listed building was likely to extend to where, or what had been, in terms of ownership and function, ancillary buildings.

21.5   THE CURTILAGE OF A LISTED BUILDING

The definition of curtilage which is frequently cited is that originating from *Sinclair Lockhart's Trustees v Central Land Board* (1951) 1 P & CR 320, which is

> ... the ground which is used for the comfortable enjoyment of the dwelling house or building ... serving the dwelling house or building in some necessary or reasonable way.

For the purposes of listed buildings, this definition has been found wanting. It is not sufficient that the building and its curtilage were conveyed or demised together (*Methuen-Campbell v Walters* [1979] QB 525; 2 WLR 113). *Dyer v Dorset CC* (1988) 3 WLR 213; (1989) EGCS 15 involved a college in large grounds, generally regarded as 'the curtilage of the college'. Within this area of grounds, it was held that a separate curtilage had been created by the fencing off of an area around a lecturer's house, even though the house shared the access to the college.

The case dealing explicitly with the definition of curtilage is *AG v Calderdale BC* [1983] JPL 310; 46 P & CR 399. In this case, a disused mill at Hebdon Bridge was linked by a first floor level 'bridge' to a terrace of three-storied cottages, the ownership of which had been severed from the mill. The contention was that the mill was physically attached to the 'bridge', which in turn was attached to the cottages and, therefore, the cottages were included in the curtilage of the mill. At the Court of Appeal, in the opinion of Stephenson LJ, the purpose of s 54(9) of the TCPA 1971 (now s 1(5) of the LBCAA 1990) was to bring within listed building control any works to objects or structures which might not individually be of any intrinsic interest, but the removal of which might adversely affect the listed building. He favoured a broad interpretation of s 54(9) and his conclusions indicated that, although at first sight it seemed unlikely that the far end of the terrace could be regarded as fixed to the mill, he thought the judge was right in concluding that this terrace was a structure fixed to the mill in the ordinary sense of the words.

In *Debenhams plc v Westminster City Council* [1987] AC 396; [1986] 3 WLR 1063; 1 All ER 51 a further case of 'linkage' was considered. In this case, several buildings were involved which were within the same hereditament for rating purposes, but only some were listed in their own right. Numbers 27 and 28 Kingly Street were not listed but had, however, been linked to the others by a footbridge at second floor level and a subway for a short period of time by an accident of history. Following the principle established in the *Calderdale* case, the Court of Appeal held that numbers 27 and 28 comprised a structure fixed to a listed building and were, therefore, part of it. This decision was overturned by a majority decision on appeal to the House of Lords. Lord Keith, in reviewing the wording of s 1(5), concluded that:

> In my opinion, to construe the word 'structure' here as embracing a complete building not subordinate to the building of which it is treated as forming a part would produce an unreasonable result ... the general tenor of the second sentence of sub-s (5) (any object or structure fixed to a building) satisfies me that the word is intended to convey a limitation to such structures as are ancillary to the listed building itself, for example a stable block of a mansion, or the steading of a farmhouse either fixed to the building or within its curtilage. In my opinion, the concept envisaged is that of principal and accessory.

In making this decision, the House of Lords did not overrule the *Calderdale* case on its facts, since it was possible, in that instance, given the history of the properties, to regard the mill and the terrace as a single unit.

This general definition was directly applied to the question of the curtilage of a listed building in *R v Camden LBC ex p Bellamy* [1992] JPL 255. The case concerned two buildings, one of which had been listed and the other, which originally formed the stable or coachhouse, had not. At the time of listing, it was within the curtilage of another property, and doubt existed as to whether it served as a garage for that property or was used separately for the repair of cars on a commercial basis. It was, however, established that the listed building and the garage/coachhouse had been in the same ownership until 1970. Nolan LJ concluded on the basis of the tests laid down by *Calderdale* and *Debenhams* that it had to be concluded that it was included in the listing, and set down the following test:

(a) the building which is itself included in the list (the principal building) must first be identified from the listing description – that is indeed the only purpose of the description;

(b) any structure (whenever it was erected) that is fixed to the principal building will be included, provided that, if it is itself a building, is ancillary to the proposed building (*per* Lord Keith in *Debenhams v Westminster City Council*, above);

(c) the curtilage of the principal building must then be identified, which will be 'quintessentially a matter of fact' (*per* Sir Graham Eyre in *James v Secretary of State (Wales)* [1991] JPL 550; 1 PLR 58); and

(d) not all the land in the same ownership as the principal building will be included (see *Collins v Secretary of State and Epping Forest DC* (1989) EGCS 150) and some land in separate ownership may be included (see *AG v Calderdale BC* above).

Nolan LJ also expressed the view that:

> This is a potentially recurring problem – being faced years after the event with the question whether or not a particular structure had to be taken to have been included in the original listing. I would hope that as a general rule it might be possible for the

description in the list, whether original or amended, to specify the main ancillary structures which are included together with the principal building.

In response to the concern expressed by Nolan LJ and others, Lord Montagu (the then Chairman of English Heritage) during a House of Lords debate on the Housing and Planning Bill, commented that:

> The practice of the Department now and of my officers who advise the Department is to consider individually all the structures and buildings on a site which can be construed as separate buildings and to list those, and only those, which qualify. The new lists will, therefore, leave little room for doubt whether a building is listed or not [*Hansard*, House of Lords, col 623, 13 October 1986].

Time will tell if the problem associated with the definition of curtilage and ancillary buildings will be resolved if or when lists are updated. In the meanwhile, the courts appear to accept a wide definition of what may constitute the curtilage of listed buildings.

21.6   OBJECTS AND STRUCTURES WITHIN THE CURTILAGE?

Any object or structure is subject to listed control (s 1(5)(b) LBCAA 1990) if it:

(a) is within the curtilage of a listed building; and

(b) it has been there since before June 1948.

The critical test is not whether the object or structure has any merit. They may be important features such as temples or grottoes, or on the other hand they could be old, dilapidated garden sheds. The test to be applied is whether an object or structure is a fixture or fitting. In the leading case *D'Eyncourt v Gregory* [1866] 15 WR 186; LR 3 Eq 382, it was held that tapestries, pictures in panels, frames filled with satin and attached to the walls, statues, figures and vases, and stone garden seats were essentially part of the house or the architectural design of the building or grounds and, however fastened, were fixtures and could not be removed. In *Dibble (HE) v Moore* [1970] 2 QB 181; (1969) 20 P & CR 898; 3 WLR 748, a greenhouse not secured to the ground was held to be a fitting.

In *Cotswold DC v Secretary of State and Pearson* [1985] JPL 407, it was held that listing did not extend to the actual ground surrounding a listed building, as the ground cannot be construed as an object or structure. However, in *Watson-Smyth v Secretary of State and Cherwell DC* [1992] JPL 451, the owner of the listed property used the stone from a 'ha-ha' to construct a new wall and filled in the original ditch. The court held that there are two component parts in the construction of a ha-ha: the ditch and the retaining wall constructed nearest to the building. The ditch and the wall were integral parts of the structure and could form part of a listed building provided the ha-ha was within its curtilage.

21.7   DEMOLITION OF LISTED BUILDINGS

Applications for the demolition of listed buildings frequently arise because of the costs involved in restoration, the difficulty of finding a suitable use for the building, or the desire to carry out redevelopment to capitalise on the development value of the site.

The economics of restoring a listed building have been recognised as a relevant consideration. In *Kent Messenger v Secretary of State* [1976] JPL 372, on appeal after the refusal of listed building consent, the inspector accepted that restoration and repair would be uneconomic, and recommended that consent should be given for the demolition of the building. The SoS disagreed but failed to give adequate reasons for doing so, and the High Court quashed his decision. In considering whether the restoration of a listed building is economically feasible, the SoS is entitled to take into account the extent to which that cost could be recouped as a result of redevelopment of the remainder of the site (see *Godden v Secretary of State* [1988] JPL 99).

The question arises whether the quality of the building to replace that demolished is a material consideration in determining an application for listed building consent. This was addressed in *Save Britain's Heritage v Secretary of State, Number 1 Poultry Ltd and City Acre Investment Trust Ltd* [1991] 2 All ER 10; 3 PLR 17. The proposal was to redevelop in Mansion House Square, London, the area known as the 'Mappin and Webb site', which included several listed buildings. These, and other buildings, were to be demolished to allow for the erection of what was described as a 'post-modern style' building. The inspector and the SoS were clearly impressed by the proposal, and in their view the design and quality of the replacement would make a greater contribution to the architectural heritage than the retention of the existing buildings. The Court of Appeal disagreed on the basis that the SoS's decision, whilst specifically agreeing with parts of his inspector's reasoning, had left his position unclear regarding other crucial parts of his own reasoning. He had failed to give sufficient justification for departing from his own policy in Circular 8/87, which provides for 'a presumption in favour of preservation'. The court's decision was reversed by the House of Lords, where Lord Ackner said:

> The determination ... depended upon the aesthetic judgment of the Secretary of State. Having exercised such judgment, the Secretary of State granted the necessary planning permission, listed building consent and conservation area consent.
>
> Your Lordships are not concerned with the wisdom of the Secretary of State's decision ...
>
> All these are matters for the aesthetic judgment by the Secretary of State and not for your Lordships. Accordingly, in allowing this appeal, your Lordships are in no way either expressly or impliedly concurring with the views of the Secretary of State which I have quoted.

Thus, the determination by the House of Lords was whether or not the SoS had given sufficient reasons to justify his decision.

This determination by the House of Lords highlights the relationship between the executive (the SoS) and the judiciary. The reversal of the decision of the Court of Appeal reinforces the fact that the courts are *not* involved in the planning merits of cases brought before them; the interpretation of planning merits is purely a matter for the SoS.

The courts have consistently held that the quality of the replacement building is a material consideration in determining application to demolish listed buildings or buildings within a conservation area (see *Kent CC v Secretary of State for the Environment* [1995] JPL 610 and *Richmond-upon-Thames LBC v Secretary of State for the Environment* [1978] P & CR 151).

21.8   DEMOLITION OR ALTERATION?

The question of whether the removal of part of a building constituted demolition or alteration of a listed building was the issue in *Shimizu (UK) Ltd v Westminster City Council* [1997] JPL 523; (1994) EGCS 205. The distinction between demolition and alteration was of fundamental importance in deciding whether compensation was payable under the then extant s 27(2) Planning (Listed Buildings and Conservation Areas) Act 1990, which was subsequently repealed by the Planning and Compensation Act 1991 (Sched 19, Part II). The significance of the decision of the House of Lords is that it determined that the whole building is to be treated as a listed building and, therefore, the removal of part of a building does not constitute demolition but rather alteration, unless the work is so extensive as to amount to the clearing of the whole site.

Listed building consent and planning permission had been granted in 1988 for the demolition of buildings between Piccadilly and Old Bond Street, London, including a listed building known as Quantas House. The consents required the retention of the facades to all the buildings and the chimney breasts and chimney stacks of the listed building. Demolition began in March 1990 and, by the following June, the redevelopment site consisted of the facades, chimney breasts and chimney stacks, as required by the consent.

An application was made for listed building consent to remove the chimney breasts, but this was refused by the SoS on appeal. This resulted in a claim for compensation under s 27, and the central issue was whether the removal of the chimney breasts constituted demolition or alteration of a listed building within the meaning of the Act. The claimants referred their claim for compensation to the Lands Tribunal, which found in their favour, having reached the conclusion that the works constituted an alteration to a listed building rather than demolition of part of a listed building. Westminster City Council challenged this decision to award compensation by way of an appeal to the Court of Appeal. The court found that the works which consisted of, or included, demolition of part of a building did not form part of a consent to alter a listed building; demolition of part of a building is not capable of being included in and treated as part of the works of alteration. In their view, the concepts of alteration and demolition were mutually exclusive to the extent of precluding the demolition of a part of the building from amounting to an alteration of the whole. In coming to its conclusion, the Court of Appeal did so on the assumption that the definition of a 'building' (s 336(1) TCPA 1990), which includes 'any part of a building', is also applied to a listed building, and that the system of control which the Planning (Listed Buildings and Conservation Areas) Act 1990 provides can be applied to any part of a listed building in the same way as it applies to the whole.

The Court of Appeal refused the claimants leave to appeal to the House of Lords, but later the Appeal Committee of the House of Lords allowed a petition for leave to appeal. The Law Lords, in their consideration of the matter, held, in allowing the appeal (Lord Griffiths dissenting), that, by virtue of the definition of 'building' (s 336(1) TCPA 1990), a listed building in the list compiled by the SoS under s 1 of the Planning (Listed Buildings and Conservation Areas) Act 1990 might be a building or part of a building, but whether the proposed works amounted to 'alteration or extension of a listed building' within s 27(1)(a) of that Act was to be considered in the context of a listed building as a whole. Whether the works constituted 'alteration' was a question of fact and degree to be determined by the Lands Tribunal. Accordingly, the appeal was allowed, and the claim to compensation under s 27 as determined by the Lands Tribunal was reinstated.

This decision of the House of Lords that, in the context of the whole building, any works which resulted in the near total destruction could be classed as an alteration resulted in a government response in the form of Circular 14/97, published at the end of August 1997. This amends the guidance in PPG 15, 'Planning and the Historic Environment', which states that consent is required for works which result in 'the total or substantial demolition of the listed building *or any part of it*' (para 3.18).

The changes in the Circular confirm that proposals which involve fabric removal, yet stop short of near total destruction of the building, will be classed as an alteration. Works will require consent only if they affect the building's character as a building of special architectural or historic interest. The demolition of a curtilage building is likely to fall into this category.

To operate successfully within the context of the circular, it would appear that it is important to define the overall character of the listed building and the relevance of its component parts. In doing so, regard will have to be taken of the building's architectural quality and its:

(a) historic and social associations;

(b) the technology of its structure; and

(c) the archaeology of its fabric,

and this will require special advice to produce a 'listed building audit'.

The question of what constitutes a significant part of a listed building was given further attention in *Sullivan v Warwick DC* [2003] JPL 1545; [2004] JPL 268. The district council issued planning permission and listed building consent allowing the demolition of part of The Regent Hotel, Leamington Spa, following advice from English Heritage. The proposal involved the demolition of the rear wing of the hotel and its replacement by a new building for retail and residential use. It was argued by Sullivan that the term "significant" had to be given a meaning which incorporated both 'quality and quantity' whereas English Nature's interpretation of paragraph 3.15A and 3.19 of PPG 15 was based upon the proportion of the building involved (this derives from the *Shimizu* case which turned on the proportion of the building to be demolished and drew a distinction between alteration and demolition) but it was clear that the planning authority were under the impression that the recommendation of English Heritage had taken into account both quantitative and qualitative aspects. Although he declined to quash the decision, Pitchford J pointed out that it is important to give the use of words such as 'substantial' and 'significant' used in the advice their full meaning. The error in this case was to give them too narrow a meaning. A small but important feature of a building can be significant; conversely a large but unimportant feature might not be.

21.9 LISTED BUILDING ENFORCEMENT NOTICES

As previously indicated (see Chapter 20, para 20.7), it is an offence to carry out work involving the demolition or alteration of a listed building without first gaining listed building consent. In *R v Wells Street Metropolitan Stipendary Magistrate ex p Westminster*

City Council [1986] JPL 903; 3 All ER 4 the Divisional Court held that the offence was one of strict liability, that is, the prosecution did not have to prove that the accused knew that the building was listed.

The effect of an enforcement notice on third parties was considered by the Court of Appeal in *Browning v Tameside MBC* (1997) EGCS 38. A listed building enforcement notice had been served on the occupant of one of a row of four listed cottages who, without listed building consent, had proceeded to demolish the front elevation of his cottage. In doing so, he withdrew restraint to the party wall between his and the claimant's cottages. The requirements of the notice were not complied with, and the council carried out the works using its powers under s 42 of the LBCAA 1990 and sought to recover its expenses of over £7,000 from the claimant. The court held that there was no liability. The notice served had nothing to do with the claimant's property and no notice was served on the claimant. Since a listed building enforcement notice carries criminal as well as financial liability, it must be construed strictly. The council had no powers to enter onto the claimant's land or to recover expenses from him, and the court awarded costs against the council.

The question of how far an lpa can use its powers to require the rebuilding of a listed building which has been demolished arose in *R v Leominster DC ex p Antique Country Buildings Ltd* [1988] JPL 554. It involved a 16th-century barn which consisted of timbers secured by wooden pegs which had been dismantled with the intention of shipping the barn to the US, where it would be reassembled. Listed building enforcement notices were issued by the lpa, and the question raised was whether the authority had the power to require the barn to be re-erected on the site. The High Court supported the lpa's action and concluded that, provided the structural components were extant, re-erection of the building could be lawfully required.

Mann J, in making this judgment, accepted that there would be cases where, after demolition, the only remains would be rubble or ash, and there was no power which would require the owner to construct a replica.

In reviewing a successful prosecution for the execution of unauthorised works to a listed building in *R v Sandhu* [1997] JPL 853, the Court of Appeal (Criminal Division) struck down the earlier decision of the High Court on the ground that the lpa adduced too much evidence. It was argued that the additional evidence was prejudicial to the defendant, who had been convicted on six counts of executing alterations to a listed building contrary to s 9(1) of the LBCAA 1990. Given that these were offences of strict liability, to adduce evidence which went beyond the level of proof necessary to establish them was not an optional extra available to the prosecution. Where the evidence was irrelevant and inadmissible and damaging to the defendant, its admission would serve no purpose other than to incline the jury to think badly of the defendant. This, in the view of the court, was such a case, and the jury might not have been swayed against the defendant had the evidence only related to the basic facts required. In prosecuting under s 9(1), the following were the only questions to be answered by the court:

(a) was the building listed?;

(b) if so, were the works specified in each of the counts executed for its alteration?;

(c) if so, did the defendant cause the works specified in each count to be executed?; and

(d) if so, were the works executed in such a manner which affected the characteristics of the building as one of special architectural or historic interest?

To go beyond these questions was unacceptable. The intent, state of mind, knowledge or motive of the defendant were irrelevant to the issue of innocence or guilt.

21.10 URGENT WORKS AND THE RECOVERY OF EXPENSES

Under the provisions of s 54 of LBCAA 1990, a local authority may execute any works which appear to them to be urgently necessary for the preservation of listed buildings in their area. Section 55 enables the authority to recover the costs from the owner of the property. In *R v Secretary of State (Wales) ex p Swansea CC* [1998] JPL 524, the question raised was, what is urgent?

The lpa was of the opinion that the works required were urgently necessary, but the SoS did not agree. The court held that the authority was entitled to be reimbursed with the cost, provided that it was acting reasonably in deciding that the works were urgently necessary. Dyson J observed:

> I would have found it surprising if Parliament had intended to allow an owner who had neglected to carry out work which was necessary to preserve a listed building to escape the liability for the costs of carrying out that work simply because the authority had decided the work was urgently necessary, when in fact it was not. What is urgently necessary may be a difficult question to determine. How urgent is urgent? Opinions may differ. As [counsel] points out, s 54 creates an emergency procedure. Authorities are expected to decide what may be a difficult question quickly.

In limited cases, the cost of works associated with an approved alteration to a listed building (the supply of goods and services) is treated as zero-rated to Value Added Tax (VAT). The building must be intended for the sole use of a relevant charitable purpose, which includes use of a building by a charity as a village hall or recreational facilities for the local community. The Court of Appeal held in *Jubilee Hall Recreation Centre v Commissioners of Customs and Excise* [1999] JPL February Update; (1998) EGCS 184 that the purpose of the exemption was to extend relief to members of the local community as users of the services and where the only economic activity was one in which they participated directly. Zero-rating was, therefore, available where a sports centre was provided and maintained by a charity; it was not available where a sports centre is a facility of a fee-paying school, whose pupils benefited, rather than members of the community.

21.11 SCHEDULING OF ANCIENT MONUMENTS

At the present time there is no compensation available for the loss development value of land where it results from the site being declared a scheduled monument. If planning permission exists prior to the scheduling compensation for loss of development value does become payable. The case *R v Secretary of State for the Environment ex p Rose Theatre Trust Co.* [1990] 1 QB 504, was the result of the foundations of the original Shakespearian theatre being discovered during excavations for the new theatre. The SoS refused to exercise his powers under the Ancient Monuments and Archaeological Areas Act 1979 to declare the site a scheduled monument as to do so would probably have resulted in compensation being payable. In dismissing the application for judicial review to quash the decision the High Court held that the risk of compensation being payable was a relevant factor for the SoS to consider. He was also entitled to take into account the developer's desire to cooperate in preserving the remains. The required re-design of the proposed building to ensure the preservation of the remains and to allow access to them is estimated have cost over £10 million. Following the development, which included these proposals, the SoS decided to include the site of the remains in the schedule of ancient monuments!

21.12 COMPULSORY PURCHASE

Under s 47 LBCAA 1990 the SoS may authorise the compulsory purchase of a listed building where it appears to him that reasonable steps are not being taken to ensure the proper preservation of the building. Such action can only be taken after the service on the owner of a repairs notice (s 48), specifying the works the authority think reasonably necessary to ensure proper preservation and the owner has failed to carry out the work. In *Robbins v Secretary of State for the Environment* [1989] 1 WLR 201, the House of Lords rejected an argument that the repairs notice could only require works to a building as it subsisted when the notice was served. It was held that the works required by the notice could require works to restore the building to the condition as at the date on which it was listed.

21.13 DESIGNATION OF CONSERVATION AREAS

The designation of conservation areas results from a resolution by the lpa. The method adopted to designate an area was the subject of a challenge in *R v Canterbury City Council ex p Halford* [1992] JPL 851 64; P & CR 513; 2 PLR 137. A planning application for 25 houses, 30 low-cost homes and a primary school in the village of Barnham was refused as the site was within the Kent Downs Area of Outstanding Natural Beauty (AONB) and a special landscape area. An appeal by way of a local inquiry opened on 10 December 1991 and that evening the council's planning committee resolved to extend the Barnham Conservation Area to include the appeal site.

Following this action, the appeal was adjourned and the owner of the site was granted leave to seek a judicial review of the council's decision. The High Court heard the case on 17 February 1992 and McCullough LJ determined that:

1 lpas are entitled to consider as an entity the whole area of the land which gives rise to special or historic interest and the setting of a village could be an important factor in defining the boundary of a conservation area. Although it had not been the intention of Parliament for 'buffer zones' to be included within conservation areas, the site in question was 'preserving the setting and immediate views of a village of special architectural or historic interest';

2 although the site was part of an AONB and a special landscape area, and trees on the site were the subject of a Tree Preservation Order (TPO), the designation of the site as part of a conservation area was a relevant issue to be considered by the lpa; and

3 in making the resolution, the council must take into account all the relevant

factors. In this case, there was no evidence to suggest that all the relevant facts were presented by the officers to the committee, particularly in terms of the TPOs placed upon trees within the site.

On the basis of this third issue, the designation of the conservation area was quashed by the court. This left the lpa with the option of redesignation of the area using the correct procedure, but to date this action has not been taken. In undertaking a judicial review, the court is concerned to ensure that the procedures laid down by statute are adhered to; it is not the duty of the court to consider the planning merits of the issue: in this case whether the area should be declared to be a conservation area.

In *R v Surrey CC ex p Oakimber Ltd* [1996] JPL B28; (1995) 70 P & CR 649, the applicants sought a judicial review of the council's designation of a conservation area of over 350 acres (141.5 hectares) at Brooklands, the site of the motor-racing track and an aerodrome. The principal ground of challenge was that the council had failed to take into account the relevant matters, including the fact that extensive modern and commercial development covered substantial parts of the area, and it also included areas of former gravel extraction. The court found that the council had carried out extensive consultations with statutory and other consultees and there had been no procedural irregularity and, therefore, the application was rejected.

These decisions highlight that an lpa may designate a conservation area with apparent impunity, provided it carries out the required statutory requirements, and the relationship between the judiciary and the executive and the discretion granted to local government in the planning system. This has led a number of commentators to question the motive of some authorities in declaring conservation areas, and has led to calls for powers to permit intervention by the SoS.

In *R v Easington DC ex p Seaham Harbour Dock Co Ltd* [1998] JPL B99, B103, the issue was the designation of a conservation area (s 69 LBCAA 1990) and whether the local authority's jurisdiction extended to a port. The court accepted that the council's administrative area was defined by the Local Government Act 1972, including s 72 which provided that every accretion from the sea, whether natural or artificial, and any part of the seashore to the low-water mark, was incorporated into the district. The court accepted that there was some conflict in case law about the status of accretions from the land into the sea, such as piers, and reclaimed land that was clearly within jurisdiction. However, the 1898 Act which set up the company provided that the docks were to be regarded as situated in the adjoining parish which now formed a part of the district and, therefore, the port was within the jurisdiction of the planning authority.

21.14 DEVELOPMENT IN CONSERVATION AREAS

The designation of conservation areas places upon the lpa the responsibility to pay special attention to the desirability of preserving or enhancing the character or appearance of the area. This responsibility clearly requires a degree of subjective judgment: what amounts to 'enhancement'? This has been the subject of numerous applications to the courts.

In the case of *Steinberg and Sykes v Secretary of State* [1989] JPL 258; 2 PLR 9; 58 P & CR 453, application for a judicial review was made by Professor Steinberg who, with others, was a member of a neighbourhood association which had expressed its views the lpa's determination to refuse the initial application and, at the subsequent appeal, against the refusal. The application was to erect a house on a piece of unused, derelict land within a conservation area. At the appeal, the inspector identified one of the main issues as whether the proposed development would *harm* the character of the conservation area. In his consideration, the present condition of the site detracted from both the visual character and residential amenity of the locality, and he allowed the appeal.

Two members of the association applied to the High Court to set aside the inspector's decision, and Mr Lionel Read QC, sitting as deputy judge, held that the inspector had misdirected himself on a point of law. The judge was of the opinion that there was a world of difference between the issue identified by the inspector of the test of *'harm'* and the need to pay special attention to the desirability of preserving and *'enhancing'* the character or appearance of the area. The concept of avoiding harm was essentially negative, whilst the underlying purpose of the legislation was essentially positive. The matter was referred back to the SoS for his reconsideration. This judgment had major repercussions on both the attitude of lpas towards development in conservation areas and the inspectorate which, thereafter, was very conscious of the need to avoid the use of the word 'harm' in their decision letters following appeals involving development in conservation areas.

As indicated in Chapter 5, para 5.5, the question of 'enhancement' within a conservation area formed part of the issue considered by the Court of Appeal in the case of the *Bath Society v Secretary of State* [1991] JPL 663; 62 P & CR 565; [1992] 1 All ER 2; 1 WLR 1303, which was once again a third party challenge. Glidewell LJ was unable to agree with the findings of Hutchinson J in the High Court that it was possible to infer from the inspector's report that he was 'paying special attention to the desirability of preserving or enhancing' the character or appearance of the conservation area. If this was spelled out in the inspector's report, it was clear that there was no suggestion in the report that the building would enhance the character or appearance of the conservation area; the inspector had said that the effect of the proposed building 'would not be unacceptably great'. This could only mean that he concluded that it would to some extent detract from the view. Having formed the opinion that the building would neither enhance, nor preserve, the character or appearance of the conservation area, he failed to carry out the necessary balancing exercise of weighing that important material consideration against such expressed benefits as would accrue from the construction of the new building. This flaw in the inspector's reasoning resulted in the appeal being allowed, and the decision of the lower court was quashed.

In making the judgment, Glidewell LJ attempted to set down guidance as to the application of s 72 and held that:

(a) where a development proposal was in a conservation area, there were two statutory duties to be performed by the decision-maker, namely, that imposed by s 72 as well as a duty to have regard to the development plan and any other material considerations;

(b) the requirement under s 72 carried considerable importance and should be the first consideration; and

(c) if the decision-maker decided that the proposal would neither preserve nor enhance the area, then it must mean that it would have some detrimental effect.

However, in his view, this would not necessarily mean that an application which failed these tests would necessarily be refused, but it did mean that it should only be permitted if it carried some advantage which outweighed the failure to satisfy the test under s 72. (See also *R v Leominster DC ex p Patricia Pothecary*, Chapter 13, para 13.10.)

In *South Lakeland DC v Secretary of State and Carlisle Diocesan Parsonages Board* [1991] JPL 654; 2 WLR 204; 1 All ER 573; [1992] AC 141, the proposition put forward by Glidewell LJ that a proposal which would neither preserve nor enhance an area must mean that it will have some detrimental effect proved not to be acceptable to the Court of Appeal. Mann LJ was of the opinion that this appeared to ignore the possibility of a 'neutral' proposal, and stated:

> ... the statutorily declared object of preserving the character or appearance of an area was achieved by either a positive contribution to preservation or by development which left the character or appearance unharmed, that is to say, preserved.

The question of 'harm' does not simply relate to proposed buildings within a conservation area but also to alteration to existing property. In the case of the *Historic Buildings and Monuments Commission v Secretary of State* (1996) ECGS 176, a challenge was mounted to the SoS's decision to uphold a householder's appeal to retain a replacement front door made from moulded plastic. English Heritage challenged the inspector's decision on three issues:

1 the SoS had taken little or no account of the Art 4 Direction which had been made in 1992 and which required householders to apply for planning permission for works which would otherwise have been permitted under the GPDO;

2 he had paid undue regard to the use of plastic and other modern materials by other householders in the area; and

3 he had failed to treat as a material consideration the danger that his decision would set a precedent for further unsympathetic developments.

The court rejected the challenge on all three grounds and made it clear that an Art 4 Direction did not in itself require special consideration; the inspector had considered, and was entitled to consider, the context of the house in its area. The door in question was in keeping with the character and appearance of that area, and the question of setting an undesirable precedent did not arise.

CHAPTER 22

TREES AND HEDGEROWS

22.1   INTRODUCTION

In this chapter, unless specified, all references relate to the Town and Country Planning Act (TCPA) 1990. The Regulations do not define the term 'hedgerow' but the *Oxford English Dictionary* defines a hedgerow as, 'a row of bushes forming a hedge with trees, etc growing out of it.'

Section 55 of TCPA does not include the planting or cutting down of trees as development. Trees make a valuable contribution to the quality of local environments whether they be a single tree or a group of trees. Under s 197 of the TCPA 1990, local planning authorities (lpas) are charged with the duty to 'ensure, wherever appropriate, that, in the granting of planning permission, provision is made by the imposition of conditions for the preservation or planting of trees'. To the public at large, trees are generally appreciated as an important element in the landscape when they are growing on land which is removed from the individual's property; there is frequently less appreciation when they are in one's own back garden or that of an adjoining neighbour.

The emphasis can only be on 'preservation', as trees have a natural lifespan and are subject to disease and decay and eventual death. The initial selection of appropriate tree species, and the maintenance required, demand that staff are employed who have the relevant expertise and Circular 36/78, 'Trees and Forestry' (para 9), suggests that this may involve sharing staff between district councils, or between the county council and several district councils.

Note: The Town and Country Planning (Trees) Regulations 1999 (SI 1999/1892) will require the updating of Circular 36/78 and this is currently awaited.

22.2   PLANTING BY THE LOCAL AUTHORITY

Local planning authorities have powers under s 89 of the National Parks and Access to the Countryside Act 1949 to plant trees on land within their area for the purpose of preserving or enhancing its natural beauty. Powers also exist under s 96 of the Highways Act 1980, which allows local authorities (other than a highways authority) and parish councils to plant trees in or on certain land acquired in connection with a highway.

22.3   USE OF PLANNING CONDITIONS

Local planning authorities are encouraged to impose conditions on planning permissions requiring the planting or preservation of trees. These conditions can be enforced by means of a Breach of Condition Notice (BCN) (see Chapter 18, para 18.3). Unlike 'normal' planning conditions, those requiring the planting of trees or other forms of flora cannot be implemented other than in the planting season, nor can the initial act of planting ensure the survival of newly planted species. Planting conditions, therefore, require careful wording if they are to result in the desired outcome, and the following model condition is set out in Append 4 of Circular 36/78:

> (Before)/(Within 12 months from the date when) (the change of use hereby permitted is carried out)/(and the land and buildings hereby permitted is occupied/first used for the purpose of ...) trees shall be planted on the land in such positions and of such species as may be agreed with the local planning authority. Any trees removed, dying, being severely damaged or becoming seriously diseased within (two) years of planting shall be replaced with trees of similar size and species to those originally required to be planted.

Note: From the author's experience, this model condition is suspect as it does not include any reference to the size of plant material which shall be planted. The lpa will be well advised to control this by amending the above condition or adding a specific additional condition to a planning permission.

It is made clear in Append 4 that it is not considered to be reasonable to use conditions to secure permanent protection of trees. This should be done by an order (see para 22.5, below).

22.4   DEFINITION OF A TREE

There is little doubt that the average lay person is perfectly capable of recognising a tree but, perhaps surprisingly, there is no statutory definition of a tree, nor is there any one agreed definition set down by the courts. In *Kent CC v Batchelor* (1977) 33 P & CR 185, Lord Denning suggested a distinction could be drawn between saplings and mature trees, the older trees having a diameter greater than 7 or 8 in (18–20 cm). However, in *Bullock v Secretary of State* [1980] JPL 461; 40 P & CR 246, Phillips J did not follow Denning and was of the opinion that a coppice of saplings could be regarded as trees. In a later case, *Maidstone BC and Kent CC v Batchelor* [1996] JPL 563, the High Court held that stools not having a stem or trunk were not trees.

The Town and Country Planning (Trees) Regulations 1999 (SI 1999/1892) do not attempt to define a tree, which is perhaps rather surprising. The exemptions for trees in conservation areas contained in Part III, para 10, do provide guidance as to the maximum size of what constitutes 'a tree' for the purpose of the exemptions (see para 22.7, below).

22.5   TREE PRESERVATION ORDERS

Under s 198(1) (TCPA 1990), if it appears to an lpa that it is expedient in the interest of amenity to make provision for the preservation of trees or woodlands in its area, the authority may, for that purpose, make an order with respect to such trees, groups of trees or woodlands as may be specified in the order.

Circular 36/78, para 40, advises that an order should be used to protect selected trees and woodlands if their removal would have a significant impact on the environment and its enjoyment by the general public. Other factors to be taken into account are their intrinsic beauty, contribution to the landscape, screening an eyesore or future development scarcity value. In addition, the importance as a wildlife habitat may be taken into account, but it would not in itself justify an order. Consideration must be given to the woodland which is managed for timber production, as this is likely to involve selective felling or thinning, and para 41 suggests the most appropriate method in such cases is to reach agreements with the landowners for the proper management of their woodlands using grants available from the Countryside Commission or the Forestry Commission.

According to s 198(6) (TCPA 1990) and Art 5 of the Town and Country Planning (Trees) Regulations 1999 (SI 1999/1892), the TPOs shall not apply to:

(a) the cutting down, uprooting, topping or lopping of any trees which are dying or dead or have become dangerous;

(b) the cutting down, uprooting, topping or lopping of a tree by, or at the request of, a statutory undertaker where the land on which the tree is situated in operational land of the undertaker and the work is necessary:

    (i) in the interests of the safe operation of the undertaking;

    (ii) in connection with the inspection, repair or renewal of sewers, apparatus of the statutory undertaker, mains, pipes cables; or

    (iii) to enable the statutory undertaker to carry out development permitted under the General Permitted Development Order (GPDO) 1995;

(c) the cutting down, uprooting, topping or lopping of a tree cultivated for the production of fruit in the course of a business;

(d) pruning in accordance with good horticultural practice of any tree cultivated for the production of fruit;

(e) the cutting down, uprooting, topping or lopping of a tree where the work is required to enable a person to implement a planning permission (not an outline permission) or under the GPDO;

(f) the cutting down, uprooting, topping or lopping of a tree by the Environment Agency to carry out development under the GPDO;

(g) the cutting down, uprooting, topping or lopping of a tree by a drainage authority in exercise of any of their functions in relation to the maintenance, improvement or construction of watercourses or drainage works; and

(h) without prejudice to s 198(6)(b) the felling, lopping or the cutting back of roots in accordance with the notice served by a licence-holder under Sched 4, para 9 of the Electricity Act 1989.

A TPO prohibits the cutting down, uprooting, topping, lopping, or wilful damage to or destruction of trees without the written consent of the lpa, which may be given with conditions (s 193(3), (2)(a)). The prohibitions contained in a TPO do not apply to trees which are dying or dead, or which have become dangerous, nor will a TPO prevent action to abate nuisance (see Chapter 23, para 23.2).

22.6 PROCEDURE FOR MAKING A TREE PRESERVATION ORDER

The form to be used for making a TPO is set out in the Town and Country Planning (Trees) Regulations 1999 (SI 1999/1892) and:

(a) specifies the trees, or groups of trees or woodlands, to which it relates; and

(b) where an order relates to a group of trees, specifies the number of trees in the group.

In addition to this form, there must be an accompanying plan to a scale sufficient to give a clear indication of the position of the trees, groups of trees or woodlands. This map is to be annexed to an order and shall be part of the order.

As soon as is practicable, after making the order, and before confirming it, the authority is required to serve on the persons with an interest in the land a copy of the order. The authority is also required to inform the parties:

(a) of the reasons for making the order;

(b) that objections or other representations may be made in accordance with reg 4;

(c) that a period, determined by the authority, but not less than 28 days, is allowed after the date of the notice, by which time objections or representations made in writing must be received by the authority;

(d) that objections or representations shall specify the particular trees or woodlands to which they refer; and

(e) that, in the case of an objection, it shall state the reasons for that objection.

As trees which are likely to be the subject of a TPO have a habit of 'disappearing', provision is made under s 201 (TCPA 1990) allowing the authority to include in the order a directive that it shall take effect immediately. This is the general rule rather than the exception. As a result, the order shall continue in force until the expiration of six months from the date on which the order was made or the date on which the order was confirmed, which ever occurs first.

A copy of the order is to be made available for inspection, free of charge, at all reasonable hours at the offices of the authority by whom the order was made and, if appropriate, at the offices of the authority on whose behalf the order was made.

The authority must consider any objections or representations duly made in respect of the order before confirming it with or without modifications (s 99(1) TCPA 1990). Where modifications are made, these shall be indicated in the order. A copy of the order must be sent to those persons with an interest in the land and to occupiers of adjoining property. All appeals to the Secretary of State (SoS) against the making of an order will be dealt with on the basis of written representation. The appeal must be lodged within 28 days of the council's decision. There is no provision for a challenge to an order except by way of an application to the High Court under s 284 within six weeks from the date of the confirmation of the order.

The lpa does not have a completely free hand in modifying orders, and, in *Evans v Waverley BC* [1996] JPL 655; (1995) EGCS 132, an appeal was lodged following a modification which included for the first time an area of woodland. It was held, in allowing the appeal, that the change from an area order to a woodland order was unlawful as it was outside the scope of s 199(1) (TCPA 1990), since the proposed modifications would affect trees not covered by the original designation and would, therefore, create an entirely different order.

Provision is also made under s 202 (TCPA 1990) for the SoS to make an order after consultation with the local planing authority should he think it expedient to do so.

22.7 TREES IN CONSERVATION AREAS

The designation of land as a conservation area (see Chapter 20) automatically affords protection to most trees within such areas, even though such trees are not protected by a TPO (s 211 TCPA 1990). Protection is *not* afforded by conservation area status for trees within five exempted cases (s 212) set out in reg 10 of the Town and Country Planning (Trees) Regulations 1999 (SI 1999/1892). The exempted cases are as follows:

(a)   the cutting down, uprooting, topping or lopping of a tree mentioned in s 198(6) or in Art 5;

(b)   cutting down of a tree in accordance with a felling licence granted by the Forestry Commissioners under Part II of the Forestry Act 1967;

(c)   cutting down of a tree in accordance with a plan of operations approved by the Forestry Commissioners under a forestry dedication covenant under s 5 of the Forestry Act 1967 or under conditions of a grant or loan under s 1 of the Forestry Act 1979;

(d)   cutting down, uprooting, topping or lopping of a tree by, or on behalf of, a local planning authority;

(e)   cutting down or uprooting of:

    (i)   a tree whose diameter does not exceed 75 mm; or

    (ii) where carried out for the sole purpose of improving the growth of other trees, of a tree whose diameter does not exceed 100 mm;

(f)   the topping or lopping of a tree whose diameter does not exceed 75 mm.

In carrying out the measurements above:

(a)   where a tree has more than one stem that is 1.5 m above ground level, its diameter shall be treated as exceeding 75 mm or 100 mm (for the purposes (e)) if any stem, measured over its bark at that point, exceeds 75 mm or 100 mm;

(b)   in any other case, the diameter of the tree shall be ascertained by measurement, over the bark, at a point 1.5 m above ground level.

22.8 DUTIES TO REPLACE TREES

When a tree which is the subject of a TPO is removed, uprooted or destroyed in contravention of an order (s 206(1)(a) TCPA 1990), or the action is authorised only because it is dying, dead or dangerous (s 206(1)(b)), then it is the automatic duty of the owner of the land to plant a replacement tree of appropriate size and species at the same place as soon as he reasonably can (s 206(1)). The replacement tree will come under the automatic protection of the TPO which formerly applied to the tree which it replaces (s 206(4)). The lpa may, however, use its discretion to relieve the person of his obligation to replant (s 206(2)).

In the case of trees within woodland which are removed because they are dying, dead or dangerous, such trees may be replaced either on the land, or near the land on which the trees grew, or on such other land as may be agreed with the lpa (s 206(3)). In woodlands, there is surprisingly no provision to require the replacement of trees which are removed in contravention of an order.

Failure of the landowner to discharge his duty to replace trees can result in the lpa serving notice to enforce the replacement of trees (s 207) within a period of four years.

The notice may be appealed against to the SoS (s 208) on the following grounds (s 208(1)):

(a) that the provisions of s 206, or any conditions subject to which the consent under a TPO has been given, which conditions the replacement of trees (s 207), are not applicable or have been complied with;

(b) that, in all the circumstances, the duty to replace trees should be dispensed with in relation to any particular tree;

(c) that the requirement of the notice is unreasonable in respect of the period within which the trees should be replaced, or in respect to the size or the species of trees specified in the notice;

(d) that the planting of the tree(s) in accordance with the notice is not required in the interests of amenity, or would be contrary to the practice of good forestry; and

(e) that the place on which a tree or trees are required to be planted by way of replacement is unsuitable for that purpose.

If the owner of the land fails to comply with a s 207 notice requiring him to replant the trees, the lpa may enter onto the land and plant the requisite trees (s 209(1)(a)) and recoup its expenses from the current landowner, irrespective of whether ownership has changed since the serving of the notice.

Where a direction is given for the felling, in the course of forestry operations, of any part of a woodland area, the authority may give the owner of the land a written direction specifying the manner in which and the time within which he shall replant the land. This may include requirements as to:

(a) species;

(b) the number of trees per hectare;

(c) the preparation of the relevant land prior to replanting; and

(d) the erection of fencing necessary for the protection of the newly planted trees.

An application for consent to the cutting down, uprooting, topping or lopping of any tree which is subject to a TPO must be made to the authority and shall in accordance with Art 6 of the Town and Country Planning (Trees) Regulations 1999 (SI 1999/1892):

(a) identify the tree or trees to which it relates;

(b) specify the work for which consent is being applied; and

(c) contain a statement of the applicant's reasons for making the application.

22.9 PENALTIES FOR CONTRAVENTION OF A TREE PRESERVATION ORDER

Any person who contravenes the provisions of a TPO by cutting down, uprooting, topping, lopping, or wilfully destroying or damaging a tree in a manner which is likely to destroy it is guilty of an offence (s 210(1) TCPA 1990). The person is liable on summary conviction to a fine not exceeding £20,000 (s 210(4)), whilst on conviction on indictment the fine is unlimited (s 210(2)(b)). In assessing the level of fine, regard may be had to any financial benefit accruing to the defendant (s 210(3)).

If any person contravenes a TPO other than in the above-mentioned manner, he is liable to a fine not exceeding £2,500.

The lpa is also able to resort to an injunction in order to prevent a possible contravention of a TPO (s 214A).

22.10 HEDGEROWS

A hedgerow as such does not constitute a tree for the purpose of TPOs, and only individual trees contained within the hedgerow can be covered by an order. Over the years, this has led to the disappearance of large lengths of hedgerows which are important features in the British countryside.

The Hedgerow Regulations 1997 (SI 1997/116) now make it an offence to remove certain hedgerows without the prior approval of the lpa. Consent can be sought by the submission of an application by either the landowner, agricultural tenant, farm business tenant or certain utilities. No fee is payable. The lpa must determine the application within six weeks and in doing so must take into consideration the applicant's reason for wishing to remove the hedge. Where such a hedgerow is removed without prior approval, the person responsible for the removal may be subject to a fine of up to £5,000 if found guilty by a magistrates' court and an unlimited fine if convicted by the Crown Court. In either case, the lpa can insist upon the replacement of the hedgerow.

Permission *is* required to remove a hedgerow either in whole or in part where it is on or runs alongside (reg 3):

(a) agricultural land;

(b) common land, including town or village greens;

(c) land used for forestry or the breeding or keeping of horses, ponies or donkeys; or

(d) a local nature reserve or Site of Special Scientific Interest.

Permission is *not* required if:

(a) the hedgerow is shorter than 20 m (unless both ends join up with other hedgerows or it is part of a longer hedgerow);

(b) the hedgerow is in, or borders, a garden;

(c) removal is required to replace an existing opening provided the original opening is replanted;

(d) removal is necessary to gain temporary access in an emergency;

(e) removal is necessary to comply with a statutory plant or forestry order;

(f) removal is necessary to comply with a statutory notice for preventing interference with electricity lines or apparatus;

(g) removal is necessary in connection with statutory drainage or flood defence work;

(h) removal is necessary to implement a planning permission;

(i) removal is necessary for reasons of national defence; or

(j) removal is necessary for works associated with work carried out by the Highways Agency.

Note: (a) gaps of 20 m or less are counted as part of the hedgerow which may be a break in the vegetation or it may be occupied by a gate or other form of access; and (b) in the case of permitted development rights most hedgerow removal *will* require prior permission.

Following receipt by the lpa of a hedgerow removal notice, the authority is required to establish whether the hedgerow is 'important', which means that it must be over 30 years old and meet at least one of the following criteria:

1   it marks a pre-1850 parish or town boundary;

2   it incorporates an archaeological feature;

3   it is part of, or is associated with, an archaeological site;

4   it marks the boundary of, or is associated with, a pre-1600 estate or manor;

5   it forms part of a pre-parliamentary enclosure field system;

6   it contains certain categories of species of birds, animals or plants (see Wild Life and Countryside Act 1981);

7   it includes:

   (a) at least seven woody species in a 30 m length (average);

   (b) at least six woody species in a 30 m length and has at least three associated features;

   (c) at least six woody species in a 30 m length including a black poplar, large or small-leafed lime or wild service tree; or

   (d) at least five woody species in a 30 m length and has at least four associated features;

Note: The number of woody species is reduced in each case by one in the northern counties.

8   it runs alongside a bridleway, footpath, road or byway and includes at least four woody species in an average 30 metre length and has at least two of the following associated features:

   (a) a bank or wall supporting the hedgerow;

   (b) less than 10% gaps;

   (c) on average at least one tree per 50 m;

   (d) at least three species from the list of 57 woodland plants;

   (e) a ditch;

   (f) a number of connections with other hedgerows, ponds or woodland; and

   (g) a parallel hedge within 15 m.

Having considered the complicated criteria listed above, the lpa is then in a position to decide whether or not the hedgerow is 'important'. If is not classified as 'important', then approval should be granted for its removal; if it is 'important', then there is a presumption against the granting of permission for its removal and the lpa will issue a 'hedgerow retention notice', which is considered to be permanent unless a later application is able to prove changed circumstances.

A hedgerow retention notice can be challenged by an appeal to the SoS within 28 days of the authority's decision. Should the lpa fail to give a decision on a hedgerow removal notice within the specified time of six weeks, or such extension of time agreed by the applicant, then the hedgerow may be removed.

Whilst the Hedgerow Regulations marked an important step in the protection of hedgerows, it is not particularly surprising that the government set up a review group in the summer of 1997 to advise on ways of providing greater protection. Included in the terms of reference are:

(a) whether the time allowed to lpas to evaluate hedgerows and respond to notices is adequate;

(b) whether the criteria for defining important hedgerows requires amendment; and

(c) how the criteria might be simplified.

The implications of a local Act affecting hedgerows in relation to the determination of a planning application was considered in *R v Solihull BC ex p Berkswell Parish Council* [1998] JPL B118, B132. A decision to grant planning permission for development that involved the removal of lengths of hedgerow was challenged on the ground that the hedgerows affected were subject to the Berkswell Enclosure Act 1802. The court found that this could not be a material planning consideration as questions regarding the legal status generally were not relevant for the purposes of the planning merits nor did the granting of planning permission override any protection that the 1802 Act might create.

22.11 UNTIDY SITES AND BUILDINGS

If an lpa considers that the amenity of any part of its area is adversely affected by the condition of any land or building, it may serve on the owner and occupier a notice (s 215(1) TCPA 1990) requiring the remedying of the condition of the land or building (s 215(2)) by taking such steps and within such timescale as may be specified in the notice. This cannot take effect within less than 28 days (s 215(3), (4)) and the period may be extended by the planning authority (s 215(7)).

The relevant s 215 of TCPA 1990 replaced s 65 of TCPA 1971, which specifically dealt with wasteland and was restricted to 'gardens, vacant sites and other open land', where it appeared to the lpa that the condition of the land 'seriously injured the amenity of any part of their area'. The new s 215 widened the definition on two counts:

1 by simply referring to 'land' rather than 'gardens, vacant sites, etc'; and

2 by reducing the level of the test to be applied from 'seriously injuring' to 'adversely affecting' the amenity of the area.

The use of the word 'land' has particular significance, as it is defined according to s 336 (TCPA 1990) to include a building. This approach to dealing with general lack of attention to land or buildings which results in an adverse affect on the general amenity of an area provides the planning authority with an alternative to enforcement action (see Chapter 18).

If the owner or occupier fails to take the requisite steps to comply with the notice, he is liable on summary conviction to a fine not exceeding £1,000. Following conviction for failure to comply with a notice, a person who does not, as soon as is practicable, do all that he can to comply with the requirements of the notice, will be guilty of a further offence, and on summary conviction is liable to a fine not exceeding £40 per day.

If a notice has not been complied with, the lpa is empowered to enter the land and take the appropriate action to comply with the notice, and to recover the costs involved from the owner (s 219 TCP 1990) irrespective of the fact that ownership may have changed since the serving of the notice.

A notice under s 215 may be appealed against in the magistrates' court, with the possibility of a further appeal to the Crown Court. The grounds of appeal are set out in s 217(1) as follows:

(a) that the condition of the land does not adversely affect the amenity of any part of the area of the local planning authority who served the notice, or any adjoining area;

(b) that the condition of the land is the ordinary result of development which is not in contravention of Part III of the Act;

(c) that the requirements of the notice exceed what is necessary for preventing the condition of the land from adversely affecting the amenity; and

(d) that the period allowed for taking the steps required by the notice falls short of what should reasonably be allowed.

In addition to the powers granted to lpas under s 215 of TCPA 1990, s 94 of the Act affords an opportunity to seek the termination of planning permissions which have been begun within that period specified in a planning condition, but which have not been completed. Provided the authority is of the opinion that the development will not be completed within a reasonable time, it may serve a notice that must be confirmed by the SoS. Notices are to be served on the owners, occupiers and anyone with an interest in the land. The notice:

(a) will not take effect until confirmed by the Secretary of State;

(b) shall specify a period of not less than 12 months for the completion of the development, failing which planning permission will be withdrawn; and

(c) the period specified in the notice to take effect shall not be less than 28 days after the date on which the notice is served.

The recipient of the notice is afforded an opportunity of a hearing before a person appointed by the SoS and such a request must be made before the date specified in the notice for it to take effect. In confirming the notice, the SoS may substitute a longer period than that specified in the notice for the works to be completed.

The following chapter deals with challenges to the use of TPOs and the question of compensation.

22.12 HIGH HEDGES

Measures to tackle the problems caused by high hedges, (the leylandii problem), were included in The Anti-social Behaviour Act 2003 (s 65). It provides local authorities with the power to intervene in high hedge disputes which neighbours cannot resolve. In such cases it is possible to make a complaint to the local authority provided that:

(a) the hedge in question comprises wholly or predominantly of a line of two or more evergreen or semi-evergreen trees or shrubs;

(b) it was over 2 m high;

(c) the hedge acted to some degree as a barrier to light or access; and

(d) because of its height, it was adversely affecting the complainant's reasonable enjoyment of their domestic property.

Local authorities are empowered to charge a fee to be paid by the complainant and for its part the authority must take into account all relevant factors, including views of the hedge-owner and the impact of the hedge on the wider amenity of the area. If they decide that action should be taken they would issue a formal notice outlining the action to be taken and the timescale for such action. This may require the reduction in height of the hedge to 2 m, or its removal, but action does not apply to roots of the hedgerow. The provisions also apply to Crown Land. The use of electronic mail for the serving of notices is specifically authorised (s 80 of the Anti-social Behaviour Act 2003). Both hedge owners and complainants have rights of appeal (s 72). Failure to comply with the notice would be a liable offence and on conviction in the magistrates' court to a fine of up to £1,000. The local authority would also have default powers to carry out the work itself and recover the costs from the hedge-owner. These default powers would be available whether or not the criminal offence was pursued.

CHAPTER 23

CASE LAW IN RELATION TO TREE PRESERVATION ORDERS AND COMPENSATION

23.1   INTRODUCTION

As indicated in the introduction to the previous chapter, trees can result in contentious issues, particularly between neighbours. A potential conflict also exists between the common law rights relating to property and the effect of a Tree Preservation Order (TPO) which is intended to preserve trees in their natural state. Tree Preservation Orders, unlike the listing of buildings (which is also designed to retain existing features), may also result in claims for compensation. This can occur when the local planning authority (lpa) is unwilling to permit action which will result in the removal, or topping or lopping of a tree which is the subject of an order.

23.2   TREE PRESERVATION ORDERS AND NUISANCE

There are many situations where a tree growing on neighbouring property not only overhangs the adjoining property but also has an extensive root system which encroaches beyond the boundary. At common law, the neighbour who is affected by the tree is entitled as of right under the tort of nuisance to cut down those branches of the tree to the extent that they overhang his property, and to remove that part of the root system, provided he adds insult to injury by returning the branches and roots to his neighbour! Such action may not only adversely affect the amenity value of the tree but may, in certain circumstances, result in its death. This raises the question: what is the effect of a TPO on this common law right?

Section 186(6) of the Town and Country Planning Act (TCPA) 1990 provides that:

> … no order shall apply … (b) to the cutting down, uprooting, topping or lopping of any trees as may be necessary for the prevention or abatement of a nuisance.

A literal interpretation of s 186(6) would, therefore, allow a neighbour legally to undertake remedial action which is not available to the owner who is responsible for preserving the tree under the terms of the TPO. In *Elliot v Islington LBC* (1991) EGLR 167; 11 EG 145, it was made clear that the ownership of a tree will remain in the ownership of the land on which the tree is planted. However, in a decision by the Secretary of State (SoS) ([1992] JPL 389), it was reported that:

> The Secretary of State is advised that 'nuisance' as referred to in s 60(6) of the Town and Country Planning Act 1971 [now s 198(6)(b)], means the tort of nuisance actionable at law, and that a tree standing on a person's own property cannot be a legal nuisance to the owner or occupier of that property.

Whilst this clarifies the situation in so far as the owner's responsibilities are concerned, a TPO is ineffective against such tree surgery as regards nuisance actionable at law by a neighbour. What constitutes an actionable nuisance has been established in a series of cases. In *Crowhurst v Amersham Burial Ground* [1878] 48 ExD 5, the poisoning of ground by a yew tree was held to be an actionable nuisance. In *King v Taylor* (1976) 238 EG 265, the extraction of water by tree roots, thus making the soil less suitable than formerly, was also held to be an actionable nuisance. It therefore appears that, if a neighbour is able to prove that the effect upon his property is nuisance actionable in law, he may take the appropriate action to overcome the problem irrespective of the fact that the tree is the subject of a TPO. If the inconvenience which results from encroachment can be held to result in unreasonable interference with beneficial use rather than a mere inconvenience, then this, too, may be a nuisance actionable in law.

23.3   NEGLIGENCE

As a result of the findings in *Barnet LBC v Eastern Electricity Board* [1973] 2 All ER 319; 1 WLR 430, a tree may be 'wilfully destroyed' by an act of negligence as well as by deliberate intent. Contractors laying cables damaged the root systems of six trees which were the subject of a TPO and, as a result, the trees were rendered less stable and presented a potential danger and their life expectancy was shortened. The council prosecuted the board, and the case was dismissed by the magistrates on the ground that the reduction of the life expectancy by an undefined time could not amount to destruction. The Divisional Court reversed this decision and held that a person wilfully destroyed a tree if he inflicted such injury that any reasonable forester would decide it must be felled.

The issue of responsibility was addressed in *Groveside Homes Ltd v Elmbridge BC* [1988] JPL 395; (1987) 55 P & CR 214, and it was held that the owner is liable for the acts of his servants but not for the actions of an independent contractor who has been instructed not to touch the tree.

23.4   DEFENCE AGAINST PROSECUTION

In *Maidstone BC v Mortimer* [1981] JPL 458; (1982) 43 P & CR 67, the respondent, who was a tree feller by profession, was charged with contravening a TPO and wilfully destroying an oak tree. He was employed by a person who honestly believed that she had received permission from the council to fell the tree. In his judgment, Park J stated that if it were the law that no conviction could be obtained under s 102(1) of the TCPA 1971 (now s 210 of TCPA 1990), unless the prosecutor could discharge the often impossible burden of proving that the accused knew of the existence of the relevant TPO, the section would have little effect. If this were to be the case, protected trees could be destroyed or felled without any appreciable risk of a penalty being incurred by the wrongdoer. The section could only be interpreted in such a manner as to create an offence only if the accused had knowledge of the existence of a TPO.

The appeal was allowed on the facts and, as the nature of the liability under a TPO was one of strict liability, the justices would be directed to convict the respondent. However, the fact that he had been misled by his employer could be reflected in the penalty imposed upon him. This case highlights the fact that the act of damaging or destroying a tree which is the subject of a TPO is an offence of strict liability.

Prosecution for the harming of trees can prove to be fraught with problems. In *Carter v Eastbourne BC* [2000] 2 P & CR 60, planning officers caught a man using machinery to uproot trees covered by a TPO. The council issued a summons against Carter but before the magistrates it was argued that the council had put forward no evidence to prove that the particular trees had been in existence when the TPO was confirmed in 1994. Although he was convicted and fined £2,000 for each offence (plus costs) the Divisional Court quashed the convictions ruling that the magistrates had not been entitled to convict on the basis of photographic evidence showing uprooted trees unless the council had also proved the age of the trees or otherwise demonstrated that they were in existence when the TPO was made.

Although the law allows protected trees which are diseased or damaged to be cut down, the Court of Appeal ruled in *R v Alath Construction Ltd* [1990] 1 WLR 1255; 60 P & CR 533, that the burden of proof for any such reason falls to the person being prosecuted.

23.5   COMPENSATION

No compensation is payable in relation to the making of a TPO, but it may be payable for loss or damage resulting from the refusal of consent to remove trees or the imposition of conditions (s 203 TCPA 1990). Under s 204(1), compensation is payable following a direction from the lpa or the SoS in accordance with Art 9, Model Order 1999. A claim must be submitted within 12 months of the authority's decision or, if appealed, the date of final determination of the appeal and any claim must be for more than £500. Entitlement to compensation is restricted to refusal for the felling in the course of forestry operations and it is limited to the owner of the land. It is also limited to any depreciation in the value of the trees which is attributable to the deterioration of the timber consequent upon the refusal. Compensation is payable should the local authority require the replanting of all or any part of a woodland for which the Forestry Commissioners decide not to make a loan.

In all other cases, no compensation is payable to a person for:

(a) loss of development value or other diminution of the value of the land;

(b) loss or damage which could not have been reasonably foreseen having regard to the statement submitted in accordance with Art 6(c) (see Chapter 22, para 22.8);

(c) loss or damage reasonably foreseeable by that person and attributable to his failure to take reasonable steps to avert the loss, damage or to mitigate its extent; or

(d) costs incurred in appealing to the SoS.

Any disputed claims for compensation are ultimately determined by the Lands Tribunal (ss 2 and 4 of the Land Compensation Act 1961).

23.6   PRINCIPLES OF ENTITLEMENT

The general principle is that any person who has suffered loss or damage in consequence of any refusal is entitled to compensation (Art 9, Model Order). In *Bell v Canterbury City Council* (1988) 56 P & CR 211; 2 PLR 69, the Court of Appeal extended this to any loss in value of the claimant's land. The court also rejected the lpa's contention that the loss was a result of the making of the order, not the refusal of consent, and took the view that it was only when the consent was refused that the loss occurred. The claimant was, therefore, entitled to compensation for the difference in value of the land in its present state and its value if reclamation to grazing land had been permitted.

In *Deane v Bromley BC* [1992] JPL 279; 63 P & CR 308, the claimant had been granted consent to prune 26 chestnut trees in his garden, on condition that the work was carried out by an approved contractor. The Lands Tribunal accepted that the nature of the work was such that the claimant could have carried it out himself but awarded compensation representing the total cost of the contracted work, less an allowance for the hire of specialist equipment.

Where consent to fell a tree was refused, as in *Fletcher v Chelmsford BC* [1992] JPL 279; 2 EGLR 213, the owner may seek specialist advice as to the effects which the tree may be having on the foundations of his house. This is a cost properly incurred by the claimant in consequence of the refusal of consent to fell the tree and is the subject of compensation.

In a similar case, *Buckle v Holderness BC* [1996] JPL 422; 71 P & CR 428, consent had been refused for the felling of a mature ash tree and the appeal was dismissed. The owner of the property sought expert advice which confirmed that the roots of the tree were damaging the foundations of the property, and he, therefore, sought compensation for the cost of remedial works to the foundations of his property which involved underpinning at a depth below the level of the root system. The lpa argued that no compensation was payable since the remedial measure would have been required in any event, even if permission to fell the tree had been granted, or that works of lesser cost were needed. The owner claimed £15,346 for the cost of remedial works and professional advice, £1,808 plus VAT for the costs of the unsuccessful appeal, and interest on the total sum. The Lands Tribunal held that it was reasonable for the claimant to pursue the appeal as it was an attempt to mitigate his loss, and awarded £13,000 payable as compensation for remedial works, as some minor works would have been required had the tree been felled. The costs of the appeal (£675.63) were also recoverable. The tribunal, in exercising it statutory jurisdiction, did not have the same powers as a court or arbitrator to award interest on the sums expended by the applicant.

In *Henriques v Swale BC* (1997) 1 PLR 1, the council refused permission for the clearance of an area of a coppice woodland sited in an Area of Outstanding Natural Beauty and an area of special landscape, on the grounds of good forestry. The claimant applied for compensation and the matter was referred to the Lands Tribunal for a preliminary ruling. The tribunal held that it was sufficient for Art 5(a) for an authority to specify 'the interests of good forestry'. Whether the decision of the lpa was well founded or not was not a matter for the tribunal but for the SoS. Furthermore, the authority was entitled to avoid paying compensation if the reasons for refusal were in the interests of good forestry.

In *Factorset Ltd v Selby DC* (1995) 40 EG 133; 2 PLR 11, the case dealt with the issue of delay in the completion of development which, it was alleged, arose from the lpa's decision to place a TPO on a tree within the development site. The site, with the benefit of a conditional permission for two dwellings, was acquired by the claimants in 1989. Later that year, the lpa made a TPO protecting a yew tree on one of the building plots. An application to lop the tree was refused by the authority, but this decision was overturned on appeal by the SoS. A revised site plan was later approved which also granted permission for the pruning of the tree in accordance with the SoS's appeal decision. Because of the delay in carrying out the development, the claimants sought compensation for the additional interest charges incurred in funding the purchase of the land and for the professional fees incurred in gaining the necessary consents.

There remained doubt as to whether the proposed lopping was 'immediately required for the purpose of carrying out the development', in which case it could not have been prevented by the order, but evidence indicated that work on the site ceased upon the insistence of the council's officers at a site meeting.

The tribunal determined that the council's officers must have been aware that a refusal of consent to prune the yew tree, with the consequential delay in the building work which they insisted upon, would be likely to give rise to losses such as those which formed the basis of the claimant's action. The tribunal, however, rejected those elements of the claim which related to the period prior to the refusal of consent by the council, but awarded compensation for the additional interest payments incurred by the claimants on the purchase price of the site, and for their expenditure on professional advice in relation to the yew tree.

The making of TPOs and their compatability with the Human Rights Act 1998 was challenged in *R (on application of Brennon) v Bromsgrove DC* [2002] EWHC 752. A dispute had arisen between the applicant and the local authority over a proposal to demolish an existing dwelling and to erect six maisonettes, and the claimant had threatened to fell all the trees on the site. The council made a provisional TPO in an attempt to prevent such action and this was challenged in the High Court on the grounds that it identified only the area of land which was a substantial garden. Before this challenge was resolved the council made a second TPO relating to the same tress but specifying them individually and by group. However, some of the trees in the first TPO had already been felled and others in the second Order were subsequently trimmed. Furthermore the claimant's redevelopment proposals had been refused on appeal, one of the inspector's reasons being the detriment which would arise from the loss of some trees. After dismissing a number of procedural challenges Richards J then addressed the Human Rights arguments. In his view there was no breach of the claimant's rights under Art 8, (rights to private property and private family life), or Art 1, (protection of private property), as the statutory provisions of TPOs represented a fair balance between the general interest of the community and the requirement to protect an individual's rights. Finally the availability of review by the High Court was sufficient to ensure that a TPO made by a council was compliant with Art 6 (right to a fair trial).

CHAPTER 24

ADVERTISEMENTS

24.1   INTRODUCTION

The control of advertisements is embodied in the Town and Country Planning (Control of Advertisements) Regulations (TCP(CA) Regs) 1992 (SI 1992/666) as amended by the Town and Country Planning (Control of Advertisements) (Amendment Regulations) 1999 (SI 1999/1810) made by the Secretary of State (SoS) under s 220 of the Town and Country Planning Act (TCPA) 1990. The definition of an advertisement is extremely wide (s 336(1)):

> ... any word, letter, model, sign, placard, board, notice, awning, blind, device or representation, whether illuminated or not, in the nature of, and employed wholly or partly for the purpose of, advertisement, announcement or direction, and (without prejudice to the preceding provisions of this definition) includes any hoarding or similar structure used or designed or adapted for use, and anything else principally used, or designed or adapted principally for use, for the display of advertisements.

The insertion of the amendment 'anything principally used, or designed or adapted for use' was introduced specifically to bring under advertisement control awnings and blinds on which an advertisement was displayed, structures such as rotating poster panels irrespective of whether or not a display was taking place and such things as gantries, pylons for free-standing drums.

The 1999 Amendment Regulations (SI 1999/1810) insert a new reg 9A which provides for the call in by the SoS of any express application for advertisement consent by an interested local planning authority (lpa). If the SoS does not call in an application, then a new reg 113A allows the local authority to determine the application themselves.

Government policy on advertisements is contained in PPG 19, 'Outdoor Advertisement Control', which amplifies the content of the legislation.

The government has declared its intention to update the system for the control of outdoor advertisement which was published in a paper entitled 'Outdoor advertisement control' (Department of the Environment, Transport and the Regions July 1999). To date, no final proposals have been forthcoming.

24.2   THE PRINCIPLES OF CONTROL

The powers of control of advertisements are exercised only in the interest of amenity and public safety (s 220(1) TCPA 1990 and the TCP(CA) Regs as amended by the Amendment Regulations 1999 (SI 1999/1810)). Local planning authorities are not allowed to operate as censors of the subject matter or the content of the design of advertisements. In terms of amenity, the lpa will take into account the characteristics of the area, and special consideration is to be given to features of architectural, historic, cultural or similar interest. Public safety involves the safety of persons using roads, railways, waterways, docks, harbours or airfields likely to be affected by the display of advertisements. Under TCP(CA) Regs, reg 4(1), particular regard is to be given to ensure that advertisements do not obscure or hinder the interpretation of traffic signs, railway signals or aids to navigation by air or water. The lpa is entitled to take account of any material change in circumstances which may occur within the period for which the consent is required when granting consent, or when considering whether to make an order revoking or modifying an existing consent.

24.3 EXEMPTIONS FROM CONTROL

The Regulations provide for three categories for the purpose of advertisement control:

1 advertisements which are not subject to prior consent;

2 advertisements which require consent but are deemed to have received that consent under the regulations; and

3 those not within the first two categories and thus requiring express consent from the lpa.

The first category includes 10 types of advertisements which do *not* require consent and cannot be challenged by the lpa. These are contained in TCP(CA) Regs, Sched 2 and are as follows:

Class A: The display of a captive balloon not more than 60 m above the ground for a maximum of 10 days in any one calendar year. This does not apply if the site is in an Area of Outstanding Natural Beauty, conservation area, national park, the Broads, or an area of special control.

Class B: Displayed on enclosed land and which is not readily visible outside the enclosure or from any land over which the public has a right of way or access.

Class C: Displayed on or in a vehicle, provided the vehicle is used for the conveying of persons or goods and is not primarily used as an advertisement.

Class D: Incorporated in the fabric of the building; but this does not include an advertisement painted on or fixed to the building. A hoarding is regarded as a building used principally for the display of advertisements.

Class E: Displayed on an article for sale or its container, provided it is not illuminated and does not exceed 0.1 square metre.

Class F: Relating to parliamentary, European and local elections. To be removed 14 days after the poll.

Class G: Required by standing order of either House of Parliament or by enactment.

Class H: Approved traffic signs.

Class I: Display of a national flag of any country, each on a single flagstaff.

Class J: Displayed inside a building not principally used for the display of advertisements and not to be illuminated and not within one metre of a door, window or other opening through which it is visible from the outside.

Note: Although the above classes of advertisements do not require prior consent, they are nevertheless subject to the standard conditions for advertisements set out in Sched 1 (see para 24.5, below).

24.4 DEEMED CONSENT

Under TCP(CA) Regs, reg 6, Sched 3 sets out 14 classes of advertisements which have the benefit of deemed consent and the conditions and limitations which apply in each case. Most of these classes are further sub-divided and it is not possible to deal with each in detail. The following selected classes provide details of the most frequent types of advertisement:

Class 1: Functional advertisements of local authorities, statutory and transport undertakers. Not to be illuminated unless reasonably required for the purpose of the advertisement.

Class 2: Relating to the premises on which they are displayed. Not to be illuminated or to exceed 0.3 sq m; no character or symbol to be more than 0.75 m in height or 0.3 m in an area of special control; no part to be more than 4.6 m above ground level or 3.6 m in an area of special control.

Class 2C: Religious, cultural, recreational, medical, hotel, club, etc. Not more than one advertisement on different road frontages and may not exceed 1.2 sq m (height, etc, as above in Class 2) but may be illuminated when related to medical or similar services.

Class 3: Located on the property for the purpose of sale or letting of property. One advertisement (maximum 0.5 sq m for residential property and 2 sq m for other property) to be removed 14 days after sale or tenancy granted.

Class 4: Illuminated advertisements on business premises with reference to the business carried on (in the case of a shop only on a wall containing a window). One advertisement parallel to the wall and one at right angles provided surface not greater than 0.75 sq m, not more than 1 m in height or two-thirds of the width of a footpath adjoining the property and not over any carriageway.

Class 5: Non-illuminated advertisements on business premises (illumination is permitted as an exception where medical or similar services are available on the premises).

Class 6: On the forecourt of business premises not to exceed an aggregate of 4.6 sq m.

Class 7: Flag advertisements in the form of a single flag attached to a flagpole projecting vertically from the roof of a building provided that it bears the name or device of the person occupying the building or refers to a specific event (other than goods for sale) of limited duration.

Class 8: Advertisements on hoardings enclosing land on which building operations are, or are about to take place but not to be erected more than three months prior to commencement of development (maximum height 3.1 m and 21.1 m in length for a period of up to three years).

Class 9: Advertisements on highway structures for advertisements authorised under s 115E(1)(a) Highways Act 1980 up to 2.16 sq m.

Class 10: Advertisements for neighbourhood watch and similar schemes.

Class 11: Directional advertisements pointing to a site where residential development is taking place (maximum 0.15 sq m in area).

Class 12: Advertisements inside buildings.

Class 13   Sites used for display of advertisements on 1 April 1974

Class 14   An advertisement displayed after the expiry of express consent unless a condition to the contrary has been imposed on the consent or an application for renewal has been refused.

The SoS may withdraw deemed consent in relation to a particular area after publishing a statutory notice and affording persons likely to be affected with an opportunity to make objections to the proposal.

The lpa also has power to challenge an advertisement displayed under deemed consent by issuing a discontinuance notice. The person on whom the notice is served may apply to the local authority for express consent and, if this is refused, there is a right of appeal to the SoS. The discontinuance notice will not come into effect until the outcome of the appeal is notified. Such a case arose in *Cheque Point UK Ltd v Secretary of State* (1995) EGCS 184. The applicants challenged the decision of the SoS to uphold a discontinuance notice served on them by the Royal Borough of Kensington and Chelsea. In 1976, express consent had been granted for the display of the advertisement, and thereafter it had the benefit of deemed consent under the TCP(CA) Regs. The lpa took the view that the advertisement was detrimental to the appearance of the building and the general street scene, and this was upheld by the SoS on appeal. He concluded that the continued display of the advertisement was 'substantially injurious to the interests of amenity and incompatible with the conservation areas status of the locality'. The court held that the SoS had used the appropriate test and, therefore, rejected the challenge to his decision.

Class 13 of the TCP(CA) Regs grants consent for the display of advertisements on a site which has been so used 'continuously' since 1 April 1974. Interpretation of the word 'continuously' was the issue in *Westminster City Council v Moran* [1998] JPL August Update. The court determined that it does not mean 'continually' and interruptions in the use of the site for the display of advertisements since 1974 does not deny deemed consent under this Class. The display of advertisements on a basis that occurs regularly is sufficient.

24.5   EXPRESS CONSENT

Unless the advertisement falls within the above classes which provide exemption or deemed consent, an application must be forwarded for determination by the lpa. As with other forms of application, the authority may grant consent with conditions or refuse consent, in which case they have to state the reasons for their action. There are, however, two essential differences from 'normal' planning consents which relate to advertisements:

1   planning consent is normally only for five years but the lpa may specify a shorter or longer period; and

2   the lpa may grant consent subject to certain standard conditions or such conditions as are considered to be appropriate.

Should the applicant appeal to the SoS against the refusal of permission, or the conditions attached to the grant of permission, the SoS may refuse to entertain an appeal which involves standard conditions. These are set out in Sched 1 as follows:

1 Any advertisement displayed, and any site used for the display of advertisements, shall be maintained in a clean and tidy condition to the reasonable satisfaction of the local planning authority.

2 Any structure or hoarding erected or used principally for the purpose of displaying advertisements shall be maintained in a safe condition.

3 Where an advertisement under these regulations is required to be removed, the removal shall be carried out to the reasonable satisfaction of the local planning authority.

4 No advertisement is to be displayed without the permission of the owner of the site or any other person with an interest in the site entitled to give consent for the use of the site.

5 No advertisement shall be sited or displayed so as to obscure or hinder the ready interpretation of any road sign, railway signal or aid to navigation by water or air, or so as otherwise to render hazardous the use of any highway, railway, waterway or aerodrome (civil or military).

24.6 AREAS OF SPECIAL CONTROL

The TCPA 1990 (s 221) and Part IV of the TCP(CA) Regs deal with definitions of areas of special control, which may be in a rural area or an area which appears to the SoS to require special protection on the grounds of amenity. It should be noted that the issue of safety is *not* a factor to be taken into consideration in declaring such areas (reg 18(6)).

Under TCP(CA) Regs, reg 2(2), all local planning authorities are under a duty to consider such definition (reg 18(1)) and to reconsider the matter every five years (reg 18(4)). The definition of an area of special control results from an order made by the lpa which must then have the approval of the SoS. An order may be challenged on a point of law by a 'person aggrieved' or by 'an authority concerned', within six weeks by application to the High Court (s 284 TCPA 1990). In 1989, it was stated that rather more than 45% of the total land area in England and Wales had been defined as being within an area of special control (Circular 15/89).

Within an area of special control, there is a general presumption against any advertisements (reg 19(1)). However, there are exceptions to this general rule (reg 19) which allows the following classes of advertisements to be displayed:

1 without express consent:

(i)   Advertisements within classes B to J of the excepted classes.

(ii) Advertisements specified as having deemed consent, with the exception of illuminated advertisements on business premises [see para 24.4, above].

2 with express consent:

(i)   Structures for exhibiting notices of local activities.

(ii) Announcements or directions relating to nearby buildings and land, for example, hotels and garages.

(iii) Advertisements required for public safety.

(iv) Advertisements which would be permitted under 2(ii) above, but for infringing the conditions as to height, number or illumination.

Advertisement regulations may be made with respect to 'experimental areas' (s 221(1)(b) TPA 1990), in order to assess over a prescribed period the effect upon amenity or public safety.

24.7 ENFORCEMENT OF CONTROL

Any person who displays an advertisement in contravention of the regulations is guilty of an offence punishable by a fine and a daily fine of £40 (s 224(3) TPA 1990). Persons displaying an advertisement include not only the person responsible for putting up the advertisement but also the person on whose land it is displayed and the person whose goods or business are being advertised.

24.8 FLYPOSTING

A large number of advertisements take the form of flyposters which are attached to buildings or virtually any other form of structure. Under TCPA 1990 s 225 and Sched 1, para 1, an lpa can obliterate or remove any flyposter without any prior notice when it is displayed in contravention of the regulations and does not identify the person who displays the advertisement. Where the advertisement does indicate the person responsible for its display, the lpa are empowered to remove it after giving two days' notice to such a person (s 225(3), (4), (5)).

24.9 LONDON: SPECIAL PROVISIONS

The London Local Authorities Act 1995 is a local Act and applies to the City and all London boroughs, with the exception of Tower Hamlets, which subsequently became a participating council by virtue of s 27 of the London Local Authorities Act 1996. Among the provision of the 1995 Act, the authorities are granted special powers for the control of advertisements. Under ss 10–13, modifications are made to s 225 of the TCPA 1990 granting new powers to require the removal of unauthorised hoardings and requiring the obliteration of any sign which the council considers detrimental or offensive to the amenity of the area.

24.10 CASE LAW IN RELATION TO ADVERTISEMENTS

The development of lighting and laser technology has resulted in two recent decisions as to what constitutes an advertisement. Two parallel decisions taken by the SoS and the SoS for Wales, who ruled that 'spaceflower' lighting apparatus, from which beams of light projected upwards to produce a floral image on the cloud cover, did not amount to the display of an advertisement (see *Great Yarmouth BC v Secretary of State, Newport BC v Secretary of State for Wales* [1997] JPL 650; (1996) EGCS 158). The High Court held that, whilst the ministers had correctly directed their attention to the beam of light, rather than the image or the equipment, they were wrong in coming to the conclusion that an advertisement had to be tangible. The role of the court was to consider the statutory definition of what constitutes an advertisement and, in doing so, to interpret the content of s 336(1) of the TCPA 1990 which defines an advertisement as:

Any word, letter, model, *sign*, placard, board, notice, awning, blind, device or representation, whether illuminated or not, in the nature of, and employed wholly or partly *for the purpose of*, advertisement, announcement or *direction* ... [Author's emphasis.]

Although the beams of light were not in themselves a representation, the court held that they were nevertheless intended to direct members of the public to the premises and, accordingly, could be regarded as a 'sign', thus falling within the definition of an advertisement.

Where an unauthorised advertisement is removed and then replaced at a later date, this is a fresh offence and, therefore, will not constitute a continuing offence for which a daily fine is payable (see *Royal London Borough of Kensington and Chelsea v Elmton Ltd* (1978) 245 EG 1011).

The display of 11 posters was held to constitute 11 separate offences (see *Royal London Borough of Kingston-on-Thames v National Solus Sites Ltd* [1994] JPL 251).

Under s 224(5) (TCPA 1990), a person will not be guilty of an offence if he is able to prove that the offending advertisement was displayed without his knowledge or consent (see *John v Reveille Newspapers Ltd* (1955) 5 P & CR 95). However, in *Preston v British Union for the Abolition of Vivisection* (1985) *The Times*, 20 July, it was held that, if an advertisement was displayed initially without the knowledge or consent of the person whose goods are advertised, that person, having become aware of the advertisement and having failed to remove it, became guilty of an offence under the regulations.

In the case *O'Brien v Croydon LBC* (1998) *The Independent*, 11 July, it was held that a discontinuance notice must be served on the persons whose specific interests are promoted in the advertisement concerned, since that person is the 'advertiser' for the purpose of TCP(CA) Regs, reg 8(2)(a).

The question of the legality of notices served by an lpa requiring the discontinuance of advertisements was considered in *Nahlis v Secretary of State* (1996) 71 P & CR 553. Kensington and Chelsea London Borough Council served notices on the owners of freehold premises requiring the discontinuance of the use of an end wall as an advertising hoarding. The appeal by the owners to the SoS was rejected, and they then applied to the High Court (s 288 TPA 1990) to quash the notices on the grounds that they were not served in accordance with s 329. The court accepted that there had been irregularities in the serving of the notices in that some had received various but not all the notices. However, the court was of the opinion that, as they were all able to appeal to the SoS within the time allowed, they had failed to show any substantial prejudice arising from the local authority's poor administration.

The courts have considered a number of cases relating to Class 8 (advertisements on hoardings) no doubt because of the advantages for large-scale advertising which they present. In *Brent LBC v Maiden Outdoor Advertising Ltd* [2003] JPL 192; [2002] EWHC 1240, it was held that a purpose-built advertisement hoarding was capable of falling within Class 8 if it performed an enclosing function. In *Postermobile plc v Royal Borough of Kensington and Chelsea* [2000] JPL 196; 80 P & CR 524, in interpretation of Class 8 it was held that the relaxing of control where building operations were about to take place required that if no building operation took place within three months there

CHAPTER 25

RURAL AREAS

25.1 INTRODUCTION

In this chapter, unless specified, all statute references relate to the Countryside Act 1968.

The countryside provides the most extensive resource in terms of production, environmental quality and as a potential for recreation. Since the Town and Country Planning Act (TCPA) 1947, all subsequent planning legislation has related to land irrespective of whether it is urban or rural in character. The same is true of orders and regulations made under planning legislation.

In general terms, the operation of planning controls in rural areas has consistently been one of restricting development. To gain planning permission, the question of need has frequently to be satisfied, particularly where policies apply to proposed development in the open countryside. This policy of restriction can be traced back to the Scott Report (1942, Cmd 6378), which was based upon a desire to retain as much land as possible in agricultural production. Over the years, it has been tacitly assumed by planning officers and elected members that any land which is not allocated for development will continue to be used productively for farming or forestry purposes, and this would ensure that the effective management of land would continue. The declaration of green belts is an obvious example of this approach to the planning and assumed future agricultural use of urban fringe land. However, in the 1990s, the issue of over-production, coupled with the EU Common Agricultural Policy, has resulted in changes in the agriculture industry which must now be taken into account in the planning of rural areas. It is essential to accept that most rural areas in Britain form part of the agriculture industry and, as such, change is inevitable. Current policies for the countryside are set out in PPG 7, 'The Countryside and the Rural Economy', which states in para 1.10:

> The guiding principle in the wider countryside is that development should benefit the rural economy and maintain or enhance the environment.

The accepted need to safeguard and enhance the quality of the rural environment has resulted in the Countryside Act 1968 and subsequent designations designed to achieve this objective.

25.2 FUNCTIONS OF THE COUNTRYSIDE AGENCY

The Countryside Commission, as from April 1999, is now re-titled the Countryside Agency. The creation of the Regional Development Agencies (see Chapter 2, para 2.5), which are now responsible for the rural regeneration programmes for their respective areas, resulted in a new Countryside Agency which arises from the merger of the old Countryside Commission with what is effectively the 'left-over parts' from the Rural Development Commission.

The Countryside Commission, which replaced the earlier National Parks Commission (NPC) in 1968 (ss 1 and 2), was at that time given extended functions relating to the countryside in general, whereas previously the NPC had been responsible only for national parks. The Commission's extended functions related to the preservation and enhancement of natural beauty and amenity in the countryside *in general*, and the provision and enhancement of facilities for public enjoyment and open air recreation (s 4(1)).

The Agency has the power to offer financial aid 'to encourage, assist, concert, or promote the implementation of any proposals with respect to those matters made by any person or body being proposals which the Agency considers to be suitable' (s 2(3)). The Agency also consults with lpas and other authorities and bodies; may offer advice or assistance; may provide publicity and information services relating to the countryside; and (s 2(8)) may carry out research and experimental projects, for example, schemes for the management of hill land (s 4). It may also undertake necessary works and, subject to the approval of the Secretary of State (SoS), may acquire land by agreement or, in extreme cases, compulsory purchase powers may be exercised (s 4(3)(a)).

It is also significant that the 1968 Act (s 11), requires that *all* ministers pay regard to the conservation of natural beauty:

> In the exercise of their functions relating to land under any enactment every minister, government department and public body shall have regard to the desirability of conserving the natural beauty and amenity of the countryside.

The Agency or a National Parks Authority (NPA) may enter into a 'management agreement' with any person having an interest in land, for the purpose of enhancing natural beauty or amenity or promoting the enjoyment of the park by members of the general public (s 45). Payments are made for the work to be carried out to achieve this object, but this is not compensation.

The Countryside and Rights of Way Act 2000 requires that the Countryside Agency prepares in respect of all land in England outside Inner London maps which will show all registered common land and all open country (see para 25.5 below). Similarly the Countryside Council for Wales is to prepare maps for Wales. Landowners have the right to appeal to the SoS or the National Assembly for Wales against the inclusion of their land in provisional maps (s 6).

25.3 NATIONAL PARKS

National parks are areas in England and Wales (and recently Scotland) which have been designated as such under the National Parks and Access to the Countryside Act (NPACA) 1949, s 6(1), (2) and (3), because of their inherent natural beauty. The official title 'national park' is a misnomer. They are not 'national' in the sense that they belong to the State; the land is owned and operated by individual landowners unlike in other countries; and they are not 'parks' as they are working environments where public access may be restricted.

National parks are designated by the Countryside Agency and the Countryside Council for Wales, and are subject to confirmation by the respective SoS. The statutory duty is that of (NPACA 1949), s 5(1)(a), (b)):

(a) conserving and enhancing the natural beauty, wildlife and cultural heritage of the areas; and

(b)   promoting opportunities for the understanding and enjoyment of the special qualities of those areas by members of the public.

The government is currently urging the consideration of National Park status for the South Downs and the New Forest. PPG 17, 'Sport and Recreation', makes it clear that, where there is a conflict between these two purposes, conservation must take precedence over recreation. There are seven national parks in England and three in Wales, namely: the Brecon Beacons, Dartmoor, Exmoor, the Lake District, the North York Moors, Northumberland, the Peak District, the Pembrokeshire Coast, Snowdonia and the Yorkshire Dales, to which the Broads was added in 1989 (Norfolk and Suffolk Broads Act 1988). The Broads have the same status as a national park, and the Broads Authority exercises similar functions within its area, with the additional responsibility of 'protecting the interests of navigation'.

The Scottish Parliament is also proposing to designate the first National Parks in Scotland which will cover the area around Loch Lomond and also the Trossachs.

The outstanding success of national parks as major centres for recreation and tourism has placed enormous responsibility on the park authorities, who now operate as planning authorities in their own right. The task of promoting the enjoyment by ever increasing members of the public has to be balanced not only against the need to enhance natural beauty but also to meet the changing employment structure and the demands of the prime land use, which is, in most parks, upland farming, the viability of which is largely determined by agricultural subsidies determined by the EU Common Agricultural Policy. National parks are essentially working environments, a fact which has determined the character which it is now sought to conserve; and any change in the level of subsidy paid to farmers may well result in changes to the character of the environment which are outside the normal powers of control exercised by lpas. For example, a reduction in the level of subsidy paid for upland cattle will almost inevitably lead to an increased level of stocking to maintain an economic balance for the farmer, and this can have a drastic effect upon the character of the flora and fauna in such sensitive areas.

25.4   FUNCTIONS OF A NATIONAL PARKS AUTHORITY

The Planning and Compensation Act 1991 requires that each authority shall prepare a local plan covering its area as well as a plan for minerals and waste policies. National parks will continue to operate within the appropriate county structure plan, except for the Lake District and the Peak District, which are granted responsibility for the preparation of structure plans for their areas.

National Parks Authorities and the Broads Authority are responsible for development control in their areas, and applications are to be submitted direct to the relevant authority, except in the case of the Broads Authority, where applications will continue to be lodged with the district councils who will pass them to the authority for decision.

In addition to 'normal' planning powers vested in NPAs, there are restrictions on permitted development rights (see Art 1(5) of the Town and Country Planning Act (General Permitted Development) Order (GPDO) 1995 (SI 1995/418), Chapter 10). Nevertheless, changes to the character of the countryside in general and the particular special scenic quality of national parks can be dramatically altered by changes which do not fall within the definition of 'development'. Encouragement is therefore given to the use of 'agreements', for example, management agreements (s 45) and afforestation agreements, which are designed to control those important elements of change. The use of agreements also extends to providing public access by means of access agreements.

Much of the national park areas cover upland areas which are suitable for afforestation which, if carried out, can have a major impact on the quality of the environment. The planting of trees does not constitute 'development' and is not subject to planning control. Agreements are, therefore, encouraged with the Forestry Commission to define areas which can be regarded as appropriate for afforestation. In addition, the SoS may make an order under s 42 of the Wildlife and Countryside Act 1968 preventing the conversion of moorland or heath to agriculture or forestry if it would be likely to adversely affect the character and appearance of the countryside. Under the provisions of s 42(2), no person shall:

(a)   by ploughing or otherwise convert into agricultural land any land … which is moor or heath which has not been agricultural land at any time in the preceding 20 years; or

(b)   carry out on any such land any other agricultural operation or any forestry operation which (in either case) appears to the ministers to be likely to affect its character and appearance …

Sub-section (2) shall not apply to any operation carried out, or caused or permitted to be carried out, by the owner or occupier of the land if:

(a) the NPA have given their consent to the carrying out of the operations;

(b) that authority has neither given nor refused consent and a period of three months has elapsed from the giving of the notice; and

(c) where the authority have refused to give consent but 12 months have expired from the giving of the notice (s 3).

The purpose of the 12-month postponement of operations is to allow the authority to offer a management agreement (s 39) to the person proposing to carry out the work, and the agreement will contain provisions as to the payments in respect of conditions required by the authority. The sum to be paid is subject to arbitration should the offeree so require (s 50). There is no obligation on the person to accept an agreement, and should he choose not to do so, he may continue with the work *but* he will not necessarily receive a farm capital grant under s 29 of the Agriculture Act 1970.

Each authority is required to prepare a map of the park showing areas of mountain, woodland, down, cliff, foreshore (including any bank, barrier, dene or beach), moor and heath, whose natural beauty should be conserved (s 43). This map must be reviewed every five years.

To assist in the conservation of the areas, the SoS or the authority, may make an Art 4 direction (see Chapter 10, para 10.2) for any part of their area. Should the direction require the use of expensive materials, for example, local stone, up to 25% of any additional costs may be claimed from the Farm Improvement Scheme Grant. Using powers under the Road Traffic Acts, limitations may also be placed upon the type, and restrictions on the time, of traffic using certain highways.

In *R v Northumberland NPA* (1998) EGCS 120, the High Court was asked to declare which body was the responsible planning authority where an application straddled the National Park boundary. Whilst the NPA had powers in relation to land within the

Park, by virtue of Sched 1, para 3(2) where the application straddled the boundary, this was a county matter. Accordingly, the determination of the application fell to be determined by Northumberland County Council.

25.5   PUBLIC ACCESS

The Countryside and Rights of Way Act (CROW) 2000 introduced the right to roam over open land in England and Wales. A right of access on foot for recreational purposes is created over 'access land' which is defined in s 1 as;

(a)   open country or registered common land shown on maps prepared under the Act;

(b)   land over 600 metres above sea level;

(c)   land subject to voluntary access arrangements under s 16 but excluding

(d)   land subject to other statutory rights of access and

(e)   'excepted land'.

'Open country' is defined as mountain, moor, heath or down but excluding improved or semi-improved grassland and large areas of open water (s 1(2)). 'Excepted land' is by its nature unsuitable for access rights and includes land:

(a) ploughed or drilled in the previous year and 'set-side' land or that used for the keeping of horses;

(b) covered by buildings or within their curtilage;

(c) within 20 m of a dwelling or a building housing livestock;

(d) used as a park or garden;

(e) used for mineral working by surface extraction;

(f) used for a railway (including light railway);

(g) used as a golf course, racecourse, training of race horses, or aerodrome;

(h) used by statutory undertakers or the military; and

(i) covered by pens for the temporary holding or detention of livestock.

Access can be excluded or restricted in certain circumstances including the right of landowners to close access land for up to 28 days a year. In addition the countryside authorities can restrict or exclude land:

(a) for management purposes;

(b) for safety reasons or to avoid the risk of fire;

(c) for the protection of nature conservation or historical heritage reasons; and

(d) the SoS for national and security or defence reasons.

In spite of the fact that s 54 of the Wildlife and Countryside Act 1981 required highway authorities to re-classify roads used as public paths as either byways open to all traffic, or bridleways or footpaths, this has not been forthcoming in many areas. The CROW 2000 creates a new class of right of way, the 'restricted byway' which gives rights of way on foot, by horse, or non-mechanically propelled vehicles, thus excluding motorcyclists and four-wheel drive vehicles (s 48(4)).

25.6   COUNTRY PARKS

The concept of country parks was given legislative backing in the Countryside Act 1968 (s 7), and they are intended to provide areas for open-air recreation and, in part, to relieve some of the pressures being experienced in national parks. Local planning authorities may create parks for the purposes of 'providing and improving opportunities for the enjoyment of the countryside by the general public'. Sites chosen must have regard to:

(a) location in relation to urban or built-up areas; and

(b) availability and adequacy of existing facilities.

Close co-operation is required between the urban and the adjoining rural authorities in the location of such parks, and contributions may be made by the urban authority to its rural counterpart to help finance such projects. The Countryside Agency is also involved in both the selection of sites and financial support for the projects. Parks may be developed on land owned by the local authority or with the agreement of the landowner and other persons having an interest in the land. Where common land exists, the local authority has power to develop the site as a country park and to provide facilities and erect buildings. Generally, the development takes the form of adequate footpath systems, parking areas, picnic tables, public conveniences, information kiosks, and possibly the provision of meals and refreshments.

25.7   AREAS OF OUTSTANDING NATURAL BEAUTY

Areas of Outstanding Natural Beauty (AONBs) must be confirmed by the SoS but there is no provision for a local inquiry as is the case with the designation of National Parks. The object of designation is to ensure that special regard is given to the appearance of the countryside and nature conservation. The SoS may by order establish a Conservation Board (s 86 (1) CROW 2000) whose functions shall be exercisable currently by a local authority or authorities. If no such board is created control remains with the relevant local authority and in either case the primary function is to take such action as is deemed necessary to enhance the natural beauty of the area. Under s 89(1) CROW 2000 every conservation board or relevant local authority is required to prepare and publish a plan formulating their policy for the management of their area. To date two Conservation Boards have been declared; The Cotswolds etc (Establishment of Conservation Board) Order 2004 (SI 2004/1716) and the Chilterns Order 2004 (SI 2004/1778). Each Board will be made up of representatives from local authorities, parish councils and members appointed by the SoS. Within AONBs, there are restricted permitted development rights under Art 1(5) of the GPDO 1995 (see Chapter 10). There are currently 541 confirmed AONBs in England and Wales, which cover approximately 14% of the total land area.

25.8   AREAS OF GREAT LANDSCAPE VALUE

In the preparation of development plans, many authorities include locally devised means of classifying land, such as areas of great landscape value, to denote areas where the quality of the landscape is such that particular policies are applied to provide additional protection. These areas have no direct statutory implications for the planning process and do *not* result in any limitation of permitted development rights or require any formal consultation with specific interests but are used by lpas to ensure a stricter use of development control powers.

25.9 GREEN BELTS

Green belts, which have become an established element of post-war in planning, are not designated by the Countryside Agency or the SoS; they are the result of policies established in development plans and, as such, they are open to review and amendment. Within such areas, there is a presumption against inappropriate development, but again there is no limitation on the permitted development rights. The government's policy on green belts is set out in PPG 2, 'Green Belts', which is to check urban sprawl, safeguard the surrounding countryside, prevent neighbouring towns from merging, preserving the special character of historic towns, and to assist in urban regeneration. Apart from the presumption against inappropriate development, there is no diminution of permitted development rights within green belts as occurs in national parks and AONBs.

Since their inception, it has always been assumed by politicians, planners and the public that green belts would remain in agricultural use, thus ensuring a continuation of their 'greenness'. This assumption is being called into question in the most critical areas of green belts as a result of difficulties experienced in farming immediately adjacent to built-up areas because of vandalism and trespass. These parts of the green belt which abut the urban area are frequently described as 'urban fringe' and, as noted in PPG 7 (para 3.13):

> ... require a positive approach to planning and management, aimed at securing environmental improvement and beneficial use of land, and increased public access, to provide amenity for the residents of urban areas.

As a result, a number of urban lpas have set up Urban Fringe Management Schemes, or carry out projects with the assistance of the Groundwork Trust, with the object of:

(a) carrying out improvements to the environment;

(b) advising and assisting landowners in conserving wildlife and landscape;

(c) providing access for persons living in urban areas; and

(d) education of the urban user of the countryside.

25.10 ENGLISH NATURE

English Nature (previously known as the Nature Conservancy Council) is responsible for designating and managing nature reserves and Sites of Special Scientific Interest (SSSIs). There are approximately 125 nature reserve sites in England and Wales, managed to provide suitable conditions for the retention and study of natural flora and fauna and geological and physiographical features. English Nature has a duty to inform landowners, tenants and lpas of the designation of such sites. The notification to landowners takes immediate effect. The reserve may be managed with the agreement of the landowner, and this will usually restrict operations and, therefore, payments may be made to the parties affected.

Sites of Special Scientific Interest are areas not forming nature reserves but having the same features or characteristics as outlined above. There is the same duty to inform the landowner, tenant and the lpa, and the SoS is empowered to make an order in respect of any land to safeguard a feature of special interest. Compensation is payable to the person having an interest in land comprising part of an agricultural unit, and this is the difference in value as a result of the order. Persons contravening the order are liable to a fine. Marine nature reserves, either tidal or up to the limit of territorial waters, may be the subject of an order by the SoS. The management of such areas is undertaken by English Nature.

The method of notification and the processes of consultation in declaring SSSIs has been the subject of two appeals to the courts: *R v Nature Conservancy Council ex p Bolton MBC* [1996] JPL 203 and *R v Nature Conservancy Council ex p London Brick Co Ltd* [1996] JPL 227. In the *Bolton* case, it was found that there had been a breach of natural justice because there had not been a fair appreciation of the objections raised by the local authority. In the second case, in reviewing s 28 of the Wildlife and Countryside Act, May J upheld the confirmation on the basis that if there were features of special interest on the site (in this case a species of water beetle), then that in itself would be a strong reason for confirmation. Further, it was not considered necessary for English Nature to be able to confirm that future conservation would be assured for the confirmation to be made. The decision to confirm the notification was held not to be perverse even though the survival of the beetle at the site probably could not be achieved.

The potential conflict between the requirement imposed by the declaration of a SSSI and other statutory requirements placed upon the landowner was the subject of an appeal to the High Court in the case of *Ward v Secretary of State* [1996] JPL 200; (1995) ELM 153. It was claimed that there was conflict between the restrictions contained in the order to declare a SSSI and the duty of the owners of the land to maintain a bridleway crossing the land as required by the Highways Act 1980 (s 40). The appellant argued that the inspector had failed to take this into account when confirming the order, but the High Court concluded that there was no irreconcilable conflict and that the order should stand.

Where an application to the Department for Environment, Food and Rural Affairs (DEFRA) for a grant for farm improvement work is objected to by English Nature, no grant shall be awarded until either the objection has been considered and, in the case of England, there has been consultation with the SoS.

Following the Council of European Communities Habitats Directive (93/43/EEC), the government has forwarded a list of 136 sites for designation as special areas of conservation (see Chapter 29).

25.11 ENVIRONMENTALLY SENSITIVE AREAS

Environmentally Sensitive Areas (ESAs) are designated by the agriculture departments in England and Wales under the Agriculture Act 1986, and particular policies and programmes apply to such areas. They cover areas of special landscape, wildlife or historic interest which are to be protected by offering financial support for the adoption of specific agricultural practices. Farmers and landowners are offered financial incentives to recreate traditional landscapes in areas declared to be ESAs, and the money is available from the Department of the Environment rather than from DEFRA. The scheme is limited to England and includes:

(a) moorland fringes, hay meadows;

(b) chalk and limestone grassland;

(c) lowland heath;

(d) coastal land (salt marshes, cliffs and sand dunes); and

(e) waterside landscapes.

25.12 NATURAL HABITATS

The Conservation (Natural Habitats etc) Regulations 1994 (SI 1994/2716) arose from the need to implement the EC Council Directive on the Conservation of Natural Habitats and of Wild Flora and Fauna (92/43/EEC). The regulations apply to sites designated as Special Areas of Conservation (SACs) and to sites classified as Special Protection Areas (SPAs) under the EC Directive on the Conservation of Wild Birds (79/409/EEC) which are referred to as 'European sites'. The Wild Life and Countryside Act 1981 (England and Wales) Amendment Regulations 2004 (SI 2004/1387) amends the definition of 'wild bird' in s 27 of the Act by including any species which is ordinarily resident in or is a visitor to the European Territory of any Member State.

Part IV of the Regulations amends TCPA 1990, in that applications for planning permission, development order, grant of deemed planning permission, approval of development proposals and other consents, are subject to the provisions of the Directive. Planning permissions which have not been fully implemented and which may significantly affect a SPA or SAC are to be reviewed and the appropriate action taken by inviting those concerned to enter into a s 106 agreement. Should no such obligation be entered into then the authority must proceed to use its powers under TCPA 1990 to revoke, or modify, the permission or require the discontinuance of the use or the removal of buildings or other works (reg 56). Regulation 60 prevents permitted development rights set out in the GPDO 1995 which adversely affect the integrity of a SAP or SAC and the opinion of the appropriate nature conservation body is to be sought (reg 61).

The lpa or the SoS may agree to a plan or project only after they have ascertained that it will not adversely affect the European site if they are satisfied that:

(a) there being no alternative solution, the plan or project must be carried out for imperative reasons of overriding public interest which may be of social or economic in nature, the competent authority may agree to the implementation of the plan or project notwithstanding a negative assessment of the implications for the site;

(b) where the site concerned hosts a priority natural habitat type or a priority species the reasons referred to in (a) must relate to human health, public safety or beneficial consequences of primary importance to the environment or

(c) other reasons, which in the opinion of the European Commission are imperative reasons of overriding public interest.

The High Court in *Newsum v Welsh Assembly Government* [2004] EWHC held that the words 'other imperative reasons of overriding public interests' were not limited by preceeding phrase 'preserving public health or public safety', since paragraph (2)(e) identifies 'social or economic nature and beneficial consequences of primary importance for the environment' as reasonable factors. Furthermore the categories described in paragraph (2)(c) are not intended to be exhaustive. The court therefore considered that public interest was capable of being served by saving a protected species which would otherwise inevitably suffer damage as a result of an existing planning permission granted before the regulations came into effect.

25.13 DIRECTIVE ON THE CONSERVATION OF WILD BIRDS

This Directive, as amended by Directive 92/43/EEC, requires Member States to take measures to ensure the conservation of wild birds and special habitats for certain species. States are required to classify SPAs for this purpose and to apply similar measures for migratory species, with particular regard to wetlands, especially those of international importance under the Ramsar Convention. The main requirements of the directive are:

(a) that it applies to birds, their eggs, nests and habitats (Art 1);

(b) measures are to be taken to maintain the population of the species at a level which corresponds to ecological, scientific and cultural requirements, whilst taking account of economic and recreational requirements, or to adapt the population of the species to that level (Art 2);

(c) to preserve, maintain or re-establish biotypes and habitats (Art 3);

(d) certain species to be the subject of special conservation measures, and Member States are required to classify the most suitable territories (Art 4);

(e) prohibition of deliberate killing, capture, damage to nests, taking of eggs, the sale or transport for sale of birds, eggs, killed or captured (Arts 5, 6 and 8);

(f) Member States may derogate from the provisions above, if there is no other solution, for the following reasons (Art 9):

    (i)   interests of public health or safety;

    (ii)   interests of air safety;

    (iii) serious damage to crops, livestock, forests, fisheries or water;

    (iv) for the purposes of research or teaching; or

    (v)   the capture and keeping of certain birds in small numbers.

The amendments introduced by the Habitats Directive (92/43/EEC) set out the criteria that Member States may take into account which will allow adverse development or proceed where there are 'imperative reasons for overriding public interest, including those of a social or economic nature'. Where a site involves a priority habitat, and/or a priority species, the only reasons which may be raised are those relating to human health or public safety. Member States must take adequate compensatory measures to ensure that the overall coherence of 'Natura 2000' is protected.

The directives relating to conservation of wild birds have become a major issue in the SoS's decision to exclude the area known as Lappel Bank from the designated

Medway Estuary and Marshes Special Protection for Birds. The conflict arises from the economic need to expand the port facilities at Sheerness on the Isle of Sheppey by reclaiming part of Lappel Bank for which planning permission was granted in 1989. The area forms part of a wetland of international importance for wildfowl and wading birds which use the area as a breeding and wintering area and as a staging post during spring and autumn migrations.

The Royal Society for the Protection of Birds (RSPB) made an application for a judicial review (see *R v Swale BC and Medway Ports Authority ex p RSPB* (1991) JPL 39; 1 PLR 6). The first application for judicial review dealt with the issue of whether there had been compliance with the Environmental Assessment Regulations, and the second application in July 1994 was on the question of whether or not the SoS was entitled to have regard to economic considerations under the Conservation of Wild Birds Directive. The RSPB argued that in designating a SPA, the SoS was entitled to have regard only to conservation issues, and that the economic issues would only become relevant once the area was designated and an application for development was submitted. His primary duty was to choose those areas most suitable for classification as SPAs.

The Divisional Court held that the SoS did have the right to take into account economic factors, and this decision was supported by a majority decision of the Court of Appeal (August 1994); but Hoffman LJ dissented on the basis that 'this would deprive the wetlands and listed species of that stringent protection which the Directive was intended to provide'. The matter was then referred to the House of Lords (February 1995), which reversed this ruling. Lord Jauncey of Tullichettle said:

> My Lords, faced with competing arguments of substance and with support for each of those arguments in conflicting judgments to two members of the Court of Appeal, I do not consider that your Lordships have any alternative but to refer the matter to the European Court of Justice under Art 177 of the Treaty, for a ruling.

The decision of the European Court of Justice (ECJ) rejected all the arguments put forward by the UK. Economic considerations can play no part in the designation of sites as being of special interest *but*, once a site has been designated, this does not prevent development going ahead on economic grounds. However, as the Advocate General pointed out, for this to happen, it must be shown that an assessment of likely effects must be made, and there are procedural safeguards including compensatory measures. If economic considerations could be taken into account at the designation stage, those procedural safeguards could be avoided.

The decision in *WWF-UK Ltd v Secretary of State for Scotland* (1998) *The Times*, 20 November, had an important impact upon UK law which incorporates the Birds and Habitats Directive. The action related to the SoS's proposal to revise proposed boundaries of the SPA to exclude parts of the northern slopes of Cairn Gorm for which planning permission had been granted, with a s 106 agreement, for a funicular railway. The court accepted that the boundaries of a SPA under the Birds and Habitats Directive had to be determined by reference to ornithological criteria alone. However, it rejected the submission that all contiguous, or linked qualifying habitats or species, had to be included in the site and that a Member State had no discretion in the boundary delineation. The court held that the SoS had been entitled to take the ski-slopes into consideration in defining the boundaries of the SPA and it was difficult to see how they could be ignored if the exercise were to be undertaken on a scientific basis. It also went on to reject the submission from Scottish Heritage to the effect that the lpa could not lawfully ascertain, as they were obliged to, that the development would not adversely affect the integrity of the proposed site.

The UK legislation designed to implement the directive was the Wildlife and Countryside Act 1981, which included prohibitions on the killing, taking or destroying eggs or nests (Part I), and the protection of special areas by designation as SSSIs (Part II). This has been followed by the Conservation (Natural Habitats, etc) Regulations 1994 (SI 1994/2716), which provides new controls in respect of the designation and protection of SPAs.

25.14 FARMING: PERMITTED DEVELOPMENT

There is no planning restriction on the type of crop which is grown, or indeed on the planting of trees, as neither falls within the definition of 'development', and this can have a dramatic effect upon the character of the landscape. Some types of agricultural activity need no permission at all, and for those GPDO 1995 is irrelevant. Section 55(2)(e) of the TCPA 1947 provides that:

> The use of any land for the purpose of agriculture or forestry (including afforestation) and the use for any of those purposes of any building occupied together with the land so used ...

does not constitute development. The definition of 'agriculture' under s 336(1) of the TCPA 1947 is also broad and includes:

> ... horticulture, fruit growing, seed growing, dairy farming, the breeding and keeping of livestock (including any creature kept for the production of food, wool, skins, or fur or for the purpose of farming of land), the use of land as grazing land, meadow land, osier land, market garden and nursery grounds, the use of land for woodlands where that use is ancillary to farming of land for agricultural purposes.

The question of what constitutes a lawful use as agriculture is demonstrated in the case of *Millington v Secretary of State* [1999] JPL 644; 1 PLR 36 (referred to in Chapter 7, para 7.14). This case revolved around what processing can be considered to be acceptable and still remain within the definition of agriculture.

Proposals to establish new agricultural units are tested against the policies contained in PPG 7, 'The Countryside and the Rural Economy', which are designed to ensure that any residential development remains linked to an agricultural activity which had the clear prospect of remaining viable. Not surprisingly, the test of viability has been a matter considered by the courts. In the case of *South Buckinghamshire DC v Secretary of State* (1998) EGCS 164, the court held that an inspector had erred in his assessment of the financial viability of an agricultural operation in terms of Annex 1 of PPG 7 because the test required an assessment of the farm as it was actually being run.

In *Crowborough Parish Council v Secretary of State* [1980] JPL 281; (1982) 43 P & CR 229, it was held that the intensification of use brought about by the conversion of land to allotment gardens did not involve operational development. It is also possible to change the use of any land, comprising any use in any location to agricultural use without planning permission (see *McKellan v Minister of Housing and Local Government* (1966) 198 EG 683). This permitted change of use also extends to buildings (see *North Warwickshire BC v Secretary of State* [1984] JPL 434; (1985) 50 P & CR 47), but does not cover 'operational' development.

Agriculture in general benefits from the permitted development rights under the GPDO 1995 (Sched 2, Part 6). The provisions of Part 6 distinguish between development on units of more than five hectares (Class A) and units of less than five but not less than 0.4 hectares (Class B).

25.14.1 Class A

Class A permits development of:

(a) works for the erection, extension or alteration of a building; or

(b) any excavation or engineering operations for the purpose of agriculture in the unit,

subject to the following limitations:

(a) not carried out on a parcel of land of less than one hectare;

(b) not related to a dwelling;

(c) involves the provision of a building or structure not designed for agricultural use;

(d) works, or other structures (other than a fence), to accommodate stock, plant or machinery, or any building erected or extended which would exceed 465 sq m;

(e) the height shall not exceed 33 m, or 3 m within 3 kilometres of an aerodrome;

(f) no part of the development is within 25 m of a metalled part of a trunk or classified road; and

(g) no erection or construction or works to a building to be used for livestock or the storage of slurry, or sewage sludge, within 400 m of the curtilage of a protected building.

Conditions relating to Class A:

(a) if within 400 m of a protected building, not to be used for livestock or slurry;

(b) extraction of minerals from land, including disused railway embankments, not to be removed from the unit;

(c) waste materials not to be brought to the site except to achieve development under Class A or the creation of a hard surface; and

(d) on Art 1(6) land (which includes conservation areas, national parks, and AONBs) the extension, alteration, etc, to a building, formation or alteration to a private way, carrying out excavations, deposit of waste, placing or assembly of a tank in any waters the developer shall:

- apply to the lpa to ascertain whether prior approval is required;
- apply to the lpa to ascertain whether prior approval is required relating to the siting design, external appearance, formation or alteration to private way, or the placing of a fish tank; and
- not carry out the development until local planning approval is given, or it is stated that no approval is required, or the lpa failed to reply within 28 days.

25.14.2 Class B

Under Class B, there are further limitations relating to agricultural buildings:

(a) the height of the building may not be increased;

(b) the cubic content of the original building may not be increased by more than 10%;

(c) the ground area of the building shall not be brought to more than 465 sq m; and

(d) in Art 1(6) areas, land is subject to the same conditions as Class A.

Certain rights apply only to Class B, and these are:

(a) development in connection with private ways;

(b) apparatus such as cables and sewers;

(c) certain waste deposits subject to limitations on area; and

(d) additional or replacement plant and machinery.

The Order has been amended by SI 1997/366 which imposes further conditions on permitted development rights and in cases where:

(a) such development for agricultural purposes ceases permanently within 10 years of its substantial completion; or

(b) planning permission has not been granted authorising development for purposes other than agriculture within three years of the permanent cessation of its agricultural use and there is no outstanding appeal.

The development must be removed unless the lpa has agreed otherwise in writing, and the land must be restored as far as practicable to its former condition unless otherwise agreed with the lpa.

This particular amendment presents potential problems for the lpa as, initially, the onus is on the developer to inform the authority within seven days of the 'substantial completion' which is the date from which the 10-year period commences. This raises the issues of:

(a) what constitutes 'substantial' completion?; and

(b) as the onus is on the developer to inform the lpa within seven days, what if he fails to do so or deliberately delays completion of the development?

A further problem which is likely to arise relates to the determination of the permanent cessation of use. The building may only be in intermittent use for the storage of grain or hay or may only be used to store old agricultural machinery. In either case it would be difficult to prove that the use for agricultural purposes had ceased and, bearing in mind the capital investment involved in its construction, there is likely be a general reluctance on the part of owners to create circumstances where the building would have to be demolished.

Although Classes A and B refer to the whole agricultural unit in relation to permitted development rights granted under Part 6, that unit has been held to be irrelevant for determining the question of whether a material change of use has taken place on agricultural land. In *Fuller v Secretary of State* [1987] JPL 854); (1988) 56 P & CR 84; 1 PLR 1, the SoS disagreed with his inspector's findings that in an enforcement appeal the agricultural unit may be a more satisfactory means of determining planning issues rather than the planning unit. The Court of Appeal upheld the SoS's decision that the agricultural unit and the planning unit were not necessarily the same, and that scattered parcels of land could not be regarded as the planning unit 'any more than, say, the similarly scattered outlets of a local chain of shops'.

25.14.3 Class C

Mineral working for agricultural purposes is permitted provided it is required for agricultural purposes within the unit, is not removed from the holding, and does not take place within 25 m of the metalled part of a trunk or classified road.

25.15 INITIATIVES RELATING TO SURPLUS LAND

The dramatic success of the farming industry in increasing productivity has ironically led to the need to take land out of agricultural production. Unlike other uses which are no longer viable, agricultural land does not easily lend itself to alternative uses because of its location and the planning policies which are designed to restrict development in rural areas. To assist in overcoming this problem, a number of initiatives have been undertaken to encourage farmers to take land out of production and, at the same time, enhance the visual amenity in rural areas, such as:

(a) The Farm Woodland Scheme is an attempt to encourage farmers to take land permanently out of agricultural production with the object of:

- reducing agricultural surpluses;
- enhancing the landscape and creating new wildlife habitats;
- contributing to supporting farm income and rural employment; and
- in the longer term contributing to the UK's timber needs.

The scheme is primarily intended for arable land, or improved grassland, but there is provision for approximately one-twelfth of the money to be spent in 'less favoured areas', that is, mainly upland areas. The scheme has to be agreed with the Forestry Commission who will then make a planting grant, which is geared to provide an incentive to plant broad-leaved species, and there are annual payments for a period of 10–40 years.

(b) Set-aside policies which, as the name implies, require that farmers rotate crop growth on their arable land in an attempt to overcome surpluses in the EU. If tree-planting takes place, there is an alternative to the Farm Woodland Scheme which provides a set-aside planting grant and an annual payment for a period of five years.

(c) Landscape conservation grants are also available from the Countryside Commission. These are available for planting trees and small woodlands, managing existing small woodlands, and conserving important landscape features.

(d) Farm Schemes operate in the upland areas of national parks under s 39 of the Wildlife and Countryside Act 1981. The problems of reducing the agricultural subsidy in the past has led, in many instances, to the over-stocking of upland moors, for example, the North York Moors experienced a 53% increase in breeding ewes between 1971 and 1986. The object of the scheme is to 'remove the pressure for increased production, encourage low intensity farming and guarantee environmental protection and enhancement whilst stimulating local employment'. Such schemes are voluntarily entered into and cover the entire farm and take the form of a five-year legal agreement between the farmer and the NPA. Annual payments are made in return for the farm being managed to an agreed prescription, and the plan also identifies works to be carried out in the five-year period for which discretionary grants are available.

25.16 FARM DIVERSIFICATION

The need for farmers to consider diversification as a means of increasing the economic base of their primary activity has resulted in grants being made available under the Farm Diversification Scheme. A grant of up to 50% of the cost of an enterprise feasibility study, up to a maximum of £3,000 to individuals and £10,000 to groups. The types of enterprises which are eligible for this form of grant aid are:

(a) processing of farm produce and timber;

(b) craft manufacturing and renovation of agricultural machinery;

(c) farm shops;

(d) direct sales of fruit and vegetables;

(e) holiday accommodation;

(f) catering;

(g) facilities for sport and recreation;

(h) educational facilities relating to farming and the countryside; and

(i) livery for horses and ponies and hiring of the same.

In addition, PPG 7 (para 2.15 and Annex D) encourages the re-use of agricultural buildings, particularly for workshop units or holiday accommodation as part of the process of farm diversification. However, it should be noted that the thrust towards diversification does not provide a *carte blanche* for the change of use, and this will require planning consent before any change can take place.

CHAPTER 26

CARAVANS AND CARAVAN SITES

26.1 INTRODUCTION

In this chapter, unless specified, all references relate to the Caravan Sites and Control of Development Act 1960.

The use of land for the stationing of caravans for residential use, whether it is a permanent use or restricted to certain times of the year, is not only controlled under planning legislation but will also normally require a site licence under Part I of the Caravan Sites and Control of Development Act 1960. The site licence is a means of ensuring that public health standards are maintained and, in a sense, is the equivalent of building regulation consent for permanent structures. A caravan site will require both a site licence and planning consent under the Town and Country Planning Act (TCPA) 1990 before it can operate (see *R v Glamorgan CC ex p Morris* [1992] JPL 374).

The use of land for a caravan site can involve a number of quite distinct forms of operation and intensity of use. The site can be used for:

(a) the siting of touring caravans, the use of which is frequently restricted to a particular period of the year, for example, March to October;

(b) occupation by static caravans which remain on the site all year, but which have planning restrictions on the period when they may be occupied;

(c) occupation by static caravans which are in permanent residential use; and

(d) occupation by gypsies and other persons of nomadic habit.

The Caravans Sites Act 1968 was primarily an attempt to deal with the issues arising from 'gypsies and other persons of nomadic habit' by placing a duty on local authorities to provide sites for gypsies and to grant powers to prohibit unauthorised camping in designated areas. The 1968 Act was later amended by the Local Government Planning and Land Act 1980 (ss 173–77), and this Part of the 1980 Act was, in turn, repealed by the Criminal Justice and Public Order Act 1994. As a result, local authorities no longer have a duty to provide accommodation for gypsies and Circular 1/94, 'Gypsy Sites and Planning', offers fresh policy advice to local planning authorities (lpas) on determining planning applications for private gypsy sites.

26.2 CARAVANS

Caravans are defined in the 1960 Act (s 29(1)) as:

> Any structure designed or adapted for human habitation which is capable of being moved from one place to another whether being towed, or transported on a motor vehicle or trailer, and any motor vehicle so designed or adapted but which does *not* include railway stock on rails or forming part of a railway system, or a tent.

Motor vehicles used for human habitation which have not been designed for that purpose, or have not been physically altered to meet that purpose, do *not* fall within the definition of a caravan (see *Backer v Secretary of State and Wealdon DC* [1983] JPL 602; 1 WLR 1485; 2 All ER 1021).

The 1960 definition was amended in the 1968 Act (s 13) to include 'twin unit caravans' (static caravans) if the dimensions do not exceed any of the following limits:

(a) length over 18.288 m (60 ft);

(b) width over 6.096 m (20 ft); and

(c) average height of the living accommodation over 3.048 m (10 ft).

A caravan site is defined in s 1(4) of the 1960 Act as 'any land on which a caravan is stationed for human *habitation* together with the land used in conjunction therewith'. A site which is used purely for the storage of caravans is, therefore, a different use in planning terms and will require planning permission in the normal way.

In *Measor v Secretary of State and Tunbridge Wells BC* [1999] JPL 182, the issue was the definition of 'development' (s 55) and whether the siting of a caravan was a building operation or use of land. The applicant had been denied a certificate of lawful use for the stationing of six mobile and 12 touring caravans for residential use on his land. The main issue was whether the appropriate period for enforcement action was four years, as a building operation, or 10 years, as a change of use of land. The court held that the meaning of 'building' required three tests, those of size, permanence and attachment (see *Cardiff Rating Authority and Cardiff Assessment Co v Guest Keen Baldwin's Iron and Steel Co Ltd* [1949] 1KB 385 and *R v Swansea City Council ex p Elitestone Ltd* (1993) 66 P & CR 422). A mobile home could not satisfy these tests with regard to the factors of permanence and attachment and the court concluded that the inspector had been entitled to find that the caravans did not constitute 'buildings'.

The change of the period of occupancy from a restricted holiday use to that of permanent residential use is an issue which concerns lpas, as the latter requires all the services normally associated with residential development, that is, schools, shopping facilities and local authority services. In the case, *Forest of Dean DC v Secretary of State and Howells* [1995] JPL 937; (1994) EGCS 138, an enforcement notice was issued alleging change of use to permanent residential use, and this was the subject of an appeal. The inspector's decision to allow the appeal on ground (c) (that is, 'that the matters do not constitute a breach of planning control' (s 174(2) of TCPA 1990) was the subject of a challenge by the local authority. The inspector's decision letter made it clear that:

> I do not regard any perceptible differences between holidaymakers and permanent residents, in the pattern of their pedestrian or vehicular movements, as having a significant effect upon the character of this land use. I do not, therefore, consider that, as a matter of fact and degree, a material change of use is involved if a holiday caravan were to be occupied as a permanent dwelling, any more than if a cottage were to be used as a second home, or made available (as many are) for holiday purposes. It follows that, if it is necessary to restrict the occupation of caravans to holidaymakers, in my opinion this can be achieved only by the imposition of appropriate planning conditions.

The court, in reviewing this decision, accepted that in this case there was no planning condition which expressly restricted the use to holiday caravans, but held that the inspector had failed to recognise the description of the development permitted in the original consent (see *Uttlesford DC v Secretary of State and Leigh* [1989] JPL 685; (1991) 2 PLR 76). On the question of fact and degree, the court accepted that the inspector was correct in looking at the effect on the site itself, but he had failed to consider the off-site effects of such a use which are relevant to whether a change of use was material (see *Devonshire CC v Allen Caravans (Estates) Ltd* [1963] JPL 47; 14 P & CR 440 and *Blum (Lilo) v Secretary of State and Richmond-on-Thames LBC* [1987] JPL 278). The decision was remitted to the Secretary of State (SoS) with the opinion of the court that he should reconsider whether, as a matter of fact and degree, the change of use, from holiday caravans to caravans for permanent residence, constituted a material change of use taking into account any relevant off-site effects.

It is clear from this judgment that, to avoid such changes taking place, and consequent legal arguments concerning matters of fact and degree, the lpa is well advised to ensure that the intended holiday use is established by restricting the use by way of a planning condition attached to any planning permission.

26.3 SITE LICENCES

In addition to the need to gain planning permission, the general rule is that no land shall be used as a caravan site unless a site licence (s 1(1)) has been issued by the relevant local authority to the occupier of the land comprising the site. The 'occupier' is that person entitled to possession of the land. If the land does not exceed 400 ssqquare yds (344 sq m), and is let under a tenancy for the use as a caravan site, the expression 'occupier' means the person who would be entitled to possession of the land but for the right of tenancy.

A site licence may only be granted following the grant of planning permission, or by virtue of a Development Order, and the licence must be granted within two months of the grant of planning permission (s 3(3)), unless:

(a) there is an agreement between the parties to extend the period (s 3(4)); or

(b) the applicant has had a site licence revoked within the previous three years (s 3(6)).

If there is no planning permission in existence, an application for a site licence must be refused (s 3(3)).

Unlike planning permission, a site licence does not 'go with the land'. The holder of the licence may only transfer it to a new occupier with the prior consent of the licensing authority. Where such transfers are accepted, the person to whom it is transferred must be the occupier of the site (s 10(1)). It is almost inconceivable that the licensing authority would refuse the transfer of a licence as, provided there is a planning consent for the site, the new occupier would simply be required to apply for a licence which must then be granted. However, if the licensing authority wishes to vary the conditions relating to the existing licence, it may be tempted to refuse the transfer which would then provide an opportunity to issue a new licence that would incorporate amendments to the original conditions.

26.4 CONDITIONS ATTACHED TO THE LICENCE

Site licences cannot be limited in time unless the planning consent is itself limited, in which case, the expiration date in both cases will be the same on both consents, but the local authority has wide discretion on other issues to which it may wish to attach conditions. These must be necessary, or desirable, in the interests of:

(a) caravan dwellers on the site itself;

(b) any other class of persons; or

(c) the public at large (s 5(1)).

In imposing conditions under s 5(6), the local authority must have regard to the Caravan Sites and Control of Development Act 1960 – Model Standards and Development Control Policy Note No 8, 'Caravan Sites' (1969). A local authority is specifically authorised to impose the conditions designed to:

(a) restrict the number of caravans which are stationed on the land and the total number of caravans at any one time;

(b) control the types of caravans by reference to size, state of repair, or any other feature but not materials of which the caravans are constructed;

(c) position where the caravans are to be sited and the positions of any other structures, vehicles and tents;

(d) ensure that steps are taken to preserve and enhance the amenity of the land including planting or replanting of trees and bushes;

(e) ensure adequate fire precautions and means of fire fighting;

(f) ensure adequate sanitary arrangements and other facilities or equipment specified by the local authority; and

(g) specify that the site licence is displayed on the site if it accommodates more than three caravans (s 5(3)).

A condition may require the carrying out of works by the occupier within a specified period, and may prevent the site being occupied by caravans until the work is completed to the satisfaction of the local authority (s 5(4)). If the works are not completed within the time specified, the local authority may carry out the works and recover the costs incurred from the occupier (s 9(3)). Unlike conditions attached to the grant of planning consent, a condition on a site licence may require the occupier to carry out works to which he is not entitled as of right. Should the occupier fail to acquire such a right, then he must forgo the use of the land as a caravan site (s 5(5)).

Conditions must relate to the physical use of the land as a caravan site. Any attempt to include conditions which seek to control the rent or security of tenure, or which would affect the social lives of the caravan users, are *ultra vires* (see *Chertsey UDC v Mixnam's Properties Ltd* [1965] AC 735).

26.5   ALTERATION OF CONDITIONS

The local authority may seek to amend existing conditions or impose additional conditions at any time (s 8(1)), and the occupier may also apply for alteration of conditions (s 8(2)). In either event, the local authority shall not consider the alteration of conditions without having regard to the Model Standards (s 8(5)).

26.6   APPEALS AGAINST CONDITIONS

The 'person aggrieved' (see *Turner v Secretary of State and Another* (1974) 28 P & CR 123) has a right of appeal to the magistrates' court against conditions within 28 days of the issue of the licence (s 7(1)). If the court is of the opinion that the condition is 'unduly burdensome', it may vary or cancel the condition, but it must first have regard to the Model Standards. This provision also applies to any alteration of an existing licence (detailed above) (s 8(4)). When a site licence is amended, the holder must surrender the original licence to the local authority (s 11(1)), and failure to do so without reasonable excuse can result in a fine (s 11(2)).

The potential for overlap between planning controls and those relating to site licences was the issue in *Goodwin v Stratford-upon-Avon DC* [1997] JPL May Update; (1996) 73 P & CR. This was an appeal against a condition imposed upon a site licence which prescribed minimum dimensions for caravans on the site and required that 28 of the permitted 34 caravans should be towable. The court was concerned about the extent to which site licence conditions could be used to reduce existing use rights under planning law and found that the justices had failed to apply their minds to the question of whether the purpose addressed by the conditions were proper purposes. The court quashed the justices' decision and remitted the matter back to them for reconsideration.

26.7 EXEMPTIONS FROM SITE LICENCES

Schedule 1 sets out cases where the need for a site licence does *not* apply. These are as follows:

1   the use of land within the curtilage of a dwelling house as a caravan site which is incidental to the use of the dwelling;

2   the use of any land as a caravan site for a period of not more than two nights by a person travelling with a caravan, provided:

   (i)   at that time there is no other caravan for human habitation on the land including adjoining land in the same ownership; and

   (ii) during the previous 12 months there has not been a caravan on the land for more than 28 days;

3   the use of land for a caravan site on land comprising more than five acres provided that during the previous 12 months:

   (i)   there has not been a caravan on the site for more than 28 days; and

   (ii) there have not been more than three caravans on the site at any one time;

4   the use of a site occupied and supervised by a recreational organisation holding a certificate of exemption, for example, Caravan Club, Camping Club, Caravan Tourists' Association, Boy Scouts, Girl Guides, Land Rover Club, etc (Sched 1, para 12);

5   the use by not more than five caravans at a time on land where a certificate has been issued to an exempted organisation for use by its members;

6   use for not more than five days for a meeting of members of an exempted organisation provided the site is supervised by that organisation;

7   use of agricultural or forestry land for seasonal occupation by workers employed on the land, or in connection with building or engineering operations, during the period of those operations;

8   use of a site for travelling showmen (members of the Showmen's Guild) either when travelling or as winter quarters, that is, October–March;

9   use of a caravan site on land occupied by district or county councils; and

10 the use of land occupied by a county council as a caravan site for gypsies.

The restrictions placed on the use of land for a caravan site under (2) and (3) above pose problems for lpas which may wish to exercise enforcement power to ensure that the stated limits are not the subject of abuse. To have any chance of enforcing the limitations placed upon the frequency of use contained in Sched 1, the local authority would have to monitor each site on a daily basis for a period of 12 months!

26.8   LOCAL AUTHORITY CARAVAN SITES

Local authorities have powers to provide, manage and charge for sites (s 24), and these powers may be used in respect of persons not living within the local authority's area (s 24(4)). Whilst they are empowered to provide sites, local authorities are *not* empowered to provide caravans. The only exception to this is power granted under the Housing Acts, which allows local authorities to provide caravan accommodation for temporary rehousing of council tenants whilst improvement works take place to their homes.

26.9   CARAVANS ON COMMONS

A local authority may prohibit totally, or accept in specified circumstances, the stationing of caravans on commons, including town or village greens (s 23(8)). The need for this provision arises because, in the case of common land, there is no single legal interest which could 'cause or permit the use of land as a caravan site' (s 1) and, therefore, no offence could be committed.

26.10 SITES FOR GYPSIES

In the *Commission for Racial Equality v Dutton* [1989] 1 All ER 306, the court held that, for the purpose of race relations, gypsies were capable of being a separate 'racial group' as defined in s 3(1) of the Race Relations Act 1976. Despite their long presence in the UK and the fact that they were no longer derived from common racial stock, they had not merged wholly with the population, but remained an identifiable group defined by reference to their 'ethnic origins'. The court also held that the definitions of 'gypsy' in the Highways Act 1980 and the Caravans Act 1968 were not of material assistance.

The question of whether it is possible to lose gypsy status arose in *Hearne v Secretary of State (Wales) and Camarthenshire CC* [2000] JPL 161. Following the issue of enforcement notices, in dismissing the subsequent appeal, the inspector had found that the appellant had given up his status as a gypsy at the time he had moved onto the land because he intended to settle there and cease his nomadic life. The High Court determined that it was not sufficient to take away a person's gypsy status based simply upon his intention to settle somewhere permanently. More was required in the way of clear evidence that he not only intended to settle, but he intended to give up the nomadic way of life altogether. In this case, the appellant's intention was supported by the production of evidence that, having obtained a job, he was undertaking further training.

Government Circular advice was aimed at gypsies and, therefore, the concept of nomadic life was crucial. Whilst it was perfectly reasonable for gypsy families to wish to have a permanent base, the nomadic lifestyle could still exist, albeit only for a short period during the year. If the evidence is clear that the only occupant of the site intends to live there *not* as a gypsy, having given up his nomadic lifestyle, the court found it was easy to decide that the site is not a gypsy site and, therefore, its status was lost and the appeal was dismissed.

The advice contained in Circular 1/94, para 22, which states, 'as with any other planning applications, proposals for gypsy sites should continue to be determined solely in relation to land use factors', gave rise to concern in *Rexworthy v Secretary of State* [1998] JPL 864. It was unclear whether 'solely' implied that the decision-maker was to ignore the special circumstances of gypsy accommodation. In quashing the decision, and holding that the inspector had taken the narrow view of subordinating the particular circumstances of accommodation for gypsies to the development plan, the court implicitly extended 'land use factors' to include personal circumstances.

The special circumstances relating to gypsies was also raised in *Delaney v Secretary of State* [2000] JPL January Update. In this case, following an appeal, the inspector upheld the decision of the lpa to refuse permission for the siting of four mobile homes for occupation by gypsies on a site which was within the green belt and was an area of special landscape character. The argument advanced was that the inspector had adopted a general approach to the case that was wrong in principle. Section 54A introduced a plan led approach to planning appeals and it was submitted that it had no relevance because the development plan contained no policies relevant to the location or establishment of gypsy sites. In dismissing the application, the court held that s 54A is couched in mandatory terms and there can be no question of it being applied or disapplied as a matter of discretion.

The special circumstances resulting from the way of life of gypsies has led to numerous appeals to the courts, particularly involving Art 8 of the Human Rights Act 1998. In a leading case brought before the European Court of Human Rights, *Chapman v UK* 27238/95 [200] JPL 1659; 1665; 1669, it was declared:

> The judgment in any particular case by national authorities that there are legitimate planning objections to a particular use of a site is one which the court is not well equipped to challenge. It cannot visit each site to assess the impact of a particular proposal on a particular area in terms of impact on beauty, traffic conditions, sewerage and water facilities, educational facilities, medical facilities, employment opportunities and so on. Because planning inspectors visit the site, hear the arguments on all sides and allow examination of witnesses, they are better situated than the court to weigh the arguments.

In *Wrexham CB v The National Assembly for Wales* [2003] EWCA 835, the issue raised was whether a traditional gypsy who is unable to travel to find work because of illness or old age nevertheless remains a 'gypsy' for the purpose of planning control. The inspector accepted that although he was no longer able to travel the appellant nevertheless retained his gypsy status. The Court of Appeal overturned the decision of the lower court and Auld LJ said:

> The whole premise of the Strasburg Court's judgment ... was that gypsies, because of their nomadic, though not necessarily wholly nomadic lifestyle, require special

consideration. There is nothing in Art 8 or the reasoning of the court to suggest that such a special consideration should continue in the manner indicated in the policies after they have given up their lifestyle, whatever the reason for doing so.

A different issue was raised in *Clark v Secretary of State for Transport, Local Government and the Regions* [2002] JPL 1365, involving the desire of Clark to live in a caravan and his opposition to living in a conventional home. The Court of Appeal upheld the judgment of the lower court where the judge had concluded that it was unclear from the inspector's decision whether Clark had a 'settled and immutable antipathy to conventional housing' which derived from his gypsy culture. Article 8 was engaged and it was not sufficient for the local authority to rely on the fact that conventional housing had been offered but refused. In remitting the case to the inspector he was directed to carry out a detailed examination of Clark's objections to living in a conventional house in order to determine the extent to which Art 8 was engaged.

The educational needs of gypsy children are often argued as presenting 'personal circumstances' under Art 2. In *Lee v First Secretary of State* [2003] EWHC 512, it was submitted that the inspector had failed to give sufficient weight to educational requirements of children. In dismissing the case Collins J said;

> there is no suggestion that the right to education had in any way been removed. Equally, the duty of the local authority to provide education wherever the appellant's families may be will continue to exist. I recognise of course that there will be difficulties created for the children if they have to move from site to site, and that is something which is obviously detrimental to their education, but such movement does take place regularly in gypsy families. The less it can interfere with children's education, of course, the better, but equally it is a factor which is taken into account when considering the personal circumstances as the inspector has done.

The question of personal circumstances as a material consideration constituting 'very special circumstances' which justified overriding national and statutory development plan policies was the issue in *South Bucks DC v Porter* [2003] 2 AC 558. The inspector concluded that Mrs Porter's status as a gypsy, the lack of an alternative site in the area and her chronic ill-health were sufficient to justify the grant of planning permission. In doing so the inspector, in addition to a landscaping condition, first made the permission personal to Mrs Porter. This decision was reversed in the Court of Appeal but on appeal to the House of Lords Lord Brown of Eaton-under-Heywood concluded that the Appeal Court had been wrong to require 'a much fuller analysis'. He concluded that there was no mystery as to why the inspector thought there were 'very special circumstances' and stated:

> To my mind the inspector's reasoning was both clear and ample. Here was a woman of 62 in serious ill-health with a rooted fear of being put into permanent housing with no alternative site to go to whose displacement would imperil her continuing medical treatment and probably worsen her condition. All this was fully explained in the decision letter and more fully still in the reports produced in evidence at the public inquiry. Should she be dispossessed from the site onto a roadside or should she be granted a limited personal planning permission? Not everyone would have reached the same decision but there is no mystery as to what moved the inspector.

CHAPTER 27

MINERALS AND WASTE DISPOSAL

27.1   INTRODUCTION

Minerals extraction, in whatever form, whether it be deep mining or surface working, is subject to planning control under the Town and Country Planning Act (TCPA) 1990, with the exception of the classes set out in the Town and Country Planning (General Permitted Development) Order (GPDO) 1995 (SI 1995/418). The responsible authorities are the county councils and the metropolitan district councils (see Chapter 2, para 2.3).

Unlike other land use allocations, minerals by their very nature can only be worked where they are found to exist in sufficient quantity, quality, and at a depth which will make it economic to extract the material. This presents a problem for the planning authorities in determining where these conditions exist, and as a result, the authorities frequently have to rely upon the extraction industries to provide the necessary information. Furthermore, the value of the commodity will dictate how far it is economical to transport the material, for example, sand and gravel are low value, heavy, bulky materials and, therefore, the market area is restricted, whereas potash or Portland stone have a national or international market.

The requirements of extractive industries create particular problems for planning. Demand may be localised or on a national scale, working may result in surface scars on the landscape, and deep mining may cause subsidence, and the workings and possible processing on or near the point of extraction may cause pollution by reason of noise, dust, water pollution or associated traffic movements of heavy vehicles. Planners dealing with minerals are also required to think in four dimensions: surface area does not take into account volume, and the timescale of operations does not relate to that for 'normal' development. Processing plants, for example, brickworks or a cement factory, involve a high level of capital investment in buildings, plant and machinery, and continuing demand for material may require the further extensive use of land in proximity to the point of production to ensure the continuation of the industrial operation.

Supply and demand for low value materials is frequently on a regional basis, and this has led to the setting up of regional working parties to deal with particular minerals. Regional Aggregates Working Parties have been established to monitor reserves, demand, over-supply or shortfall within the region, and where applicable, the contribution the region should make to ensure adequate supplies in other parts of the country. Consideration is also given to the contribution synthetic and waste materials can make to meet future demand.

27.2   DEVELOPMENT PLAN

In accordance with s 16 of the Planning and Compulsory Purchase Act 2004 (PCPA2004) a county council, in respect of any part of their area for which there is a district council, must prepare and maintain a scheme to known as a minerals and waste development scheme. In doing so the scheme must specify;

(a) the documents which are to be the minerals and waste documents;

(b) the subject matter and geographical area to which each document relates;

(c) which documents are Development Plan Documents (DPDs);

(d) which documents (if any) are prepared jointly with one or more lpas;

(e) the timetable for the preparation and revision of the documents;

(f) such other matters which may be prescribed;

(g) submit to the SoS at such time as prescribed or directs;

(h) send a copy to the Regional Planning Board (or, if a London borough, the Mayor of London)

27.3 DEVELOPMENT CONTROL

Mineral and waste disposal applications form a specialised area within the development control functions undertaken by shire counties and metropolitan districts. Outline applications (see Chapter 12, para 12.5) are not appropriate for proposed mineral extraction, and the EU Directive on Environmental Assessment 85/337/EEC requires that environmental impact is to be taken into account in determining such applications. The environmental statement is to be submitted as part of the planning application.

Where surface minerals are to be extracted, this can result in a scar on a hillside, for example, slate or limestone quarrying, or when the removal of material is from a relatively flat area, the working may result in a hole, and there may be a requirement to restore the land to the previous surface level on the completion of extraction. To achieve this, it may be necessary to import material and this will require a waste disposal licence which is issued by the Environmental Health Authority in addition to planning consent. The grant of a licence will control the type and quantity of material to be brought to the site and public health safeguards in the operation of the disposal of waste material. It is particularly important that the deposited material does not pollute natural water courses, and this may restrict or prevent the tipping of household refuse, which is the only form of material which can provide a consistent source of supply. If the form of material to be used to fill the void is restricted to inert matter, for example, builders' rubble (excluding asbestos), then it may prove difficult to restore the site in any pre-determined timescale because of lack of suitable material. The location of the mineral site is also a major factor in determining the availability of material to be used as 'fill', as it is uneconomic to transport waste over long distances. There are, however, circumstances where there is a surplus of overburden after the cessation of workings; this particularly applies to opencast coal operations, where the depth of the seam of material removed creates a void which is less than the bulking-up factor related to the replacement of overburden. This occurs because it is not possible to achieve the degree of compaction of the overburden which existed prior to the operations.

The TCPA 1990 (Sched 5, Part I(3)) suggests that, under normal circumstances, a consent for the extraction of minerals shall be for a period of 60 years, although this may be varied according to particular circumstances. This timescale is far beyond the horizons of plans prepared by lpas, and this may cause difficulties in determining the after-use of the site. The restoration of the site is usually phased to allow it to take place in stages during the actual operations of extraction, and it is important to establish an after-use at the time at which consent is granted. In the case of a wet quarry, would an area of water be a valuable resource in 60 years' time, or is the land likely to be required for some form of development? For example, in the case of a wet quarry, for example, sand and gravel or brick shale, the answer will determine not only the form of restoration but whether it is necessary to import material to fill the void created. Sixty years is a long time span, but as the minerals are a finite resource, the actual removal of the material can only be regarded as a 'temporary' use of the land.

Schedule 5, Part I(5) directs that, any permission for the winning or working of minerals or the deposit of waste granted on or before 22 February 1982 which was not time limited, will expire on 22 February 2042: a note for your diary!

The 'normal rule' is that the grant of planning permission will lapse after a period of five years unless implemented but, in the case of minerals, the period is extended to 10 years. The commencement of development is taken to be the earliest date on which any mining operations to which the consent related have been carried out and, in *Thomas David (Porthcawl) Ltd v Penybont RDC* [1972] 3 All ER 1092; 1 WLR 1526, Lord Widgery described '… each shovel full or each cut by the bulldozer [as] a separate act of development'.

In *Staffordshire CC v Riley and Others* [2001] JPL 1325; EWCA 257, the quarry owners claimed that the removal of topsoil from the site between 1952 and 1953 amounted to the commencement of development. The Court of Appeal upheld the judgment of the lower court that the removal of topsoil alone did not amount to the winning and working of minerals. There was no evidence to indicate that the removal of 12 in of topsoil had rendered the marl accessible and therefore working had not commenced and there was no longer an extant permission for the working of minerals.

Early planning consents for minerals extraction frequently included a condition which required that the land be restored to its original level, or the level of surrounding land. There was no requirement to maintain or care for the land after restoration. In 1982, lpas were granted additional powers to ensure that in future adequate aftercare took place once the original condition had been satisfied. This 'aftercare condition' may require that such steps are taken as may be necessary to bring the land to the required standard for agricultural use, forestry use or use for amenity.

The Planning and Compensation Act (PCA) 1991 (Sched 1) applies these provisions to development involving the deposit of refuse and waste materials.

This is a further reason for establishing the intended use of the land in 60 plus years, one which simultaneously can create problems for mineral operators due to their legal interest in the land. Mineral operators can negotiate a right to extract minerals either by:

(a) having a freehold interest in the land surface and the minerals below;

(b) negotiating a right only to the minerals from the freehold owner, either on the basis of outright purchase or the payment of a sum for each tonne extracted; or

(c) in some circumstances, where there is third party ownership of the minerals, for example, parts of Durham and Northumberland where the minerals rights are vested in the Church, the operator may be required to negotiate the mineral rights with both the freehold owner (in order to gain access to the material) and the Church authorities (in order to acquire a right to work the material).

As the operator's interest is the mineral below the surface, there may be reluctance to acquire a freehold interest in the land unless this is absolutely necessary, as the operator, in many instances, does not wish to become the long-term surface landowner, with little or no interest or expertise in farming, forestry or recreation. It is this fact which has led in the past to the now defunct Open Cast Coal Executive creating golf courses and country parks resulting from an agreed plan of restoration and then handing them over to the lpa or some other agency to maintain and operate.

27.4   THE RIGHT TO WORK MINERALS

The Mines (Working Facilities and Support) Act 1966 provides a mechanism whereby the right to work minerals can be obtained, but this right does not pre-empt consideration of the proposal by the Minerals Planning Authority (MPA). Under the 1966 Act, the prospective operator must first approach the relevant government department and, if there is a *prima facie* case, the matter will be referred to the High Court. The court may make an order granting the applicant the right to work minerals if it is satisfied that:

(a) the applicant has an interest in the minerals, or minerals adjacent to those which it is intended to work;

(b) there is a danger that the minerals will be left unworked;

(c) it has not proved to be reasonably practicable to gain the necessary rights by private negotiation; or

(d) it is in the national interest that the minerals should be worked.

27.5   PERMISSIONS UNDER THE INTERIM DEVELOPMENT ORDER

Old permissions which were originally granted between 1943 and 1948 under an Interim Development Order (IDO) for the extraction of minerals or the deposit of mineral waste were deemed to be granted permission under TCPA 1947 (s 77). These permissions remained in operation and could be reactivated at any time and therefore presented a potential problem for MPAs. This unsatisfactory situation was resolved in the PCA 1991, which introduced a registration scheme. Any person who was the owner or who had a legal interest in the land to which the old permission relates was required to register the permission with the MPA not later than 24 March 1992 (Sched 2, para (1), (2) and (3)). Failure to register by that date resulted in the permission lapsing without the payment of compensation (s 22(3), (4)).

Where an application for registration is granted, the MPAs are entitled to impose conditions and must impose a condition which ensures that the development should cease not later than 21 February 2042. In the case of inactive sites, working cannot recommence unless the site has been registered and conditions approved by the MPA (s 22(3) PCA 1991). With active sites, the permission will cease to have effect unless conditions are approved by the MPA within 12 months of the date of registration, or such period as may be agreed with that authority (Sched 2, para 2(4)).

In *Platt (Daniel) Ltd v Secretary of State* (1996) 71 P & CR 90; EGCS 113, the requirement under s 22 to register IDO permissions questioned the validity of the workings which had taken place on land for at least 85 years for extraction of clay and marl for the manufacture of tiles. The owner's application to register a 1947 IDO permission was rejected by the SoS on the ground that the owners had failed to comply with the conditions attached to the 1947 permission. It appeared that the permission was akin to an outline consent (not an appropriate type of application for minerals permission), and that the plans and details required were never submitted to the lpa; the owner had acted since 1947 on the basis of a full and unconditional permission. The court upheld the SoS's view that development had been carried out in breach of the condition that satisfactory plans and details be first submitted and, therefore, the development was unlawful. Accordingly, the permission could not be regarded as having been implemented before 1 April 1979, and as a result, the permission was not registrable under s 22.

The issue of conditions and the procedure for imposing conditions was set out by Lord Hoffman in *R v North Yorkshire CC ex p Brown* [1999] JPL 616. Once an application for registration had been granted the owner was entitled to apply to the mineral authority to determine the conditions which should be attached to the permission. To activate the consent under registration an application had to be made within 12 months of the grant of registration or the determination of an appeal against its refusal. Failure to apply to the MPA within that period results in the permission ceasing to have effect. The mineral authority is entitled to include

> any conditions which may be imposed on a grant of planning permission for development consisting of the winning and working of minerals or involving the depositing of mineral waste.

The minerals authority is also required to impose a condition that working shall cease not later than 21 February 2042. Once the conditions have been finally determined these are to be registered and the old permission has effect on the basis of these new conditions. Their Lordships also held that EC Directive 85/337 (The Assessment of Certain Public and Private Projects on the Environment) applied to the determination of the council under s 22 (PCA 1991) since that decision was the equivalent of a competent authority which entitles the development to proceed. As the council had not considered whether an environmental assessment was required at that time, the Court of Appeal had been right to reverse the decision of the High Court and quash the determination of the conditions.

The Court of Appeal upheld the judgment of the lower court in *Earthline v Secretary of State* [2003] JPL 715; 1 P& CR 224, which held that a local authority could not impose a condition requiring the early cessation of gravel extraction from a site in Berkshire. The council, in registering a mineral permission originally granted under an interim development order in 1946 in accordance with PCA 1991, had required that all extraction should cease in 2000. The quarrying company's appeal requesting a longer period was rejected. The High Court ruled that the council had no basis for limiting the period of extraction since this would breach the terms of the Act which allowed all minerals permission to remain valid until 2042.

A second challenge to the regime for updating conditions was considered in *R v Oldham BC ex p Foster* [1999] JPL December Update. Planning permission had been granted in 1953 for the mineral extraction but, by virtue of the Environment Act 1995 (Sched 13), this was treated as a dormant site. An application was subsequently made for the determination of conditions and was granted. The proceedings arose from an application by adjoining neighbours for a judicial review of that decision. The court found that none of the operations that had taken place under the original permission were lawful. Condition 1 required the applicants to have submitted to the lpa a detailed scheme for the continuation of workings on the site by 31 March 1953. No such scheme had been submitted and, therefore, the permission had lapsed.

The court noted the ruling of the House of Lords (see above) and accepted that it was theoretically possible for the lpa to determine conditions which themselves would require all the remaining environmental information. However, this was not the actual case here and, in a number of aspects, the conditions would not achieve what was required by the Directive.

27.6 WASTE MANAGEMENT

The PCA 1991 introduced a new statutory requirement for local plan coverage of development involving the depositing of refuse or waste materials (other than mineral waste) and this requirement remains as an element of the new plan-making system (see Chapter 3). County councils are responsible for producing Minerals and Waste Local Development Frameworks and Development Schemes, and likewise unitary authorities' minerals and waste policies may form part of a DPD or comprise a separate DPD.

In producing plans to deal with waste materials, account must be taken of the European Directive on Waste (75/442/EEC) which came into force in 1977, since when it has been amended by Directive 91/156/EEC. The measures to be undertaken by Member States, as set out in the Directive are:

(a) to prevent or reduce waste production (Art 3(1)(1)(a));

(b) to ensure the recovery of waste by recycling and the use of waste as a source of energy (Art 3(1)(b));

(c) to ensure the recovery of waste without harm to the environment (Art 4);

(d) to establish waste disposal installations using the best available technology not involving excessive costs (Art 5);

(e) to establish or designate a competent authority to implement the Directive (Art 6);

(f) to draw up waste management plans

(g) to ensure adequate measures for the handling of waste (Art 8);

(h) to require any establishment carrying out waste operations to be licensed by the appropriate body (Art 9);

(i) to carry out periodic inspections of the licensed operations (Art 3) and;

(j) to ensure that the cost of disposing of waste by the operator or the producer of waste is borne in accordance with 'the polluter pays' principle (Art 5).

A reduction of disposal of waste by means of landfill sites and the growth of the principle of re-cycling is a prime object of the government in complying with European Directive 75/442/EEC, as amended by 91/156/EEC (see Chapter 29 para 29.3). The waste plan prepared is required to give consideration to the land use implications of the authority's waste policy including the need for sites and facilities in particular areas. The assessment should be based upon the following principles (see PPG 10);

(a) consideration of the Best Practicable Environmental Option for each waste;

(b) regional self-sufficiency;

(c) the proximity principle; and

(d) a waste hierarchy.

The role of the planning authority in the production of a waste plan is that of involvement with land-use implications and must be distinguished from the plans drawn up for waste regulation authorities under the Environmental Protection Act 1990. The Landfill (England & Wales) (Amendment) Regulations 2004 (SI 2004/1375) amend the regulatory regime governing landfills for the purpose of implementing Council Decision 20003/33/EC which specifies detailed criteria and procedures for the acceptance of waste at landfills.

The modification of a waste management licence granted under the Waste Management Licensing Regulations 1994 (SI 1994/1056) and the lack of an environmental assessment resulted in a challenge in the High Court: *R (Friends of the Earth Ltd) v Environment Agency* [2003] EWHC 3193. Sullivan J held that the Environment Agency was wrong to have amended the conditions on a waste management licence without complying with the requirements of the Habitat Regulations (92/43/EEC) (see para 25.12).

The Household Waste Recycling Act 2003 (s 1) inserts a new s 45A into the Environment Protection Act 1990 which imposes a general duty on every waste collection authority to arrange for the collection of waste in its area and to ensure the collection of at least two types of recyclable waste together or individually separated from the rest of household waste.

27.7   CONTAMINATED LAND

The first trial under Part IIA of the Environment Protection Act 1990 in *Circular Facilities (London) Ltd v Sevenoaks DC* [2004] JPL 1319 was held in June 2004. Under s 78F(2) of the Act a person is liable for the costs of remediating 'contaminated land' if that person;

> ... caused or knowingly permitted the substances, or any of the substances, by reason of which the contaminated land in question is such land or be in, on or under that land.

Such a person is known as a Class A person and s 78F(3) provides that;

> ... a person shall only be an appropriate person by virtue of subs (2) above in relation to things which are done by way of remediation which are to any extent referable to substances which he caused or knowingly permitted to be present, on or under the contaminated land in question.

And s 78F(9) provides that

> A person who has caused or knowingly permitted any substance (substance A) to be in, on or under any land shall also be taken for the purposes of this section to have caused or knowingly permitted there to be in, on or under land any substance which is there as a result of a chemical reaction or biological process affecting substance A.

If, after reasonable inquiry, the authority has not 'found' a Class A person then the owner or occupier of the land becomes an appropriate person.

In this case the land in question had been a brick and tile works and after operations ceased sometime between 1909 and 1938 the clay pits became ponds and the remainder of the site became marshland. In 1964 the owner began to fill the clay pits which already contained vegetable matter and other non-putrescible matter, and the filling continued intermittently until about 1970. In 1972 Mr S, who did not own the site, applied for and was granted planning permission for the construction of eight houses on the site which he subsequently bought. Fly tipping continued on the site and in 1979 Mr S sold the site to Circular Facilities (CF). In 1980 a geotechnical report was submitted to the lpa based upon five trail pits. The entry for trail pit 3 showed, '... black organic matter with bricks, roots, iris leaves and plastic sheeting, water entering the excavation at this level and gasses bubbling though it.'

CF sold eight houses to private residents and no evidence was submitted during the trial that the residents had been informed of the organic matter remaining below their houses, or the generation of gases from that matter. In the early 1990s Kent County Council Waste Management Department carried out a review of landfill sites and, in particular, those that had been infilled and developed. Methane and carbon dioxide were found to be present in significant concentrations and Sevenoaks District Council, at its own expense, incorporated gas protection measures to each house. In 2000, following an independent survey, the planning authority issued a Record of Determination that the site was contaminated land and in 2002 served a remedial notice on CF which it identified as the Class A person. CF lodged an appeal claiming that it was unreasonable that the firm was the appropriate 'person' and that the authority had unreasonably failed to determine that another person, that is, the former owner of the site, was the appropriate person. Whilst the appeal was pending the local authority determined there was imminent danger to the occupants of the houses and carried out remedial works at a cost of over £46,000.

District Judge Kelly found that the 1978 geotechnical report must have been available to CF and aware of the risk posed by landfill sites and in terms of the Class A 'person' he stated;

> I am satisfied that Sevenoaks DC complied with the statutory guidance as a result of which the former owner was excluded form the class of appropriate person.

NB At the time of publication CF had won the right to a retrial.

The findings in this may prove to be significant as it was found that:

(a) It is not necessary for a person to introduce contaminants onto land in order to be liable under Part IIA of the Environment Protection Act 1990. It is sufficient that the person knows about the presence of such contaminants and fails to remove them;

(b) it is not necessary for the person to know the specifics of the presence of contaminants; it is enough that he is aware that they are in, on or under the land; and

(c) the requirement that a remedial notice is suspended during an appeal is likely to create problems for the enforcing authority.

27.8 REVIEWS OF MINERAL AND WASTE DEPOSITS

Because of the long timescale of operations, and the fact that in some instances mineral operations have not taken place for a number of years on what now appear to be semi-derelict sites, PCA 1991introduced a new s 105 into TCPA 1990, which requires that a MPA shall undertake periodic reviews of mineral and waste disposal sites in its area. The MPA must review every site within its area in which operations are being carried out, or have been carried out during the previous five years, or which have the benefit of a planning consent which has not yet been activated. Having carried out the review, the MPA should then consider whether it would be appropriate to make any one of the following three orders.

27.8.1 A discontinuance order

A MPA may impose a discontinuance order (s 102 TCPA 1990) in respect of mineral working or the disposal of waste which can require the use to cease, or may require the removal of buildings, plant, etc, or impose conditions relating to restoration and aftercare. Such an order cannot take effect unless confirmed by the SoS, and there are the usual procedures for the making and hearing of objections (see Chapter 16).

27.8.2 A prohibition order

Prohibition orders (Sched 9, para 3 and 4 TCPA 1990) prevent the resumption of mineral working or the deposit of waste material where there has been no working for at least two years and the MPA may reasonably assume from the evidence available that it is not intended to continue operations on the site. In addition to preventing the resumption of working, the order may also require:

(a) the removal of any plant or machinery;

(b) that specific steps are taken to remove or alleviate injury to amenity;

(c) compliance with conditions of the original planning permission; and

(d) compliance with a restoration condition.

A prohibition order must be confirmed by the SoS, and there is the usual right of objection and provision for the hearing of objections.

27.8.3 A suspension order

Where the MPA has reason to believe that operations are likely to recommence on the site at some time in the future where there has been no substantial working in the previous 12 months, it may issue a suspension order. The order will specify action which is to be taken to achieve:

(a) the preservation of amenities of the area during the period of suspension;

(b) the protection of the area from further damage during that period; and

(c) the prevention of further deterioration in the condition of the land.

Provision is also made for making supplementary suspension orders (Sched 9, para 6 TCPA 1990) which would impose further requirements, or revoke the suspension order. Suspension orders must be confirmed by the SoS before they can take effect.

A suspension order does *not* prohibit the resumption of mineral extraction or waste disposal, but the person intending to resume the activity must first give notice to the MPA (Sched 9, para 10). The MPA is required to review suspension orders and supplementary orders every five years.

The question of the use of suspension orders (and as a result of the judgment, their possible uselessness) was considered by the Court of Appeal in *R v Secretary of State for Wales ex p Mid-Glamorgan CC* [1995] JPL 1146; EGCS 23; 2 PLR 38. The county council, as MPA, made an order to prevent the resumption of quarrying at what it regarded as an inactive site. The court held that the SoS was entitled to take into account, not only the factual situation at the time at which the order was made, but also subsequent events. To prevent him from doing so would mean that he was shutting his eyes to reality. As a result of this interpretation by the court, the way is open for the owner of such a site to recommence operations on the site or take such other steps to establish the likelihood of the resumption of working.

27.9 COMPENSATION

It is possible that any of the orders referred to above (see para 27.8) may result in claims by the operator for compensation. Imposing a restriction on an extant planning permission normally automatically incurs a liability for compensation, and mineral development is subject to this general rule. However, in the case of minerals, this requirement to pay compensation has been modified to take account of the fact that mineral consents last for such a long period of time, and circumstances may change during the period covered by the permission. The complicated details for assessing the amount of compensation payable are set out in MPG 4, 'The Review of Mineral Working Sites' (Annexes 2, 3 and 4).

27.10 CONDITIONAL CONSENT LEADING TO GRANT OF PERMISSION

The granting of permission for surface mineral working frequently has a condition attached which requires the excavations to be filled in and the land restored to its previous level or the level of surrounding land. In *R v Secretary of State ex p Walsall MBC* (1997) EGCS 23, the court, in following *R v Derbyshire CC ex p North East Derbyshire DC*[1980] JPL 398; (1979) 77 LGR 389, held that such a condition attached to the original consent could be taken as effectively constituting planning permission for the deposit of waste on the site. (*Note*: This planning permission would nevertheless require a site licence for the tipping of waste materials before the operation to restore the land could be undertaken.)

27.11 SURFACE SOIL

The removal of surface soil is a form of 'extraction' and constitutes development. Under the Agricultural Land (Removal of Surface Soil) Act 1953 (s 1), the removal of soil without prior planning consent constitutes an offence if:

(a) a person removes surface soil from agricultural land with a view to the sale of that soil;

(b) the removal of soil is undertaken without the grant of permission required under TCPA 1990 (Part III); or

(c) the quantity of soil removed in any period of three months amounts to more than 5 cu yds.

Planning permission is deemed to be granted under the GPDO (1995) for engineering operations reasonably necessary for the purposes of agriculture, and the cutting of peat and the removal of turf, including the removal of surface soil necessary to carry out these operations.

For the purposes of the Act, agricultural land includes land the use of which has been discontinued prior to the intention to remove surface soil.

27.12 MINERALS DREDGING

The growing importance of marine dredging as a source of minerals, particularly sand and gravel, has resulted in a government review of the procedures to control the activity. The SoS is to become the regulatory and enforcement authority, and DEFRA will be consulted prior to any grant of permission and will have responsibility for monitoring the effects of dredging activities. New dredging permission will normally be valid for 15 years with reviews every five years to determine whether the permission should be renewed. All areas of the seabed below the low-water mark will be covered irrespective of ownership. In most instances, the ownership is vested in the Crown Estate who had previously acted as both landowner and quasi-planning authority.

27.13 MINERALS POLICY GUIDANCE NOTES

MPG 1   General Considerations and the Development Plan System

MPG 2   Applications, Permission and Conditions

MPG 3   Coal Mining and Colliery Spoil Disposal

MPG 4   Review of Mineral Working Sites

MPG 5   Stability in Surface Mineral Workings and Tips

MPG 6   Guidelines for Aggregates Provision in England

MPG 7   England Forestry Strategy: A New Focus on England's Woodlands

MPG 8   Planning and Compensation Act 1991: Interim Development Order Permissions – Statutory Provisions and Procedures (September 1991)

MPG 9   Planning and Compensation Act 1991: Interim Development Order Permissions – Statutory Provisions and Procedures (March 1992)

MPG 10   Provision of Raw Material for the Cement Industry

MPG 11   Environmental Impacts and Mineral Working

MPG 12   (replaced by PPG 14, Development on Unstable Land)

MPG 13   Guidelines for Peat Provision in England

MPG 14   Environment Act 1995: Review of Mineral Planning Permissions

MPG 15   Provision of Silica Sand in England

MPG 17   Oil, Gas and Coal Bed Methane

MMG   Extraction by Dredging of Sand, Gravel and other Minerals from English Seabed

CHAPTER 28

COMPULSORY PURCHASE AND COMPENSATION

28.1 INTRODUCTION

The confiscation of an individual's right of land ownership is a denial of a basic right, but there are occasions when, in the interests of the general public, a reluctant owner must be forced to release his interest in the land, in which case the owner must be compensated. In the case of *AG v De Keyser's Royal Hotel Ltd* [1920] AC 508, it was stated:

> It is a well established principle that, unless no other interpretation is possible, justice requires that the statutes should not be construed to enable the land of a particular individual to be confiscated without payment.

The denial of the basic right of ownership of land which results from action by the state is justified by the action being in 'the common good'. It is a means of ensuring that the reluctance on the part of an owner does not prejudice development proposals which are in accordance with the planning objectives of the local authority. In a large number of situations, the *threat* of compulsory purchase is sufficient in itself to ensure that an owner agrees to sell his interest in land and compulsory purchase action is unnecessary. The power to acquire land does, however, ensure that the local planning authority (lpa) can use its power to assemble sites for development, redevelopment and improvement which may involve a multiplicity of ownerships. The power of compulsory purchase is not available to the private developer and, therefore, the local authority may well use its power to assemble sites in the single ownership of the authority and then enter into a partnership scheme with a developer who is responsible for financing the project.

28.2 COMPULSORY PURCHASE POWERS

The power to acquire land by compulsory purchase for planning purposes is contained in ss 226, 228 and 231 of the Town and Country Planning (TCPA) Act 1990, as amended by the Planning and Compulsory Purchase Act (PCPA) 2004. Section 26, as amended by s 99, empowers local authorities, having being authorised to do so by the Secretary of State (SoS), to compulsorily acquire and in their area;

(a) if the authority think that the acquisition will facilitate the carrying out of development, re-development or improvement on or in relation to the land; or

(b) which is required for the purpose necessary to achieve the interests of the proper planning of an area in which the land is situated,

provided the local authority thinks the use of these powers will contribute to the achievement of one or more of the following objectives and will result in the promotion or improvement of:

(a) the economic well being of the area;

(b) the social well being of their area; or

(c) the environmental well being of the area.

(NB The 'planning considerations' referred to in s 226(2) TCPA 1990 are omitted in s 99(4).)

Using these powers, adjoining land may also be acquired if required for the purpose of executing works or where land is acquired to provide for an exchange of land where the proposed development, re-development or improvement involves part of a common, open space or garden allotment. It is also possible, with the authorisation of the SoS, for a local authority to acquire land within the area of another authority.

Once the land is acquired it is immaterial who should undertake the work to achieve the object of the acquisition. For example, in terms of redevelopment, the lpa may well seek to use its compulsory purchase powers to facilitate the purchase of land required for the assembly of a large site for comprehensive redevelopment, and then transfer an interest in the land to a development company to carry out the work.

Although Crown immunity from planning control has been removed by PCPA 2004 it remains outside the amended compulsory purchase provisions.

28.3   ACQUISITION OF LAND

The procedure for the compulsory acquisition of land is undertaken by the issuing of an order (s 226(7) TCPA 1990) which may be the subject of an appeal to the SoS. Any such appeal will be conducted in accordance with the Compulsory Purchase by Non-Ministerial Acquiring Authorities (Inquiries Procedure) Rules 1990 (SI 1990/512), which follow the lines set out in planning appeals (see Chapter 16, para 16.4). Compulsory purchase also includes the power to acquire an easement or other right over land (s 228).

Once the order has been confirmed, the acquiring authority may obtain the ownership of the land which is the subject of the order by making a general declaration under s 1 of the Compulsory Purchase (Vesting Declarations) Act 1981. If the authority takes possession of the land using its powers under s 1 of the Compulsory Purchase Act 1965 before the completion of the purchase, it must pay the vendor interest on the purchase money (s 11(1)).

28.4   CHALLENGE TO COMPULSORY PURCHASE ORDER

Any application to the High Court to challenge a confirmed compulsory purchase order must be within a period of six weeks from the date on which the notice of confirmation was published (s 23(4) of the Acquisition of Land Act 1981). In the two cases, *R v Secretary of State ex p Okolo* and *R v Secretary of State ex p Omoregei* [1997] 2 All ER 911, the applicants applied to the court challenging the validity of each order. The time period relevant for the lodging of the challenge was a period of six weeks from Tuesday 18 June 1996. Both challenges were issued on 30 July 1996, and the SoS applied to the court to strike out the applications since it was submitted they were one day out of time and the Act did not permit an extension of the statutory time period of six weeks.

The issue considered by the court was whether the statement 'within six weeks' allowed an application on the sixth Tuesday after the notice of confirmation or whether the time expired at midnight on Monday 29 July when a full six weeks, each of seven days, had passed. The court accepted Mrs Omoregei's interpretation, which was that if on a Tuesday one was asked to do something 'within a week', it could be done at any time up to *and including* the following Tuesday. It was held that the common sense and non-technical approach to calculating time was sound, and accordingly the application by the SoS was dismissed.

In *Miles v Secretary of State and the Royal Borough of Kingston* [2000] JPL 192, challenges were made to a compulsory purchase order (s 226(1)(b) TCPA 1990). The applicant also argued that the council's action was in breach of Art 8 of the European Convention on Human Rights (ECHR) in that it breached her right to respect for her home.

The applicant owned the property but had not lived in the house for 19 years as a result of which the property and the garden were in a badly dilapidated condition. After unsuccessfully attempting to compel the owner to take action under s 215 TCPA 1990 (see Chapter 22, para 22.11), the council eventually decided compulsorily to acquire the property on the basis that the land was required for a purpose which it was necessary to achieve in the interests of the proper planning of the area. The applicant argued that s 226(1)(b) only applied to the 'proper planning of an area' and not 'proper use'. Furthermore, there was no policy in the Unitary Development Plan (UDP) directly related to the property, nor was there a 'plan'.

In dismissing that part of the appeal, the court held that lack of maintenance leading to continuing decay did real harm to the character and appearance of the neighbourhood and, therefore, the action was to achieve a planning purpose. The second issue which fell to be considered were the implications, if any, of Art 8 ECHR. The court found that, even if the order had related to property that was the applicant's home, there had been no breach of Art 8 in light of the decision in *Buckley v UK* [1995] JPL 633; JPL 1018. It was clear that the appropriate procedures had been carried out and action was necessary for the preservation of the environment in the interest of the community. The order related to property which was not the applicant's home and, therefore, there had been no interference with her right under Art 1 of the Protocol of the ECHR which states that 'every natural or legal person is entitled to the peaceful enjoyment of his possessions'.

28.5   COMPENSATION FOR COMPULSORY PURCHASE

The PCPA 2004 made a number of changes relating to the payment of compensation. A new s 5A is introduced into the Land Compensation Act 1961, specifying the 'relevant valuation date' (RVA) after which no adjustment is made in respect of anything which may happen after that date. The valuation is undertaken by the Lands Tribunal and is based on market value, that is, what a willing seller may expect in the open market. If the land is subject to a notice to treat, the RVA is the earlier of:

(a) the date when the acquiring authority enters on and takes possession of the land; or

(b) the date when the assessment is made.

If the land is subject to a general vesting order the RVA is the earlier of

(a) the vesting date; or

(b) the date on which the assessment is made.

Provision is made in PCPA 2004 for advanced payment for land that is subject to mortgages (s 104) and basic loss payments (s 106). The latter applies to owners and tenants of property (provided they have held that interest for at least one year) and such payment is in addition to any payment for the value of the land and disturbance payment. Section 107 provides for payment to occupiers of agricultural and other land (who have held that interest for at least one year).

Sections 108 and 109 make provision for details of arrangements for making a claim and importantly exclude from the entitlement to loss payments of persons who have neglected their property after one of a variety of statutory notices has been served. This exclusion has bee introduced to prevent those whose neglect would otherwise allow them to benefit from that neglect.

28.6   CERTIFICATE OF ALTERNATIVE DEVELOPMENT

The question of the market value of land is inextricably tied to the nature of the use which would be permitted in accordance with the plan and planning policies for a particular area. A problem occurs where the development plan does not have any firm proposals and it is assumed that the existing use will continue during the plan period. This is frequently known as 'white land', and it cannot be assumed that the lpa would refuse all applications for development in such areas simply because the plan does not envisage development proposals. Similarly, there is a presumption against development in green belt land, but this does not mean that development will not be permitted. It is, therefore, unreasonable to assess compensation on the basis of the existing use when there could be an opportunity to increase value if the grant of planning permission is forthcoming.

Under the Land Compensation Act 1961 (s 17), the landowner may apply to the planning authority to issue a certificate of development. In doing so, the lpa is required to answer the hypothetical question: what in all the circumstances, would be the kind of development for which planning permission might reasonably be granted if the land were not being compulsorily acquired and an application for development is assumed to have been lodged in respect of the land?

The applicant for such a certificate is required to specify one or more classes of development which he considers would be appropriate for the land in question, in accordance with the Local Government Planning and Land Act 1980 (s 121), were it not to be compulsorily acquired. This is *not* a planning application; it is a method of ascertaining the use, if any, which could take place on the land. The lpa must issue a certificate indicating the class or classes of development which it would accept, or that no alternative use would be accepted. The applicant for such a certificate can claim the costs incurred by him in making such an application as part of the compensation due to him on the acquisition of the land.

Any person aggrieved by the certificate issued by the local authority has the right of appeal to the SoS and must be granted an opportunity to be heard by a person appointed by the SoS (1961 Act, s 18(3)). The SoS may confirm, vary or cancel the certificate.

The Planning and Compensation Act (PCA) 1991 amended the certification procedure (s 65 and Sched 15, paras 15–18) by allowing its operation in the case of land designated on the development plan as either an area of comprehensive development or an area allocated primarily for residential, commercial or industrial uses, or a combination of such uses, which had previously been excluded. It is also made clear that, where a certificate is issued, its content overrides any contrary planning assumptions made in the development plan. For example, the development plan may include provision for a school site, and the lpa is required to consider alternative use(s) for the purpose of issuing a certificate, and as the surrounding land is likely to be in residential use, the alternative use would be residential, thus establishing a value purely for the purposes of compulsory acquisition.

28.7 PLANNING BLIGHT

Planning blight occurs where the proposals contained in the development plan effectively prevent the owner of land or property selling his interest in the open market because of the implicit threat of a compulsory purchase notice by the local authority or other statutory agency. In such cases, a blight notice may be served on the local authority (s 149(2)(3) TCPA 1990) by:

(a) the resident owner-occupier of any hereditament;

(b) the owner-occupier of any hereditament with a net annual value not exceeding the prescribed limit (currently £18,000 as set out in the Town and Country Planning (Blight Provisions) Order 1990 (SI 1990/465)); and

(c) the owner-occupier of an agricultural unit.

This right of the owner to serve a blight notice is dependent upon two main factors: (i) the land is shown for some other purpose in the development plan; and (ii) the local authority, or other agency granted compulsory purchase powers, will exercise its right to purchase the land or property. The problem of the landowner is highlighted in the case of *Elcock and Elcock v Newham LBC* [1996] JPL 421; 71 P & CR 575. The Lands Tribunal acknowledged that the neighbourhood had been blighted for a number of years by the gradual acquisition of properties within it by a neighbouring polytechnic. Whilst the local plan for the area stated an intention that the land would be required for the development of the (then) North East London Polytechnic, following the Education Reform Act 1988, the council was no longer the responsible authority for the polytechnic. The 1988 Act granted existing polytechnics the status of universities and, as a result, the prime source of funding was from central government and not the local authority as had previously been the case. As a result, future development proposals might be carried out by the university, private enterprise, or the local authority, or any combination of these three. As the claimant had failed to show that land was allocated in the local plan for the purposes of functions of the local authority, it could not be regarded as qualifying land for the purpose of the blight notice procedure.

The scheme provides no protection to a person whose land may depreciate in value as a result of the threat of a compulsory purchase order relating to adjoining land. For the purpose of s 149 TCPA 1990, an 'owner-occupier' includes a lessee with at least three years to run in addition to the freeholder of property (s 168(4)), and a 'resident owner-occupier' is defined as 'an individual who occupies the whole of the hereditament' (s 168(3)). Following what may be regarded as a harsh decision of the Lands Tribunal in *Webb v Warwickshire CC* (1972) 23 P & CR 63, which determined that the interest terminated on death and that a personal representative could not serve a blight notice, this anomaly was corrected by s 161. It is now possible for a personal representative to serve a notice if the deceased owner been entitled to serve a notice prior to his death, provided one or more individuals shall benefit from the proceeds of the sale.

Under the present blight provisions, a notice can only be served on a local authority in respect of a business if the annual value does not exceed the figure of £18,000 (see above), or if the owner occupies part of the premises. This provision excludes investment owners on the basis that it is impossible to ascertain whether the value has changed because of the blighting effect of proposals by the lpa, or because of changes in the property market. The investor may regard this as an opportunity to sell to the authority merely because changes in the property market at a particular time may make it more profitable to sell, and to place the proceeds in a more profitable investment.

Blight notices may be served on the local authority in the following circumstances:

(a) after the preparation and submission of structure plans, local plans and UDPs, where land is required for government departments, local authorities, statutory undertakers, or public telecommunications operators, or the land is included within an 'action area';

(b) where land is affected by resolution of the local authority or directions from the SoS;

(c) when land is to be compulsorily acquired under a special Act, for example, Channel Tunnel Act 1986;

(d) when land is within the area designated for a new town;

(e) where land is included within a slum clearance area;

(f) land which the local authority proposes to acquire as a part of a General Improvement Area;

(g) where new highway proposals are contained in a development plan, including the alteration and improvement of an existing highway;

(h) when land is affected by new street orders;

(i) where land is within an urban development area; and

(j) where land is subject to a compulsory purchase order and the notice to treat has yet to be served.

In relation to the acquisition of land for highway proposals ((g) above), in *Norman v Department of Transport* [1996] JPL 513; 24 EG 150, the Lands Tribunal was required to rule on whether the highway subsoil formed part of the hereditament of an adjoining property to enable a blight notice to extend to the whole of the property. By presumption of law, the claimants owned the freehold interest in the subsoil under half the width of the A35 trunk road where their cottage abutted the road. The tribunal concluded that the highway subsoil was included within the claimant's hereditament. They were in one ownership; they were in the same curtilage or were contiguous, and the subsoil could not be separately let. The tribunal also stated that the onus fell on the highway authority which had made a compulsory purchase order to acquire the subsoil, to prove that it was not part of the hereditament, that is, land to which the persons have title. In the tribunal's opinion, the authority had failed to do so and the burden of proof had not been discharged. The deemed notice to treat was, therefore, for the whole of the claimant's hereditament.

The blight notice must be served upon the authority which is likely to acquire the land, using the appropriate form which is set out in the General Regulations. This will state that part of the hereditament which is affected by blight, and must provide evidence that the claimant has made reasonable efforts to sell the property and that this resulted in a substantially lower price. This provision does not apply where the property is authorised to be acquired by a special enactment or where a compulsory purchase order is in force. In the case of a hereditament, the notice must require the authority to acquire the whole of the claimant's interest, irrespective of the fact that only part may be blighted. The rules are different for farms, and the claimant is restricted to that area of the farm which is blighted, unless he is able to prove that the remainder of the farm cannot be sold at a reasonable price.

If the authority is not willing to purchase the land specified in the notice, it may, within two months, serve a counter notice specifying its objections (s 151) on the basis of one of four grounds:

1   that the conditions laid down in the 1990 Act have not been satisfied;

2   that they do not intend to acquire any part of the land or hereditament;

3   that it does not intend to acquire any part of the land or hereditament within the next 15 years; or

4   that, in the case of agricultural land, it proposes to acquire only part of the affected area.

An aggrieved claimant may refer the matter to the Lands Tribunal and it is his responsibility to prove that the objection is not well founded. If no counter notice is served, the authority is deemed to have served a notice to treat.

In *Smith v Kent CC* (1995) 44 EG 141, the applicants served a blight notice on Kent County Council as highway authority, seeking the acquisition of the whole of their property which was affected by proposed road-widening works. They challenged the counter notice issued by the authority served under s 166(2)(b) TCPA 1990 which provides that:

> ... in the case of a park or garden belonging to a house, the part proposed to be acquired can be taken without seriously damaging the amenity or convenience of the house.

The Lands Tribunal was of the opinion that, in terms of amenity, such was the level of noise experienced that the case was marginal. However, taking into account the broader issues, which included the loss of privacy arising from the loss of trees on either side of the dwelling, there would be a serious effect upon the amenity of the dwelling house following the implementation of the scheme. For this reason, the tribunal set aside the counter notice and upheld the blight notice.

The question arose in *Carrel v London Underground Ltd* (1996) 12 EG 129 as to whether a blight notice served following the publication of safeguarding plans for the proposed alignment of Crossrail was deemed to have been withdrawn as a result of the claimant's sale of his property. The Lands Tribunal noted that the only express case in which the rights under the notice would pass to another person was under s 161, dealing with the powers of personal representatives upon the claimant's demise. Otherwise, once the claimant's interest had been lost, there is nothing to compel a local authority to purchase the land. The claimant could not use the blight notice procedures as a means of obtaining damages or compensation for having sold his property at a significant discount from its unblighted value.

28.8 REVOCATION OR MODIFICATION OF A PLANNING PERMISSION

Compensation is available to landowners as a result of actions by the lpa to revoke or modify an extant planning consent (ss 97 and 102 TCPA 1990). Such situations may be rare, but they can occur where there has been a change in planning policy at either a national or local level. For example, Alnwick District Council has recently been informed by the SoS that a consent granted, but yet to be activated in accordance with the then national policy on the siting of supermarkets, no longer accords with current policy and, therefore, should be revoked. If this action is taken, then the cost of revocation will fall to the lpa.

28.9 PURCHASE NOTICES

Where a planning permission has been refused, or granted subject to conditions which result in the land becoming incapable of beneficial use in its existing state, the landowner may serve a purchase notice on the local authority (s 137(2), (3) TCPA 1990). Similarly, if a discontinuance order has been made, a purchase notice may be served if the land has become incapable of reasonably beneficial use or if the land cannot be made capable of reasonably beneficial use by carrying out the development for which planning permission has been granted, whether by that order or otherwise.

Decisions as to whether land has, or has not, become incapable of reasonably beneficial use falls, in the first instance, to the lpa, with a right of appeal to the SoS. Policy guidance contained in Circular 13/83, para 13 states:

> In considering what capacity for use the land has, relevant factors are the physical state of the land, its size, shape and surroundings, and the general pattern of land uses in the area; a use of relatively low value may be regarded as reasonably beneficial if such a use is common with similar land in the vicinity ... profit may be a useful comparison in certain cases but the absence of profit (however calculated) is not necessarily material; the concept of reasonably beneficial use is not synonymous with profit.

The operation of these provisions are dependent upon a definition of the term 'beneficial use' and this was explained by Widgery J in *Adams and Wade Ltd v Minister of Housing and Local Government* (1965) 18 P & CR 60 as follows:

> The purpose of s 129 (1962 Act) is to enable the landowner whose use of his land has been frustrated by a planning refusal to require the local planning authority to take the land off his hands. The reference to 'beneficial use' must, therefore, be a reference to a use which can benefit the owner or a prospective owner, and the fact that the land in its existing state confers some benefit or value upon the public at large would be no bar to the service of a purchase notice.

This definition requires further refinement as the legislation refers to a '*reasonably* beneficial use' which is a matter to be determined on the basis of fact and degree. This issue was addressed in *General Estates Co Ltd v Minister of Housing and Local Government* (1965) 194 EG 202, where the applicants owned a site half of which was let to a sports club at a rent of £52 per year, and the remainder of which was vacant but could be let as grazing land for about £20 per year. The minister, supported on appeal to the High

Court, concluded that the land was capable of reasonably beneficial use and dismissed the application.

'Reasonably beneficial use' would appear, in most cases, to refer to economic factors. In *R v Minister of Housing and Local Government ex p Chichester RDC* [1960] 2 All ER 407, the Divisional Court considered whether land is considered incapable of reasonably beneficial use if its existing state is of less value than if permission were granted for Sched 3 development (for details of Sched 3 PCA 1991, see para 28.10 below). The case involved coastal land that was subject to erosion which could only be curtailed by the expenditure of a large sum of money. There were 14 bungalows on the land and the remainder housed 17 caravan sites let as holiday homes during the summer under temporary planning permissions. The owner was refused permission to develop the land for residential purposes, and on receipt of the refusal notice, served the local authority with a purchase notice. This was confirmed by the minister on the ground that the value of the land in its existing state, with the benefit of temporary planning permissions, was substantially less than if planning permission had been granted for the rebuilding of the buildings which formally stood there and which were demolished in 1937. Chichester Rural District Council applied to the High Court to have the minister's confirmation of the purchase notice quashed. The court quashed the decision and held that the question was whether the land had become incapable of reasonably beneficial use in its existing state and *not* whether the land was of less use to the owners in its present state than if it had been developed.

Subsequently, in the case of *Brookdene Investments Ltd v Minister of Housing and Local Government* (1970) 21 P & CR 545, it was held that a comparison with Sched 3 values may be made, provided it is considered along with other relevant factors, but the weight given to the valuation is a matter to be determined by the SoS.

28.10 SCHEDULE 3 TO THE PLANNING AND COMPENSATION ACT 1991

The PCA 1991 (s 31) repealed compensation restrictions on new development and for restrictions on Sched 3 development, leaving Parts I and III in operation.

Part I, for which no compensation is payable, relates to:

(a) the rebuilding of properties in existence on the appointed day (1 July 1948) or any building before that date which was destroyed or demolished after 7 January 1937, including the making good of war damage;

(b) the carrying out of maintenance, improvement or other alteration of any building which affects only the interior of the building, and are works for making good war damage so long as the cubic content of the original building is not substantially exceeded; and

(c) the use of two or more separate dwelling houses of any building which, at the material date, was used as a single dwelling.

Part III (Supplementary Provisions) relates to:

(a) buildings, works or use of land, after 1 July 1948, where there is a condition limiting the period for which they may be retained, and states that the provisions shall not operate except for the period specified in that condition;

(b) an increase in the cubic content, and specifies that in the case of a dwelling house, this shall not exceed one-tenth, or 1,750 cu ft, whichever is the greater; and

(c) in any other case, if it is increased or exceeded by more than one-tenth.

These provisions, which originated in the TCPA 1947, to allow rebuilding of war-damaged buildings, resulted in the replacement of offices in most major cities, and particularly in London, where the original cubic content, plus the 10% allowance, meant that the old style Victorian offices with high ceiling heights were replaced by modern buildings, which dramatically reduced the height of rooms and thereby increased the available floor space.

28.11 OTHER CLAIMS FOR COMPENSATION

Reference should be made to the earlier chapters which deal with compensation payable under certain circumstances, for example:

(a) listed buildings (see Chapter 20);

(b) mineral working (see Chapter 27);

(c) Tree Preservation Orders (see Chapter 22); and

(d) stop notices (see Chapter 18).

CHAPTER 29

PUBLIC INVOLVEMENT

29.1 INTRODUCTION

Planning has evolved since the Town and Country Planning Act (TCPA) 1947, as has the public interest and desire to be involved and to influence the outcome of planning policies and decisions. Many reasons have been advanced for this growing public interest, particularly in relation to their local environment, for example, better education concerning environmental matters; a reaction against the bureaucratic decisions of the 1960s which saw large areas 'suffer' the consequences of redevelopment; the loss of familiar features in the local area; and an increasing awareness of the principle of conservation. The growth of pressure groups in the 1960s which startled the Western world with urban riots, both in the US and France, led to a political reaction designed to improve the involvement of individuals in local affairs. It can also be argued that the recent worldwide movement to safeguard natural resources, including flora and fauna, is largely the result of public pressure on governments.

Members of 'the public' cannot be regarded as having a consensus view on issues which are raised as a result of planned change. National and local pressure groups, as well as individuals, frequently seek to influence the decisions of locally elected representatives who have the responsibility for planning decisions within an established legal framework. The function of planning is to meet the future needs of society as a whole. In doing so, there is no single answer to a complex series of interrelated issues; for example, residents in a village may support the need for a bypass, although the local traders frequently resist such a proposal on the ground of loss of potential trade, and conservationists may regard a bypass as a threat to the natural beauty of the area and to wildlife habitats. Each group pursues its own laudable objective and the relative weight of contradictory evidence is a matter for the elected representatives advised by their professional officers.

When considering identical planning applications, an individual will inevitably express opinions which accord with his 'role' in a particular set of circumstances; the objector who seeks to influence the planning decision on a neighbour's proposal to carry out development may in turn become a developer in his own right, and decry any attempt by 'the public' to intervene in his proposed activity.

29.2 INVOLVEMENT IN PLAN-MAKING

The combination of changes to the planning legislation in the 1960s and social attitudes towards authority effectively ensured that 'the genie was out of the bottle' in terms of public involvement in planning. The Planning and Compensation Act 2004 places great emphasis on 'front loading' in the preparation of the new style of plans and requires, as an integral part of the submitted documents, a Statement of Community Involvement (SCI). The Government's intentions are set out in Planning Policy Statement 12 (PPS12), 'Local Development Frameworks' and the paper 'Community Involvement in Planning: The Government's Objectives'. The paper states in para 2.5 that, 'the community must be able to put forward and debate options and help mould proposals before they are settled.'

PPS12 (para 3.4) sets out the principles for community involvement which are:

(a) Community involvement that is appropriate to the level of planning.

(b) Front loading of involvement. This should provide opportunities for participation in identifying issues and debating options from the earliest stage.

(c) The methods used to encourage involvement and participation should be relevant to their experience. Consideration should be given to how people are most likely to get involved and what facilities are available to them, including working with Planning Aid. It is stressed that there is no 'one-size-fits-all' solution.

(d) Clearly articulated opportunities for continuing involvement. The process should allow local communities to see how ideas have developed at various stages. These must be part of continuous programme and not a series of one-off disjointed steps.

(e) Transparency and accessibility. People should know when they will be able to participate and involvement should extend beyond those who are familiar with the planning system.

(f) Planning for involvement. Community involvement should be planned from the start of the plan-making process.

An important feature of the SCI is its legally binding effect, and once adopted it must be complied with in the preparation of other Local Development Documents (LDDs). It is also the subject of independent scrutiny but the presumption is that it is sound unless it is shown to be otherwise as a result of evidence considered at the examination. In assessing 'soundness' the inspector will determine whether the local planning authority (lpa) has complied with the minimum requirements for consultation as set out in Regulations:

(a) the lpa's strategy for community involvement links with other community involvement initiatives for example the community strategy;

(b) the statement identifies in general terms which community groups or other bodies will be consulted;

(c) the statement identifies how the community and other bodies can be involved in a timely and accessible manner;

(d) the method of consultation to be employed are suitable for the intended audience and for the different stages in the preparation of LDDs;

(e) resources are available to manage community involvement effectively;

(f) the statement show how the results of community involvement will be fed into the preparation of development plan documents and supplementary planning documents;

(g) the authority has mechanisms for reviewing the SCI; and

(h) the statement clearly describes the planning authority's policy for consultation on planning application.

The Planning and Compulsory Purchase Act 2004 and accompanying government advice places great emphasis on the requirement to ensure that 'the community' is involved in plan-making but no attempt is made to define 'community' other than to suggest that it is made up of many diverse groups, no doubt with conflicting aspirations. The paper, 'Community Involvement in Planning: The Government's Objectives' makes it clear in paragraph 1.12, which states that:

> But participation cannot substitute for proper decision-making through accountable institutions. To be legitimate, that process must allow communities to feel that they had a real influence. The process for community involvement, enshrined in the SCI, are designed to help achieve that and provide real opportunities to shape the critical decisions about their future.

The question remains as to how far people can be allowed to have 'real influence'.

The Freedom of Information Act 2000 came into effect on 1 January 2005 together with the Environmental Information Regulations 2004 (SI 2004/3391). Whilst the Act has general application 'environmental information' has been singled out for a special statutory regime. Under s1(1):

> any person making a request for information to a public authority is entitled to be informed in writing by the public authority whether it holds information of the description specified in the request, and if that is the case, to have that information communicated to him.

There is no obligation on a public authority to charge any fee but it may charge what is regarded as a reasonable amount. The basic requirement is that the public authority makes information available as soon as possible and no later than 20 working days after receipt of the request, unless a charge is to be made, in which case the period runs from the date of the charge being paid.

This right is not confined by subject matter; it is not confined to persons who may exercise it, nor is it confined by some recognised need to know. Whilst there are certain exceptions to disclosure in the Regulations those relating to 'environmental information' are not circumscribed. The new definition of 'elements of the environment' are 'air, water, soil, land, landscape and natural sites including wetlands, coastal and marine areas, biological diversity and its components, including genetically modified organisms'.

Following the Act, the public should in future be fully aware of information relating to the environment in order to assist in their involvement in the process of plan production.

29.3   INVOLVEMENT IN PLANNING APPLICATIONS

Persons notified, or any other persons who become aware of a planning proposal, are entitled to see the application file and to make representations to the authority within 21 days of receipt of the notification letter. The lpa is also required to keep a register of all planning applications, and this must be made accessible to members of the general public. When granting planning permission lpas are now required to provide a resume of the reasons supporting the grant of permission.

Both the applicant and the interested parties may use the democratic system by lobbying their elected local authority members. Matters brought to the attention of the officers as a result of public reaction to a proposal must be brought to the attention of the elected representatives before a decision is taken on the proposed development. This requirement for comments or objections is to be regarded as material considerations and was reinforced by the decision in *R v Rochdale MBC ex p Brown* [1997] JPL 337 (see Chapter 13, para 13.5).

Nevertheless, within the democratic structure of government, the final responsibility for decisions lies with the elected members. Planning decisions are not taken as a result of local referendums, and it is the weight of argument rather than the weight of the petition which is the relevant factor!

At the relevant committee meeting at which the proposal is to be determined, the general public may attend as observers and, in the case of some authorities, may be allowed to address the committee at the discretion of the elected members. This opportunity to address the committee is not generally available and will depend upon the standing orders of the particular council. Where there are a number of members of the public who share a common attitude towards the development, it is usual for the committee to request that they appoint a spokesperson to express their views.

The European Council Directive 90/313 and the British Transposing Regulations, the Environmental Information Regulations 1992 (SI 1992/3240) on the freedom of access to environmental information were considered in *R v Secretary of State ex p Alliance Against the Birmingham Northern Relief Road* [1999] JPL 231. The objectors applied for an order compelling disclosure of the concession entered into between the Secretary of State (SoS) and the Midland Expressway Ltd under the New Roads and Street Works Act 1991. The court rejected the submission that the regulations conferred a subjective discretion upon the decision-maker as to what information was required to be disclosed. In the view of the court, whether information relating to the environment is capable of being treated as confidential was to be tested against the factual questions contained in reg 4(3). The one exception occurs when the information falls within reg 4(1)(a) which relates to confidentiality. The general purpose of Art 3.4 of the Directive (reg 3(2)(c)) is to enable an individual who is refused information to ascertain whether the refusal is well founded in fact and law. That purpose is not satisfied by a bare assertion that the document is confidential and it should be possible to provide some explanation as to why the information sought is considered to be confidential.

The court inspected the concession agreement to assess to what extent, if any, it should be regarded as confidential and decided that, with substantial blanking out so as to mitigate the loss of confidentiality, it should be made available to the applicants' legal advisors.

The High Court, in *R v North West Leicestershire DC ex p Moses* [2000] JPL January Update, raised issues of proximity and also possible implications arising from European law. The applicant sought to set aside a planning permission granted in 1994 for the extension of a runway at East Midlands Airport on the ground that it was obtained without compliance with the requirements of an Environmental Impact Assessment, and a declaration that a further permission in 1996 was unlawful. The court rejected her application on the grounds of insufficient *locus*. Since lodging her application, she had moved house to a new home six miles away and the court held that it should not grant leave unless it considers the applicant has sufficient interest related to the time at which the application came to be determined. The court referred to the judgment of Sedley J in *R v Somerset CC ex p Dixon* [1997] JPL June Update, where it was held that the threshold at the point of application to leave was set only at the height necessary to prevent abuse. Scott Baker J preferred a higher threshold which was that the court should not be burdened with a case that was bound to fail.

Although it was easier to identify a sufficient interest than to define it, he considered that it was important not to lose sight of the purpose of the provisions which ensured that those who have no real or justifiable concern do not take precious time from the Crown Office or subject other parties to unnecessary costs. The court also dealt with the submission that European law required a more liberal approach. The court was satisfied that there were no deficiencies in the domestic procedure that would open up an issue of Community law application.

29.4   INVOLVEMENT IN PLANNING APPEALS

As explained in Chapter 16, only the applicant can take action to appeal against a decision of a lpa to refuse consent or grant consent subject to conditions. The planning authority is not required to give reasons for the grant of permission, and at present there is no provision which would allow a third party to challenge the decision. The public's involvement in planning appeals can, therefore, only result from an action by the applicant. This situation could change as the Labour Party has indicated that it intends to 'create a new right of appeal for residents against developments which fly in the face of their local plans' but adds '... tightly defined rules would be necessary to restrict the right to *bona fide* objectors'.

Once an appeal is lodged, the lpa is required to renotify those persons informed of the original application and any other persons who have notified the authority of their interest in the original application. The method adopted to deal with the appeal will determine the manner of the public's involvement (see Chapter 16). Hearings are not regarded as a suitable means of determining an appeal if there is likely to be a significant number of the public who would wish to attend. Appeals determined by written representation will require (as the name implies) the submission of a written statement which will be considered with the statements prepared by the appellant and the lpa. In the case of a local inquiry, those persons who have submitted evidence are entitled to address the inquiry, and others who have not expressed an earlier concern may be allowed to address the inquiry at the inspector's discretion.

29.5   JUDICIAL REVIEW

In most cases, the decision of the lpa cannot be challenged in the courts. Similarly, following an appeal to the SoS, his decision is also final unless there is a successful legal challenge on a point of law. It is stressed that the challenge *must* be on *a point of law*; the planning merits of the case are *not* a matter for the courts. The constraint placed upon the courts is summed up by Connor LJ in *R v Haringay LB ex p Barrs and Flaherty* (1988) unreported:

> We are not a Court of Appeal from the Planning Committee. We cannot substitute our views on that of the Planning Committee.

If a third party, that is, a party other than the lpa or the appellant, is to mount a challenge to the decision by means of a judicial review, he must establish *locus standi*, that is, prove a direct interest in the matter. The Supreme Court Act 1981 (s 31(3)) states:

... the court shall not grant leave to make such an application [for a judicial review] unless it considers that the applicant has sufficient interest in the matter to which the application relates.

Provided the third party establishes *locus standi*, this is the only legal entitlement which exists to enable a challenge to be made by an individual, or a group of persons, to ensure that both local and central government act according to the law. The critical need is for the third party to establish his 'interest' if he is to be afforded the opportunity to challenge a decision by way of a judicial review. Where the challenge relates to a particular site or area in which the challenger lives or works, this may well provide that opportunity. In *R v Stroud DC ex p Goodenough* [1982] JPL 246; 43 P & CR 59, it was held by Woolf J that the applicants had standing to initiate a review of the council's alleged inaction over maintaining listed buildings, at least partly because they were local business people in the vicinity of the buildings in question. Also, in *R v Her Majesty's Inspectorate of Pollution ex p Greenpeace* (1993) 5 ELM 183; [1994] All ER 329, it was significant that a number of Greenpeace members lived in the Cumbria region in which the pollution had occurred.

The degree of connection to the area in establishing *locus standi* to bring about a judicial review is a matter for the courts and, in *R v Hammersmith and Fulham LBC ex p People Before Profit* [1981] JPL 869; (1983) 45 P & CR 364, Comyn J suggested a very wide and loose connection when he stated:

... a person is entitled, in my judgment, to object to a planning matter who has a legitimate *bona fide* reason. He does not have to be a ratepayer, he does not have to be a resident; but he must *not* be an officious bystander or an officious busybody. He must have what any reasonable person would say was a legitimate interest in being heard in objection. I do not think that one can set down elaborate and comprehensive rules about that because each one of us may have a legitimate *bona fide* interest in places far removed from where we live. They may be places in which we holiday; they may be places where we go for sporting events; they may be places that we feel are so much in the national interest that we ought to be heard about them as citizens of the country.

This wide interpretation was not shared in *R v Secretary of State ex p Rose Theatre Trust Co* [1990] JPL 360; 1 QB 504; (1991) 1 PLR 39. This case arose following the discovery of the remains of the Rose Theatre by developers during the construction of an office block. The site was regarded as a valuable archaeological site of national importance with particular significance to Shakespearean scholars. The SoS refused to schedule the site under the Ancient Monuments and Archaeological Areas Act 1979 for financial reasons, and the Trust attempted to have the decision reviewed. Although the Trust included local residents and a local MP amongst its members, Schiemann J did not accept that it had *locus standi* to initiate judicial review proceedings, and regarded their interest to be 'a mere intellectual or emotional concern'. The Historic Buildings and Monuments Commission probably had standing but declined to challenge the refusal to schedule the site.

A further case, *R v North Somerset DC and Pioneer Aggregates (UK) Ltd ex p Garnet and Pierssene* [1997] JPL B134, involved an application for leave to challenge a decision of the council to grant planning permission to Pioneer Aggregates for an extension to an existing quarry at Ashton Court, Bristol. The applicants described themselves as local residents and environmentalists and members of Friends of the Earth who had been active in making objections to the proposal when it was considered by the local authority. The proposed quarry extension involved land known as Top Park Field which was owned by the council and which was designated as a site of nature conservation in the approved Avon County Structure Plan. The site included a wildflower meadow which it was proposed to translocate to another field as part of a proposal to restore the entire quarry complex. The applicants lived some four miles from the application site and the public has no right of access to the area. The respondents pointed out that applicants were not the owners of the land, they had no rights over the land, they were not neighbours, they had no commercial interest and they had no rights of consultation. They were in the same category as any other ordinary members of the general public. In exercising its discretion, the court concluded that a 'sufficient' interest had not been shown, and Popplewell J ruled that leave should not be granted.

This ruling on *locus standi* was followed one month later by the ruling of Sedley J in *R v Somerset CC ex p Dixon* [1997] JPL June Update, who rejected the challenge by the county council to the *locus* of an applicant who lived 4.8 km from the site and had no special interest in it other then membership of various environmental bodies and the local parish council.

The question of establishing *locus standi* remains problematical, but guidance from Lord Diplock in *R v Inland Revenue Commissioners ex p National Federation of Self-Employed* [1982] AC 617 suggests that:

(a) standing should not be treated as a preliminary matter, but should be approached in the legal and factual context of the whole case;

(b) the merits of the challenge were an important, if not dominant, factor; and

(c) significant factors pointing to the conclusion that the applicants had sufficient interest were the importance of vindicating the rule of law, the importance of the issue raised, the likely absence of any other reasonable challenger, and the nature of the breach of duty against which relief was sought.

Although judicial review forms part of the participatory mechanism, it is important to understand that, by its very nature, it is challenging procedural irregularities rather than the decision itself. Legal proceedings are costly, and often the parties are ill matched in terms of financial resources and expertise. Nevertheless, successful challenges are frequent in relation to planning decisions, and particular reference should be made to the examples contained in, for example, *Steinberg and Sykes v Secretary of State* (Chapter 21, para 21.14) and *R v Sheffield City Council ex p Russell* (Chapter 11, para 11.13).

29.6 PLANNING PERMISSION AND THIRD PARTY RIGHTS

In *R v City of London Corporation and Another ex p Mystery of the Barbers of London* (1996) EGCS 101, the High Court held that a local authority which carried out development in accordance with a planning permission was authorised to interfere with third party rights where it subsequently developed the site in accordance with that permission. The authority had acquired land by compulsory acquisition, and granted a building lease to a mutual insurance society to construct a building known as Shelley House, and at the same time it granted land to the applicant and covenanted not to erect any form of structure which would obstruct the passage of light.

Later, the city decided to demolish Shelley House to provide a redevelopment site for commercial purposes. Planning permission was granted, and it was acknowledged that the form of redevelopment would interfere with the right to light enjoyed by the applicant's land. The court held that the right was not confined to the first development, but to all subsequent development of the land. As the safeguard of the need to gain planning permission existed, and the necessary permission had been granted for the redevelopment, the authority was authorised to interfere with the third party right, but compensation was payable for loss or damage resulting from the interference with that private right.

The granting of planning permission does not in itself allow the implementation of that permission. The following chapter deals with the interaction of private land law rights and also those of common law which may prevent implementation of planning permission.

It has also to be borne in mind that third parties may, in limited circumstances, be liable to pay costs to either or both of the main parties following a planning inquiry. In *Meacock v Richmond-upon-Thames LBC* (1998) unreported, the court agreed to award costs against an unrepresented third party applicant, not only in favour of the lpa, but also in favour of the developers. A serious allegation of impropriety had been made, for which there was no justification in substance, which the developers clearly needed to refute.

CHAPTER 30

NON-PLANNING CONTROLS

30.1   INTRODUCTION

There is a temptation, when considering the law relating to town and country planning, to assume that it is the only form of control exercised over the development of land and buildings. This is certainly not the case. This chapter deals with other forms of control which exist quite independently of planning control, and situations where there is an apparent degree of overlap with planning control which may give rise to potential conflict.

Planning effectively has a dual role in controlling land use change. The first is pre-emptive, that is, to consider the likely impact of proposed development on the environment. In so doing, the local planning authority (lpa) has to decide whether that impact is acceptable or not in making its decision as to whether it should be allowed to proceed with or without limitations by way of planning conditions. The second role is to enforce against breaches of planning control, and this action may have the effect of duplicating controls which are available in common law.

30.2   LEGAL RIGHTS OF THE OWNER

The legal rights of the land or property owner are circumscribed by the town and country planning legislation, the most important element of which is the removal of the owner's right to carry out development without first gaining planning consent. Nevertheless, the owner retains rights which may impact upon the granting of planning consent, either to himself or others. These natural rights include the right of support for land (buildings are not included, and the right must be acquired by an easement or covenant) and a right to an unpolluted free flow of air across property. Although the owner can acquire an easement to establish right to light from adjoining land, he cannot claim to have the right to a view, although this is frequently the basis of objections against the granting of planning permission. The only opportunity available to a person who may wish to retain the enjoyment of an existing view, is to acquire the land which would ensure that the view is preserved.

Although no action can be taken in respect of aircraft that pass over a property at a reasonable height under the Civil Aviation Act 1949, the owner can seek an injunction to prevent others from using the air space above his property. In the case of *Anchor Brewhouse Developments Ltd v Berkley House (Docklands Developments) Ltd* (1987) 3 BLR 82, an injunction was granted to prevent the jib of a crane swinging over adjoining property as this was held to amount to trespass. This right may not prevent redevelopment in built-up areas, but it will certainly make it more difficult to carry out the construction!

In the exercise of his rights over his property, the owner must not interfere with the legal rights of others, otherwise a consequential liability in tort may arise. This follows the long-established common law principle in private nuisance which is described as the unreasonable interference with another's use and enjoyment of his own property or unreasonable interference causing physical damage. Where a nuisance is caused, for example, noise or smells, the person affected is entitled to seek an injunction to prevent the continuation of the nuisance. As explained in Chapter 19, para 19.18, local authorities may also take action through the courts to seek an injunction to prevent the continuation of an unacceptable activity.

The converse situation is whether the granting of planning permission can confer immunity from an action of nuisance by a third party. The courts have been called upon to determine this issue, and the following four cases indicate the changing legal interpretations. In *Gillingham BC v Port of Medway (Chatham) Docks Co Ltd* [1992] JPL 458; 3 WLR 449; [1993] QB 343 planning permission for commercial development of a former Royal Navy dockyard resulted in heavy goods vehicles using the single access which ran through a residential neighbourhood. The council had been aware at the time of granting planning permission that the development would involve the movement of heavy goods vehicles which would change the character of the neighbourhood. The hardship on local residents had been played down in favour of the job opportunities which the development afforded. The decision of the High Court accepted that the implementation a planning permission will inevitably gradually change the character of the neighbourhood and this may alter the standards by which to judge whether an activity is a nuisance. Buckley J stated that:

> Parliament has set up a statutory framework and delegated the task of balancing interests of the community against those of individuals and of holding the scales between individuals to the local planning authority.

In so saying, he appears to suggest that once the balance has been decided, private rights as well as public rights may be negated.

In a subsequent Court of Appeal decision in *Wheeler v JJ Saunders Ltd* [1995] JPL 619; 1 PLR 55, the *Gillingham* decision was heavily qualified by the court. It was noted that, unlike Parliament, a lpa had no jurisdiction to authorise a nuisance save in so far as it had a statutory power to permit a change in the character of a neighbourhood. Hence, a planning permission would not normally confer any immunity from an action in nuisance. The claimants made a complaint in nuisance in the form of smell emanating from the defendant's pigs which were kept in premises which had been granted planning permission in 1989. Gibson LJ pointed out that, prior to the *Gillingham* decision, the general assumption appeared to have been that private rights to a claim in nuisance were unaffected by the grant of planning permission. Whilst he could see that, in the case of major development it might be inappropriate to grant an injunction, whether that should preclude any award of damages *in lieu* might require further consideration. The court was unwilling to accept the extinction of private rights without compensation as a result of an administrative decision which could not be appealed against by the objector.

This approach was followed in *Delyn BC v Solitaire (Liverpool) Ltd* (1995) EGCS 11, where the council sought an interlocutory injunction against a Saturday market which opened 3 miles from the council's own statutory Saturday market. The defendants argued that they had been granted planning permission for the market in 1983 and therefore had a statutory right to run their market. The High Court dismissed this defence, holding that planning permission merely removed the impediment on use or development of land imposed by planning laws, and did not override any other rights relating to the land. It did not confer a market right which was a franchise, nor did it confer immunity from action in nuisance.

In a later action, two separate appeals were heard together, and the issues were whether interference with television reception, and damage caused by excessive dust from road construction works, were actionable in private nuisance. *Hunter and Others v Canary Wharf Ltd* (1995) EGCS 153; [1996] 1 All ER 482; [1997] 2 All ER 426 resulted in a final determination by the House of Lords. The Law Lords rejected the claimants' claim that the construction of a large tower block built under a planning permission granted by a statutory scheme (the London Docklands Enterprise Zone scheme) which resulted in interference with television reception in their homes constituted an actionable private nuisance. In making the judgment, the court held that the interference with television reception caused by the mere presence of a building was not capable of constituting an actionable private nuisance. Subject to planning control, a person is free to build on his own land unrestricted by the fact that the presence of his building might itself interfere with his neighbour's enjoyment of his land. Accordingly, in the absence of an easement, more was required, such as nuisance *emanating from* the defendant's land, than the mere presence of a neighbouring building to give rise to an actionable private nuisance. The appeal was dismissed. Nevertheless, although the building itself may have the benefit of immunity from an actionable private nuisance, the activity within the building does not necessarily enjoy that immunity. Lord Cooke of Thornton, in examining the relationship between planning and nuisance, made the following observation:

> Control of building height is such a common feature of modern town planning control regimes that it would be inadequate to say that at the present day owners of the soil generally enjoy their rights *usque ad coelum et ad inferos* [up to the heavens and to the bowels of the earth]. Although the primary responsibility for enforcement falls to the administering authorities, I see no reason why neighbours prejudicially affected should not be able to sue for nuisance if a building does exceed height, bulk or location restrictions. For then the landowner is not making either a lawful or a reasonable use of landowning rights. This is to treat planning measures not as creating rights of action but in denoting a standard of what is acceptable in the community.

In giving judgment on a second case, *Hunter and Others v London Docklands Development Corporation* [1997] 2 WLR 687, relating to an alleged nuisance resulting from the deposit of dust from the construction of a road near the claimants' property, the Lords also dismissed that appeal on the basis that the alleged nuisance was temporary and the works were carried out reasonably (see *Andreae v Selfridge & Co Ltd,* below).

Three general principles emerge from these cases:

1 the defence of statutory authority is inapplicable to a planning permission whether granted by a lpa or under a statutory scheme;

2 where a lpa has granted planning permission which would alter the character of a neighbourhood, then for the purposes of determining whether or not an injunction should be granted, the question of nuisance should be decided by reference to the neighbourhood as changed by the permission; and

3 the grant of planning permission has no effect on other private rights, for example, a market franchise or a restrictive covenant affecting development. (For details of restrictive covenants, see para 30.3 below.)

In referring to 'the character of the neighbourhood' (point 2 above), the question of what is unreasonable enough to amount to a nuisance varies with the locality. This was established in *Sturges v Bridgman* [1879] 11 Ch D 852 where a doctor obtained an injunction to stop a confectioner grinding sugar in premises next to his surgery in the medical area of Wimpole Street, London. Thessiger LJ commented that 'what would be a nuisance in Belgrave Square would not necessarily be so in Bermondsey'. The doctor had only recently built his surgery, but succeeded in his action against the confectionery business which had been in operation for 60 years.

Changes due to planning policy may turn an established activity into a nuisance. In *Leeman v Montague* [1936] 2 All ER 1677, a new housing estate was built adjoining a farm, and the crowing of cockerels was held to be a nuisance because altering the running of the farm would reduce the noise. As the problem could be at least partially overcome by an action which was comparatively easy to implement, it was held to be nuisance for this reason. In allocating land for new uses, and thereby changing the character of the neighbourhood, planning authorities may effectively prevent the continuation of existing uses in the area.

Activities which are only temporary, such as construction work involving noise and dust, may not be regarded as nuisances provided they are carried out reasonably and at hours which cause minimum disturbance (see *Andreae v Selfridge and Co Ltd* [1938] Ch 1). The temporary use of land or buildings which is permitted under the Town and Country Planning (General Development Procedure) Order (GDPO) 1995 (SI 1995/419) Part 4 (see Chapter 10) can be challenged where they are of an anti-social nature.

Because a particular activity may be of interest to the general public, this does not necessarily mean that the courts will refuse to treat it as a nuisance. In *Kennaway v Thompson* [1981] QB 88, the Cotswold Boat Racing Club expanded their activities on Mallam Water after Miss Kennaway had built a bungalow near the lake. In spite of the popularity of the racing, an injunction was granted by the court to restrain the activity to its previous level. However, this approach was not accepted by the Court of Appeal in *Miller v Jackson* [1977] QB 996; 3 WLR 20; 3 All ER 338. The Millers had moved into a house which overlooked a cricket field and complained that cricket balls were frequently hit into their garden. The trial judge awarded damages for broken windows and granted an injunction preventing the future playing of cricket. The Court of Appeal quashed the injunction, Lord Denning saying there was no nuisance at all, Lane LJ saying there were valid grounds for issuing an injunction, and Cumming-Bruce LJ holding that, whilst he agreed with Lane LJ, it would be contrary to the public interest to grant an injunction. (See also *Adams v Ursell* [1913] 1 Ch 269, which related to the public utility in the case of a fish and chip shop in a residential area.)

The case of *Wallington v Secretary of State for Wales* (see Chapter 7, para 7.17) raised major questions concerning the role of planning enforcement where there was apparently no attempt by any party to take action to seek an injunction on the basis of nuisance. The machinery of planning took over the traditional role of the courts in dealing with what in this case can only be assumed could have constituted an alleged nuisance.

It is becoming more likely that action in connection with alleged statutory nuisance will be based upon the Environment Protection Act 1990 (s 79) as they share the same characteristics of common law nuisance, for example prejudice to health, smoke, fumes, gases, dust, smell and noise. The prosecution may be brought by an aggrieved person under s 82 or by the local authority under s 80 and, if it is satisfied that a statutory nuisance exists or is likely to reoccur, the local authority has a duty to act by the service of an abatement notice. Potentially this could lead to embarrassment on the part of the authority if it has granted planning permission for the activity which is causing the nuisance. In such cases the only defence under s 80(7) is that best practical means were used to prevent or counteract the effects of the statutory nuisance.

30.3 RESTRICTIVE COVENANTS

The decision in *Tulk v Moxhay* [1848] 18 LJ Ch 83 created what are now described as restrictive covenants, that is, the right of an owner to place restrictions on the future use of land or rights. This case involved land in Leicester Square, London, the use of which was restricted to a garden. This was enforced against the owner who was aware of the covenant at the time of his purchase of the land.

Where restrictive covenants exist, they are incorporated in the deeds relating to the property, and a potential purchaser is thereby made aware of their existence. In recent years, it has become relatively common for housebuilders of large estates to place restrictive covenants on each house prior to sale which are designed, for example, to ensure that the property is not used for any commercial purpose, caravans and boats are not be stored on the premises, and that front gardens are not to be enclosed by walls, gates or hedges. The latter restriction was very popular in the 1960s, largely as a result of the 'open plan' housing estates pioneered in new towns, and this particular restrictive covenant was frequently duplicated by a planning condition attached to the planning permission for the whole estate, which removes the permitted development rights under the GPDO.

The Lands Tribunal has the power to waive a restrictive covenant if it has implicitly been abandoned 'by reason of changes in the character of the property or the neighbourhood, or other circumstances of the case which the tribunal may consider material'. The findings of the tribunal can, therefore, be of direct interest to planners involved in development control. Planning policies may allow for the conversion of large houses into flats only to find that the tribunal upholds a restrictive covenant which prevents such a change from taking place. A planning policy designed to achieve land use change does not in itself allow the development to go ahead if there is a restrictive covenant in force which precludes that use of the land. In *Truman Hanbury v Buxton Co Ltd* [1956] 1 QB 261; [1955] 3 WLR 704 London Road, which is part of a large estate at Leigh-on-Sea, was built in 1848 with covenants against non-residential uses, and specifically forbidding premises to be used as hotels, inns, or for the sale of wines or spirits. By 1950, the road included shops, and an application was considered to discharge the restriction in relation to hotels and associated uses on two plots. The Court of Appeal upheld the decision of the Lands Tribunal, and Romer LJ stated: 'I cannot see how the covenant is obsolete when it is still capable of fulfilment and affords real protection to those entitled to it'. In the case of an application to the tribunal by Bailey (1981) 42 P & CR 108, planning permission had been granted and activated for the change of use of a cottage and adjoining land to a riding school. The tribunal refused to discharge a covenant which forbade non-residential and non-agricultural uses which was designed to protect the adjacent home of the original vendor.

It is important to appreciate that the formulation of planning policies and the grant of planning permission do not in themselves provide a legal authorisation for the changes proposed or accepted by the lpa.

In *Hunt's application to the Lands Tribunal* [1997] JPL 159, a restrictive covenant provided for the erection of one house only on each of 54 plots, and each house had to be within a building line. The applicant bought an area of garden belonging to one of the plots and gained planning permission following an appeal to the Secretary of State (SoS). He subsequently built a house in advance of the building line in accordance with the planning permission. No one objected until he received a letter from the council which was responsible for the building scheme drawing his attention to the covenant requesting a payment of £12,500 (plus VAT) to release the covenant. The council later withdrew the objection but five objectors appeared at the tribunal at which the applicant sought to have the restriction modified or discharged to allow the house to be retained. The tribunal held that the objectors would not suffer any loss of view; the alleged increase in traffic was not well founded; and the increase in density was insignificant. At this point, Mr Hunt was no doubt jubilant, but the tribunal refused his application on the ground that the house was well in advance of the building line, and presented a generally cramped appearance which was obtrusive in relation to the surrounding area, and the relaxation of the scheme of covenants would result in the creation of an undesirable precedent for the further subdivision of plots. The tribunal was satisfied that to prevent the erection of a house on the plot, or if necessary, to pull a house down where it had been erected, was acceptable in the public interest.

30.4   BUILDING REGULATIONS

Building regulations are designed to ensure adequate standards of building work for the construction of domestic, commercial and industrial buildings. They are laid down by Parliament, and are supported by technical guidance on compliance known as 'Approved Documents' which set out the legal requirements. There are minimum standards which are designed to secure the health and safety of people within or about buildings, energy conservation, and access facilities for disabled persons.

Building regulations are applied over and above the need to gain planning consent. It is quite possible that planning permission can be granted for a building form which will not meet the requirements set down under building regulations, or vice versa. The permitted development rights granted under planning legislation may, nevertheless, require building regulation consent prior to the carrying out of the development, for example, permitted extension to a dwelling house granted under Part I (GDPO) will require building regulation consent unless it is a porch or conservatory of less than 30 sq m floor area, provided the glazing complies with the safety glazing requirement of the Building Regulations (Part N).

Internal alterations which do not normally require planning permission may require building regulation consent and, in the case of a listed building, listed building consent. In the case of listed buildings, it may well prove impossible to meet current standards as set down in the regulations without destroying the intrinsic character of the building, either internally or externally. In such cases, it may be possible to waive the standards in the interest of retaining the character and use of the listed building, but the essential needs of protection against fire will remain paramount. It is also possible that a change of the use of a building which is permitted under planning legislation will first require building regulation consent even though construction work may not be intended. In such cases, the requirement arises because the change of use may involve different requirements of the regulations.

Unlike planning applications, there is no statutory requirement to inform the occupants of neighbouring properties of the intention to carry out building works requiring building regulation consent. It may be prudent to do so if the building operation is likely to require access to a neighbour's land, as this could lead not only to animosity but also to a possible civil action for trespass.

The Access to Neighbouring Land Act 1992 makes provision for an application to the courts for an access order (s 1) if consent is not forthcoming from the owner of neighbouring land. This may be granted under s 1(4) in specific circumstances which relate to:

(a) the maintenance, repair or removal of any part of a building or other structure comprised in, or situate on, the dominant land;

(b) the clearance, repair to removal of any drain, sewer, pipe or cable;

(c) the treatment, cutting back, felling, removal or replacement of any hedge, tree, shrub or other growing thing which is so comprised and which is, or is in danger of becoming, damaged, diseased, dangerous, insecurely rooted or dead; and

(d) the filling in, clearance, of any ditch.

The court will not make an order (s 1(3)) where it is satisfied that if it were to make such an order:

(a) the respondent or other person would suffer interference with or disturbance of his use or enjoyment of the servient land; or

(b) the respondent or other person in occupation of the whole or any part of the servient land would suffer hardship.

30.5 HAZARDOUS SUBSTANCES

The title of the relevant legislation, the Planning (Hazardous Substances) Act 1990, is misleading. The legislation does not relate to development, but concerns itself with the control of hazardous substances 'on, over or under land' (s 4(1)). Local planning authorities can exercise a degree of control over the siting and use of hazardous substances through the development control system, but there are situations where hazardous substances can be brought onto land, or used differently within it, without there being any associated development which requires planning permission. Controls under the Planning (Hazardous Substances) Act 1990 are specifically intended to regulating the storage and use of hazardous substances. The requirement for hazardous substances consent does not apply to the transportation of material or to temporary storage unless the material is unloaded (s 4(3)) or when it is less than the quantity prescribed in regulations made by the Secretary of State (s 4(2), (4) and (5)). The current regulations are contained in the Planning (Hazardous Substances) Regulations 1992 (SI 1992/656).

The regulations specify 71 types of hazardous substances which are classified under three headings:

1   toxic substances;

2   highly reactive substances and explosive substances; and

3   flammable substances other than in (1) and (2).

The quantities of material for which consent is required vary according to the degree of hazard it is likely to produce, for example, 1,000 tonnes of ammonia nitrate-based product to 1 kg of 2,3,7,8 tetrachlorodibenzo-p-dioxin (TCDD).

Deemed consent is granted (reg 3) for hazardous substances:

(a) contained within an aerosol dispenser, provided the capacity does not exceed 1,000 ml, subject to certain exceptions;

(b) contained in an exempt pipeline or service pipe; and

(c) unloaded from a ship in an emergency until the expiry of 14 days.

There are two further occasions when deemed consent may be claimed:

(d) where a hazardous substance was on, over or under the land for a period of 12 months prior to 1 June 1992 (the date at which the Act came into force) and a successful claim is established by application to the local authority (s 11(1)); and

(e) where development of land is to be carried out by a local authority or by a statutory undertaker under government authorisation (s 12(4)).

The authorities responsible for controlling hazardous substances are the lpas and the Broads Authority except for land which is:

(a) in a National Park;

(b) used for mineral working; or

(c) land in England used for refuse disposal.

In the above cases (b) and (c), the responsible authority is the county council acting as the Minerals Planning Authority. Applications are to be submitted on the appropriate form (see Sched 2 of the Regulations) accompanied by a site map showing the location of the substances. The application has to be advertised (s 7 and reg 6(1)) by means of a notice in the local press and the placing of a notice on the site. The application must include a certificate (s 8) which confirms that the applicant is the owner of the land or that he has taken steps to inform the owner. These certificates are the same as those required by the planning authority when dealing with a planning application (see Chapter 12, para 12.4).

The application may be approved by the authority unconditionally, or subject to such conditions as it thinks fit, or refused (ss 9(1)(a), (b) and 10). In dealing with the application, the authority must have regard to any material consideration, including:

(a) any current or proposed use of the land to which the application relates;

(b) the way in which land in the vicinity is being used or is likely to be used;

(c) any planning permission which has been granted for the development of land in the vicinity;

(d) the provision of the development plan; and

(e) advice given by the Health and Safety Executive or the Health and Safety Commission.

Unlike planning consent, a hazardous substances consent does not 'run with the land'. The consent is automatically revoked when any change takes place in the person in control of the land to which a consent relates (s 17) unless a successful application has been submitted to the local authority for a continuation of the consent. Should the original consent be revoked or modified following this application, the authority becomes liable for compensation payable to the person who was in charge of the land (s 19).

The enforcement of control is by the issue of a hazardous substances contravention notice to be served on the owner of the land, any other person who appears to be in control of the land, and other persons having an interest in the land (s 24(4)). The notice must specify the steps needed to remedy the contravention (ss 24(1)(b) and 24(5)(b)) which may require that the substances are completely removed from the land (s 24(6), (7)). The notice must also specify a date when it comes into effect, which shall not be less than 28 days from the date of service (s 24(5)(a)).

There are provisions for an appeal to the SoS against a refusal or the imposition of conditions in the same way in which appeals are lodged in relation to applications for planning permission (see Chapter 16) and a right of appeal to the SoS against a hazardous contravention notice. Following an appeal, the notice will not take effect until the appeal is determined (s 25(2)). However, should the authority consider it expedient to do so, it is entitled to seek enforcement by means of an application to the court for an injunction (s 26A).

30.6 POLLUTION CONTROLS

The relationship between planning control and other means of control of potential pollution to the environment provided by the Environmental Protection Act (EPA) 1990, the Water Resources Act 1991, and the setting up of the Environment Agency under the Environment Act 1995, has required a review of the role of the planning authority as one of the agencies involved in the control of activities which may result in pollution of the environment.

In reviewing the Use Classes Order (UCO) 1987, the government consultation paper proposed the special industrial use classes, that is, noxious uses contained in the then use classes (B.3–B.7) should be extinguished and subsumed into the general industrial class (B.2). The arguments in favour of this action were, first, that the industries involved are generally in decline and, secondly, that it was considered that the new pollution control legislation would not weaken control over such industries. These proposed changes were put into effect in the revised UCO (see Chapter 8), and planning control now operates on the basis that any industrial process which is likely to cause pollution is within Class B.2.

Where the responsibility lies in controlling potential pollution was the critical issue in the case of *Gateshead MBC v Secretary of State and Others* [1995] JPL 432. The case arose from an application for planning permission to erect a clinical waste incinerator. The application provoked a great deal of public interest and planning permission was refused on six grounds, which included:

1 that the proposal is contrary to the provisions of the approved development plan;

2 that the use conflicts with the allocation of neighbouring land;

3 failure to supply sufficient information to demonstrate that the plant could be operated without causing nuisance to the surrounding locality, including the possible release of noxious substances; and

4   failure to demonstrate the overall effects in terms of long term health risk.

The SoS allowed the appeal and, in doing so, overruled the inspector and an assessor, both of whom accepted that the appeal should be rejected on environmental grounds. The SoS accepted that it was necessary to have regard to environmental considerations, but stated it was not the role of the planning system to duplicate the controls which existed under EPA 1990 which provide stringent controls over potential emissions. This decision of the SoS was challenged by the lpa in the High Court where Mr Jeremy Sullivan QC sitting as Deputy Judge upheld the SoS's action.

The matter was then referred to the Court of Appeal, where Glidewell LJ again upheld the SoS's decision, stating that the existence of a stringent regime under the EPA 1990 for preventing or mitigating that impact was also a material consideration. The appellants argued that this 'stringent regime' required the application of the test of 'the best available techniques not entailing excessive cost', and that this could not guarantee that any problems would be totally eradicated. This, in the view of the lpa, could leave emissions of harmful substances being released at unacceptable levels. Furthermore, they saw no real possibility that (the then) Her Majesty's Inspectorate of Pollution (HMIP) would refuse to give permission for the operation of the plant. The Court of Appeal rejected these arguments and determined that the matters which led the inspector and the assessor to recommend refusal were matters which could properly be decided by HMIP. Glidewell LJ took the view that:

> If it had become clear at the inquiry that some of the discharges were bound to be unacceptable, so that refusal by the HMIP to grant authorisation would be the only proper course, the Secretary of State, following his express policy, should have refused planning permission. But that was not the situation. At the conclusion of the inquiry, there was no clear evidence about the quality of the air in the vicinity of the site.

Following the outcome of the *Gateshead* case, the government published PPG 23, 'Planning and Pollution Control', in July 1994 in an attempt to clarify the apparent confusion arising from the duplication of controls. Whether this Policy Guidance Note actually achieves its objective to clarify the situation is a matter of considerable debate in both the legal and planning professions. PPG 23, para 1.3 states:

> The planning system should not be operated to duplicate controls which are the statutory responsibility of other bodies (including local authorities in their non-planning functions). Planning controls, except where they are applied in the context of hazardous substances consents, are not an appropriate means of regulating the detailed characteristics of potentially polluting activities.

The definition of 'pollution of the environment' is that contained in Part I of the EPA 1990. Pollution is defined as occurring following:

> ... the release (into the environmental medium) from any process of substances which are capable of causing harm to man or any living organisms supported by the environment. 'Harm' means harm to health of living organism or other interference with the ecological systems of which they form a part, and, in the case of man, includes offences caused to any of his senses or harm to his property. Harm would include, for example, harm caused by offensive smells. Noise, however, would not normally be pollution.

(*Note*: For further consideration of noise, see reference to PPG 24, below.)

It is, however, apparently recognised that the planning system has a wider role in protecting the environment than is available under the pollution control system, as para 1.35 goes on to state:

Under the planning system, 'harm' can have a wider meaning than under Parts I and II of EPA 1990, extending for example, to unsightly development and loss of amenity in the wider sense.

Paragraph 1.34 acknowledges that 'the dividing line between planning and pollution controls is not always clear', and the Court of Appeal, in upholding the High Court's decision in the *Gateshead* case, accepted the statements by Mr Sullivan QC that:

Where two statutory controls overlap, it is not helpful, in my view, to try and define where one control ends and another begins in terms of some abstract principle ... it is clear beyond any doubt that the environmental impact of emissions to the atmosphere is a material consideration at the planning stage.

(*Note*: The reference in this case was to the atmosphere, but it may be assumed that the statement may be generally interpreted as applying to 'the environment'.)

The anticipated role of planning, as a mechanism for controlling pollution, is outlined in para 1.33, which makes it clear that planning should be concerned with:

... whether the development itself is an acceptable use of land rather than the control of the processes or substances themselves. Material considerations are likely to include:

location;

impact on amenity;

risk and impact of potential pollution;

prevention of nuisance;

impact on road and other transport networks;

need; and

the feasibility of restoring the land.

In the *Gateshead* case, the reasons for refusal of planning permission included consideration of some of the matters listed above, but these were not held to be material considerations warranting the refusal of planning permission in that instance. The critical factor in the *Gateshead* case appears to have been that the HMIP had an unrestricted right to refuse to accept the proposal irrespective of the grant or otherwise of planning consent. This is not the case with most other forms of overlapping controls.

The problem of overlapping environmental controls was considered once again by the Court of Appeal in *R v Bolton MBC ex p Kirkman* [1998] JPL 787; NPC 80; Env LR 560. In this case, the Court of Appeal dismissed, but with certain qualifications, an appeal against a decision by Carnwath J not to grant an application for judicial review. Schiemann LJ did not accept that the lpa had been in breach of its duties in allowing the details of environmental control to be handled by the integrated pollution control authorisation process operated by the Environment Agency and stated:

In my judgment, this is unarguable and, while the dual system of control permits a local planning authority to exercise greater control and conduct a greater degree of investigation that this authority saw fit to do, it does not render this legally obligatory.

Nor was the lpa obliged to have made a determination as to what was the Best Practical Environmental Option (BPEO) in relation to a particular stream of waste; they were entitled to take a general view on the BPEO, and did not have to base it on specific figures.

The definition of pollution acknowledges that 'harm in the case of man, includes offences caused by any of his senses or harm to his property. Harm would include, for example, harm caused by offensive smells'. This begs the question: what is an offensive smell? One individual may find an 'agricultural smell' to be quite acceptable, another may find it offensive to his senses. The Public Health Act 1936 (s 91(1)) requires that the odour constitutes a statutory nuisance, and to do so it must be either prejudicial to health or a nuisance. A smell which simply causes annoyance will not suffice; it must be an actionable nuisance in tort, that is, it must amount to a public or private nuisance at common law (see *NCB v Thorne* [1976] 1 WLR 543).

Public nuisance arises from an activity which prejudices a substantial section of the community, although it is actionable in suit of a private individual if he can show some special damage over and above that suffered by the community in general. In *Benjamin v Storr* (1874) 9 LR CP 400, the claimant's coffee shop was adversely affected by the smell from the defendant's horses. The courts, in attempting to strike a balance, have insisted that the defendant's conduct must be substantial or unreasonable, and in *Walter v Selfe* (1851) 4 De G & Sm 315, it was stated by Knight-Bruce J that inconvenience must materially interfere '... with the ordinary comfort physically of human existence, not merely according to elegant or dainty modes and habits of living, but according to the plain and sober and simple notions among the English people'.

Harm to property arising from smell which may cause a diminution in the value of that property was considered to arise in *Benjamin v Storr* where the smell acted as a deterrent to persons using the coffee house. However, where the smell simply interferes with the use and enjoyment of land, the general character of the area may prove to be a deciding factor in determining whether a nuisance has occurred. In *Shoreham UDC v Dolphin Canadian Proteins Ltd* (1972) 71 LGR 261, Donaldson J said:

> I have to remember that this is an industrial area. The local inhabitants are not entitled to expect to sit in a sweet-smelling orchard. They chose to build their houses or buy them ... in an area where a tallow factory had been established for many years, where there are other factories. There has been a mushroom factory and jam-making factory ... There was a chemical works across the river and there are the usual smells from a dock area. So this is certainly not an area where one should impose very tight and strict standards of smell.

However, if the smell amounts to an actionable nuisance, it is no defence to claim that the claimant came to the nuisance. In *Bliss v Hall* (1838) 4 Bing NC 183, the claimant moved to a house near the defendant's tallow factory which gave off 'divers noisome, noxious and offensive vapours, fumes, smells and stenches'. It was held to be no defence that the business had been operating for three years before the claimant arrived since he 'came to the house ... with all the rights which the common law affords, and one of them is the right to wholesome air'.

Although noise is specifically omitted from the definition of pollution in the EPA 1990, PPG 24, 'Planning and Noise', provides advice on how lpas should seek to minimise the impact of noise which can have an adverse impact on the environment and individuals. In addition to general advice on the siting and control over development which is likely to result in unacceptable levels of noise, the guidance note also draws attention in Annex 7 to the powers granted to a local authority under the EPA 1990 and the Noise and Statutory Nuisance Act 1993.

The question of overlapping controls was considered in the case of *Black (WE) Ltd v Secretary of State* [1996] ELM 123, where the High Court found that it was lawful for a planning authority, when granting planning consent for housing development, to impose a condition on the granting of planning consent preventing the occupation of houses until the completion of works necessary for surface water attenuation and storage. It was held that the condition did not involve duplication of other statutory controls and was not inconsistent with the scheme of objectives of the Water Industry Act 1991.

30.7 LICENSING CONTROLS

The grant of planning consent or the permitted changes of use under the UCO in certain instances cannot be implemented without the further grant of a licence to operate that activity. As explained in Chapter 26, the grant of planning permission must be followed by the grant of a site licence to operate a site as a caravan site. This automatic grant of a license does *not* apply in other circumstances.

Examples of uses which require an independent judgment on the part of the licensing authority include premises in which the sale of alcohol takes place, places of entertainment, places for gambling (including bingo and amusement centres) and sex shops. Thus, whilst it is possible to change the use of premises in the UCO without the requirement to seek planning permission, that use may not be authorised by the licensing authority. Where planning permission is required, the lpa cannot take into account competition with established uses of the same or similar kind, nor can it take into account moral issues in making its determination. The licensing authority is not fettered in this way, and may well determine to refuse a licence on the grounds of 'enough is enough' in relation to a particular use, for example, they do not wish to see a further proliferation of public houses or amusement centres.

The added requirement placed upon an applicant for planning permission allows that person a choice of whether he seeks planning permission prior to applying for a licence or vice versa. There is no legal requirement that planning permission be granted prior to an application for a licence to operate, although many developers regard the granting of planning permission as a positive factor which will be in their favour and taken into account by the licensing authority.

30.8 REGISTERED COMMON LAND

A town or village green may be registered under the Commons Registration Act 1965 and this prevents development because s 29 of the Commons Act 1876 regards encroachment on or the enclosure of such land as a public nuisance. Section 22(1) of the 1965 Act defines a town or village green as;

Land which has been allotted by or under any Act for the exercise of recreation of the inhabitants of any locality or on which the inhabitants of any locality have a customary right to indulge in lawful sports and pastimes or which falls within subsection (1A) of this section.

(1A) Land falls within this section if it is land which for not less than twenty years a significant number if the inhabitants of any locality, or of any neighbourhood within a locality, have indulged in lawful sports and pastimes as of right and either-

(a) continue to do so, or

(b) have ceased to do so for not more than such a period as defined.

Application to register common land is made to the relevant county council, unitary authority or to a London borough council (the registration authorities). In the event of objections being lodged to the proposed registration it has been determined in *R (on application by Whitmey) v The Common Commissioners* [2004] EWCA 951 that the decision is that of the registration authority and it is neither obliged nor permitted to refer the issue to the Commissioners. The question of the acquisition of rights on village greens was the issue in the decision of the House of Lords in *R v Oxfordshire CC ex p Sunningwell Parish Council* [1999] JPL September Update, the outcome of which is of major significance to developers.

Planning permission had been granted for two houses on glebe land and the parish council applied to the county council to register the glebe as a town or village green under the 1965 Act. The application was refused on the ground that the use of the land by the villagers had not been shown to be 'as of right' following the findings of *R v Suffolk CC ex p Steed* [1996] 75 P & CR 102. In that case, 'as of right' was interpreted as a right enjoyed by the inhabitants of the village to the exclusion of all others. Such a restrictive view was not argued by the villagers of Sunningwell who claimed to have a right to use the land but not to the exclusion of all others.

Lord Hoffman accepted that activities conducted on the green, which included walking, tobogganing and family games, were of the nature of 'sports and pastimes' within the Commons Registration Act (s 22(1), Class C) which refers to land 'on which the inhabitants of any locality have indulged in sports and pastimes of right for not less than 20 years'. There was no need to show that the land had been used for regular sporting events. Whilst there was little evidence to show that persons other than villagers had used the land for games or pastimes, it was sufficient that villagers had been the predominant users.

APPENDIX I

TOWN AND COUNTRY PLANNING ACT 1990
DEVELOPMENT PLAN SYSTEM
INTERIM ARRANGEMENTS

1   PLANS UNDER THE TOWN AND COUNTRY PLANNING ACT 1990

1.1 The hierarchy of plans prepared in accordance with the requirements of the Town and Country Planning Act (TCPA) 1990 involved regional planning guidance prepared by central government and, in two-tier authorities, the preparation of structure plans by the county councils and more detailed district-wide local plans by the constituent district councils which were in accordance with the policies contained in the structure plan. Single-tier authorities were responsible for the production of a 'hybrid' unitary development plan, Part I of which was akin to a structure plan in terms of broad policy statements and Part II to a district plan. County councils were, in addition, responsible for minerals and waste disposal plans.

1.2 Structure plans were subject to the approval of the Secretary of State (SoS) following an Examination in Public. Local plans were subject to a local plan inquiry following which the inspector appointed by the SoS made recommendations relating to the amendment of the plan as prepared by the local planning authority.

2   PLANS UNDER THE PLANNING AND COMPULSORY PURCHASE ACT 2004

2.1 The new plan system is detailed in Chapter 3 and it provides for a Local Development Framework (LDF) which is a folder-based collection of documents including a core strategy, Local Development Scheme (LDS), adopted proposals map, site specific allocations and a statement of community involvement (SCI). It may also include action area plans and supplementary planning guidance (SPG). The LDF will also be the subject of an annual monitoring report to be carried out each December which is intended to bring about transparent scrutiny of policy and the progress toward key milestones set out in the local development scheme.

2.2 Regional spatial strategies (RSSs) will replace regional planning guidance. It had been anticipated that the regional guidance would be prepared by new elected regional assemblies but following the overwhelming 'no vote' on the setting up of the first of these assemblies for the north east of England, it seems unlikely that the government will pursue any further attempt to create any such elected assemblies. The current unelected regional bodies are likely to remain but will retain a major role in setting out regional policies.

2.3 Local development schemes were to be submitted to the SoS by 28 March 2005, that is, within six months of the commencement of the Act, and are to show what milestones in the preparation of LDSs will be achieved by March 2007. The milestones included are:

    (a) start of preparation of all local development documents (LDDs);

    (b) public participation on preferred options and sustainability appraisal report forming the development plan document (DPD) (or draft SPG and SCI);

    (c) submission of DPD/SCI;

    (d) pre-examination meeting (DPD/SCI);

    (e) start of examination (DPD/SCI);

    (f) adoption and publication of all LDDs;

3   INTERIM PROPOSALS

It is acknowledged by government that the new system will take time to become fully operational and therefore a series of interim policies have been set out in the Town and Country Planning (Transitional Regulations) (England) Regulations 2004 (SI 2004/2205). Following the commencement order:

(a) all adopted development plan policies are 'saved' for three years;

(b) plans with an inspector appointed will continue to adoption under the old arrangements. (NB the inspector will continue to make 'recommendations' on the content of the plan;)

(c) plans that have reached at least 'first deposit' stage will continue to adoption under transitional arrangements. They will require a further deposit and inquiry with a binding report from the inspector;

(d) plans that have not reached first deposit stage will lapse; and

(e) current regional guidance will continue until replaced by RSSs.

The new Public Service Agreement target for the Office of the Deputy Prime Minister is that, 'the planning system to deliver sustainable development outcomes at national, regional and local levels through efficient and high quality planning and development management processes, including the achievement of best value standards for planning by 2008.'

The status of an emerging local plan in relation to the new style local development framework was tested in *Martin Grant Homes Ltd v Wealdon District Council* (2005) (unreported). Martin Grant Homes and Taylor Woodrow, who wished to object to housing allocations, claimed that the council was obliged to hold a local plan inquiry into objections to its local plan review in accordance with the interim provisions set out in the Planning and Compulsory Purchase Act 2004. The District Council held the view that, as the new Act required it to prepare a local development framework by 2007, holding a local inquiry would result in wasted costs totalling approximately £400,000. The High Court ruled that unless there were 'exceptional' reasons for withdrawing the draft plan the statutory requirement to hold a local plan inquiry must be followed. The fact that it may be more economical not to hold an inquiry did not qualify as an exceptional circumstances. Accordingly it was ordered that the council hold an inquiry.

APPENDIX II

RESUMÉ OF THE GENERAL (PERMITTED DEVELOPMENT) ORDER 1995 (SI 1995/418)

SCHEDULE 2: PERMITTED DEVELOPMENT

PARTS 1 and 2

See Chapter 10.

PART 3   CHANGES OF USE

Note: Also refer to Town and Country Planning (Use Classes) Order 1987 (SI 1987/764)

Class A   Change of use to Class A1 from Class 3 or from a use for the sale, or display for sale of motor vehicles.

Class B   Change of use to Class B1 from B2 or B8 and

Change of use to B8 from B1 or B2.

Not permitted within B8 if change relates to more than 235 sq m floorspace.

Class C   Change of use from Class A3 to A2.

Class D   Change of use of premises with a display window at ground level from A2 to A1.

Class E   Change of use of land or building from use granted planning permission to a use specifically authorised when it was granted.

Not permitted if:

(i)   application for planning permission was before 5 December 1988;

(ii)   carried out more than 10 years after the grant of permission; or

(iii)   would result in a breach of any condition.

Class F   Change of use to mixed use of single flat above ground floor Class A1 or A2.

Conditions:

(i)   A1 or A2 retained on ground floor;

(ii)   ground floor not to be used in whole or part as a single flat;

(iii)   occupancy of the flat by a single person or people living as a family; and

(iv)   not more than six residents.

Class G   Change of use from mixed use to A1 or A2 where there is a display window at ground floor level for that purpose.

Condition: prior use of part of the building as a flat.

PART 4   TEMPORARY BUILDINGS AND USES

See Chapter 10.

PART 5   CARAVAN SITES

Class A   Use of land other than a building as a caravan site in accordance with the provisions of the Caravan Sites Act 1960, Sched 1, paras 2–10.

Class B   Development required by conditions of a site licence under the 1960 Act.

PART 6   AGRICULTURAL BUILDINGS AND OPERATIONS

Class A   Development on units of 5 ha or more.

Permitted:

(i)   erection, extension or alteration of a building; and

(ii)   excavation or engineering operations necessary for agriculture.

Not permitted:
(i)   on a parcel of land of less than 1 ha;
(ii)   related to a dwelling;
(iii)   not designed for agricultural purposes;
(iv)   works or structure (other than a fence) to accommodate stock, plant or machinery or any building erected or extended would exceed 465 sq m;
(v)   height exceeding 33 m. Within 3 k of aerodrome maximum height 12 m;
(vi)   any part of the development within 25 m of metalled part of a trunk or classified road;
(vii)   erection or construction, or works of a building, or excavation to be used for livestock or the storage of slurry/sewage within 400 m of the curtilage of a protected building; or
(viii) excavations or engineering operations on or over Art 1(6) land connected with fish farming.

Conditions under Class A:
(i)   if within 400 m of a protected building not to be used for livestock or slurry;
(ii)   extraction of minerals on land including disused railway embankments not to be removed from the unit;
(iii)   waste materials not to be brought to the site except when used to achieve development under Class A or the creation of a hard surface;
(iv)   on Art 1(6) land the extension, alteration, etc, to a building, formation or alteration to a private way, carrying out of excavations, deposit of waste, placing or assembly of a tank in any waters the developer shall:
        (a) apply to the local planning authority to ascertain whether prior approval required relating to siting, design, external appearance, formation of or alteration to a private right of way or placing of a tank;
        (b) development shall not commence until the local planning authority have given approval, state no approval is required, or has failed to reply within 21 days.

Class B Units of less than 5 ha but more than 0.4 ha.
        Permitted:
(i)   extension or alteration of an agricultural building;
(ii)   installation/replacement of plant/machinery;
(iii)   provision/replacement of sewer, pipe, etc;
(iv)   provision/replacement of private right of way;
(v)   creation of a hard surface;
(vi)   deposit of waste;
(vii)   repairing ponds/raceways, replacement of tanks for fish farming.
        Not permitted if:
(i)   carried out on a parcel of land forming part of a unit of less than 0.4 ha;
(ii)   external appearance materially effected;
(iii)   development within 25 m of metalled part of a trunk or classified road;
(iv)   if used for livestock or slurry/sludge within 400 m of protected building;
(v)   creation/extension of fish ponds other than the removal of silt;
(vi)   if height of building increased;
(vii)   if cubic content of building increased by more than 10%;
(viii) any part of the new building would be more than 30 m from original;
(ix)   the ground area of the building extended would exceed 465 sq m (calculated on the basis of the original building and any extension carried out in preceding two years any part of which would be within 90 m of the proposed development);
(x)   would involve the extension/alteration or provision of a dwelling;
(xi)   any part of the development would be within 5 m of any boundary of the unit;

(xii)   the ground area would exceed 465 sq m; or

(xiii) the height exceeds 12 m or 33 m within 3 k of an aerodrome.

Conditions under Class B:

(i)   that permitted by Class B within 400 m of protected building shall not be used for the accommodation of livestock or storage of slurry/sludge;

(ii)   in the case of Art 1(6) land, prior notification to the local planning authority required as above under Class A.

Note: If no other buildings are available 400 m or more from a protected building to accommodate livestock and the need arises then permitted based upon quarantine requirements, alternative damaged by fire, flood or storm, and animals that are sick, giving birth or extreme weather conditions.

Class C   Mineral working for agricultural purposes.

Permitted: any mineral necessary for agriculture within the unit of which it is a part.

Not permitted: if excavation within 25 m of metalled part of trunk or classified road.

Condition: not to be moved outside the land which is held for agricultural purposes.

PART 7   FORESTRY BUILDINGS AND OPERATIONS

Class A   Permitted on land for forestry/afforestation:

(i)   erection, extension, alteration of (subject to 10% maximum based on cubic content of the original building and no increase in height);

(ii)   formation, alteration and maintenance of private ways;

(iii)   obtaining minerals for the purpose of (ii) above; and

(iv)   other operations (not including mining and engineering operations).

Not permitted:

(i)   involving a dwelling;

(ii)   height above 3 m within 3 k of aerodrome; or

(iii)   within 25 m of metalled part of trunk or classified road.

Conditions:

(i)   developer required to inform the local planning authority to determine whether any prior approval required regarding siting, design and external appearance and materials to be used;

(ii)   plan and fee to be forwarded to the local planning authority;

(iii)   site notice to be displayed;

(iv)   the local planning authority has 28 days to comment and failure to do so grants deemed consent.

PART 8   INDUSTRIAL AND WAREHOUSE DEVELOPMENT

Class A   Extension or alteration to buildings.

Not permitted:

(i)   if not used for the same purpose (includes the provision of employee facilities which are not to be used between 19.00 and 06.30 hours by employees other than those working during that period); not permitted where hazardous substances are kept on the premises;

(ii)   height exceeds the original building;

(iii)   cubic content of original building exceeded by 10% on Art 1(5) land and 25% in other cases;

(iv)   floorspace exceeded by 500 sq m on Art 1(5) land and 1,000 sq m in other cases;

(v)   external appearance is materially effected;

(vi)   development within 5 m of the boundary; or

(vii)   would lead to a reduction in space for car parking or the turning of vehicles.

Class B   Development on industrial land.
          Permitted: replacement, installation of machinery, pipes sewers, etc, provided does
          not materially affect the external appearance or exceeds 15 m from ground level or
          height of that which it replaces, which ever is the greater.
          Note: Industrial land does not include land adjacent to a mine.
Class C   Permitted: the creation of a hard surface.
Class D   Deposit of waste.
          Permitted: deposit of waste resulting from an industrial process on site on 1st July
          1948 irrespective of extension of superficial area or height.
          Not permitted:
          (i)   if waste includes materials resulting from the winning of minerals; or
          (ii)   use on 1 July 1948 was for waste from the winning of minerals.

PART 9   UNADOPTED STREETS AND PRIVATE WAYS

Permitted: repairs to unadopted streets and private ways.

PART 10   REPAIRS TO SERVICES

Permitted: works for inspecting, repairing, renewal of any pipe, sewer, cable or other
apparatus.

PART 11   AUTHORISED BY PRIVATE ACT, ORDER OR HARBOURS ACT 1964

Not permitted:
(i)   erection, alteration, etc, to building, bridge, aqueduct, pier or dam;
(ii)   involves formation, alteration of mans of access to a highway;
Unless prior approval by the relevant planning authority.

PART 12   DEVELOPMENT BY LOCAL AUTHORITIES

Class A   Erection, construction, maintenance, improvement of buildings.
          Permitted:
          (i)   small ancillary buildings related to a function carried out by the authority;
          (ii)   lamp standards, information kiosks, refuse bins, barriers, etc.
Class B   Deposit of waste by local authority on land used for the purpose on 1st July 1948
          irrespective of increase in superficial area or height.

PART 13   DEVELOPMENT BY HIGHWAY AUTHORITIES

Permitted:
(i)   on land within the boundaries of the road; and
(ii)   on land outside the boundary but adjacent.

PART 14   DEVELOPMENT BY DRAINAGE AUTHORITIES

Class A   Permitted: development in, on, or under any watercourse or land drainage works in
          connection with improvement, maintenance or repair.

PART 15   DEVELOPMENT BY THE ENVIRONMENT AGENCY

Class A   Permitted:

(i)   development not above ground;

(ii)   development in, on or under a watercourse or land drainage;

(iii)   building plant or machinery or apparatus for survey or investigation; and

(iv)   maintenance, improvement, etc, of works for measuring flow.

Not permitted:

(i)   construction of a reservoir;

(ii)   alteration/extension to a building which would materially affect appearance, existing height exceeded, cubic content more than 25% of original or would exceed 1,000 sq m;

(iii)   erection of plant not to exceed 15 m or height of the original whichever is greater.

PART 16   DEVELOPMENT BY OR ON BEHALF OF SEWERAGE UNDERTAKERS

See Part 15

PART 17   DEVELOPMENT BY STATUTORY UNDERTAKERS

Class A   Railway and light railway undertakings.

Permitted: development of operational land required in connection with movement of traffic by rail.

Not permitted:

(i)   construction of a railway;

(ii)   erection of a hotel, railway station or bridge;

(iii)   construction/erection other than wholly within a railway station of an office, residential or educational building, building used for industrial purposes, car park, shop, restaurant, garage or petrol filling station.

Class B   Dock, pier, harbour, water transport, canal inland navigation.

(See Class A above.)

Class C   Works to inland waterways.

Permitted: improvement, maintenance, repair (other than commercial or cruising waterway) (see s 104 Waterways Act 1968).

Class D   Dredgings.

Permitted: use of land by statutory undertakers for the spreading of dredged material.

Class E   Water and hydraulic undertakings.

(See Class A above.)

Class F   Public gas transporters.

Permitted:

(i)   laying underground mains, pipes, etc;

(ii)   construction of storage area, construction of boreholes;

(iii)   placing and storage of pipes and other apparatus;

(iv)   erection on operational land of building solely to protect machinery; and

(v)   any other development on operational land.

Not permitted:

(i)   structure for housing apparatus exceeding 29 cu m if at or above ground level, or under a highway used by vehicular traffic;

(ii)   in the case of boreholes any machinery would exceed 6 m in height;

(iii)   in the case of a building when the design and external appearance would be materially affected; and

(iv)   plant or machinery not to exceed 15 m in height or height of the original whichever is the greater.

Class G   Electricity undertakings.

(See Class F above.)

Class H   Tramway and road transport undertakings.

Permitted:

(i)   installation of posts, wires, transformer boxes, etc;

(ii)   installation of tracks, telephone cables, signs, etc;

(iii) passenger shelters, barriers; and

(iv)   any development on operational land.

Not permitted:

(i)   structure exceeding 17 cu m in the case of (i) above;

(ii)   erection, alteration, reconstruction of building materially affecting design or external appearance;

(iii) plant or machinery exceeding 15 m in height or height of the original whichever is the greater; and

(iv)   development not wholly within tram or bus station.

Class I   Lighthouse undertakings.

Permitted: development under the Merchant Shipping Act 1894

Class J   Post Office.

Permitted:

(i)   installation of post boxes, self service machines; and

(ii)   development on operational land.

Not permitted: (as for Class H above).

PART 18   AVIATION DEVELOPMENT

Class A   Development at an airport.

Permitted: on operational land the erection/alteration of operational building connected to the provision of services.

Not permitted:

(i)   construction/ extension of a runway;

(ii)   passenger terminal exceeding 500 sq m;

(iii) extension/alteration to a terminal as existing on 5 December 1988 or if after that date the building as built would exceed 15%; and

(iv)   alteration other than to an operational building where external appearance would be materially affected.

Class B   Air navigation development at an airport.

Permitted:

(i)   provision of air traffic control services;

(ii)   navigation of aircraft using the airport; and

(iii) monitoring of aircraft movement.

Class C   Air navigation near an airport.

Permitted:

(i)   on operational land outside but within 8 k of the airport;

(ii)   provision of air traffic control services;

(iii) navigation for aircraft using the airport; and

(iv)   monitoring of aircraft movements.

Not permitted:

(i)   any building other then those for equipment for items above;

(ii)   any building exceeding 4 m in height; and

(iii) installation/erection of radar, radio masts, antenna or other apparatus which exceeds 15 m in height or height of that replaced whichever is the greater.

Class D   Development by Civil Aviation Authority (CAA) within an airport.

Permitted: within the perimeter, air traffic control, navigation and monitoring requirements.

Class E   CAA development for air traffic control and monitoring.

Permitted: subject to restrictions (see Class C above).

Class F   Development by CAA in an emergency.

Permitted: use of land for moveable apparatus or to replace unserviceable apparatus.

Condition: Period limited to six months and land to be restored.

Class G   Development by CAA for air traffic control.

Permitted: use of land to provide services in connection with:

(i)   air traffic control;

(ii)   navigation of aircraft; and

(iii) monitoring of aircraft.

Condition: limited to six months and land to be restored.

Class H   Development by CAA for surveys, etc.

(As above.)

Class I   Use of airport buildings by operators.

Permitted: use of buildings within the perimeter managed by operators for air transport services or other flying activities.

PART 19   DEVELOPMENT ANCILLARY TO MINING OPERATIONS

Class A   Erection, extension, replacement repair, etc, of:

(i)   plant and machinery;

(ii)   buildings;

(iii) private ways or railway, or sidings; and

(iv)   sewers, pipes, cables, etc.

Not permitted:

(i)   in relation to land which is an underground mine which is not an approved site or unless a plan was deposited with the mineral planning authority before 5 June 1989;

(ii)   unless for the purpose of winning and working of minerals;

(iii) if external appearance materially affected;

(iv)   height above 15 m or original whichever is the greater;

(v)   any building erected exceeds 1,000 sq m; and/or

(vi)   the cubic content replaced, extended or altered would exceed 25% of the original.

Conditions:

(i)   within 24 months of ending operations or such period agreed with the planning authority, buildings shall be removed; and

(ii)   the land shall be restored.

Class B   Operations for the erection, installation, extension, rearrangement, repair or other alteration with the prior approval of the mineral planning authority.

(Aee Class A above.)

Class C   Development required for the maintenance or safety of a mine or disused mine for ensuring the safety of the surface of the land adjacent to the mine.

(See Class A above.)

PART 20   COAL MINING DEVELOPMENT BY COAL AUTHORITY and LICENSED OPERATORS

Class A   Development by a licensee in a mine started before 1 July 1948.
Permitted:
(i)   winning and working of underground coal and related minerals in a designated seam area; and
(ii)   development underground to gain access to coal and related minerals.
Conditions:
(i)   unless there is an approved restoration scheme, or the operations have permanently ceased the operator shall, before 31 December 1995, or such time agreed with the mineral authority, apply for approval of such a scheme;
(ii)   restoration to be carried out within 24 months or period specified;
(iii)   aftercare for a period of five years following restoration;
(iv)   if no restoration scheme approved all buildings, etc, to be removed; and
(v)   land shall be restored as far as practicable to original form and use.

Class B   Development by licensee of British Coal started before 1 July 1948.
(See Class A above.)

Class C   Development required for authorised mine by licensed operator.
Not permitted:
(i)   external appearance of the mine materially affected;
(ii)   any building/plant, etc, including waste exceeds 15 m;
(iii)   re-arranged, repaired, replaced not to exceed 15 m or height of original;
(iv)   building not to exceed 1,000 sq m;
(v)   cubic content exceeding 25% increase over the building replaced; and
(vi)   if to create a new surface access or improve existing non-active access.

Class D   Development by licensee of mine with prior approval of mineral authority.
(See Class C above.)

Class E   Carrying out by Coal Authority or licensed operator of development required for the maintenance or safety of a mine or disused mine with the prior approval of the mineral authority.
Permitted:
(i)   provided external appearance not materially affected;
(ii)   buildings, plant, machinery, etc, not over 15 m in height or height of original.
Note: Only to be refused (when application required) if it would injure amenity of the neighbourhood and modifications cannot be reasonably imposed.

PART 21   WASTE TIPPING AT MINE

Class A   Deposit on land used as a mine or ancillary land of waste from the mine.
Not permitted:
(i)   where waste deposited in an excavation the height of waste deposited would exceed that of adjoining land, unless provided for in a waste management scheme; or
(ii)   in any other case the area of height of the deposit (measured at 21 October 1988) would increase by more than 10% unless provided for in a management scheme.

Class B   Deposit on land comprising a site on 1 July 1948 for waste from coal.
Not permitted: unless in accordance with scheme approved by the minerals authority before 5 December 1988.

PART 22   MINERAL EXPLORATION

Class A   Development on any land not exceeding 28 consecutive days.
Permitted:
(i)   drilling boreholes;
(ii)   seismic surveys; and
(iii)   making excavations.
Not permitted:
(i)   if for petroleum;
(ii)   within 50 m of residence, school or hospital;
(iii)   within a National Park, AONB, SSSI or archaeological area;
(iv)   explosive charge of more than 1 kg;
(v)   more than 10 excavations in any 1 ha within 12-month period; and
(vi)   any structure would exceed 12 m or 3 m within 3 k of aerodrome.
Conditions:
(i)   no operations between 18.00 and 07.00 hours;
(ii)   no trees to be felled or damaged;
(iii)   topsoil and subsoil to be kept separate; and
(iv)   within 28 days of cessation land to be restored.
Class B   Development of structures for exploration.
(See Class A above.)

PART 23   REMOVAL OF MINERALS FROM MINERAL WORKING DEPOSITS

Class A   Removal of material from stockpiles is permitted.
Class B   Removal of material from any deposit other than a stockpile.
Not permitted:
(i)   unless notified to the minerals authority in writing;
(ii)   covers a ground area exceeding 2 ha unless the mineral deposited on the land more than five years before the development; or
(iii)   the deposit derives from operations permitted under Part 6 of this Schedule
Conditions: relate to the restoration of the site.

PART 24   DEVELOPMENT BY TELECOMMUNICATIONS CODE SYSTEMS OPERATORS

Class A Development of land controlled by operator under licence.
Permitted:
(i)   installation, replacement, etc, of telecommunication apparatus;
(ii)   emergency use of land for up to six months by moveable apparatus; or
(iii)   ancillary to radio equipment housing.
Not permitted:
(i)   apparatus excluding antenna would exceed 15 m in height;
(ii)   replacement equipment exceeding 15 m above ground level or height of original;
(iii)   installation/replacement, etc, on a building; height of apparatus not to exceed 15 m on a building which is 30 m or more in height;
(iv)   installation, replacement, etc, on a building the apparatus would exceed the height of the highest part of the building or structure by more than:
(a)   10 m when building is 30 m or more in height,

(b) 8 m when the building is more than 15 m but less than 30 m in height;

(c) 6 m in any other case;

(v)   installation, alteration or replacement of any apparatus other than a mast, antenna, public call box, not projecting above the surface and the ground area not to exceed 1.5 sq m;

(vi)   where located lower than 15 m above ground;

(a) antenna to be located on a wall or roof slope if highway within 20 m of structure;

(b) dish antennas not to exceed 0.9 m or aggregate size of all dishes 1.5 m;

(c) antennas other than dishes, not more than two on a building;

(d) the building is a listed or scheduled monument;

(vii)   where located higher than 15 m above ground level:

(a) dish not to exceed 1.3 m or aggregate size of 3.5 m;

(b) not more than three antennas;

(c) not on listed building or scheduled monument;

(viii) in the case of Art 1(5) land;

(ix)   if within 3 k of the perimeter of aerodrome the CAA to be informed.

PART 25   OTHER TELECOMMUNICATIONS DEVELOPMENT

Class A Microwave antenna on buildings over 15m in height.

Not permitted:

(i)   on dwelling house or other structure within the curtilage;

(ii)   consists of development described in Part 24;

(iii)   more than two antenna;

(iv)   exceeds 90 cm;

(v)   in the case of terrestrial microwave antenna, exceeds 1.3 m or the highest part of the antenna would be more than 3 m above the building; or

(vi)   is on Art 1(5) land.

Conditions:

(i)   should be sited to minimise the impact as far as possible;

(ii)   when no longer required to be removed as soon as practicable.

Class B Satellite antenna on building of less than 15 m in height.

Not permitted:

(i)   on dwelling houses or other structure within the curtilage;

(ii)   consists of development described in Part 24;

(iii)   dimensions which exceed 90 cm on a building on Art 1(4) land and 70 cm in any other case;

(iv)   exceeding the highest part of the roof;

(v)   more than 1 antenna;

(vi)   would consist of installation on a chimney; or

(vii) on wall or slope of a roof fronting a highway (waterway in The Broads).

Conditions:

(See Class A above.)

PART 26   DEVELOPMENT BY HISTORIC BUILDINGS and MONUMENTS COMMISSION FOR ENGLAND

Class A Permitted:

(i)   maintenance, repair, restoration of any building or monument;

(ii)   erection of screens, fences or covers to protect building or monument;

(iii)   works to stabilise any cliff, watercourse or coastline required to preserve a building/monument.

PART 27   USE BY MEMBER OF CERTAIN RECREATIONAL ORGANISATIONS

Class A Permitted use of land for recreation or instruction and erection of tents.

Not permitted: within the curtilage of a dwelling house.

Note: Recreational organisations are those holding a Certificate of Exemption under s 269 Public Health Act 1936.

PART 28   DEVELOPMENT AT AMUSEMENT PARKS

Class A Permitted:

(i)   erection of booths or stalls, installation of plant and machinery; and

(ii)   extension, alteration, replacement of booths, stalls, etc.

Not permitted:

(i)   if on land or pier within 3 k of aerodrome not to exceed 25 m;

(ii)   in the case of an extension if exceeds 5 m from ground level or height of original building whichever is the greater.

PART 29   DRIVER INFORMATION SYSTEMS

Class A Permitted: installation, erection replacement of apparatus.

Not permitted:

(i)   other than on a building, the building base area exceeds 1.5 sq m or 15 m in height;

(ii)   the highest part of the apparatus would exceed the highest part of the building by more than 3 m;

(iii)   would result in more than two microwave antennas.

Conditions:

(i)   sited to minimise the effect on the external appearance of the building;

(ii)   when no longer required to be removed as soon as practicable.

PART 30   TOLL ROAD FACILITIES

Class A Permitted:

(i)   setting up, improvement, etc, of facilities for toll collection; and

(ii)   provision of hard surface used in connection with these facilities.

Not permitted:

(i)   if not within 100 m of the boundary of toll road;

(ii)   height of building exceeds 7.5 m or 10 m where sloping roof; or

(iii)   where aggregate area (excluding booth) of building exceeds 1,500 sq m.

Condition: local planning authority to be informed and will decide if prior approval required for siting, design and external appearance.

PART 31   DEMOLITION OF BUILDINGS

Class A Permitted: any operation consisting of the demolition of a building.

Not permitted:

(i)   building rendered unsafe/uninhabitable by action/inaction of owner; or

(ii)   where it is practicable to secure safety/health by repair or support.

Conditions:

(i)   if demolition required on grounds of health/safety justification must be sent to the local planning authority;

(ii)   in other cases application to the local planning authority as to whether prior approval required as to method of demolition and restoration of the site; and

(iii)   site notice required and development not to begin within 28 days to allow determination by the authority as to whether approval is required.

Class B   Permitted: operation consisting of the demolition of whole, part of any gate, fence, wall or any form of enclosure.

PART 32   SCHOOLS, COLLEGES, UNIVERSITIES and HOSPITALS

Class A   Permitted: erection of building for the purpose incidental to the use of the above.

Not permitted:

(i)   where more than 10% of the cumulative floor area;

(ii)   where cumulative total volume would exceed 250 cu m;

(iii)   where any part of the new building is within 20 m of the boundary of the site; and

(iv)   as a result any land used as a playing field could no longer be used.

Condition: in the case of Art 1(5) land materials used shall be similar to those used in the construction of the original buildings.

PART 33   CLOSE CIRCUIT TELEVISION CAMERAS

Class A   Permitted: installation, alteration, replacement when used for security purposes.

Not permitted:

(i)   on a listed building or scheduled monument;

(ii)   dimension of the camera and housing exceeding 75 x 25 x 25 cm;

(iii)   less than 250 cm above ground level;

(iv)   protruding more than 1 m from the surface of the building;

(v)   any part of the camera or housing be in contact with the building at a point which is more than 1 m from any other point of contact;

(vi)   would be less than 10 m from any other camera installed on a building;

(vii)   not more than four cameras on the same side of the building; or

(viii) more than 16 cameras on the building.

Conditions:

(i)   to be sited so that it minimises the effect on the external appearance; and

(ii)   removed as soon as practicable after it is no longer required.

INDEX